J. C. Levenson is Edgar Allan Poe Professor of English and Charles Vandersee is Associate Professor of English, University of Virginia. Ernest Samuels, Pulitzer Prize–winning biographer of Henry Adams, is Professor of English, Emeritus, Northwestern University. Viola Hopkins Winner has published books on Edith Wharton and Henry James.

THE LETTERS OF
HENRY ADAMS
Volume III

1886–1892

Henry Adams

The Letters of

HENRY
ADAMS

VOLUME III : 1886–1892

Edited by
J. C. Levenson, Ernest Samuels
Charles Vandersee, Viola Hopkins Winner

with the assistance of
Jayne N. Samuels, Eleanor Pearre Abbot

The Belknap Press of
Harvard University Press
Cambridge, Massachusetts
and London, England

1982

Preparation of these volumes was made possible by grants from the
Program for Editions of the National Endowment for the Humanities
and from the Seth Sprague Educational and Charitable Foundation.
Publication of the volumes has been assisted by a grant from the
Publications Program of the National Endowment for the Humanities.

Library of Congress Cataloging in Publication Data
Adams, Henry, 1838–1918.
The letters of Henry Adams.

Publication of the letters sponsored by
the Massachusetts Historical Society
Bibliography: v. 1, p.
Includes index.
Contents: v. 1. 1858–1868—v. 2. 1868–1885—
v. 3. 1886–1892.
1. Adams, Henry, 1838–1918.   2. United States—
Civilization—1865–1918—Sources.   3. Historians—
United States—Correspondence.   I. Levenson, J. C.
(Jacob Clavner), 1922–   . II. Massachusetts
Historical Society.   III. Title.
E175.5.A2A4   1982   973'.072024   82-14673
ISBN 0-674-52685-6 (set)

Contents

Illustrations

Henry Adams' South Seas Route

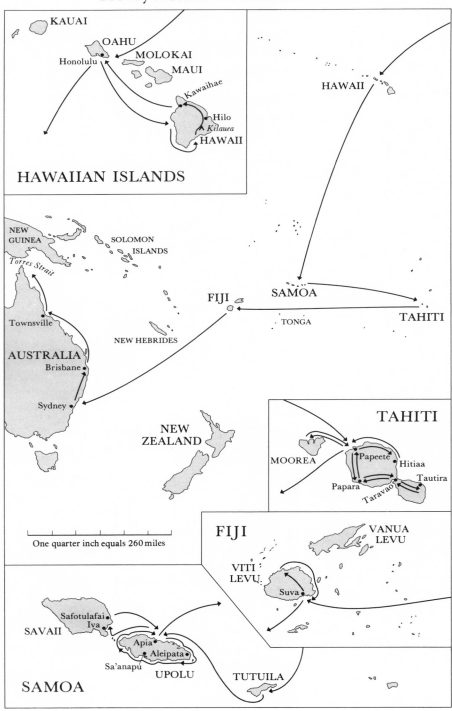

KAUAI

OAHU
Honolulu
MOLOKAI
MAUI
Kawaihae
Hilo
Kilauea
HAWAII

HAWAIIAN ISLANDS

HAWAII

NEW
GUINEA
SOLOMON
ISLANDS
Torres Strait

FIJI
SAMOA
TONGA
TAHITI

Townsville

AUSTRALIA
Brisbane

Sydney

NEW HEBRIDES

**NEW
ZEALAND**

TAHITI

MOOREA
Papeete
Hitiaa
Tautira
Papara
Taravao

One quarter inch equals 260 miles

FIJI

VANUA
LEVU

VITI
LEVU
Suva

Safotulafai
Iva
SAVAII
Apia
Aleipata
Sa'anapú
UPOLU
TUTUILA

SAMOA

Henry Adams' South Seas Itinerary

August 23, 1890, sails from San Francisco on the *Zealandia*.

Sandwich Islands, August 30–September 27, 1890

August 30, Honolulu; September 5, Nuuanu Valley, Pali; 12, leaves for the island of Hawaii; 13, leaves Kailua on the *W. G. Hall;* 14, Kilauea; 17, Hilo; 20, Laupahoehoe; 22, Kawaihae, boards the *Kinau;* 24, Honolulu; 27, sails for Samoa on the *Alameda.*

Samoa, October 5, 1890–January 29, 1891

October 5, Tutuila; 6, leaves for Upolu; 8, Apia; 24, Satapuala; 25, Manono; 26, Apolima, Iva in Savaii; 28, Papalii; 29, Safotulafai; November 1, Apia; 27, Lauli'i, Falefa, Fagaloa; December 2, Aleipata; 3, Nuutele; 4, Le-pa; 5, Falealili; 6, Vao-vai; 8, Sa'anapu; 9, Satapuala; 10, Apia; January 29, sails for Tahiti on the *Richmond.*

Tahiti, February 4–June 5, 1891

February 4, Papeete; 24, Papara; 27, Taravao; 27, Tautira; April 3, Papara; 9, Papeete; 12, Opunohu, Moorea; 24, returns to Papeete; June 5, sails from Hitiaa on the *Richmond*; 9, Rarotonga.

Fiji, June 16–July 23, 1891

June 16, Suva; 26, leaves Suva for interior; 28, Vuni Ndowa; July 5, Siga-toka River; 6, Mata-kula; 8, Wai-kumbo-kumbo; 9, boards the *Clyde* at Vanua-kula; 10, Mba River; 11, Marriott's Station; 13, leaves Nailange and Mba, grounded at Tonga-vere; 14, Viti Levu Bay; 16, returns to Suva; 23, sails for Australia on the *Rockton*; 25, New Hebrides Islands.

Australia, July 31–August 15, 1891

July 31, Sydney; August 7, Brisbane; 8, boards the *Wodonga;* 11, Townsville, sails for Java on the *Jumna;* 15, Thursday Island, clears Torres Strait.

Java, August 21–August 29, 1891

August 21, Bali; 23, Batavia; 24, Buitenzorg; 25, Garoet; 27, Batavia; 29, leaves for Singapore; 31, Singapore; September 1, leaves for Ceylon on the *Melbourne.*

Ceylon, September 6–September 21, 1891

September 6, Colombo; 7, Kandy; 12, Anuradhapura; 14, Dambolo; 15, Kandy; 17, Colombo; 21, sails for France on the *Djemneh.*

October 9, 1891, arrives at Marseilles.

THE LETTERS OF
HENRY ADAMS
Volume III

1886–1892

I.

Resuming Life
1886–1887

Crushed by his wife's suicide, Henry Adams recognized almost from the moment of shock that he must rally his will to survive. The one way to do so, he decided, was by "going straight ahead without looking behind." So on December 30, 1885, he moved as planned into the splendid house at 1603 H Street that Richardson had designed for him. Knowing the peril of isolation, he asked Theodore Dwight, a clerk at the State Department, to move in with him as librarian-secretary-companion, and he continued to see old friends. As for the greater peril of idleness, he worked again at his *History* and gradually caught his old stride.

In the summer of 1886, instead of going back to Beverly Farms, Adams traveled to Japan. Less than twenty years after the Meiji Restoration modern customs and comforts were found there mainly in the few open ports. To the land beyond the commercial cities Adams brought an informed interest in Buddhism and Japanese art. Guided by his companion, John La Farge, and his expatriate-Bostonian instructors, Ernest Fenollosa and Sturgis Bigelow, he went in for sightseeing and curio-buying with something like his old energy.

The trip was indeed restorative. After his return, Adams found work and society easier. In the summer of 1887, which for the first time in twenty years he spent at Quincy, history proved its power to elicit even greater energy. At one point his five-hour-a-day stint worked up to almost ten, and by the end of August he was dictating to a "caligrapher," whose typing helped him to speed completion of his third draft volume, on Madison's first administration. He claimed to feel less enthusiasm for skewering "defunct statesmen," and as he lost his relish for work, he dwelt on travel as incentive. But in the fall of 1887 he gave up a projected trip to Mexico and settled for the lesser distraction of setting up a greenhouse and growing roses. History and engagement with life held their own against withdrawal and wanderlust.

To John Hay

Washington. 10 Jan. 1886

Dear John

The hall stair-case seems finished, and the fire-places are also done, except perhaps the library hearth. Up stairs the floors are oiling, which is the last touch, I believe. I see no reason why you may not carry out your plan. Next Sunday I want to see you and Mrs Hay taking your dinner with me. My own establishment is still in embryo and likely to smell of everything unsavory; but you shall have some dinner to eat, and I deny further responsibility.[1] The man has not yet come to put up my shades, and I can only hope that you will be better provided for. Your gas-fixtures are up. Archer & Pancoast's man has been hard at work on them these two or three days past.

My days pass in hanging pictures. You have no conception what a vast resource this offers. I remember me that Theodore Tilton was wont to do it in his domestic nocturnes. Theodore knew the human mind.

Therefore come along. 'Tis cool, Therm. 14° at eight this morning; with snow and wind; but a sun that howls for shades, and the man on a spree between here and Boston.

Ever Yrs   Henry Adams.

MS: MHi
1. HA moved to 1603 H Street on Dec. 30, 1885.

To John Hay

Sunday, 17 Jan. [1886]

My dear John

Your house yearns for you. The carpenters are fairly out, or seem to be. Before another week, everything except the dining-room must be as ready as it can. Come quickly, or you will have no one to welcome you. If anything in life or death had still the power to shock me, it would be the catastrophe of Katey Bayard.[1] I know how you liked her, and how few old friends are left. Washington is a new place; I no longer recognise it; I am getting it on my nerves. Come quickly, and make a change.

If Mrs Hay will send a few children temporarily to me, or will come herself, with a baby or two, I shall be pleased and proud. You will have to pass a few days somewhere, I suppose, while your furniture is going in. I am first in rank and position. My new cook is not bad. My floors are nearly finished. My bed-rooms shall be supplied with anything you bid. My whole establishment stands at the disposition of your seniory. The dogs bark welcome to all the children, and ask only to help them move.

I suppose King is back again, but he has not been here as I hoped.

Ever Yrs   Henry Adams.

MS: MHi
1. Katherine Bayard died of a heart attack Jan. 16.

To Thomas F. Bayard

20 January, 1886.

My dear Mr Bayard

I have hesitated long before writing, for I knew that you would be overwhelmed with sympathy; but I cannot forget that sympathy has been a relief to me; and in all the world I doubt whether another person exists, beyond your family, who sympathises with you more keenly than I do. Life is grim. Yet we are under a sort of compact with society to take, without complaint, whatever comes; and within the last few weeks I have learned that, in the mass of human distress, trials like yours and mine can be endured, since so many men and women do endure them.

Ever truly Yrs   Henry Adams.

Hon. T. F. Bayard.

MS: DeHi

To John Hay

Washington. 22 Jan. 1886.

Oh, western Star[1]

Your letter filled me with joy. Your house has not more than a hundred workmen engaged on it, and is way ahead of mine except in a few details like rugs. You know how I bought out Sloane's shop. Whether Whitney bought eight hundred, and I eight thousand, or *vice versâ*, I have quite forgotten; but anyway I must have eight thousand more; and have decided to go to Japan next summer for no other object than to buy kakimonos for my gaunt walls.

If you bring with you only one or two children, you had better put up with me till your household is running. I can't take in Mrs Hay and the baby at the same time, but I presume you mean them to go at once to their palace. In any case you will find advantages in being with me, even if only to study how my flues smoke. My counsel and Dwight's wisdom are both useful, and my servants can give you much advice. Come straight to my house, letting me know at about what hour to open the doors. When Mrs Hay comes, we will, if so advised, take her in here, and send you into the attic next door.

The sun brightens at expecting you, and the snow faints with the warmth of its expectation.

Ever Yrs   Henry Adams.

MS: MHi

1. An echo of Whitman's "When Lilacs Last in the Dooryard Bloom'd" (1865).

To John Chipman Gray

Washington. 25 Jan. 1886[1]

My dear John

Thanks for your kind note.

As yet I have not succeeded at all in overcoming the feeling that I have no further interest, except as a by-stander more or less amused, in the struggle and anxieties of the world; and it is in this frame of mind that I wished for you as a trustee, not so much on my account, or on my wife's—though the selection would have naturally come from us both,—as on account of Ned and his children, whose future is much more on my mind than is my own.[2] I want to leave things in such a shape that there shall be no possibility of my doing anything more for their protection and interests. This done, I leave the whole matter to Edward, sincerely hoping that neither you nor I may be obliged to concern ourselves further, but that Edward will make his own arrangements, knowing exactly where he stands and what his children will have to depend upon.

As for me, I am going on, in the hope that sooner or later the future will get to look natural again. I am surprised to find how easy it is to go on under such circumstances. When one cares for nothing in particular, life becomes almost entertaining. I feel as though I were at a theatre—not a first class, but a New York theatre.

Ever Yrs   Henry Adams.

J. C. Gray Esq.

MS: MH

1. HA misdated this letter 1885.
2. On Jan. 30, HA, Gray, and Edward W. Hooper were designated trustees and Hooper's daughters beneficiaries of MHA's estate.

To George Bancroft

Washington. 11 Feb. 1886.

Dear Mr Bancroft

I have read the Plea, and am exceedingly grateful to you for saying, with dignity and weight such as no one else can command, what history requires should be said.[1]

Although we are quite aware that the path of "sovereignty"—which our grandfathers called tyranny—cannot be longer blocked or impeded, we are bound to record, as the government moves, the distance it has gone, and the shorter stage that remains before it.

Our *Peau de Chagrin*—once called Liberty—has shrunk uncommonly fast; but the future will doubtless find compensation.[2]

Ever truly Yrs   Henry Adams.

Hon. George Bancroft.

MS: MHi

1. In *A Plea for the Constitution of the U.S. of America Wounded in the House of its Guardians*, published Feb. 5, Bancroft argued that the Legal Tender decision of 1884 threatened "a death blow to the constitution" (p. 6).

2. In Balzac's novel *La Peau de chagrin* (1831) a magic piece of leather shrinks with every wish it grants.

To Henry Holt

8 March [1886]

Dear Holt

Thanks for your letter. I am almost amused at the idea of my caring now for anything that so-called critics could say. When the only chapter of one's story for which one cares is closed forever, locked up, and put away, to be kept, as a sort of open secret, between oneself and eternity, one does not think much of newspapers.

What a vast fraternity it is,—that of 'Hearts that Ache.' For the last three months it has seemed to me as though all society were coming to me, to drop its mask for a moment and initiate me into the mystery. How we do suffer! And we go on laughing; for, as a practical joke at our expense, life is a success.

Source: Cater; MS not found.

To Eli Thayer

1603 H Street. Washington. D.C.
14 March, 1886.

Dear Sir[1]

I have to thank you for your favor of the 12th inst.

I am sure that I could do nothing better than what you suggest; but, as yet, no one has attempted to give us any tolerable history of our country since the Revolution, and such work as I can do must be devoted to a time more remote than that which you recommend. Whatever comes within human memory is subject for memoirs rather than history. You have a duty to perform in telling the facts of your experience, before history can make good use of your material. I trust that you will not neglect so serious a task, which is more important than that of the historian; because historians will grow in all ages, but the men who make history are limited to the period of the history they make.

I am very respectfully your obedient servant

Henry Adams.

Hon. Eli Thayer

MS: RPB

1. Thayer is best known for his founding of the New England Emigrant Aid Company, which settled Free-Soil families in Kansas. His short book on the subject appeared in 1887.

To Paul Leicester Ford

1603 H Street Tuesday, 22 March 1886.

My dear Mr Ford[1]

I send back the manuscript you were so kind as to lend me.

A great mass of material is almost as troublesome to a biography as a short allowance. I should like, for my own part, to see it all published, so that I could make my own choice of what interests me; but the public would not look at it. About half will have to be admitted, if the material is fully used; about half may be omitted without risk of hurting the book.[2]

I am surprised at the immense labor and perseverance shown in collecting, copying and arranging the material, and at the quantity of the material itself. I am gratified, too, at discovering that I can claim a family interest in the Dictionary. Weary and worn in the paths of history and biography, I admit having been more seriously interested in the Greenleaf genealogy than in the politics or philology; but genealogy has a curious, personal interest, which history wants.[3]

I have made memoranda of general suggestions as I went along. You can burn them. The page is enclosed.

Of course the book must be published. What remains to be done is easy, now that the material is in a shape to be handled in detail. The author has only amusement before her.

Yrs truly   Henry Adams.

MS: NN

1. Paul Leicester Ford (1865–1902), already a serious scholar, later edited *The Writings of Thomas Jefferson* (10 vols., 1892–1894) and wrote popular novels, including *The Honorable Peter Stirling* (1894).

2. The material was compiled by Ford's mother, Emily Ellsworth Fowler Ford, for a biography she was writing of her grandfather Noah Webster.

3. The Adamses were related to Noah Webster through his wife, Rebecca Greenleaf Webster.

To Emily Ellsworth Fowler Ford

1603 H Street. 30 March, 1886.

My dear Mrs Ford[1]

Nothing would gratify me more than to be of use in an undertaking like yours; but, in such work, one can rarely be as useful as one would wish, for, in literature, the author must in the end carry his own load, and finds this course easiest. You have much pleasure before you, in preparing the book. If you are like the rest of us, you will find much criticism a greater annoyance than failure itself.

My criticisms are always simple; they are limited to one word:—Omit! Every syllable that can be struck out is pure profit, and every page that can be economised is a five-per-cent dividend. Nature rebels against this rule; the flesh is weak, and shrinks from the scissors; I groan in retrospect over the weak words and useless pages I have written; but the law is sound, and every book written without a superfluous page or word, is a master-piece.

All the same, no one cares to apply so stern a law to another person. One has a right to be severe only with oneself.

I am very truly Yrs   Henry Adams.

Mrs Ford.

MS: NN

1. Emily Ellsworth Fowler Ford (1823–1893), wife of the bibliophile Gordon L. Ford. Her uncompleted book was edited by her daughter Emily Ellsworth Ford Skeel and, titled *Notes on the Life of Noah Webster,* was privately printed in 1912.

To Charles Milnes Gaskell

My dear Carlo

If I have not written these three months past, it is only that I did not want to impose myself on my friends. As one of my associates, himself not ignorant of suffering, remarked to me some time ago: The worst of our troubles is that they are bores! Whatever happens, I do not intend to be a bore, and I would not write, till the danger was somewhat less pressing.

At last this winter has passed, and I am obliged to look about me. With its usual exasperating coolness, the world has gone on, carrying me with it, as though I were a stray monkey floating down Niagara on a hand-organ. Furious as I am at the thought of being smashed about, and able to do nothing to help myself, still, if one is to float at all, one might as well float so as not to be offensive to society, which is all, more or less, in the same case. So I have decided to get myself quite out of the way. All winter I have never left my house except to ride, or for a short walk; nor seen society except for the old friends who came to see me. Luckily for me, John Hay and his family came in January to take their new house next mine; and this gave me a resort that I needed; but the winter has been dark with deaths among my oldest and closest friends, and we have had a long struggle with the saddest circumstances.[1] Fortunately Washington is a cheery place where people take life gaily, and I have been by no means solitary or deserted. As the summer comes on, I groan at the need of departing; but as there is no choice, I have decided to pass it in Japan. I leave here about June 1, to return in October; and shall amuse myself by two long sea-voyages, which I abhor; and by two months among the Japanese whom I do not in the least pine to see. I can't go to Europe. It is full of ghosts.

Probably, by the time I get back here in the autumn I shall have so far recovered the tone of my mind as to feel once more some practical concern in the world's affairs. As I see matters now, I am bothered by the conviction that the world really has suddenly made a great change; and that it is not merely I who have had a mental shock. Both here and in Europe a vast revolution seems to have occurred within a year past. Our politics are already old-fashioned—quite thrown aside by new social movements. As for your affairs, I venture to have no opinion. Your liberal movement has been dragged aside by the Irish difficulty, in which I feel no interest, and which I do not expect to understand. I can only surmise that if you are to legislate on Gladstone's theory that an Irishman differs from an Englishman only by the results of bad government, you will need some experience very different from ours in America to bear you out. Rather than set up such a system of bickering as Gladstone suggests, I would call an Irish parliament at once, and leave it to decide what connection with England it wanted. Absolute independence might be not the worst result.[2]

Luckily I feel no concern in the matter; yet it is certainly a vast change, and makes the England of today a very strange country to me. I have become an old man in a twelvemonth. The future no longer belongs to us. I care not a silver dollar, even at its future value of eighty cents, what kind of society the world is to have; but I feel sure that it will be so different from ours that our generation will find it a bore. As you know, this settles it. We become *ganaches*,[3] and that is a role like another,—rather amusing to such as like to look on. I accept it. I always did like the theatre, though my only ambition was to write the play.

I mean to write to Robert before I sail. Give my love to your wife and to such friends as still hobble about. "Either tomorrow or some other day,"[4] we shall doubtless meet.

Ever Yrs   Henry Adams.

MS: MHi
1. Mrs. Thomas Francis Bayard, aged 51, died on Jan. 31, fifteen days after the death of her daughter Katherine. Mrs. George Bancroft, aged 83, died March 15. H. H. Richardson was fatally ill with Bright's disease; he died April 27.
2. Gladstone's Home Rule Bill, then before Parliament, provided for an Irish legislature empowered to deal with domestic affairs only. The bill was defeated June 7.
3. *Ganaches:* old fogies.
4. Arnold, *Empedocles on Etna,* I, II, 471 (1852).

To Carl Schurz

1603 H Street. 28 April, 1886.

My dear Friend

I should certainly have come to see you and your family in New York if I had not felt a strong dislike for going anywhere. Waiting for time to pass, and well aware that the passage of time must set me again, though I cannot see how, in some working relation to a world that now seems to me singularly preposterous, I have preferred to remain within my own house, seeing only old friends, and avoiding all effort or form of society, until my points of compass became right of their own accord, and I do whatever I like, without a sense of having no concern in what I am doing. You doubtless know the experience as well as I do. With the confidence that another six months will set me right, I am going to pass four of them in Japan, in the hope that where everything is upside-down, I shall find myself in keeping with the rest.

I wish you had come on to the meeting of the Historical Association this week.[1] It is now going on quite successfully, and is a good place for asking conundrums. I could, too, have shown you some interesting early letters of Henry Clay's. As for his age in 1806, I suspect it to have been usual to raise no question when the required year was actually begun. Clay wanted but three or four months of completing it; and Congress was not exacting.[2] Above all, the press did not make a business of interviewing the uncles and grandfathers or even the female cousins of the young women said to be about to marry government officials.

Please give my love to Agatha and the others. Some day I shall see you all again.

Ever Yrs   Henry Adams.

MS: ViU

1. George Bancroft presided at the third annual meeting of the American Historical Association in Washington, April 27–29, and HA attended; a paper on "Jefferson's Use of the Executive Patronage" provoked "some comment by Mr. Henry Adams, of Washington" (*Papers of the American Historical Association*, II [1887], 47).

2. Schurz was writing the biography of Henry Clay (1777–1852), who entered the Senate when still 29. *Henry Clay* (1887), American Statesmen series.

To Paul Leicester Ford

1603 H Street. 18 May, 1886.

My dear Mr Ford

I have to thank you very much for the kindness with which you have copied Harrison's letters for me.[1]

No one can ever tell what documents will be of service. One must have everything. Sometimes a mere date is very valuable.

Should you ever come across a copy of Jo. H. Daveiss' pamphlet—"View of the President's Conduct,"—published in Frankfort, Ky., please fasten on it for me.[2] It is the only pamphlet of the time that I have failed to find. If I am away, Mr Dwight will take charge of it, and pay for it.

Very truly, and with many thanks   Henry Adams.

Mr Paul Ford.

MS: NN

1. William Henry Harrison (1773–1841), ninth president of the United States, as governor of Indiana territory figured in the sixth volume of HA's *History*.

2. Joseph Hamilton Daveiss (1774–1811), killed in the battle of Tippecanoe, appeared mainly in the third volume as the prosecutor of Burr. *View of the President's Conduct Concerning the Conspiracy of 1806* (1807).

To Theodore F. Dwight

Palace Hotel [San Francisco]. 11 June, 1886.

My dear Dwight

Your letters of the 4th and 5th reached me today. La Farge and I arrived yesterday, after a brilliant run in our luxury of a private car all the way from Albany.[1] La Farge is quite upset about your coat, which is with us, and which I commonly wear. I hope he will make it good on his return. I tell him he must paint you a Japanese water-color.

I know you will want to know what I have to say of your favorite city. On the whole I wish you would not ask. Even you, I think, would find it a disappointment. Perhaps the season adds to the general effect, but the city looks to me as though its glories had passed; and everyone tells me that the two Oregon lines have diverted a large part of Californian trade, and that the last three years have been very hard ones. To my eye the city looks a little seedy; but I have wasted a whole day trying to find Dumas' novels, and La Farge has struggled for painting materials with the same fate; so our eyes may be jaundiced.

We have been too busy to see anything or go anywhere except to bed. Not an acquaintance, big or little, has come within our range; we are not positively anxious to be sea-sick, but I admit that even moderate seasickness is better than delay. Tomorrow at one o'clock we shall go on board our ship, and I hope by tomorrow sunset to be out of sight of the United States.[2] We have the ship to ourselves. All the cabins are at our disposal, and we look forward to twenty days of our own company. Fortunately La Farge is good company. As for me, I can only hope I am better company to others than to myself.

I am sorry that your head troubles you; but don't worry about it. You are too young to break down yet. As for what you say about gratitude, I am inclined to laugh at it. You have done and are doing far more for me than I for you. As for being "a burden," whenever that event happens, we will talk it over. I find burden enough in myself to make other people's burdens rather a relief to me, and I am not so amusing that I expect the world to corus[cate for my pleasure.][3]

John Hay writes most affectionately from Cleveland, and Ellen Gurney telegraphs that the last medical examination still develops no disease in Gurney. Yet he fails steadily, and I am more anxious than ever about him.

I suppose the Bancrofts and Fields will have gone before you get this letter; and you will be alone. I rather envy you. After all, I should not be tearing about the world, seasick and uncomfortable, if I were able to keep still.

This huge caravansary is uncommonly quiet, and the big halls seem empty. I imagine them to have been once crowded and noisy, but you know all about it. All the same, I doubt your being happy here now, though the roses are beautiful.

12 June. On board. Your telegram just come. We shall be off in half an hour. Fine weather, and all well. But it is great fun to run a genius. La Farge is a perpetual delight and study.

Love to all. Good-bye.

MS: MHi

1. La Farge accompanied HA to Japan as his guest. They crossed the country in the Union Pacific directors' car, at the disposal of CFA2, president of the railroad.
2. The Pacific Mail line advertised the departure of its S.S. *City of Sydney* for Hong Kong via Yokohama on June 12 at 2 P.M.
3. Source for bracketed words is Cater. The MS page ends with "corus-" and the second leaf of the folio sheet (which has been torn in half) is missing.

To John Hay

San Frisco. 11 June [1886]

My son John

My ship is in the bay, all ready at the quay, but before I wend my way, good-bye to thee John Hay; or words to that effect, for I have not my usual facility at verse today. San Francisco looks dusty, wintry and seedy, as I look over it at 8.30 A.M, from the fourth story of the Palace Hotel. Sea-sickness lies before, and the alkali desert behind this town. I have no choice between the two; but I find the town an unhappy medium.

Our journey was a glorious success. As I got into my train at Boston on Thursday the 3d, to start for New York, my brother Charles came down to tell me that his directors' car had unexpectedly arrived at Boston that morning, and would return to Omaha the next day. So I went to New York rejoicing; passed a delightful day with King, St Gaudens, &c, and at 6 P.M. dragged poor La Farge, in a dishevelled and desperate, but still determined mind, on board the Albany express. Never listen to the man who says that Corporations have no souls! At Albany I tumbled into the U.P. car at eleven o'clock at night, and from that moment till we reached here yesterday, we had nothing to think about except to amuse ourselves. The U.P. fed, clothed and carried us, as affectionately as though we had money to lend; and landed us at last, not at Omaha, but in the court of this Palace, just like two little Aladdins from school.

La Farge's delight with the landscape was the pleasantest thing in the journey. While I read Buddhism and slept, he tried to sketch from the moving car. His results were a sort of purple conglomerate, but the process amused him. On the Humboldt river our thermometer stood at 98° inside the car; but I am the creature of habit, and you will not be surprised that, even under these circumstances, I had Mme Modjeska and her husband to twelve-o'clock breakfast.[1] C'est plus fort que moi! Clearly I am a breakfasting animal.

Adventures we discard, for we are old and no longer vain; but La Farge makes a delicate humor glimmer about our path. Among other people whom he left in New York, likely to tear their hair on hearing of his departure, was the agent of Cassell, for whom he is illustrating Shelley's Sky Lark.[2] To this unhappy man, La Farge telegraphed from Poughkeepsie: "The purple evening melts around my flight."[3] I know not how meek the spirit of that man may be, but the evening of most men, under such conditions, would have been purple with oaths. At Omaha a young reporter got the better of us; for when in reply to his inquiry as to our purpose in visiting Japan, La Farge beamed through his spectacles the answer that we were in search of Nirwana, the youth looked up like a meteor, and rejoined: "It's out of season!"

We went yesterday afternoon to see our steamer. So far as we could learn, we were the only passengers. We were given the two best staterooms, with the promise of as many more as we might ask for. If you and King were with us, we would capture the ship, turn pirate, and run off to a cocoa-nut island. As it is, we shall be sea-sick without crime. If La Farge sees anything he wants, I will buy it for you, as it will probably be good. If not, I will spend it for myself, and send you whatever you don't want.

As for what you say about my hospitality, it is full of delicate humor. You well know that had it not been for you and yours, I should probably by this time have settled up my little account with the Hotel Company Unlimited, and cleared for a new chance. Perhaps you have not done me much of a service, but who knows? I mean to get out of the rest of life every new flavor it has. Our best love to Mrs Hay and the babes.

Ever Yrs   Henry Adams.

MS: MHi

1. Helena Modjeska (1840–1909), Polish-born actress, and her husband (also manager), Karol Bozenta Chlapowski.

2. Cassell & Co., the British publishing firm with a New York office, probably wanted the illustration for one of its reprint series. No such illustration by La Farge has been found.

3. "The pale purple even / Melts around thy flight"; Shelley, "To a Skylark" (1820).

To Theodore F. Dwight

Pacific Ocean. 28 June. [1886]

My dear Dwight

You and Clarence King and Arnold Hague deserve to be keel-hauled for telling me that the Pacific Ocean is different from other oceans. I have been over it, north, south, east, west, up to latitude 46°, and it contains nothing but head-winds, chopping seas, rains, cold and seasickness. Four quiet days in sixteen; the rest all kick and plunge, shiver and groan. We are at last within a thousand miles of Yokohama,—should be there in four days,—but have not yet seen a blue sky, or a fair wind, or a long swell. We have been sea sick from the first hour out, when that vile shore-wind sent us to bed. We have been more miserable by the linear inch than ever two woe-begone Pagans, searching Nirvana, were before. Today is a brief let-up. We have got to warmth if not to sunshine. We have come down from the Arctic circle as far as lat. 40°, long. 158°. We have crossed the 180th meridian and dropped a day, without solving Carroll's problem.[1] I begin this letter, so as to give you the sea-flavor while it still lasts.

We have the ship to ourselves. Only four female missionaries divide our realm, and to them I have not spoken. They sing and talk theology, two practices I abhor. La Farge and I are under the captain's special protection, and we abandon the cabin to religious exercises. A youthful Prussian named von Deich, and a U.S. engineer named Pemberton, going out to join the Monocacy,[2] are also on board; but, even with them and a fat commercial traveller, the smoking-room is not filled. La Farge and I have it almost for our own.

I cannot read—even Dumas. Your kindly package was duly delivered, and touched me even to tears; for I was in bed, very sea-sick, and the tears were permanent, more or less, for a week; but the same cause interfered most seriously with my benefitting by your thoughtfulness, for when one does not eat, one has nothing to digest. I am still very shaky; but in calm weather do manage to sit at table, and even to eat a bit.

From this painful picture, you will judge that we are sorry we came, and wish we were at home. Not a bit of it! We are gay as petrels. We chatter, laugh, swear, and even—sometimes—smoke. We are bored like men who know all that ennui can tell us, and we live in it, at home. La Farge is a charming companion, who never complains or loses his temper, or makes a foolish remark; but in the despair of seasickness and cold and wet, is just what he is at the dinner-table. I wish I could say as much for myself; but even I am kept to the mark by him.

2 July. Just arrived, and not yet gone ashore; but I send this, because the Belgic is starting back in an hour. We have had a nasty voyage, with four days quiet weather, but have had no other trouble, and are here ahead of time. I am sorry to send such a letter, but you will at least know that we are all right.

MS: MHi
1. Lewis Carroll was considered instrumental in the movement to standardize time, which culminated in the International Prime Meridian Conference in 1884. More recently, he had set forth the problem of precisely where and when the day changes its name in circumnavigating the globe in "Knot X," *A Tangled Tale* (1885).
2. A U.S. warship in the Asiatic Squadron.

To John Hay

Yokohama. 9 July, 1886.

My son John

We have been here a week. Between the wish that you were with us, and the conviction that you would probably by this time be broken up if you had come, I am distraught. Amusing it certainly is—beyond an idea,—but comfortable or easy it is not by any means; and I can honestly say that one works for what one gets.

We have devoted the week to Tokio, and you can judge what sort of a place it is from the fact that there is neither hotel nor house in it where we can be so nearly comfortable as we are in a third-rate hotel at Yokohama, twenty miles away. Here we have rooms directly on the bay, with air as fresh as the Japs make it; and here we return every evening to sleep. Sturgis Bigelow acts as our courier and master of ceremonies, but La Farge has mastered Mandarin Chinese, and hopes soon to be a fluent talker of Daimio Japanese.[1] As for me, I admire.

Fenellosa and Bigelow are stern with us. Fenellosa is a tyrant who says we shall not like any work done under the Tokugawa Shoguns.[2] As these gentlemen lived two hundred and fifty years or thereabouts, to 1860, and as there is nothing at Tokio except their work, La Farge and I are at a loss to understand why we came; but it seems we are to be taken to Nikko shortly and permitted to admire some temples there. On secret search in Murray,[3] I ascertain that the temples at Nikko are the work of Tokugawa Shoguns. I have not yet dared to ask about this apparent inconsistency for fear of rousing a fresh anathema.

The temples and Tokugawas are, I admit, a trifle baroque. For sticking a decisive bit of infamous taste into the middle of a seriously planned, and minutely elaborated mass of refined magnificence, I have seen no people— except perhaps our own—to compare with the Japs. We have the future before us to prove our capacity, but they stand now far ahead. Some of the temples are worse than others, but I am inclined to let Fenellosa have his way with them, if he will only let me be amused by the humor. Positively everything in Japan laughs. The jinrickshaw men laugh while running at full speed five miles with a sun that visibly sizzles their drenched clothes. The women all laugh, but they are obviously wooden dolls, badly made, and can only cackle, clatter in pattens over asphalt pavements in railway stations, and hop or slide in heelless straw sandals across floors. I have not yet seen a woman with any mechanism better than that of a five-dollar wax doll; but the amount of oil used in fixing and oiling and arranging their hair is worth the money alone. They can all laugh, so far. The shop-keepers laugh to excess when you say that their goods are forgeries and worthless. I believe the Mikado laughs when his ministers have a cabinet council. The gilt dragon-heads on the temples are in a broad grin. Everything laughs, until I expect to see even the severe bronze doors of the tombs, the finest serious work I know, open themselves with the same eternal and meaning-less laughter, as though death were the pleasantest jest of all.

In one respect Japan has caused me a sensation of deep relief. In America I had troubled myself much because my sense of smell was gone. I thought I never should again be conscious that the rose or the new-mown hay had odor. How it may be about the rose or the hay I know not; but since my arrival here I perceive that I am not wholly without a nose. La Farge agrees with me that Japan possesses one pervasive, universal, substantive smell,— an oily, sickish, slightly fetid odor,—which underlies all things, and though infinitely varied, is always the same. The smell has a corresponding taste. The bread, the fruit, the tea, the women, and the water, the air and the gods, all smell or taste alike. This is monotonous but reassuring. I have rea-soned much and tried many experiments to ascertain the cause of this phenomenon, but it seems to be a condition of existence, and the accompaniment of Japanese civilisation. Without the smell, Japan would fall into dissolution.

I am trying to spend your money. It is hard work, but I will do it, or succumb. Kakimonos are not to be got. Porcelain worth buying is rare. Lacquer is the best and cheapest article. Bronzes are good and cheap. I want to bring back a dozen big bronze vases to put on the grass before our houses in summer, for palms or big plants, so as to give our houses the look of a cross between curio shops and florists'. Tokio contains hardly anything worth getting except bronzes. A man at Ozaka has sent up some two hundred and fifty dollars worth of lacquers, sword-hilts, inlaid work, and such stuff. As he has the best shop in Japan we took the whole lot, and have sent for more. Inros[4] are from ten to fifteen dollars. I shall get a dozen for presents. Good cloisonné, either Chinese or Japanese, is most rare. Fine old porcelain is rare and dear. Embroideries are absolutely introuvable. Even books seem scarce. Japan has been cleaned out.[5] My big bronze vases will cost from fifty to two hundred dollars apiece, but these will be good.

We called on our minister, Falstaff of Texas, who puffed himself up and caused me an agony of suppressed laughter by repeating your exact diplomatic formula that he had consented to come here merely to oblige the President, who wished him to take charge of an important negotiation.[6] He also warned us against sunstroke—"what the French call 'coup de seal.' "[7] Such a perfect specimen of American rococo I have never seen, which led to the remark that on one day we had bagged four Showguns of the Tokugawa dynasty, and one Showgun of the Tobacco-chawer dynasty, and we could not decide which Showgun was the best specimen of the lot.

I have not presented my Japanese letters of introduction, as I found it would imply a course of entertainments which I would rather avoid. Tokio is an impossible sort of place for seeing anyone. It is a bunch of towns, and the Europeans live all over it, so that one goes five miles or so to make a call or to see one's dearest friend for five minutes. The thermometer today is anywhere between 90° and 200° in the streets, and calling on formal ministers of state under such conditions is not amusing.[8]

I shall go to Ozaka and Kioto in September, unless the country is absolutely closed by cholera. Indeed I should do many other things if I were not anxious to spare La Farge the risk of illness. He continues to be the most agreeable of companions; always cheerful, equable, sweet-tempered, and quite insensible to ideas of time, space, money or railway trains. To see him flying through the streets of Tokio on a jinrickshaw is a most genial vision. He peers out through his spectacles as though he felt the absurdity as well as the necessity of looking at the show as though it were real, but he enjoys it enormously, especially the smell, which quite fascinates him. He keeps me in perpetual good humor except when we go to see anything. I am a rusher, and an hour of sight-seeing tires me out, legs and eyes, brain and feet. I want to catch the first impression and stop before it is driven out by fatigue. La Farge cannot stop at a cheap bric-a-brac shop less than an hour.

At a museum or a temple he gives the first hour to the first room; then, when I am already used up, he devotes two hours more to a microscopic examination of every detail, and comes away at last with a cracking headache, an hour late to his positive engagement, and scaring me for fear he might be ill. This continues day after day. I am lost in wonder how he ever does work; but he can be energetic, and his charm is that whether energetic or lazy he has the neatest humor, the nicest observation, and the evenest temper you can imagine. When he loses the trains, I rather enjoy it. After all, who cares?

Of startling or wonderful experience we have had none. The only moral of Japan is that the children's story-books were good history. This is a child's country. Men, women and children are taken out of the fairy books. The whole show is of the nursery. Nothing is serious; nothing is taken seriously. All is toy;—sometimes, as with the women,—badly made and repulsive; sometimes laughable, as with the houses, gardens and children; but always taken from what La Farge declares to have been the papboats of his babyhood. I have wandered, so to express it, in all the soup-plates of forty-eight years' experience, during the last week, and have found them as natural as Alice found the Mock Turtle.[9] Life is a dream, and in Japan one dreams of the nursery. Give my love to yours and its mistress

Ever   Henry Adams.

La Farge thinks it would interest the children to know that *ma* in Japanese is a horse.

MS: MHi
1. The language of educated people (*daimio:* feudal baron).
2. Ernest Francisco Fenollosa (1853–1908) arrived in Tokyo in 1878 to teach Western philosophy and political economy at the Imperial University; he remained in the country, studying, collecting, and restoring Japanese art. He favored the aristocratic, Buddhist art of medieval Japan over the more popular art that flourished under the Tokugawa shoguns.
3. Murray's *Handbook for Travellers in Japan* was first published in 1884.
4. *Inros:* small, compartmented cases, originally used to hold seals and ink.
5. Not least by HA's fellow Bostonians. The Museum of Fine Arts (Boston) owes a large part of the riches of its Japanese holdings (some 5,000 paintings, 60,000 prints, 7,700 ceramics) to the pre-1884 collecting of Edward S. Morse, Ernest Fenollosa, and William Sturgis Bigelow. In 1884 Japan began restricting export of national treasure.
6. Richard Bennett Hubbard (1832–1901), the former Democratic governor of Texas, was appointed minister to Japan (1885–1889) as a reward for his services in the presidential campaign. Shakespeare's Falstaff, with his face-saving lies, amused listeners who were in the know.
7. *Coup de soleil:* sunstroke; *coup de ciel:* a special providence.
8. Apparently because he had said much the same thing earlier, HA deleted the following opening to the next paragraph: "At this moment a man has come up from the best curio dealer in Japan, at Ozaka, with curios to the value of $250, including inros, sword-guards, and pipes, a promiscuous lot which Bigelow declares to be first-rate. So we took it all and sent for more."
9. *Alice in Wonderland*, ch. 9.

To Theodore F. Dwight

Nikko. 17 July, 1886.

My dear Dwight

If you feel curious to know where we are, take some map of Japan, and, after starting from Yokohama, go north twenty miles to Tokio, then north again about fifty miles to a town called Utsonomia, then towards the west some twenty miles further, where, among mountains, is a village named Nikko. If you will look into Murray's Japan, you will see that Nikko is famous for certain large temples* built in the 17th century in honor of two or three Shoguns of the ruling dynasty. They are the sights which all travellers are expected to see; but we did not come here solely on their account. Nikko lies high and is cool, with beautiful scenery, and has been chosen as a summer residence by Sturgis Bigelow who lives here with his friends, Mr and Mrs Fenellosa, and who hired a little Japanese toy-house near by, for us.[1] Ten days of Yokohama and Tokio were more than enough for us. Tokio is amusing, but, with the thermometer above 90°, a somewhat cloying joy. For smells it has no known rival. Every house is a cess-pool; the water is from surface wells; and the surrounding country is one vast, submerged rice-field, saturated with the human excrement of many generations of Japanese. Another drawback to the low country was the cholera which was all about us at Yokohama, and promised, as the heat increased, to become uncommonly lively. It was still worse in the south, at Ozaka and Kioto, where we ought later to turn our steps. Finally, ten days of Japanese or hotel food made us curious to learn how clean Mrs Fenellosa's table might be; for a pervasive sense of oily nastiness characterises every article of ordinary consumption.

In spite of all this, I have not often been more amused than I was by our stay in Yokohama and Tokio. Everything was new, and opposite to all fundamental principles. La Farge and I went about under Bigelow's guidance, and had our little joke about all we saw and did, always ending in the conviction that we were playing baby, and living in doll-land. Just now we are established in our doll-house with paper windows and matted floors, the whole front open towards ridiculously Japanese mountains; and as it is a rainy day we expect our child-owners to come and play with us; for we think ourselves rather clever dolls as dolls go. As to the temples, I will enclose you a photograph of one. You will see that it is evidently a toy, for everything is lacquer, gilding, or green, red and blue paint. I am still in search of something serious in this country, but with little more hope of success. Nothing which is held as serious elsewhere seems to be taken

* I enclose the photograph of one, to save description.

seriously here. The religion is a high old joke to them. Death itself is treated as a pleasant conceit. The only solemn fact of life is what is called Ocha-no-yu, or the ceremony of making the Honorable Tea;—what we call five o'clock tea.

I have delivered only one of Mr Kuki's letters, and shall deliver no more, as it would be a mere form, and the various ministers are already seeking their summer retreats. I did not care to be entertained *en diplomate,* and to be entertained *à la Japonaise* would be too much for my stomach which is none too steady even against fried eels and rice. We arrived here quite used up, literally poisoned in Bigelow's case, and something like it in ours; and nearly a week of mountain air, clean quarters, good food, and quiet, has not yet wholly set us up. Mrs Fenellosa has rescued us from our trials; but I cannot imagine what we should have done without her; for, with Tokio, Yokohama, Ozaka and Kioto shut against us, we should have been terribly cornered. In the north there is nothing to see, and only the pure Japanese mode of life to live. I am rather surprised to find that no European, however hot may be his Japan-mania, and even when he is a Buddhist in profession, makes so much as an attempt to live after the manner of the country. By tacit consent this is admitted to be out of the question. Even a journey is a severe trial, and one carries food, sheets, flea-powder, and if possible drink. Our one night's experience in an excellent Japanese hotel, though infinitely droll, was more than sufficient for a life-time. Even Japanese rice is unappetising, and after ten days of Japanese tea, I cherish the packages of my own tea, brought from Washington, as a luxury not to be had for money or love in this country. Your Acid Phosphate, too, is now my steady tipple.

As yet we have found little to buy, and nothing very well worth getting; but we are doing our best to spend our money. Here at Nikko are no shops to speak of. Kioto is the place for purchases, and we do not feel confident of getting there. Fenellosa and Bigelow are the highest authorities on lacquers and kakimonos; but they can only pick up a good thing now and then. We shall probably stay at Nikko at least a month, and the dealers are to send us what they have. La Farge will sketch. I shall make excursions and kill time. The rainy season has begun today, and there is no temptation to move.

No letters since I arrived. Take care of yourself and you will take care of me.

Ever Yrs   Henry Adams.

MS: MHi
1. Fenollosa's first wife, the former Lizzie Goodhue Millet of Salem, Mass.

To Sir Robert Cunliffe

Nikko. 21 July, 1886.

My dear Robert

I have long owed you a letter. Buried now for some weeks in the heart of Japan, I find myself with time to think of my friends. I do not know whether you heard that I ran away from America six weeks ago. Life there had become intolerable. My own existence was knocked to pieces, and I could do nothing with it. My father and mother were suffering under a variety of trials, very different from mine, but not easier to bear. Add to this that my brother-in-law Gurney had broken down, and that the greatest anxiety was felt on his account; and that I could do absolutely nothing for any of them, while I was in a fair way to break down myself. You will see from all this, why I am now writing to you from Nikko, among the mountains of Nipon, where I see as little as possible to remind me of myself, and can gain three or four months of hardening to my difficulties. The journey alone, which took a month of steady motion, and three weeks of infernal seasickness, was a relief from my other forms of sickness.

So much by way of explanation. As for Japan, it is very amusing, not to say absurd; and I am delighted to have seen it; but I do not think I care to become a Japanese. I have laughed without stop, ever since landing. Everyone does the same thing; the joke seems to go round; and nature herself refuses to be serious, but persists in mimicking dinner-plates and nursery-screens. I went into a convulsion the other day at a thunder-storm which sounded so like poor gongs that I could not believe it natural. I am travelling with John La Farge, a New York artist; and we live here in a doll-house, with two rooms, paper-windows, and ladder-staircase, so like a toy that we have come to accept it as a fact that we are children once more, making believe at imaginary travels. Nothing agrees with one's formulas. One feels like sitting down in the street, and making mud-pies.

This is more or less what I am doing. Driven into the mountains by heat and cholera; disgusted with Japanese food and inns, and the smells of Tokio and the rice-fields, I am waiting in comfort to see what is to be done next, and am in no hurry to find out. Heavy rains have come. The mountains are lost in mist. The temples and tombs of the Shoguns drip with moisture. When the sun comes out, the sudden heat gives one a vapor bath. I wrap myself in my Japanese dress, and lie on my verandah, reading and sleeping, while La Farge sketches our little temple-garden, with its toy water-fall, miniature rocks and dwarf trees. The shaven priest trims his shrubs or sits on his heels in his house behind us. We take our meals with some American friends near by, who are officials in the University at Tokio, and have a house here in summer. They are more or less frequented by other Japanese officials, who talk English, and tell us about Japanese art, literature, history, religion and everything we want to know. Dealers come with bric-à-brac for sale. There is some society, but I have not sought it. Your minister is here, with his wife who is an old American friend of mine; but I have not been to see them.[1] I have official letters from the Japanese minister at Washington to all the authorities of Japan; but I have not delivered them. Summer is no time for formalities, and one does not want to put on a frock coat to drink bad tea and exchange solemn phrases, through an interpreter, with cabinet ministers who can do nothing to amuse one.

Tokio is beastly; nothing but a huge collection of villages, scattered over miles after miles of flat country; without a building fit to live in, or a sewer to relieve the stench of several hundred thousand open privies. I was greatly amused, and still more disappointed by it; amused by the people and their customs; disappointed at the want of anything else to see. Not even a tolerable hotel exists there. We had to sleep at Yokohama twenty miles away. As for the rest of the country, all that is specially interesting is about Kioto, in the south; and we are still in doubt when and how to get there, for the heat and the cholera are much in the way. We cannot attempt it before September. We are uncommonly lucky to have a retreat here at Nikko.

Our steamer sails for San Francisco on September 23, and I should be established once more at Washington by October 20. By brief telegrams we hear of your political doings in England, but I know nothing of your personal share in them. As I have no concern and no opinions about Irish matters, I have nothing to say. The world seems to me to have suddenly changed, and to have left me an old man, pretty well stranded and very indifferent to situations which another generation must deal with, as it best can. Both in Europe and in America, and even here in this rococo Japan, total change is the order of this time. I have been thrown out of the procession, and can't catch up again.

My best love to your wife and all our friends. Write to me to Washington in October, and tell me all your news.

Ever Yrs   Henry Adams.

MS: MHi
1. Sir Francis Richard Plunkett (1835–1907), secretary of legation at Washington 1870, minister to Japan 1883–1888, and Lady Plunkett (May Tevis Morgan, d. 1924) of Philadelphia.

To John Hay

Nikko. 24 July, 1886.

My son John

Do you happen to know where Nikko is? If not, I cannot tell you. All I know is that it is in a valley among some green mountains in the insides of Japan; that it is pretty; that the hour is 8 A.M. of a sweet morning; that I am lying, in a Jap *kimono* on the upper verandah of the smallest doll-house your children ever saw; that La Farge is below, in the bath-room, painting our toy-garden, with its waterfall and miniature mountains; and that at nine o'clock we are to step down to the Fenellosa's to breakfast.

Since Monday, July 12, we have been here, and here we are likely to stay. The shortest possible experience of Japanese travel in its most favorable form satisfied me that pleasure lay not there. We had but six or eight hours between Tokio and this place. Four hours were by rail, rather pleasant though hot. I enjoyed looking out at the ridiculous landscape, though it was mostly a rice field, where numerous Japs with immense round hats, and little else, paddled about, up to their knees and elbows in black dirt which I compliment in calling mud. Here and there were groves about temples, or bamboo thickets about cabins. As night came on, bonfires smoked, to keep away mosquitoes; and, by the shade of Yeyas, they were not built without reason; for, although I saw no other four-footed animal, except three pack horses and three dogs, in fifty miles, the skeets restored a liberal average for beasts of prey. We reached at 9 P.M. a town, called Utso-nomyia. So I was credibly informed, at least, and I believe it; for I know that we got into a wagon, and were driven two miles, at a full run, through a street thronged with infant children and paper lanterns. I know not how many we immolated; I soon wearied of counting; but I do know that our driver shouted, at intervals of flogging his brutes; that a devil at his side blew a penny trumpet; that another devil ran ahead and yelled; and that at last we were dropped not at a door, but, as usual, at a counter, and were told to take off our shoes. We were then led across a miniature court, past several open privies (which smelt), and an open bath-house where naked[1] men and women were splashing, up a ladder staircase, to three rooms which were open to each other and to the air and moon. We were pleased. La Farge and I gamboled in the sprightliness of our youth and spirits. The rooms were clean and adorned with kakimonos and bronzes. We lay on the floor and watched our neighbors below, while Bigelow concocted food out of a can of Mulligatawny soup and boiled rice. After eating this compound and smoking a cigar I would have wished to sleep a little, and in truth our beds and mosquito nets were built. At midnight I wooed slumber; but first the *amidos* or sliding shutters of the whole house below had to be slammed, for twenty minutes; then all the slammers had to take a last bath, with usual splashing and unutterable noises with their mouth and throat, which Bigelow assured us to be only their way of brushing their teeth. I have never known at what hour these noises ceased, but they ended at last, and we all fell asleep.

Presently I was waked by a curious noise in the court. It was a man, moving about, and stopping every few steps to rap two bits of wood together—clack-clack—like castanets. He interested me for twenty minutes. I understand he was the watchman on pattens, and that he thus notifies thieves to be on their guard. During this part of the entertainment I became aware that all was not well with myself; in short that I had an attack of cholera of the worst sort; a pain internal, passing into desperate nausea; then into drenching perspiration, and lastly into a violent diarhoea. With these afflictions I struggled for an hour or two, and at last crept back to bed, weak as the moonlight which illuminated my sufferings, and hoping only for an hour of forgetfulness; when, long before daylight, the *amidos* began to slam again, the bath began to splash, the bathers choked and coughed, and chaos came.

Towards nine o'clock we consulted. Then it seemed that La Farge was suffering just as I did. Both of us were in a miserable state of weakness, trusting only that the end of our mortal career might arrive soon to bring repose. I was reduced to laughing at La Farge's comments to a point where exhaustion became humorous. Bigelow brewed for us some of my Chinese tea,—for Japanese tea was nauseous. We managed to dress; and at half past eleven we were stuffed into a cart and rattled off over roads that we remember. That wagon understood jouncing. We hung on to any handy rail, and, when we could, we fell in the wagon rather than in the rice-fields. Ten miles of these gaieties brought us into a road between rows of huge cryptomerias, which seem to be a kind of giant pine; and when our horses struck this region, the ways being heavy with mud and mending, they refused to go at all. For ten miles, they balked every hundred yards, and if an ascent intervened, they balked there besides. Changing horses made the matter worse; the fresher the horse, the more vigorously he balked; while our two drivers beat them over the head and withers with a heavy club. On experiment I found that I could stand—when not laughing,—and I thought walking less fatigue than sitting to see the brutes beaten. I crawled up the hills, and perspired freely with a temperature of 90°, but in course of the day I had four cups of tea, and walked about as many miles. At six o'clock we reached Nikko; I climbed up a long stone stair to our small house; and went energetically to bed.

We have never found out what upset us, nor has Bigelow found out what poisoned his arm and laid him up for a week at the same time. All we know is that our drive to Nikko did us no harm, and in a few days we were all right again, with a fancy for staying quiet and not immediately indulging in the luxuries of Japanese hotels. Our small palace of two rooms, with paper windows and two hospitable shaven priests who say only *Ohio,* satisfy our yearnings. I have had cholera enough for the present.

I admit that Mrs Fenollosa's table has a share in our Sybaritism. The fact that, if we travel, we have nowhere to go where there is anything to see, except to Kioto and the south, is also an element. Kioto and Osaka are hotter than the future life; they are overrun with cholera; so is Yokohama where we had it common, and it has now extended to Tokio. No one seems ever to travel in the north and west, or to go to Kui-sui even for Satsuma ware.[2] Nikko is the prettiest part of Japan; here are the great temples of Yeyas (Iye-yasu) and Iye-mitsu, the first and third Shoguns; here, if it were not for show waterfalls, I can be content, and La Farge can sketch.

In truth the place is worth coming to see. Japan is not the last word of humanity, and Japanese art has a well-developed genius for annoying my prejudices; but Nikko is, after all, one of the sights of the world. I am not sure where it stands in order of rank, but after the pyramids, Rome, Mme Tussaud's wax-works, and 800 16th Street,[3] I am sure Nikko deserves a place. Without forgetting the fact that the temples are here and there rather cheap grotesque, the general result of temple and tomb, architecture, ornament, landscape and foliage, is very effective indeed. When you reflect that the old Shoguns spent twelve or fourteen millions of dollars on this remote mountain valley, you can understand that Louis Quatorze and Versailles are not much of a show compared with Nikko.

Photographs give no idea of the scale. They show here a gate and there a temple, but they cannot show twenty acres of ground, all ingeniously used to make a single composition. They give no idea of a mountain-flank, with its evergreens a hundred feet high, modelled into a royal, posthumous residence and deified abode. I admit to thinking it a bigger work than I should have thought possible for Japs. It is a sort of Egypt in lacquer and greenth.

When I am here I feel sorry you did not come. The walking is all up and down steep hills, to be sure; and Mrs Fenollosa drags us to see waterfalls day and night. You can find consolation in reflecting on this.

I have, in all, bought six or eight hundred dollars worth of things no better than you can see every day in New York, and no different. You can select what you want. I have bought nothing expressly for you, and will take it all if you do not care for it. No first-rate thing has yet offered itself. Fenollosa tried to get the refusal of a pair of screens, six leaves each, on gold; which he averred to be the greatest work he ever saw of Okio, a celebrated painter of flowers in the last century.[4] The price asked was large; eight hundred dollars. I could not buy it without seeing it; and I believe it has been bought by Mori, the minister of education.[5] Nothing else of first-rate work has been offered. I despair of bringing back anything good.

27 July. Yesterday arrived from Ozaka a large lot of kakimonos, sent up by the great curio-dealer, Yamanaka.[6] I gleaned about two dozen out of the lot. They are cheap enough, but I fear that Fenollosa, who is in Tokio, will say they are Tokugawa rot, and will bully me into letting them go. He is now trying to prevent my having a collection of Hokusai's books.[7] He is a kind of St Dominic, and holds himself responsible for the dissemination of useless knowledge by others.[8] My historical indifference to everything but facts, and my delight at studying what is hopefully debased and degraded, shock his moral sense. I wish you were here to help us trample on him. He has joined a Buddhist sect; I was myself a Buddhist when I left America, but he has converted me to Calvinism with leanings towards the Methodists.

Love to Mrs Hay, Del and Alice. Yesterday I came near buying two baby monkeys for them.

Ever Yrs   Henry Adams.

30 July. Your telegram of June 26 arrived this morning, with other pleasant news.[9]

MS: MHi
1. HA wrote "naken" for "naked."
2. Kyushu, the southernmost island, where Satsuma ware was still being produced.
3. The address of Hay's new house.
4. Maruyama Ōkyo (1733–1795), founder of the naturalistic Maruyama school of painting.
5. Mōri Arinori (1848–1888) had been a diplomat in the U.S. 1870–1873, China, and Great Britain before becoming minister of education in 1884.
6. Yamanaka Kichirobē (1845–1917), art connoisseur and dealer.
7. Katsushika Hokusai (1760–1849), painter and wood engraver of the Ukioyo-e or Popular School. His sets of prints, including the famous "Hundred Views of Mount Fuji" (1834–1835), were much admired by the French Impressionists.
8. St. Dominic (c. 1170–1221) proselytized among the Albigensian heretics; Fenollosa tried to convert Westerners from the belief that Hokusai was the greatest of all Japanese artists.
9. The telegram, which has not been found, probably sent news of the birth June 25 of a daughter to Elizabeth and J. Donald Cameron.

To Theodore F. Dwight

Nikko. 30 July, 1886.

Dear Dwight

Your two letters, June 22 and July 2, arrived together this morning, and I scratch a line to acknowledge them by tomorrow's mail.

Please tell the Secretary that I am greatly obliged for his kind introductions. I had already made my call on Minister Hubbard (you need not add that he is the pompousest dodgasted old Texan jackass now living) at Tokio. At present he is in the mountains, and I am in the mountains, but we are a long way apart, and unless the mountain comes or goes to Mahomet, Mahomet is not likely to meet the mountain again. On the new Consul General I will call when I next return to Yokohama.[1]

Your news is all good, and has given me much repose of mind. As we sail homewards on September 23, it is a great thing to reach August without drawback.

Since my last, nothing has changed here. La Farge and I are still lords of our little house, its paper windows and its waterfall. He avers that he is Huckleberry Finn and I am Tom Sawyer. We certainly feel like those models. La Farge tries to sketch. I try to photograph. Our joint success leaves a margin for Tom Sawyer's imagination to fill in. Nikko is fascinating, but I am safe from one kind of bric-à-brac, at least; if not from the best. The one kind, of which I have seen no specimen possible, is still the women.

Our time passes very rapidly in doing nothing. We have not even a Shakespeare to read. We have a friendly flea at times, and mosquitoes, horse-flies, black flies, and waterfalls. Of the lot I prefer the mosquitoes, but the fleas have points. Your Acid Phosphate holds out till the hardened sinner return in six weeks. The cholera seems rather letting up. I still hope to reach Kioto early in September, but pretty nearly all the curios in the south have been sent up for me to choose from.

Please send my love to the Fields, and say that I hope to write to them by the next mail. By the time this reaches you, we shall be thinking of our return voyage. We have a pair of infant monkeys here which I would like to bring to the Department, if I thought there were vacancies for them; but perhaps our owl would have more chance. Take care of yourself. Good-bye.

Ever Yrs   Henry Adams.

MS: MHi
    1. Clarence R. Greathouse (1845–1899), consul general at Yokohama 1885–1889.

To John White Field

Nikko. 4 August. 1886.

My dear Mr Field

My knowledge of the world comes down no later than to the point of your arrival at Ashfield.[1] About a fortnight after you reached that mountain valley, I reached this one, and I am fixed here about as firmly as you are. Heat, and bad food, bad water, bad roads, bad conveyances, and bad fleas, check energy of travel. I hardly count the cholera, though it has also a share in producing content; but I do reckon among the difficulties a marked liability to attacks, of a colic—if not of a choleraic—nature, which have bothered us a good deal. In short I am very well satisfied to have a comfortable retreat, while the rice-fields round Tokio and Ozaka boil in a tropical sun.

Dwight will probably have told you where we are, and what we are doing here; but, to make it clearer, I enclose a photograph I took from my balcony, to show the Japanese garden under our sway. La Farge and I occupy a baby-house, of four rooms. We sleep in the two upper rooms, which are open to the air, when we do not draw our paper windows together. Our next neighbors are Sturgis Bigelow, and Mr and Mrs Fenollosa, who live in a more imposing Japanese house below us. All of us being more or less in the same line of tastes and feelings, we have a sort of common establishment which is controlled by Mrs Fenollosa.

My life here is not very different from what it might be at the Baths of Lucca or at Thun. Pretty mountains, clothed with dense woods and tangled vegetation, surround us, and, curiously enough, are wilder than European mountains, for the Japanese live only in the low country, and leave these superb mountain flanks to monkeys, deer and Americans,—or

English, as the case may be. I have nothing to occupy me; but still time seems to fly faster than is quite convenient. Now and then, early in the morning, I start off with a boy carrying Sturgis Bigelow's camera, and I photograph a temple or some accident that interests me; but the great consumers of time are the bric-a-brac dealers who bring huge cases from Tokio or even from Ozaka, and consume day after day in opening and displaying stuffs, lacquers, metal-work, books, pictures, crystals and all the curios of Japan. I buy pretty nearly everything that is considered good by Bigelow and the Fenollosas; but as yet I have seen nothing that seemed necessary to my existence, and my purchases are mostly for commissions or presents.

Of the Japanese I see only those who are about us here, mostly friends of Bigelow and Fenollosa. They are a curious people. I should think them a very fair counterpart of the ancient Egyptians. They are not so quick as I expected, and have nothing that suggests energy; but they are friendly as monkeys, and they laugh day and night, especially when they are serious. Their language is a bar to all real contact with them, and their abominable rice destroys all hope of living among them; but their little wooden houses are seemingly clean, and the country swarms with babies to an extent that leaves no doubt of their domesticity. They wear very little clothing, to be sure. In fact, many of them wear none. The children especially go stark naked. This lends only a slight interest to the landscape, for I see little to admire in their figures except their legs, which are extraordinarily powerful.

Here at Nikko we are among a simple mountain population which has little to show except its primitive habits. The great temples are the shows of Nikko; and these are wonderful works, chiefly, I think, for their novelty as landscape-architecture. If I could satisfy myself that one quite perfect line or conception existed in Japanese architecture I should be quite satisfied; but my conscience protests while my eyes admire; and the aggressive bad taste of a part, hurts the triumph of the whole. I can find little to photograph that wholly satisfies one's hunger for something neither gorgeous nor grotesque.

Yet the place is so well worth seeing that in many ways nothing in Europe rivals it. I should class it very high among the sights of the world. If architecture falls short of perfection, nature steps in to give the perfection wanted; and the result is something quite by itself. Sky, mountains, and trees are exquisite.

I am glad I came, though the country still keeps to me its first peculiar aspect of a toy-world, where all the picture-books and tea-cups of childhood are animated with a clever imitation of life. The imitation is not perfect. Especially the women are wooden, jerky, and mechanical; evident dolls badly constructed. The children are much better, and in a toy-shop would bring five dollars apiece, if in good repair.

The weather is the chief drawback to activity, for it is a perpetual exaggerated dog-day; lovely mornings; drenching rains in the afternoon; and moisture that recalls a hot-house. The slightest effort drenches one with perspiration, but on the whole I prefer the effort to the oppressiveness of quiet. The nights up here are cool, but at Tokio they are like the hottest nights at Washington.

We have had no adventures. So far as I can see, travelling here is much like ordinary travelling in Europe. I have had no chance to deliver Mr Kuki's letters of introduction, for the summer disperses society here, as it does with us. Anyway I should only have had various dinners, with European forms, to decline. Official society has no charm. Japanese modes of life are by no means suited to us. Even the foreign residents here, like the Fenollosas, who go freely into society, have little to tell of it except its forms. I dislike sitting on my heels, which causes me extreme anguish; I cannot gracefully touch the ground with my forehead, or suck my breath; or follow the formalities of the *Cha-no-yu,* or five-oclock tea, which is the only serious labor of Japanese life. Even the theatre, after a few hours of sitting cross-legged, seems to me a pleasure not to be lightly challenged. I prefer my country walks; my wayside shrines; and the cottages of the poor, which I need not enter.

La Farge is trying hard to paint and sketch, but thus far with little result except the taking or buying of countless photographs. He is a charming companion, with oddities enough to be a constant amusement, and humor that never fails to make us gay even in our worst sufferings. Whether seasick, or choleraic, he is always on the level of the occasion. Bigelow is an angel of good-humor and unselfishness. If I am not seeing much of Japan, I am at least seeing it pleasantly.

We sail either September 23 or October 3. As soon as the weather grows cooler we must go down to the inland sea, and visit Kioto. That done, we pack up, and launch.

My best love to Mrs Field. Please let her consider whether she likes best a choice of lacquer, stuffs, metal work, or paintings.

Ever truly Yrs   Henry Adams.

MS: MH
1. In the Berkshire Hills of Massachusetts.

To Theodore F. Dwight

Nikko. 10 August, 1886.

Dear Dwight

I enclose you a letter which I wish you would forward to John Field. Human life being what it is, I prefer to avoid the chance of my letter finding no address.

Nothing new has happened here since my last; but the weather gets hotter and hotter, or at least more doggy, and we are already talking of putting off our departure till October 3 in order to get ten days chance for cooler travelling. La Farge wants to sketch. I am lazy. The Fenollosas talk of sailing on the same steamer. In short, everything unites to delay us.

Japan has the single advantage of being a lazy place. One feels no impulse to exert oneself; and Buddhist contemplation of the infinite seems the only natural mode of life. Energy is a dream of raw youth.

In case you are curious to know the objective conditions of my Buddhism, so that you may recognise them in your next incarnation, I inclose a photograph of the view westward from our balcony, looking up the valley.

Some seven miles up, and five thousand feet above sea-level, is a pretty lake, buried among green mountains and untouched forests, as wild as any in the Sierras. In an access of absurd vivacity I mounted a wooden framework called here a *mma*, or horse; but as little like a Christian horse as our favorite monkey, So-sen, is to Possum. Along with a swarm of pilgrims, clothed in white, with round straw hats, I wandered up to the lake, and swam in its waters. I did not climb the sacred mountain, Nantaizan, as they did; but I eat soup with chop-sticks, which I thought more difficult. With this exception I have made no serious effort of late, except to lunch of Sunday with the British minister and his wife, who are old acquaintances. This is my only social experiment, if I except a visit this moment from my landlord, the high-priest, Suzuki, of Iye-Mitsu's temple, who has been sitting on the floor, looking at my picture-books, but unable to make me understand a word he said. The high priests seem to be the only Japanese of any position hereabouts, and they are not stately figures, but dirty and doubtful.

I think as little as I can about America and my affairs and friends. If the thing sinks and disappears, I shall sail over it, and learn the fact. But from time to time I do feel some anxiety to know how you get on.

Ever truly Yrs   Henry Adams.

MS: MHi

To Elizabeth Cameron

Nikko. 13 August. 1886.

My dear Mrs Cameron

Thanks for your kind little note which Dwight forwarded, and which gave me real pleasure in my Japanese retreat. In return, I can only tell you that Japan is a long way from America, but that it is not far enough to prevent my thinking too much about home matters. I have heard but once from there, since I sailed, and luckily all my news was pleasant. In six weeks more I shall be starting for home. Shall I bring you an embroidered *kimono* for a dressing-gown, or would you rather have a piece of lacquer? or a sword?

La Farge and I have found shelter in the mountains from the heat and hotels of Japan. We have a little box of a Japanese house, where we look out on a Japanese temple-garden, and on Japanese mountains, all like the pictures that one sees on plates. We are princely in our style. The dealers in *curios* send us, from far and wide, whatever they can find that we like, and our rooms are full of such rubbish. La Farge sketches. I waste time as I can, sometimes walking, or going over the hills on rats of pack-horses; sometimes photographing in the temple-grounds; sometimes sitting cross-legged, and looking at bales of stuffs or lacquers; sometimes at tea-houses, watching the sun when it kindly sets behind the big mountain Nan-tai-zan, and leaves us in a less perspiring condition than we are by day. The scenery is very pretty; not unlike that of the Virginia springs; and the temperature much the same though very moist. Of interesting people I see nothing. I doubt whether there are any such. The Japanese women seem to me impossible. After careful inquiry I can hear of no specimen of your sex, in any class of society, whom I ought to look upon as other than a *curio*. They are all badly made, awkward in movement, and suggestive of monkeys. The children are rather pretty and quite amusing, but the mammas are the reverse; and one is well able to judge at least the types of popular beauty, seeing that there is little clothing to hide it, and that little is apt to be forgotten.

This branch of my historical inquiries has not proved rich; but, though the people are not a success in regard to personal attractions, they are very amusing indeed, and have given us infinite varieties of laughter ever since we saw our first fishing-boat. I do not advise you to come to Japan for comforts, and if you do come, I advise you to allow yourself three months leisure in order to get used to various pervasive smells, and to forget all your previous education in the matter of food, houses, drains and vehicles. If you can live on boiled rice or stewed eels, or bad, oily, fresh tea; or in houses without partitions or walls except of paper; or in cities absolutely undrained, and with only surface wells for drinking water; or if you can sit on your heels all through five hours at the theatre, and can touch the floor with your forehead when I call upon you; and say *Hei* and *Ha*[1] at stated intervals, you will do very well in Japan. I do all these things with less success than is to be desired, for I cannot sit on my heels at all, and I suffer to the extent of anguish even in sitting cross-legged; Japanese food makes me sea-sick, and the smell of Tokio seems to get into food, drink, and dreams; but I have not yet had my three months education, and have even evaded it by flying to the mountains and by getting myself fed and protected after the American manner. After ten days of modified Japanese experiments I was content with what I had learned. Nothing but necessity would induce me to try another Japanese article of food or to pass another night in a Japanese inn, for the first experiment proved nearly fatal; and although I did not fear death, I shrank from dying of Japanese soup in a Japanese inn, with Japanese women to look at as my last association with earth. This weakness on my part shows the sad effects of too long life. One ought to enjoy poisonous mushrooms fried in bad oil, and to delight in looking at wooden women without any figures, waddling on wooden pattens.

Our faculty for laughing has been greatly increased, but we try in vain to acquire the courteous language of the country. No European can learn to track out the intricate holes and burrows in which Japanese courtesy hides itself. I wish I could master, in order to teach you, the ceremony of the *Ocha-no-yu,* or honorable five-o'clock tea. I declined to buy a book which contained paintings showing fifty arrangements of the charcoal to boil the kettle on this occasion; and as many more of the ways in which a single flower might be set in a porcelain stand. My friend Bigelow bought the pictures and is professor of the art. Simpler tasks satisfy me. Seeing the woman, who had charge of our horses, eating hard green plums, I requested Bigelow to tell her with my compliments that she would suffer from stomach-ache. Her reply, profoundly serious, was to the effect that my remark had truth; her stomach did respectfully ache. I learned much from this attitude of respect which even the digestive apparatus of a Japanese peasant-woman assumes towards a stranger.

I have bought *curios* enough to fill a house, but nothing that I like, or want for myself. The stuffs are cheap and beautiful, but I have found no really fine embroidery. The lacquer is relatively cheap, but I do not care for it. I can find no good porcelain or bronze, and very few wall-pictures. Metal work is easy to get, and very choice, but what can one do with sword-guards and knife-handles?[2] I am puzzled to know what to bring home to please myself. If I knew what would please you, I would load the steamer with it.

I enclose a photograph of our garden-waterfall. It splashes a great deal, with very little water.

Remember me to Mr Cameron and believe me very truly

Henry Adams.

MS: MHi
1. Both words meaning "Yes, indeed" or "Well, I see."
2. La Farge considered "the little piece of Japanese metal-work—for instance, the sword-guard or the knife-handle—an epitome of art, certainly a greater work of art than any modern cathedral" (*An Artist's Letters from Japan* [1897], p. 140).

To John Hay

Nikko. 22 August, 1886.

My son John

I have still to report that purchases for you are going on, but more and more slowly, for I believe we have burst up all the pawnbrokers' shops in Japan. Even the cholera has shaken out little that is worth getting. Bigelow and Fenollosa cling like misers to their miserable hoards. Not a kakimono is to be found, though plenty are brought. Every day new bales of rubbish come up from Tokio or elsewhere; mounds of books; tons of bad bronze; holocausts of lacquer; I buy literally everything that is merely possible; and yet I have got not a hundred dollars' worth of things I want for myself. You shall have some good small bits of lacquer, and any quantity of *duds* to encumber your tables and mantles; but nothing creditable to our joint genius. As for myself, I have only one *Yokomono,*—or kakimono broader than it is long,—and one small bronze, that I care to keep as the fruit of my summer's perspiration.

For Japan is the place to perspire. No one knows an ideal dogday who has not tried Japan in August. From noon to five o'clock I wilt. As for travelling, I would see the rice-fields dry first. I have often wondered what King would have done, had he come with us. I've no doubt he would have seen wonderful sights, but I should have paid his return passage on a corpse. For days together I make no attempt at an effort, while poor La Farge sketches madly and aimlessly.

By the bye, a curious coincidence happened. Bigelow announced one morning that King and Hay were coming from Tokio with loads of curios for us. La Farge and I stared and inquired. Then it appeared that Bigelow and Fenollosa employ two men—Kin, pronounced King,—and Hei,—pronounced Hay,—to hunt curios for them, and had sent them word to bring up whatever they could find. I thought this one of the happiest accidents I ever heard, and I only wish that Messrs King and Hay had brought better things, as their American namesakes expected. They meant well, but they lacked means. Nevertheless they brought a few nice bits, to sustain the credit of their names.

Fairly bored by sweltering in this moistness, I stirred up Mrs Fenollosa to a little expedition last Tuesday. Fenollosa is unwell; La Farge is hard at work; but Mrs Fenollosa, Bigelow, and I, started to visit Yumoto, the Saratoga, or White Sulphur, of Japan. Yumoto lies just fourteen miles above us among the mountains, and with one of my saddle-horses I could easily go there and return on the same day; but such a journey in Japan is serious. Only pedestrians, coolies, or Englishmen, work hard. Mrs Fenollosa summoned five packhorses. All Japanese horses known to me are rats, and resemble their pictures, which I had supposed to be bad drawing; but these packhorses are rats led by a man, or more often by a woman, at a very slow walk. Mrs Fenollosa mounted one; Bigelow another; I ascended a third; a servant and baggage followed on a fourth; the fifth carried beds, blankets, linen, silver, eatables, and drinks. At half past eight the caravan started, and at half past ten it arrived at the foot of Chiu-zen-ji pass, where one climbs a more or less perpendicular mountain side for an hour. I preferred my own legs to the rat's, and walked up. So we arrived at Lake Chiu-zen-ji, a pretty sheet of water about seven miles long, at the foot of the sacred mountain Nan-tai-zan. On the shore of this lake is a temple, where pilgrims begin the ascent of the mountain, sacred to Sho-do Sho-nin, who devoted fifteen years of his valuable existence, in the 8th century, to the astounding

"Somentaki. My favorite deserted temple buried in forests and unworried by tourists. I photographed it for the little gate, and the bamboos. Nikko. Aug. 1886."

At Mount Vernon, October 24, 1887
Left to right: William C. Endicott, Mrs. Endicott, Lady Herschell, Lord
Herschell, Mary C. Endicott, Nannie Macomb, Mrs. Wright, Henry
Adams; seated: William C. Endicott, Jr., Cecil Spring Rice

feat of climbing it.[1] As it is very accessible, and only 8000 feet above the sea, Sho-do Sho-nin is a very popular and greatly admired saint, and some five thousand pilgrims come every August to follow his sainted steps. Next the temple are some inns, but not a farm or a human dwelling exists on the lake or among the mountains; for if the Japanese like one thing more than another it is filthy rice-fields, and if they care less for one thing than another, it is mountains. All this lovely country, from here to the sea of Japan, is practically a dense wilderness of monkeys, as naked as itself; but the monkeys never seem out of place as a variety, though I have not met them in society, and speak only from association. We stopped at an inn, and while lunch was making ready, Bigelow and I went out in a kind of frigate for a swim in the lake. After lunch, sending our beasts ahead, we sailed to the next starting-point, just the length of a cigar. Another two miles of rise brought us to a moor for all the world like Estes Park and the Rocky Mountains. Crossing this, we climbed another ascent, and came out on an exquisite little green lake with woody mountains reflected on its waters. Nothing could be prettier than the path along this shore, but it was not half so amusing to me as our entrance into the village of Yumoto, with its dozen inns and no villagers; for, by the roadside, at the very entrance, I saw at last the true Japan of my dreams, and broke out into carols of joy. In a wooden hut, open to all the winds, and public as the road, men, women and children, naked as the mother that bore them, were sitting, standing, soaking and drying themselves, as their ancestors had done a thousand years ago.

I had begun to fear that Japan was spoiled by Europe. At Tokio even the coolies wear something resembling a garment, and the sexes are obliged to bathe apart. As I came into the country I noticed first that the children went naked; that the men wore only a breech-clout; and that the women were apt to be stripped to the waist; but I had begun to disbelieve that this disregard of appearances went further. I was wrong. No sooner had we dismounted than we hurried off to visit the baths; and Mrs Fenollosa will bear me witness that for ten minutes we stood at the entrance of the largest bath-house, and looked at a dozen people of all ages, sexes and varieties of ugliness, who paid not the smallest regard to our presence. I should except one pretty girl of sixteen, with quite a round figure and white skin. I did notice that for the most part, while drying herself, she stood with her back to us.

When this exceptionally pleasing virgin walked away, I took no further interest in the proceedings, though I still regard them as primitive. Of the habits and manners of the Japanese in regard to the sexes, I see little, for I cannot conquer a feeling that Japs are monkeys, and the women very badly made monkeys; but from Mrs Fenollosa and other ladies, I hear much on the subject, and what I hear is very far from appetising. In such an atmosphere one talks freely. I was a bit aghast when one young woman called my attention to a temple as a remains of phallic worship; but what can one do? Phallic worship is as universal here as that of trees, stones and the sun. I come across shrines of phallic symbols in my walks, as though I were an ancient Greek. One cannot quite ignore the foundations of society.

23 August. My poor boy, how very strong you do draw your vintage for my melancholy little Esther. Your letter of July 18 has just reached me, and I hardly knew what I was reading about. Perhaps I made a mistake even to tell King about it; but having told him, I could not leave you out. Now, let it die! To admit the public to it would be almost unendurable to me. I will not pretend that the book is not precious to me, but its value has nothing to do with the public who could never understand that such a book might be written in one's heart's blood. Do not even imagine that I scorn the public, as you say. Twenty years ago, I was hungry for applause. Ten years ago, I would have been glad to please it. Today, and for more than a year past, I have been and am living with not a thought but from minute to minute; and the public is as far away from me as is the celebrated Kung-fu-tse, who once said something on the subject which I forget, but which had probably a meaning to him, as my observation has to me.[2] Yet I do feel pleased that the book has found one friend.

25 August. I can't say, "let's return to our sheep," for there are no sheep in Japan, and I have eaten nothing but bad beef since landing.[3] As for returning to my remarks on Yumoto as connected with the sexes, I decline to do it. In spite of King, I affirm that sex does not exist in Japan, except as a scientific classification. I would not affirm that there are no exceptions to my law; but the law itself I affirm as the foundation of archaic society. Sex begins with the Aryan race. I have seen a Japanese beauty, which has a husband, *Nabeshame,* if I hear right,—a live Japanese Marquis, late Daimio of Hizo, or some other place; but though he owns potteries, he has, I am sure, no more successful bit of bric-a-brac than his wife is;—but as for being a woman, she is hardly the best Satsuma.[4]

You did not say whether you liked porcelain. I have met only a few little bits, not better than you see in New York everywhere; and not cheap. I have bought one or two on the chance you might fancy variety, but they are not very amusing.

28 August. We go down to Yokohama tomorrow. A week from today we sail for Kobe, Ozaka and Kioto. At Ozaka I shall find your gong. We return to Yokohama, Sept. 23, to sail on the City of Peking for San Francisco on October 2. I should be in Washington, October 25.

Best love to all yours. Mrs Don's letter has rather upset me; but I wrote to her before receiving it.[5]

Ever Yrs   Henry Adams

Yokohama. 31 August. Having today completed purchases of curios to the amount of about $2,500 dollars, I have drawn out your letter of credit. This pleasing news I hasten to communicate, for fear of receiving or inflicting a shock in the future. I can't say when the articles will reach America, as most of them will go by Suez to New York. Some time next spring you will perhaps hear that they have arrived somewhere.

It is hotter than blazes here, but we are supposing ourselves to go to Kobe on Sunday next per Messageries steamer "Volga."

Ever Yrs   H.A.

MS: MHi
1. Shōdō-Shonin, the Buddhist monk who built the first shrine at Nikko in 766, was said to have founded the shrine at Lake Chiuzenji in 816.
2. Kung-fu-tse, original form of the latinized "Confucius."
3. The French saying "Revenons à nos moutons," from an anecdote about sheep-stealing, in which a digressive lawyer is repeatedly prompted by the judge to return to the subject of the sheep.
4. Nabeshima Noahiro (1846–1921), English-educated lord of the Hizen clan, minister to Italy 1880, member of Senate 1882.
5. Mrs. Cameron in a July 15 letter to Mrs. Hay (enclosed in Hay's letter to HA, July 18) wrote that they had wanted to call their baby, born June 25, Marian, "but Mr. Adams was so far away there was no means of knowing whether he would like it or not, and I dared not give her the name without his permission. So Mr. Cameron, to gratify his father, gave her the old-fashioned name of his grandmother—Martha Cameron—which I like very well, but which has no association as the other would have had."

To Theodore F. Dwight

Yokohama. 31 August. 1886.

My dear Dwight

Your letter of July 23, which arrived a week ago, was very grateful to me except as to your health. I shall have to take you in hand on my return.

La Farge and I have got along well, so far. We came down from Nikko two days ago. Yokohama is hot and uncomfortable, but very pretty, with Fuji behind us, and the great bay in front. We expect to sail for Kobe next Sunday, and to have three weeks of hard travel. The weather is still broiling.

We have changed our passages to the City of Peking on October 2. If all goes according to programme, I should reach Washington before November 1. Please inspire some beneficent female to inquire about a cook for us. You know about what we want. Mrs Sims has not head enough. Perhaps Miss Dodge would consent to help you, or Miss Markoe might aid. The cook must be colored, or willing to live with colored servants.

The Fenollosas sail in the same steamer. Mrs Fenollosa will probably bring her Chinese nurse. As Fenollosa is a Japanese official, travelling under Japanese orders and credentials, he ought to have no trouble at the Custom House with his Chinese servant; but to prevent all possible objection it would be well to get the Treasury to notify the Collector that Fenollosa's nurse is not to be bothered.[1] Mrs Fenollosa is, I think, a cousin of the

Endicott's. I advised her to write to the Secretary of War about it. Anyway, if you can manage to fix the matter securely, I should be glad. The San Francisco custom-house is so great a terror to everybody, that with one accord all my acquaintances, *official* and private, advise me to keep clear of it, and send all merchandise by Suez to New York. You can judge for yourself how troublesome this must be. As for me, I have some tons of curios, and between the high rates of the Pacific Mail, and the severity of the San Francisco custom-house, I am forced to send most of my things by a tramp-steamer round to New York.

The cholera has bothered us by disorganising the workmen who ought to have made my reflectors. I have only today received the first pair, and the rest are not yet begun. Otherwise, although the cholera is active all about, we have paid no attention to it. If it catches us, it will kill us, for it is virulent; but as I don't care, and La Farge seems not nervous, we go ahead like the thirty million people who are in the same situation. About thirteen deaths yesterday here and a hundred and fifty or two hundred at Tokio. At Kobe and Ozaka there is plenty of it. At Kioto, not more than here. By the time this reaches you, we shall be either dead or clear.

I have bought about 2000 dollars worth of curios, half for Hay. Would Miss Dodge prefer an embroidered kimono for a dressing-gown, or a piece of lacquer?

Ever Yrs   Henry Adams.

MS: MHi
1. Fenollosa was commissioned by the Japanese government to study American and European methods of art education. HA wished to avert an embarrassing enforcement of the Chinese Exclusion Act (1882).

To John Hay

Kioto. 9 Sept. 1886.

My son John

Kioto at last! La Farge and I made an impressive entry at nine o'clock last night, with our suite, by moonlight; and this morning—at half past six o'clock,—we are sitting on our verandah, looking out over the big city, he sketching, and both of us incessantly wishing that you and King were with us, for there is no kind of doubt that Japan is *omoshiroi,* a word we pronounce *amushroi,* which means amusing, and is always in use. Kioto is *omoshiroi* as we look over it; a sort of Japanese Grenada. For two months we have heard and talked of nothing but Kioto, and here we are! Think of it, dissolute man! It is like being in the new Jerusalem with a special variety of Jews. You see at once why La Farge and I are up and active at six A.M.

Before recovering from this active state, I proceed to business, to which our last two days have been devoted. I may have mentioned that the great *curio* dealer of Japan is at Osaka. His name is Yamanaka, and has some philological or other relation with *Jammer* (German) and *nigger,* (Amer. vulg.). La Farge and I, after six days of boiled and furious activity at Yokohama, trying to get things done, which is something the Japanese never do, gave it up; but I would have given you a present if you could have seen us on our expedition last Friday to what the old books called the *Dye boots.*[1] This remnant of the vanished splendor of Kamakura is about twenty miles from Yokohama, and, next to Kioto and Narra, we have damned it persistently for two months because of the heat. I bought—for you or others— various specimens of so-called Kamakura lacquer, the only instance in human history where *nacre* has been used with success; and every time I saw the stuff, I cursed it because I had not had energy to see the Dai Butsu. Last Friday we saw it, and as La Farge says it is the most successful colossal figure in the world, he sketched it, and I, seizing the little priest's camera, mounted to the roof of his porch, and, standing on my head at an angle of impossibility, perpetrated a number of libels on Buddha and Buddhism, without shame at the mild contempt of his blessed little moustache, which is ächt Japanesisch of today. This is not my story. I mention it in passing Kamakura, for we saw no more of the city which is no longer existing or visible; but having lunched at a tea-house, and watched a heavy shower make the roads hopeless, we were persuaded by the *Ho*—Howo, Japanese phoenix, an acute disease known as a travelling servant whose death in torture is a matter only of hours,—to return by way of the beach of Enoshima. Although we knew that all view of Fuji,—the only object of such a trip— was hopeless, we let ourselves in for what proved to be an hour's walk over a soft sand-beach in a steam-bath. In half the distance La Farge fell into his jinrickshaw exhausted, and I tumbled into the Pacific ocean and swam or waded to the next village. When I tried to come out of the water, the surf covered me with black sand; my clothes were so wet that I could not get them on, and my boots were full of water. So I put on my coat, tied a yellow oil-paper rain-cover round my waist, and seating myself in my kuruma, stuck my naked legs over the footboard, and was whirled through the village like a wild Indian.[2] The curious part of the matter was that in a mile of transit to the nearest tea-house, not even a child raised an eyelid of surprise, whereas La Farge who followed later, in complete European costume, was received with enthusiasm. Evidently my out-fit is the one expected from Americans in this country. We drove back to Yokohama afterwards in the dark, and I could not wonder at the calmness with which my legs had been received. As we drove through mile after mile of village without front walls, every house offered a dimly lighted study of legs in every attitude. My eyes still whirl with the wild succession of men's legs, and of women's breasts, in every stage of development and decomposition, which danced through that obscurity.

On Sunday we took a French steamer for Kobe. Of course we were seasick. We are always sea-sick on the Pacific because King said it was always smooth with a long swell, whereas it is always rough, with a short, choppy sea, straight up and down. I was acutely miserable for twenty-four hours, and this means thousands of years. The inland sea was better, but much like other seas. At Kobe we began to pick up. Kobe is only the European settlement for Osaka and Kioto; a kind of waiting-room to Yamanaka's, towards whose shop I am leading you.

Seven hours were devoted to Yamanaka on Monday; seven more yesterday. The total result is that he has nothing good. I bought or ordered six or seven hundred dollars worth of things, and not one which I thought creditable to me. Bigelow said that your gong must sound for two minutes after being struck, and must have a clear, pure, melodious ring. I found only one that met the requirement; and none of the usual chinese gongs begin to approach it. You are the possessor of a bell-gong on a stand; total cost, twelve yen, say ten dollars. I hope you will like it. We rather did. Indeed I saw nothing else I liked, except two large six-leaved screens, painted by Chinnan-pin, a Chinese artist who came to Japan about 1680.[3] Deer covered the six leaves of one; storks, the other. Price 1500 yen. As I could not afford this amount without drawing on you, I bought two pairs, equally large, but less expensive. These cost 80 yen for the whole twenty-four panels. One is birds; one fishes. I thought you might fancy one pair, so I bought two to select. Not a kakimono did we find, though we were shown them till we fairly kakimoaned. Only one lesson was impressed more deeply than ever on my heart; which was that, if I want good things, I must buy Chinese. In porcelain there is no comparison; in embroidery, none; in kakimonos, not much. The best Chinese is always out of sight ahead, as in cloisonné, and, I think, even in bronze, though bronze is *the* Japanese metal. Only in gold lacquer and small metal work, like sword-guards, or perhaps small ivories, like netsukes, where Japanese humor and lightness have the field to themselves, the Japanese excel.[4] They are quite aware of their own inferiority, and the prices they pay for good Chinese or Corean work are out of all proportion to their own.

The prices are not what stagger me, at least in most cases. I have not found the best work to be more costly than the second-best. Indeed, the best things I have got were positively cheap. My trouble is in the temptation to buy masses of indifferent work, which is the best I can get. Tons of porcelain, pottery and bronze will go home, which I have bought only in the hope of bringing out one good bit. Freight and duties will double the cost; and I shall want not one in ten of them at any price. None of the things are large. Except for temples or gardens the Japs make few large things for themselves. Their small houses and low rooms are not suited to big ornament. Everything you see of that sort, especially tall bronzes, porcelains and lacquers, unless it comes from temples or gardens, is made for export and is not true Japanese. Things like *Inros;* lacquer boxes a few inches long; *netsukes* of ivory or wood; *fukusas,* or embroidered and woven stuffs like my eagle-and-ocean screen; swords; small kakimonos; tea-jars from two to twelve inches high; flower vases, porcelain or bronze, from two inches to eighteen in height; in short, anything that will go on a table, or is easily handled, is Japanese domestic decoration. The big vases, especially the big grotesque bird-flower-and-dragon vases, are *never* seen out of the shops in Yokohama. No Japanese ever dreamed of such decoration, except perhaps for a temple or some public-place. All his best, choicest and Japasneeziest work is in little things to be worn, or to be shown to guests at his Cha-no-yu, or Tea-party, in a bare little room, about ten feet square, with walls of Chinese simplicity; white plaster and wood unplaned.

This idea was new to me, and has altered my notions of what is good bric-à-brac. Except some porcelains and bronzes, which are coarse work, I have bought nothing of any size. On the other hand, I am driven mad by having to make lists of hundreds of small duds that go by scores into one's trouser-pockets. For you I have wanted to get large things to fit your scale, but except a pair of screens, I have found nothing. The large, old Kutani and Imari-jars are always broken, and the new are not good.[5] One large lacquer box you should have, to stand on a parlor table, and contain embroideries; I have seen such very good, old and decorative, but the one I wanted for you, though only my modest preference, is held at three thousand yen.

Sunday. 12 Sept. This travelling is taking hold of my system. We cannot stand the pace. At our age occasional repose is a benefit. La Farge and I have jounced in kurumas; rattled through temples; asked questions, and talked Japanese, or listened to it, till we cower in fear before every new suggestion. We are nauseated by curios; I detest temples; he is persecuted by letters of introduction, and I who have delivered only one of mine, pass all my time trying to escape hospitality. At last I understand the duties of life. Never be hospitable to a traveller. He is only happy in freedom. Damn him, and let him go.

One Japanese interior is highly amusing, but the joke is not rich enough for two. I find myself here with La Farge; T. Walsh, of Walsh, Hall &Co; two interpreters; a travelling servant; the Governor of Kioto's secretary; three Kioto merchants; and madness! The temples are ordered to produce their treasures for us; the houses drag out all their ancestral properties, and very curious they are; the artists in porcelain, the dealers in curios, and even the *schools,* we are expected to inspect as connoisseurs. Today we had three hours at the house of Kassiobawara San, an elderly merchant here, who happens to live in the oldest house in the city; then at noon we started in kurumas, with a stewing heat, for a river twelve miles off; then we shot what the *Ho* calls "rabbits" for an hour, in a boat; we got through the rapids only to jounce for another hour or two in kurumas back to Kioto, where two makers of porcelain and a big curio dealer were sitting at the door of my room, and a Japanese gentleman was waiting to call on La Farge. The Japanese gentleman sat till half past eleven, thereby driving us to wish ourselves in bed or somewhere.

All the same, since leaving Nikko, we have just piled in the impressions. If we do not soon become masters of the Japanese science, we shall at least learn something of our own to take its place. We will turn out a new Japan of our own. La Farge has bought materials enough,—vast mounds of rubbish—to construct a world of decoration, paint forests of pictures, and exhaust the windows of Christianity. I have learned so many new facts of which I am ignorant, that I could fill winter-evenings with my want of knowledge. The only branch we have not yet exhausted is that of the dances, and we intend to begin today on this sphere of usefulness. Geishas are ordered for this evening. If they please me as little as most of their Japanese sisters, I shall not want further acquaintance. I am in hot pursuit of the Butterfly Dance, and have started a chace through the temples in search of it. On the whole, Ozaka and Kioto pan out well.

Wednesday morning. 15 Sept. I close this despatch by reporting that we had our Geisha ball, in all the forms, last night. No words can give you an idea of the drollness. I am lost in astonishment at this flower of eastern culture. I cannot quite say that it is like an imaginary theatre in a nursery of seven-year-old girls, or that it is absolutely and disgustingly proper; because all my Japanese friends got drunk on saki; and some of the singing-women were highly trained; but for an exhibition of mechanical childishness I have seen nothing to equal it, except a Japanese garden, or a batch of Japanese wooden dolls. Absolutely the women's joints clacked audibly, and their voices were metallic.

I will tell you all about it when we meet; but La Farge is so much more amusing about it than I can be, that you had better wait till our book comes out, in which he will write the story, and I draw the pictures.[6]

Ever Yrs   Henry Adams.

16 Sept. A letter from King, ordering a Jap. house, has just arrived. Will nothing short of a house content him? Also one from Mrs Don in my own house, which pleased me much.[7]

MS: MHi
1. The Daibutsu, or Great Buddha, bronze statue over 40 feet high, cast in 1252.
2. *Kuruma:* colloquial name for jinrikisha.
3. Shên Nan-p'in, Chinese painter in Japan 1730–1732, not 1680.
4. *Netsuke:* a carved toggle on the sash from which the cords of inros and pouches are suspended.
5. Old Kutani, the original porcelain made in the late seventeenth century. Old Imari, wares made prior to 1868.
6. In dedicating *An Artist's Letters from Japan* to HA, La Farge wrote: "If anything worth repeating has been said by me in these letters, it has probably come from you, or has been suggested by being with you—perhaps even in the way of contradiction. . . . And you alone will know how much has been withheld that might have been indiscreetly said."
7. In an undated letter King had proposed that HA join with him and the Hays in colonizing Sunapee, New Hampshire. "To that end look over the Japan houses & pick a jewel of artistic design & find out what it could be duplicated for, shipped to Boston & put up." The Camerons were staying for the summer in HA's house at Beverly Farms.

To Theodore F. Dwight

Kioto. 16 Sept. 1886.

My dear Dwight

As I expect to be only ten days behind this letter, I shall cut it short, and only say that La Farge and I have pursued our journey successfully, and have had ten days of great amusement and hard work in this ancient capital of the Mikados. We have delivered at last one of Kuki's letters, and although the Governor of Kioto to whom it was addressed, is ill, and we have not seen him, a secretary was detailed to attend us, and we have had everything opened that is openable. We brought also private letters, and go about followed by a train: Ourselves; the Secretary; four Japanese friends; our interpreter, and our servant. The procession is imperial. We gave a ball, night before last, with dancing- and singing-girls. Our Japanese friends all got very drunk on saki, and the Secretary went to sleep in the middle of the room; but I suppose they thought themselves obliged to honor our hospitality in that way. I am far from admiring the Geishas, who were not even improper; but I was greatly entertained by our American legs, which tend to sprawl, in Japanese dress. This morning I have been down to Ozaka to settle up our account for *curios,* which amounts to about a thousand dollars for the last ten days. This afternoon we give another entertainment; the Butterfly dance; in an adjoining temple. Tomorrow we go to Nara, about thirty miles, in jinrickshas, to see the original capital of the empire. On Monday at latest, we start over-land for Yokohama, and home.

Kioto is a very pretty place indeed. I hardly know any inland city, except Grenada, so charmingly situated. The hotel is good, and overlooks the city and mountains, with the best chance for La Farge to sketch, but we have been too busy for much sketching. Very few foreigners are here, and none seem to be living here. We have it to ourselves, and circulate wholly among Japanese as an ornament to their city. Indeed we are fast becoming adopted citizens, and if I could only get to think the Japs real live people, and not dolls, or could tolerate the women, I should feel like one of them, and eat fish and soup with chopsticks.

As I make no progress in this direction, I am as ready to come home as I ever shall be; and if the City of Peking reaches San Francisco at all, you may assume that we are there. The idea of the voyage is a nightmare. We had another wretched experience of the Pacific ocean from Yokohama to Kobe, and I look forward to the worst of all for our homeward voyage.

I shall come directly to Washington to look after things there, and set the household going. In November I must go to Boston for a week. Although I have bought what seems to me an enormous mass of things, not more than a tenth part of them are intended for our own establishment. The rest are commissions or presents. Only half a dozen pieces of bronze, porcelain or kakimonos, are to adorn our charms.

8 P.M. Yours of July 24 and August 14 have just arrived. Many thanks for your care of Mrs Don. I am much pleased at her taking the house; and have a letter from her there, dated Aug. 16. La Farge and I have just returned from our Temple Dance, after a grand, imperial farewell to our Jap friends.

Ever Yrs   Henry Adams.

MS: MHi

To Theodore F. Dwight

Palace Hotel. S.F. 21 October, 1886.

My dear Dwight

We arrived yesterday morning at about three o'clock, and the first official who boarded us gladdened the very soul of Mrs Fenollosa by announcing that orders had been received from the Treasury to admit the Chinese nurse without question. She had been very anxious about it, with good reason; and I was extremely pleased to carry the point, as I am under uncomfortable obligations to her for hospitality and attentions. This balances the account, thanks to you.

My brother was here waiting our arrival, but the first news he had for me was that of Gurney's death, and this, of course, was a savage blow.[1] I had hoped to find him well.

I must go to Boston first to see Ellen Gurney and the children.[2] My brother is to take me round to Southern California and home by the Atlantic & Pacific. We expect to reach Boston in a fortnight. I shall stay a few days there, and then shall bring the dogs on to you.

I hope you will have found a cook. We shall also want a first-rate laundress. You know I was not satisfied with Beckley, and do not want to take her back. Please make inquiry, and even engage anyone who seems very satisfactory.

Probably two cases will arrive at the Georgetown custom-house for me, before my arrival. If the collector sends notice, please ask him to retain the cases till I arrive, and then let them be opened and appraised, or examined, at the house.

Your letters, received yesterday on board the "Peking" and at the hotel, were, as they always are, very welcome and interesting. I had also a long one from Ellen Gurney, and one from John Hay. My friends are certainly loyal. They give me no excuse for going back on myself. Sad as much of the news is, and indifferent as I am to most things that used to interest me, I can follow the procession as long as the rest stand by it; but the gaps are becoming fearful to think of.

Anyway, here we are again, after a long, and, at times, stormy voyage. I know not whether it was the phosphate, which I religiously took, or my greater habitude of seafaring, but I suffered less than usual from sickness, and was less eager to get ashore. The "Peking" was comfortable, and our party large. We were regular at our meals, and had plenty of room. I could sit in my cabin with the port open, except in very rough weather, and could smoke there. These were unaccustomed comforts at sea.

I hope to find you better for the cold weather, but shall try to take your health in hand. You must be made to become robust.

My love to everyone till I see them.

Ever Yrs   Henry Adams.

San Francisco has improved. We run down to Monterey this afternoon and return tomorrow to dine with Holden.[3] The Cliff House is seedy, but the seals still grunt.

MS: MHi
1. Gurney died of pernicious anemia Sept. 12.
2. The Gurneys were childless; the children were the Hooper nieces.
3. Edward S. Holden, president of the University of California 1885–1888, director of Lick Observatory 1888–1897.

To John Hay

Palace Hotel. San Frisco
21 October, 1886.

Dear Hay

Your letter arrived just as I did. We had a long voyage, a rather severe gale, obstinate and strong head-winds, and a ship in poor sailing order, but I was much more comfortable than usual, and not disposed to hurry. Certainly I should have been still more contented to remain out of the world, had I fully foreseen the gloomy news that waited for me. I must now go to Boston. My brother Charles, who has been here expecting our arrival, is going east by way of southern California. I go with him, expecting to reach Boston in about a fortnight, and Washington in another week or ten days; say the middle of November. By that time I hope to find you and Mrs Hay and the children established in permanence.

Then I will tell you the end of our Japanese travels, and our adventures in returning by land to Yokohama from Kioto. I am still in doubt whether you would have done well to go with us. La Farge is certainly the better for his journey, and bore the fatigue and exposure of the Tokaido quite as well as I did, though we had eleven consecutive days of the most difficult travelling I ever did, chiefly on account of weather. Perhaps the amusement kept him going; it certainly kept itself going to the last. I have never laughed more idiotically than from beginning to end of Japan; but I have learned something; and among the chunks of wisdom I have picked up is that which I have so persistently written to you; viz: there are no good curios for sale in Japan, and it is cheaper and quicker to buy them in New York or Paris. Another nugget of golden learning acquired by me, is the certainty that Japan and its art are only a sort of antechamber to China, and that China is the only mystery left to penetrate. I have henceforward a future. As soon as I can get rid of history and the present, I mean to start for China, and stay there. You will hear of me then only as of a false pig-tail pendant over eighteen colored suits of clothes; which, I am told, is the swell winter dress of a Chinese gentleman. In China I will find bronzes or break all the crockery. Five years hence, I expect to enter the celestial kingdom by that road, if not sooner by a shorter one, as seems more likely to judge from the ways of most of my acquaintances at home.

In two hours we start for Monterey, to return tomorrow. I wish you were with us. The weather is beautiful, and the air delicious. My love to Mrs Hay.

Ever Yrs   Henry Adams.

MS: RPB

To Charles W. Eliot

1603 H Street. Washington 13 November, 1886.

My dear Sir

Mrs Gurney asks me to advise and help her in deciding what shall be done in the way of a memorial for Gurney. Of course such a request cannot be declined, and even if I had no other relation to Gurney than that of scholar, I should feel bound to help in a matter so delicate and difficult, if help was asked. I have thought over the subject as carefully as I could and have given Mrs Gurney the following advice.

Gurney's life offers not enough material for a studied and formal biography. I cannot advise her to attempt it, nor to try for such an object.

In my opinion his life does afford material for a valuable and interesting sketch or series of sketches, in which his friends and associates could share. If they are willing to assist, I feel sure that a small work of much value could be made.

I propose to ask three or four of them to write each a short account of Gurney's share in the movements best known to them; and of course my first thought is of you, for such a sketch as I should ask you to do, would have a double value as regards the College and all the men who shared in your efforts. You are more interested than anyone else in having your ideas and objects correctly stated. In arranging Gurney's life in sections or chapters, the most serious section, you will quickly see, must be that which deals with the reforms effected in the College through what we may almost call the revolution of '68. Such a chapter must be written to explain what were the objects proposed, the difficulties in the way, and the share taken by the instructors in originating and carrying the reforms against these difficulties. I have no hesitation in advising Mrs Gurney to ask you to write such a sketch. You have the facts in your mind; you can tell the story with more authority than would be possible for any other man; you need not introduce your official action at all, if you object to it, for the story may stop with your election as President; and you can easily bring it within the scope of thirty moderate pages. As for time, a few hours will answer. A stenographer can come out, and take down from dictation whatever you like, which can be put in type and altered, arranged, enlarged or shortened at your leisure.

If you do this, I shall advise Mrs Gurney to ask either Prof. Peirce or Prof. Dunbar, or both, to carry on the story through the administrative period since 1868.

I hope that in this way the book may be what Gurney would have wished, a serious contribution to the history of the College, and a useful weapon for strengthening the reforms he had at heart; but the story, to be effective, must be told by the actors; it must in a sense have the interest of autobiography; the only interest that lasts forever, and holds its own in history. I am willing to do the work of editing, introducing, filling gaps, and furnishing material, if necessary, but I cannot do more; and I expect his associates to do for him what he would surely have done for them, as he showed in the case of Chauncey Wright.[1] They owe it to him, if not to themselves.

Upon your cooperation the whole plan must depend. No one busy man can be asked to do any large share of such a work. Several must divide the labor in order to make it easy to each. Your example would decide the result; without you, the book would carry less authority, and the other collaborators would be more hard to obtain, and would find their tasks more serious.

I need hardly add that my own effort is perhaps the greatest of all. To break through a long paralysis of thought and interest is far more difficult than to divert an energy. I am willing to do what I can; but I cannot do it alone, even for Mrs Gurney's sake.[2]

Ever very truly Yrs   Henry Adams

Pres. C. W. Eliot.

MS: MH-Ar

1. Ephraim Whitman Gurney contributed a commemorative sketch of Wright to the privately printed *Letters of Chauncey Wright* (1878).
2. Nothing came of HA's proposal.

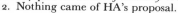

To Elizabeth Cameron

1603 H Street.
Friday morning. [19 Nov. 1886]

My dear Mrs Cameron

Your note reached me as I was going to dine with the venerable historian at six o'clock. After dinner I called again to see you, but once more failed.

Your invitation is seductive to a cookless wanderer on what Mr Longfellow was pleased to call life's solemn main, meaning probably that the voyage was always serious when the wanderer was unfed.[1] My trouble, however, is not so much one of food as of a sentimental wish to see you again, and hear of your welfare, you being more or less the only friend whose meeting I have not dreaded for fear of hearing ill tidings. I hope my harvest of thorns is now gathered in,[2] and I can enjoy the few flowers there are.

I—or we, if you prefer it—should of course delight in taking you—and your cuisine—at your word to its full extent; but if we did, we should never get a cook; the inducements to delay would be irresistible, and Dwight would see untold blemishes in every new candidate. On the other hand, we—or I—or he—are, am or is delighted to accept any invitation you will send us. We will come to dinner, breakfast, tea, lunch or supper, either in the parlor or the nursery.

Therefore, if you will have me, him or us, to dinner today, or tomorrow, or any other day, you have only to ask Martha to stop and tell me so. This will give me the additional advantage of admiring the young person herself. I am equally obedient to a summons for any other meal, but cannot speak for Dwight who is absent.

Very seriously Yrs   Henry Adams.

MS: MHi
1. "A Psalm of Life" (1839).
2. "They have sown wheat, but shall reap thorns"; Jeremiah 12:13.

To Theodore F. Dwight

Union Club   Boston Wed. 24 Nov. 1886.

Dear Dwight

Thanks for your note of the 22d and for your many struggles with our household affairs.

I reached Boston at 10.30 Monday night without hitch. On the whole everything was as little painful as could be expected.[1] My various errands

will keep me here till Sunday, when¹ I shall bring Molly on with me.² We shall leave here on Sunday. I must stop a day in New York—perhaps two. You can expect us either Tuesday or Wednesday.

I hope Okakura is with you, but I have not been able to learn where he is.³

The cook is the main thing. If necessary we must get a temporary one from Mme Demonnet or somewhere.

                                        Ever Yrs   Henry Adams.

MS: MHi
1. CFA had died Nov. 21, aged 79. HA attended the funeral Nov. 23 at the First Church in Quincy and the interment at Mount Wollaston Cemetery.
2. Mary Ogden Adams, eldest of CFA2's five children, aged 19.
3. Okakura Kakuzo (1862–1913), art scholar who came abroad with Fenollosa on the Japanese government study mission. As curator of Oriental art at the Museum of Fine Arts, Boston, 1910–1913, he had charge of collections which he had helped form in the 1880s.

To Albert Bushnell Hart

                              1603 H Street. Washington. 3 Dec. 1886.

Dear Sir¹

I have to thank you for sending me the Outline of your historical course.²

I will not attempt to offer any opinion on so considerable an extension of the methods of teaching a subject which hardly admits of being satisfactorily taught. Probably Cambridge has long since forgotten my experiments and—as I judged them—failures, in the field you are toiling over. Every man must beat out his own path, and I wish the utmost success to yours; but above all I hope that you will discover and fix, what I tried and failed to do—some system of teaching history which should be equally suited to a fixed science and a course of *belles lettres*. Between the two conditions I found compromise impossible, and separate handling impracticable. In other words, I found that a system which taught history as a science, could not be satisfactorily combined with a system which taught history as a branch of *belles lettres* or popular knowledge. For six or seven years I tried experiment on experiment, hoping to satisfy myself by creating a sound historical method for the college, and I spent time, labor and money freely in the effort. I am glad to see you working so vigorously in the same direction; and I wish I could offer you help, but your only valuable help will be in your own energies and your scholars' qualities.

                         I am yours truly   Henry Adams.

A. B. Hart Esq.

MS: RPB
   1. Albert Bushnell Hart (1854–1943), historian at Harvard 1883–1926.
   2. The printed syllabus of Hart's course in American political and constitutional history (*Methods of Teaching History,* 2nd ed. 1885), which included recommended readings in HA's *Gallatin, Randolph,* and *New England Federalism.*

To Charles Milnes Gaskell

1603 H Street. 12 Dec. 1886.

Dear Carlo

Thanks for your letter of Nov. 26. My father's death came at last as quietly as his long decline had come gently. I had been back from Japan about a fortnight, and had at once gone on to see him. I thought him failing so slowly that he might well survive the winter; but he was liable at any moment to give out, and the end could not be far. My mother got over the last agitation fairly well. Her own health is so much broken that I am far from easy about her.

On landing at San Francisco I was received by the news of Gurney's death, which was a much more serious blow, because Gurney stood in the full centre of active interests. When I married in 1872, my wife's family consisted of seven person's, myself included. Only three of us are left, and if I survive either of the other two, I shall have to accept some pretty serious responsibilities and cares. As I am situated, no one could be much less fit for assuming charges which involve minors and women. Apart from this, Gurney was a person so necessary to the working of affairs about him that his place cannot be filled. His death paralyses us in many directions, and of course makes us anxious in others, especially about his wife. Three months have now passed; she has stood them unexpectedly well; but such a steady run of bad luck shakes one's nerves, and I feel no sort of confidence in anything. If the moon were to wander off to another planet, I should no longer be surprised.

My journey to Japan had at least the advantage of consuming five months, and of doing it in a very amusing way. I suppose I may call myself rather an old traveler; but I never made any journey half so entertaining. My sense of humor developed itself so rapidly that I was in a broad laugh from the time I landed at Yokohama, and can't help laughing whenever I think of the droll island and people. I took with me a well-known New York artist, John La Farge, an old acquaintance, and a very unusual man, who stands far away at the head of American art, but who interests me more as a companion than as a painter, for he kept me always amused and active. We were three months on shore, and became quite Japanned. If it were not that the country and people are now as familiar to everybody as though they were a part of Clapham, I should be half tempted to tell you something about them; but the traveler has at last learned his own rank in boredom, and has the sense to hold his tongue. The only practical result of the trip has been to make me earnest to close up everything here, finish history, cut society, foreswear strong drink and politics, and start in about three years for China, never to return. China is the great unknown country of the world. Sooner or later, if health holds out, I shall drift there; and once there, I shall not soon drift back. You may find me there with a false pig-tail, and a button on the top of my head as a mandarin of a new class.

The world here has become wholly uninteresting to me. I cannot pump up any enthusiasm about politics, poetry or science, and political economy is the worst bore yet invented. As for your English, or rather Irish, affairs, I have given up the effort to follow them. They are local to an extent inhuman to outsiders. I have had at times a vague notion of running over to see you, but I should be a true Rip Van Winkle, and a bore of the Noachian epoch. I know no one except your uncle Frank who would be my contemporary, and I enclose you a letter for him to tell him that I have read his book, and recognise him as my long-lost brother.[1] To get out of the world's stream seems to me easy enough, but to get back into it a pure impossibility. You would think me a miserable nuisance if I turned up, twenty-five years behind the age, wondering what you are talking about, and regarding all your society as insane. The fact is, I am going crab-wise, and shall soon get so far off that you wont be able to see me. I can't make out what anyone wants to quarrel about, for there seems to be nothing worth it.

For next summer I have unformed plans for the western mountains, but the Hays are going abroad again, and offer a temptation to go with them. If I can manage to worry out this winter here, I may feel energetic enough for a sea-voyage, but it is possible that, before spring, the instinct of restlessness may carry me to Mexico, and, once there, I may wander for months. On the other hand, if you will get up a war in Europe, I shall half fancy a distant sight of it.

I am trying to boil up my old interest in history enough to finish my book, but the fuel is getting scarce. I think the chances about even whether it will ever be published or not. Society is getting new tastes, and history of the old school has not many years to live. I am willing enough to write history for a new school; but new men will doubtless do it better, or at least make it more to the public taste.

Give my love to your wife and all the antediluvians.

Ever Yrs   Henry Adams.

MS: MHi
1. Sir Francis Doyle, *Reminiscences and Opinions* (1886).

To Thomas H. Dudley

1603 H Street. Washington. 15 Dec. 1886.

Dear Sir[1]

I am, unfortunately, too far from my father's papers to be able to prepare any sketch of his life. I could do this only at Boston or Quincy. Probably my brother Brooks, who was with my father at Geneva, could furnish the material most easily. His address is at 23 Court Street, Boston. Yet I doubt whether, for your purposes, the sketches printed in the Springfield Republican and Boston Advertiser, at his death, might not be more useful than anything we could furnish you. They gave, I presume, all the facts you would care to know. Of that period which you would naturally treat most fully, you are yourself perhaps better informed than any other living man. You are familiar with his official papers, and know why they were written, and whether or not they were useful to you. I should be very far from feeling inclined to substitute anything of mine in the place of criticism and appreciation so much more valuable. Indeed I could furnish only dates and facts, which have already been printed; the critical treatment would in any case have to come from some other source.

I trust that time has treated you gently; but it is, at best, not respectful.

I am very truly Yrs   Henry Adams.

Thomas H. Dudley Esq.

MS: CSmH
1. Thomas Haines Dudley, former consul at Liverpool, published his personal recollections of CFA's diplomacy in "Three Critical Periods in Our Diplomatic Relations with England During the Late War," *The Pennsylvania Magazine of History and Biography* 17 (1893), 34–54.

To John Quincy Adams

1603 H Street. 16 Dec. 1886.

Dear John

I return the papers in regard to the Church bequest. For God's sake let it be paid.[1]

Yrs ever   Henry Adams.

J. Q. Adams Esq.

MS: MHi
1. CFA's estate of $1,250,000 went to his family, except for $10,000 to the Adams Temple and School Fund, created by JA for the building of the Stone Temple (First Church) in Quincy and for educational purposes. JA and JQA and their wives were buried in the Stone Temple, and the Adams Academy opened in 1872.

To Charles W. Eliot

1603 H Street. 30 December, 1886.

My dear President

Your letter of Dec. 27 I have kept one day unanswered. Knowing that you are soon to sail for Europe, I am unwilling to keep it longer.

I am more sorry than I can tell you to be obliged to decline the very flattering invitation your letter conveys. I will not trouble you with my reasons, which are without interest from the moment they become absolute; indeed I think there is a certain impertinence in offering reasons at all. If I could come back, I would do so with the greatest pleasure. I cannot; but I regret it with all my heart, and I know of no position, professional or political, which I should have regarded as more dignified or more useful than that of McLean Professor.

Please convey my thanks to the President and Fellows; and express my warm sense of the kindness and compliment which I am obliged to decline.

With my best wishes for the success of your holiday I remain

Very sincerely Yrs   Henry Adams.

Pres. C. W. Eliot.

MS: MH-Ar

To James Russell Soley

[1887]

Dear Soley[1]

Do you think you could find out for me whether the archives of the War Department still contain the correspondence between Secretary Eustis and William Henry Harrison, Governor of Indiana, during the year 1811, on the world-renowned campaign of Tippecanoe?

I want copies if the originals exist.

Yrs truly   Henry Adams.

J. R. Soley Esq.

MS: MSaE

1. James Russell Soley (1850–1911), professor of history and law at the U.S. Naval Academy 1872–1882, Navy Department librarian and supervisor of naval war records 1882–1890.

To Sir Robert Cunliffe

1603 H Street. 17 January, 1887.

Dear Robert

You are a good boy to write me such long and pleasant stories.

I have nothing to tell you in return. Our public affairs are very dull. My private affairs are still duller. I have not yet recovered interest in the world's doings, but am willing to hope that I shall, although the world seems to understand itself as little as I understand it, and, except for a few discontented people or classes, seems to blunder on with no distinct idea where it wants to come out. Your politics are a specimen. Europe altogether is a specimen still more to the point. As for America, so far as I can see, no one has any ideas at all except to feed, clothe and amuse oneself.

You know that I have for years looked on your political question as simply that of selecting between the democratic and the aristocratic standpoint. Sooner or later all of you will have to range yourselves on one side or the other, and the old Whigs must end by taking the conservative side at last. The present apparent impasse seems to me due only to the inevitable slowness of large bodies of men to shift their ground. You can hardly fail to act with the conservatives if only because you are within sight of your fifties. Men of fifty ought not, and generally are not able, to be revolutionists.

Old Tennyson is an instance. I cannot easily understand how an artist, as he was, can put himself in a frame of mind so artistically bad, as that of his last poem, or can consent to abandon that repose which he knows to be the highest art. Still, he has written an unmelodious shriek which, although it would be undignified even if the universe were shrivelling, contains passages equal in my opinion to his best, as far as energy of expression goes. I suspect some of these verses will live, in spite of the poem.[1]

Sir Francis's book gave me great amusement though it is disfigured by the same fault. Old men should know how to make their exit with grace and good-humor. If the world has treated them well, they owe it as much in return. I am far from denying that mankind is on the high-road to destruction, and I cannot understand how any churchman, with the Thirty-nine Articles in his teeth, can help asserting it; but I do not think that art or manners require us to fling the fact constantly in our neighbors' faces. We don't tell our invalid friends that they are going to die in tortures; we tell them pleasant anecdotes, and fairy-stories about King Arthur and Queen Guinivere.[2] The Carlisles and Ruskins are bores.

Heaven knows that I say this without meaning anything disrespectful to them. Their motives, apart from the egotism, are all that the Archbishop of Canterbury could wish; but either they are artists or they are not; and, if they claim to be artists, they ought to obey what they know to be fundamental laws of art.

Japan gave me so much to think about that I am eager to start again, not for Japan but for China. As it happens, I have several years of literary work to do before I can wholly close up and dismiss my past life, and set out, after the manner of Ulysses, in search of that new world which is the old.[3] Nothing whatever attaches me any longer to the spots I expected to die in. Neither public nor private relations detain or much concern me. To one who wants nothing, that he can conceive of as a part of his future life, the instinct of wandering is strong, and every day I pass at my desk is passed in the idea that it is so much out of my way. If I can get off, about the year '90, I may, with health and strength, wander ten years before being driven to cover by age; so you need not despair of hearing that I am a Mandarin or an Arab.

Hay and his family, my only stay, go to England in May. You will of course see them. His great work is done, and is now publishing. Very good it is.[4] I am not certain how long they will stay abroad; they say, only till autumn.

King is struggling with destiny in New York. I hope to see him in a few days.[5]

My mother, though old and broken, has got through the shock of my father's death as well as was rationally possible. The death was of course not a surprise, and was quiet and peaceful.

My love to all yours.   Ever truly   Henry Adams.

MS: MHi
1. The speaker in "Locksley Hall Sixty Years After" (1886) comments stridently on the shibboleths of progress, equality, and universal peace. Tennyson was 77.
2. The last of Tennyson's *Idylls of the King,* which had been appearing since 1859, came out in 1885.
3. " 'Tis not too late to seek a newer world"; "Ulysses."
4. Serial publication of *Abraham Lincoln: A History* began in the *Century* in November 1886.
5. At the annual meeting of the Anglo-Mexican Company, stockholders led by Agassiz forced King to resign the management of the Yedras mine.

To Houghton, Mifflin and Company

1603 H Street. 22 Jan. 1887.

Gentlemen

In further reply to your letter of 14 Jan., I beg to inform you that Mr Morse will receive every assistance that may be necessary to enable him to write the volume you suggest on the Life and Public Services of my father.[1]

On application to my brother, Mr J. Q. Adams, he will be able to make whatever arrangements may be needed.

I am very truly Yrs   Henry Adams.

Messrs Houghton, Mifflin & Co.

54

MS: RPB

1. The proposed biography for Morse's American Statesmen series finally appeared in 1900, written by CFA2.

To Harriet Taylor Upton

1603 H Street. 16 Feb. 1887.

Dear Madam[1]

The only person who can give you the information you want is Miss Elizabeth Adams, now in Florida, whose exact address I do not know, but can procure for you. Or I will forward any letter that you may send me for her.

So far as I know, the Adams boys were always very like other boys, and very certainly no better behaved. In the New England of that day, there was little divergence of condition, and not much of character.

I am truly Yrs   Henry Adams.

MS: RPB

1. Harriet Taylor Upton (1853–1945), journalist, was seeking information for her Children of the White House series, published in the Boston children's magazine *Wide Awake,* Feb. 1888 (JA) and Nov. 1888 (JQA), and as a book in 1892.

To Charles Francis Adams, Jr.

1603 H Street. 25 Feb. 1887.

Dear Charles

I have received the Town Records, and have devoted some hours of study to them.

The only evidence of Susanna Boylston's second marriage is on "Oct. 17, 1766, John Hall and Susanna Adams, both of this town." I suspect this to be our great-great-grandmother. Perhaps you can find some record of her death in 1797.

Can you explain to me on what principle our grandfather ("Life of John Adams," p. 7) gave the following dates as equivalents:[1]

17th day of	8th month	— 17 Oct.
2d " "	9th "	26 Nov.
5th " "	6th "	5 Aug.
23d " "	4th "	23 June
11th " "	9th "	11 Nov.
24th " "	10th "	24 Dec.
11th " "	12th "	15 Feb.
8th " "	9th "	8 Sept.
3d " "	7th "	3 Sept.
25th " "	12th "	25 Feb.

That the year should be measured from March 1, is perhaps proper; but what is the proper date among the following:

J.Q.A.	Records
25 Feb. 1667.	25th 12th, 1667.
7 " 1669.	7th 12th, 1669.
31 Jan. 1671.	31st 11th, 1671.
4 Jan. 1689	4 Jan. $168\frac{8}{9}$
28 Jan. 1691	8 Feb. $169\frac{1}{0}$
18 Feb. 1696.	18 Feb. $169\frac{5}{6}$

I gather from these and other instances that though J.Q.A. corrected for the numbers of the months, he did not correct for the year, and that some one has been very careless in transcribing. I can make nothing of his date for the first John Adams's birth. He says twice (pp. 9, 11) it was 28 Jan. 1691. The Record (p. 669) gives 8 Feb. $169\frac{1}{0}$. Can he have tried to correct for New Style? If so, not only does the change betray the want of correction everywhere else, but it is wrong in the number of days, and seems corrected the wrong way by subtracting instead of adding.

As I am not in the habit of reading records, I take it for granted that the muddle is my own; but as I want to make my table correct, perhaps your antiquarian mind will some day go over the dates and tell me what they mean.

For instance (Records, 630)

———

John Adams . . . was borne
the (11) mo (12) 1656.

———

Then (p. 637)
John Adams . . . . dyed
the (27) (11) 1656.

———

I take this to read that my indefinitely grand-uncle John Adams first, brother of our second Joseph, was born on Feb. 11, 1656; which I take to be (corrected) Feb. 22, 1656, (seeing that his elder brother Joseph was born only about a year before, Dec. 24, 1654, and no correction can be made for Joseph's year unless man is mad.)

Now then! This John Adams, son of Joseph and Abigail, dies 27 Jan. 1656, which, corrected to new style, ought to be 8 Feb. 1656, and is just a fortnight before he was born; which was a clever thing to do, and explains the family wrong-headedness.

Add to this that J.Q.A. (p. 7) says this poor John was born Feb. 15, 1656; and I leave you to figure out the probable margin of error all round.

I would not unduly perplex your accountants in view of a Congressional enquiry,[2] but I do also observe that John Adams, according to the Brookline town records, married Susanna Boylston Nov. 23, 1734; but according to J.Q.A., on Oct. 31.

Also John Adams married Abigail Smith Oct. 25, 1764, and had daughter Abigail July 14, 1765. This was prompt, though correct.

Finally J.Q.A. (p. 12) says (note) that the first John died May 25, 1760. John the second says (Diary, p. 128, note) that his father died May 25, 1761. The record does not mention the death.

Yrs lovingly but confusedly Henry Adams.

MS: MHi

1. Britain (and the American colonies) did not adopt the Gregorian calendar until 1752. Under Old Style, the year began on March 25. Also, to make the vernal equinox fall on March 21, eleven days had to be added to Old Style dating, so that Jan. 1, 1690, became Jan. 12, 1690/1, or Jan. 12, 1691.

2. A new investigation of Union Pacific finances, voted by the Senate later this day, again delayed funding of the railroad's debt to the United States government.

To Elizabeth Cameron

1603 H Street. 10 March, 1887.

Dear Mrs Cameron

Brent takes over the fish-screen. If you think, after trying it, that you would prefer the birds, you have but to say so.

Of course I would rather you should take it as a gift; but if you are tired of gifts, I am willing you should take it on what terms you like, if you want it. Everyone ought to have everything one wants. I presume there is no objection to my acting on this liberal rule in applying it to you.

The pair cost 38 yen, which is exactly 30 dollars. Mrs Hay took one, paying, I think, twenty dollars for it, the duty being 30 per cent. If you take the other, you shall certainly not be required to pay more than Mrs Hay did.

As for the other trifle, it is hardly the equivalent of a bunch of violets. Please call it one, and oblige

Yrs truly Henry Adams.

MS: MHi

To Elizabeth Cameron

1603 H Street. Wednesday. [16 March? 1887]

Dear Mrs Cameron

If you thought of coming here today, don't carry it into effect, for I am going with my dear Chang Yen Hoon to Baltimore.[1] Tomorrow you ought to come to matronise some one,—I forget who—whom Suzanne said she intended to bring in, to breakfast.

If the imperial crysanthemum can be made to serve for wall decoration, I would use it so, though it would be better for a ceiling. The trouble with me was that I had no space for it. I have a magnificent piece of gold and red, but only some ten yards; not enough even for a full portiére.

Ever Yrs   Henry Adams.

Mrs J. D. Cameron.

MS: MHi
1. Chang Yin-Huan (1837–1900), Chinese minister simultaneously to the United States, Peru, and Spain 1885–1889, had resided in Washington since April 1886.

To Theodore F. Dwight

57 Mount Vernon Street.[1]
Sunday, 10 April, 1887

Dear Dwight

Thanks for your's of the 7th. The stamps have been amicably distributed among the three youths, and were received with respectful emotion. They commissioned me to present their thanks to John Chew, and to express their gratitude. This means, of course, that I wish you would tell him that his kindness is appreciated.

I find things here as bad as I feared. I am long since beyond complaint or distress; but a few years ago I should have thought the world impossible on such conditions as I see about me. The fun of the show may become evident with time; as yet I see little to laugh at, and the prospect of next summer is not among the most amusing parts of the comedy.

Molly and I start for New York on Tuesday afternoon, and after passing Wednesday there, we hope to reach Washington by the limited on Thursday. If the weather is fine, Brent can come down in the Victoria for us. If not, he can bring a coupé.

My brother Brooks is going to Vienna, and wants an introduction to some one who can put him in the way of living like a gentleman, and seeing the cavalry schools, stables &c. If you meet Lippe, ask him if he knows a proper person to trust with so precious a young flower.[2]

Ever Yrs   Henry Adams.

MS: MHi
1. The Boston home of ABA.
2. Count Lippe-Weissenfeld, counselor at the Austro-Hungarian legation. BA had just published his anti-Puritan *The Emancipation of Massachusetts* (1887), and now intended to learn German, at HA's suggestion, as preparation for further historical work.

To Samuel L. M. Barlow

1603 H Street. 17 April, 1887.

My dear Mr Barlow

Allow me to introduce to you my friend Mr Kuki, the minister of Japan. Mr Kuki is a connoisseur, and wishes to see some of the New York collections. I should be greatly obliged if you could help him to do it.

Very truly Yrs   Henry Adams

S. L. M. Barlow Esq.

MS: CSmH

To Samuel L. M. Barlow

1603 H Street. 17 April, 1887.

My dear Mr Barlow

Mr Kuki, the Japanese Minister, is going to New York on Wednesday, and is emulous of Chang Yen Hun, for whom John Hay has opened the doors of the collectors. I have ventured to give Kuki an introduction to you, not that I want you to entertain him, but that you might show him your things, and ask Mr Dana, Brayton Ives, H. R. Bishop, or any collector with whom you are on friendly terms, to open their doors to the oriental.[1] As Kuki has always been very friendly and useful to me, and may be still more so in the future, I want to show him every civility. His English is a trifle chaotic, but he is intelligent and a gentleman. His strong point as a connoisseur is Chinese and Japanese paintings, but he is a good judge all round.

If you are unable to attend to him yourself, perhaps you could send him an introduction to Dana or some of the fraternity.

My love to Mrs Barlow.

Ever yrs   Henry Adams.

What is the address of the man who mends your porcelain so well?

MS: CSmH

1. Charles Anderson Dana (1819–1897), owner-editor of the New York *Sun* 1868–1897; Brayton Ives (1840–1914), stockbroker and banker; Heber Reginald Bishop (1840–1902), sugar merchant and railroad financier. They all had notable collections of Chinese and Japanese art objects.

To Elizabeth Cameron

1603 H Street. Sunday. [17? April 1887]

Dear Mrs Cameron

I shall certainly come. Though not a promising figure for a fairy God-father, I shall not be the one who staid away.[1]

Ever Yrs   Henry Adams

MS: MHi
1. The fairy-tale allusion is to "The Sleeping Beauty." The christening of Martha Cameron (1886–1918) took place April 24.

To John Hay

1603 H Street. April 17, 1887.

Dear Hay

I find Washington tolerable only under pressure, and I catch myself gazing at your windows with perpetual wonder at your absence; but the more I gaze, the less I find to say about it. Molly and I arrived safely and duly. I wasted Friday in making calls, but missed Chang, and caught Mrs Don only, as it were, by what is left of her hair, which was too short for a holt.[1] Kuki came yesterday with tidings of the Fenollosa-Okakura expedition, and sat an hour talking Chinese. Chang goes today, I think. I hope he will have energy to see the show in New York; and I have promised Kuki to give him, too, the means of improving his mind on Sung and Han antiquities. If we are not laying up for ourselves treasures in China, put no trust in Yellow imperial porcelain.[2]

Except the usual gossip peculiar to this nigger paradise I hear nothing worth your august attention. Not even a new beauty has been advertised. Only Mrs Larry Hopkins is on show at the Whitneys, much to Archy's distress. His moral nature is all broken up by this outrage on his purest aspirations. I find that I was asked to the Christening, and got a pink card from Dorothy.[3] Old grandpapa Bancroft has gone to Nashville, leaving Suzanne with the other mice to play. Mice rhymes with Rice, and reminds me that Molly has asked them both to dinner on Monday,—Spring, not Autumn, Cereal.[4] The Burlingames dined here Friday, and we talked heavenly of Peking, an earthy Paradise if Burlingame ever was of it.[5] Today is Sunday, and we miss you. I never felt duller.

My love to Mrs Hay and the babes. Dwight's and Molly's too.

Ever   Henry Adams.

MS: MHi

1. Mrs. Cameron, who had been ill with typhoid fever that spring, had lost most of her hair. It had grown back, but was still short.
2. Hay had arranged for Chang to see the Oriental collections of Heber Reginald Bishop and Charles A. Dana.
3. Minnie Dunlap Hopkins was divorced from Amos Lawrence Hopkins, son of the educator Mark Hopkins and brother of Archibald Hopkins. Mrs. Whitney had testified for Mrs. Hopkins at the divorce trial. The well-reported christening of Dorothy Whitney (1887–1968), born Jan. 23, took place Easter Monday, April 11, at St. John's Church.
4. Cecil Arthur Spring Rice (1859–1918), secretary at the British legation with intervals 1887–1895, ambassador 1913–1918.
5. Edward Livermore Burlingame (1848–1922), private secretary 1865–1867 to his father, Anson Burlingame, at the U.S. legation in Peking, on the New York *Tribune* with Hay in 1871, editor of *Scribner's Magazine* 1886–1914.

To Paul Leicester Ford

1603 H Street. 1 May. 1887.

My dear Mr Ford

I return the two curious pamphlets for which I thank you very much. This ephemeral literature is like autumn leaves. One would think the whole world would in time be swamped by it, but it disappears, and as far as I can see, the result for historians is as blank as though no pamphlets or newspapers were written. One would like to use them, but they contain not enough evidence of humanity to supply an epigram. Carlyle used to wail and shriek over his piles of dusty pamphlets, but he was given to noise. My own feeling is only of regret that they are not usable by me.

Many thanks for them. I am still unable to find some that were once well known, especially western imprints. Even our public libraries fail on American history.

Very truly Yrs   Henry Adams.

Paul L. Ford Esq.

MS: NN

To John Hay

1603 H Street. Sunday, 1 May, 1887.

Dear Hay

Thanks for your letter of the 25th with your news of the Mexican greaser.[1] I wish I had news to return; but except the refrain "Good-bye, Mrs Helyer," this place has sung nothing since you left. Molly has been here on a wild round of gaieties, ending up with a dinner which Mrs Whitney very kindly gave for her; but as she sat between Roustan and Walter Berry, I came in for little profit at third hand. Marian Howland has not been here. At least, if she has, she must have kept herself in a dark room without newspapers.[2]

I see that Eli Thayer has gone for Nicolay.[3] I have gone for your poem in the Century of today. If this is fruit of your mature vine, I think you are happy in preserving the flavor of your vine-yard. 'Tis pretty, Nay, 'tis much! Perhaps the conclusion is a little weak; but I would not care to strengthen it.[4] King says we ought to publish our joint works under the title of "The Impasse Series," because they all ask questions which have no answers; but nothing has any real answer, and when one walks deliberately into these blind alleys where Impasse is stuck up at every step, one cannot, without a certain ridicule, knock one's head very violently against the brick wall at the end. Victor Hugo did this, to the delight of Frenchmen; but, for our timider natures, let us go on, as before, and, when we see the brick wall, take off our hats to it with the good manners we most affect, and say in our choicest English: Monseigneur, j'attendrai. You have done it charmingly. Please say it some more.

Yes, Angell was my scholar, but I prefer his visits—Basta! you are exempt from such worn jests.[5]

Our love all round.   Ever Yrs   Henry Adams.

MS: MHi

1. King had taken direct charge of developing the Sombrerete mine, in central Mexico, but was temporarily in San Francisco to supervise the building of new mill machinery.

2. Marian Howland, King's half-sister.

3. In a letter to the Boston *Sunday Herald,* April 4, Eli Thayer reproved Nicolay and Hay for casting doubts on the usefulness of the Free-Soil settlement of Kansas. His letter, in response to the April installment of *Lincoln* in the *Century,* attracted attention in the press. HA knew, as Thayer did not, that this part was written by Nicolay.

4. The poem "Israel," based on Jacob's wrestling with the angel, expresses the futility of metaphysical quest. Hay reported that it had been "kicking about the place for twelve years" and that since there would be "no fresh ones—once in a decade I may fish out an old one" (Hay to HA, May 12).

5. Elgin Adelbert Angell (1849–1898), Harvard '73, a Cleveland lawyer. "His appropriate name is Angell—and he is our only Mugwump in Ohio. . . . He gave me to understand that your principal worth in life had been the formation of his lofty character—which he thinks does you the highest credit" (Hay to HA, April 25, 1887). HA alludes to the proverbial "Like angel-visits, few and far between"; Thomas Campbell, *The Pleasures of Hope* (1799).

To Charles Milnes Gaskell

1603 H Street. 8 May, 1887.

My dear Carlo

Your letter of April 9 finds the usual May struggle here; a divided empire between all sorts of seasons, and no kind of objects. Our want of country occupations is a serious thing. With us, one must be either cit or lout; no happy medium exists; one cannot be country squire and city gent at the same time.

My summer is to be passed at Quincy with my mother who is now near eighty, very much broken, and alone, owing to my brother Brooks's taking a vacation in Germany. Four months at Quincy are to me what four months of solitary prison in Ireland might be to you; but it matters very little, and I shall be able to accomplish a deal of heavy work. As I never go into society, or pay visits, I am relieved of the worst burdens of the seasons. The summer will pass, in time; next year I am going to Hawaii for the summer; and two years hence I shall take my first run to Peking; so that the summer question will not bother me again.

Your Irishification is not amusing, and to escape it I have stopped reading English news. Our newspapers are wholly run by Irish for Irish, and the quantity of Irishism is even more obnoxious than the quality. From time to time I see the headlines of some news that makes me wish you had fallen on a pleasanter Parliament; but I console myself by hoping it amuses you. We are doing our best to restore prosperity to your farmers by raising railway rates all over our country; but if your squires can hold on another generation, or perhaps fifty years, I have a strong notion that things will come right for them. Last summer I got a sort of an idea how very small the really cultivable world is, and how fast it is filling. Fifty years more will bring it near the explosive point. I am rather sorry for your children, but I think your grandchildren may find occupation worth having. As for investments, I don't know how the widow and orphan are to live. As trustee, I think it lucky if I can net four per cent for those whom I protect; soon it will be three. To be sure, the nominal capital rolls up; but one gets very little for a million. When I was a boy, and until the last fifteen years, six per cent was the rule. I can take good western mortgages now at that rate, but, for trusts, I fear going so far from home.

Europe will some day become interesting if it does nothing long enough. Heaven only knows how long it is since I have read a new European book, or seen a picture or heard a story from there. By the bye, an intelligent and agreeable fellow has turned up here at your Legation; about the last place one looks for such. His name is Spring Rice, and he has creditable wits. Mad, of course, but not more mad than an Englishman should be. Unluckily he is here only for a short time, and goes back to the Foreign Office in the autumn. He drops in at times on me for meals, and pays in a certain dry humor, not without suggestions of Monckton Milnes's breakfasts five-and-twenty years ago. Other Englishmen twain or more have been here, and, for some unintelligible or unremembered object, have sat at my table; but I forget me as to their names or looks.—Except the Yates Thompsons, who were scourging the land with a wilde, verwegene Jagd.[1] The statistician does not improve with age, and newspapering.

News grow not. Life is dull to scare a Chinese mandarin. I am well, as far as I know; with everything in the world, except what I want; and with nothing to complain of, except the universe. I wish you the exact reverse of my situation; you will find it more amusing if not more to your taste. My love to your wife and children.

Ever Yours   Henry Adams.

Please find out and tell me in your next letter whether old Thomson Hankey and his wife are still living and in their senses. My mother wants to know.

MS: MHi

1. Henry Yates Thompson (1838–1928), owner of the liberal *Pall Mall Gazette* 1880–1892, and collector of illuminated manuscripts; his wife Elizabeth (d. 1941) was the daughter of publisher George Smith. "Wilde, verwegende Jagd" (wild, foolhardy chase) comes from "Lützows wilde Jagd" (1813) by Theodor Körner, from which Karl Maria von Weber made a rousing patriotic song.

To John Hay

1603 H Street. Sunday, 15 May 1887.

My dear John

Thanks for the Kingian letter, which I return. On the whole, the youth seems better than I feared six weeks ago. I hope the earthquakes have not upset his Hacienda.

Decidedly *no* is my answer for you about the alley. You don't use it, and Tuckerman does not expect you to share costs. I would take no notice of the letter.[1]

Molly and I were all packed and ready to start on Tuesday, and see you off on Wednesday, when your letter clipped our little plan. Molly has had a gay month of it, flying about with wings of spring to the farm every afternoon, or to Mt Vernon with Queens, or to old Bancroft's with Presidents.[2] She and Suzanne have done their little gilded wings quite brown by sheer flitting. As for me, my bronze flower-tank is out; so are my awnings; my breakfast table is crowded to suffocation and famine; Mrs Don is tender, and is going to Beverly, and has taken me to call on Mrs Cleveland; Miss Lucy is sympathetic, and comes to breakfast at one o'clock; Rebecca Dodge is affectionate; Sally Loring bright; Miss Thoron, Catholic; and they are all as one family; but Oh, my blessed Virgin! they feed my soul with but thin nectar. I would that you were back, for I find solitude oppressive. The prattle of sparrows, even in H Street, becomes monotonous.[3]

The measle business pleases even less than twitters. I shall wait with anxiety to hear that the babes and you are on your path; but if I were you, I would come on by way of Washington and pass a day or two with Dwight and me. I will go with you to New York on the 30th. I dismiss my cook, and close up here, on June 1, and start for Quincy on or about the 5th.

The world, we hope, is happy, for it is dull enough to have leisure for anything. Try some more poetry. My own winter-work is ended, and China so much nearer.

Ever Yrs   Henry Adams

MS: MHi

1. "After we have made Papas Corcoran and Tuckerman a present of some hundreds of feet of land in alleys, must we now regrade for them?" (Hay to HA, May 12, 1887).

2. On May 5 Mary Adams was one of fourteen guests at a dinner party given for the president and his wife by George Bancroft; on May 6 she went to Mount Vernon with a large party escorting Queen Kapiolani of Hawaii.

3. President Cleveland married Frances Folsom (1864–1947) on June 2, 1886. Marie Louise Thoron (1864–1958) was newly added to HA's list of sparrows.

To John Hay

1603 H Street. Monday, 23d. [May 1887]

Dear J

Please let me know by telegraph whether you are to sail on June 1. I may go on with Molly as far as New York next Monday. In this case we might casually meet. Your letter received today says nothing on the subject, which inspires doubts in a suspicious nature.

Molly hangs on here till she is fired out. Apparently the fascinations of Quincy leave room for soberer tastes.

The young women still drop in to breakfast, but are becoming scarce. Mrs Don has departed to Harrisburg, with Martha. The roads are dusty. My own horse Prince is dead lame. The national drill is in progress, and camps surround the monument. Altogether, I have a hard time of it, and want to start for China soon. Meanwhile I am translating the Beatitudes into English. Disciples are called "school-produce" and the first Beatitude runs: "Pure heart of man is possess blessing of, for has God kingdom approach are of kingdom." What it means I can't say. Love to the pink-faced ones.

Ever   Henry Adams.

MS: MHi

To Theodore F. Dwight

Hotel Brunswick, New York, 7 June 1887

My dear Dwight

If no other difficulty exists than danger of robbery, I think Mrs Field may feel safe. Not only can the building be made strong, but it can be so connected by bells and alarms that theft would be as difficult in Ashfield as in Philadelphia, and much more so than in Washington, where we have no protection that would disturb a sensible burglar. The difficulty of carrying a picture away is much greater in Ashfield than in a city. It can be more easily traced, and the chance is less of a robber who is a connoisseur.[1]

Edward Hooper telegraphs me that he can't meet me here, so I shall not see him this week.

I passed the morning with Schurz who wants to read my two volumes. Please wrap the two that Mr Ward had—still in paper covers—and make a parcel of them. Direct to Carl Schurz, 175 West 58th St. and send by express.

La Farge says he has sent the butterfly Sphynx.[2] Hay meant you to have charge of it, so you had better open and enjoy it.

Please add my name to your own in enquiring after Mr Corcoran.

Ever Yrs   Henry Adams.

P.S. I think I forgot to lock my corner-desk. There is nothing in it to steal, but you might as well close it, and put the key in my writing-table drawer.

MS: MHi
1. Mrs. John Field, whose husband died March 17, was moving art works from Washington to her home in Massachusetts.
2. *Sphinx: A Phantasy*, a watercolor by John La Farge, probably an illustration to Emerson's poem "The Sphinx." It was owned by Hay.

To Theodore F. Dwight

Direct to Quincy.   Adams Building, 23 Court St. Boston.[1]
Tuesday 14 June, 1887.

My dear Dwight

Yours of the 12th arrived this morning.

The dogs arrived safely yesterday morning, and are now making things lively for their grandma. They are very happy to be back, and show it by indifference to me, and devotion to my mother who pretends to hate them.

Daisy is also at Quincy, resting after four days on her legs. Prince is at Busigny's school, to see what ails him.

Brent has started back. On his return you will have to dismiss Roper. On July 1, pay Brent thirty dollars. If he finds no work, let him do Roper's work, and keep the stable in order. For this, pay him fifteen dollars monthly, August 1, Sept. 1, and October 1. Soon after October 1 he is to come back here for the horses.

Brentano's bill *is* mine, but the articles were a parting railway gift to Mrs Don. Hence their frivolity. Please send Brent down with the money.

I found the Siebold at D. G. Francis's for $60, being half its value.[2] I had been long in search of it. If you can find me a copy of Stanislas St Julien's China equally cheap, I would like it.

Everything is as usual at Quincy. I am this moment starting out to Cambridge. Hooper avers that Mrs Gurney is better.[3]

La Farge and I were together the better part of four days in New York; but otherwise I saw very few people.

We had a comfortably warm day yesterday at 80°. Today a sharp frost, or what feels like it.

Ever Yrs   Henry Adams.

T. F. Dwight Esq.

My mother sends her remembrances, and expects you later. She is wretchedly—as usual.

MS: MHi
1. HA was writing on JQA2's office stationery.
2. One of the several books on the ethnology and natural history of Japan by the German scientific explorer Philipp F. von Siebold (1796–1866).
3. Ellen Gurney, sister of Edward Hooper and MHA, did not recover from the nervous illness brought on by her husband's death in late 1886. Wandering on the railroad tracks near the West Cambridge depot, she was struck by a train and died from the injuries on Nov. 20, 1887.

To John Hay

28 June, 1887.

My dear John

Your letter arrived last evening. I should have written if my way of life had given matter suitable to a serious man like you; but what has a butterfly and a trifler to do with a sage who dines with the Lord Mayor. I have been at Quincy since the 11th. My gaiety has been exhausting and continuous. I have called on two old ladies of eighty or more, and have frequented various invalids and persons in bad condition. Dr William Everett has called upon me. I have returned the civility. I have given rifles to my two twin-nephews, with which they are as certain as possible to kill each other, or some one else; but I don't care, because they have a big new sailboat which will drown them if they escape shooting. They are twelve years old. My nieces all prefer jack-knives, an amiable taste, showing refinement and literary propensities.

In the entire horizon that bounds my cell, I see nothing that would bear shipment to London. Dwight must be ill. He has not written at all. Sturgis Bigelow has come home to nurse his father who is either dying or pretending to die; I think the former, though the doctors have hinted the latter, because H.J.B. is so bent on his own way that they can never tell what else ails him.[1] I write history as though it were serious, five hours a day; and when my hand and head get tired, I step out into the rose-beds and watch my favorite roses. For lack of thought, I have taken to learning roses, and talk of them as though I had the slightest acquaintance with the subject.

In short, the summer is just what I expected, with a few details better and a few worse.

Mrs Don has not yet come on, though Beverly waits her. I have not heard a whisper of her plans. Ned Hooper, Sturgis Bigelow and I are planning to run down for an hour to North Easton to see La Farge's new window. That to Mrs McKim in Trinity is very successful in its way.[2]

My love to milady and the babes. Also to Cunliffe, the Clarkes and the world, especially vanity Fair.

Ever Yrs   Henry Adams.

MS: MHi
1. Henry Jacob Bigelow (1818–1890), professor of surgery 1849–1882.
2. Completed in January, the "Angel of Help" window in Unity Church, North Easton (20 miles south of Boston), is one of La Farge's most ambitious works. Julia Appleton McKim (1859–1887) was the wife of the architect Charles Follen McKim. The memorial window in Trinity Church, Boston, derives from Titian's *Presentation of the Virgin* at the Accademia in Venice.

To Theodore F. Dwight

Quincy. 30 June, 1887.

Dear Dwight

I was glad to get your letter. Clifford Richardson told me you were not ill, or I should have been anxious. He told me also of Mrs Lippitt's illness. I will write to Miss Dodge.

If Quincy is not ornamental, it has other qualities more obnoxious. Of all things I dislike most to be useful; but evidently I am needed here. My poor mother, besides her other troubles, has jammed her foot in an elevator, and is laid up with an extra cause for anxiety in a crushed toe;—a mighty serious thing. My twin nephews have to have rifles, and as I am the only relative they have not struck this year for presents, I am the one to fit them out. William Everett needs one of the family to attend his school-celebration, and I am the fresh hand needed.[1] Somebody must look after the children's fireworks, and I have nothing better to do. Three old ladies, over eighty, ought to be called on; and octogenarians are my specialty.

The library is quiet, the roses are exquisite, and the weather is just settling down to summer. Time manages to get itself along. One month of four is past. I am not eager to have it go—or stay; but I think you would be better off at this season here than where you are.

Mrs Gurney is about the same, but gaining, I think. I go over once a week to pass the day with the children and to see her.

If you are not satisfied with Durkin, deal with him as you would with your own. Beveridge's bill is right I suppose. Let Brent pay it.

Mrs Field has a wide world before her. I hope she may find more rest in it than I think she ever will.

My mother sends her regards, and the dogs their barkings. They are very popular and even my mother does not complain except when I punish them.

Ever Yrs   H.A.

What is John Hay's *banker's* address?

MS: MHi
1. Everett was headmaster of Adams Academy, Quincy, 1877–1893.

To Theodore F. Dwight

Quincy, 6 July, 1887.

Dear Dwight

Tell Brent to buy the necessary hose. Tell the amiable Spring Rice that I shall have to see my papers at Washington before I can say what I need to verify; but I may have occasion to write him on the subject.

My mother is getting on pretty well. Of course her condition is a very trying one.

Will Everett's Eulogy is very good. I will send you a copy when printed. You can tell Sidney that we are all pleased with it.[1]

The Chinese books have arrived. If I don't learn the Kuan-hua soon, the want of books will not be my excuse.[2] The only difficulty with them is that they all pronounce and spell differently.

The revision of the history makes progress. I hope to get half a volume ready by October.

I went to Cambridge yesterday, and found things unchanged.

Drought here, and, last week, very oppressive heat.

Ever Yrs   Henry Adams.

T. F. Dwight Esq.

MS: MHi
1. The tribute to CFA was delivered in Quincy, July 4.
2. *Kuan hua:* Mandarin Chinese.

To Theodore F. Dwight

Quincy, 10 July, 1887.

Dear Dwight

Please thank Mrs Fairchild on my account. I am not earnest to buy any more ancestral property. I have here a vast deal too much of it for my comfort. If she renews the subject, please say that for the present I can't attend to it.

We are burned up. No rain, and scorching sun. Luckily sea breezes have cooled us when the interior was roasting alive.

I work near ten hours a day, and shall soon finish the cosmos at this rate. I believe any criminal confined in Quincy could talk Chinese in elegant Mandarin within three months.

My mother is getting well, but the toe-nail will be months in growing. She is not positively radiant with youth or spirits, but she passes time. The dogs are just the happiest human beings that ever barked at a strange cur outside. Marquess in this hot weather finds bathing in the brook a real tonic.

I wish you would come. I have a vast collection of old international law for you to look over; not to speak of MSS. and typography.

Yrs ever   Henry Adams.

T. F. Dwight Esq.

MS: MHi

To Theodore F. Dwight

Sunday 24 July, 1887.

My dear Dwight

My mother asks me to say that your room is ready for you, and that she will be much pleased to see you. I can testify that the Jus Gentium, Elzevirs and Plantins are moulding for want of you.[1]

We go on like old Father Time. I work frantically. If my eyes hold out, they will really do themselves credit. As yet they grumble but march.

Everyone has gone away. My brothers and their family are either at the Glades or on the plains.[2] My sister is down at Wareham on Buzzard's Bay, where Miss Baxter is making her a visit.[3] My mother and I are taking dog-days solid and solitary.

We escaped all the heat, which seemed to stop somewhere near the State line all round. I doubted whether you would ever be seen again except as roast Librarian.

Should you come direct here, I wish you would hunt up, and put in your trunk Books IV and V of my MS. which you will find, I think, in one of the drawers of the big desk. I think I left the MS. in the black carton or box in the second drawer next my seat, but it may be somewhere else in another drawer. Don't send me the MSS of Vol. IV by mistake. If you don't come direct, I would like to have you send the MS. by express. I think I have written only Book I of Vol. IV.

William and Maggy are to have their board-allowance monthly. By the bye, how shall we arrange to pay them on Sept. 1.? You had better talk with them on the subject. If they want it, they can have their pay till October 1 from you, when you come away.

You are right in paying the $5.50 for Julia Jones.
Auf wiedersehen! The dogs are happy all day.

Ever Yrs   Henry Adams.

MS: MHi
1. Among the fine old books that Dwight was coming to Quincy to catalogue were imprints from the Elzevir (Dutch) and Plantin (Flemish) presses.
2. The Glades, at Strawberry Point in Scituate, Mass., had been built as a summer hotel in the 1840s but never flourished. After the Civil War half a dozen families clubbed together to make it a private resort. JQA2 and CFA2 bought into the club in 1880.
3. The Adamses' friendship with Lucy W. Baxter (1836–1925?), daughter of George Baxter of New York City and younger sister of Sarah Baxter Hampton, began before the Civil War. The Baxters figure in an account of Thackeray in the *Education*, ch. 9. Lucy Baxter at this time was ABA's companion.

To Theodore F. Dwight

Friday 4 Aug. 1887.

My dear Dwight

The History arrived yesterday. Many thanks.

Clarence King looked in on me yesterday for a few hours. He was burying Arnold Hague's father in Boston.[1]

Hay writes from Scotland. Poor fellow, he has been staying with Carnegie.[2]

We have had no heat here that you would not think coolness. Thermometer never but once up to 90°, and only oppressive for dogginess. You had better take the next train.

Make what arrangements you please at the house. If the money gives out, let me know. I hope I shall myself be back by October 1.

King wants a house in Washington for the winter for his mother and sister. What becomes of the Fairchild's old place? I suppose Hopkins would know.

Things grind on here, especially history. I shall hurry it up with a typewriter after September 1, so as to have a volume to print this autumn.

Yrs ever   Henry Adams.

T. F. Dwight Esq.

MS: MHi
1. William Hague (1808–1887) of Boston, a Baptist minister.
2. The Hays had visited Andrew Carnegie (1835–1919), the Scottish-born industrialist, in Perthshire. Among Carnegie's sixteen other guests were HA's bête noire James G. Blaine and Blaine's ally Sen. Eugene Hale.

To John Hay

Quincy, 4 August, 1887.

Dear Heart

Your letter of July 20 arrived here two days ago, and King followed it yesterday. He combined his hour here with an hour burying Hague's father in Boston, and a day at Sunapee buying land.[1] He wanted me to go up to Sunapee with him, but crowbars wont start me from here till my brothers return.

The ruffian seems well and bright. He says that his operation worked like a charm, and that he has been very well since, but it will have to be repeated. He has no news except that La Farge is to do W. Reid's half-moons and suggests a Japanese tea-party.[2] La Farge is some wilted by the heats, but pulls himself together every day or two, and to use his own expression, "whacks in a whole apostle."[3]

King took oath that he had not heard from you since you sailed. I thought this more unlikely than any story I ever heard him tell; but he stuck to it. As he had nothing more to say to me and was pining to bury Dr Hague, I dropped him into the cares and let him go.

I work six hours a day on history, and am making it just dance. Two hours are devoted to Chinese. I learn two new characters every day, and forget them, and two more, the next day. My knowledge is becoming extensive and accurate, but I am not yet quite ready for a tutor.

Dwight, or what is left of him, will be here soon. I expect to leave here myself on October 1, either to go to Washington, or with King to Mexico; I hope the latter, for I want a planet or two for variety after this summer. Of course you will give my love to the Britishers. Gaskell and Cunliffe have both written to me since you have been there.

Mrs Don is at Beverly. Martha is sick, knocked up by the journey. I have a note from her abusing Bar Harbor.

Love to Mrs Hay and the babes.

Ever Yrs   Henry Adams.

MS: MHi

1. King did not buy land in New Hampshire, but Hay did—1,200 acres for a summer retreat.

2. Whitelaw Reid engaged La Farge to paint allegorical murals (*Music* and *Drama*, completed 1888) in the lunettes of the music room of his New York house.

3. La Farge was working on *The Ascension*, a large mural for the chancel of the Church of the Ascension in New York City. He had received the commission just before leaving for Japan in June 1886 and finally completed it in December 1888.

To Elizabeth Cameron

Quincy, Saturday [6 Aug. 1887]

My dear Mrs Cameron

I have waited with impatience to hear of your arrival, because I had no opinion of Bar Harbor, and, as I never saw it, I felt sure it was not suited to Martha's education. Beverly is a place that will do her no harm. Its distractions will leave her time for self-improvement.

I wish you had told me whether the young lady's illness preceded the journey, or was only a consequence of it. Also, if you can ever spare a moment, let me know if she and her mother are quite well.

Much as I want to see you, I can't quite make up my mind to go to Beverly; not because it would give me pain so much as because I am no longer able to feel it. Pain is not so bad as some other things, and just now I have my hands full. Yet if you ever come up to town, and want to go shopping, I will escort you, and we will do Boston. You shall tell me whether Boston or New York or Philadelphia is the best place to buy table-clothes. I will show you the State House and Trinity Church, and we will lunch at Young's.

My mother wants you to come here. As she is now a cripple, growing deaf, losing her sight, and horribly disgusted with her eighty years, she is bored to frenzy by her ails and her solitude here. You would do her a mercy to come over for a night, and if only Martha could come, my mother would be gay for a week. Clarence King stopped here an hour the other day, and quite made her young.

Please order anything that you want at Beverly, and send me the bills; or let me know, and I will order it. Ober will build you a new house if you prefer one. Only tell him what to do.

Ever truly Yrs   Henry Adams.

MS: MHi

To Justin Winsor

Quincy 16 Aug. '87.

Dear Sir

I called at the Library yesterday to ask a renewal of the favor I have had in former years, of using the newspaper files of the College. I want those of 1810, 1811, 1812, if possible of the New York Evening Post, and, if not the Post, then the Philadelphia Aurora. As the wicked and vicious are the only people who conceal nothing, and the good are worthless to historians, I prefer for my purposes the wickedest papers there are.

Very truly Yrs   Henry Adams.

Prof. Winsor.

MS: MHi

To Justin Winsor

Quincy, 17 Aug. [1887]

Dear Sir

Many thanks for the volume of newspapers.
Dwight is with me, and will soon be over to see you. Just now he is trying to freshen his roses a bit, after a Washington summer.

Very truly Yrs   Henry Adams.

Prof. Justin Winsor

MS: MHi

To Elizabeth Cameron

Quincy, 18 Aug. 1887.

My dear Mrs Cameron

I was fast becoming uneasy about you, but still hoped that you were flying about to lunches and dinners, when Dwight undertook to seek you out. His report leaves much to be desired. I am sorry not to be nearer, where I might see to things a little, and run a few errands. As it is, I shall only worry myself with thinking what I would have done if I had been there. If Curtis does not satisfy you, send for Haddock at Beverly; not a polished, but a stout party in sickness. Today is so gloomy that I feel as though you must be as low as the weather, and I am the last person yet invented for encouraging any one.

Dwight will have told you the little there is to say. Quincy is not enlivening. I hope your friend Okakura the Jap will pay me a visit next week. We will ask him to send over some of the more recondite portions of a lady's wardrobe to make the kimonos useful. Kuki has never yet received the calico patterns.

I have letters from Hay, La Farge, and English friends, full of nothing. Not even an anecdote to amuse you. I wish you might be able, some fine day, to go down to North Easton with me to see La Farge's window there, and Richardson's buildings.[1]

My best regards to your husband. Can I do anything for him?

Ever Yrs   Henry Adams.

MS: MHi
   1. Under the auspices of Frederick L. Ames, Richardson built five buildings in North Easton between 1880 and 1884: the public library, town hall, railroad station, gate house for the Ames estate, and a small gardener's cottage.

To Elizabeth Cameron

Quincy 19 Aug. 1887.

Dear Mrs Cameron

Thanks for the note, which has greatly relieved my mind. I was getting to be worried about it. If I had known how bad the trouble was, I should have been down on you long ago; but I always imagine young infants like Martha and you to be well and frisking.

If Martha is well enough to let you come to town, we will go to Cambridge any Monday, and you will delight the children. Let me know what train you come up, and I will meet you at the station.

If Okakura comes, won't you join us on a lark to North Easton, returning here for the night, and staying as long as you can. We want a fine afternoon for North Easton, and, as the Ames's are in Europe, we must take our dinners before starting. If Okakura does not come, you will have to stand our society alone. It is not gay, but you will make it so. My mother is very earnest to see you here, but she will be broken-hearted not to see Martha, who has more charms to the grand-maternal heart than any other and older form of humanity.

I have told Blanchard to see that the expressman gets you vegetables and fruit from Boston regularly if you want them. The expense is trifling, and the trouble to you all saved by sending a written order to Quincy market.

Yrs faithfully   Henry Adams.

MS: MHi

To Elizabeth Cameron

The Homestead, Quincy, Mass.
Tuesday. [31 Aug. 1887]

My dear Mrs Cameron

Martha is a great anxiety to me, but I hope to bring her teeth through all right now that the hot nights are gone, and we have begun to freeze again. Give her my love and whatever else she wants. With your letter came one from Okakura quite breaking my heart by saying he cannot come, and appointing Pekin as our place of meeting. Also Clarence King telegraphed me yesterday to come to him at Parker's, and when I went today, he was gone.[1] These disasters have broken me up a good deal.

Dwight has gone to Auburn. I have brought two of my nieces from Cambridge over here, to make us feel young. I caught the two Higginsons in Boston yesterday, and they quieted my anxieties that you might be perishing of hunger or cold. I am dreadfully harrassed by shyness, and hate to impose an extra note on you to keep me posted.

If my nephews get back from Bar Harbor, I shall send them over in the "Papoose" to get you and Miss Cameron out for a cruise.[2]

Whenever you mean to go shopping in Boston, try and do it of a Monday, so that I can act as footman.

Ever truly Yrs   Henry Adams

MS: MHi
1. The Parker House, a Boston hotel.
2. George Caspar Adams and CFA3, sons of JQA2, owned a new 44-foot cutter, the *Papoose.*

To Theodore F. Dwight

Quincy 31 Aug. 1887.

Dear Dwight

Your umbrella is lost. My enquiries of the cab-driver led to nothing; and I think he would have told the truth. I asked at the Boston station, and inspected several hundred umbrellas with the same result. I know not what more to do.

We go on here as usual. I have got my caligrapher at work, and am watching to see whether she will succeed in writing as fast as I require. Looly and Polly Hooper are staying here, teaching Possum type-writing.[1] Okakura has failed me. Martha Cameron is getting on as well as four new teeth allow. Clarence King has come and flown. Without waiting till I could catch him. Other news I have none.

Of course you will give our regards to your mother. If Alward is able to talk, tell him that we think much about him. I wrote to Mrs Field on Sunday.

My mother is fretting to hear, and scolds at you as faithless; but I don't think you need be uneasy.

Ever Yrs   Henry Adams.

MS: MHi
1. HA's calligrapher was a typist. The first shift-key typewriter, having both upper and lower cases, had appeared in 1878; earlier models had only capital letters. Louisa and Mabel Hooper were 13 and 12.

To Theodore F. Dwight

Quincy, 2 Sept. 1887.

Dear Dwight

The enclosed is all I have to report.

We go here as usual. I am making terrific play with my type-writer,[1] who gets through nearly a chapter a day. The work is hard, and keeps me on the intellectual jump.

Your vacation promises to make your return to Washington a pleasure. I shall myself not be sorry to see the first of October arrive.

My regards to Alward. I should be glad to know what else to send.

Ever Yrs   Henry Adams.

MS: MHi
  1. *Type-writer:* typist, a usage first recorded in 1884.

To Elizabeth Cameron

Quincy 7 Sept. [1887]

My dear Mrs Cameron

I am homesick to see you, but unless you take matters into your own hands with all that grasp of conquest which characterises you, I shall see nothing of anyone. I am tied like a lamb. Miss Baxter, who practically looks after my mother to the relief of the family at large, has just gone away for ten days to see her Hampton nieces in New York. I am alone here, and my mother is not a good subject for masculine care. Also I am victim to a female called a caligraphess, or some such classical title, meaning a type-writer; whom I am slowly killing with five hours a day of type-writing, in order to hurry my journey to the Celestial Empire. Human victims should always be sacrificed before beginning a journey. This keeps me busy. If you could only come over for Sunday, you would make life another thing, and I would come to town Saturday afternoon to get you. But I know you are too much occupied. I want to see Martha, but I am afraid to urge her to come until you have seen the place, and whether she can be made comfortable; but any responsibility you should take, I should applaud.

Of course *I* stands for my mother.

A letter yesterday from Hay. His children have got a colley pup.

Ever Yrs   Henry Adams.

MS: MHi

To Elizabeth Cameron

Quincy, Sunday [11 Sept. 1887]

My dear Mrs Cameron

Tell Martha that I know all about it, and distinctly remember my sufferings at her early age. Perhaps she won't believe it, but you must assure her that I never hesitate to tell a lie.

For once I will tell the truth in saying that we shall be delighted to see you here any day you will come. I wanted to propose that you should bring Rebecca Dodge with you, but I am to take her out to Cambridge on Monday, and will tell her your trials, unless she has already got to you; in that case, she can tell me.

My brother Brooks will be back from Europe on Oct. 1, and on that day I shall fly to Washington, and perhaps further. Frosts are excellent for babies, but I prefer other milk for men. Be sure the furnace is in order, so as to give you a little warmth these cool mornings. Half an hour of furnace will make the house comfortable all day. Perhaps you would like to go to Mexico. If King will take us with him, we can have a republican time. I must explode into space somewhere, after this summer of galley-slave toil. My comfort is to think that the public shall suffer for it, and any number of defunct statesmen will howl, in the midst of their flames, at the skinning they are getting this season, owing to my feeling cross.

Ever Yrs   Henry Adams.

MS: MHi

To John Hay

Quincy, 13 Sept. 1887.

My dear Prodigal[1]

As you must be now approaching these shores, and probably enjoying a nasty storm we have sent you, I write this line to meet you on your arrival, and to make you regret the princes you have left behind you.[2]

I shall be in New York on October 1, or soon afterwards, and thence to Washington direct, where I am to wait for King. He will tell you what we mean to do, for I shall be guided by him. You would do well to join us. You will have to make a good many jokes to brighten up the last half dozen centuries, and you should lay in a supply in Mexico.

I too have been working, like a Buffalo Bill, all summer, and I carry back to Washington a whole new volume prepared for the printer since June 15.[3]

At last I have bowed my meek head[4] to the caligrapher, and weeping I dictate. With this vile modern innovation I shall spoil my work, but I shall either be in my pleasant grave on this day two years, or my history will be done and out. I have notified the Japanese government to begin operations in China at that date.

Meanwhile, if King has not found a house at Washington, you had better buy him one. While you are about it, buy a rose-garden also for winter use.

I saw Mrs Don yesterday for the first time. Martha has had a close call, and is still under the weather.

Spring Rice will rejoice over your fatted calfs. So shall I. My love to Mrs Hay and the babes.

Ever Yrs   H. Adams.

MS: MHi
1. An allusion to the parable of the prodigal son (Luke 15).
2 The Hays had left Cowes on the Isle of Wight, finding it "infested with princes" (Hay to HA, Aug. 25). Cowes was the headquarters of the exclusive Royal Yacht Club, and fashionable regattas were held there.
3. This is the third "draft volume" of the *History* (on Madison's first administration).
4. An allusion to Henry H. Milman's hymn "Ride On! Ride On in Majesty!" (1827).

To Elizabeth Cameron

Quincy. Wednesday. [14 Sept. 1887]

My dear Mrs Cameron

Your letter came so late last evening that I thought it safer to send you a telegram this morning. You are, of course, the nearest reasonable approach to an angel—assuming angels to be like you,—and I shall, for that reason, have no conscientious scruples about sparing my blonde type-writer's life for one day, and letting a Senator and General or two go till Friday when I shall bang 'em again; but do get Billy Big to send me a message to say when I am to come and matronise you ladies at his house. He is a dangerous fellow, and very Japanese, but he has pretty things if we can only make him give them to us.

Thanks to you and Rebecca Dodge I enjoyed my rainy Monday more than anything for these many moons. You were arch-angelic to come up, and amuse those infants and me. I wonder whether I could set up for five years old at Washington, and have a nursery to receive lady-visitors? It would be rather fun if G.B. and I had a doll-house together, with Suzanne as a nurse; but the dolls would need much mending.

Ever Yrs   Henry Adams.

MS: MHi

To Elizabeth Cameron

Quincy, Friday [16 Sept. 1887]

Dear Mrs Cameron

Thanks for your business letter. When you pack up your things, if you send a trunk to Washington, please put into it half a dozen of the best table-cloths, or all nine if they are equally good; and three dozen breakfast napkins. If you are not sending boxes to Washington, please give the linen to Blanchard, and tell him to get the Obers to express it to 1603 H St. Next spring, if you go to Philadelphia or New York, and will let me go shopping with you, I will, with your assistance, make up the supply for Beverly.

Great enjoyment is very pleasant, except for the reaction. I hate every kind of mood equally, but the reactionary mood I hate most. I enclose you a letter from King just received. You see, the Mexican trip can begin at any time, and go anywhere. I will start on any provocation any day after Oct. 7.

The North Easton train leaves the Old Colony station at 2.15 P.M. I can come in, and meet you, or I can join the train at South Braintree, just below here. You can have two hours at North Easton, return by the 4.53 train, reaching here at 5.30, and send your ball-dresses ahead per Winslow's Quincy Express.

As the newspapers announce Suzanne's engagement, I suppose the match has failed. She would surely have written to some of us. Yet to be Vicomtesse is a great joy.[1]

Ever Yrs   Henry Adams.

MS: MHi
1. Suzanne Bancroft's fiancé was Vicomte Albert de Chaunnac Lanzac. The match that supposedly had failed was with Charles Carroll, son of the former governor of Maryland John Lee Carroll.

To Theodore F. Dwight

Quincy 20 Sept. 1887.

My dear Dwight

I am glad to think you are back again. In another ten days I shall start after you.

Please send Brent on by rail, to get here on the 29th. I have taken passage for the horses on the steamer of October 1, which will require Brent to pass the 30th here.

I suppose the Hays will come to Washington soon. If Hay will only go to

Mexico with me, we shall amuse ourselves. I shall start at some indefinite time in October, and be gone till December.

Maggy had better not put up curtains, carpets or anything, until further orders. I wish you would, if you happen to stroll towards Georgetown, along Pennsylvania Avenue, stop at Moran's stove-shop, between 20th and 21st (I think), south side; and ask him to come at once and continue experiments on the parlor (library) fire-place. He can take out the temporary work he put in, and can try any other scheme he thinks of, either altering the opening of the flue, or enlarging the flue itself, if he can; or putting whirligigs on top.

We shall also want two new Refrigerators, one large and one small, which he can supply.

All seems quiet here. Miss Baxter returned from New York yesterday. The children are coming up. Brooks has sailed. My volume is done, all but one chapter.

Ever Yrs   Henry Adams.

MS: MHi

To John Hay

Quincy. 20 Sept. 1887.

Dear Heart

I take for granted that you will go to Mexico with us. No man can write history without going to Mexico. If only to expunge Europe from your mind, and recover your sense of American native nobility, you must go among the greasers. I shall start at any time, with anybody, for anywhere. Tell Mrs Hay that I will take care of her, and we will bring back a Mexican cuisine, peppers and gumbo-filet for breakfast all winter. I know she will go, if properly cared for.

I leave here on Oct. 1 for New York and Washington. When shall you join me there? Dwight pines without you; but he finds solitude and labor easier than a vacation devoted to nursing the moribund Alward, who bounces out of bed and writes letters when he should be singing hymns at Heaven's gate.[1]

If, as I surmise, you are already at Cleveland or near it, you must be already ready to come back again, so don't delay.

My type-writress, toiling over the last chapter of my new volume, distracts my attention, but I have no more to say than that I want to hear your English gossip, and to see your papooses again. Give them my love.

Ever Yrs   Henry Adams.

John Hay, Historian & Poet.

MS: MHi

1. Shakespeare, Sonnet 29.

To Theodore F. Dwight

Quincy. 22 Sept. [1887]

Dear Dwight

Will you please enclose to me a pattern cut of the lamp-wick.

The volume is done; the beautiful-writer is dismissed; the family is nearly reunited; I am packing; and in ten days shall be sliding on to New York.

I wish it were to be sooner, for I like cold weather here less than warm.

More or less boxes will arrive by express before I do, which you will tell William to pay for. My stay in New York will hardly exceed one day. Probably by Wednesday, the 4th you may look for me.

Ever Yrs   Henry Adams.

T. F. Dwight Esq.

Miss Baxter sends her regards. So does my mother, in intervals of disgust at not feeling well.

MS: MHi

To Elizabeth Cameron

Quincy, 27 Sept. 1887.

My dear Mrs Cameron

As I can't hear anything from you before I get to Washington on Oct. 5, or 6, I hope you will write me a line there. I expect to be at the Brevoort House on October 4 (Tuesday, a week from today) in case I can be of any service. Of course I am anxious to know about your mother, to say nothing of yourself.

I am very cold and uncomfortable, and want sunnier lands. But I wish I could find somebody pleasant to go with me as far as Los Angeles, El Paso, San Francisco, or the next world, if the trip is to be a pleasant one. I dislike solitude, as few do. Lend me Martha, and I will bless you, for notwithstanding her last experience, I am sure she will occupy my time and attention.

The Hays are at a town in the west called Cleveland, and will stay there till winter. What induces them to waste a happy life like theirs at such places, I do not know.

The little girls still sing your praises. They are to come on in December

Yrs ever   Henry Adams.

Mrs J. D. Cameron.

MS: MHi

To John Hay

Quincy, 29 Sept. '87.

Bless your digestion, my father, I never dreamed you could go to Mexico. It's only the lunatics, like La Farge, who can afford to be wise, and do what's best, without care whether the planets reel. All I meant was that it would be uncommon pleasant if the bounds of space and time had allowed themselves to be so far broken as to admit you to such lunacy.

As neither space nor time exist for me, I shall join King in October if I can find him. I rather fancy joining him at San Diego, if he wants me; but he has given no hint how to find him, and I wait in doubt whether he means to be found. A solitary pull-man across the continent is not a gay preparation for immortality, but if it were really solitary I could be content. I dread the autumn invalid.

I quit this gravel-pit next Monday for New York. On Wednesday I go on to Washington. After that, I am ready to start anywhere. The chance of my appearing at Cleveland is small, but you must bring the drawings to Washington. We will perpend upon them there.[1]

Mrs Don has deserted me, and bolted for Richfield Springs to nurse her mother. What disturbs the mamma?[2]

My brothers and sisters are once more at their posts. Brooks returns today from Germany, and he is the last. I have earned a vacation, and a long one; but probably I shall see you by December 1, at latest.

Love to the family   Ever Yrs   Henry Adams.

MS: MHi
1. Hay brought back from Europe "some drawings by Old Masters which will make your teeth curl" (Hay to HA, Sept. 23, 1887).
2. Richfield Springs is a resort in Otsego Co., N.Y. Mrs. Cameron's mother was Eliza Williams Sherman (1822–1893). It was actually her grandmother who was ill.

To Elizabeth Cameron

1603 H Street. Washington 6 Oct. 1887.

My dear Mrs Cameron

I fear you gained little by hurrying through New York. I must have arrived just as you were leaving, and of course I was more than sorry to find that you had gone; especially as I saw afterwards that the Owl Train, in which I supposed you to be, was blocked for several hours on the road.

I wanted you to give me some aid and council in New York about shopping; and to see La Farge at dinner on Tuesday; but these are among the might-have-beens which make life an incessant delusion. Now that I have got back here, I don't know why I came, or why I stay. The first days of return to this place are always hard work to me; and I am already longing to start again; but King neither writes nor telegraphs, and I wait to learn when and where that fire-bug means to let me catch him. Anyway I shall hardly see you before December, and unless you want an escort to the World's End or to the White House, I can hope to be of no use.

I am sorry; for time does not seem to clear away the wreckage of life, or to show how to climb over it; and I find no amusement so satisfactory, on the whole, as that of distributing what I can, among my friends. My only trouble is that they are too few to take it all.

Ever truly Yrs   Henry Adams.

MS: MHi

To Elizabeth Cameron

1603 H Street. Monday, 10 Oct. 1887.

My dear Mrs Cameron

Washington is still too warm for Martha. Today the thermometer is 83°. I delight in it, but Martha's roses would fade, to say nothing of your own, which are nevertheless worth preserving for your many adorers, one of whom, Spring Rice, passed last evening with me, chanting your hymns. He is certainly better worth having in your train than most of us others who are there. He has more of the charm of the most agreeable English society than any Englishman we have had. He has also another quality which is worth considering, for he is a gentleman, and the species has become rare in his profession.

I have also seen Miss Rebecca and Mlle Suzanne. The latter is more kinds of a woman than ever, and the former is prettier than ever, having filled out a bit since last spring. Why don't the idiot man insist on that girl's marrying? After the trials she has had, such a temper and disposition ought to be equal even to marriage, which seems to be the final test of angels. Suzanne says that your adorer No. 1, her grandpapa, is more and more buzzy in the head; but these old men are not to be trusted, for Suzanne also declares that, when she called to see Mr Corcoran, who receives in bed, he showed a youthful ardor of affection that scared her; though Suzanne ought not to scare easily.

I expect to hear from King today, and shall probably be gone before you arrive. Don't set me up for a melancholy recluse, or sacrifice your own cares for mine. We mostly have enough, without betraying them. I have a sort of idea that your late notes have not been so cheerful as they might be; and I am almost afraid to suspect it. The mushroom plantation is under way, and some roses with them. You shall see them when they are paid for.

Truly Yrs   Henry Adams.

MS: MHi

To Theodore F. Dwight

Dear Dwight

Will you send me over by Brent the volume of the Biographie Universelle which contains the life of Serurier, French minister at Washington in 1810–1816.

H.A.

13 Oct. 1887.

MS: MSaE

To John Hay

1603 H Street. Sunday, 16 Oct. 1887.

Dear Heart

You see before you a wilted Virginia creeper. Yesterday I got a telegram from King at El Paso saying that we must give up our trip on account of unprecedented floods.

The process of being knocked down faster than one can get up does not grow on one; but let us dismiss it, for it's a bore. I wish you were here. Washington is never so enjoyable as in this wonderful weather, and without the New Yorkers and their amusements. Dwight and I are deadly lonely, but Spring Rice strolls in at every hour, and Suzanne comes often to discuss whether she shall be married. Mrs Cameron is still, I suppose, at Beverly, but she writes that Martha is flourishing; and as poor Mrs Don has had a devilish year, what with the narrowest shaves of Martha, herself, and her [grand-] mother,[1] I am glad to hear that one of the trio is doing well. If you were here, we could be comfortable. Come and stay with me, or at any rate take your meals here, if Mrs Hay declines to come with you. I will get a cook now, and put my rugs down. Tell Mrs Hay that we need her more than Cleveland can. I am heart-broken about Lossie.[2] A few weeks ago I came within a hair's-breadth of letting Marquis drown. I thought no such trifle would disturb me, but I've no nerves left, and the danger shook me up like a scrambled egg.

Ah! I had nearly forgot! I have bought the winter-garden on New York Avenue, $6,400, or 58 cents a foot, 54 feet front by 200 deep. My gardener Durkin is refitting it, and I shall stock it. I mean to have a Japanese tea-house there, and give Marshall Niels as rewards to beauty.[3] You had better buy the corner, and we can run a summer-garden as well.

Love to Mrs Hay and the babes. Come quick.

Ever Yrs   Henry Adams.

MS: MHi
1. HA's brackets.
2. The Hays' collie had run away. Hay reported on the dog's return in his next letter to HA, Oct. 22.
3. Maréchal Niel roses.

To Elizabeth Cameron

1603 H Street. 20 October, 1887.

Dear Mrs Cameron

Seeing your windows at last open, I just called at your house to ask whether you had come. I got no good for my impertinence. "The end of this week, or the beginning of next," was all my profit, though I am as solitary and melancholy as Possum himself who is lying on the floor, drenched with the rain and disappointment at finding you still away. Rebecca Dodge has gone to Charleston. Hay is still in some barbarous western haunt. Clarence King is, or was, at El Paso, whence he telegraphed me last Saturday that we must give up our Mexican trip on account of floods unparalleled for a generation. Of course I had nowhere else to go, and no one to go with me, so here I am, and here I must stay until some one frees me. If you were here—I don't know. Probably I should never see you.

I suppose this sort of life is bearable because one bears it, but the cook-question wilts me. I can't face ordering breakfast and dinner, and poor Dwight is in consequence losing his health and hurrying to a premature grave at a boarding-house table. I see him grow yellower day by day, without complaint; but though my heart is touched, I do nothing. That cook kills *me*.

Spring Rice has returned from New York with all the Wests of the compass[1] and twentytwo trunks—or was it thirtytwo? The Endicotts asked me to dinner tonight to meet the Herschells, but I go to no dinners, even at home.[2] People are beginning to come. You should see Suzanne's ruby and sapphire. She can't make up her mind whether to be married or not. We must raise our present another five dollars. Please give my love carefully to Martha. To her mother I suppose I must be only sincerely hers

Henry Adams.

MS: MHi
  1. The British minister Sir Lionel Sackville-West and his family.
  2. Farrer Herschell (1837–1899), 1st Baron Herschell, lord chancellor 1886, 1892–1895, and his wife, Lady Agnes Adela Kindersley Herschell (d. 1902).

To Elizabeth Cameron

1603 H Street. Sunday, 23 Oct. '87.

Dear Mrs Cameron

Your note came just in time to tell me that my worst fears were true, and that I had expected you too soon, after all. I am glad, though, that you found Beverly tolerable, and are not discouraged by it. In that case you can take care of it many years, and you wont part with it. You have no business matters to arrange, either with Hooper or with me. How many times shall I tell you that the house is yours; and one does not pay rent to oneself for one's own house, or to anyone else? If you say more about it, I shall be angry, and when angry I am quite terrible.

My first cook comes tomorrow, an Irish lady who has cooked for the whole diplomatic corps, including the Gerolts, Schlözer, Thornton, and Aristarchi. I suppose she drinks, or has fits; but I liked her voice. Will you come and dine with the Chinese Minister, who will be my only dignitaried guest this winter? He has some rare porcelain, and I want him to divide it between us. Tomorrow we are to have a storm and I am going to Mt Vernon with the Endicotts and Herschels. This is the alternative to dinners. If this melancholy procession does not finish me, I shall try to survive till you come.

I know of nothing that I want in the way of shopping, unless you happen to see a chimney that doesn't smoke. If so, buy it for me if not too dear, as James Lowther said of the tooth-brush. If you are going to get dresses in New York, I shall not expect you before Thanksgiving, which is the worse for me as I shall never see the dresses. Your diplomatic flock is scattering. I suppose you will see Jenisch in New York on his way to the journey I did not make.[1]

Please let me know when you are to get here.

Ever historically   Henry Adams.

MS: MHi
  1. Rücker Jenisch, attaché of the German legation.

To Henry Cabot Lodge

1603 H Street. October 25, 1887.

My dear Cabot

My grain-dealer is John Tynan, corner of 16th and L Streets.

My horse-shoer is Banville, 409 13½ Street, below the Avenue.

My journey to Mexico has had to be given up, according to King's report of floods, &c. I hope to go somewhere in January.

Washington is brewing its usual winter deviltries, but is now quiet, decent and fit for gentlemen and ladies. You would find November passable here.[1] I hope your wife may take the notion of coming soon.

Ever Yrs   Henry Adams.

H. C. Lodge Esq.

MS: MHi

1. Lodge, elected in November 1886, was U.S. representative 1887–1893; the new Congress convened Dec. 5, 1887.

To Charles Milnes Gaskell

1603 H Street. 30 October, 1887.

Dear Carlo

If I have not written since your last letter three months ago, my reason was that I had nothing to say. I passed the whole summer at Quincy taking care of my mother; and during those four months I never left the place for a night. On leaving Quincy four weeks ago, I meant to make a trip to Mexico; but at the last moment was stopped by telegrams which announced floods, fever and broken roads, so that Clarence King, who was to be my companion, would not go. Of the world I see and hear nothing; but I have worked very hard, and have completed a third volume; so that only one more volume remains to be done, and I hope in two years to close up my life as far as literature and so-called usefulness go. I have got to the point where they bore me.

Winter is beginning again. To make a little fresh interest I have bought a green-house, and have taken to forcing roses and things. The amusement is rather more expensive than a good-sized yacht, but it is an aristocratic occupation, and I am singular in following it, for in this city no other gentleman cultivates flowers or fruits. As long as I have roses to give away, no one will comment on my gray hair or bald head, or the crows-feet that are deep as wells under my eyes. The women at least will see nothing but ambrosial curls. As I never dine out or go into society, I cannot introduce the fashion of wearing garlands, but I can look at them, which must be pleasanter. My table is loaded with flowers, and I have to buy Chinese vases, at God knows what cost, to show them. Flowers and bric-a-brac are refined tastes, but, when combined with history, would ruin Ferdinand Rothschild.[1]

Of news I have very little. The Hays have come home, and are to be here next week, but I have not seen them or heard their English budget of news. Lord and Lady Herschell were here last week. As I declined to dine with them, I was asked to join a party for them to visit Mt Vernon, and did so. He seems a pleasant man. Some Aclands, too, have been here. Chamberlain is expected; and Spring Rice tells me that Mrs Dugdale is coming or come over. I would rather like to know Chamberlain, who strikes me as the strongest man in English public life; but a politician is a poor lot anyway, and not a comfortable acquaintance.[2] Our own politics are too mean for notice. As far as I can understand them, your's are no better. I have often told you that I no longer follow them, and I'll not repeat it; but if you can follow ours, I'll follow your's. I am much in hopes that our government, under the fisheries pretext, may have the good sense to seize Canada. We need a war to clear away this Irish and socialist rubbish; and a war between England and America would be interesting, especially as our generation could look on. I have urged it all I could, not only on my own government but also on your Legation; but Secretary Bayard and Minister West have no sense of fun or grand politics. I can do no more unless I offer to raise an Irish legion for the capture of Quebec.

I hear of new things nothing. Books are many and few. We have neither poet, philosopher nor wit. Even I qui vous parle visibly baisse. I have only wit enough left to wish the world had more. London doubtless scintillates. I see that even old Venables still survives; and every now and then I chuckle over some column of the Saturday which would not have pleased me much twenty years ago, but which has now an octogenarian flavor as of rain-water Madeira.[3] If there is newer wit, I do not hit upon it, unless Myers can be considered to have opened a new vein, or adit, in ghosts.[4]

I owe Robert a letter, and am waiting to hear his news from Hay. My affectionate regards to your wife. What school is the small boy at?

Ever Yrs   Henry Adams.

MS: MHi

1. Ferdinand James de Rothschild (1839–1898), Liberal Unionist M.P. 1885–1898, art collector.

2. Joseph Chamberlain was in the U.S., November 1887 to March 1888, negotiating a treaty concerning North Atlantic fisheries.

3. George Stovin Venables (1810–1888), a contributor to the *Saturday Review* from its first number in 1855 to his death.

4. Frederic Myers, one of the founders of the Society for Psychical Research in 1882 and coauthor of *Phantasms of the Living* (1886).

To John Hay

1603 H Street. Sunday 30 Oct. '87.

Dear Heart

I am pretty well tired out waiting for you, and am mighty glad you're coming. The last month has been as hard work as I've known, thanks to King, who writes at last from El Paso a letter to explain what happened. I've got through, and after you get here the sense of hanging by one's finger-nails will be less. Mrs Don also promises to return tomorrow. My only consideration for a month of dry-rot is that Volume III is getting printed; but as I am seasick every time I see a proof, the sense of its being a baby becomes overpowering. You have missed Lord & Lady Herschel, whom I accompanied to Mt Vernon the other day, and found her ladyship so agreeable that after an hour's work I fled to Mrs Wright and Nanny Macomb as to a corps de ballet.[1] The British female whacks me silly. Chamberlain will just arrive for your delectation, and Spring Rice says that Mrs Dugdale will stay with you in December; but I believe you are his informant. She can't stay with me, for I am going to have Ned Hooper's three daughters, and shall expect Del and Helen to entertain them. You see that Whitney is broken up. I have heard nothing about it, and don't know what it means.[2] Even Suzanne was unsuspicious of it two days ago. This disposes of all the set of the two last winters, and probably some one new must do the monkeying. No simian arrivals are announced.

I have got a new cook at last, and feel as though poor Dwight had a chance. Your house seems all right; but once more, at the risk of impertinence, I aver that you ought not to let the children take their meals down stairs unless malaria is a very decided object. I would kill and mutilate anyone who let children of mine do it. Yet chills and fever are a good American complaint, and perhaps suit our civilisation, so I don't find fault. Of course King does not say when he returns.

My love to all yours

Ever   H.A.

MS: MHi

1. Nannie Rodgers Macomb (b. 1864), daughter of Rear Adm. John Navarre Macomb and Ann Rodgers Macomb.
2. William C. Whitney turned over his duties to an acting secretary of the navy and was rumored to have suffered a severe nervous breakdown.

To Elizabeth Cameron

1603 H Street. Saturday evening [4 Nov. 1887]

No, I will not be bullied to that extent! I should not dare look anyone in the face and admit that I had let you pay me such an absurd price for a few weeks in a house I would be glad to get occupied for nothing. All Beverly would be down here in a week offering you any house on the shore at fifty per cent off my charges. Mrs Brimmer would give you no peace till she had got you to take her house for taxes and water-rates.

If you insist on paying rent, I suppose I must stand by Hooper's estimate of last year, which, I think, was $400. Or you can exchange checks with me for $1,000,000 or any other round sum.

The poor greenhouse is very sad, with no roof, and plants all tumbled on the ground. I am afraid to show it tomorrow, though I would much like to go there with you and Martha. Another week will get it going, I hope, but until then I can't recommend it as a show place.

I enclose the plat of the ground with the prices asked. Please keep it. I want to make Hay buy some. He shall have no roses if he doesn't. They shall all go to you.

Yrs truly   Henry Adams.

Mrs J. D. Cameron.

MS: MHi

To Elizabeth Cameron

1603 H Street. [Nov. 1887]

Oh, don't, don't, don't, PLEASE don't! You don't know how hard it is. Besides I have already declined to dine at Endicott's, and shall refuse Bayard's invitation if he sends me one. Let me off, and I will love you like a—niece! Poor Spring Rice was having a nasty, faint turn just as your card came last night; and we were dosing him with boiling water on the sofa.

Please send your guests here! I will dose them with anything,—indigo is handiest;—but don't make me meet the Endicotts and Bayard.

H.A.

MS: MHi

To Lucy Baxter

1603 H Street. 5 Nov. 1887.

My dear Miss Baxter

I want to learn from the friendly Patterson whether he can find for me, and send me, some rose-plants of a size for immediate forcing, and at a reasonable rate: say $4 to $6 a dozen. All the nurseries hereabouts sell mostly small plants; but I am in a hurry, and want flowers by Christmas. Of course I want the best and newest, though I do not run after roses like

Her Majesty, for size; but I want them also eighteen inches or two feet high; and if I can get them of that size, I would take almost any good kind of the Teas or Hybrids. The number would be less important. I will take any number from a dozen to a thousand if they are cheap enough, but at present I would like to try the plants, and, for an experiment, five or six dozen would do. Even a dozen very choice or new and amusing ones would be exciting. Will you ask Patterson about it? If he knows he can find the things, he could write an order to the nursery to have plants and bill sent to me.

The greenhouse is at present a chaos of glass and timber. I expect your aid to run it. Please visit all the greenhouses there are, more or less, and tell me if you see anything without which no respectable greenhouse could be.

We are still much interested in your negotiation. Dwight watches it as though it were his own.[1]

Ever truly Yrs   Henry Adams.

MS: ScU

1. The negotiation, presumably concerning Thackeray's letters to Lucy Baxter and her family, was with E. L. Burlingame of Charles Scribner's Sons. He had just published Thackeray's letters to Mrs. William Brookfield serially in *Scribner's Magazine* and as a book. *Thackeray's Letters to an American Family*, edited with an introduction by Lucy Baxter, was published by Century and did not appear until 1904.

To Elizabeth Cameron

1603 H Street. Sunday [13 Nov? 1887]

My dear Mrs Cameron

I am very much pleased that you should have been troubled by so delightful a cause as not dining with me. You have discovered a new way of giving pleasure by absence. Some people can give it only in that way, but in you it is a *tour de force* that I admire and wonder at. As for its cause, it is, I suppose, only a "Spring Rice." If I were tolerably sane or sensible I should have done as he and Endicott wished, and should have dined with you all, which would have saved you annoyance. The fault was wholly mine, and I am as much ashamed of it as I ought to be; but having long since given up all attempt to defend, excuse or justify in any way my own conduct, I can only hold my tongue and not make the matter worse by talking. You shall reprove me to what extent you please, if you will only come to dinner to do it. I wish you would come this evening when Langley dines here alone.[1]

Ever gratefully Yrs   Henry Adams.

Mrs Cameron

MS: MHi

1. Samuel Pierpont Langley (1834–1906), astronomer, physicist, director of the Allegheny Observatory at Pittsburgh 1867–1886, secretary of the Smithsonian Institution 1887–1906.

To Lucy Baxter

1603 H Street. 15 November, 1887.

Dear Miss Baxter

Thanks for your two letters. I was much gratified by your remarks on my second volume, and shall begin to think myself an artist if I make on other people, as on you, the impressions you describe. Did you ever see Shakespear's King John acted? I saw old Phelps act it in Berlin in 1858, and it left on my mind only the impression of the art of the dramatist and actor who succeeded in giving something noble and sympathetic to one of the worst scoundrels recorded among rulers.[1]

Thanks also for your labors on the green-house question. Patterson's views on the subject of immediate forcing are final. I must buy here the roses I need, if I can find them at moderate rates in the greenhouses. Such roses as are for next spring and winter, I can still buy wherever they are best, and I would like to have Patterson keep his eyes about, and if he sees a *very* good lot, cheap, he can snap them for me. You know I don't care for size but for sentiment, and the old Glorie de Dijon and Safrano are prettier to me than La France or Her Majesty. Neither am I eager that my roses should look professional. I have only a winter-garden, and seek no prizes at shows. Yet I want whatever is best in taste, and shall be glad to try the new.

At this moment, as quickly as possible, I want water-lilies. Do they flower in winter under forcing? Do they propagate by seed, bulb, cutting or roots, and can I set them going at once? At least, can I not start them? I want the white, pink and blue water-lilies, not the lotus, which is too big and coarse. Any lily that is refined and amusing would be a joy to the babies whose perambulators will frequent my empty glass halls. Whatever Patterson can supply, I want quick; for next week my new roof will be finished; my new heaters will be started, and I can begin to get the plants going. As yet we have had no frost below 32 °, but the shrubs have been so chilled as to be thrown out of bearing, and have been knocked about till they are almost destroyed. The agony of mind has been too much for me, and I have nearly taken to my bed.

I want also to know something about grapes. I mean to indulge in some vines, but unless I can steal them from Mrs Jack, I fear getting poor ones.

Dwight had a letter from Burlingame the other day, written as by one in a steam-engine, saying much about the letters. Dwight will write to you, I suppose. Burlingame seems to have been a little scared to find them so much more than he expected, and he is like a hen who has hatched ducklings.

Did I write that Mrs Dugdale was to be at the Brunswick? If I did, I was just about that-sized idiot that I always knew myself to be. She is at the Vendome, and has been there a week.

If you drive out with my mother, stop in Cambridge and see how my children are. They are coming to me in three weeks, I hope; but I fear their father may be unable to get away.

I do not know that you can do anything else for me, unless you will go to De Busigny's and ride my horse. Daisy has been laid up for a fortnight with a cough, and I have not ridden except on my greenhouse which requires a manège more difficult than any Busigny can teach.

History languishes under all these trials, but by the blessing of Heaven I manage to torture at least one statesman a day.

Very truly Yrs   Henry Adams.

Miss Baxter.

MS: ScU

1. Samuel Phelps (1804–1878) of the Sadler's Wells company of London, which visited Germany March–May 1859.

To Lucy Baxter

1603 H Street. Monday, 19 Dec. 1887.

My dear Miss Baxter

I ought to have written to you long ago, but all my proceedings have been affected by the illness of Edward Hooper, which has left me, since December 1, in doubt as to all my doings. Even now I am puzzled. I don't want to come on until he is better, for fear of exciting and upsetting him, yet I have not an idea whether he is really improving.[1] Anyway I have given up Christmas;—partly on Dwight's account, who is in low spirits that is actually a pleasure to see. I hope to start in the first week of January, after paying my bills,—or before, if the bills are as big as I expect.

Burlingame's letter is the usual story. Publishers are all vile, and the English worse than the American. Whenever the wretches come to terms among themselves, everything will go on, and you will be cheated duly. Burlingame writes to Dwight that he is disappointed not to have heard from you. You had better write and tell him that you were never so delighted with anything in your life.

The greenhouse is now our daily resort. Generally it is a shower-bath; but the season there is about March, and the roses shoot merrily in long red streamers, while one gold-fish and a frog swim in the tank, expecting the lillies which are just beginning to show life. I have nauseated all my women-friends with camelias; but my roses and violets obstinately refuse to flower, and the more fire I make in the steam-engine, the colder and bluer my violets and Bennetts and Brides are. Just now I have on my table one or two Niels, and tiny Papa Gontiers, and a Duchesse de Brabant, about the size of a hazel-nut, but so exquisitely delicate that I think it makes even the pure white of the camelias a little gross; while it is my sole memento of the late Suzanne who made me order it, and whose name it now bears on the gardener's label. As Mrs Charles Carroll, this blusher has a great future in my affections.[2]

My various Queen-regents go down to their domain occasionally, and order everything changed; and as each has a particular dislike to everything that anyone else likes, and as they all disapprove what I like, we have great success. Martha Cameron does best, for she only wants to be carried about. Her mamma shows desperate energy, but as yet only misguided. We have had a snow-storm of late, which has cast a solemn gloom over our interior, somewhat as though we were under water, besides dripping us with ice-water wherever we go; and this incident has prevented our official Sunday-morning meeting, so that we are behindhand with business. I want half a dozen low wicker-work chairs, of the cheapest kind, and can't get them here. Do you know whether Boston produces them? I want also a great many other things, but, until I can get some flowers, it seems to me I needn't hurry.

I hope you are beginning to find Boston familiar, and that the routine is growing natural. I cannot say that Dwight or I give you a good example; for two homesicker men I never saw, especially as neither of them know what they are homesick for; but we shall be glad to take you in, at any time you think a change agreeable.

Give my love to my mother. I am sending off Christmas presents to the Florida baby today.[3] For this time the little girls at Cambridge must go unpresented. I shall try to find something in New York as I go through.

Very truly Yrs   Henry Adams

Dwight says he is going to write.

MS: ScU
1. Hooper suffered from depression brought on by the death of his sister Ellen Gurney on Nov. 20.
2. Presumed to be still engaged to the Vicomte de Chaunnac Lanzac, Suzanne Bancroft married Charles Carroll privately on Nov. 15. HA was one of three guests at the wedding dinner given by George Bancroft.
3. Marian Fell (1886?–1935), daughter of Edward Nelson Fell and Anne Palmer Fell, was named after Marian Adams.

To Elizabeth Cameron

1603 H Street. Christmas, 1887.

Dear Mrs Cameron

Martha's aesthetic education is too much neglected. She must be taught in easy lessons. I send you a bit of La Farge's water-color to begin.

Ever Yrs   Henry Adams.

MS: MHi

To Elizabeth Cameron

1603 H Street. [1887?]

My dear Friend

You never in your life said or did anything that gave me so much as a twinge. How can you imagine such an outrageous fiction? I thought you understood better my weaknesses. On the contrary if it weren't for you I should have no spirits at all, and if I am ever more than usually low in my mind, it is because I don't see you to keep me up. You have quite enough to worry you without inventing more, so please don't class me among the burdens. If I have any cause of complaint, it is only that I can't relieve you of some of your worries. My mother used to send me over Europe to get maids, cooks, servants in general, hats and clothes for her. Why don't you utilize me in the same professional way?

Ever Yrs   Henry Adams.

MS: MHi

2.

Working Toward the End
1888–1889

At the beginning of 1888 ties to life seemed to multiply. Cecil Spring Rice, an attaché at the British legation who was still in his twenties, proved to be very like the young Englishmen who had become Adams' close friends twenty years before. Spring Rice was literary, political, social, high-spirited, and possessed of a gift for friendship to which Adams immediately responded.

An even greater imaginative leap of years marked his growing closeness to Martha, Elizabeth Cameron's baby daughter. Martha brought out a great and growing love for children which Adams expressed in person and in easy, fanciful letters.

Other evidence, however, shows that beneath the surface lay depression and world-weariness. The surviving fragment of diary, with its record of progress on the *History,* also shows how concentrated work could thrust out gloom, for a time at least. (The diary, in effect Adams' notes to himself, is printed here in italics.)

Another vigorous summer's work at Quincy brought Adams through the fourth, and last, draft volume—on Madison's second administration. Then, after three months' holiday spent shepherding his friend Sir Robert Cunliffe on a coast-to-coast tour of the United States, he began in January 1889 to prepare copy-text for publication. He rewrote from the beginning and, even at this late stage, sought new sources—in Ottawa and, through Cunliffe, in London. Finally, in October 1889, the first two printed volumes, on Jefferson's first administration, came from Scribner's.

To Lucy Baxter

1603 H Street. 1 Jan. 1888.

My dear Miss Baxter

Thanks for your letter of the 30th. I expect to leave here next Thursday, the 5th and to reach Boston the next day, probably by the late train, between ten and eleven at night. I shall stay a week. Unless I hear to the contrary, I take for granted that my mother wishes me to stay with her, so I shall come to Mt Vernon Street.

You should have been here to see my Christmas presents. The Chinese minister sent me a tea-cup, four hundred years old, to teach me what Ming porcelain ought to be. In order to show its beauties, he had an expensive jeweller's box made for it, of awful yellow silk and velvet, best American style. I knew not which most to admire, but my visitors preferred the box. They thought they could buy the tea cup anywhere for ten cents, but the box was beautiful.

The greenhouse, after barely escaping a freeze, is today under water, drenched in snow and rain. My roses are coming into flower in quantities, but will come out just as I start for Boston. The lilies are struggling up; but I have not yet succeeded in warming the tank as I wish. The cold water and cold air between them are enough to disgust any Lily unless a Jersey one.[1]

Very truly Yrs   Henry Adams.

MS: ScU
1. Lillie Langtry, born on the island of Jersey, was known as the Jersey Lily.

To Elizabeth Cameron

1603 H Street.

My dear Mrs Cameron

Last evening Spring Rice, in a wholly unjustifiable manner, violated the laws of hospitality by writing what he pleased to call a sonnet on the greenhouse. As it seems to refer chiefly to you, I send you his original draft, illustrated by the poet, and also a translation in Dwight's best hand. The poetry will not give you fame like that of Laura or of "Mr W. H." whom Shakespeare complimented in the same form of verse; but barring want of imagination, vigor of expression, and choice of language, I do not see but that it is as good as some of Shakespeare's and all of the magazines'. If you will have it,—so! If not, you can write the next sonnet yourself.[1]

Please let me know if I may get your seats and tickets for Thursday, or run to the dressmaker's for you, or do your packing, or take care of Martha.

Dwight and I went to Baltimore yesterday and bought plants—more roses. I send you a few camelias which have just come in.

Yrs truly   Henry Adams.

3 Jan. 1888.

MS: MHi

1. Spring Rice called his sonnet "H.A. to E.C." The Dwight copy, not the original draft, survives:

> When all the world is cold and blank and bare—
> When like a stricken victim nature cowers
> When winter drags its slow reluctant hours—
> Midwinter on the earth and in the air—
> Seek we the haunt where all that's bright & fair
>> In summer teems sweet scents & tangled bowers
>> There all the glory of the south is ours
> Deep green and gold and creamy white and there
>> The genius of our flowery paradise.
> She waits, the fair magician who can bring
>> To weary loiterers under weeping skies
> In Wintry ways forlornly wandering
>> Spring in her smile & summer in her eyes
> A sweeter summer and a softer spring.

To E. L. Godkin

Boston, 13 Jan. 1888.

Dear Godkin

Edward Hooper is recovering from a long and trying nervous illness which has kept him more or less in bed for six weeks. I am here for the purpose of seeing whether I can get him to Washington, but we are still a little afraid to risk the fatigue, and I shall return next week without him, hoping that he will follow in another week or two.

I am also in attendance on my mother who is very infirm and complaining. A week of these pleasures is more than I hanker after, and is calculated to impress on one's mind what our friend Zola calls *la joie de vivre,* but not a passionate wish to prolong it.[1] Of other matters I know nothing, and I have at last reached the stage so much deprecated by you in old days, where not only I never read a newspaper, but feel additional pangs of ennui whenever I see one. Next summer I am intending a trip to the Fiji islands where they eat missionaries, and may, if they like, eat me, but at least will not elect a President.

Give my love to your wife, and believe me

Ever Yrs   Henry Adams.

MS: MH

1. Emile Zola (1840–1902), *La Joie de vivre* (1884), one of the Rougon-Macquart novels.

To Martha Cameron

1603 H Street.

Mr Dobbit has much pleasure in accepting Miss Martha Cameron's very kind invitation for this afternoon, and begs to send a few flowers for her table.[1]

3 Feb. 1888.

MS: MHi
1. Dobbit (Dobbitt, Dr. Dobbitt), Martha's name for HA.

1888. Washington.
Sunday, 12 February.[1]

The winter drags along about as miserably as it began. I am still quite off my balance, and have been peculiarly depressed by an attack of what seems malaria, perhaps the growth of my greenhouse. Our labor and expense there have been rewarded by a deluge of Niel roses; but the hybrids I bought have made no progress. Sturgis Bigelow made his appearance this week. My brother Charles has been here on railroad business. Lucy Frelinghuysen has come in and out. Martha Cameron comes for biscuit and books, and howls if she is not allowed to enter the house. My little knot of friends are steady in their allegiance, and Mrs Cameron is more winning than ever; but Clarence King telegraphs that he will be ready to start next Thursday, and I hope a week from today to be in Charleston, on my way to Cuba. I am weary of myself and my own morbid imagination, but still more weary of the world's clack and bustle, and the dreary recurrence of small talk. History is in Chap. VI of Book II. No proofs of Vol. III this week.

1. HA appears to have kept a continuous diary, in several volumes, beginning in 1852 at the age of fourteen. The single portion known to survive (after his methodical rereading and destruction of it in 1888 and other possible winnowings) consists of forty-eight entries running from Feb. 12, 1888, to July 7, 1889. This fragment has not previously been published in full. The entries are integrated with the letters in chronological order but are italicized to distinguish HA's private notations from what he wrote for the eyes of others. When entries occur successively, footnotes are gathered at the end of the sequence. The manuscript diary is at the Massachusetts Historical Society.

To Lucy Baxter

1603 H Street. 16 Feb. 1888.

My dear Miss Baxter

I start south tomorrow with John Hay and Dwight. I do not know where we are going or how long we shall stay, but I mean to go as far as I can, and stay till I get warm. I have not a notion of any future address, or how anyone can communicate with me. I will try to write a line or two from somewhere, but my notions of geography are misty.

I have written to your niece, but when I wrote, I supposed Dwight would stay here to acknowledge anything she sent. Please explain to her the change in arrangements.[1]

I know of nothing here to amuse my mother unless it is the death of Mrs Frank Emmons. She died of whiskey, a quart a day. A post-mortem examination showed three points of advanced disease of the brain.[2] Frank was devoted to her, and has felt her death acutely. As my own brain is diseased in a good many more than three points, I am only surprised at her temperance. If I took to drink, nothing short of a hogshead would answer.

My Niel roses are gone, which is the reason I go. We expect to reach St Augustine (Hotel Ponce de Leon) next Wednesday. I know no more.

Ever Yrs   Henry Adams.

MS: ScU
1. The niece, Lucy Hampton, was sending HA rose plants from South Carolina.
2. Waltha A. Emmons died Feb. 12 of "general debility" (*New York Times,* Feb. 13).

To John Hay

Havana. 4 March [1888]

Dear Hay

At last I have bought a straw hat, and you can tell Mrs Hay that as this was Sunday, I went this morning to mass at two churches, and am going this afternoon to a bull-fight. As I attend these religious functions wholly out of regard for her, I wish to receive proper credit. We miss you sadly. Our trip to Narcoossee would have been perfect if you had been with us to shiver in the furious rigor of the Florida cold; and you would have given gaiety even to Tampa, although the place taught us only the origin of the phrase "to tampa with," meaning doubtless to put a stopper, or head, on anyone inclined to effervesce. We had a good voyage, and fine east winds, and arrived here yesterday morning.

Havana is just my affair. I swagger about in a big straw hat, and wallow in Cuban dirt. The place is more Spanish than Spain. The women at church are just lovely in their black mantillas. I have gone silly over ten ancient negresses who were so classically draped about their faces and shoulders, and knelt and sat on the church pavements so mediaevally that life seemed sunless where they were not to be. The palms in the Governor's garden have better figures than I imagined. I am so much pleased with the squalor and possible fleas of Havana that I doubt whether we shall go further especially because careful inquiry seems to prove that I can go nowhere but to New York. By way of New York, I can in time reach Jamaica. I might also reach Jamaica by way of Mexico, but New York seems rather the most direct, unless we paddle over in a row-boat. Tomorrow I may learn more about my movements. With the fear of King before me, I want to find out whether Cuba has any ancient art to steal, but as I am a taciturn and shrinking animal, and have not an idea how to set about it, I fear that the original Velasquezs and things will lie about till he comes.[1] The look of the houses shows that once good things were understood here. They knew and still know how to make arches. Every old building has a fine arched court. Here and there one sees a good façade. They built as bad rococo too as any Spaniards that ever lived, and the cathedral front is a triumph of the school. With all these advantages they must have had bric-a-brac; otherwise they were little better than civilised Christians or Lutherans; but I cannot make up my mind which bell I had better ring first, to ask, as King would do: "Tiene usted por hazardo algo de bric-à-brac adentro."

Dwight and I had a captivating dinner at the Restaurant de Paris last evening, and became quite glorified over a bottle of Burgundy. Upon my little life, you would have enjoyed it, for it was muy Espagnol; more so than Dwight's internal economy today. We went afterwards to two Spanish theatres, and closed up with a Baile,—the Andaluz. My soul is divided with emotions whether I shall close up tonight with a masked ball, after the bull-fight and opera. Ask Mrs Cameron what she would advise. Perhaps, to make sure of being right, I had better go; but I have no one to tell me how to misbehave.

We still expect to be back in a fortnight. Love to all yours.

Ever truly   Henry Adams.

MS: RPB

1. Diego Rodriguez de Silva y Velázquez (1599–1660), the Spanish painter.

To Elizabeth Cameron

Vedado. Wed. 7th [March 1888]

My dear Mrs Cameron

I have got your fan. Let me nourish the hope that it will be what you want, for the price it cost was ruinous—not in money, but in morale. As far as money is concerned, the only trouble was to find anything good enough for you to carry; but your responsibility for moral expenditure is beyond calculation. Of course I could not select the proper thing without assuring myself that it was beyond criticism, and the day after our arrival at Havana I found an altogether unexpected chance of educating myself, so that I might defy all the Spanish attachés in Washington to carp at your outfit. A great bull-fight was to take place. Six Andalucian bulls, and three famous Espadas—among them the celebrated Guerrito, of whom you have heard as much as I—were brought over at great expense, for the occasion.

Never was such a splendid function in Habaña! I had hitherto refused to see a Corrida de Toros. Even in Spain I carefully kept away from the show, not so much from motives of delicacy for the bull, as from long experience that the consequence of such a spectacle to me would be a more or less violent and sudden attack of sea-sickness; but I was so deeply convinced of the steadiness with which I could face anything in pursuit of your fan, that I only wonder I did not, like the bold but ill-mannered gentleman of the German ballad, accoutre myself as a banderillero, and jump into the arena before the whole circus.[1] I did the next best thing, for I made Dwight go with me. We got the best seats, in the front row, just where the bull enters; but I doubt whether any one of the six bulls was half as much astonished as I was at our meeting. Even after I was fairly seated, I could not shake myself back into a certainty that I was I anyhow, and I began to feel that my mission in life was to be an Andalucian espada with an Astracan cap and a purple jacket. The show was just thrilling, but what turned my poor old addle-brain on end was the dozen or two ladies in more or less soul-moving costumes. One exquisite creature in the costume of an Andalucian bull-fightress,—a feminine adaptation of the matador's dress—reduced me to a pitiable state of imbecile adoration. She was a vision, and I wished I were a picadero or a peccadillo, or anything to her. The thousands of men howled with delight as she entered. Her black Astracan cap and blood-red dress looked, I admit, a little warm for the season; but we hot-blooded Spaniards pay no thought to such trivial details as that. The other ladies wore the white mantilla mostly, which is also fatal to any man with a soul. I was still lost in gazing at these dreams of Roman delight, and watching their fans—the Andalucian vision carried one such as you wanted,—when the barrier opposite was thrown open, and the procession of fighters, headed by the three Espadas, marched across, loaded with costumes of color and gold. If I was enthusiastic before, I was classically sublime at this last vestige of the Roman arena; and the Captain General assumed the proportions of Heliogabalus. I felt that life was still left in the worn-out world. My true archaic blood beat strongly in my heart. I wished for Clarence King to be with me that we might enjoy together the revival of our strong, young lives. Just then the bull rushed in, close by me, and the fight began. He was a handsome animal; but certainly he looked a little out of place; too natural and domestic, and rather Yankee than Roman. From the first I could not impress myself with the idea that he was dangerous. He did not seem to want to hurt anybody. He dashed at the red cloths, but not at the men. Presently they stuck things into him till long patches of blood streamed down his shoulders, and he dashed at a poor, old cab-horse, whose eyes were bandaged, and whose rider held him still, close to the barrier. The bull struck him square on the shoulder, and I saw the horse fall over, feebly kicking, while the bull strolled away. I looked at Dwight. He was blue, purple and streaked. I felt that I looked worse. I turned my glass on the Andalucian beauty. If she felt any pleasure at that moment, she showed none in her face. She looked bored. The fight went on. As I measured it, the time taken to kill that bull was two hours and three quarters. He gored three more horses in the same cool way, without seemingly enjoying it. He fought without enthusiasm, doggedly, as though he were bored, like the Andalucian beauty. Twice he leaped clean over the five-foot barrier, and I could almost touch his back, and might almost have washed my hands in his blood, while he stood at my feet. At last, the Espada came forward, and missed his first *coup*. The next time, I knew by the cries that he succeeded better. I saw the bull trot forward a few steps, the sword sticking up from his shoulder. Then he stopped and began to shake himself. Then a torrent of blood began to pour out of his mouth and nostrils. I judged this to continue fifteen minutes. I watched my Andalucian beauty, who looked straight forward without a sign of interest. The other women mostly looked away; or uneasily about the place. None seemed excited or carried into regions of frenzy. I should say they were all wishing themselves elsewhere. The men howled more or less, but on the whole I was too unwell to watch long; and the moment the bull was dragged out of the arena, I told Dwight that I would keep company with the bull. Dwight acquiesced with some energy. We dropped down a ladder, got our cab, and drove back to town. On arriving we happened to notice the time. The entire fight had not consumed half an hour. I was feeling critically unwell, and if it had not been for a sort of general carnival that afternoon and evening, I should have hardly recovered my balance.

Yet I am not disposed to say that I will never go to another bull-fight. On the contrary I will not only go, but I will carry Martha in my arms, and order for you a whole Andalucian costume, if you will go with me. Nothing would give me more entertainment than to see how you would get through the show; but I admit I should expect to get the fun from you rather than from the bull direct. My offer holds good for a year.

Cuba is fascinating, in the bull-fight way. Habaña is as romantic as anything in Spain, but it is excessively Spanish. Dirt and noise and heat have driven us out three miles to a summer restaurant kept by a Frenchman named Petit, close on the water. Here, looking out over the surf and rocks, and the blue-green-purple sea, I am passing a morning writing to you, with the thermometer at 90° and no appetite for breakfast. I like dirt, and adore heat, and care little for sleep, and prefer the worst possible smells; so I am in Paradise, after a manner; but Dwight is sad and hankers for Washington and Possum. My only trouble is that I can go no further. We cannot get to Jamaica by any means at all that would bring us back in time for Dwight's leave of absence. We cannot even go to St Iago at the other end of the island except once a week, by steamer, and only by starting Sunday which is too late. Tomorrow we shall go to the baths of San Diego to see the western end of the island. Monday we shall go to Matanzas. Wednesday we must start back to Florida, and I suppose we shall be in Washington by Saturday the 18th. I am, of course, eager to return; but probably should come back by way of Panama and New Zealand if my own choice were to guide, so great is my haste.

Habaña seems to devote itself to perpetual masquerade. Last Sunday was nothing but driving, riding, masking and balls. I have passed all my evenings at the opera, selecting the handsomest woman in the boxes for distant adoration. They are fascinating, but I cannot ask them to breakfast, for I foolishly forgot to bring introductions, and my romantic imagination breaks down in the effort to introduce myself. To my surprise I find also the men as handsome as the women. Accustomed to regard men as ugly animals, I never recover from the surprise of having to admit their good looks. I have ransacked the shops, but have found nothing to buy. Cigars and fans are the only exceptions. Not even a Spanish toy for Martha has shown its head. Unless I bring her a cocoa-nut, or a string of bananas, I can do nothing for her esthetic education. I have not even found plants for the greenhouse. Where the whole show is a greenhouse, flowers are scarce and poor. Unless I bring over the whole botanical garden, with its avenues of eightyfoot palms, I must leave empty-handed.

Hasta mas ver! Give my love to Martha.

Ever truly Yrs   Henry Adams.

MS: MHi

1. In Schiller's literary ballad of 1798 "Der Handschuh" (The Glove), a lady throws her glove into the lions' cage to test her lover; he retrieves it but then throws it at her face.

To Charles Milnes Gaskell

Los Baños de S. Diego 8 March 1888.

My dear Carlo

In the course of aimless wandering I have drifted for a day to this Spanish hole in the middle of Cuba, and bethink myself that I owe you a letter. An evening with nothing to do at a Cuban sulphur-bath tends to recall one's friends to one's mind. While the chattering Cubans are playing loto at the next table, I will try to write a few pages to bore you.

I forget where or when my last letter was written. I can only remember that I had a more than usually unsatisfactory winter at Washington. I have got into a bad way of never leaving my house except to see one or two intimates like John Hay. Society scares and bores me, and I have wholly dropped it. During the cold weather I pass an hour every afternoon at my greenhouse and watch my roses. If it were not that friends are very goodnatured, and come in unasked to breakfast and dinner, I should be a hermit. One of my most valuable allies is a young fellow of your Legation whose name I have already mentioned to you,—Spring Rice,—who not only comes two or three times a week to dinner, and keeps me posted about the world's doings, whether I care for them or not, but also brings

Englishmen with him if he thinks them worth knowing. Among others he brought Mr Chamberlain, who took kindly to my habits, and asked himself several times to dinner without other company than ourselves. Chamberlain amused and interested me. He talked much and well, very openly, and with a certain näiveté that I hardly expected. He was a success in society, and was received with an amount of attention that seemed to puzzle him, considering how little favor he got from newspapers and politicians. He flirted desperately and openly with the young girls, and especially with one of my own little flock who come to breakfast with me.[1] On the whole he made a decided mark, and held more than his own against all comers. His opinion of America is not a high one, and he took little trouble to disguise it; but as he studied it only on the political side, he did not disturb our complacency. His chief objection was that we cared little for statesmen and orators.

By way of contrast to Chamberlain, Charles Robartes turned up. I am sorry to say that he was considered to be *the* bore. He was obliging enough to do me some small services which I hardly repaid. I hope the government will promote him to a lucrative office at a distance.

Ferguson of Novar was also at Washington with his sister and Mrs Dugdale.[2] Probably Mrs Dugdale has told you her travels. We all liked Ferguson who became intimate in our narrow little set, and we were sorry when he went home. He and Spring Rice and I had a common tie in devotion to Mrs Cameron, who took Ferguson into her house to nurse him through a fever.

I have been particularly well all winter, but the disease of restlessness is quite as trying as most fevers. Clarence King was ordered by his physicians to these absurd baths for rheumatism. I made every arrangement to come with him. John Hay, who has some chronic inflammation of the vocal chords agreed to be of the party. At the last moment King's physicians would not let him go; but I was bound to go somewhere so I took my companion, Theodore Dwight, and started with him and Hay for Florida three weeks ago. Hay left us after a fortnight, to return home, but Dwight and I rambled on, crossed from Florida to Havana, and have been a week in Cuba. I like summer, and palms, Spain and garlic; I do not much object to dirt or smells; and this time I thought my stomach so strong that I went even to a bull-fight which was declared to be the most splendid ever seen in Havana. Splendid it certainly was, but one bull settled my stomach so effectually that I left the other five to the mercies of the rest of their admirers. Havana is a gay ruin, but after being kept awake five nights by the noise and smell, I thought that country air would do us good, so we came about a hundred miles into the western end of the island. Next Wednesday I expect to start back in order to reach Washington on the 18th.

Meanwhile history has made little progress. I want to go to the Fiji Islands next summer, a five months affair; but am in doubt whether I can fairly get away. The object of such long expeditions about the Pacific is to tire myself out till home becomes rest. If I can do this within two years, things will be simplified. Otherwise there is no help but to start then for good, and go till I drop. You can have no idea of the insanity of restlessness. Reason is helpless to control it.

War in Europe might affect my movements, and I am watching for its outbreak with more interest than I have felt in public affairs for years.[3]

My mother, at last advices, was rather well. I hope you and yours are all right. Give my love to Robert when you see him. Read Froude on the West Indies. It is rather true.[4]

Ever Yrs   Henry Adams.

MS: MHi
1. Mary Crowninshield Endicott, daughter of the secretary of war.
2. Ronald Craufurd Munro-Ferguson (1860–1934), later Viscount Novar, Liberal M.P. 1884–1914, governor-general of Australia 1914–1920. His sister was Emma Valentine Munro-Ferguson (d. 1897). Their father was Col. Robert Munro-Ferguson of Raith, Fife.
3. Russian intervention in Bulgaria threatened to set off a European war involving all the major powers.
4. Froude's *The English in the West Indies* (1888) includes chapters on Cuba.

Tuesday, 20 March.

Back again after a month of wandering in Florida and Cuba. If it was not happiness, it was at least variety. King broke down after all, and could not go; but Hay, Dwight and I started on Friday, Feb. 17; passed a day in Richmond; another at Charleston, and a third at Savannah; arriving on the evening of Tuesday, Feb. 21 at the wonderful Ponce de Leon, the palace just built for a hotel by the Cleveland standard-oillionnaire, Flagler.[1] We stayed there till Saturday. Hay had swarms of acquaintances, and was delightful company. Friday evening we gave a dinner. All our guests belonged in the house. Brayton Ives and his wife; an Alexander with a Californian heiress-wife of the Crockery clan;[2] Mrs Gus Hayes, pretty, silly and dubious as ever, with a female friend; Captain Black and his wife, once Daisy Derby;[3] and Mrs Patterson, once Medill.[4] I knew none of them, but selected Mrs Black and Mrs Patterson as my neighbors, and found them charming. While at the Ponce, we had also the amusement of witnessing President and Mrs Cleveland's reception, and I watched Mrs Cleveland's splendid vigor in handshaking. From St. Augustine we went, Saturday, 25, to Winter Park and stayed two days. There we parted from Hay with deep regret. Dwight and I went on to Kissimmee, Tuesday, 28, and drove seventeen miles to Narcoossee where the Fells live. Here we passed a day and saw Anne Palmer, and the baby, whom she named after Clover. A stranger establishment I have seldom seen than theirs, dropped in the middle of a Florida lake, and surrounded by forest and swamp, with a colony of young English wanderers two miles away, trying to grow oranges in the sand. Yet Anne is happy and contented and an important personage, with a brick house and comparative wealth. Marian is a quiet child who gives no sign of marked character as Martha Cameron does. I cannot guess what she will make. We left Narcoossee after noon on Wednesday, 29, and went down to Tampa where we passed a rather dreary day, and sailed for Havana, in the Olivette, late Thursday night, reaching Cuba early Saturday morning. Havana proved amusing but uncomfortable. Sunday, March 4, we went to a great bull-fight, and managed to sit through one out of the six bulls. Chacun à son gout!

The bull-fight was followed by a carnaval mascarade and I had much amusement watching the costumes and people. I went to the opera three nights in succession. An atmosphere of ruin overhung everything in Cuba. Poverty and brigands pervaded the island; but the picturesque flourished all the more. Driven by the heat, smells and noises, from the city, we took up our quarters at Petit's restaurant at Vedado, where we had the sea under our eyes and the sea-air in our faces. We went a hundred miles westward to the Baths of San Diego, and tried the volante and Spanish cooking. We went near as far eastward to Matanzas. We ransacked Havana. We remained nearly a fortnight in Cuba, and started north on Thursday, 15, in the Mascotte. The Florida channel was as bad as the Calais-Dover trip, and I was excessively uncomfortable, but revived on reaching Key West, and had a pleasant voyage to Tampa. We took the mail train; were stopped a day at Waycross by a railway accident; and reached Washington yesterday noon. Mrs Cameron and Martha met us at the station and took us to her house to breakfast. So I am back again. I can hardly say that I find myself worse than ever; but the return brings only depression. At Vedado, Thursday morning, before starting, I looked out seawards and asked myself whether honestly I wanted or not to return. As near as I could tell my real feeling, I had not one wish ever to see Washington or home again. My only instinct was to run away. Here this instinct is stronger than there. I have got to find new servants; I must soon get a new gardner; my mother writes supplicating me to pass the summer with her; society seems more ghastly and dreary than usual. If it were not for Mrs Cameron and John Hay, I should turn and run.

Sunday 8 April.

After a week at Washington, and writing one small chapter of history, I went down to Norfolk with King and Hay. We passed five very pleasant days, especially one at Williamsburg and one at Fredericksburg. On returning here I set up my establishment last Monday, and dined at home for the first time in six weeks. Winter has gone. I have begun to ride once more. My breakfast table is rarely deserted. Travel has done me good. I have not suffered much from depression, and not at all, of late, from excessive and alarming turns of temper. Not that I am really able to reconcile life with limitations; but the day-by-day work runs without positive distress. Of the world, little or nothing makes itself heard within my reach. My brother Charles is now with me. My mother is poorly and seems breaking. Edward Hooper and the children come next week.

Sunday, 15 April.

At work again on history; Book III, Chap. I. Spirits much better, and almost no acute depression; only indifference and tedium. Edward Hooper has not come, as little Ellen makes slow recovery. Visitors drop in as of old. I see most of John Hay and his children; Mrs Cameron and Martha; Spring Rice. No society outside my house, and no care for what goes on. My mother is better again. Brooks is going to Europe, and I suppose I must go again to Quincy.

1. Henry M. Flagler (1830–1913), then involved in Florida real estate and railroads, had worked with Hay's father-in-law, Amasa Stone, in 1872 to double the capitalization of the Standard Oil Co.
2. Charles Beatty Alexander (1849–1927), New York lawyer, and his wife, Harriet

Crocker Alexander, daughter of Charles Crocker, Southern Pacific Railroad president. Other Crockers were influential San Francisco bankers.

3. William Murray Black (1855–1933), with the Army Corps of Engineers, and Daisy Derby Black.

4. Elinor Medill Patterson (1855–1933), daughter of Joseph Medill, owner and editor of the Chicago *Tribune* and former mayor of Chicago.

To Elizabeth Cameron

1603 H Street. Saturday 28 April 1888.

My dear Mrs Cameron

I enclose you Matthew Arnold's last article so that you can at your leisure get up your conversation with Spring Rice and Sir Lionel for the next country-club breakfast,—if they know at the Country Club that Matthew is dead.[1] The article is open to the objection of being commonplace beyond even our own American standard; but even if it were not all as true as Matthew's own Philistinism, you would find satisfaction in the exquisite touches of Arnoldoxy which I have underlined. These are *interesting*, if America is not.

I have to thank you for the kindness of your infant daughter to my nieces. Martha was with them both morning and afternoon yesterday, and made herself charming. She found my horse Daisy rather alarming, in the general circuit among pigeons and stables, but she behaved with becoming composure. My girls left me this morning, and I am alone again. Your establishment is altogether deserted today, as Miss Mary Cameron last evening advised me. I have just seen your daughter, with a huge banana in her clutches, wandering away with her two nephews to accompany them a space towards the Bradley mansion.[2] She smiled graciously on me, but preferred, as was just, the society of younger men. John Hay and I who were all I could offer her, bowed as meekly to her will as we do to that of her mother. After all, the relation is not so very different.

If anything has happened since your departure, I do not know it. Spring Rice, Herbert, Winthrop Chandler and Endicott clattered away yesterday afternoon towards Harper's Ferry.[3] The other Endicotts have gone to Boston. The Chinese Minister has asked Hay and me to dinner, and I am going. I shall try to engage him in return for about the 12th and shall count on you.

Ever truly   Hy. Adams.

MS: MHi

1. Arnold died April 15. "Civilisation in the United States," *Nineteenth Century* 23 (April 1888), 481–496.

2. Mary Cameron was Senator Cameron's fourth daughter. His eldest daughter, Eliza, married William H. Bradley, son of Supreme Court Justice Joseph P. Bradley.

3. Michael Henry Herbert (1857–1903), counselor at the British legation 1888–1889; Winthrop Astor Chanler (1864–1926), grandson of Samuel Ward, married Ward's niece Margaret Terry in 1886.

To Lucy Baxter

1603 H Street. Sunday, 29 April 1888.

My dear Miss Baxter

Thanks for your letter or letters, for I think I have two to acknowledge. Since the middle of February I have felt waif-like, and have postponed letter-writing as well as everything else. Brooks and Charles kept me informed about my mother's condition, but I wish I had felt easier on account of your own health.

My state, though somewhat like that of the lark at break of day uprising[1] not because he likes to rise but because he can't sleep, is much what it was a year ago, but even more bothered to know what to do. I meant to draw a long breath of relief and cast all my old clothes into the Pacific ocean with a lunatic hope that I might find an excuse for not coming back in the autumn, for I find my mode of existence more intolerable than ever. My mother's wail of despair at Brooks's departure obliged me to give up these hopes in order to comfort her. I turned my thoughts to Quincy, but this summer I need to have Dwight with me, and I could not impose him on my mother. Then I pitched on Beverly. I would rather roast myself over a red-hot gridiron than go back to my house at Beverly, and I doubt whether, when the moment comes, I can make up my mind to do it; yet it has the advantage of comfort and convenience for work, and freedom from daily worries. Probably I should be best off if I went there; but as far as my mother and you are concerned I might as well be in Fiji as I intended. At Beverly I am altogether out of the way; further than John and Charles at the Glades, and able neither to relieve your cares nor my mother's troubles. So I see little good in my going to Beverly, unless it consists in getting a fit of depression that will drive me wholly away next winter. Perhaps I might quarter Dwight somewhere in Quincy, but for this purpose I must be on the spot. Meanwhile summer is coming, and I become more and more perplexed what to decide. Of course I can't talk to my mother about it, as it would only fret her; and I can't do, what I should naturally do, bring Dwight with me, because it would seem to her a burden. Under these circumstances I rather revert to Fiji as the best alternative, and wish that the Lord would kindly show me what to do, as it's not my funeral anyhow, and I never took any such contract.

All this is for your private ear. I don't ask you to do anything because I don't see what you can do; but if you notice indications of insane conduct in me, you may know the reason, and may calm my mother's anxieties by assuring her of my total loss of intellect. The result will be happy, but the process is aberrant.

I warmly hope that your health is improving. From this point of view, and the general question what conduct on my part would most alleviate your burdens, I would like to know what course you would rather have me take.

If profanity, under the most beneficent conditions, tends at times, as philosophy teaches, to smooth our paths through life, I have little doubt that it is acting well on mine at present. Everything is out of joint. I am bothered by a whole bramble-bush of difficulties, and see no resource but to run away, like Marquess, who was always a reflective animal with an eye ahead. The greenhouse bothers me. I must get a new gardner and spoil it at large cost. My little nieces have just left me, and I am not in the least pleased at the state of the eldest's health. My history is slower than ever and more deadly wobbly. The young women have all deserted me, and my house is as dull and gloomy as a comic theatre. Add to these and other comforts of a home, that I am more kinds of a fool than Gladstone, Boulanger[2] and Marcus Tullius Cicero rolled into one; and you will forgive this carol of my lark-notes in the dawn of a sweet day.

Really I am much more interested to know how you are than in my own affairs. Please confide in me with the same cheery optimism which I show in my confidences to you. I can doubtless do much to cheer you up, for I often notice the effect of my society to be decisive on others by calling out all their powers of self-preservation.

If I were you, I would burn this letter, but the recommendation is wholly on your own account. As for me, I could easily write lots as pleasant as this.

Ever Yrs   Henry Adams.

MS: ScU
  1. Shakespeare, Sonnet 29.
  2. Gen. Georges Boulanger (1837–1891), leader of a nationalist movement that attracted Bonapartists, militarists, royalists, and the extreme left, was dismissed from the army in March and was elected to the Chamber of Deputies on April 15. He fled the country in 1889 and was convicted of treason in absentia.

To Edward Sandford Martin

1603 H Street. 29 April, 1888.

My dear Mr Martin[1]

I have too long delayed thanking you for your little volume for the rich. You have hit the vein of humor of our time; rather an American vein, I suspect; a kind of reaction likely to spread with the increase of our society, which does not yet fairly know whether to take itself seriously or not, and is more doubtful on the subject than it ever was before. The amiable satirist has a large field of popularity before him, and I don't know that anyone can do better than to play in it, though it produces no gold and little subsidiary currency. You may at least console yourself with the reflection that it costs you less than history would do, and is on the whole quite as likely to interest.

Many thanks for your kindness in sending us the volume. Dwight joins me in regards.

Yrs truly   Henry Adams.

E. S. Martin Esq.

MS: MH

1. Edward Sandford Martin (1856–1939), Harvard '77 (a founder of the Harvard *Lampoon* and, in 1883, of the humor magazine *Life*), *A Little Brother of the Rich and Other Poems* (1888).

Sunday 29 April

Last Sunday I was in New York where I went to meet Edward Hooper and his three older daughters who were coming to make me their long-planned visit.[1] At New York I saw La Farge and St Gaudens, and made another step in advance towards my Buddha grave. Nothing now remains but to begin work, and St Gaudens hopes to play with it as a pleasure while he labors over the coats and trowsers of statesmen and warriors.[2] My time has been otherwise given up to the children. Little Ellen is very fragile and needs great care. To my great relief she gained strength while here, and yesterday they all went back after a pleasant week of lovely spring weather. I am much bothered about many things; chiefly about my summer and my greenhouse which I find a severe drain and care. Brooks has started for Europe.

1. Ellen, sixteen years old; Louisa, fourteen; Mabel, thirteen.
2. As early as 1886 in Japan, HA had advised with La Farge in planning a monument for MHA's grave in Rock Creek Cemetery and later with the Japanese scholar Okakura on the symbolism of Buddha figures. When commissioning Saint-Gaudens, HA deliberately gave him only his general idea. Saint-Gaudens wrote on an early sketch of the figure: "Adams. Buddha. Mental Repose. Calm reflection in contrast with the violence or force in nature." In addition, HA suggested that the sculptor not read books for inspiration but talk instead with La Farge and keep about him objects such as photographs of Michelangelo's frescoes in the Sistine Chapel; later HA lent him photographs of Chinese statues of Buddha. From these sources Saint-Gaudens developed his idea of a seated, hooded figure, "sexless and passionless," expressing philosophic calm. Work on the monument, which was curtained off in a corner of his studio, gave Saint-Gaudens a rare break from the limitations of realistic portraiture (*The Reminiscences of Augustus Saint-Gaudens* [1913], I, 356–362).

To Elizabeth Cameron

1603 H Street. 1 May, 1888.

My dear Mrs Cameron

Your letter of yesterday, which has just come to enliven me, seems to want historical treatment; and I take a moment from the famous battle of Lundy's Lane to tell you that your promising daughter passed an hour with me yesterday, with the thermometer near ninety, looking at the pigeons and indulging in chocolate, ginger-snaps and Caldecott.[1] She had a short intermediate flirtation with Baby Hay, leaving him quite broken up and desperate; and was restored to her baby-wagon at six o'clock, as fresh as a dang yion. I had also on Sunday a period of her society equally happy in spite of the heat.

I took her to see Hay's preparations for Kennan's lecture to the Fortnightly Club, but neither she nor I attended the festivity, although I had solemnly promised to do so.[2] Dwight went and found it as hot and crowded as the occasion required. Mrs Hay threatened to introduce me to Mrs Hobson, which shook my nerves. The Mexicans had also a great affair last night, so you see what you have lost in the tropical season.[3] I have less than my usual frenzied gaiety on hand, but am going to the Higginson orchestra on Friday.[4] Do you want me to keep a ticket for you? Frank Higginson dined with me Sunday, badly cut up by your absence and the report that you would not come to Beverly.

I am getting lovely roses from the greenhouse every day, and the place grows always prettier, but I am also more than ever bothered by it, and have decided to make no change there till autumn. This is sheer cowardice in the hope that either it or I may burn up before that time. As I am still doubting where to pass the summer, my hope has some slight foundation.

Please read Harry James's Liar in the May Century. He has hit on a nice study of femi-nature. I have known such men, and have pondered in like perplexity about their wives.[5]

Ever truly Ys   Henry Adams

MS: MHi
1. Randolph Caldecott (1846–1886), English illustrator of children's books.
2. George Kennan (1845–1923), journalist, explorer, engineer, recently returned from Siberia, lectured at the April 30 meeting of the Fortnightly Club, a women's group, held at the Hays' house.
3. A ball inaugurating the new building of the Mexican legation to which 1,200 people had been invited.
4. The Boston Symphony Orchestra, founded by Henry Lee Higginson in 1881 and underwritten by him, was giving two concerts in Washington.
5. In Henry James's "The Liar," the narrator detests a habitual but harmless teller of lies and wonders if the liar's wife condones the lies or masks an aversion.

Sunday, 6 May.

My chapters I and II on the Niagara campaign are at last finished; the only pleasant chapters to write, in the whole work. Edward and the children having gone, I have made love to Martha Cameron and by dint of incessant bribery and attentions have quite won her attachment so that she will come to me from anyone. She adores Del Hay's pigeons! and takes a fearful joy in visiting Daisy in my stable. Her drawer of chocolate drops and ginger-snaps; her dolls and picture-books, turn my study into a nursery. My roses are becoming handsome again. My brother Charles and his wife are now with me. Gericke's concerts this week.[1]

Sunday, 13 May

Finishing the northern campaign of 1814 in Chapters III and IV. I have been social this week, dining Tuesday with the Chinese Minister in a company of statesmen: Ingalls, Evarts, Bayard, Roustan, Justice Miller, Aliunde Bradley, and such old ghosts of a life once almost real.[2] The same day Lucy Frelinghuysen brought Mrs John Davis and Adele Grant the professional to breakfast. Miss Grant exquisitely pretty and well-broken.[3] Miss Thoron and Mrs Cabot Lodge also came to breakfast. Mrs Patterson-Medill, Miss Thoron and May Cameron came to dinner. Mrs Cameron has come back and was here yesterday to breakfast. Nevertheless I am low-minded, though since Cuba I have had hardly any jim-jams. Everyone is going away. I want to go and stay; but have got to repeat the old desperate Quincy effort.

Sunday. 20 May.

Energetic work on history this week, nearly finishing Chap. V of Book III, on the campaign of Washington. The last month has shown great progress, and I see the day near when I shall at last cut this only tie that still connects me with my time. The Hays have gone north. Spring Rice sails for England tomorrow. I am almost alone except an occasional visit from Martha or her mother, and I have been sad, sad, sad. Three years!

1. Wilhelm Gericke (1845–1925), conductor of the Boston Symphony Orchestra.
2. John James Ingalls (1833–1900) of Kansas, Republican senator 1873–1891. Samuel Freeman Miller (1816–1890), Supreme Court justice 1862–1890, Republican member of the electoral commission that settled the disputed presidential election of 1876. Joseph P. Bradley (1813–1892), Supreme Court justice 1870–1892, called "Aliunde" (Lat.: from the outside) because he was placed on the electoral commission as a nonpartisan but invariably voted with the Republicans.
3. Adele Grant (d. 1922), daughter of Mr. and Mrs. Beach Grant, had made her debut in 1883; she was a "professional beauty," a fashionable celebrity.

To Sir Robert Cunliffe

1603 H Street. 27 May, 1888.

My dear Robert

I wonder whether you or I wrote last. I have quite forgotten, but I know it is a very long time since I heard from you, and a letter yesterday from Carlo recalls the curious thing called Time which impresses me as being the most ridiculous of all political absurdities. Carlo sends a new batch of old acquaintances who are dead or dying. The feat is so common now that I wonder why anybody should still think it worth his doing.

As for me, the pyramids are jealous. I write history by the aeons, and cease to read newspapers. For the first time in my life I have no knowledge of what is doing in what is supposed to be creation; and I have no doubt that the star Gamma Aquarii, if there is one, might disappear from the Heavens and I never know it unless Langley dropped in to dinner and told me. Carlo's letter gave me more news of you all, and of public affairs, than I should ever have had without it. To balance the account, I send you back by mail, my only British counsellor on this side, young Spring Rice, who is returning to his cheery desk at the Foreign Office for life-imprisonment. If you meet him, by chance, be good to him for my sake. Not that I harbor sentimental attachments, but because the youth is clever, and I wish him to do me credit. Also remember me tenderly to my honorable friend Joseph Chamberlain if you ever see him. I do not know whether he is to marry my other friend, Miss Endicott, but if he does, I trust you will show a tender attachment to his wife, for my sake also, or for your own still more.

News of myself is poor and scarce. My last long volume draws to a close. I have maligned all the statesmen of the civilised world until the supply is exhausted, and I must go to the East for more. Another year of moderate work ought to set me free forever from my duties in life, as men call the occupations they are ashamed to quit, but are sorry to follow. Once free, I shall begin a new life, in which the old one can hardly have any sequence. I say that I *shall* do it; but I mean that if I still feel then as I do now, and if nothing prevents, I shall cross the Pacific within two years for an absence which will last as short or long a time as may be.

So much egoism for news' sake. The Hays have gone from Washington for the summer, and Hay has found a new malady which gives him fresh interest in life; a chronic inflammation of the vocal chords. He enjoys it, and makes it a pleasure to his friends. Clarence King has the same affection along with many others equally entertaining. King works hard to support royal tastes, but lives like a vagrant. Hay thinks he is to take his family to Colorado for the summer, but he hankers for London. If he does not come over, you had better join him in Colorado. I must nurse my mother in Quincy as I did last summer. She is now eighty, much broken and requires a son or two in constant readiness.

Of politics and affairs I know as little as any living man, and of society not much more. A man who never leaves his own house gets ideas of society only at second-hand, and society this year has been particularly quiet. I have no new acquaintances and no Americans to commit to your tenderness. Our public men are uninteresting, as poor Matthew Arnold justly observed, and our society is, as he also noticed, flat. Curious that a poet and philosopher like Arnold should have wasted his last hours in writing common-places that every society fribble has long since got tired of talking about. He might have found new things to say, for there are many new things to observe here, but he was past the age of observation and reproduced only his old formulas.

I go north in about ten days and expect to remain fixed at Quincy till October.

Many thanks for the exquisite photograph of the children. Love to them all and to your wife.

Ever truly Yrs   Henry Adams.

MS: MHi

To John Hay

1603 H Street. Sunday, 27 May. 1888.[1]

My dear Hay

Your royal yness did not deign to say whether your royal yness meant to go direct from Sunapee to Cleveland or return to New York, wherefor I write to Cleveland to say that if you like New England at this season, I am glad of it, but that Washington is quite bad enough for me. Rain and clouds all this week, and bad weather pretty much ever since you left, have calmed my restlessness to that extent.

I have worked like Possum over an old carrion bone he has picked up in the street, only my work has been gnawing the bones of statesmen and heroes which rattle in a dull and sodden way when I kick them. I have now ransacked pretty much the whole graveyard, and see the glimmering landscape fade on my sight, while the moping owl, whom I take to be a critic, is getting ready to complain.[2] He will have cause.

Washington, without you and Mrs Hay and the children, is but a town like other haunts of imbeciles. Even Mrs Cameron has been at Harrisburg, but had the sense of decency to leave Martha for me. An occasional lost reveller drops in and wails that Spring Rice should have to wear Bishop Doane's spare coat and breeches all the way over; but Springy would look well in anything, and if Miss Leiter can be induced to think that all his *good* clothes went by the other steamer, she may not notice the condition of his actual wardrobe. My question is; how would papa Leiter's shoes fit Spring Rice?[3]

Thanks for the invite to Tuxedo! I shall leave here say June 6. Whether I shall stop in New York I cannot yet say. I have got to pull my house down to put in flues 13 x 20, and have also got to build a new greenhouse. Why stop in New York to see shops and landscapes? A bank account would be a gayer outlook than that from the Brunswick breakfast-room.

With love to all yours   Henry Adams.

MS: MHi
  1. HA misdated this letter April 27.
  2. Thomas Gray, "Elegy Written in a Country Churchyard."
  3. Spring Rice, the victim of lost baggage, was notoriously careless about his clothes; William Croswell Doane (1832–1914), Episcopal bishop of Albany, was known for splendor of dress. Sailing on the same ship to England, May 21, were Mary Victoria Leiter (1870–1906), later Lady Curzon, and her father, the Chicago merchant Levi Ziegler Leiter (1834–1904). Leiter retired in 1881 and moved to Washington, where Mary Leiter came out in 1888 and was the star of the season. Spring Rice was courting her.

Sunday, 27 May.

Finished Chapter VI of Book III, and all my searches in the War Department. Nothing but New Orleans remains to be told of military affairs. The weather has been wet and dull. I have worked hard, without distractions except an occasional hour with

Martha Cameron or a stray guest to breakfast or dinner. Only once on horseback, in mud and showers. My brother Charles has been here, once more disappointed in getting his legislation.[1]

1. With some $50,000,000 in government loans, the Union Pacific was subject to recurrent congressional efforts at regulating its operations. CFA2, as its president, hoped to reduce such interference by issuing new securities that would enable the railroad to repay the loans on a fixed schedule. The bill to authorize this procedure brought him to Washington for the "hopeless and repulsive work" (*Autobiography*, p. 192) of making political deals. Congress put off voting until the next term.

To James Clarke Davis

1603 H Street. [May 1888]

Dear Davis

Nothing to say[1]

Yrs ever   Henry Adams.

MS: MH-Ar
1. Davis, secretary of the Harvard class of 1858 since 1883, was gathering information for a new class report.

To John Hay

1603 H Street. 3 June, 1888.

Dear Hay

I started Wednesday, and, a week from today, shall be in Quincy wishing myself among the angels of Paradise—who have sense enough to go anywhere but there. I hope vaguely to see King in New York; but lay no unction either to soul or body on that chance.

Washington is now deserted. Count Sala and I saw Mrs Cameron and Martha depart yesterday.[1] My cook also has gone, and seeks other bonanzas, I presume, for she gave no sign of return. The Club is odious; worse than ever was known. I am making farewell calls, and have been down the river on the Despatch at last.[2] If a man lives long enough, his destiny overtakes him.

Weary as I am of it, Washington never was so beautiful, and the season is perfect for enjoying it; but the fiends drive, and Quincy yawns. I have done what I could to ruin you, and shall write a ghastly sum on the blank check you left with me. As yet I can not accurately forbode the precise number of thousands I shall insert; but I enclose a sheet of memoranda which will give you an idea of your impending ruin. Durkin has made beds of roses and chrysanthemums and honeysuckle for you that are so much better than mine as to make me decide to tear down my houses and grow only a summer-garden. You are fenced in, all about, like youthful virtue, and I mean to buy for you about fifty thousand square yards of glass sashes to force our lettuce next spring. This will be an autumn task. Meanwhile my table is as pink as my first ball-dress with your roses.

Sunapee never smiled upon me greatly, for I too was in Arcadia born[3] and know from long experience how insoluble the Arcadian problem of summer is; but if the children like it, all is well, for summer was made for children, and only the späte Herbst at Washington for us. I hope you will build your house, if only to bring you once towards my hermitage.

You should see Springy's successor! His name, he says, is Berkeley or Barclay. He is fresh—but so fresh—from Harrow, I conceive, and drinks only dry champagne at the club; plays tennis, of course, and, within twenty-four hours, after asking Rebecca Dodge who wrote Henry Esmond, asked me whether I had read Matthew Arnold's Light of Asia, and told Mrs Cameron in the sweetest English schoolboy humor, to "shut up." Il ira loin, ce butor![4]

What is the news? Since you left, the world has not once kicked me to wake me up. My love to Mrs Hay and the babes.

Charges against J.H.

May 19.	Back fence	$42.94
" 26.	Labor (digging)	15.00
June 2	Front fence	52.00
" "	Labor	17.50
" "	Gas bill	16.75
" 4	Saul's bill for chrysanths. &c.	5000.
" "	Extras	1245.37½
		$1,738,500.00

Say one million, seven hundred and thirty eight thousand five hundred dollars more or less.

With this sum I hope to clear your embarrassments before I leave so that you will be fairly free from care.

MS: MHi
1. Count Maurice Sala, secretary to the French legation 1884–1890.
2. HA went with the Lodges to Mount Vernon on the naval vessel *Despatch* May 31.
3. From the Latin motto "Et ego in Arcadia," a tag phrase for stylized nostalgia.
4. George Head Barclay (1862–1921), from Eton and Trinity College, Cambridge, minister to Persia 1908–1912. *Light of Asia* (1879), a poem on Buddha, was by Sir Edwin Arnold. *Il ira . . . butor!:* He'll go far, the boor!

Sunday, 3 June
Another long season ended, and all ready to begin the Quincy trial. I have had a gloomy week, not quite so desperate and wild as in my worst days, but, so far as I can

remember, equally hopeless and weary. I long for travel, but must imprison myself for another year. I went, last Thursday, with the Cabot Lodges and a small party, down the river to Mt Vernon on the Despatch. The dissipation cost me three days of despondency. Mrs Cameron and Martha left yesterday for Harrisburg, and cost me another day of low spirits. I have written part of a new chapter and have labored to get my greenhouse and household arranged for the summer. Dwight has left the State Department and come into our family service.[1] I start Wednesday.

1. Dwight had resigned as State Department librarian to give full time to organizing the Adams family papers and library.

To Elizabeth Cameron

1603 H Street. 4 June, 1888.

Dear Mrs Cameron

If you and Martha were to ask me to turn back-double-somersaults all the way to Harrisburg, I suppose I should do it, such being the natural feebleness of my character, and the acquired idiocy of my mind. You may therefore expect to see me arrive by the 9.50 A.M. train on Wednesday, and to pass the night; although the Blessed Damozel alone knows how I am to manage it.[1] I have several engagements in New York for Thursday; but I owe one piece of inspired wisdom to La Farge, worth all his painting:— When you want to do a thing, *do it!*—Following his great example, I shall cut my engagements.

Miss Amélie Rives is engaged to Winky Chandler's younger brother.[2] This is official. I know not whether he wears a silk shirt now; but we shall see whether he wears a hair one hereafter.

Yrs in haste   Henry Adams.

MS: MHi
1. In Dante Gabriel Rossetti's poem "The Blessed Damozel" (1850), the lady envisions a heavenly union which her earthly lover fears he will not attain.
2. Amélie Rives (1863–1945), of a distinguished Virginia family, created a stir with her "passionate" novel *The Quick or the Dead?* which first appeared in *Lippincott's* in April. She married John Armstrong Chanler, June 14.

To Elizabeth Cameron

The Homestead, Quincy, Mass.
Sunday 10 June 1888.

My dear Mrs Cameron

Once more, thanks for my little holiday! I enjoyed it all the more for its coming between two railway-trains, with a framing of railway tracks. For the first time I see that even railways may be, in some degree, useful, since they serve to make a charming contrast for Martha and you. Yet when I bade you good-bye and climbed your Vestibule Train, with a mind which, as you may have observed, was for once quite bird-like for cheerfulness and anticipation of pleasure, I could not help a slight depression at finding that astonishing creation of man's genius and luxury to be entirely intended and used for the conveyance of Chicago German Jews. Why did Matthew Arnold see nothing to interest him in our civilisation? I saw, between Harrisburg and New York enough in a single Vestibule Train to interest the remainder of my life in answering a single conundrum,—why the German Jew should be the aim and end of our greatest triumphs in science and civilisation. I offer this to Martha for a prize Essay on taking her Degree of Virgo Artium at Wellesley College. If she solves the riddle, she should set up for a Sphynx and marry a Presidential candidate.

The atmosphere of Abou Meshec Shadrach ben Isaacs seemed to reduce me lower and lower until I arrived at the Brunswick and took a solitary dinner, after which I found myself fairly desperate in a ghastly solitude.[1] Under more favorable conditions I could have taken, like my friend whose name I've forgotten in Musset's Caprices de Marianne, to a bottle of wine, and tobacco, till stupefaction should bring back content;[2] but after June 1 I drink no wine till October, so this resource was barred, and at half past nine at night, I took to solitaire. Degrading as the confession is, I had nothing better to do, and I wasted immortal time trying to think how cards should be put one on another. Five years ago, I should have treated with proud consciousness of superiority the suggestion of such a fall; but I was glad, last Thursday night, to shuffle cards and wish for October when wine would be allowed. Yet in the midst of my most interesting combination, a knock came at my door, and Clarence King appeared. Soon afterwards La Farge came in. They taught me all the nothingness of art, science and society till after midnight, and I was with them all the next day and evening, when King and La Farge became so exhausted by the prolonged mental effort that both went to sleep, one on the bed, the other on the sofa, where I left them, at King's room, while I resumed solitaire. So it is that, as civilisation ends in the Chicago Jew, the society of our most amusing friends leads back to shuffling of cards. Yet you wonder that I long for the Cannibal Islands.

After a tedious hot day in the train I arrived here at seven last evening and began the summer gaieties. My mother has sensibly failed, physically and mentally, but is still rather stronger than I am. Miss Baxter has grown used to the burden and carries it better than I feared. All else is as it was a year ago. Summer is barely begun. The air is still a little cool, and the garden looks as if winter had squeezed the lilacs close. I want Martha here, and should feel quite contented if she were with me, but she would certainly catch cold. I feel my own membrane rasped at Worcester, and never fairly soothed till I get south of the Statue of Liberty. Still, send Martha on to me if she wants to come. I won't mind her schnupfen.

Ever Yrs   Henry Adams.

The west side of the Old House and the nearby Stone
Library, Quincy, Massachusetts

Lucy Baxter

Interior of the Stone Library
The portrait of Charles Francis Adams on
the balcony railing was painted by
Frederick P. Vinton, 1879

The Hooper sisters and their father at Maplewood
Left to right: Mary, Mabel, Fanny, Louisa, Ellen (seated), and
Edward W. Hooper

Cecil Spring Rice

Mabel Hooper

MS: MHi
1. Shadrach, Meshach, and Abednego were the stubborn nonconforming Jews who infuriated Nebuchadnezzar and were consigned by him to the fiery furnace; Daniel 3.
2. Octave in Alfred de Musset's play *Les Caprices de Marianne* (1833) takes refuge from the emptiness of life in drunken revelry.

Sunday, 10 June

Without further incidents at Washington, I left at 9.50 Wednesday morning by the train for Harrisburg. Very hot and wilted I arrived there at two o'clock, and found Mrs Cameron waiting for me. I passed twentyfour hours at their farm Lochiel on the edge of Harrisburg, with foundries, railways, canals and factories at their door, but though I cared not at all for the place, I greatly enjoyed being with Martha and her mother.[1] This is my summer's holiday. I left again at two, Thursday, and reached New York at seven; passed a day with King and La Farge; called at the Evening Post for a dividend, and was laughed to scorn; and yesterday came on here, where I find all things as they were a year ago, except that my mother has sensibly declined in body and mind. Still she may last another year. A quick and easy end would be a great blessing for her, and would save her much suffering. I might say the same for myself. I would certainly be quite willing to go with her.

Sunday, 17 June

Once more settled into the deadly routine of last year. The acute depression has left me, and I am growing dull and indifferent and selfish. Exertion is hard. My poor mother is in a state that excuses me from social effort, and I sit in the library, and write history. Book III, Chap. VIII.

1. Made up of three farms bought before the Civil War, Lochiel was the earlier and smaller of two estates in the Harrisburg area assembled by Simon Cameron.

To Martha Cameron

Quincy, 23 June, 1888.

My dear Martha

I am afraid of boring your mother with letters, so I have not acknowledged your photographs though I received them nearly a fortnight ago; but as your birthday is coming, and I have no present to send in exchange, I think the least I can do is to thank you for your kindness in sending me the pictures, which now stand against the books by my desk, and make me very homesick. I wish you were here in my library with Possum and Mr Dwight and me and two or three other dogs. I should be much more contented, and the roses would look quite happy this warm day to see you looking at them. Since coming here I have seen no one except my old mamma, who is quite a different-looking person from your mamma. I have been to Cambridge to see your friend Noony who asked many questions about you. She is going to Beverly about July 10, and hopes you will soon be there. If you were here I should take you to see my niece Dorothy who is six months older than you.[1] I never saw her but once, and then she howled until I left the room, but you would teach her better. I should get some gum-drops for her and you. Gum-drops are better than chocolate in hot weather.

Please tell your mamma that history is getting on, some ten hours a day, and promises to be soon fairly finished. This is all the news I have, except that Dwight arrived this morning from a round of visits to fashionable people, and has begun work as *Archiviste.*

Ever affectionately   Henry Adams.

MS: MHi

1. Dorothy Adams Quincy (1885–1952), born Dec. 4, daughter of MA and Henry Parker Quincy.

Sunday 24 June

The roses are out. Yesterday was hot, 95°. Dwight arrived in the morning and went to work with me in the library. My mother rather gains than loses in the hot weather. I have begun Book IV, and am at Ghent. Dwight has arranged with Burlingame of Scribner &Co for publication.

To John Hay

Quincy, 27 June, '88

Dear John

Distraught with sadness at hearing nothing from you since your departure from Washington or thereabouts I begin to fear something wrong.[1] I was particularly sorry to leave New York before you came, but Quincy pressed, and *j'y reste.*

Dwight has also arrived and has taken charge. He seems happy though he goes today to Commencement. We are at the height of our rose season, and in an ocean of roses; but I think rather better than I did of our own.

I sent you an approximate account covering the expenses of fencing, bedding and draining your garden; a flower-bill, and a gas-bill for twenty dollars or so. The amount of the check at last was $175. I now receive the enclosed letter from the Commissioners. Shall we wait, or go ahead? If funds are not available before August, we had better go ahead; but I don't understand whether $252. covers the whole square or only our 200 feet. Anyway we must have the sewer. Please return the letter.

I have nothing gladdening to write for the better encouragement of your vices. My mother has gained steadily of late, and seems almost as strong as last year. I am fixed again for the summer as though I were a pinned Maikäfer.[2] Hooper will be obliged to take little Ellen and the other children to Bethlehem for the summer. He goes next week. Ellen shows a tendency to catarrh. My nephew Charley has built a new yacht which he calls the Bab-boon. Suzanne was at Class Day.

My love to you all. Tell Helen or Alice to write to me if you are too serious.

Ever Yrs   Henry Adams.

MS: MHi

1. In Chicago at the Republican national convention Hay was a strong supporter of Sen. John Sherman, who, after leading for six ballots, lost to Benjamin Harrison, June 25.

2. *Maikäfer:* Ger., May bug, a beetle that feeds on foliage in the spring.

To Wayne MacVeagh

Quincy 6 July, '88

My dear McVeagh

Will you now do me the kindness to send me by express here (care of Mrs C. F. Adams, Old House, Quincy, Mass.) the two volumes of my history which you have. I want all the marginal notes, suggestions, corrections and general vituperation you can annotate them with, and do not mind your keeping them a few days if you profit by the time to make yourself obnoxious; but I am now gathering myself for a fatal attack on the publishers, and in a few weeks more must begin to print. So I must call in my circular notes.

I was sorry to hear that you were out of sorts in the winter. Take to growing roses in a winter-garden as I do. It will give you more dyspepsia and keep you poor for life, which is, I take it, what you want. Apparently it is what I want, for I have lost account of time and place, and no longer know whether I am living in the past or future. The present I know I do not live in; but I still have views on Asia and Polynesia.

Give my love to your wife, and believe me

Ever Yrs   Henry Adams.

MS: PHi

To Elizabeth Cameron

Quincy 8 July, 1888

My dear Mrs Cameron

Your letter of July 2 relieved me of vast and crushing nightmares of imagining that you and Martha had taken to agriculture, or started for Fiji in advance of me,—all because I had heard nothing of you for three weeks.

The discipline is good, and in future, like Shakespeare, I will not question in my jealous thought where you and Martha may be, or your affairs suppose, but like a sad slave stay and think of nought save where you are, how happy you make those.[1] Shakespeare probably used poetic license in these remarks, and when he said he thought of nought, he meant that he wrote Romeo and Juliet, or Othello. I have only the resource of writing history, but even at that infinite disadvantage I feel greatly comforted to find that Shakespeare and I are a pair, at least in our common regard for you. Now that I have recovered from my anxieties, I have really nothing but that to say. The daily troubles of a nervous invalid of eighty are familiar enough to bear passing over. My little nieces, instead of going to Beverly have been taken to Bethlehem or Maplewood, in the White Mountains. Little Ellen showed a tendency to catarrh, and the physicians wished to stop any habit of hay-cold. So they all started last week, and have set up a house on the hills. I hope it will do Hooper good, and my hopes are rather greater for him than for the girl. Meanwhile Dwight has been to Beverly and reports all ready for you there. Give Blanchard time enough to warm and dry the house; otherwise come when you like as though it were your own. I suppose you could take either the Gurneys' or mine, at choice, as you preferred, and we should be equally pleased to see either opened.

Dwight seems still happy and has his own way at last with everything. I am working very hard indeed and very fast. Of the world I hear and know nothing, but am extremely dyspeptic and homesick whenever I think that I can't see you and Martha.

Ever Yrs   Henry Adams.

MS: MHi
1. Shakespeare, Sonnet 57.

To John Hay

Quincy 8 July, 1888

Dear John

I would give a ream of ruled law cap, written full of history, to be going with you to Colorado; but yet a while I must abide here, and, to admit the truth, the frenzy of finishing the big book has seized me, until, as the end comes nigh, I hurry off the chapters as though they were letters to you. I think that five more chapters will pretty much finish the story. A concluding Chapter or Book must be still written on topics and tendencies, but I shall begin printing next autumn.

I am glad to see your hand again on the Lincoln. Criticism is not needed, but I have now gathered about me an epidermis of nerves sensitive at peculiar and arbitrary points. I know that my sensitive points are no more properly sensitive than a million others, but I trust to the devil to be good enough to spare me more, or I shall never get through a proof-sheet at all. My last axiom, invented within three months, is that the present tense must never be employed in historical writing, and can never under any circumstances be so good as the past tense; while the word *now* should be ruthlessly struck out wherever it occurs, no matter under what apparent necessity it is used. I communicate this satanic idea to you on Mark Twain's theory of getting rid of it. Perhaps if you take it up, I may forget it. Anyway it is sure to make you uneasy which is always good for a middle-aged and indolent protectionist.

I have ordered the sewer to be made, and have hired Mrs Philip's lot, as she seemed inclined to think I used it for base purposes without recompense. Dwight is now installed as literary owner of the Adams family, and seems happy in his property. I imagine that the world is going on elsewhere, since it seldom stops spinning, but I know nothing about it, and cannot even tell you whether Mr Grant's death will remove the beautiful Adèle from Washington. Edward Hooper has taken his children to Bethlehem under medical advice, and started a house there.

Love to all yours.   Ever truly   Henry Adams.

MS: MHi

Sunday 8 July
Steady work without break. Chapter III, Book IV. Nothing to distract me.

To Charles Scribner

12 July, 1888.[1]

Eight volumes, five hundred pages each.

Every pair of volumes to make a separate work, with titlepage and index.

Maps and plans where necessary, say half a dozen in each volume on an average, but more in the last two, where the war requires them. No folding maps. All such plans &c, to be contained within the size of the page.

Printing to begin by October, preferably by John Wilson.[2]

The whole work to be printed and ready, before any portion is published.

No steel engravings. If any illustrations are thought necessary, the author to prescribe their nature and quality; also the cloth binding.

The author prefers an arrangement by which the publisher should pay no royalty until the sale shall have reimbursed all expenses. After the expenses of publication are repaid by the sale of any fixed number of copies, the author would like to know what share of the proceeds of future sales is supposed to belong to the author. He has never yet been offered, in cases of former publications, more than ten per cent, if he remembers correctly; but he has always thought and still thinks the author ought to share equally with the publisher.

Henry Adams.

MS: ViU

1. This memorandum by HA was sent to Charles Scribner (1854–1930), head of Charles Scribner's Sons, by Dwight, who conducted preliminary discussions on HA's behalf. Dwight's covering letter summarized progress thus far. Six copies of Volumes I and II (584 and 601 pages) had been privately printed, to give HA a draft to circulate privately and a clear text for revision. Volume III was "now being put in type," and Volume IV, "now being written," would not be "printed in advance of the edition for publication," but would come as manuscript copy. These four big volumes were to be divided into eight, and eventually the second Madison administration was extended into a ninth volume of the Scribner edition.

2. John Wilson & Son, Cambridge, Mass., printed HA's private draft copies of the *History* and the completed version published by Scribner.

To Elizabeth Cameron

Quincy, 15 July, '88.

Dear Mrs Cameron

Have I thanked Martha for her charming letter? My imagination has never equalled the amount of interest which she puts into a page. Nothing could be more natural and simple than her style, and I see signs of humor in every line.

She ought to come here and be my secretary, and relieve Dwight, who is now a sort of literary factotum, and will soon be in general charge of the establishment, from the kitchen to the barn. I don't know how he can manage a farm, but I do know that neither my brothers nor I can do any better, so you may yet see him milking a cow, and reading an old MS. at the same time. We none of us know our whole genius till we've been tried.

I am horribly annoyed that you should be growing thin. As a choice, perhaps I prefer thinness to its opposite, but I object to having need to choose. Please think better of it. Miss Sally Loring does not do so, and I see no excuse for you. Apparently Miss Sally has left the step-maternal abode, for good. I understand she is passing the summer by herself, and I fear she is not wildly happy.

Midsummer has come, the strawberries and roses have dropped and faded, my last half-dozen chapters are begun, and my nephew Charley has beaten everything with his new cutter the Babboon; I am as cold as usual in a Boston summer, and my brothers are taking their families to the Glades in order to be colder; Stanford White has sent me a salmon from the Ristigouche,[1] and John Hay has gone to Colorado; my mother is still eighty years old or more, and Miss Baxter is in New York; I see or hear dimly that some new political jackanapes is set up for President, and that Congress is likely to be in session for two months yet; but I am still waiting to know when you are to be at Beverly. I shall not see you, but I want to send Martha a wooden pail and shovel to dig in the sand on the beach. I have no news from my nieces at Bethlehem, and for a fortnight have seen no one, and not left my desk except to exercise my horses; so forgive my imbecility.

Ever Yrs   Henry Adams.

MS: MHi

1. Stanford White (1853–1906), architect, partner of McKim and Mead, friend of La Farge, Richardson, and Saint-Gaudens; the Ristigouche Salmon Club, Matapedia, Quebec.

To Charles Milnes Gaskell

Quincy, 15 July, 1888.

Dear Carlo

My eye happened to fall on a newspaper paragraph yesterday mentioning the funeral of Sir Francis Doyle.[1] Your last letter somewhat prepared me for this, but I had not supposed his death to be so near. My old and dear friend Mrs Russell Sturgis died only a month before. I suppose some one may still be alive, but the number of ghosts already exceeds the number of living, and I find myself more at home with them.

I am very sorry, for your sake, for Sir Francis' death must leave a great gap in your sympathies. This process of growing old is infernal torture. One is conscious of dying with one's friends; a joint falls off with every friend that dies,—as though one were leprous.

I have nothing very hilarious to write from here, where I am once more, to my infinite weariness, doing nurse, when I meant to be on the Pacific ocean. My brother Brooks is in London, which accounts for my being here. The imprisonment gives me six hours a day at my desk, and, with this spur, history comes on so fast that I can now see the end of it. Another eighteen months ought to close my literary activity for life, and start me behind the sun.

Your friend Cotes has not come within my range. Everyone is now so scattered that I might not hear of him if he were under my eyes. John Hay, my usual companion, has taken his family to Colorado; much as you might take yours to Siberia for the summer. The world belongs to my nephews and nieces, children in their teens and twenties, who sail boats and think of dress, and wonder what life is to be for them. The worst of a childhood's haunt like this place, where I am, is that it forces on one's mind the passage of time. Once I get to a new place, I feel as young and as lively as at twenty.

Probably you read the papers and know more than I do about American as well as European affairs. We are electing a President this year. I care little which is chosen, but favor the man in office. He is not Moses, but he is better than the other fellow.

My love to all yours.

Ever   Henry Adams.

MS: MHi
  1. He died June 8.

Sunday, 15 July.
  Finished Book IV, Chapter III. Proofs of Vol. III very slow; four more chapters to come.

To John Hay

Quincy 22 July, 1888

Dear Tenderfoot

The guaranty is in my possession, therefore be not uneasy about it. I wish you had bought Mrs Philip's lot as well as Voorhis', for first she says I must rent it, and then she says she has two purchasers and means to sell it, which is not my affair; but I am a pauper, owing to the triumph of my party and principles, while you wallow in the fatness of defeat.

My fury about the historical present was a long-penned but always forgotten volume of irritation at your collaborator's extravagant and exuberant indulgence in that obscene habit. I am not aware that you sinned. Yet I object even to saying in my favorite phrase: "The greatest of all philosophers, the wise and polite Kung-fu-tse, observe*s*." The assertion is ridiculous on its face, for Kung died more than two thousand years ago.

I do want your mountain *muchissimo,* but I run a greenhouse, and have got to rebuild and reheat and restock it, besides paying printers' bills for masses of history, and pulling the whole side of my house down for a new chimney. I must sign some portentous I.O.U. this autumn, but China is near, and damn the Jews.

A telegram from King yesterday summoning me for a week to Tuxedo. Of course I cannot go. My mother's condition obliges me to be here day and night till released. Yet I am glad to know where the outlawed ruffian is.

Deep am I in the peace of Ghent. I am haunted by the idea that no general historian has given a detailed account of a negotiation. Bancroft slurs the Treaty of 1783. I know no model for such a narrative, yet it interests me more than war. Is a foreign ideal on record?

Dwight's love and mine to all. How I wish I could ride up the mountain with the children.

Ever Yrs   Henry Adams.

MS: MHi

To Wayne MacVeagh

Quincy 22 July, 1888

My dear McVeagh

Many thanks for your kind invitation to Bar Harbor. I am tied here by attendance on my mother whose infirmities have become so great as to require the constant presence of some of her sons. I am the one in residence during these four months, and I shall not venture to pass a night away until I am relieved. So I have had to decline all invitations.

I want the volumes, but I want more the greatest possible number of marginal corrections. Quere: Am I right in saying in Marbury vs. Madison that the marshal of the Supreme Court could be stripped of his legal character by the President? I believe the Court appoints its own marshal. Can the President affect his tenure?

In a week or two my third volume will be ready for reading. My fourth is within ten or twelve chapters of the *Finis*. Another year will see me, I trust *accouché*. No more instruments than the file will be used on the occasion. The knife I have no longer the energy to use.

I grow old with a certain steadiness and regularity that wins my own admiration, for I can measure my motion from year to year, like that of the planets. Sidereal motion it is not, but gross and dull, hardly even sensual for the senses grow blunted. I profess not to like it, and hope that you and your wife know not what it means.

Ever Yrs   Henry Adams.

MS: MH

Sunday, 22 July.

Deep in Ghent negotiation, Book IV, Chap. V. Interesting to me more than most.[1] Lucy Baxter away since 10th. My mother rapidly failing, especially in mind and voice; conscious of it, and painfully distressed at times. Her eyes now beginning to be subject to illusion. She can hardly survive the year, or retain consciousness of our identity beyond the time of my stay here. She may die at any moment if the heart should stop action. I suppose I can go through the fresh experience, for nothing affects me now; but it does not make life more tolerable.

1. The five U.S. commissioners in the negotiation to end the War of 1812 included JQA and Albert Gallatin.

To Elizabeth Cameron

Quincy, 29 July, 1888.

My dear Mrs Cameron

The rule that nothing matters much, does not apply to you. According to what I understand to be the teachings of my master, the great Chinese philosopher, Lao-tse, the small is infinitely great and the great infinitely small, and no truth exists of which the opposite is not equally true. I would not have this doctrine vulgarly promulgated, lest, like George de Barnwell's, it might chance to do harm;[1] but in your case I freely admit that I am very sorry you are not coming to Beverly, and still more sorry that you should be sorry. As for the house, you need not waste a thought upon it. I keep it only to lend to friends, and no friend but you has ever wanted it. Of course the house would be better for occupation, and I would gladly hire some friend to pass a month or two in it; but no one wants it, and it is not singular, for the Gurney house is also empty, and, as far as I know, the whole shore is half deserted. Indeed I think you might walk into almost any house there, and have not only house but household as long as you want it, without paying even in thanks, as long as you do not send in your butcher's-bill to the owner.

My philosophy goes no farther than the reflection that I should see no more of you at Beverly than at Harrisburg. My summer is passing, thanks to the dynamic necessities of time, and I suppose some other condition will follow, which I like still less; but, as I have no one within reach whom I care for, and no possibility of seeing such a person, nothing matters much,—not even rheumatism which has caught me directly in the back, and causes me to howl as I ride, for the good of the youth of this neighborhood. My mother is no worse than when I came—perhaps better,—but the best is bad enough. Edward Hooper writes cheerfully from Bethlehem. Clarence King writes despondently from Tuxedo. The Hays are rambling on Colorado mountains. If I had Martha here I could do beautifully. Please send her on.

Ever truly Yrs   Henry Adams.

MS: MHi
  1. This sentence is an almost exact quotation from Thackeray's "George de Barnwell" (1847).

To Charles Scribner

Quincy, 1 Aug. 1888.

Dear Sir

Mr Dwight has handed me your letter of July 27, and I will answer it myself to save time.

Your offer is perfectly liberal and satisfactory, but for certain reasons I would rather alter it a little, as I understand it, in your favor.

First, I wish you to understand my position as you would regard it in a business point of view. If I were offering this book for sale, I should, on publishers' estimates, capitalise twelve years of unbroken labor, at (say) $5000 a year, and $20,000 in money spent in travelling, collecting materials, copying, printing, &c; in all $80,000, without charging that additional interest, insurance, or security per-centage which every business-man has to exact. This book, therefore, costs me $80,000; and on business principles I should make a very bad affair if I did not expect to get ten per cent per annum from it for ever. If I bargained according to publishers' rules, I should demand eight thousand dollars a year secured to me; and if I got it, I should still get less than I could probably have acquired in any other successful business.

As I am not a publisher but an author, and the most unpractical kind of an author, a historian, this business view is mere imagination. In truth the historian gives his work to the public and publisher; he means to give it; and he wishes to give it. History has always been, for this reason, the most aristocratic of all literary pursuits, because it obliges the historian to be rich as well as educated. I should be sorry to think that you could give me eight thousand a year for my investment, because I should feel sure that whenever such a rate of profit could be realised on history, history would soon become as popular a pursuit as magazine-writing, and the luxury of its social distinction would vanish.

I propose to give the work outright to the public and the publisher, but I have some objection to admitting the publishers' share in producing it to be greater than my own. This may be a fad, but I have seen the author squeezed between the public and the publisher until he has become absolutely wanting in self-respect, and I hold to preserving the dignity of my profession.

I propose therefore that you shall take all the profits of the book. Having published a number of volumes, and being somewhat familiar with the history-market, I am fairly safe in saying that a twelve-dollar book, in eight volumes, cannot expect a sale of two thousand copies. A sale of fifteen hundred copies will secure the publisher. For still greater security I will add five hundred copies, or a thousand, or ten thousand, if you like; but in making the contract I wish to let it run thus: "After the sale of [say]¹ 2000 sets, the author shall receive one half the proceeds, after deducting only the charge for printing, binding, and paper."

I know not what this would come to, but I presume about thirty five cents a volume, and you offer me 22½ cents on all sales over 1500. The difference is not much. In any case the author can hope to receive nothing for two years or more, and in the case of selling three thousand copies, which I regard as an extravagant idea, within three years, the author would be no better off than by accepting your proposal. I intend by my plan to secure you, as far as is in my power, from all loss or risk, and to make over to you whatever profit may be conceived as possible; and all I ask in return is that you shall admit the author to have half the credit, if there is any credit, of the work. For this reason I want expressly to exclude from the cost of the volume the publishers charges of advertising, rent, salaries, putting on the market &c.

With this alteration, I see nothing to interfere with in your plans.[2]

Very truly Yrs   Henry Adams.

MS: ViU
1. HA's brackets.
2. On Aug. 7 Scribner protested against HA's reasoning and raised his offer from a royalty of 15 to 20 percent.

Sunday, August 5.
Finished the battle of New Orleans; Book IV, Chapter VI. False alarm about my mother, due to action of bromide. She is about as well as last year, but much more nervous.

To Rebecca Gilman Dodge

Quincy, 6 August. [1888]

My dear Señorita

You were angelic to write. I sometimes wonder what goes on in the world, and how people amuse themselves; for the sensation of feeling outside comes strange even to the most aged; but when I hear from you butterflies and humming-birds accounts of the way you fly and hum, I begin to wonder whether there still is any world. Down here in this hole, I sit day after day at my desk from morning till night, while Dwight sits at another table, and muddles his brain over family papers, and at intervals my mother sends for me to consult what she is to order for dinner or whether she shall drive at four or quarter past. Nothing else happens. My little nieces have gone to Bethlehem in the White Mountains so that I make no more visits to Cambridge and never go to Boston. Two of my brothers are at the Glades, and your own dear one, Brooks, is in England. John Hay and all his brood are in Colorado, dancing on mountain tops. Mrs Cameron and Martha are I know not where; but are *not* to be at Beverly, I know not why. Everyone seems occupied more or less as I am, and, as no one professes to want anything else, I also am as happy as they.

This is my news. I wish I were at Berkeley Springs with you, and could see your palace and park, and swim in the tank which I have heard exists thereabouts. Shall you come north? I can give you no news of friends or enemies. My nephews are sailing their new yacht Babboon (be sure of the two B's, for luck) far away on the ocean, while Molly looks yearningly after them over the blue waves from the Glades. I am rebuilding the greenhouse at Washington, and pulling down the side of my own house. My history is nearly finished. Before New Year I hope to complete it. Then I shall have to make presents to all my young and beautiful friends. What can I give you?

My love to your mother and to you.

Ever truly Yrs   Henry Adams.

Dwight sends as much love as you will accept.

MS: MH

To John Hay

Quincy 6 Aug. 1888.

Dear Jan

Ives's line is as mysterious to me as bankers' accounts are apt to be, but I know that what I got, I spent; and what I spent, I have; therefore the $7.87 belong to you, and are none of mine.

Thoron's treatment of your instructions does credit to his sense of your literary merits.[1] By the bye, I've not read the August instalment; but feel real sympathy with poor Kennan.[2] As for my own drivel, I have finished the battle of New Orleans and, with it, the War of 1812. Ten chapters more will finish me too. I find that my Chinese stills most complaints, and I am making all arrangements for departure with you to Yokohama, June 1, 1890. Mrs Hay and the children shall follow as soon as our Pekin palace is ready, the following autumn.

King writes very despondingly, whether to make me gay or to suit his own feelings, I may not guess. Robert Cunliffe writes of coming over in the autumn, and I have replied that if he will come in September, I will try to get King; and all come out to Cleveland, pick you up, and go on to San Francisco, Los Angeles and Mejico, for a grand indulgence in pulque and short-cake. I feel but the faintest shade of idea that the baronet will come; but if he be seized by the sudden madness, you may pack your portmanteau and mount your mule, for the caravan will doubtless go somewhere.

You have read Boswell, which is creditable. I am reading for novelty Cardinal de Retz and Bolingbroke; the one in search of an anecdote, the other in search of style.[3] Both are good reading for the purposes. De Retz is quite charming. Of all things left in this life, the only thing I want is to be a Cardinal.

I am rebuilding my house and greenhouse; both are now level, more or less, with the ground. The question of heater is all-pervading. I am going to try a new hot-water boiler of Boston invention. Your new ground, I hear, is enclosed; but I hear nothing from Mrs Philips.

Give my love to Mrs Hay and the infants, and the burro.

Ever Yrs   Henry Adams.

MS: MHi
1. Ward Thoron (1867–1938), who was looking after HA's house and affairs in Washington, had indiscreetly passed on to Corcoran's executors a paper on the back of which Hay had, in ribald terms, expressed his opinion of them.
2. "My Meeting with the Political Exiles," Kennan's article in the August *Century*.
3. Paul de Gondi (1614–1679), Cardinal de Retz, French churchman, politician, and diplomat, *Mémoires* (1717). Henry Saint-John (1678–1751), Viscount Bolingbroke, friend of Pope and Swift, *The Idea of a Patriot King* (1749).

To Ward Thoron

Quincy, 11 Aug. [1888]

My dear Thoron

Thanks for your telegram and letter which gave me the only intelligible account I have received of the great disaster. I telegraphed you yesterday authority to settle and wind up the bankrupt concern. Try and not let me be bled any more for it, and I will with extreme pleasure pay you what I hope will be your first professional honorarium.[1]

Please also abstain as far as you can from bothering me with objections or difficulties raised by the parties interested. I intend to rid myself of the whole affair in regular process of time, and under no circumstances shall I build or rebuild the greenhouse or any part of it. If neither Saul nor any other gardener will take the camelias, orchids, &c, they can freeze. Durkin may remain for the present to preside over such hardy plants as are left, and the sewer will drain off the water that otherwise would swamp us; but the land is to be like Hay's, clear and free for sale.

With these instructions I hope you may be able to clear away wreck, plants, contractors, rubbish and laborers without getting me into law-suits or damages.

Ever Yrs   Henry Adams.

MS: Faith Thoron Knapp
1. Thoron was reading law in James Lowndes's office.

Sunday. August 12.
No change in this dreary existence. I have taken up my Chinese again and find I recover it fairly quick. I mean to make a new attempt to learn a thousand characters thoroughly. The week is devoted to filling up holes in work done on Vols. III and IV. Correspondence with Scribner about publication. Received Thursday telegram that my greenhouse-roof had fallen while rebuilding, crushing plants, and requiring at least $1000 repairs. I telegraphed Friday to Ward Thoron to stop building and turn the place into a summer garden.

To Elizabeth Cameron

Quincy, 19 Aug. 1888.

My dear Mrs Cameron

Thanks for your letter of the 14th. I hardly know which is worse,—to hear, or not to hear, from you; for when I do not hear, I am uneasy, and when I do hear, I am homesick; but at least I am glad to know that Martha is digging in the sand, and that you are once more swimming in fashion. Even when one is made seasick, at sea, one likes to see it afar off; and I, who am always made very seasick by society, like to hear about it from you.

As for my own drowned-rat-ship, I have been to Bethlehem, or rather to Maplewood, to see my small nieces. I found them capering about a big hotel among five hundred people, and acquiring a healthy feminine taste for gossip about their elders. Now that I have floated in the wake of the hotels from Tampa to the Canada line, I consider myself a craftsman in frivolity and can look on undisturbed while three asthmatic young men try to amuse thirty voracious young women, and the ubiquitous boy of ten plays base-ball on the verandah, trying to shave my nose with his noble skill. This too shall pass away. Meanwhile, little Ellen is stronger, has more color, and continues to gain. She is still below the safety-mark, but I feel no immediate anxiety. The rest are all right.

Did you, or not, leave any plants in my greenhouse? The question is one which I would gladly hear answered in the negative, for, ten days ago, I received a series of telegrams and letters from Washington, from which, among a mass of incoherent details about contractors, storms, plants and Mrs Durkin's bonnet, we eliminated the central idea that, in the process of rebuilding the greenhouse, the contractor had removed the sides while he loaded the top, and one morning, while Mrs Durkin was putting on her bonnet, he had come in to announce that the whole greenhouse roof was flat on the ground, with the plants and Durkin under it. Durkin must have got out, for he wrote me the same day a letter in which the i's and h's played hide and seek in the least expected corners, but except to inform me that the contractor was Bosh, and that I must rebuild the whole place on a new plan, he furnished no information even about his own sense of wrong. I telegraphed to Ward Thoron to stop building, wind up the concern, sell the plants, and convert the place for the time into a summer garden. So there is an end of the greenhouse; but I hope you had nothing in it, or that whatever you had has not been crushed or sold. For the present a garden will remain there, but only for spring and autumn purposes.

I admit to being greatly pleased with this catastrophe, for I wanted to have liberty for some newer folly, and the garden was beginning to be a bore. Martha can still come down in the autumn for chrysanthemums, and I shall hope to have roses for May, and plants for the outside of my house; but I shall have no retreat for my winter afternoons, which is my only regret. Probably you and John Hay will be the chief sufferers for my ennui; although I can see no easy way of imposing more of my society on either of you than I have done in the past.

I am going to send you a little book presently, when I next go to town; a remarkable sketch of eastern hareem life, probably the best ever given. I want you to see what I mean to become when I am Sultan and Imâm, as my plan is.

Ever truly Yrs   Henry Adams.

Mrs J. D. Cameron

MS: MHi

To Charles Scribner

Quincy 19 Aug. [1888]

My dear Sir

Thanks for yours of the 14th.

On further reflexion I see that I cannot begin printing much before November 1, as I must have some little time in Washington to prepare copy. You need not hurry your preparations more than you like; but I presume you will instruct me as to the rate at which you wish the printing to proceed after it is once begun. I care not how much the publication is delayed,—the longer, the better, for my objects;—but I would much prefer to be free of the whole job as soon after January, 1890, as possible, so that I can go abroad in that year. If you issue the first two volumes a year or so hence, and the others at six months, or four months, intervals, I suppose I may be allowed to clear out as soon as the plates are finished without waiting for the publication. In that case I will furnish copy as fast as the printers will take it, and you can publish when you please. I have only two wishes: one is to be free, and the other to escape the annoyance, which to an old author is considerable, of infuriated grandsons and patriotic women-critics crying for redress.

Yrs truly   Henry Adams.

MS: ViU

Sunday, Aug. 19

I have been to Bethlehem to see Edward Hooper and his children whom I found pretty well. Little Ellen has not recovered all her strength, but is tolerably well. I have now broken the heart of the summer, and hope only for four or five weeks more work. On the whole, if that time is successfully used, I shall have done enough. Scribner has undertaken to publish for me. My third volume will soon be wholly printed.

Sunday, August 26.

Eight hours of work every day this week, either on History or Chinese. Book IV is finished. Only eight chapters remain to be written, and of these only four are narrative. Vol. III is slowly printing. Another month will complete it. I have left my desk only to exercise my horses.

Sunday, September 2

Clarence King was here one day this week. Have reached Chap. II, Book V. Contract made with Stanford White for stone-work of Buddha monument at Rock Creek. Have written to St Gaudens to send his contract for signature.

To Martha Cameron

Quincy 9 Sept. 1888.

My dear Martha

I love you very much, and think of you a great deal, and want you all the time. I should have run away from here, and looked for you all over the world, long ago, only I've grown too stout for the beautiful clothes I used to wear when I was a young prince in the fairy-stories, and I've lost the feathers out of my hat, and the hat too, and I find that some naughty man has stolen my gold sword and silk-stockings and silver knee-buckles. So I can't come after you, and feel very sad about it. If you would only come and see me, as Princess Beauty came to see Prince Beast, we would go down to the beach, and dig holes in the sand; and would walk in the pastures, and find mushrooms, which are the tables where the very little fairies take dinner; and we would feed Daisy with apples; and go to visit some nice old fairy aunts—very, very old, who would give you beautiful cake;—and Possum and Marquess would be so glad to see you that they would sit up all day on their hind legs, and bring you balls to play with. Then you should help me to write beautiful history in my big library, and build houses with the books, where we would live with the dogs. I am very dull and stupid without you; and have no one but old people to live with.

Please come to Washington as early as you can, if you can't come to me here. Take care of your mamma, for poor mamma does not know very well how to take care of herself, and needs you to look after her, and keep her out of mischief. I know it's a great care to have a mamma to look after, for I have one of my own, and she gives me almost as much trouble as your's gives you; though she is so lame and old that she can't go to parties or walk much, while your mamma can still go about by herself, even if you are not helping her. My mamma has to be wheeled in a chair, and is very cross because she can't walk, or read, or write to her little grandchildren, like you. Give my love to your mamma, and tell her all about me; and that I expect to leave here in about a month for Washington; and that Clarence King has again promised to take me to Mexico in November; and that my history will be finished tomorrow; and that she must take great care of herself, so as to be well and strong when I next see her. I know she must have been in some mischief, because she has not written to me for a month, and I have always noticed that when ladies do not write to me, they are in mischief of some kind. Be sure you write often, so that I may not think you naughty or unwell.

I have sent Mr Dwight up to Lenox to look after you, and he writes me that you have not forgotten me. Be sure to keep on loving

Your affectionate   Dobbitt

MS: MHi

To John Hay

Quincy 9 Sep. 1888.

Dear Don Juan

I enclose you a letter from Hyde, which will, I hope, calm your mind on the subject of that venerable imbecile. Stevens belongs to Dwight. His scalp will doubtless also adorn your letter-file in due course of time.

Nothing has occurred here which deserves the sad tribute of a passing letter, and I have nothing to tell you until Dwight returns from Lenox where he is gathering social gossip for us from the lips of Sam Ward and Miss Thoron. I sit at my desk six hours every day, and spin my web with the industry of Anthony Trollope. I can hardly believe my own ears when I say that tomorrow my narrative will be finished; all my wicked villains will be duly rewarded with Presidencies and the plunder of the innocent; all my models of usefulness and intelligence will be fitly punished, and deprived of office and honors; all my stupid people, including my readers, will be put to sleep for a thousand years; and when they wake up, they will find their beards grown to their waists, and will rub their eyes, and ask: "Do the crows still fly over Washington?"

By the bye, I wish you would give me a copy of your verses on that subject.[1] I find them hanging in a horrid way in my memory, like poor Jack in Miss Porter's Original Poems, caught under the chin on a meat-hook.[2]

In another week, all my brothers and sisters will be reassembled here within call. I do not know when I shall get away; probably in a month.

My love to the children and their mamma.

Ever Yrs   Henry Adams.

MS: MHi
1. "The Crows at Washington," in *Poems by John Hay* (1890).
2. The fate of Harry in Jane Taylor's poem "The Little Fisherman" in Jane and Anne Taylor, *Original Poems for Infant Minds* (1806): "But as he jumped to reach a dish/To put his fishes in/A large meat-hook that hung close by/Did catch him by the chin."

Sunday, September 9.

Nothing but hard work this week which has brought me towards the end of Chap. IV, Book V, which closes my narrative, March 4, 1817.[1] Tomorrow I shall reach that point. Four economical and literary chapters remain to be written, and I hope to have these in shape before I return to Washington.[2] I think I never before wrote eight chapters in less than two months; but I have now nothing else to do. Life is at least simple. If I have no satisfaction, I have little interest. I am nearly Buddha.

1. The date of Madison's retirement and the inauguration of James Monroe.
2. The concluding chapters covered "Economical Results"; "Religious and Political Thought"; "Literature and Art"; and "American Character."

To Sir Robert Cunliffe

Quincy, Mass   10 Sept. 1888.

Dear Robert

I am more than delighted. You are a very well-behaved fellow (for a Britisher), and you can tell your wife and children that you are highly esteemed beyond the Atlantic.

When you reach New York, seize a carriage (which will probably cost you two dollars, confound 'em; *I* always go on the elevated road for five cents) and drive to the *Brunswick Hotel,* Fifth Avenue and Twenty-seventh St. On arriving there, ask for letters and take bath, breakfast, dinner, supper, or go to the bar-room and take a *Whiskey-sour,* while reading your instructions. I cannot yet say what I shall say then, for I don't know; but if I can't meet you in New York, you must come here, which is easily done.

Until you know more of your movements, order letters, &c, to be sent *Care of Mrs Charles Francis Adams, Old House, Quincy, Mass. U.S. America.*

You shall be put in immediate nomination for the Presidency or any other office you want. I didn't know there was to be an election, but perhaps it may be so. We don't run for offices; only for money.

Ever Yrs with love to miladi and the young   Henry Adams.

As I write on the spur of the moment, half an hour after receiving your letter of Aug. 31, I say only what is pure necessity. The whole of it merely amounts to this. On landing, go to THE BRUNSWICK (mind you, *not* the Brevoort) and ask for letters.

P.S. Bring clothes of all sorts and lots of them. At sea and in the north you will want rough, heavy things for cold weather. In Mexico, if we go there as is my present intent, you will be in the tropics and will want white flannel or the thinnest stuffs. As I mean to show you all there is to see, perhaps you will have to visit the North Pole yet.

Of expenses I say nothing because I know little. Having no money, I don't care what I spend, but will try to leave you a pittance for regard of Sir Foster, your successor.

MS: MHi

To John Hay

Quincy, Mass. 10 Sept. 1888.

Dear Don Juan

I wrote you a letter yesterday to Cleveland with nothing in it. Today I write you another to New York, where you once said you were to be the 12th, and give you due and legal notice, by authority of Anthony Hyde, James Lowndes, Ward Thoron, Lucius Tuckerman and Henry Stevens, that I have received a letter from Sir Robert Alured[1] Cunliffe, Baronet, of the Welsh Peerage, saying as follows, videlicet, to wit, viz:—

That he sails in the Germanic, September 26, and is due at New York October 5.

I have written him to go to the Brunswick and ask for his letters which will guide his tottering steps. Will King be there then? My purpose holds to take the Baronet to Mexico if King will go. In that case we will stop over a train at Cleveland and pick you up. Be ready to start on receipt of telegram. I do not know what to do with the Britisher in the interval of three weeks. Advise, oh Wise One!

Ever Yrs   Henry Adams.

MS: MHi
  1. *Aluredus:* Latin for Alfred, Cunliffe's middle name.

To Charles Scribner

Quincy, 14 Sept. 1888.

Dear Sir

I return the agreement, signed.

My copies of the history (the two earlier volumes) are filled with criticisms and marginal notes by the various readers, which I have got to consider in preparing for the reprint. On my return to Washington I can perhaps select one, and, after examining its notes, send it to you; but I think John Wilson has one or two copies in sheets of all three volumes (the third just finishing the last sheets), and he could let you have the whole. The fourth will be printed directly from MS. and is finished in first draft, just the size of the third. Neither the third nor the fourth will exceed five hundred and fifty pages.

I would like to see Wilson myself on the subject, but hesitate to do so before you have taken whatever steps you think proper.

Yrs truly   Henry Adams.

Charles Scribner Esq.

MS: ViU

To Elizabeth Cameron

Quincy, 16 Sept. 1888.

My dear Mrs Cameron

I was glad to see your handwriting again, for I feared you had forgotten the hermit of this vale, if one may call such a gravel-drift a vale. I shall soon quit my cave, and you may expect serious work in trying to keep me amused, for you will have double duty, as I have just received a letter from one of my oldest and most agreeable English friends to say that he sails Sept. 26, only ten days from now, and expects to arrive at New York Oct. 5. Clarence King and John Hay are both to be there to meet him. Perhaps I shall go on. Where shall you be at that time? If you are still at Lenox then, and Miss Frelinghuysen is also there, perhaps I will bring, or send him up. Please ask Miss Frelinghuysen whether she would like to take charge of an intelligent, good-looking, agreeable English baronet, whom she must address as Sir Robert, about the usual age, who has left his wife and children at home in Wales near the vale of Llangollen, where she can stop to rest after landing at Liverpool. I know Miss Frelinghuysen would like him, and that he would be popular at Lenox, as he has been everywhere.

Dwight has not yet returned to report about you, and Miss Baxter failed to find your name at the Sloane ball. So I do not yet know well what you are doing or how severe the sprain is, or how it happened. Evidently you have genius for accidents, and Martha will have all her intelligence required to look after you some sixty years hence. If you would take Martha, and join King, Hay, Cunliffe and me on a trip to Mexico in October, I should have all my little world together, and we needn't come back at all, but take a cocoa-nut grove by the seashore, in the tropics, and do nothing but eat bananas and look at the sea. Martha should play with the tarantulas. Just now Mexico is deluged with rain, and one cannot go there, but in six weeks perhaps we shall have better luck, and by that time,—oh, but I'll be ready to go! Four months of prison would satisfy an armadillo.

My brother Brooks arrived yesterday from England, full of recent impressions of that watery Paradise. I do not know what Miss Abigail Hamilton née Dodge, said about it, but I imagine that Brooks and she would find common ground on English soil. He reports Spring Rice as very low-spirited, and very much devoted to Will Endicott. Probably the latter gentleman writes you his movements, and you know enough of him to tell me some day how the youth Rice (Spring) really takes his London.

Brooks's return, with that of my other brothers, nearly releases me. By October 1, I shall begin to start the caravan for Washington again, and probably open house on the 15th if the lady who cooks for the crowned heads of Europe condescends to save you the trouble of finding me another cook. I carry back the last volume of my history, finished; and I begin at once to print the whole affair. China looms in the distance. I believe your husband and the other gentlemen who haunt the Capitol, have been trying to pick a quarrel with China so as to get me shut out, or massacred when in; but it won't matter.[1] If shut out I shall set up an empire of my own on an island by itself, and if massacred I shall go straight to Heaven or somewhere else with the missionaries. The Senate means well, but it is too well-intentioned for its supply of human weaknesses.

I wish I had more news, but perhaps the last remark is news enough. Give Martha my tenderest love. Propriety forbids me to send as much to her mamma, so I remain only conventionally hers,

Henry Adams.

MS: MHi
1. On Sept. 7, before China could ratify a treaty restricting labor emigration, the Senate hastily passed a Chinese Exclusion bill more stringent than that of 1882.

To John Hay

Quincy 16 Sept. 1888.

Dear Juan

Your letter relieves me of a load. If you and King will amuse the Baronet for a few days, I am all right. Perhaps I will join you on the 6th. I can't yet decide, for I am unable to fix my departure. I have written to Lenox to learn whether anyone takes in baronets there. If King or you will show him Tuxedo, and Hewitt will board him for a few days, so that I can bridge over the 15th when my establishment will be ready to run, we can hang on for our trip to Mexico. Had I best write to Hewitt?

I fancy that Cunliffe, like other English baronets, is by no means rolling in wealth just now, and that the less we drain his purse, the better he will be pleased. He seems also, according to my brother Brooks, to intend a short visit.

Mind that you go with us to Mexico, if we go. If we can't go, I don't mind. You can then stay at home. I wish I could find out with certainty how long it will take to print eight volumes of five hundred pages octavo. On that depends my departure for China. I am trying to find out; but I can already see that I shall have hard work to get away within two years, as I intended. I still think I can do it; but all depends on John Wilson's supply of type. How are your prospects, and what your intentions? Perpend, and have it clear when winter comes. I will not desert you at Washington as long as our loads are on our backs, but when I come to the Delectable Land, or wherever the pack falls off, then—let us wander to the New Jerusalem.[1]

Ever Yrs   Henry Adams.

MS: MHi

1. A pun on the Celestial City (New Jerusalem) in John Bunyan's *Pilgrim's Progress* (1678) and the Celestial Empire (China).

Sunday, September 16.

The narrative was finished last Monday. In imitation of Gibbon I walked in the garden among the yellow and red autumn flowers, blazing in sunshine, and meditated.[1] My meditations were too painful to last. The contrast between my beginning and end is something Gibbon never conceived. Spurred by it into long meditated action, I have brought from Boston the old volumes of this Diary, and have begun their systematic destruction. I mean to leave no record that can be obliterated. Of the four concluding Chapters, I have already written one third, and all are in my mind, outlined and partially filled in. Brooks has returned. Dwight has been a fortnight at Lenox. John and Charles with their families return tomorrow from the sea-side. Robert Cunliffe is coming over, to arrive October 5, and I shall then depart. Signed contract with Scribner for publishing. He is to take two thousand copies besides those for the press, for himself. Afterwards he is to allow 20 per cent, or thirty cents a volume, which is $2.40 a set. I expect no afterwards, but if my book has the large sale of five thousand copies, I shall receive twelve thousand dollars for twelve years work, or a thousand dollars a year. I have spent more than that on it. Nothing yet from St Gaudens whose contract is the only serious undertaking now left.

1. HA refers to the passage in Gibbon's *Autobiography* in which Gibbon recounts the completion on June 27, 1787, of his history of Rome.

To John Hay

Quincy, 23 Sept. 1888.

My dear John

I have written to Hewitt. I shall not get on for your dinner, though I would do so if you needed me. As you will have King's help, and, I hope, will drop Cunliffe at Tuxedo or Ringwood without needing aid, I will pick him up when he drops. What the deuce can I do with him. The season will be too late for Lenox; I know not a solitary cannibal at Newport; and Washington will be hopeless for him. He will want to see political meetings, torchlight processions, common-schools and dynamite explosions, while I haven't so much as a notion whether dynamiters explode regularly, or only, like historians, at the close of undeterminate epochs. Anyway, give my love to Mrs Dick Derby whom I've not seen since I loved her twenty years ago.[1]

I have composed the last page of my history, and the weather is so wet that for a week I've been in vain trying to do Gibbon and walk up and down my garden. I wish Gibbon had been subjected to twelve inches of rain in six weeks, in which case he would not have waited to hear the bare-footed monks sing in the Temple of Jupiter, and would have avoided arbors as he would rheumatics. I am sodden with cold and damp, and hunger for a change. All because I was filial, and gave up Fiji to nurse my mother whose health is as good as my own.

Ever Yrs Henry Adams.

MS: MHi
1. Sarah Alden Derby (1850–1907) had made her debut in Washington the winter before HA's return there in 1868; she married Dr. Richard Henry Derby in 1877.

Sunday, September 23.

No sunshine since last Sunday, and floods of rain. In the midst of gloom and depression I have come to the last page of my history. I wish I cared, but I do not care a straw except to feel the thing accomplished. At the same time I am reading my old Diaries, and have already finished and destroyed six years, to the end of my college course. It is fascinating, like living it all over again; but I am horrified to have left such a record so long in existence. My brain reels with the vividness of emotions more than thirty years old.

To Elizabeth Cameron

57 Mt Vernon St
Monday [24 Sept. 1888]

My dear Mrs Cameron

The children have only Wednesday afternoon at home, after two o'clock. If you would like to go out, I could take you, say at one o'clock on Wednesday, to lunch with them; or Miss Baxter, who is a sort of sister in my mother's household, could take you. Miss Baxter will call on you. If you happen to be out, you can write me a line in case you want to go; if you are too busy, as you are sure to be, you need not even write the note. I shall know by not hearing. I wish you would give me something I could do to make your visit pleasanter, but I know that, at the Higginsons, you have no opening for outside assistance. They will make any other services hopeless. All my family live in caves and log cabins and feed on roots compared with them.

Ever Yrs Henry Adams.

MS: MHi

To Elizabeth Cameron

Tuesday evening. [25 Sept. 1888]

My dear Mrs Cameron

I should have named Saturday rather than Wednesday, except that you had ordered your departure for that day. I have no idea that you will be able to keep clear of engagements for Saturday, and shall not count on your getting to Cambridge; but if you do, I will take you, or send you, or meet you there as you may ordain. The children will be charmed to see you.

I am almost afraid to tell you that there is no Sunday morning train. The Sunday trains are at 3.30 by the N.Y.&N.E. road; and at 4.30 by Springfield. One brings you to New York at 9.30; the other at 10.30 in the evening. Frank Higginson can advise you which to take. I strongly hope to carry my brother-in-law, Edward Hooper, back with us, and am not sorry to go in the afternoon for his sake, as he is still weak from a long nervous illness; but I am at your orders, and will engage a special at a million dollars an hour, if you tell me to do so.

You are quite right to fall in love with my brother John. He is the only one of the family who can make one laugh when one's ship is sinking. I am glad you have found him. Never mind about Brooks, who is only a kind of exaggerated *me*, and could at best only give you another edition of a book you have read.

I can cure your cold but only by sending you to Florida. Please nurse it carefully till then. Perhaps I shall send Edward Hooper with you.

Here comes a note from Mrs Higginson asking me to lunch on Saturday at the hour when you should lunch at Cambridge if you go at all. What shall I say?

Yrs faithfully   Henry Adams.

MS: MHi

To Elizabeth Cameron

Thursday. 10 A.M. [27 Sept. 1888]

Dear Mrs Cameron

The children will be delighted. Miss Baxter and I will call for you at one o'clock on Saturday. My craven spirit assures me that you will be in bed, all broken up, by that time; and if I find you unfit, I shall make you stay at home to rest.

My mother was all in pieces at learning that her servant had turned you away yesterday. The old lady, it seems, was particularly curious to inspect you, having heard your name recur so often of late; but she forgot to give special orders for your admission. Hence an explosion. Knowing how busy you must be, I could only comfort her by saying that it was probably clear gain to you.

Please take note and report to me whether my nephew George is properly devoted. Please teach him discipline. Make him run all your errands, and see that you have the best partners. If he does not keep up to his work, I will cut him off with a licking. Tell him to introduce to you George Agassiz, my companion to Fiji and Thibet.[1]

If you and Edward Hooper do not both go to pieces on the way to New York (as I fully expect) I should recommend the 4.30 train

Yrs faithfully   Henry Adams.

MS: MHi
1. George Russell Agassiz (1862–1951), son of Alexander and Anna Russell Agassiz.

Sunday, September 30.

Steadily working ahead towards my demise. My third volume is at last printed though I have still a second revise of the last chapter to correct. I have read and destroyed my diary to the autumn of 1861. Nothing in it could be of value to anyone, but even to me the most interesting part was my two closing College years. Much is unpleasant and painful to recall. Have sold at a sacrifice of two thirds all the railroad stock I still own, and am beginning to provide twenty thousand dollars for St Gaudens and Stanford White. The world still steadily narrows towards a point two years distant. My nephews George and Charley sailed for Europe yesterday on the "Pavonia." On the same day, Sept. 29, 1858, just thirty years ago, I sailed first for Europe in the "Persia." I took my niece Elsie to see them off at East Boston. Raw afternoon; poor ship, and rather unsatisfactory leave-taking in the crowd. Frost in the night; the third in this cold month.

To Elizabeth Cameron

Quincy 2 Oct. 1888.

Dear Mrs Cameron

Cunliffe reaches New York next Friday, and goes to the Brunswick where King and Hay will take care of him for a week. They are to quarter him on Hewitt for a few days, and either at Hewitt's, or at Tuxedo, or at the Brunswick, I intend to join Cunliffe on the 13th.

My next movements are uncertain. If Cunliffe wants to travel, I shall go with him wherever he likes. Otherwise I shall return to Washington and mope till you come. Possibly the Baronet may prefer a round of visits. In that case I shall try to pass him about, but shall not join the vortex.

Dwight passed Sunday at Salem with the Lorings who were very kind to the extent of Sarah giving him her photograph. From Rebecca Dodge we have heard nothing since her grandmother's death. Please give Martha my love. I wish she would come to Washington and make me a visit. My whole acquaintance is slowly shrinking to her.

Ever Yrs   Henry Adams.

MS: MHi

To Sir Robert Cunliffe

Quincy, Mass. 3 October, 1888.

Dear Robert

Welcome! You will be received by Hay and King, and will leave yourself entirely to their direction. Probably I shall join you in about a week after your arrival, and in the meanwhile you will look about and reflect on the best way of employing your time. Travel, visiting, politics, fashions or vice. I am ready for travel or vice; the rest shall be kept cold for you, iced, to serve when called for.

Keep me informed of your whereabouts, and be obedient to your guardians. Britishers cannot be allowed to run alone in this country; it's too big, and they would get lost.

Ever Yrs   Henry Adams.

MS: MHi

Sunday 6 October.

Preparing to print. Saw Wilson last Tuesday and Wednesday about a specimen page. Continue reading old diary, but I hesitate to destroy much of the record since 1862, not that I think it valuable, but that I may want to read it again. Portions are excessively interesting to me; nothing to anyone else. I suppose Robert Cunliffe has arrived in New York, and I expect to join him next Friday.

To Sir Robert Cunliffe

Quincy, Mass. 8 October, 1888.

My dear Baronet

If you poor old doddering Britishers try to play tricks with our weather, we shall have to talk with you—gently but affirmatively. Wait a few days and I'll show you weather enough to take your few remaining hairs and teeth out, and preserve them for a geological epoch like the Siberian buffalo.

Meanwhile I'll treat you gently as beseems your callow youth. I will be at Albany Friday night. There I will take you in charge, and if you dare to ask a question where or when you are going, or who or what you are to see, I'll have you made an American citizen and obliged to attend primaries and vote, till your premature demise after a few months of a living death. We will, after a becoming and decorous manner, paint our war-path red; but if I choose to carry you round the globe diagonally on a telegraph pole, you will have to go, and not talk to me about families, or brothers or grand-nephews at home. We are free American citizens—we are—and we mean to wallop our own niggers, law or no law.

I shall write about details to King. Keep up your courage! Be firm, though seasick! Few terrors are so awful as a London dinner,—except a New York one. That past, you are safe.

Ever affecly   Henry Adams.

Sir R. A. Cunliffe.

MS: MHi

To Franklin MacVeagh

Quincy, Mass. 8 October, 1888.

My dear McVeagh[1]

I expect to start next Friday on a trip to California with an English friend of mine, Sir Robert Cunliffe; and we shall probably stop a day to show the Baronet the beauties of Chicago. Of course I shall bring him to call on you and your wife, but if you and Mrs McVeagh happen to be absent, I want at least to see your house, and the 'oofs of the 'orses generally.[2] Therefore, unless you are in Siberia or Sandusky or some other place where nothing ever reaches you, I wish you would give orders that I may not find your portal resolutely closed. As we are off on a youthful lark, and mean to be once more in our 'teens, I expect to show the poor Britisher a severe gait.

With my best regards to Mrs McVeagh I am very truly Yrs

Henry Adams.

Franklin McVeagh Esq.

MS: RPB
1. Franklin MacVeagh (c. 1842–1934), Wayne MacVeagh's younger brother, founder and head of a Chicago wholesale grocery firm.
2. Emily Eames MacVeagh. The MacVeagh house, commissioned in 1885, was built by Richardson's firm.

To Elizabeth Cameron

U.P. Car 010. On the Platte River
17 October, 1888.

My dear Mrs Cameron

Here I am again, in your old quarters, still warned that God hates a liar, and that the Truth is mighty.[1] This time I am taking my baronet where the sunset beckons. Beyond the night, beyond the day, that happy baronet follows me,—the most delighted and astonished baronet that ever was, because the old car happened to be returning empty from Boston, and picked us up at Chicago to carry us over the U.P. territory. No Duke ever felt so grand as my modest Sir Robert in his own particular car.

We shall go up to Portland by the Short Line, and then down to San Francisco by the new Shasta route. There we shall become mortals again, and knock about California for three weeks, before returning by way of New Orleans and St Augustine to Washington, about November 27. I hope we shall find you there, and shall pray for it. If you want anything from the Pacific coast, send word to me at the Palace Hotel in San Francisco. I will fetch you the whole Yosemite if you think Martha would like it.

Jimmy Parker is as ubiquitous as ever, and asks to be remembered to you. The weather is, even here, cloudy, cold and raw, the plains dull and brown, and the wind rough. We shall grumble if the sun fails us tomorrow, for we have pursued it as though we were still as young lovers as when we pursued the British maidens whose age is now as doubtful as that of the geologic reptilians whose bones Marsh digs from these weary plains. As yet our mistress, the sun, has shone but two days since we left the coast. I suppose it is because we are growing old. Anyway I object. No amount of physical comfort atones for such neglect.

At Chicago Frank McVeagh devoted himself to us, and Mrs McVeagh threw open her exquisite house, to which mine is a cheap log-cabin, and asked charming young persons to dine, who made the venerable British lion curl his mane and purr with pleasure. I asked each of the fascinators to share our car and our hearts, such as they were; but as usual they trampled on us, and we were obliged to wander on alone, like the last buffalo. I am now trying to replace them with a person slightly less beautiful and perhaps not quite so ornamental—Arnold Hague, after whom I am racing by telegraph into the wilderness towards Shoshone, but with few hopes.

What is to become of my household during this adventure, I do not know, and naturally I do not greatly care; but you will do it a kindness as well as an honor by making use of it, in case you go to Washington and want quarters or dinner. The Swedish Crown-princess will treat you, I am sure, with every honor and culinary respect.

I expect that my baronet will be pretty well educated by the time I bring him back, but not so polished that he cannot still receive instruction, and I shall be greatly disappointed if you are not there to instruct him for the few days he will devote to mastering our political and constitutional system in Washington. Thus far he has shown shocking indifference towards common-schools, sewers and elections, but I feel sure he can do better if well directed. My dependance is on you.

I gave to Dwight your message about Robert Elsmere, but I doubt his ability to do what you ask.[2] I have even tried to read it myself, but have stranded at the p. 137, with 540 pp. still before me. Of all human characters, I think the British parson and the British virgin amuse me the least, and I find 137 pages quite as much as I can manage on such a subject, especially as the whole 137 pages could much better be condensed into 37. Nevertheless I would not prejudge even the British parson or the British maiden, and I have sworn a terrible oath to read the whole book, although the most trivial American maiden in flesh and blood would probably fatigue me less.

The valley of the Platte glides by, with a cold gray sky, while I waste your time with these futilities, and the baronet writes to his baronette, or brunette. Lady Cunliffe is a jovial Welsh matron, and I hope she will derive great instruction from a description of the Plattitudes, but I'll not weary you with more. Tomorrow we shall reach Salt Lake. Please wish us a pleasant return to Washington, and be there to ensure it.

Truly Yrs   Henry Adams.

MS: MHi
  1. The motto "God is Great:—then, why lie?" had been painted on the mirror of the car by Francis D. Millet, CFA2's friend.
  2. Mrs. Humphry Ward, *Robert Elsmere* (1888), a novel on a religious theme.

To Charles Milnes Gaskell

Union Club San Francisco
28 October, 1888.

My dear Carlo

Robert's arrival broke the long stilness of the summer, and started me off, on the 13th, to take him wherever he wanted to go. Since then we have wandered steadily westward, four thousand miles, through all sorts of scenery and people; stopping at Salt Lake; visiting the Shoshone Falls, which tourists have hardly yet discovered in the lava-deserts of Idaho; descending the Columbia River in Oregon; and turning south seven hundred miles down the Pacific coast till we arrived here yesterday morning. I took Robert out to see the sun, setting in a hazy summer light over the Pacific; and I offered to take him on, still westward, as far as the sun went; but he showed at last the effect of age and travel; he refused to go further, and turned his face eastward. Apparently we are at the end.

I think he has enjoyed the trip, though the work is certainly hard, and the fatigue more steadily exhausting than one at first suspects. As for me, I am always contented when in motion, and ask no better than to wander on. Tomorrow we start for the Yosemite; and when we are done with this part of California, we shall go south to the Mexican border, and home to Washington by way of New Orleans. We expect to reach Washington about Nov. 25, and Robert sails December 12 for Liverpool.

Robert is the same pleasant traveling-companion that he was twenty years ago, and takes life as gaily and with as much appreciation as ever. I am heartily glad to have this outing with him, for the chance is small that we should ever renew our youth in any other way. We sometimes speculate whether you would enjoy our adventures, such as they are; and whether you would be intolerably bored by suffocating dust and jouncing carts; vast sand-deserts, and barren sage-brush plains, over which one has to travel, day and night, without much sleep, till one's ideas of the world become altogether upset, and even the solidest Yorkshire valet gets tired of wondering where the country-seats are. Fortunately Robert brought no valet, and we carry our own dust, inch-deep, with a green reflêt, in patience, without being obliged to dust a servant too. I expect to find Robert quite ground away, as by a sand-blast, before I get him across the great southern plains.

For one Sunday we are resting in luxury at San Francisco, with nothing to do, much bent upon doing it. The baronet is fairly tired, and so am I. The Club is very fine, and the city as bright as sun and movement can make it. Robert has gone to get his hair cut; then we shall breakfast, at noon, and then—I know not what. Some amusement is sure to turn up.

Of course Robert has given me a deal of information about matters in England, and I feel myself almost as well up as I ever was, though this is perhaps no great thing. I am very sorry to hear of Gifford Palgrave's death, which met us on our arrival here. Otherwise we have seemed to strike nothing in the way of news. At this distance I think even Ireland seems a less overpowering element in the cosmos than it seems nearer home; and one finds the Chinaman take the place of the ubiquitous Irishman, politics and all. Both are rather a bore; but the Chinaman bores one in a new way, as Dr Johnson said of the poet Gray.[1]

Robert has returned, and is ordering breakfast. He is wrestling with the California cuisine, and wants me to tell him about all the game-birds he sees, and all the trees. As though I knew! My only labor is to sit on his inquiring mind.

Ever Yrs   Henry Adams.

MS: MHi
1. "He was dull in a new way, and that made many people think him great"; Johnson, in Boswell's *Life.*

To Elizabeth Cameron

Yosemite Valley. Sunday, 4 Nov. 1888.

My dear Mrs Cameron

With the deepest contrition for having disobeyed and offended you, I must still confess that here we are in the Yosemite Valley, and, unlike the ambitious youth Rasselas, we are anything but eager to leave it.[1] Last night a little rain fell,—the first since April,—and today all the hills are white, and the pines powdered with snow. I have just returned from a long day in the mountains, where the fresh snow was about us, and where I felt myself a modified, though deteriorated, black bear, with strong prejudices against civilisation. In this spirit, inflamed by an atmosphere of third-rate Britishers created by a party of belated globe-trotters who have drifted here to our perdition, I am trying to reconcile myself with my fellow-man by writing to you, who are the chief reconciling element. For the moment the Yosemite is a good enough Gobi for me; but, though I feel ashamed to say so to you, it is true that the other day, arriving at San Francisco, I took my baronet out to the Cliff House, where the Pacific was rolling in its long surf in the light of a green and yellow sunset; and there I pointed to the Golden Gate and challenged the baronet to go on with me. Ignominiously he turned his back on all that glory, and set his face eastward for his dear fogs; and I, too, for the time, submitted; but the longing was as strong as ever, and, if I had not wanted to see Martha once more, I am not quite sure that I would not, then and there, have run for it.

Forgive this bit of selfishness and egotism, which is due only to your reprovals, and to the Britishers. My baronet has enjoyed his journey, which has indeed been a succession of rapid and fantastic changes such as even I, who have travelled in America occasionally, could hardly take in. When I wrote to you from the Platte Valley we were already well shaken up to new sensations. We had—or he had—seen Tuxedo, Chicago, and U.P. Car 010 which was the loftiest emotion of all; but the next day he learned what sage-brush was; the third, he saw Salt Lake and passed an afternoon wandering along its shores; next he had a sensation watching the Utah Mountains for a whole day, which ended by bringing us to Shoshone. You should have seen us two animated dust-heaps driving across twenty-five miles of fluid dust and solid lava to see Shoshone Falls, and clambering down and up that pleasing ravine, much as though one slid down from Table Rock by a rope. My legs ached for a week, and my very hat stood on end with terror, but this was a trifle compared to its condition when the mainspring of our wagon broke, on the way back, and the baronet and I were bumped for twelve miles of solid lava blocks in a solider dust, till we regained our car. Then we struck a furious storm on the summit of the Oregon mountains, and ran twenty miles down-hill over trees corduroying the track; but

I preferred this to running over cows, as in Idaho, though the cows are perhaps a softer road-bed. We went down the Dalles by steamer, with a rain-accompaniment, and saw Portland through a water-fall heavier than the Shoshone. The day passed in running by Mt Shasta in northern California was another sensation worth having; but we found San Francisco dull in spite of its swell club-house; and we lost our glory when we left our car.

Last Monday night we started for the Sierras and arrived here Wednesday afternoon. Since then we have passed a year or two in the amusement of climbing the face of cliffs three thousand feet high, and standing on their edge afterwards. This sensation certainly takes away one's breath, if that is its object, and at last I have struck on the edge business, leaving it to the baronet on the principle that his son may just as well succeed now as later to the baronetcy. I prefer to break my own neck short of three thousand feet, not requiring so much time as the Britisher for reflection in the air. Tomorrow we go after the big trees, another sensation. Then we go back to San Francisco; thence to Monterey, Santa Barbara and New Orleans, and finally to Washington on or about the 25th where we hope to have our last and best sensation in seeing you. Our journey has been such a spendid success that I cannot realise the possibility of any disappointment in its climax at the end.

My baronet is a charming companion, and I am but an indifferent one whose only virtue is a willingness to go anywhere and stay as long or as short a time as he likes, and whose chief vice is to discuss geology by the hour without understanding the first principle of it. If I bore him, he does not bore me, but is appreciative, and quite hostile to all useful information. Even the lurid figure of Mr Gladstone has been temporarily overshadowed in his mind by the cliffs and forests of the Yosemite, and we shall cast our votes on Tuesday among the big trees, indifferent to what political party they belong. I do not believe them to be republican, democratic or Gladstonian, but if they are either, more's the pity, and they may yet live to forget it. I know you would like to be with us on this solemn occasion, and I shall select one of the prettiest Sequoias to take back to Martha for a plaything. She can grow up to it. To her, at her age, a few hundred feet, more or less, are nothing.

I am sorry to quit the bears and other society of the mountains, and have hoped in vain for a storm that should shut us in for the winter, but the skies remain blue and the waterfalls empty. Since the memory of man the valley was never so dry, and as I hate waterfalls, having been dragged to see them in every quarter of the globe till hydrophobia is imminent, I rejoice in a state of things which leaves only pebbles and pools to look at. The Indian summer is enough for me, and a brown desert is my delight, but our guides mournfully point out where the waterfalls ought to be, and treat with speechless resentment my rejoicings over their absence. We shall reach San Francisco, I hope, next Thursday, and I trust to escape the annual deluge which is overdue there, so as to see southern California in its romantic dust.

Do not disappoint us at Washington, and then our journey will be a long success.

Ever Yrs   Henry Adams.

San Francisco. Nov. 8. Just arrived and received yours of Oct. 30. All flourishing. Thanks for your milder views of my conduct.

MS: MHi

1. The hero of Samuel Johnson's romance *Rasselas* (1759), bored by the peacefulness of his "happy valley," leaves it to search for perfect happiness in another condition of life.

To Theodore F. Dwight

San Francisco 8 Nov. 1888.

Yours of the 28th Oct. from Washington has just reached me on my arrival here. I don't care for shutters, as I prefer burglars, but you had better order all the small things to be done, and have the Turner glassed if it can be finished before my return on the 25th. This seems to me improbable, and as I must have some company while Cunliffe is with me perhaps the Turner had better wait. Of course let William have his glass and china if you can find it; but I think I shall have to attend to it myself, as I probably know the only shops where those things can be got. Fruit knives are a delicate matter. I want none of the fruit knives of commerce. Perhaps they had better wait.

I want Brent to find out at the riding-school whether I can get a good horse for Cunliffe to ride for the days he is with me.

The chimney is a great relief.

MS: MHi

To Abigail Brooks Adams

Santa Barbara 14 November, 1888

Dear Mamma

Your letter reached me just as I was leaving San Francisco the other night. The hotel-clerk let it lie several days undelivered, till I looked through the letter-pile before leaving. Day after tomorrow we start for New Orleans, and, after two or three days there, shall go on to Washington, so that within a short time after you receive this letter, I shall be at home again.

I stayed an extra day at San Francisco in order to go with a young Boston architect named Coolidge, one of Richardson's men, to see the University buildings which Gov. Stanford is putting up, at Menlo Park near San Francisco. The buildings are going to be the prettiest and most artistic in America, or perhaps in Europe; and I was anxious to see them, though they are not quarter finished.[1] I afterwards, the next day, went to see Gov. Stanford's house in San Francisco, which is big enough for a University, and astonishing beyond the Yosemite or all the wonders of the wild west. The world never saw such glory. An insane tomcat would be sobered by the Governor's furniture.[2] My poor baronet caved in. I felt proud of my fellow-citizen, and thought better than ever of the United States Senate to which Gov. Stanford belongs.

We arrived here at Santa Barbara, last night, and have passed the day driving about, in a foot of dust, to see the place, which is a sort of Sorrento, only it looks south instead of north. We drove out to several villas and orange-groves above the town, and I found the roses in splendid flower, among oranges, lemons, bananas and palms, so that you can tell Miss Baxter I have found summer at last. To be sure the thermometer was only about sixty, which I call quite cool enough; but at least no rain has fallen here since last April, and I may still find warmth at El Paso where I shall be next Sunday, as Miss Baxter will be pleased to know.

I would like to stop here, and buy a villa on the hills, and grow roses; which would be much pleasanter, looking out over the Pacific Ocean, than to sit in your house at Washington and look at snow-storms and politicians; but my baronet, in spite of my advice, refuses to settle here, and persists in sailing for England on December 12; so we are to start next Friday for the east. Our journey has been very pleasant, and I have been constantly surprised to find how much we have to see in America, and how amusing it is. The desert alone is worth the money. I never get tired of looking at it, and the deserter it is, the more it amuses me, especially these southern deserts with devils standing over them with arms stretched out, calling themselves some kind of cactus, I believe.[3] A great stretch of sand, inhabited at long intervals by these devil-trees, is very lively. I think we have about four days of it between here and the nearest cultivated country. Then there is always the chance that my baronet may be robbed or shot in going through Texas, which would be still more entertaining.

If we reach Washington safely, you will hear of us in time. Eight thousand miles is not much of an excursion, and I shall not be able to stop at once, until I have run a few thousand more.

Ever affecly   Henry Adams.

MS: ScU

1. Charles Allerton Coolidge (1858–1936), of Shepley, Rutan, and Coolidge, Richardson's successors and architects of the original quadrangle, completed 1891, of Stanford University. Leland Stanford (1824–1893), railroad builder, governor of California 1861–1863, and Republican senator 1885–1893, founded the university in 1885.

2. Stanford's two-million-dollar palace on Nob Hill had an Indian room, a Pom-

peiian room, and a Chinese room. A feature of the art gallery was a circular velvet seat with plants filling the center and, perched on the plants, mechanical birds that sang at the touch of a button.

3. The saguaro cactus, which reaches a height of seventy feet.

To Charles Scribner

1603 H Street. Washington. 26 Nov. 1888.

Dear Sir

On returning to Washington, I find yours of November 13, which I hasten to answer.

John Wilson, at my request, set up a page for me, as I was not satisfied with that he set up first, and which you enclose to me. I enclose the specimen. My only doubt is whether the quotation should be put in smaller type for more contrast. I calculated with Wilson that this page was not only the most elegant, but coincided most closely with my wish to have volumes of five hundred pages each. If you are satisfied, I do not care to alter this specimen unless to reduce the size of type for quotation.

My taste rather inclines towards simplifying the page. I think that the reader who has a table of contents at the beginning, chapter by chapter, and an index for each pair of volumes, besides one for the whole, at the end, would neither need nor look at chapter- or page-headings. If you assent, I propose to drop the arrangement in books, and run the chapters through the volume. Each volume then serves as a Book. Under any circumstances I cannot retain my old arrangement, as the new volume would begin in the middle of a Book; and I can discover no other satisfactory division, suited to the new volume I want. Therefore I propose to number the Chapters consecutively, (except the Introduction, which will make eight chapters) and to make no change in page-headings except for chapters, dates and paging. The result will be such as you see on the specimen, after striking out the Book 1, and enlarging the type of *Chap. 1.*[1]

I want no marginal notes. They were never of use to me in any book, (except Coleridge's Ancient Mariner.)

I infer from your letter that your chief doubt will concern Chapter-headings, and that you regard them as more important than page-headings or marginal notes. I regard them all as quite superfluous. Neither Macaulay nor Mahon used Chapter-headings.[2] The beauty of a page is its absence of all that disturbs the eye. Usage is arbitrary, but one cannot go wrong by being simple. My only doubt is about quotations, for I think the whole page should be in one type; but I must put references in foot-notes, and if one must use small type anyway, one might as well use it in the text. Therefore I yield to this variation from abstract rules, but I see no reason for disturbing the page with unnecessary changes, either before Chapters or elsewhere. I should use the same heading for odd and for even pages, except that the Chapter in one corner would interchange with the date on the other.

Of course you must understand me as expressing only preferences, not fixed prejudices. If you are very decided on any of these points, I do not care to hold out, least of all, about page-headings. I regard them merely as work thrown away. I never regard them in reading, and I do not believe any reader would notice their presence or absence in a history more than in a novel, where uniformity is very common, or in very old books, where it is, I think the rule.

My chief difficulty concerns the maps and plans. These should be nicely engraved to suit the page, as in Napier's Peninsular War.[3] I dislike all the patent processes I have seen. All thicken the lines. Supposing them to be engraved satisfactorily, ought they to be printed on a page, or inserted as in Napier? I care little, but I suppose the insertion to be less troublesome, though more liable to error.

Anyway the engraving must, if possible, precede or at least accompany the printing. The earlier volumes need few plans, but the later or war chapters will require a number. I must furnish them, and must find my engraver. Do you wish to take charge of this matter, or do you prefer that I should find my own man? I know only enough about the subject to dislike every method I ever saw, especially all photographic processes.

I am ready to print as fast as you please, and Wilson can turn out the plates faster than I can correct proof. Whenever you give the order, I will start.

Yrs truly   Henry Adams.

MS: ViU

1. The draft volumes of the *History*, with HA's revisions, became copy-text for the first edition. In the draft volumes, on the same line as the running titles and at the inner margin of the facing pages, the printer had given book and chapter numbers and the date of the narrative topic. To balance the pages, "Book I" and "Chap. I" were bracketed one above the other in reduced type. HA's suggestion for simplified format was followed, including the adoption of arabic numerals.

2. Philip Henry Stanhope (1805–1875), Earl Stanhope, published his *History of England, 1713–1783* (1836–1863) under his previous title of Viscount Mahon.

3. *History of the Peninsular War* (1828–1840) by Sir William Francis Patrick Napier (1785–1860), general and historian.

To Charles Scribner

1603 H Street. 29 Nov. 1888.

Dear Sir

Your letter of yesterday has just arrived. We may consider all the details settled. Your wish for a chapter-title for odd pages, coinciding, as it does, with my own doubts, disposes of the matter. If you were undecided between the various possibilities of page-headings, I might have asked your opinion whether the same page-heading might not run through a volume, or even two volumes, as a sufficient division of subject: E.G; JEFFERSON'S FIRST ADMINISTRATION instead of a chapter-heading often awkwardly expressed; but if you are clear in preference of the chapter as the proper subject-division, I assent without further delay.

I think we need hardly employ two kinds of illustration. Some of the campaign-maps will have to be somewhat complicated, and one or two boundary-maps will require nice work to look well. As these should be engraved and inserted, we might as well engrave the rest, and keep the letterpress unbroken. In no case shall I require a folding-map, but the engraving should be all the nicer on the smaller scale. If you can glance at Napier (Boone, 1841) you will see what I want. I will enquire of the Survey here about map-engravers, though I know that Julius Bien has always done their work.

If you will write to Wilson and settle your arrangements with him, I will go to Cambridge next Wednesday or Thursday, when I shall be in Boston; and will then agree with Wilson about the regular supply of copy. He can begin printing within ten days.

Yrs truly   Henry Adams.

MS: ViU

Friday, November 30.

I left Quincy on Friday, October 12, and joined Robert Cunliffe and John Hay the same evening at Albany, going on through Cleveland, where Hay left us, to Chicago which we reached Saturday night. At Chicago we passed two days, Frank McVeagh taking charge of us, and giving us at last a pretty dinner in his exquisite house. My brother Charles's car caught us at Chicago and we started, Tuesday 16, westward. After weeks of rain and clouds, I was glad to meet the sun at Laramie, and we arrived at Salt Lake City late at night, October 18, to find extreme drought and perfect skies. At Salt Lake Bishop Sharpe took us in charge and carried us down to the Lake in a special train Friday afternoon, and up to Ogden in his own car Saturday morning.[1] All Saturday we ran over the narrow-guage Utah Northern, through a charming country, until we changed to the Oregon Short Line, and regained our own car. Saturday night we reached Shoshone, and on Sunday, 21, drove over twentyfive miles of lava and dust to the Falls. After a day there, we returned to Shoshone, Monday, 22, and that night went on, entering Oregon the next morning, and reaching the Dalles Tuesday night. Wednesday, 24, was passed on the Columbia, with some storm, reaching Portland in time to dine at the club, under charge of General Manager Holcombe. Thursday, 25, we saw Portland in a flood of rain and started for San Francisco. All day, Friday, 26, we skirted Mount Shasta, as beautiful a bit of scenery as heart could desire, and superb skies. Saturday morning, October 27, we reached San Francisco, and rested, finding the Union Club a reposeful spot, and no one in town. Monday, October 29, we started for the Yosemite, slept Tuesday night at Wahwona, and Wednesday in the valley. We delivered a letter of introduction to old Galen Clark who took us in charge and showed us the whole valley for near twenty miles up and down and sideways, till I think I know it thoroughly. The weather was superb, and the drought unprecedented. We returned to Wahwona, Monday Nov. 5, and passed Tuesday in majestic repose under the great trees, riding on good ponies up and down. On Wednesday we returned to Raymond and the railway. Thursday, Nov. 8, we were again at San Francisco where I found George Howland, Clarence King's half brother, and took him with us for a night to Monterey, returning Saturday. Passed Sunday, Nov. 11, at Menlo Park with Coolidge the architect, inspecting his University Building. Monday, 12, Cunliffe and I started again, but without our car, and reached Santa Barbara Tuesday night. Wednesday and Thursday, 14 and 15, we were at Santa Barbara. Friday we ran on to Los Angeles, caught the Southern Pacific train, reached Yuma the next morning, El Paso Sunday noon, and at last after four weary days, got to New Orleans Tuesday, Nov. 20. Remained three days, and visited the battle-field, but knew no one to show us society or introduce us at the Club. Friday, 23, we started again, and reached Washington Sunday evening, November 25. We travelled in all about nine thousand miles with perfect success.

1. John Sharp (1820–1891), Mormon bishop and a major railroad builder in Utah, was a director of the Union Pacific.

To Mary Endicott Chamberlain

1603 H Street. 10 December '88.

My dear Mrs Chamberlain

On my return from the Pacific coast, I found you gone, and only your very kind note to tell me what had happened.[1] You are already so far advanced in your new world that you must have begun the curious second stage which we all reach, when we are constantly wondering which is most unreal, the present or the past, and I can do no better than send you, as a sort of compromise, my friend Sir Robert Cunliffe, to make a sort of double connection, for he will talk to you almost with equal familiarity of America and England. He is one of my oldest and closest friends. I am sure you will like him, and will want to hear of all he has to tell you. He carries with him a little wedding-gift on my behalf, rather late for the occasion, but worth your acceptance because it is American, and brought by us all the way from El Paso for your favor. Opals were once thought unlucky; but I shall certainly not think anything unlucky which prevents your wholly forgetting me. Give my best regards and wishes to your husband, and believe me most sincerely yours

Henry Adams.

MS: MHi
1. Mary Endicott and Joseph Chamberlain were married in Washington, Nov. 15. Their engagement in February had been kept a secret to avoid alienating the Irish vote in the presidential election: her father was in Cleveland's cabinet and Chamberlain had left the Liberal party in protest against Irish home rule.

Sunday, 10 December

Another week of absence, this time at Boston which Cunliffe wanted to see. Glad of any excuse for escape from my haunting anniversary, I set off with him and passed the week at New York and Boston, seeing all my friends and family, and actually dining with my old friend Sarah Alden, now Mrs Derby, in New York. In Boston everything was going as usual, my mother about the same, and at Cambridge all well. On returning to New York I went yesterday to see St Gaudens who has begun the Buddha. We discussed the scale, and I came away telling him that I did not think it wise for me to see it again, in which he acquiesced. Molly has returned with us to Washington. Cunliffe leaves us next Tuesday. At Cambridge I saw John Wilson, and gave him the first sheets of copy.

To Sir Robert Cunliffe

1603 H Street. 16 Dec. 1888

Dear Robert

I write a line only to say that I miss you, and do nothing but wonder whether you can really get home alone. I was quite horrified to find that you had undertaken to go aboard the steamer by yourself, and both Hay and I are very anxious to hear that you succeeded. The weather has been fine here, and by this time you are so near the other coast that I cease to calculate storm-centres.

Your visit has been a boon to me, and I feel it the more as I settle back upon routine. My heart still reproaches me for being so unsympathetic to you about your political interests, but you ought to reflect that I am positively brutal to my own people about ours, and that, considering my feelings on the whole realm of politics, I was not altogether so much to blame as though I were simply malevolent. To me, politics have been the single uncompensated disappointment of life—pure waste of energy and moral. I hate to see other men hope, where I think myself wiser. It reflects on my character for veracity.

Yet I shall be keen to hear your adventures, political, nautical and domestic. As my own are limited to the preparation of copy for the press, I think you can guess them without telling. Constant and uninterrupted profanity would be the entire material of my history, if the proof-sheets contained the spirit of their copy and corrections.

My love to miladi and the young ones, and a pleasant Christmas to you all.

Ever affectionately   Henry Adams.

The Washington newspapers have raised you to the peerage.

MS: MHi

Sunday 16 December
Cunliffe sailed last Wednesday. I have since worked desperately to prepare my first chapters for the press. Gradually I am beginning to rewrite the whole first volume.

To Charles Scribner

1603 H Street. Washington. 19 Dec. 1888.

Dear Sir

Wilson writes me that he has sent you the sample proofs of the first eight pages. I see they have overlooked the alternate Chapter-heading which I substituted in the copy. With this correction it seems to me satisfactory, and whenever you approve, I will send to Wilson the copy for steady work.

My only doubt regards the introductory chapters which will be eight in number, and will fill near half a volume. Ought these chapters to be set apart and headed *Introduction,* or ought they to run directly into the narrative? The question has greatly perplexed me. I do not fancy Introductions. I see that most of the historians had the same feeling. Gibbon ran his introductory chapters into his narrative, and Macaulay actually broke off his narrative to insert his introductory chapter. On the other hand I admit that my first seven or eight chapters are wholly introductory, not only to my sixteen years but also to the century. They ought to stand by themselves.[1]

I will follow your opinion if you have a decided one either way.

Yrs truly   Henry Adams.

MS: ViU
1. The six introductory chapters—on the condition of the United States in 1800—were not set apart from the succeeding narrative chapters.

Sunday 23 December
Very hard work preparing copy for the press. Received the first eight pages of proof from Wilson, and, after waiting to hear from Scribner, returned them yesterday with copy for the whole first chapter. At last I am launched and must take my final course. I am pleased with the new page, which is that of Froude's cabinet edition; but I am

troubled about the form of my introductory chapters, as I am in effect rewriting them, and can no longer meditate over choice of changes. Molly is still here.

Sunday 30 December

Still busy with copy. No more proof. Beautiful weather, and horseback. Molly brings more gaiety to the house, but I see rather less of my own friends. Box of stuffs arrived from Sturgis Bigelow in Japan.

To Lucy Baxter

1603 H Street. 6 Jan. 1889.

My dear Miss Baxter

As I suppose you will have returned, I send you a check for Roche's bill. I know nothing about it, but presume it's all right. Gallagher can tell best.

As though I had done no work in the summer, I am now toiling day and night to get my poor old history into condition to stand up. Never did I try such a job. As fast as I plaster and whitewash one chapter, those behind and before crumble and tumble. The printers howl for copy, and I must let the poor old asthmatic, rheumatic, astigmatic, but not even dogmatic, pre-historic wreck totter into the world. I always said I was Casaubon, and shall be easier when other people know the secret.

Molly seems to drag out a prematurely youthful existence in a half-awake kind of maze. I suppose she bores herself less here than at some other places, for she stays; but the temptation to shake her is not to be resisted. She has the family character. Everyone of us has to be fired out of a cannon to be roused into consciousness of anything but ourselves.

I am sure you enjoyed your Xmas, so I'll not wish it. Apparently Mt Vernon Street was no worse for the vacation. I was astounded to receive a letter announcing a visit to Gloucester Street.[1]

If you see Dwight, tell him I have nothing for him.

Ever truly Yrs   Henry Adams.

MS: ScU

1. Mt. Vernon Street refers to ABA. Presumably she and Lucy Baxter had visited CFA2 at the house he had built in 1887, at 20 Gloucester Street in Boston's Back Bay.

Sunday 6 Jan. 1889.

Another year nearer the end, thank time. Copy, copy, copy! Disgusting labor. I can write faster than I can prepare for the press. Luckily the printers send me no proofs. Dwight has gone to Boston. Edward Hooper has been here. The Hays have scarlet fever and we are all quarantined, as I am much there. Fine weather till yesterday, and regular horse-back. Little society. Frank McVeaghs to breakfast and dinner.

To Charles Scribner

1603 H Street. 9 Jan. 1889.

Dear Sir

Your's dated yesterday has just arrived.

You know best, but I rather dislike to run chapters through more than one volume. A volume seems to me a good division, and chapters a good subdivision. I always feel a little shock at seeing a volume begin with anything but Chapter I. None of these volumes will contain more than Chapter XVIII, and I think we can find room for that.

Why use Roman numerals? CHAPTER 38 looks quite as well as Chapter XXXVIII, which strikes me as rather clumsy. I notice that Longmans, in their edition of Froude, adopted both abbreviations, and used [CH. 27 as though they had been in difficulty on the same point. If you think the abbreviation necessary, I would do the whole thing, and make sure. If you think that the Chapters may run with the volumes, I shall be quite pleased.

For the first volume I shall have to be exceptionally careful in proofreading. Everyone criticises first volumes. No one cares much afterwards. Do not feel uneasy if I seem at first over-fussy in requiring revisions.[1]

Yours truly   Henry Adams.

Charles Scribner Esq.

MS: ViU

1. Henceforth, until Sept. 20, Dwight conducted HA's negotiations with Scribner's on various aspects of the *History*—maps, binding, paper, index, proofreading, publication schedule. Dwight's 24 letters appear in Massachusetts Historical Society, *Proceedings* 71 (1953–1957), 24–36.

Sunday, 13 January

Still fine weather. Horseback every day. Shocking labor over first volume of history which has to be rewritten. I have only sent about one fourth of it to the printer, and received half the first chapter in proof. I am troubled at the amount of time the thing promises to take in printing. My brother Brooks is here. Molly's young friends make my society, except the Hays who are still quarantined.

To Theodore F. Dwight

1603 H Street. Wednesday [16 Jan. 1889]

Dear Dwight

Nothing presses for you here. I am hard at work, and Molly hard at play. The Hays are still in quarantine, and Mrs Cameron shut up with roseola or rash of some sort. Still uncooked, we wail for daily bread. Tom Lee and Linda Lawrence go with us to the concert Friday.[1] Belinda is desperate and wants to join you and become archiviste. The Dept. seems to threaten reforms that don't suit.

No hay novedades.[2] Miss Leiter breakfasted with us last week and was very charming. I felt angrier than ever with Springy.[3] Printing has not got beyond first chapter nor finally disposed of that. The labor of rewriting does not diminish.

Give my love to everybody, and tell Molly's mamma that her daughter was here when I last heard of her, and as she seemed to be going somewhere, I guess she's well.

Ever Yrs   Henry Adams.

T. F. Dwight Esq.

MS: MHi
1. Thomas Lee (1858–1936), former law student and stockbroker, whose hunting and fishing trips HA liked to join. The concert was that of the Boston Symphony Orchestra.
2. *No hay novedades:* I have no news.
3. For not pursuing her successfully.

Sunday 20 January.

Work on the history is easier now that I have got into diplomatic affairs. Nearly all the copy for my first new volume is ready. No more proof comes. Society is active, and I passive. Yet I took a little party to Gericke's concert Friday, and went to a supper given by John Bancroft afterwards. Gericke, Adamoski, Burnett, and the three diplomates, Rosen, Tavera, and Arco, the new German.[1]

Sunday, 27 January.

Warm, moist weather still. Always hard at work preparing copy, and have done about 350 pages of the old volume which contains 580; another week or two ought to complete it, and then I can begin rewriting my last volume. The work is trying; when I quit it, at three o'clock in the afternoon, my nerves are raw, as though I had scraped them. Ch. II and Chap. VI in type.

1. Timothée Adamowski (1858–1943), Polish violinist with the Boston Symphony Orchestra and founder of the Adamowski Quartet in 1888. Edward Burnett (1849–1925), Democratic representative from Massachusetts 1887–1889. Baron Roman Romanovich Rosen (1847–1921), Russian chargé d'affaires at Washington 1886–1890, ambassador to the United States 1905–1911; Ernst Schmit von Tavera (b. 1839) of the Austrian legation; Count Ludwig von Arco Valley (1845–1891), minister to the United States 1888–1891.

To Marie Louise Thoron

1603 H Street. 28 Jan. 1889.

My dear Miss Thoron[1]

Nothing could please me more than to know that you are happy, and I am quite sure you are and always will be happy with a man whose character and temper are like those of William Endicott. You have my approval and warm wishes at the start, and I am sure you have those of every one. At the same time I must complain a little that the only young ladies who seem to get married are those who belong to my breakfast-table, and that it is becoming really impossible for me to keep the supply equal to the demand. This is a subject on which you ought to have reflected seriously before taking a decision.

As I have not seen Molly today, I have not given your message, but I suppose you gave it yourself last evening, and Molly on her return from your house, told me of your announcement. Please give my love to your grandmother, and tell her that I have given my approval to you, although both she and I regard ourselves as making a great sacrifice.

Ever truly Yours Henry Adams.

MS: MHi
1. Marie Louise Thoron was engaged to William Crowninshield Endicott, Jr. (1860–1936), Boston lawyer, son of the secretary of war.

To Paul Leicester Ford

1603 H Street. 29 Jan. 1889.

My dear Mr Ford

The papers are worth keeping. I shall have much to say about Prevost, and feel some concern about doing him the regular percentage of injustice. He got his share in his time, as your newspaper remarks. I think I am familiar with the contents of the two papers, but I am surprised that you got the Dearborn document from London. It must have come from the Dearborn sale at Boston, a few years ago.[1]

Very truly Yrs Henry Adams.

P. L. Ford Esq.

MS: NN
1. Sir George Prevost (1767–1816), governor-general of Canada, recalled to London in 1814 as a result of his military fiasco at Plattsburg, N.Y. Henry Dearborn (1751–1829), Jefferson's secretary of war 1801–1809, senior American general in 1812, retired in 1813 because of his fiascoes in the Niagara and lower Canada campaigns.

To Theodore F. Dwight

New Albemarle House
Elizabeth City, N.C., 6 Feb. 1889.

Dear Dwight

Tomorrow morning, as we imagine, we are to start on a steam-ship for somewhere. I am told it is to carry us to a lighthouse. The ship is a fine one, about the size of an express wagon. We have chartered it for a cruise, and will call it the blizzard. Phillips is quite stalwart, and I still hope he will survive the voyage, unless the steam-flat sits on him too heavy.[1]

I beg you will send my mail to Washington, North Carolina, to be called for at the Post Office. Probably we shall not arrive there before next Wednesday, but you had better send the whole mail Saturday evening. As we may find the weather or other causes hasten our movements, I won't look for anything later than Saturday.

We may go on to Charleston. Our movements are very liable to unexpected variations. Meanwhile we are mariners and sail the mighty deep, which looks very cold, raw and rough today.

Ever Yrs Henry Adams

MS: MHi
1. William Hallett Phillips (1853–1897), lawyer, specialist in international law. *Steam-flat:* a flat-bottomed tender for carrying passengers to and from a ship, or for river navigation.

To Elizabeth Cameron

Charleston Club 23 February, 1889.

My dear Mrs Cameron

I am very doubtful whether I can ever return to Washington. My decline in morals and manners, owing to the evil influences of Tom Lee and Willy Phillips has been so rapid as to leave little hope of ultimate recovery. I am afraid to look Martha in the face, and dare not meet you until I am purified by the moral atmosphere of the new administration. My two companions have led me into wild excesses. We succeeded in getting, with much difficulty, to a lighthouse where Tom Lee was to shoot ducks, and Phillips was to enjoy perpetual summer. The summer began by landing in an open boat, after breaking a quarter of a mile of ice with oars, and then wading through a mile of half frozen swamp. Tom's shooting consisted in chasing ducks over ponds; and, as ducks fly rather faster than lightning, we had nothing but cold boiled pork and potato to eat. Getting tired of this sport, we tried to escape from North Carolina, but escape was impossible. After long imprisonment we seized an open boat, and made a perilous voyage in Arctic cold, to Roanoke island. There we were detained a week or two, searching for the lost colony of Sir Walter Raleigh. A steamer at last passed near, and we hailed her at midnight from the shore. She took us aboard and carried us to Little Washington, a sweet tranquil spot, but one from which no man was ever known to come away. By this time—which was just a week ago, we were reduced to extreme despair, and my two companions could only sustain themselves by obliging me to learn euchre and poker, by means of which they took away all my money, leaving me no resource but to follow them as long as they would pay my expenses. They dragged me on board a small steamer at three o'clock one morning, and carried me fifty or sixty miles up the Tar River. There, at a spot called Tarboro, they landed, and after another night of anguish, owing to Tom Lee's aversion to drummers, we caught the first train that came by. It happened to be bound south on the Atlantic Coast Line, and I found myself at Charleston the next morning, in a drenching rain, cold as Archangel, and dirty as an Esquimaux.

Tomorrow these savage men are to take me to Savannah. From there I know not what to expect. I have overheard Tom Lee talking of a ball, with which your name was coupled, and which seemed to be expected for the week after next. Perhaps I may be carried back to Washington, if he wants to go to the ball; or perhaps I may be sent to some spot still more awful than North Carolina, if there is one. I am at their mercy, and shall continue to play euchre and eat shad as long as life holds out. Only, if Tom Lee does come back to a ball with you, pray intercede for me in the intervals of your thoughtless gaiety. Think of what I have suffered, and send me hope.

You are too busy to think of outlaws like us, so I write to prevent your forgetting us. Would you like a sharks-tooth? I have seen nothing else to bring home to you.

Ever Yrs   Henry Adams.

MS: MHi

To Theodore F. Dwight

Oglethorpe Club Tuesday 26 Feb. [1889]

Dear Dwight

I see among the advertisements of the Revue des Deux Mondes a volume of "Lettres inédites de Talleyrand à Napoleon, 1800–1809. Par Pierre Bertrand." I shall have to see this before letting my first volumes go. Will you try to find a copy at New York, or if necessary send to Paris for it. I guess the New Yorkers must have it.

The weather is so bad that we can do nothing. Savannah is pleasant enough. We all went to a ball last night and stayed till two or three o'clock. You can imagine the eccentricity of our appearance at a midnight dance in Savannah. I was almost amused, the thing was such lunacy on our part; but some of the girls were pretty, and the supper was excellent. I am deadly sleepy today, and have sent Lee and Phillips off to take berths for Washington next Friday. If we could hit a tolerable day, we might find amusement here, but we see nothing but raw rain.

No mail here yet. I suppose something will arrive tomorrow.

Ever Yrs   Henry Adams.

MS: MHi

Sunday, 3 March.

I have been away all the month of February, wandering with Tom Lee and Willy Phillips along the coast of the Carolinas and as far south as Savannah. Phillips was sent off for his health, and we went with him. We started by way of Baltimore to Fortress Monroe; thence to Norfolk, and Elizabeth City; there we chartered a little steamer, and went in one day to Manteo on Roanoke Island, whence we crossed to Body Island Light. After four days vainly trying for duck, we beat back to Manteo in an open boat, and passed four days more investigating Roanoke island and Raleigh's lost colony. Saturated with shad-fishing and marshes, we took steamer to Little Washington and passed a day on the Tar river in a steamer that set us down at Tarboro. Our life in North Carolina was pretty rough and quite beyond society of any sort; but we went to Charleston, arriving Feb. 21, and thence to Savannah a week ago. Phillips introduced us into society, and we were amused and dissipated. I did not want to return to the inauguration, but my companions were bent on it, and we arrived here yesterday noon.[1] The weather has been gloomy and wet; otherwise we have done well enough.

Sunday, 10 March.

Inauguration week. I shut myself up and worked. March weather, windy and raw. A few guests and callers came in, but my society has been chiefly little Martha Cameron.

Sunday 17 March.

Printers have finished twelve chapters. At this rate they will consume years. I am rewriting the concluding chapters of my last volume. Very quiet season. Brooks has been here. He goes to Europe again, and I to Quincy for the summer. John Hay is deep in Blaine and Harrison office-distribution; Whitelaw Reid and what-not.[2] My society is wholly Martha Cameron and her mother.

Sunday, 31 March.

Wilson is very slow in printing. I have as yet received only four hundred pages since he began in January. Chapter XV came yesterday. I have prepared all the copy for the second volume, and am rewriting the eighth. Very quiet otherwise. Dwight has rheumatism. Mrs Cameron is in bed with a touch of pneumonia. The politicians are wrangling over their offices. President Harrison is amusing me by developing the characteristics peculiar to Indiana politicians. Hay's private account, derived from Blaine, of Harrison's behavior, is convulsing.

Sunday, 7 April

Having hurried the printers I have got to Chap. I of Vol. II. Revisal of last volume goes on rapidly. I have set a type-writer to work at the beginning, while I write back from the end. The world still tedious and flat.

1. President Benjamin Harrison took office March 4.
2. James G. Blaine was Harrison's secretary of state 1889–1892. Acting for Harrison, Hay persuaded Whitelaw Reid to accept the post of minister to France, whereas Reid had wanted the English mission.

To Charles Milnes Gaskell

1603 H Street. 21 April, 1889.

Dear Carlo

Time runs off without notice in these days of middle-aged common-place. Your letter of February 28 seemed to arrive only yesterday. I have been less than usual in quarters this winter, and have been more than usually busy when here. Robert and I ceased our wanderings only in December, and I started again in six weeks to pass the month of February knocking about an unknown region called the North Carolina Sounds, a vast wilderness of sand, mud and forest, populated by wild ducks and a genial fish called the shad. When March began, I had to return, for the printers could no longer be neglected, and I have made my contract for publishing the eternal history which has been the bore of my friends and myself for ten years. The first two volumes are pretty nearly ready, and will appear, I suppose, either in the summer or autumn, to be followed by the rest as fast as the publisher pleases. The printing and preparing tie me down quite tight, so that I shall not run away again till all is finished. The summer is to be passed with my mother again. My brother Brooks sails for Europe at the beginning of May, and I shall take his place. I suppose you will see him in London.

We have had a change of administration here which has interested many people, but makes little difference to the world or society. I know not a man in the new lot, high or low, and for the first time in thirty years, have not an acquaintance in the cabinet. Acquaintances grow somewhat scarce, at best, as one becomes more exacting with age. The dread of a bore grows to horror. John Hay remains my only companion, but he too starts for England in three weeks, and I hope you will see him in London where he will quarter himself and his family for a time.

Our new minister to London, who is known familiarly here as Bob Lincoln, will, I hope, be liked. He is a good fellow, rather heavy, but pleasant and sufficiently intelligent. I have known him slightly for some years. Hay has known him since childhood, and is very intimate with him.[1] Unless Hay himself were to have the place, Lincoln was as good a man as was likely to be sent, and you had better ask him to dinner. If you were not on the other side, I should also recommend Mrs Chamberlain to your regards. She is one of my breakfast-table, and does me credit.

You ask about our railroads. They are not encouraging for investment and never will be so, in my opinion. They are too much exposed to hostile legislation, taxation and competition. I have long ceased the effort to increase my investments there, or indeed anywhere. Such property as I am concerned with, is chiefly in city real-estate or in conservative bonds, bank-stock &c, and produces barely four per cent. My wants are not great, and are likely to be less rather than greater, so I have little knowledge of affairs.

My mother, though more and more broken, still shows much strength. The rest of us are middle-aged people, not ornamental and far from amusing.

My love to all Ys.

Ever   Henry Adams.

Tell Robert I have delayed writing only for his sake. I shall write soon.

MS: MHi

1. Robert Todd Lincoln (1843–1926), son of Abraham Lincoln, had been secretary of war 1881–1885; he served as minister to Great Britain 1889–1893.

Sunday, 21 April.

The printers have sent me foundry proofs of the whole first volume. The last proofs of Chap. IV, Vol. 2, were returned yesterday, and the first proofs of Chapter VII. Have rewritten the Battle of New Orleans. My Hooper nieces have been here this week.

Sunday, 28 April.

Chap. X of vol. II went back to the printers yesterday. I am working hard preparing vol. III for the press. The Hoopers went home Wednesday. Everyone is going to Europe: Hays, Camerons, brother Brooks and God knows who. Pumpellys, Hay and Mrs Cameron to dinner last night.

To Sir Robert Cunliffe

1603 H Street. 29 April, 1889.

My dear Robert

I have postponed writing ever since the year began in the idea of sending you the two small drawings you know of. La Farge sent me his little green meadow long ago, but Edward Hooper brought the Winslow Homer only last week.[1]

I sent the La Farge by express last Saturday. As La Farge considers it mine, owing to some old pecuniary relations between us, you need not be troubled about accepting it. He wanted me to change its frame, which is only an old one not intended for it; but Hooper and I thought the frame quite happy, and not likely to be improved; so I send it as it is. Take the glass out to wash the paper and paste off.

The Winslow Homer I placed, an hour ago, in one of Mrs Cameron's trunks. She sails tomorrow in the "City of New York," for Liverpool, with her husband and little daughter Martha. Unless something occurs to prevent their departure, they will reach Liverpool before this letter reaches you. She expects to stop at Chester. I have told her to write you a note, and, if you are at Acton, to run down to take lunch with you. She is, as you know, my special ally, and if you can guide her in the path of rectitude and travel, pray do for my sake. If she does not turn up, write her a line, to the care of J. S. Morgan &Co in London, and get your drawing.

The Hays sail on the 15th, I think, and go to London direct. If you are in town, look them up, and, by the way, introduce them to Carlo if they don't know him.

All America is on its way to Europe this month, including my brother Brooks who leaves me to nurse my venerable mamma at Quincy till his return. I am not eager to revel in the charms of Quincy, but I am still less disposed to see Expositions,[2] so I remain and mope over proof-sheets in solitude.

Since you departed, the winter has followed you, but I have little to tell about it. In February I rambled off with two friends and knocked about the southern sea-coast in queer places and discomfort, but, with that exception, I have done nothing except what I was doing when you were here. My mind is absorbed in the amusement of printing my history, which is now well under way, and will burst upon the world this year. The business of printing is like that of chopping straw or sawing wood, monotonous and fatiguing, but it absorbs one's mind, which is a gain when one's mind is reduced to so small a grease-spot as mine.[3]

Of society I know nothing, of politics less. I do not even know what has been doing in England, and have not heard the word Ireland since you left. King has been all winter occupied in nursing his mother through a terrible illness, and has not left her room. Hay has been mostly here, and what little I have heard of the cosmos has come to me through him. Now that he is going, and Mrs Cameron is gone, I am more helpless than ever, but I shall probably hang on here till June before going to the North.

I am told that a new minister has arrived from your honorable government.[4] Hay dines him this week. I am little likely to meet him, and he is not positively certain to rush to me. Let us hope he will like it.

Carlo wrote me that he had seen you and heard your wondrous tales. He seemed pleased to be an alderman or seneschal or terrapin or something. I hope you like county government, and stand on granite foundations.

Give my love to Lady Cunliffe and the infants. Take some of it yourself, and believe me

Ever Yrs   Henry Adams.

MS: MHi

1. Edward Hooper was an early collector of the watercolors of Winslow Homer (1836–1910). Cunliffe's interest may have been stimulated by a Homer painting which HA owned.

2. The Paris Exposition of 1889, for which the Eiffel Tower had recently been constructed.

3. HA, who had just received the first sample pages from Scribner's, was beginning the process of choosing paper and binding, which he finally completed, with La Farge's help, in August.

4. Sir Julian Pauncefote (1828–1902), minister (after 1893 ambassador) to the U.S. 1889–1902.

To Elizabeth Cameron

1603 H Street. 2 May, 1889.

My dear Mrs Cameron

Your letter from Sandy Hook has just reached me. I thought at first that you must have been prevented from sailing, and then was quite overcome by your report. I have been making myself quite too-too ridiculous by thinking about you and Martha, and am amused not only by my own idiocy but by the apparent assumption on the part of my friends that I must be humored and gently soothed about it. The receipt of your note, after I have gone through two melancholy days of rain and sympathy, is like seeing the sun again. I am infinitely grateful to you for writing it, and feel quite as though I were on board.

By dint of sticking to my desk ten hours a day, I am trying to forget that your house is empty. Tomorrow morning Molly is to arrive, in charge of Mrs Cabot Lodge, and I suppose the flies will somehow gather again where the sugar is, as heretofore, and I shall be enlivened by the buzzing. Dwight dined out last night, and made himself miserable by drinking Burgundy, so that this morning he is plunged in gloom and gout. Never mind! Even paying my tax-bill will not depress me now that I know you are, or were, off all right. Actually the sun has come out this morning, and winter returns, to make things gay.

I write this line, not to send it, but only to show that I properly appreciate your parting note. A week hence I shall do something new in my life. I shall send every day for a newspaper, until I see that you have arrived.

William Endicott has just come in, full of surprise at your departure. I did not tell him I had this instant heard from you. That detail seems more valuable when kept for my own use. I would put it into my history for safe-keeping if I could; but, though safe there from publicity, it would be too interesting for the rest of the work.

Sunday, May 5. You are half way, and I wish you had as lovely a morning as this. We have been cold since you left. I thought it was because you had gone; but Molly, who arrived Friday, complained that it was because Boston was warm. A ghastly vivacity prevails here; the last before dissolution. I hear of races, dinners and parties to Luray.[1] I have an Englishman on my back, a young Clough, sent by Sir John Clark. He comes and dines and irritates Dwight who launches on him avalanches of thin-disguised vituperation. The Hays fed Punchfoot[2] last night with Blaines, Hitts, Cabot Lodges and—Molly. The latter, on returning, averred that Punch was stupid—but I know not; she had not much of his society. Clarence King is here for a spare epoch as his way is, coming by a way-train, and leaving by the next express. So I am surrounded by gay young people, and went yesterday afternoon to see a theatrical show at the Hays, given by the children and attended by all the other children. Mrs Hay and I sat in the front row, and admired Del and Helen, various Johnsons, youthful McCauley and Eugene Hale the younger, who were severally and unitedly more excellent and insufficiently admired than Mrs Cleopatra Curlew Potter. Helen is fascinating and had masses of lilacs, buttercups and peonies thrown to her. Most of the gilded youth (female) were there from Constance Lodge to Baby Hay.[3] I enjoyed the amusement. Afterwards I strolled with Clarence King and noticed that he was quite gray, almost like myself. Strange how suddenly the young turn gray nowadays.

All this is only to say that I am glad you are half-way over. My mother is already sending word that I must come to Quincy at once. The ball in Boston was pretty, Molly says, but Mrs Jack's jewels quite outshone by the splendor of other women's stage jewelry. Jeff Coolidge was the successful beauty.[4]

Thursday, 9th. 8.30 A.M. The Hays tell me you have arrived; they heard it last night from Mrs Cabot Lodge. I am glad, and I will close these remarks and drop them into the box as I go to the War Department to rummage old papers. We are roasting after our wont at this season. I look for 90° in a space; at this hour the mercury is 75°. Your club had its reception yesterday, and every one was there and said it was pretty.[5] Suzanne came here afterwards to dinner with Charley, and the Herbert episode. Molly is flying about, finding late worms to pick up, after the other sparrows have departed. A Britisher—one Clough, a poet at one remove—has been here with letters—one to me—and has been but a qualified success. I pass your house sometimes, always with a pang, wondering whether Martha was seasick or homesick, but hoping you have been really getting thorough satisfaction from your ocean, and enjoyment from your summer. I wish I were with you, for my accounts from home are anything but agreeable, and I do not find Quincy an oasis in the desert. Indeed I greatly prefer the desert to any oasis I know. I must go there as soon as I can. Everyone leaves here next week. The Hays too, and after their departure I am little better than a schoolmaster without scholars—nary child to my back, and nothing to talk about. At best I have no news even to tell you, for we are still waiting to hear from May Clymer, and Horace Grey will not be married till June 5.[6] Mrs Lodge will write news. I write only to say how we miss you and are homesick for you.

Ever Yrs   Henry Adams.

MS: MHi

1. The Luray Caverns in Virginia, about ninety miles from Washington.
2. Sir Julian Pauncefote.
3. Eugene Hale, son of Sen. Eugene Hale and Mary Chandler Hale. Cora Urquhart Brown-Potter (1859–1936), after much success in amateur plays for charity, went on the stage professionally in 1886. Constance Lodge (1872–1948), daughter of Rep. and Mrs. Henry Cabot Lodge. Clarence Hay, the youngest of the Hay children, was 4½.
4. Thomas Jefferson Coolidge, Jr. (1863–1912), Boston banker.
5. Senator Cameron was president of the board of governors of the Country Club.

6. The anticipated marriages: Sen. Thomas Bayard of Delaware to Mary Willing
Clymer, Nov. 7; and Associate Supreme Court Justice Horace Gray to Jane Matthews,
daughter of Associate Justice Stanley Matthews, June 4.

Sunday 5 May.
*Mrs Cameron left here last Tuesday and sailed for Europe the next morning. I went
to Baltimore with them. Molly arrived here Friday. Clarence King is here. Central
Asian talk.*

To Lucy Baxter

1603 H Street. Sunday 12 May 1889.

Dear Miss Baxter

Your letter to Dwight, adding to the details Charles gave us of your difficulties, makes me anxious to give you what aid I can. I will hurry my
preparations so as to leave here June 2 instead of June 10, and reach
Quincy by June 5 at latest. If you think it useful, I will break off here at
once, and come on. In either case you had better say nothing about it to
anyone, but just tell me what *you* would prefer. My object is not so much to
be of use to my mother, who is not now likely to be benefitted by anything I
can do; but rather to relieve you, as far as I can, of unnecessary care. On
this matter I am not able to form a clear judgment. If I were in your place I
should certainly not want unnecessary people about, or anyone who did
not positively take some share in carrying the load. Indeed I gave my
brother Brooks distinct notice that as long as I should be at Quincy I did
not want *him* there on any terms. I have no right to suppose that I should
make things easier by my presence, and I might easily make them worse.
You must act as commanding officer, and issue your orders to suit your
wants. I will obey them, and so will Dwight.

Ever Yrs   Henry Adams.

MS: ScU

To Elizabeth Cameron

1603 H Street. Wednesday, 15 May 1889.

My dear Traveller

I am beginning to hope for a letter, since eight days have passed after
your arrival at Queenstown. The Hays departed two days ago and are now
tossing on the briny deep. Dwight went to Quincy yesterday to nurse Miss
Baxter and my mother. Molly and I are left solitary, and I am liable at any

moment to be called to Quincy. Washington consists of Mrs Cabot Lodge with whom I dine tomorrow. Last evening Suzanne in a pink dress suddenly appeared to dinner with Sigourney Butler and Lowndes.[1] I thought the latter seemed in low spirits, and today we learn that Miss Tilly is to marry Mr Gray tomorrow.[2] I suppose you know all these things by intuition so I will not dilate on the charms of bride or groom; but at least you must be proud to know that the Bayard-Clymer alliance is at last officially announced and another of these awful sexagenarians is settled. I think this must end them. No other man of that age will have the courage to face the music. Apparently none but the aged marry, and the prospect of the next generation is decidedly limited. The world will be quite habitable when populated by such means.

I pass seven hours a day over proof-sheets, and try to forget my solitude. Yesterday I called on Rosen to discuss Central Asia with him. He seemed delighted to think that a civilised being could want to see Central Asia which he characterises as dirty. I hope his government will make me an Emir or some such thing—say a jaguar. Ward Thoron and Rebecca Dodge came to breakfast with not a jot of gossip even for you. Mary Leiter comes also to my poor table at times, and Molly seems chiefly to reside under the protection of papa and mama Leiter.[3] She defends papa. I am willing, as there is no immediate Leiter to figure as my nephew. Punchfoot goes to Mt Vernon on the Despatch next Saturday. Aren't you sorry to be away?

P.S. No he didn't, because of Allan Rice.

Sunday, 19 May   No one seems to have heard from you yet, except for some telegram said to have announced your departure to drive somewhere in the north. I hoped some one would have heard yesterday. Perhaps I shall find that a letter has come, when I go to Mrs Lodge's lunch at Grasslands this afternoon. Now that society has gone away, and Washington is empty I have emerged from my web, and become gay. I have dined with Mrs Lodge and been to three concerts. At the dinner I was told of Allan Rice's departure on a diplomatic mission, very far, I imagine, from his taste.[4] I could not help shocking the company by wondering whether he was already at work worrying the Holy Ghost to write an article against the Prime Minister of the Heavenly Kingdom, and if so, whether he would be instantly sent to add to the terrors of the Inferno. Yet how comfortable it must be for a man who is dead, to know it, and not to go round like so many dead men, getting married and dining out.

Theodore Roosevelt was at Lodge's. You know the poor wretch has consented to be Civil Service Commissioner and is to be with us in Washington next winter with his sympathetic little wife.[5] He is searching for a house. I told him he could have this if he wanted it; but nobody wants my houses though I offer them freely for nothing. I went to talk Central Asia with Rosen the other day, and Rosen complained of the rents charged at Beverly. I told him I had two houses there, either of which he might have for nothing; but he will go on, just the same, scolding about rents. Luckily he

offers no objection to our Asiatic Mystery, and I expect to make a sort of
Marco Polo caravan. History bids fair to get quickly out of the way. By
next January I hope it will be finished. Just now I must go to Grasslands,
and Molly is cross because it rains.

26 May, 1889. We went to Grasslands and it did rain. No one there but
the Lodges, Edwards, Miss Blaine Endicott and Miss Thoron who was to
depart the next day. Then Endicott, Dwight and Hewitt Morgan went off
on a trip to Richmond and Williamsburg, and left me alone to work. The
splinters and shavings of history have whizzed so fast this week that I could
not see out of my windows. Molly went home last Tuesday under the
charge of papa Leiter, Miss Leiter and the little Leiters, while Baron Speck,
Ward Thoron and I wept on the platform.[6] Constance Lodge brought one
of her girl friends to breakfast Friday. My old cousins, Miss Lizzy and Hull
Adams, dined here last evening with Tom Lee. There you have my news,
such as it is,—little but my all. I went up to sit an hour with Mrs Lippitt
yesterday afternoon, as Rebecca Dodge came in a lamentable state of mind
to say that her mother had taken a turn to depression and was beginning to
entertain them with an account of their sins and her own.[7] Miss Rebecca
will get used to it in time, but I was obliged to admit that sometimes
mamas were not entertaining. My own has been having a terrible time, and
has worn out two or three relays of the most vigorous assistants. I am to go
on, a week from today to take my turn at the wheel. So, please direct to
Quincy. In the words of the poet, "I wish and I wish that the spring would
go faster nor warm summer bide so late, and I could grow up like the fox-
glove and aster, for winter is ill to wait."[8] No matter! yesterday your letter
came, as I was becoming anxious for fear something had gone wrong. I am
sorry the Cunliffes were away, but of course I half-expected it. I am much
more sorry that I was not with you at Shrewsbury, for that is the part
of England I know best, and I could have amused you there for a week.
Tell Martha that I love her, and she must not be silly-billy. I was afraid
she would be homesick on the steamer, and make travel a true weariness.

The Mt Vernon picnic comes off tomorrow at last. So I am told. I suppose Mrs Lodge writes to you, so I will not double her reports. We have
rain every day, and picnics are risky.

Please get Martha to send me a letter.

Ever Yrs   Henry Adams.

Mrs Lodge tells me that my Hooper nieces have acted a play with their
friends at Cambridge. It was Samson Agonistes if you please to buy a Mil-
ton and read it!

MS: MHi
1. Sigourney Butler (1857–1898) of Boston, legal and political associate of JQA2,
held a treasury post under Cleveland.
2. Tillie Frelinghuysen; Winthrop Gray.
3. Mary Carver Leiter (1845–1913).

4. Allen Thorndike Rice, who had turned the *NAR* into a popular and profitable enterprise, had been appointed minister to Russia by Harrison; on May 16, just before his scheduled departure, he died suddenly in New York City.
5. Theodore Roosevelt (1858–1919) and his second wife, Edith Kermit Carow Roosevelt (1861–1948). The young Theodore had been with his family on the upper Nile in 1873 when the Roosevelts picknicked with the Adamses. Roosevelt's first year at Harvard was the last year of HA's professorship.
6. Baron Hermann Speck von Sternburg (1852–1908), German military attaché 1885–1890, ambassador to the U.S. 1903–1908.
7. Eliza Gilman Lippitt (1827–1903) was Rebecca Dodge's mother.
8. Jean Ingelow (1820–1897), "Seven Times Two," *Songs of Seven* (1866).

Sunday, 19 May.

The Hays have gone. I am left without my usual haunts. Even Dwight is in Boston. Yet Molly remains, and I see rather more society than usual. Dinner at Mrs Cabot Lodge's. Sinfony concerts. Breakfasts and dinners at home. Fine weather and horseback. Much work on printers' copy and proofsheets. Rapid progress. Call on Rosen, Russian chargé, to give information of our intent to visit Central Asia.

Sunday 26 May

Molly has gone, and I go next Sunday. Hard work and rapid progress on history to Chap. 7 of Vol. III. Rainy weather. Little riding. Picnic last Sunday at Grasslands, farewell to Lulu Thoron.[1] Hull and Lizzy and Tom Lee to dinner yesterday. Lizzy for the first time old and feeble.

1. Marie Louise Thoron.

To John Hay

1603 H Street. 1 June, 1889.

My dear Hay

Everything is closed up; the house sounds hollow and deserted, and I start for New York tomorrow. As far as I know, nothing has happened in this town since you left; unless deluges of rain count. I have nothing to tell you of myself; except that I shall see King tomorrow at dinner, and that he goes to Mexico next Tuesday. The few people still here seem determined to start next week. Even Mrs Cabot Lodge is to be dragged away unwillingly to Nahant, and Judge Gray is to be married on the 8th. Sigourney (or Sigourny, which is it) after being removed from office, was nearly drowned, or his throat cut, by Mrs Cabot Lodge, on a boat-picnic where he practised jumping ashore on a slippery rock, with six bottles in his hands, and was brought back to town by Cabot in a tug, pretty near bled to death, having cut an artery under the thumb or somewhere. Mrs Cabot has been very good to me in my solitude. Molly departed ten days ago in charge of Leiter père, and in company with the Leiter demoiselles. Ward Thoron is at this moment writing reams of legal cap for his admission to the bar. I presume that the other people in the world are also doing something, but I know not what, and as no one tells me, I presume further that no one cares.

You are, I hope, going to the Derby or to Marlborough House, or doing something equally foolish and entertaining to tell me about hereafter. Give my love to Spring Rice, Robert Cunliffe, the Clarks, and everyone else whom I don't know. Write to me at Quincy when you have nothing to say, so as to suit my negative condition. I forgot to ask your own address, and trust to luck to hit it. Mrs Hay and the infants will, I hope, be homesick for my sake, as I shall be for theirs.

Ever Yrs   Henry Adams.

Quincy, Sunday, June 9. I kept my letter to get your address from King, and then kept it to speak of him; but on reaching Quincy last Tuesday I was received by the unexpected announcement that my mother within three days had suddenly sunk into lethargy and was not expected to live through the night. She lived in fact two days, and died at last on Thursday evening at half past ten o'clock. The funeral occupied us the next two days, and today is the first of return to regular thoughts.

I shall remain here till the autumn without in any way changing my arrangements. Miss Baxter will continue in charge of the establishment, and Dwight will run his department into regular habits. You can continue to address me simply *Old House, Quincy, Mass.*

King seemed fairly well. His mother is in Newport, and so far all right. He has by this time started for Mexico, and will return broken up as usual, I expect; but if he gets his machine to work he will at least be one step nearer to needing fewer journies. Lafarge was very bright and infantile; quite childlike in his views of men, women and painting. We ran about and saw Shugio and the American artists, and had much discussion over Kenyon Cox's saffron-stomached model, and Sargent's Mrs Marquand.[1] We dined and smoked and talked, but I don't know that we said anything. In these days I have lost even the habit of remembering a jest unless it hits me like a catapult.

I left Washington under water, though I regret to hear nothing of drowning among the occupants of our opposite house. I think the Potomac had better be dammed at Harper's Ferry. Perhaps some day it will bust when Congress is in session. Lately I have read three newspapers to learn what happened in the flood, and you may freely impart your suspicions that I shall read no more. The reporter, alas, is never the one to be drowned.

Nearly through my third volume! I am scrambling over my MS. closing.

Ever Yrs   Henry Adams.

MS: MHi
1. Heromich Shugio, New York importer of Japanese goods and art work. At the Society of American Artists Exhibition in New York (May 11 to June 15), Kenyon Cox's nudes—"A Nymph," "Brune," and "A Yellow Rose"—were the most controversial entries. Kenyon Cox (1856–1919), son of Jacob Dolson Cox, became a respected mural painter and art critic. The portrait of Mrs. Henry Gurdon Marquand by John Singer Sargent (1856–1925) was highly acclaimed.

To Elizabeth Cameron

1603 H Street. 2 June, 1889.

My dear Mrs Cameron

In half an hour I must start for New York and Boston, and I intend to amuse myself for the last half-hour by writing a word to you. The town is at an end. Everyone except Justice Gray and Secretary Bayard has got married or gone, and those two Arcadians are to get married and go next week. By way of celebration we have had rains,—oh, but real rains that you read about. At the first glimpse of sunshine yesterday I started off on Daisy to see what was left of the universe. I found all the old bridges gone on Rock Creek, and had to come down to our new bridge to cross, where Martha's little waterfall quite roared. Rock Creek tumbled like the rapids at Niagara. I came across, and down to the Potomac about half way to the Chain Bridge. The whole thing was running loose. The canal was busted and running like an insane mule. The river was quite superb. I raced with casks and beams, but they beat me, though Daisy was going an easy seven miles. This morning, Pennsylvania Avenue is flooded and the trains and steamers can't run. I am going to try the B. & O. train at noon, for I must meet King and La Farge at dinner at seven, but I doubt whether even the B. & O. will get me through. Meanwhile I am going without having received the Japanese case, though it is somewhere near, and I don't know how to distribute the stuffs. Yours are in it. I shall take care of that till you arrive. Mrs Lodge and Constance will get theirs as well at Nahant. By the bye, did Mrs Lodge write you that she had nearly killed Sigourney Butler on a picnic; not so much by the picnic which is rather suited to kill Cabot; but by leading him to slide off a slippery rock into the river with six bottles of ale in his hands. The boy cut an artery and almost bled to death.

Quincy, 9 June. On arriving here last Tuesday evening I found my mother already unconscious and rapidly sinking. She died Thursday night, without recovering consciousness or speech. The decline was so rapid that I knew nothing of it till I arrived, although we were aware that it was likely to happen at any time.

I am left here with Dwight for a solitary summer, but I have stipulated that Miss Baxter shall stay also. As I expect it to be the last, and am absorbed in publishing, the punishment is not severe;—at least, I hope not. We shall be quite alone, for my brothers and sister will all go away.

Apparently I am to be the last of the family to occupy this house which has been our retreat in all times of trouble for just one hundred years. I suppose if two Presidents could come back here to eat out their hearts in disappointment and disgust, one of their unknown descendents can bore himself for a single season to close up the family den. None of us want it, or will take it. We have too many houses already, and no love for this. My countryhouse at Samarcand requires my immediate attention, and the claims of society in Bokhara, Kashgar and Yarkand permit me to entertain no thought of Beacon Street. I shall leave Dwight to guard the family archives, and shall turn the key in the door. After all, my many houses are not half so dead and dull as their owner—that's me!

I passed successfully across the floods, and arrived at New York last Sunday evening by B. & O., an hour late, but in time to find King and Lafarge waiting for me. I passed a day with them very playfully. I wish you had been with us. We had a little glass, a little studio, a little Japan, a little— cocktail; a little dinner, and much comment on the universe not altogether complimentary to it, but not so severe as it deserved.

I am beginning to hope for another letter from you. A long one came this week from Cunliffe about you and the pictures.

12 June. Your letter of May 27 has just arrived, so I will send the enclosed sheets to the post-office by way of acknowledgment. You are angelic to tell me so charmingly of your doings. I wish I could tell you of mine, but life in Quincy offers only comments on the growth of the grass or the relative merits of roses. We have each our favorites among the roses which are now in full bloom; and I hope you'll not fail to see the rose-show in London and send home anything very new and lovely. Be sure also to get Martha a nice dog. I should recommend a young Skye as probably the gentlest and best suited for her handling, but for you I should say that a watch-dog was the proper thing, to make you take care of yourself. Possum is unwell, please tell Martha; and takes Nux Vomica three times a day. Martha will like to know that I hold his mouth open while the coachman pours the medicine into it.

Our household runs quietly on, Miss Baxter a good deal upset by reaction, and Dwight a good deal flustered by tons of proof sheets tumbling upon him from everyone who happens to be printing a book. Looly and Polly come today for a little visit. Looly says she was a giant in Samson Agonistes. Dwight has been staying with the Tuckermans at Oyster Bay where he saw all the clans. Molly goes down soon to stay with Mary Leiter "quietly." Apparently quiet is all we have to offer since everyone has gone to Europe. Even my Japanese box has not arrived, and nothing but printers remain to make life endurable.

I hope you got some information from Woolner, or bought some of his pictures. I always walk off with some of his things when I am there, and a bit of Turner or Gainsborough would do you good when you squander millions on Fanning.[1] Dwight is having your Fannings framed, and I am framing your photographs—you and Martha in Japanese silk. Miss Baxter and I decided on red for you, and green for Martha.

H.A.

MS: MHi
    1. Solomon Fanning (b. 1807), an obscure painter of portraits and murals.

Quincy. 9 June.

Left Washington last Sunday flooded. Passed a day in New York with King and Lafarge. Arrived at Quincy at half past six Tuesday evening, and was received by my sister Mary Quincy with the announcement that my mother had suddenly sunk into lethargy and was not expected to survive the night. She was unconscious and speechless. The next two days passed in watching her slowly sink. She died at half past ten o'clock, Thursday evening, June 6. I was present. We buried her yesterday (Saturday) afternoon by my father's side at Mt Wollaston. I shall remain here this summer with Miss Baxter and Dwight.

To Rebecca Gilman Dodge

The Homestead. Quincy, Mass.
16 June, 1889.

My dear Friend

Thanks for your kind letter and your mother's. Even those who cling most to life seem glad at last to leave it; and I think my mother was thoroughly weary. She was unconscious when I arrived, and she never moved or spoke afterwards during more than two days that she lived.

For the summer I find myself here the head of a big establishment, with Miss Baxter and Dwight for colleagues. Our lives are devoted to printers, and our minds to proof-sheets and copy. Of the world and its doings we know next to nothing; but I have had letters both from Mrs Cameron and from John Hay in London, where they seem chiefly engaged in meeting Mrs Robert Elsmere at dinner.[1] Although Mrs Elsmere is an acquaintance of mine and an intelligent female as regards early ecclesiastical history, I prefer staying at home. Your friend Molly I see occasionally riding horseback alone in the twilight with the mosquitoes. Various other nieces and nephews are hanging about the place, chiefly in the strawberry patches. Looly and Polly Hooper have made me a little visit this week for three days, highly educated because they have acted Samson Agonistes and Looly was the giant Harapha.

Ever Yrs   Henry Adams.

MS: MH
1. Mrs. Humphry Ward.

To Eliza Gilman Lippitt

Quincy 16 June, 1889.

My dear Mrs Lippitt

Many thanks for your kind note. My mother's death severs, I think, the last tie that binds me to my old life, and probably another year will find me fairly at the end.

One learns to regard death and life as much the same thing when one lives more in the past than in the present. Indeed, when the present becomes positively repulsive, and the past alone seems real, I am not sure but that death is the livelier reality of the two. My poor mother suffered more and more, during the last three years, until life became excessively burdensome to her, and enjoyment of what she had was impossible. I do not doubt but that I have inherited her disposition, for I cannot see anything in life worth having except the things one wants to have. When one has reached this stage, life is over.

I dare not say that I hope you are better, and have reached Berkeley, for fear that you may not be better, and may still be in Washington. Here the roses and strawberries are just on the wane, and with them the freshest part of summer. The weather, too, is becoming warm, and it is time for us all to keep cool and quiet. I trust that you are both.

Ever Yrs   Henry Adams.

MS: MH

Sunday 16 June.
Looly and Polly Hooper have been here for three days this week. I have worked less than usual but get on. The roses have had their week, and today are beginning to fade.

To Anna Cabot Mills Lodge

Quincy, 18 June, 1889.

Dear Mrs Lodge

Many thanks for your kind letter.

I return brother Sturgis's remarks, which were evidently meant for feminine sympathies rather than for criticism. Of course *I* sympathise, but can't tell him so. Our conclusions are too far apart. Sturgis is, like everyone else, bound to find Paradise in this world, and seems to be in dead earnest. Thousands and millions of men have taken his road before,[1] with more or less satisfaction, but the mass of mankind have settled to the conviction that the only Paradise possible in this world is concentrated in the three little words which the ewig Man says to the ewige Woman.[2] Sturgis calls this the Fireside, and thinks he knows better. He looks for his Paradise in absorption in the Infinite. Probably the result will be the same. Sooner or later, fate commonly gets bored by the restless man who requires Paradise, and sets its foot on him with so much energy that he curls up and never wriggles again. When Sturgis cant squirm any longer, and suddenly realizes that Paradise is a dream, and the dream over, I fear that he is too sensitive a nature to stand the shock, and perhaps it wouldn't be worth his while to try.

I am very hard at work for the summer, and still looking for that Japanese box which comes not though it should. Thanks for your kind invitation. If I go anywhere I shall certainly come to you. Tell Constance I am in despair about her dress.

Ever truly Yrs   Henry Adams.

MS: MHi
1. Sturgis Bigelow was returning to the United States from Japan as a convert to Buddhism.
2. Echoing the final two lines of Goethe's *Faust*, Part II: "Das Ewig-Weibliche / Zieht uns hinan" (The eternal woman-spirit / leads us on).

To Elizabeth Cameron

Quincy 27 June, 1889.

Dear Mrs Cameron

Your letter from Raith, written at the news of my mother's death, reached me yesterday, and today I see the announcement of your father-in-law's death, and hardly know whether to write to you in England, or to expect your return.[1] On the whole I imagine that, even if your husband should be obliged to come, you will probably wait till September; so I write all the same.

Not that I have anything to tell you! I know that Mr Cameron's death must be an event of very serious consequences to your husband and his family, but I know too little what consequences to expect, to be able to say anything about it. I have been through all these experiences recently, and know only that nothing is to be said.

A million thanks for your kind sympathy with me. The world has some slight compensations for its occasional cruelties. I suppose, for instance, that in gradually deadening the senses it cuts away the unpleasant as well as the pleasant. As I walk in the garden and the fields I recall distinctly the acuteness of odors when I was a child, and I remember how greatly they added to the impression made by scenes and places. Now I catch only a sort of suggestion of the child's smells and lose all the pleasure, but at least do not get the disgusts. Life is not worth much when its senses are cut down to a kind of dull consciousness, but it is at least painless. As for me, waste no sympathy. My capacity for suffering is gone.

Quincy is dull and dusty, but not unendurable. It has not the peace of the cloister, but has to some extent its solitude. Miss Baxter, Dwight and I are very cheerful and contented, as though we were politicians who had got a comfortable office for a single summer,—a kind of William Walter.[2] We play poker of evenings. I won two thousand dollars from Miss Baxter last night, and one thousand the night before—in chips. I write history or correct proofs every day, or go to Boston on errands. You and Martha are my chief companions,—you in red Japanese silk, Martha in green—and you smile at me on my toilet table, to my great comfort and enjoyment.

Sturgis Bigelow reminds me of the broomstick in the Ingoldsby Legends—start him and he wont stop.[3] He has sent me, as I desired, one big box of Japanese cottons and stuffs, which has not arrived; and yesterday I got an invoice of another, containing about two thousand dollars' worth of varied exquisiteness in oriental luxury. Your stuff, it seems, is in box No. 2. I suppose you must go into mourning, and will hardly want it; but apparently all Washington will have to buy Bigelow's goods, and you shall establish a modisterie in my hall, and act as chief-agent for the firm. What young ladies do you wish as assistants? I have no doubt they will all be glad to assist you, and I will notify them betimes to be ready at the autumn opening.

Your account of yourself at Raith was delightful, and your idea of a house in Scotland shows no end of good sense. Scotland is the best place I know for the dog-days. I hope you will do it. Dont come home before September,—unless you come to Beverly, which still awaits you. Edward Hooper goes down there tomorrow with the children to occupy the Gurney house for a month or six weeks. Then he takes them to Maplewood. The children are very well, and next year go to school in Boston. Looly is as tall as Polly. My Adams nephews and nieces are promiscuously about the place, along with various dogs, horses and other stock. I wish Martha and you were here, and it would be quite sociable. Willy Phillips and Lowndes are to visit us presently. We have a rambling shebang of a house, capable of packing a dozen or two people, and nobody in it. History runs ahead like a limited slow freight-train, but will git thar.

My regards to your husband, and love to Martha.

Ever Yrs   Henry Adams.

MS: MHi

1. Simon Cameron died June 26, at the age of 90.
2. On March 18 William Walter Phelps was appointed commissioner to the Berlin conference on Samoa, and on June 26 minister to Germany.
3. Richard Harris Barham, "A Lay of St. Dunstan," *The Ingoldsby Legends* (1840–1847), comic tales based on traditional material.

To John Hay

Quincy 30 June 1889.

Dear Hay

Thanks for yours from Raith, which was accompanied, as once before, by one from Mrs Cameron. I am really besummered by your summer, and enjoy your visits much more than I should my own. Of the world I would gladly send you news worthy yourself and the refined Elsmerian society you frequent; but midsummer in Boston is not the time for letter-writing. True, I had a flash of half an hour the other morning from Mrs Jack Gardner and Jack[1] who drove from Brookline to see me; but one Mrs Jack does not do for you. I must have a professional beauty or two on toast. By the bye, my Japanese box of spring dresses arrives tomorrow; and the spring chickens are already dressed. More by the token, Bigelow sends me an invoice for a second case, containing silks, linens, cottons, &c, valued at seventeen hundred dollars, now on their way from San Francisco. Will you kindly order no clothes in London? I shall expect you and Del, as well as Mrs Hay, Helen, Alice and the baby, to buy my figured Japanese stuffs, and wear them straight through till the supply is exhausted. You will find blue Japanese trowsers, à la cigogne, a happy emblem.

Vol. IV, Chap. 4.—So far, oh Lord! I shall pass the half-way post about August 1, and am working like James G. Blaine and W. E. Gladstone to get my two last volumes ahead of the printer.[2] In August I must go to Ottawa to seek more useless rubbish. Who is there that one should have heard about. I know not even the Governor General's name.

Lowndes writes that a parcel of Corcoran's garden on I Street opposite Riggs's house has sold for $6.00 a foot. The Judge—Lowndes to wit,—is coming here for a visit in a few weeks. I keep a hotel open, but no guests offer, even with all bills paid. Lowndes and Will Phillips alone threaten to profit by this unequalled chance which will never occur again. Miss Baxter, Dwight and I are reduced to playing poker every evening. The weather is hot and relaxing, and my nephews threaten to take me to sail.

Love to all yours   Henry Adams.

MS: MHi
1. John Lowell Gardner (1837–1898).
2. Blaine followed his two-volume *Twenty Years of Congress* (1884–1886) with *Political Discussions* (1887). Gladstone was publishing his nine-volume *Gleanings from Past Years* (1879–1890).

To Elizabeth Cameron

Quincy 6 July 1889.

Dear Mrs Cameron

I wrote you a long letter a week ago in the belief that you would not return, and I still hope, in spite of your note of the 25th, that you have not come. You must have heard of Mr Cameron's death before you sailed. Still, I write this line to tell you that we—that is, all your friends—are very glad to have you here again, and will do wonderful things to make you regret Scotland as little as possible. You can send Martha to me if Lochiel does not suit her. I need not say that Martha's mother may be sent with her; but I may remark that Beverly is wailing for some one to occupy it, and though I can't do like Edward Hooper, who pays a friend a thousand dollars a quarter to occupy one of his spare houses, I should still consider myself under great obligations to anyone who would run the house a month or two, so as to keep it dry and free from squirrels. If you will consent to go there, I will offer every inducement, and am not sure but what I would offer to pay a handsome premium. Creditable tenants are worth something at Beverly. In Quincy we have given up the hope of ever seeing one.

I have dressed all my friends and acquaintance à la Japonaise. Nothing but a pair of black silk stockings seems to be left for you, but they are very nice.

Yrs truly   Henry Adams.

MS: MHi

Sunday, 7 July.
Vol. IV, Chap. 6. Vol. VII, Chap. 17. Steady work and rapid progress. All day in the library, and a ride at the end.[1]

1. The final entry of HA's extant diary.

To Martha Cameron

Quincy 14 July, 1889.

My dear Martha

Your letter was beautiful. It told me about your journey; the steamer; and how you drove from Chester; and all about London; and how long the sun stays up at night in Scotland when it ought to be in bed. I wish I had as much to say as you have to tell me. Don't you think you could make me a

Elizabeth Cameron

Martha Cameron

visit at Quincy, and tell me what you have been doing? I have a garden and a pond, and a brook where Possum chases the frogs; and I have Prince and Daisy in the stable, and cows; and you can come and play with me in the library, and have as many dolls and playthings as you want. Then I have a whole house for you at Beverly, and you can go and dig sand on the beach, and bathe perhaps, if its not too cold. My niece Dorothy who is only six months older than you, bathes already, but she is at Wareham where the water is warmer. Beverly is very cool and comfortable. We have had no warm weather yet, till today, when the thermometer is 79. I think you had better first come and see me; and then go down and pass the rest of the summer in my house at Beverly. Looly and Polly and the other girls are staying at Beverly now.

I shall write to your mamma next week, but you can tell her that I have dressed all her acquaintance in Japanese clothes, and I think you ought to have one. Tell her that Mr Dwight is passing Sunday at Mattapoisett with Miss Sally Loring; and that your friend Niggy Butler was out here this week. I have been to see a base ball match, and play poker every evening; so I shall soon be as old as you.[1]

MS: MHi
1. Instead of signing this letter, HA drew a sketch of a curly-haired dog with long ears.

To Sir Robert Cunliffe

Quincy, Mass. July 14, 1889.

Dear and Eminent Barnet

I want you to do something for me—something of the utmost importance.

I want you to go to the Record Office and obtain from the keeper a copy of the letter of *Earl Bathurst to Sir George Prevost, dated June 3, 1814,* and to be found in the Canada correspondence from the War Office. (I believe Bathurst was then principal Secretary of State for War.)

My object is to get the instructions in regard to the invasion of the U.S. in 1814. Perhaps the guardian of the reading-room at the Record Office (if he is my friend who was there in 1880) will let you glance at the record-volume, and see if there were any other instructions issued to Prevost in June, July or August, 1814, and let me have copies.

I want also the instructions given to General Ross about the attack on Washington in August, 1815, if any orders were given.

I want also the instructions to General Pakenham about the expedition to New Orleans in 1814. Probably the War Office Records will contain these, and they were doubtless brief.

As I enjoy a special privilege, granted in 1880 by Lord Salisbury and his colleagues, for the perusal of all papers down to 1815, and have already copies of everything most [*The rest of the letter is missing.*]

MS: MHi

To Elizabeth Cameron

Quincy, 17 July, 1889.

My dear Mrs Cameron

The wedding-present for Miss Thoron has arrived—many thanks for your kindness in acting as Adams's express agent—and so have the water-colors, an hour ago. Dwight will be charmed and will write you. At this moment he is at work in Boston, dismantling the house.[1] When he comes out, he will be soothed by the drawings. The Bonington is an exquisite little glimpse into heaven, and you should look at it only when you are particularly happy.[2]

I have nothing to send you in return that could possibly suit your present situation unless it is a pair of Japanese black silk stockings which Bigelow put into his box like a cadeau de noce, as though I wore ladies' hose. I will send it to you as a present, and I would tell you the cost if I knew it, for I suppose Bigelow wished to get orders for his dear Jap's; but he forgot to tell me what the stockings cost. If they don't fit you, I authorise you to dispose of them to the lady most likely to encourage the trade. Honi soit, &c. I regret that I cannot, like King Edward, send also the garter. You must ask Bob Lincoln for that.

Our present occupation here is base-ball. Miss Baxter, my brother John, Dwight and I, go in with a covey of brats, to see Boston play this, that and the other club. I am getting my real education, and shall know some of the true swells by sight. We can't go to yacht-races, for a little Scotch cutter is beating our heads off.

History howls. I finish today Volume 7 in manuscript. Volume 4 is finished in type. I hope to get all the writing done by the time I return to Washington. Then its you who must read the eight volumes, while I skip to the Feejee Isles.

You need not fear heat if you come our way. I almost envy you in being warm. As yet we just escape shivers.

Ever Yrs   Henry Adams.

MS: MHi

1. The Adams house at 57 Mount Vernon St.
2. Richard Parkes Bonington (1801–1828), English painter of landscapes and street scenes. Mrs. Cameron sent her pictures to HA to let him see what she had purchased and, probably, to have Dwight catalogue and frame them.

To John Hay

Quincy 21 July, 1889.

My dear John

Will you greatly thank Mrs Hay on my account, for the salver, which was sent to me by Mrs Cameron and is now at the silversmiths being marked. I hope it will be as satisfactory to Miss Thoron as it is to me. For this I owe you monies as well as gratitude. I will pay both, but as for the first, unlike the last, I shall pay best after knowing the quantum.

By this time you are on the Eiffel Tower or Mont Blanc or some such treiffel, enjoying the change of climate, and the cotelettes à la Boulangère. I can not follow you. My range of vision does not extend beyond Nahant. My excitement is going to Baseball matches with my nephews and nieces. We saw your Cleveland heroes beat our Boston swells, and Chicago get a severe rebuke from us. Unfortunately I have not seen John L. Sullivan, though I would go far to do so, nor have I read the reports of his famous battle,[1] nor heard a word of Clarence King, nor been to stay with Mrs Cabot Lodge, though I see that both Cabot and Teddy Roosevelt are on the shop-counters in apparent self-satisfaction, which makes me as sick as Possum to reflect that I too can no longer avoid that disgusting and drivelling exhibition of fatuous condescension.[2] All books should be posthumous except those which should be buried before death, and they should stay buried. I am struggling in a sea of Japanese calicoes and silks which Bill Bigelow has sent me to the enrichment of the U.S. customs. My only satisfaction is that Mrs Hay will soon return and have to wear them all. My nieces, a dozen, more or less, are already clothed in them, except Molly, and she has had to go to Alaska with her good papa and mamma to escape, but not for long. Mrs Cameron is at Harrisburg, broiling in black clothes and fever germs. Dwight is toiling in the line of his many labors, and tries to play poker every evening with melancholy want of success though he wins all our chips. Possum and Marquis are all that is lively about the place, and they are astonishingly rheumatic and blind.

With love to you all   Ever Yrs   Henry Adams.

MS: MHi
    1. John L. Sullivan (1858–1918), "the Boston Strong Boy," boxing champion 1882–1892, won a 75-round match against Jake Kilrain in Richburg, Miss., July 8.
    2. Lodge, *The Life of George Washington* (1889); Roosevelt, *The Winning of the West* (1889), the first of four volumes.

To Henry Holt

3 Aug. 1889

Dear Holt

Do as you please. Let him have what information he wants, provided it does not point in any close direction.[1] I think if you collected all the imputed authors, you could give general information which would take them all in—authors, I mean, not public. The whole thing is now dead and forgotten, and will not be resurrected by such devices.

As for the money, send me your own check, and give your own receipt to yourself. Your books already run so.

Yrs truly   A.D.[2]

Source: Cater; MS not found.
    1. Edmund Clarence Stedman (1833–1908), Wall Street broker, poet, and critic, was including an excerpt from *Democracy* in *A Library of American Literature*, 11 vols. (1888–1890), edited with Ellen M. Hutchinson. It appeared in volume 10 (1889).
    2. *A.D.*: Author of *Democracy*.

To Elizabeth Cameron

Quincy 4 August, 1889.

My dear Mrs Cameron

You would not have found Beverly very charming this past week, for the rain has drowned everything, and we are mildewed. I went down with Miss Baxter Friday to see the children. Every thing looked green and fresh, but more like Scotland than America, the water oozing all about. I have set Looly to work with stern orders to prepare everything at your house for you, and see that nothing is forgotten; but the children think it a grievous injury that you should not come till after they go; for they are to leave for Bethlehem the 14th or 15th.

I am also going there on or about the 25th for a Canadian excursion, and I am going to take the children on it. I shall carry Dwight, and Mrs Baxter, and perhaps Elsie Adams, Molly's sister, and three of the Hooper children, with their father; a party of eight; and we are to go to Niagara, Ottawa, down the St Lawrence to Montreal and Quebec, and then perhaps up the Saguenay. I do not know how long we shall be away, and if the weather is tolerable, I shall take it easily.

Meanwhile I have sent them a trunk full of Japanese stuffs. Did I write you that Bigelow's ark had arrived, containing as well as I can calculate material for at least one hundred and twenty five ladies' dresses of silk, cotton and linen, crêpes, printed, of all the colors known to the gorgeous east, and of prices suited to every station in politics from baby McKee to Willy

Wally Phelps.[1] They are very amusing. I wish they had come three months earlier so that you might have helped me to open them. As it is, I think you and Mrs Lodge must come over on a picnic some day before the 25th to look at them. One or two of them, which I consider distinguished, I mean to keep for my own feminine society. Your crêpe is among the rest, but as you can't wear it at present, I have left it in a drawer with the other things. My niece Elsie had one of the cottons made up, and for a cheap dress I thought it very successful. Molly was to have chosen one for Miss Leiter, but could not find anything sufficiently startling. Molly is now rolling down glaciers in Alaska, but will be back, I suppose, by the 20th.

What are you to do with Martha while you are at Newport? Why not send her on to us here? You can pick her up in passing, and make your picnic then? We will give you quarters for a night, if it is proper; and as far as I can see we are much too dull, too solemn and too old to be suspected of impropriety. You can consult Newport in case of doubt, and I should like to know the decision; but you can send Martha along anyhow, for I presume no question of propriety affects her until it ceases to affect her mother. Martha shall ask all the questions she likes, and shall pass her time in the library tearing up all Dwight's favorite manuscripts. You can then come and get her whenever you please, or leave her here on your way to Newport viâ Boston. My niece Dorothy, six months older than Martha, is now at Wareham; but, though gracious, she is so serious that I dare not indulge even in such distant approaches as I ever make to levity, without a sense of rebuke which I am not strong enough to support. I earnestly pray that Martha may retain her infantile capacity to take a joke which won my young affections.

Dwight has written about the picture-gallery. The drawings are a kind of Secrétan affair and you should have a sale.[2] They make a collection quite like the Louvre when you see them together.

Ever Yrs   Henry Adams.

MS: MHi
   1. President Harrison's infant grandson, Benjamin Harrison McKee (1887–1958), was so much in the news that people joked about his having more political influence than a cabinet member.
   2. Mrs. Cameron's recently acquired drawings did not quite rival the Secrétan collection, sold in Paris, July 1–2, for over a million dollars.

To Henry Holt

Quincy. Mass. August 8, 1889

Dear Holt

S.[1] wants to know whether A-of-D is American born. Tell him: Yes!

I do not understand that he asks for more. If he writes to ask other questions, such as whether the person or persons is or are already in his list, tell him that the question is not pertinent, for certainly the person is not in his list in that connection, even if he or she is a professional, like Harry James or Mrs. Burnett.[2] If he presses further you can say that the person or persons in question are certainly not in his list of novelists,—after careful study of the list.[3]

I think the thing had better stop there. In his own interest, the riddle is more amusing to his readers than the solution would be.

I guess your bookkeeper will have regard enough for the firm not to talk of its affairs at street-corners. Nothing but an official advertisement would be likely to call much attention now to an affair so old. Yet I want it to remain forgotten, in order that a certain interest may still attach to it, and that the author may avoid the sort of notoriety which is the curse of authorship as it is of politics.

Source: Cater; MS not found.
1. Stedman.
2. Frances Hodgson Burnett (1849–1924), author of *Little Lord Fauntleroy* and other popular novels.
3. "The Author of 'Democracy'" appeared anonymously in Stedman's work, but HA appeared under his own name for two excerpts from the *History* in volume 11 (1890).

To John Hay

Quincy 18 August, 1889.

Dear John

I have nothing to tell you, so I write a line to tell it. Your's from London of August 4 arrived the other day, as letters will, conjointly with letters from all my other correspondents, just as people come to breakfast when I have none. Robert Cunliffe, John La Farge, Mrs Cameron and Miss Thoron deluged me with information in one cloud-burst—whatever a cloud-burst may be, but I am never sure about these recent newspaper inventions. Lulu Thoron professes to be satisfied with the offering: "It is *so* what we wanted!" Let us hope that it is really *so* what she wanted, and that you and Mrs Hay and I may be always successful in wedding presents, a career in which success is rare and confers the highest diplomatic rank. Mrs Cameron had been to Newport, and says that "Mary Leiter was resplendent in a Japanese gown with blue lightning flashes over it. It was a great success and looked original." I shall soon be the fashion. I have already sold, by means of my nieces at Beverly, about a dozen Japanese gowns, silks, linens, cottons and crêpes, and have a hundred more for sale. I paid six hundred dollars duties on the box, which will make the Georgetown custom house pay its expenses for the first time in history. Does Mrs Hay appreciate what she loses by getting clothes in Europe when the first modiste in the solar system lives next door in Washington? Mrs Cameron goes to my house at Beverly next week, and I expect her with Mrs Cabot Lodge here next week to breakfast. Daisy Davis who was dining here yesterday, said that her sister was doing the Baby McKee rôle in the Presidential party at Bar Harbor; but I think Cabot is probably the only original and successful Baby McKee. We shall know, when the Boston collector is appointed, which I take to be the ultimate and final end and efficient cause, or *natura naturans,* of all Babies McKees.[1] La Farge accouches this month of his Japanese paper in the Century and seems much reduced by it.[2] I have invited him to go with me and a dozen or two nieces to Canada on the 26th but I doubt whether he cares to load up more infants than his own which appear to satisfy him. He has worked hard this summer in order to go to Europe, and,—as one always shows a striking likeness to oneself,—he stays at home while St Gaudens and Stanford White are over there. King is back, and wrote me a telegletter suggesting "a few hours" at Quincy. I promptly sat upon that idea, and replied that if I was not good for a few days, I was not worth keeping anyway, and would not be put up without that reserve price. Since then he has been silent, and I know not even whether he is like to speak again.

I have now given you all the private gossip that my attentive ears have caught of late, and will add only that I have entertained our learned counsel James Lowndes a week, and have taken him to see Plymouth Rock. My brother Brooks, Dwight, Miss Baxter and I are boarding in the family shebang, and trying to think we are, as Byron says, green and wildly fresh without though worn and gray as well as bald both without and within.[3] The only young female I have seen has been, as I have somewhere historically observed, Mrs Cabot Lodge's sister, who is a rival of Mrs Cabot McKee herself in my affections and esteem. I have sold dresses to Mrs Jack Gardner, but have not seen her. My brothers are, all but Brooks, in Alaska or the Yo Semite or North Scituate or elsewhere. Edward Hooper and his callow brood are at Maplewood. Mr Justice Field is not, where all Supreme Court justices ought to be, in the nether pit; but thanks to the efficiency of Marshall's Deputy Assistant Nagle, the only truly competent man connected with the United States government, the hardened old law-calf has the pleasure of dancing on his enemy's grave. I propose to organise a new political party, and to nominate Nagle for the Presidency.[4] Yet as sure's your born, he will be beaten on the popular vote by Harrison and we shall have to depend on the Supreme Court to put him in.

This country is on its way to H [cap.][5] but I can't help it, and am glad you're coming back. I go to Washington October 1. Perhaps I may get warm for once.

Ever Yrs   Henry Adams.

Love to the Cunliffes. Glad to hear that miladi is so's to be about.

MS: MHi

1. Evelyn ("Daisy") Davis (1853–1926), sister of Anna Cabot Mills Davis Lodge, was engaged to marry BA. Lodge was prominently in the news as he opposed (unsuccessfully) President Harrison's nominee for Boston collector.

2. La Farge's series "An Artist's Letters from Japan" did not begin until February 1890.

3. "All green and wildly fresh without, but worn and grey beneath"; "Stanzas for Music" (1816).

4. In 1888, Supreme Court Justice Stephen Johnson Field (1816–1899), on circuit duty in California, had found David S. Terry in contempt of court. Despite Terry's threat to assassinate him, Field returned to California the next summer. On Aug. 14 Terry, appearing ready to assault Field, was shot and killed by Field's bodyguard, U.S. Deputy Marshal Davis Nagle.

5. HA's brackets.

To Elizabeth Cameron

Quincy 23 August. [1889]

My dear Mrs Cameron

I sent you today two boxes containing vast hordes of oriental gorgeousness, viz:

One crêpe à la crème to order. Cost.	$46.00
One white crêpe ribbed like the sea-sands, costing	$36.00
Two linen dresses each costing $28	56.00
Three linen rolls making one dress	$12.
And five cotton rolls costing	$7.50

In all, I think $157.50. In the box are also the three rolls of queer crêpe, but these belong to my own importation, and are not sold but offered as presents to encourage high living and thinking. Two more patterns are reserved till Lowndes's box can be attended to, probably tomorrow.

Send back anything you don't want, and advise me of errors. As I start for Canada early Monday morning, you had better wait till I return before attempting to settle anything.

I can't even give you an address, for I do not know when I shall be anywhere. Perhaps, if I find that I can't get along without hearing from you, I shall write to beg for a line. Try and make yourself comfortable, and if the place needs attention, order the proper thing to be done in my name. You can't be wrong.

Love to Martha, and my best remembrances to mademoiselle.

Ever truly   Henry Adams.

MS: MHi

To Anna Cabot Mills Lodge

Ottawa. Tuesday. [3 Sept. 1889]

Dear Mrs Lodge

With the usual perversity of travel, I find myself at the beginning of my labors when I ought to be ending them. The heat and dust drove us first to the Saguenay instead of Niagara. We travelled hard, and without stop, but on our return from the Saguenay arrived here yesterday afternoon too late for me to begin my archives. This morning I sent the rest of my party to Alexandria Bay in the Thousand Islands, and promised to follow them this afternoon, but after a long day's work I found that I must stay over tomorrow and catch them at Toronto on their way to Niagara. I cannot leave them, as Edward Hooper must go back to Boston, and I must take charge of the children.

So I must give up the hope of being with you next Saturday.[1] If this were my fault I should feel very much troubled by it. As I am not to blame, I hope Daisy will not like me the less for being absent. Tell her that I will obey her wishes in everything, just as much as though I were present, and that as for loving and honoring I need no church service to make me do it. I authorise Brooks to act as my attorney to make any promise that Daisy shall think proper to require.

Of course I have heard not a word from home since starting, and am fairly wound up to nervous agitation by the wish to know how you are doing. In the somewhat sultry solitude of a hotel bedroom in this unbaked though sunbaked town, I can only wear away a long evening by wishing I could have a half-hour's talk with you; but I suppose you are too busy to have time to waste in answering my questions. I will talk to the gas light, and listen to the cabs. The entertainment wants vivacity, without offering repose; but I must make it do, till I have a chance to see you.

We shall be at the Clifton House on Thursday, I suppose. I hope to be in Quincy in a week. Thus far our journey has been successful, and except for the heat and smoke and dust on the railways, we have had no annoyances.

I shall never forgive Daisy if she thinks I don't think enough of her. This is my chief anxiety. Give her all sorts of love and believe me

Ever Yrs   Henry Adams.

MS: MHi
1. Mrs. Lodge's sister and HA's brother were to be married on Saturday, Sept. 7.

To Elizabeth Cameron

Ottawa. Tuesday evening. [3 Sept. 1889]

My dear Mrs Cameron

I have just written to Mrs Lodge to say that I cannot get home to the wedding. I address the letter in ignorance whether Boston still exists; for the last week has been a long one, of much change. I am almost ashamed of writing to you now, for I cannot deny that you have a right to think such a letter a bad compliment. I am quite alone in my hotel bed-room in this Canadian Paris, with nothing to do but to play patience. I sent the children, Miss Baxter and Hooper to the Thousand Islands this morning, that I might enjoy my archives all to myself. I have worked seven hours today, and must work seven more tomorrow in the hope of catching them at Toronto by travelling tomorrow night. Under such conditions a letter is dangerous, and has an odor of archives. Yet I risk boring you, because I never have found the limit of your good nature, and am quite curious to know whether any limit exists.

I have only the regular story to tell. We have been to Montreal, Quebec and the Saguenay. I think the children have enjoyed it, and I hope Miss Baxter, who likes travelling, has not been bored; but we have had no adventure of any sort, and have seen only tourists in swarms. The tourist is an animal of a nature that never roused my sympathy even when I was anxious to sympathise; and at present I positively prefer other society. So vitiated do one's tastes become that I am ruthless enough to sacrifice even you, rather than sit in a hotel corridor.

If I were at a supper after a theatre party I should not have less to say. Even there I should at least be sleepy, but here I have not the satisfaction of excusing myself on that account. My only excuse for writing is that I really must imagine you to be somewhere about. My only surviving notion of happiness is the sense that some one, to whom one is attached, is sitting in the next room. In the Russell House at Ottawa such a sensation is not within bounds of sanity; but a letter is a sort of substitute for it.

All the news I can offer, which does not relate to archives, concerns our future movements. We expect to reach the Clifton House Thursday, and to start on our return as soon as I have looked at three or four battle-fields. Probably we shall reach Quincy a week from tonight, but possibly in less or more time. I am tempted to take the train to Vancouver, but shall doubtless be foolish enough to return home. My single hopeful idea is the thought that you are in the house at Beverly and will make it cheerful. I hope the mosquitoes are gone or going. Kiss Martha for me and tell her that I eat a bear yesterday for dinner, but Looly and Polly would not.

Ever Yrs   Henry Adams.

MS: MHi

To Rebecca Gilman Dodge

Clifton Hotel. Niagara 7 September, 1889.

My dear Friend

I am delighted. What can I say more? You know all that I think about it.[1] I have told you again and again that life is not worth having unless one is attached to some one; and I am sure that you will not find a better or a more affectionate fellow than the one you have attached yourself to. Give him my warmest regards, and tell him from me that he has certainly found the dearest young woman for a wife that the world could give him.

I expect to be early in Washington, and to see you before long. Please hurry the wedding. My brother Brooks who marries Daisy Davis today, has been engaged only three weeks. I cannot attend his wedding, much as I would like to be there, because I have brought three nieces on a journey and cannot leave them; but I strongly approved the rapidity of the proceeding, and also its privacy. I want to secure my new sister before she has time to get tired of me. I want to see you settled and happy so that you will be ready to love even Brooks and Molly.

You must write to Dwight. I shall not see him for some time. Your letter has only just reached me, and I shall not return to Quincy yet. Give my love and congratulations to your mother, and believe me your very affectionate and approving friend

Henry Adams.

MS: MH
1. Rebecca Dodge had just become engaged to Lt. Charles Whiteside Rae, U.S.N. (1847–1908).

To Sir Robert Cunliffe

Quincy 14 Sept. 1889.

My dear Robert

After much cogitation on the Prevost instructions I have bethought myself that in 1815 the Prince Regent ordered an inquiry into the causes of Prevost's defeat at Plattsburg the preceding year. Prevost was recalled from Canada, and the Court Martial was organised, witnesses notified, &c; but Prevost died before the trial began.

I suspect that all the official papers bearing on the Plattsburg campaign, including the instructions, were then handed over to the Law Department, or Judge Advocate General, or whoever was to draw the charges, and, as often happens, were never returned to the proper sources.

Perhaps this suggestion may give a hint to the keeper of the records which would enable him to recover the papers. He might know where to look for them. Certainly they must exist.

Hay has arrived, but I have not seen him, as I have been travelling in Canada, and returned only last night. He has gone today with King to New Hampshire to build a house or two for future summers. I have come back only to close up my affairs here, which will take a fortnight or three weeks. Then I return to Washington. I expect to be there after October 10, and letters to arrive at that date should be addressed to me there—1603 H Street—as usual.

My brother Brooks is thoroughly married. I sincerely hope he will stay so. His wife is every way a charming person, and suits me perfectly—which I presume to be a brother-in-law's first requirement.

My love to all yours.

Ever Truly   Henry Adams.

MS: MHi

To John Hay

Quincy 14 Sept. 1889.

My dear Prodigal Son

When I arrived here last evening, after three weeks absence in Canada, I found your telegram summoning me to dinner at half past seven. Had I arrived an hour earlier I could have managed it, but it was then too late, and I had to let it go. I had come from Maplewood that morning, and by a variety of chances, did not reach this house till after seven o'clock in a condition which could not be palliated by any measure short of entire undress.

I was more sorry than the cold world would believe, but I hope it is only a few weeks delay. I mean to break up my quarters here as soon as possible after October 1, and shall look for you in Washington as soon as the frost touches your vast prairies at Cleveland.

While you have been closing up the British account, and bidding a fortune or two for the favors of the aristocracy, I have been taking a small army of nieces up and down the St Lawrence, and hunting archives at Ottawa. This labor is now accomplished. My brother Brooks is married and settled. You have returned. Corporal Tanner is removed.[1] The world is evidently resting from its labors, and needs repose. I think with astonishment of all this recent activity. Even my friend Rebecca Dodge is to be married to Charley Rae.

Give my love to Mrs Hay and the Écrévisses. I look forward to finding Alice a sort of lobster at least.

Ever Yrs   Henry Adams.

John Hay Esq.

MS: MHi

1. James Tanner (1844–1927), a corporal in the Civil War, was appointed U.S. commissioner of pensions by Harrison. His liberality on behalf of Civil War veterans led to his resignation on Sept. 12.

To Elizabeth Cameron

Sunday 15 Sept. 1889

Dear Mrs Cameron

We reached Quincy Friday evening; Miss Baxter, my niece Elsie Adams and I, for Dwight could not go with us. Our journey was quite successful, especially at Niagara. Of course you, being from Cleveland, have never seen Niagara, and I ought to have thought of this when I mentioned the Clifton House, which would be as well known to you as the Falls, if you were not from Cleveland; but in any case I could not have received a letter, had you sent one there. I had time to write to Rebecca Dodge in terms of becoming encouragement. Is it not curious to see how my breakfast-girls get married? Next winter I must really find some new ones, and with the prospect of immediate husbandry my table ought to be crowded. I fully expect that Miss Leiter will go next, for I am told she has cut a great figure at Newport, and there are always octogenarian statesmen in Washington.

No, I was not at the wedding. The fault was not mine, for my journey had been fixed long before the engagement took place; but I was sorry, for I always like to do the correct conventional thing, and I ought to have been there. The refinement of satire in being conventional would not have been my inducement in this case, as in some conceivable weddings. Rather I should have enjoyed seeing Brooks submit to the conventionalities which he has hitherto made a business of swearing at. I ought now to go down to Beverly and see them. She wrote me a very sweet note last week asking me to come. The worst of it is that I would rather be moderately roasted alive. Nothing but a hydraulic ram could ever drive me to go anywhere; and just now, with the approach of autumn, my spirits are a good bit below their usual point of hilarity. In this state of reluctance I am disposed to encourage the sacrifice of some of your neighbors as useless for better objects. Don't risk your own life, but incite one of the Coolidge's or Higginsons or any ignorant neighbor, to call on the bride. Doubtless the first half-dozen will be either killed or maimed, but the rest will recover, and my proposed visit will be forgotten.

Robert Cunliffe writes that you carried away all the fair weather when you left England. Miss Baxter has discovered in English papers that the Queen is going to have a reception at Acton Park, in a visit to North Wales. Poor Cunliffe will never get over it. You will have baby McKee at Beverly if such examples are to be set. The Hays have returned. John Hay and

Clarence King were in Boston Friday evening on their way to Sunapee to build houses; but I arrived just too late to see them, or to hear the tale of the Ferguson wedding.[1]

Miss Baxter and I are now alone here, preparing for the general break-up which is fixed for October 1 or thereabouts. Dwight is away on business. I am full of book-printing, house-breaking and estate-settling. My brother Charles returns tomorrow from the west, and will make it lively for us. I shall start for Washington as soon as possible after October 1, and if you were to be there, I should think of going with undiluted satisfaction. As you would not be there in any case, I hope you will find Beverly tolerable, and will stay as long as you can for the sake of the house which is more in need of you than even I am. If you have a chance of letting me see you as you move about, please don't forget me. I am satisfied to know that you are there, but I would like all the same to see you once in a lifetime or two.

When Dwight took down your pictures, he took also a trunk filled with linen for the house. The linen Blanchard was to take out, and the trunk he was to return. As the trunk was not returned I wrote to him about it; and now I find here an elegant little box evidently suited to carry Martha's best clothes. I cannot consent to rob Martha; so, perhaps you will hunt up my trunk—of leather, canvas-covered, marked H.A.—and send it back by Austin & Winslow's Quincy Exp.

My love to Martha. I wish I could dig with her on the beach.

Ever Yrs   Henry Adams.

MS: MHi
   1. Ronald Munro-Ferguson married Lady Helen Hermione Blackwood (d. 1941), daughter of the first marquess of Dufferin and Ava, on Aug. 31, 1889.

To Charles Scribner

Quincy 20 Sept. [1889]

Dear Sir

I have asked Wilson to print for my personal use, at my expense, a dozen copies of my Vols. 1 and 2 on thin paper. I presume that you will have no objection, as the copies are to take the place of so many of the regular edition, and to be used only by myself or family and a few special friends; but if you see any objection, let me know. Otherwise do not trouble yourself to answer this letter. I will go on and order the copies to be printed unless I hear from you to the contrary.

Very truly Yrs   Henry Adams

Charles Scribner Esq

MS: ViU

To Elizabeth Cameron

Tuesday Oct. 1 [1889]

Dear Mrs Cameron

The tickets are taken. Soon after nine o'clock Thursday morning I shall be at the Providence R.R. station awaiting you. You know where it is—near the corner of the Common, not far from Trinity Church.[1]

In return I want you to do me the favor to look for a book in the study. Two volumes (i & ii) of Parton's Life of Andrew Jackson. Please throw them into some receptacle—Martha's tub—and bring them to me at Washington. They are worthless, but I have the third volume there.

I am eager now to get away and to find myself under your protection again. Don't fail!

Ever Yrs   Henry Adams.

MS: MHi
1. The station of the Boston and Providence Railroad, near the southwest corner of Boston Common at what is now Park Square.

To Theodore F. Dwight

1603 H Street. October 8, 1889.

Dear Dwight

I shall be in running order tomorrow, cook and all. I have taken Mrs Bugher's cook (is that her name?) from Emily Beale McLean, and as she is sworn to be good-natured, and I am sure she's black, I hope for peace if not for entrées. You will be fed somehow when you come.

Please get my medicine box from the office where John says it is; and pay Gordon for it, if you can find from him the charge.

I fell into a myriad of freemasons here last night who caused me much profanity and some delay. Today the streets are like an Inauguration with their procesh.[1]

Have met only Rebecca's young man, who seems happy. I am going now to see her.

I will tell you a joke on my historical capacity. I have been perplexed all summer to know where I saw the Ripley's "Facts" which I used. I find that *I own it.*[2] After that, you will believe my account of my own memory.

Ever Yrs   Henry Adams.

P.S. You may tell Charles his window is or was in Paris.[3]

MS: MHi
1. The Knights Templars, a masonic organization, held a national convention in Washington Oct. 6–13. Their parade on Oct. 8, in which some 25,000 knights marched, was reviewed by President Harrison and his cabinet.
2. E. W. Ripley, *Facts Relative to the Campaign on the Niagara, 1814* (1815).
3. John La Farge's *Peacock and Peony* window for CFA2's house in Boston was shown at the Paris Exposition of 1889.

To Lucy Baxter

1603 H Street. Washington 10 Oct. 1889.

Dear Miss Baxter

Your letter arrived yesterday while I was wondering how you were; and I was delighted to see it. As for its contents, I shall not take them too seriously. My friends are all down on their luck. At New York I found La Farge and King in depths of low spirits. Their troubles are chiefly financial, but when we haven't such gross and vulgar causes for distress, we take to the lighter forms of homesickness. I don't blame. I can't honestly do it, for I am myself the most abandoned heimwehist living, and have quite lost the faculty of seeing the world from any other point of view; but I do not see that it makes much difference as long as we can do nothing about it. Perhaps I might be homesick even for Quincy if I were not already homesick for Beverly. Things twist about in this queer way, and the result is that we grin and say we like it.

Clarence King and I passed Sunday at Tuxedo. I was amused. The place was quiet, and rather old fogy for the occasion, but I felt that I saw the 'oofs of the 'orses. I drove over to Ringwood to lunch with the Hewitts. George Rives also drove over, with his wife and Mrs Pierre Lorillard.[1] They came in an open trap; we in a sort of four-wheeled Herdic with a pair of horses. After lunch heavy rain came on, and Mrs Hewitt asked me to take the two ladies home in my wagon. You would have been amused to see me making myself agreeable to Mrs George Rives and Mrs Pierre Lorillard, in close, not to say crowded juxtaposition, for an hour or more, with their husbands in the rain; but I did it as well as I knew how, leaving my companion to strike the gait. I liked Mrs Lorillard, who is a very pleasing person. I can't say the same thing altogether of her companion.

My journey was very pleasant from Boston, with Mrs Cameron and Martha. Don was ready to receive them, and I saw them again only for a short time the next day when La Farge and I took Mrs Cameron to the Art Museum to see the Rembrandts.[2] La Farge was very entertaining, and we chiefly listened to him. La Farge, King and I trifled away our evening at the theatre seeing young Sothern as Chumley; idiotic, but suited to our mental condition.[3] I saw nothing worth having in New York, not even a bonnet, or a wedding-present for Daisy, unless she wants glass or cigars.

I arrived here Monday night among a million free-masons with cocked hats and drawn swords which stuck into one's eyes all along the railway platform. Washington was deserted except for Knights, and the Knights belonged to Little Alice's kind.[4] The Club was a dreary stye. I met only Charley Rae who beamed and comes with Rebecca to dine this evening. Also William Endicott and his Lulu come to lunch today. The bride business is chiefly amusing to the bride, but I shall at least get it over quick. With unexampled celerity I have got a cook and set my house going with as many servants as cockroaches, and much too many of both.

The dear Chang Yen Hoon, who left here a week ago, sent me a present of farewell, with a sweet note inviting me to China. And I sent him nothing, and did not know he was going. I am puzzled what to do.

Remember me to Miss Hovey, and write soon.[5]

Ever truly Yrs   Henry Adams.

MS: ScU

1. George Lockhart Rives (1849–1917), lawyer, historian, assistant secretary of state 1887–1889, and his second wife, Sara Whiting Rives (d. 1924). Emily Taylor Lorillard (d. 1925), wife of Pierre Lorillard (1833–1901), tobacco merchant, race-horse breeder, and developer of Tuxedo Park, N.Y. Opening in 1886, it became the playground of fashionable New Yorkers and gave its name to the tailless dress coat popularized there.

2. In January, the Metropolitan Museum had been given the Henry Gurdon Marquand collection, which included two Rembrandts and other major works.

3. Edward Hugh Sothern (1859–1933), American actor, in *Lord Chumley* (1888), by David Belasco and Henry C. De Mille.

4. That is, the Knights Templars seemed as absurd as the White and Red Knights in Lewis Carroll's *Through the Looking Glass*, ch. 8.

5. Marian Hovey (1835–1898), of Boston, was the daughter of George O. Hovey and sister-in-law of John T. Morse, Jr. Lucy Baxter became her companion after ABA's death.

To John Hay

1603 H Street. Friday 18 Oct. '89.

Dear Hay

What the deuce has become of you? Here be I and Spring Rice and three score Admirals and others waiting your appearance with perfect confidence from day to day, and you never come;[1] and there was King at New York, in a mess, expecting you to be there instantly, and console him. Yet you come not, and I'm little better than an Admiral myself if I can understand it. Your letter of the 11th certainly led me to imagine you were already near the next railway station.

I know nothing of duties, neither of receipts. No political menial has come to me about duties. I suppose he prefers to steal the whole shop this time. Allah il-Allah!

Hurry up! I want you bad tonight for an Admiral Molyneux who is all that is left—except the other descendents—of Sir Thomas More.[2] I had to send for Langley to fill your place.

Love to Mrs Hay and the Ecrevisses.

Ever Yrs   Henry Adams.

MS: RPB
1. Spring Rice returned to Washington, Oct. 10, as secretary to the International Marine Conference.
2. Admiral Sir Robert H. More-Molyneux (1838–1904), delegate to the marine conference.

To Sir Robert Cunliffe

1603 H Street. 20 Oct. 1889.

Dear Baronet

Why the dogs didn't you tell me that you had H.B.M. to breakfast?[1] Do you fear my fierce democracy? One humbug is as good as another. You should not go back on yours. (Don't repeat this to miladi.)

The papers have arrived from the F.O. and I am under just a million obligations. I cannot say that they prove your wicked government to be any blacker in heart than we all knew it to be; but they calm my mind as to the investigations of the next fool who undertakes to write on the subject. At any rate I have garrotted him. I yet hope they will find the Prevost papers for me. To keep them active I enclose a list of naval reports I want. Not that these are very essential, but some other idiot will say they are.

I presume some one will send me a bill for the copying.

John Hay has not yet arrived here, nor are his traps clear of the Custom House so your caddo is still wasting its charms. I shall write on its arrival.

Spring Rice is again here with eight or ten admirals whom he brings to dinner from time to time. Otherwise I am quite alone this last fortnight, working hard. I suppose my first two volumes will be out next week, but I shall not send them to you until I find some one to read them here. The sixth is now passing through the slow grind of type-setting, and the seventh and eighth are finished except for the slight changes that your fresh material may cause. I am not anxious to be read in England. I don't want to make you feel as though you wished you were dead. So I send no copies there. At least, I believe not; though publishers are capable of any crime.

La Farge and King were in New York a fortnight ago, and King took me to Tuxedo for Sunday. I found both of them down on their luck, and very low in mind. Apparently money is the source of all happiness; at least, art and science seem to be as dependent on it as landlords and historians.

My days are passed in regularity quite calculated to induce despair. Six hours at a desk; three on a horse; and the rest in wishing I were in bed, or in being there. Dwight is still at Quincy; Hay at Cleveland; Mrs Cameron at Harrisburg; and not even a pretty girl is near enough to come to breakfast. Luckily the weather is fine, and the winter hard by.

I have wholly forgotten whether Carlo or I wrote last, but I shall write to him soon. Meanwhile give my love to everyone, especially to your wife and Fossy if the future baronet permits me to be so familiar as to address him in that style.

Ever Yrs   Henry Adams.

MS: MHi

1. Her Britannic Majesty (Queen Victoria).

To Elizabeth Cameron

1603 H Street. [after 20 Oct. 1889]

Come, come, oh come! Dwight has just returned and John Hay may be with us if not too seedy after dining here yesterday with sixteen Russian Admirals. I want painfully to come over to you now, but know you would find me in the way.

Ever   Henry Adams

MS: MHi

To Charles Scribner

1603 H Street. 23 October, 1889.

Dear Sir

I have to thank you for the six sets of vols i and ii which arrived this morning. For the great interest and constant attention you have given to the book, not merely in regard to its appearance, but in every other respect, I feel deeply obliged; and can only hope that you may not be doing for it more than it deserves.

As soon as the copies of my little private edition of twelve sets come from the binder, I shall give myself the pleasure of sending you a presentation copy, if it seems worth your acceptance.

I am very truly Yrs   Henry Adams.

Charles Scribners Sons.

MS: ViU

To Lucy Baxter

1603 H Street. Sunday 27 Oct. '89.

Dear Miss Baxter

I hoped to send you by this time a copy of my own private *ladies* edition of my two volumes, of which I had a dozen sets printed for private use, on special paper; but Hathaway has not yet sent them to me, and as the binding is as serious as the subject, I am obliged to wait. You will get them in time.[1]

Dwight has arrived here. So has John Hay, though not his wife and children. So has Mrs Cameron. Martha has come to look over her books and dolls; and Dwight has hung Mrs Cameron's pictures. Rebecca Dodge has selected her trousseau or a part of it, or I have selected it for her. Among the rest, the blue gauze silk with white flower-figures, and the blue haute nouveauté, I meditate adding the linen crape of seagreen-white-blue. Spring Rice has also come, personally conducting a band of admirals who are a surprise to me. They never damn their eyes or shiver their timbers. They have apparently never been at sea. At least they never tell sea-stories. They have had no adventures or escapes. They never mention battles. They only come and eat their dinner and talk about the Teutonic, in which they made the voyage over.[2] They are well-behaved; and a Russian admiral who comes to dine also under Spring Rice's guidance, has a sweet black moustache that sticks out like a Russian bear.

Everyone is coming home. Even Sturgis Bigelow writes that he shall soon be here to gladden the children's hearts. Mrs Johnny Davis has been left behind for a short time, but is expected soon. Tilly seems to have run herself into the usual state of nerves which adds so much interest to women's lives, and Lucy is trying to do the same. Gossip filters but slowly to these remote parts so early in the season, and I hear little news except that the Bayard-Clymer wedding is to take place on the 7th. No new young women are yet on hand to take the places vacated by marriage at my table, and I hear a fearful rumor that even the Leiters are to desert. Papa Leiter is said to have taken a big house in New York besides giving half a million for his Newport place.

I watch with the greatest interest for news from you and your struggles from the cosmos. I know not why one daily round is not as good as another, and when I sit down at my desk every morning, knowing precisely what I am to do all day, I wonder whether I should be more or less peaceful if I tried to do something desperate, like scalping a member of Congress, or frying my cook on her own kitchen-range. On the whole, the passionless peace business seems to be nearest the average course of nature and I fancy that the fish which sticks in his pool is as well off as the one that cuts about in the waterfall. For myself I prefer Fiji and the Desert of Gobi; but only because I've not been there. You have your desert of Gobi on Beacon Street and I always found it sufficient. Your idea that you appreciated *me* is melancholy. I am only a ghost, dead as the great Pan (by the bye, Charles has sent Dwight sixteen volumes of Browning),[3] and live only because I appreciate a few others,—you among the rest. Don't reverse the correct process.

Ever truly Yrs   Henry Adams.

MS: ScU

1. The private, or so-called "ladies edition," consists of the first two volumes of Scribner's trade edition printed on thin paper and bound in dark red morocco by F. P. Hathaway, Boston bookbinder.

2. The newly launched *Teutonic,* one of the first ships with twin-screw propulsion, was not only a luxury liner, but was armored and fitted to double as a warship.

3. Elizabeth Barrett Browning, "The Dead Pan" (1844). *The Poetical Works of Robert Browning* (1888).

To Lucy Baxter

1603 H Street. Tuesday. Nov. 5 [1889]

Dear Miss Baxter

I write one line in haste, on receiving yours of Sunday to say that I shall be greatly annoyed if you do not come to pass at least one full day with us here. Perhaps I shall not be in a situation next year to entertain you unless you happen to stop at Pekin or Fiji; so come now! Tell Miss Hovey that Dwight and I are invalids too, and need your attendance.

Constance Lodge is with us now, and Martha comes in, two or three times a day. Today she left her doll Gretchen for me to mend.

The volumes are to arrive this week. If they come too late, I shall keep your's till you make your visit here.

Yrs ever   Henry Adams.

MS: ScU

To Sir Robert Cunliffe

1603 H Street. November 10, 1889.

Dear Robert

Did I thank you for the picture? I have written so many notes to you lately that I forget the last. If I have not acknowledged the picture, I will; and if I have, I will do so again. Miss Cooke is charming. Everyone has been delighted with her, and she has been quite as much a belle here as her self-esteem could permit; for I am sure she was a shy beauty. She has gone to Boston to be framed, and I expect her back forthwith.[1]

The sheets of copy have also arrived, but again no bill. I have been engaged, working the new material into my text. The more, the better, if it is not in print. I would like a copy or photograph of Gen. Lambert's plans of the battle grounds at New Orleans and Mobile Point. I think I have the Canadian correspondence, especially for 1812–1813; but Prevost's letters, after all, are chiefly valuable for their enclosures, and those I must see, to select. The unpublished naval reports are most valuable now.

You can tell Miss Byrne. I shall still have time to use new material. My two introductory volumes are out; but I have sent none to England, and mean that none shall go there. If you want to see it, you must come here; but I do not imagine you will hear of it otherwise. As I never read a newspaper, and do not allow the book to be mentioned in my hearing, I am not certain that anyone has yet read it, except three or four people who were given copies, and had to acknowledge them. I feel as though I had had a baby and had got to have three or four more. You can ask all the mammas of your acquaintance whether under such circumstances the subject is the one they most enjoy.

No great news here! Spring Rice comes in pretty nearly every evening, either to dinner or in the evening to play cribbage. Hay arrives tomorrow from Cleveland, but the family comes not yet. Mrs Cameron is very well, and I depend almost wholly on her for feminine society. Other friends are coming or returning, and my small set promises to be rather larger than common this winter. I am told that my brother Brooks and his wife are much married, and all my other family connections seem to flourish. Peace be with them.

I wonder whether I owe Carlo a letter. Somehow I have lost count, and must write to ask him. Give him my love when you see him. Give the same to miladi and the infants.

Ever Yrs   Henry Adams.

MS: MHi
1. *Miss Cooke,* one of the many faintly tinted portrait drawings by John Downman (1750–1824) of Wrexham (near Cunliffe's place). The sitter's identity is unknown.

To Charles Milnes Gaskell

1603 H Street. 24 November, 1889.

My dear Carlo

I have lost count of our letters, and remember only that I have heard nothing from you for a very long time. Luckily time no longer affects me. I have become as indifferent as the Egyptian Sphynx to the passage of centuries, and my friends always remain young because I don't see them. You can't imagine how pleasantly I remember England, and how very much alive you all are, though you have been dead or quarreled these twenty years.

I am as dead as a mummy myself, but don't mind it. As a ghost I am rather a success in a small way, not to the world, but to my own fancy, which I presume to be a ghost's world, as it is mine. Things run by with spectre-like silence and quickness. As I never leave my house, and never see a newspaper, and never remember what I am told, the devil might get loose and wander about the world for months before I should meet him, and then I should not know who he was. You can have no idea how still and reposeful, and altogether gentlemanly a place the world is, till you leave it.

Spring Rice has come back again with a dozen or so of admirals whom he is personally conducting about the dangers of youth and ocean. Occasionally he shelters them with me for a while, to rest a bit and doze over my dinner-table. They seem a temperate set, and I don't fear their dozing under it. The town is filled with all sorts of foreigners on all sorts of conferences about the most ridiculous trifles, such as trade with Patagonia, and fog-horns. Spring Rice runs the fog-horns, and so I hear them. He has broken down Admiral More Molyneux and one tough old sea-captain by dissipation, and has packed them off to sea to get well. In another fortnight he will have worn out the lot, and will be the only admiral left.

My brother Brooks has settled into married life, and a new house in Boston, where I trust he will stay quiet till he finds his way to a better world. His wife is extremely nice, and he has every reason to be a contented oaf for ten years at least. The rest of my family haunts the old holes, growing grayer year by year, with furrows like railway cuttings across their faces, expressing a choice variety of middle-aged respectable vices; avarice, gluttony and the like. Even the young generation is no longer so very young. My two nephews George and Charles Adams, who have just returned from the grand tour abroad, are older than you and I were, when we haunted London together.

I have thrown upon the cold world two children in the shape of volumes, the first of eight or ten of which I am to be delivered. As they lost all interest for me long ago, I cannot believe that they would interest my friends, so I have sent no copies about. If any American should ask if I sent them to you, say Yes,—and that you have read them with much pleasure. The conversation will not go further, and both of us will have made a proper appearance before posterity.

The Hays brought me back a little gossip about England, and the baronet occasionally writes me a line on business. Stray Englishwomen wander about here, and occasionally a man, but none that inspire a passion.

My love to all your family.

Ever truly   Henry Adams.

MS: MHi

To Lucy Baxter

1603 H Street. Sunday 8 Dec. 1889

My dear Miss Baxter

I have a mind to get you to go to Hathaway and seize my books, but Dwight has already asked Shriver to do it, so you are exempt, and can feel as I did the other day when I was summoned on jury duty, and succeeded in convincing the Chief Justice that I was not a fit person for the purpose. Since you were here, Washington has not changed. I am still hammering at proofs and indexes, and going for five o'clock tea with Martha. Next week I go to New York to meet Molly. John Hay and I go together, and I suppose I shall arrive just as you leave. Otherwise I would suggest your taking me to the Barye show.[1] Edward Hooper and John La Farge have been here this week, steeped in paint, after a prolonged debauch in the New York galleries. La Farge was evidently pleased at being decorated. Ribands are better than nothing, I suppose, but they bring little currency to him.[2]

St Gaudens writes that he shall come on today. I never believe these artists, yet I always order their rooms to be got ready. John Hay threatens to give a Bohemian dinner at the Knickerbocker to Abbey, Millet and Parsons who arrive Thursday from Europe; and he wants to know if I will attend. When I say yes, he pitches in such Bohemians as William Waldorf Astor and Loyd Brice, as though that was fit company for a gentleman who has passed his life in avoiding them. At that I kick.[3]

My small flock flourishes. Mrs Cameron, Mrs Lodge, Miss Leiter and Rebecca Dodge all dropped in unexpectedly to breakfast last Thursday, with Spring Rice and Hay, and made a very gay crowd. I have quite as much society as I can manage. Last evening for the first time in weeks Dwight and I dined alone, and sat down afterwards to a quiet game of cribbage. We are now just even on games. Since he came on we have played 115 games, and with frightful difficulty he won the odd game last evening. On points he is about two hundred ahead.

Mrs Lodge also goes to New York next week, leaving Cabot to run Congress. Cabot has elected his Speaker and become a man of the future. I think he is as much disliked as most rising statesmen, but perhaps no more so; and his friend Reed, the new Speaker, has gone far with an equal load of unpopularity. The attitude of the Grand Panjandrums, Blaine and Harrison, towards these young assassins is as amusing as their attitude towards each other. Reed and Lodge really have some ideas of usefulness, which never entered the heads of B. & H. Blaine detests Reed and Lodge; Harrison detests the whole lot, and Blaine and Harrison detest each other, while Reed and Lodge hate them all.[4]

Naturally I see nothing of such people, but I hear not a little, and I do not envy the future historian. Yet I suppose that the history of a pole-cat government would interest polecats.

Fortunately Martha is still gracious, though at times tyrannical.

I wonder whether Daisy found a tea-pot to suit her. I had some sent on.

Ever Yrs   Henry Adams.

MS: ScU

1. The American Art Galleries exhibition of the French animal sculptor Antoine-Louis Barye (1796–1875) and his contemporaries, Nov. 10–Jan. 15.

2. La Farge received the ribbon of the Legion of Honor from the French government for his innovations in stained glass; he also won a first-class medal for his window in the Paris Exposition.

3. The three artists had all won medals at the Paris Exposition. Edwin Austin Abbey (1852–1911), illustrator and watercolorist; Francis Millet; Alfred William Parsons (1847–1920), English landscape painter. Lloyd Brice (1851–1917) of New York was the newest proprietor of the *NAR*.

4. Thomas Brackett Reed (1839–1902) of Maine, Republican representative 1877–1899; Lodge managed his election as speaker. Blaine was secretary of state under Harrison 1889–1892.

To Charles Scribner

1603 H Street. Washington 15 December, 1889.

Dear Sir

I send you by express tomorrow a copy of my "ladies' edition" for your acceptance. I had intended it as a compliment to your taste in books, but unfortunately could get no paper good enough for the purpose. Had I been able, I should have printed on such paper as Macmillan used for his Globe Shakespeare. My paper is lighter, but less opaque and blue in tone.

I had also meant to cut down the margins in binding, and have a flexible cover, so as to make a pocket-edition, but Hathaway has run away with me, and in consequence his work is more conspicuous than my intentions.

At all events the two volumes will serve to show how trivial a thing history may be made.[1]

Very truly Yrs   Henry Adams.

Charles Scribner Esq

MS: ViU

1. The books are 4⅞" by 7⅜", approximately the same size as the trade edition. The first volume was inscribed: "Charles Scribner / with the regards of Henry Adams, December, 1889."

To Charles Francis Adams, Jr.

1603 H Street. 22 Dec. 1889

Dear Charles

I have meditated with due solemnity over Mr Balch's document and your epistle.

As a simplifier you appear to me to be a failure.

I see no special advantage in using so much machinery in order to create a trust contrary to law which any court would instantly declare void.[1]

If simplicity is an object I think we should do better to instruct our executors to reserve so much money for so many years, and pay the interest to the Adams Trust, or some one else.

As the bequest must in any case depend wholly on honor, a letter of instruction will answer as well as anything in the form of a deed or legal act.

Nevertheless I don't care, and if you have a taste for creating impossible trusts, and reciprocal obligations to do illegal acts, I am just as ready to proceed in that way as in any other.

Yrs ever   Henry Adams.

Charles F. Adams Esq.

MS: MHi
1. CFA2 wanted to establish a trust to provide income to maintain the family library in Quincy after his and HA's deaths. On the illegality of the trust, see HA to CFA2, July 3, 1890.

To Evelyn Davis Adams

1603 H Street. 23 December, '89.

Dear Daisy

Your wedding present should arrive (from Doll & Richards) by Christmas. You will understand that I intend you a great compliment by sending you what most people would think a meaningless daub. It is one of La Farge's sketches for a window never carried out.[1] I chose it because, incomplete as it is, I thought it rather the most important of his small sketches, and the one which showed his color most strikingly.

Hang it where it will have light, but not near anything else. It will kill most water-colors I know. Small as it is, it needs space.

A happy Christmas, and as many of them as you want! Sturgis Bigelow has just left me, on his way home. Your sister dined here last night, but Constance has deserted me. She says she has a cold. I am going to see.

Affectionately Yrs   Henry Adams.

Mrs Brooks Adams.

MS: MHi
1. *Moon Passing through Clouds*, a watercolor.

3.

Waiting to Depart

1890

Adams had come to regard work on the *History* as his last tie to Washington, an old routine in which he was only going through the motions. He looked forward to escape, but the first volumes, now in hand, covered only a quarter of his story. He was bound to his Washington life for some time yet. The energy that went into the last rewriting he eventually geared down to an unrelenting attention to maps and charts and index and questions of volume division.

A new circle of intimates, almost as close as the Five of Hearts, filled more of Adams' time and thoughts, but did not distract him from thinking of Fiji or the Gobi Desert as the goal toward which he labored. La Farge agreed to accompany him on his travels once more, and the itinerary became more definite. They were to sail for Samoa in July, but La Farge's work created delays for more than a month. With his own work complete, Adams' restlessness grew unchecked. Also, his affection for Mrs. Cameron, as we learn from later letters, became complicated by new intensity. Departure, when it came, was more than welcome.

To Lucy Baxter

1603 H Street. 4 Jan. 1890

Dear Miss Baxter

Dwight said he should write to you last Sunday, so I waited. Nothing in particular is going on, and I am bored only by people's conversation, which consists in saying that they have, or have had, what they please to call the grip. No other excitement has penetrated Washington. I sit in my ark, and send out my doves—Dwight, Hay and Molly—to pick up information at dinners, but the result is hardly one olive-branch. Never did I know the world to be so sleepy and indifferent. Even my breakfast table is broken and bankrupt. Molly finds all her friends gone, and no one come, while Miss Leiter, radiant as the Princess of Trebizonde if there was one,[1] comes in only to say that she is going off. Mrs Cameron has retreated to Fortress Monroe, and Martha says I'm a fool, and is not pleased with me because I laugh disrespectfully at her dignity.

Molly is decidedly bored and took to her bed yesterday with feverishness. She dined at the Cameron's where Rachel, the débutante, gave a festa.[2] Hay went to bed also yesterday. Rebecca Dodge and her young man dine here tonight for fasting and prayer before their marriage on the 9th. I can find no one to dine with them, so shall treat them as family. I have been to the theatre to see the Senator, and sat between Mrs Cabot Lodge and Mrs Theodore Roosevelt, sweetly cared for, and laughed wildly at the usual rubbish rather more than usually usual; but it made me more or less regret that I had ever been born to write history about senators for a race that laughs at such pictures of itself.[3] Well, we are a feeble and benevolent generation, bless our little hearts!

I am gradually accomplishing all the great objects of my life. Imprimis I have sent Brooks his wedding-present. Mine is but a modest and unfinished water-color daub of La Farge; but Charles has given a piece of Chinese porcelain fit for an Emperor. You must go and pray to it. I have not seen it, but Dwight and La Farge were very enthusiastic.

My next life-work has been to have the Schönberg Roth Schönberg née Wards to dinner, which I accomplished the other evening with the help of John Hay, Jeff. Coolidge and Miss Leiter.

My third effort is to organise my Gobi expedition on which I am now engaged.

In the intervals of these serious undertakings I am hurrying out the rest of the History, which is all on end. I cannot help you to notices, either newspaper or other. Dwight reads and keeps them all, and I never see them. I know nothing about the book except what people write or say to me, and that is very little; but as yet I have heard no severity or harshness. This is of course a great relief, but sooner or later I expect to pay for it.

You ask about the pictures? I thought the Angelus was well worth five thousand dollars.[4] As painting, I preferred almost all the others.

Ever truly   Henry Adams.

MS: ScU

1. In Offenbach's *La Princesse de Trébizonde* (1869) a traveling showman's daughter wins by her beauty the hand of a prince. The princesses of Trebizond, a medieval empire on the Black Sea, were fabulously beautiful and married off to form important alliances.

2. Rachel Cameron, youngest daughter of J. Donald Cameron and his first wife, Mary McCormick Cameron.

3. *The Senator,* by David Demarest Lloyd and Sidney Rosenfeld, is based on a historical case involving a 70-year delay in the settlement of claims for damages incurred during the War of 1812. The play was especially well received in Washington for its "very interesting insight into social, political, and diplomatic life in this city" (Washington *Post,* Dec. 29, 1889).

4. *The Angelus* by Jean-François Millet, which cost the American Art Association $115,000, was drawing huge crowds in New York.

To Sir Robert Cunliffe

1603 H Street. 4 Jan. 1890.

My dear Robert

Miss Byrne has sent me the enclosed bill. As I can't well draw a bill of exchange to so general an address as "Miss Byrne" I enclose a draft for the amount, and will thank you for endorsing it properly to her, and sending it.

At the same time I wish you would thank her and express my warm thanks for her services. She has sent me a series of papers which are most valuable to me, and which will complete my series of MSS. quotations in a most satisfactory manner. No one can glean much in that field after I have done with Miss Byrne's gleanings.

I have no news to send you. As usual I am solitary in my society, and sit in my den week after week, seeing no one but John Hay and Martha Cameron. Just now I have a niece staying with me who helps to tell me gossip. The doves go out of the ark every night and return with dinners to tell about, but they bring astonishingly little food for Noah at home.

Spring Rice is still here, having sent home all his admirals. He will probably stay here for the winter, to help out the minister with a copyist. I do not know the minister or his family, but hear them very highly spoken of.

I am deeply grateful for your assistance about the Record Office. You have shed lustre on your time. My love to Lady Cunliffe.

Ever Yrs   Henry Adams.

MS: MHi

To Charles Scribner

1603 H Street. 12 Jan, 1890

Dear Sir

I am at last forced to admit that I cannot conveniently bring my last four years, 1813–1817, within the compass of two volumes. The war would in any case swell the size of the volumes, and besides the increase of text, I shall have a score of plans, and at least a hundred pages of index. I shall have to take three volumes or make uncomfortably thick ones.

At present I am inclined to close the second volume with the battle of New Orleans, and make the third a small one with the mere conclusion and winding up of the story. I shall have four chapters in the nature of an epilogue. Altogether, with the index, the last volume may approach three hundred and fifty pages.

As I do not know how such an addition may strike you, and as I am especially unwilling to throw any extra burden or risk on you, after you have done everything I asked, I shall be glad to hear your views about the matter.

Very truly Yrs   Henry Adams.

MS: ViU

To Charles Scribner

1603 H Street. 15 Jan. 1890.

Dear Sir

The problem is this:—Of MS. narrative I have, according to my closest calculation, one thousand printed pages more or less, but probably somewhat less,—say .... 975 pp.
—Index for all nine volumes, probably .... 100 pp.
—Plans, maps &c, in bulk perhaps equal to .... 50 pp.
I cannot squeeze my calculation within eleven hundred pages, and I suspect it should be nearer twelve hundred. At all events I dare not allow for less than twelve hundred.

A volume of six hundred pages would be troublesome. Accordingly I was disposed to suggest three volumes of four hundred pages each. Unfortunately this division cut the battle of New Orleans in half, and left internal arrangement senseless. Of course I feel the proprieties of the internal arrangement more decidedly than I feel any other; and I could devise no better solution of the problem than this:—

Vol. vii. 16 chaps: say 384 pp. with charts; in all probably near 400 pp.

Vol. viii. 14 chaps: say 375 pp, as the chapters are long, with charts; in all probably equivalent to 395 pp.

Vol. ix. 10 chaps; say 235 pp. With Index to the whole work, say 100 pages, or 335 pp. in all.

Of course I cannot be certain of not making an error of twenty or thirty pages, but no possible error would make much difference. The last volume must in any case be made to contain the whole index, and, if this is the case, will not the problem be simplified by inserting the whole index at first, rather than an index for the three volumes at first, and then altering the size of the last volume in the final issue. I assume that the whole nine volumes must have a general index. The annoyance of consulting four indexes to one series would be very unpleasant to general students. In rearranging the nine volumes with a consecutive title-page (if you like), you can either retain or omit the two-volume indexes. I should say, omit them, and leave only the general index; but purchasers of the separate sets from the beginning are also entitled to the general index. Therefore in any case the ninth volume ought to contain a general and not a special index.

So I came to the result of having Vol. vii about 400 pages; Vol. viii about 395 pages; Vol. ix about 350 pages, including the General Index.

The alternative seems to be two volumes of 550 pages each, at least, and possibly more.

I am indifferent. The copy is ready, and Vol. vii goes to Wilson this week. Until we get about ten chapters in print, say about a month hence, we are not obliged to decide. I need to know only where to end volume I.

Yrs truly   Henry Adams.

Charles Scribners Sons.

I ought to add that the internal arrangement naturally brings the whole campaign of 1814 together in Vol. viii. The battle of New Orleans includes the entire southern campaign of that year, and fills three chapters, or seventy printed pages with four or five maps.

If these three chapters are carried over to Vol. ix, they swell that volume above 400 pages.

If two chapters are carried over, at least one must be brought from Vol. i to Vol. ii, which completely destroys the subject-unity of all three volumes.

I might add a couple of chapters, but the ten chapters of conclusion are sufficient, and the reader would be bored.

Presentation copies.

Vols. iii & iv.

The same list as before (for Vols. i & ii) but with such changes of addresses as are required. For example, William M. Evarts, *Washington, DC.* Abram S. Hewitt at his house in *New York City.*

Please send two dozen copies to me here.

MS: ViU

To Lucy Frelinghuysen

1603 H Street 20 Jan. 1890

Dear Miss Frelinghuysen

If I did not know that at moments of great distress nothing matters much, I should be sorry to have sent you my stupid offering when I did. I had no idea you were in trouble. As for me, I consider my troubles in life as over, and I sit on the shore and watch the sufferings of others with a pleasant sense of selfishness and pity, as though I were a shipwrecked mariner with nothing to lose. I have much time for sympathy, and you have had no stinted share.

You are very kind about my poor, stupid maunderings in print. The public must be pitiably bored if it is really amused by such writing. From time to time I am obliged to refer to it, and seldom fail to wonder whether it is possible that anyone can have patience to read it through. Nothing will ever convince me of a thing so improbable.

The season has begun, and as usual I am left deserted by the *monde qui s'amuse,* till amusements are over, when they will return to me for dust and ashes in Lent. Surely you might come on. Influenza is no worse here than elsewhere, and your friends are even more numerous than influenzial.

Ever Yrs   Henry Adams.

MS: Henry Cabot Lodge

To Charles Scribner

1603 H Street. 23 Jan. 1890

Dear Sir

Can you tell me the greatest number of pages you could conveniently allow to a volume? Could the paper be so far reduced in weight as to allow of 525 pages in the thickness of Vols. i & ii?

Yrs truly   Henry Adams

Charles Scribner Esq.

MS: ViU

To Lucy Baxter

1603 H Street. 26 January, 1890.

My dear Miss Baxter

I began to fear that you had become as much of an invalid as Miss Hovey, when your letter of last Sunday arrived. Dwight has got another of his bilious fits, and adds little to the hilarity of life; and if I were not myself the gayest and most active of butterflies, I think the world would probably produce no more honey or flowers. Even I want to go to Mexico. If you will only provide a car, and come through, picking up Hay and me and Mrs Cameron and Mrs Lodge and Constance and Helen as you pass, we can have some variety still. Indeed I am not sure but that I shall go anyway. Printers send no proof. I am way ahead of the publishers. Gobi comes nearer day by day, and if I do not see Mexico now, I shall have to wait till next time.

Washington is dull, I am told. With a thousand persons hunting for amusement, I should think it likely that they would scare their game; but they scare it mostly into my house, I think, for my monthly bills show constant increase of eating. My table—at least the table of my entire she-bang—costs me five hundred dollars a month, which I think large for two persons who eat little. Neither Dwight nor I can consume sixteen dollars worth of beef a day. I am led to think that others must share the task; yet I never have parties—only beauties, who eat little. The mighty Smalley of the Tribune dined with me twice last week.[1] Yesterday Rebecca Dodge, as she calls herself, though I went to her wedding a fortnight ago, brought her pretty bridesmaid, Miss Matty Mitchell, to breakfast; and today Ward Thoron brings his girl, Carry Storey, to the the same entertainment. The Roosevelts and Mrs Cameron come to dinner. I have just been taken by Martha to the greenhouse where the camelias are all in flower. The day was springlike, and the crocuses in flower. Your niece's Cherokee rose is now in the open air, and is doing nicely. I am watching for flowers on it, and meanwhile my table is adorned with my own orchids from another greenhouse, while I am running a third for profit. To be sure Hay owns and runs the camelia house, but in Mrs Hay's absence, I take the flowers.

Thanks for your cutting, which goes into Dwight's menagerie. I was greatly pleased the other day to receive one dated from the "House of Representatives, State of Washington." As I did not know the existence of such a State as Washington[2] I felt as though I had struck posterity at last. I glanced at enough of it to find out that the critic, while extravagantly complimentary, thought that, if I had a fault, it was that of being a bigoted Virginia republican. Posterity ceases, after that, to inspire wonder. "Compare me with the bettering of the time."[3]

The history has not raised a ripple in my existence, and if the two coming volumes escape shipwreck, I shall start for Gobi without further thought of them. I believe the next pair is to appear in February, and I have the fifth and sixth ready. The seventh and eighth are with the printer, and will be done in May. John Hay finishes his great work at the same time, and is beginning to wonder what Gobi he can find to make an occupation for the rest of his life.

Nikisch came, and had an audience which for Washington was large. I tried in vain to see the difference between the playing, but my memory or perception was too weak. I should not have known the change except from seeing the leader.[4] This would be humiliating if I were not already beneath humiliation; but the story has become stale from use.

I am glad you saw the babes.

Ever truly Yrs   Henry Adams.

MS: ScU
1. George Washburn Smalley, European news editor of the New York *Tribune* 1867–1895, based in London.
2. Washington was admitted to the Union, Nov. 11, 1889.
3. "Compare them with the bett'ring of the time"; Shakespeare, Sonnet 32.
4. On Jan. 17 the Boston Symphony Orchestra gave its first performance in Washington under its new conductor, Arthur Nikisch (1855–1922), formerly of the Leipzig Opera.

To Charles Scribner

1603 H Street. 30 Jan. 1890

Dear Sir

After the most careful calculation I have squeezed the text of my narrative, in the concluding volumes, down to 920 printed pages. I allow roughly 100 pages for index. I do not yet know how many maps and charts are required, but I am confident they will not much exceed 30 pages. 920+100+30=1050. By dividing into volumes of 525 pages I think I could promise to come out right. I like light volumes, but I do not like an unnecessary number, and am quite willing to stick to the original plan if possible. The Index is the only real difficulty, and perhaps the Index may not exceed seventy-five or even seventy pages. I have made a blunder already in Volume 6, about the Index, which will be corrected only when the Index for that volume is dropped. I do not want to make another in the final shape of the last volume.

I think there are no charts in Vols. iii & 4. Which map do you refer to?

Yrs truly   Henry Adams.

MS: ViU

To Charles Scribner

1603 H Street. 1 February, 1890

Dear Sir

The closest calculation I can make on the proposed three volumes is as follows:

Vol. i.	370 pp.	10 maps (?)
Vol. ii.	340 pp.	14 "
Vol. iii.	210 pp.	text.
	100 "	index
	310 pp.	
Total	1020 pp.	24 maps.

I may add a little to the text, but not much. The chief possibilities of error are in the maps and index. Some of the maps are single pages; some are double. I may want to insert more, especially single-page plans of battles.

As for the index, my last (Vols. iii & iv) is twentyfive pages. The next (Vols. v & vi) will not be less. That for Vols. vii, viii & ix will be longest of all, as it will cover many new subjects like the war. In rearranging the four indexes, the first will be amplified. On the whole, the general index is likely, in spite of shrinkage on repetitions, to reach at least one hundred pages.

At a pinch I might to advantage work another chapter in; but I would rather not.

You must decide. I assent to anything.

Yrs truly   Henry Adams.

MS: ViU

To Charles Scribner

1603 H Street. 8 Feb. 1890

Dear Sir

Your decision seems to me wise; but if there is no occasion to act until we reach Chap. xvi in printing, I should prefer to leave the matter open till then. I am not quite certain how the chapters will run, and a page or two on each chapter makes the whole difference. At twentyfive pages a chapter, forty chapters would give a thousand pages, which exceeds my limit, and would, with maps and index, require a volume between five hundred and sixty pages, and five hundred and seventy.—At twentyone pages a chapter, forty chapters would give eight hundred and forty pages, and would allow a volume not exceeding four hundred and ninety pages.

My chapters have averaged 23⅓ pages till now. Forty chapters at 23⅓ pages make 934 pages. This would make my previous estimate of a volume not exceeding 525 pages.

Owing to some close differences in footnotes and material between these volumes and their predecessers, as well as to their MS. copy, (the others having been already printed), I cannot be sure of keeping the chapters within 23⅓ pages on an average. I have some reason to fear they may average 26 pages, and until I see how the ten early chapters run, I cannot pledge myself to the size of the volumes within a limit of error so narrow.

Yrs truly Henry Adams.

MS: ViU

To William D. Shipman

1603 H Street. 11 Feb. 1890

Dear Sir[1]

As you have been so kind as to take an interest in my work, I enclose you a copy of the two latest volumes.

Many thanks for your kind letter of the 9th. Having now said all I care to say about President Jefferson, the persons who have courage to labor through the four volumes must consider themselves as its authors as well as owners, and must put into the work whatever is wanting, as well as omit whatever is wrong. A book once given to the public ceases to belong to the writer of it, who neither can nor should interpose further between readers and their property. I hand over one copy at least to a reader in whose knowledge as well as judgment I can feel entire confidence.

Very truly Yrs Henry Adams.

Judge Shipman

MS: RPB
1. William Davis Shipman (1818–1898) of New York, law partner of Samuel L. M. Barlow.

To Charles Scribner

1603 H Street. Friday, Feb. 14, 1890

Dear Sir

The only objection to stopping the printers is that I intend to sail, on or before July 1, from San Francisco for the east, and the date of my return is a matter altogether doubtful. I am quite indifferent when the last four volumes are to be published, but if they are to be published at all, they will have to get clear of *me* before July 1.

I did not mean to convey the idea that the MS. is incomplete. On the contrary, it is quite ready, and nothing but the General Index remains to be done. This Index I must do, chapter by chapter, as the printers complete the last volumes. I am for that reason anxious not to be caught at the last moment with half the Index undone. It would be awkward to correct proofsheets at Kashgar[1] or Tahiti.

The six earlier chapters are coming out fairly well for length; at least, within twentyfive pages on the average. In a week or two more, I shall be able to form an opinion about the whole.

The vols iii & iv arrived safely. Thanks for the trouble you have taken. If I want more copies I will ask for them.

Yrs truly   Henry Adams

MS: ViU
1. Kashgar, in Chinese Turkestan. HA still hoped to travel in central Asia.

To Lucy Baxter

1603 H Street. 16 Feb. 1890

Dear Miss Baxter

Sure enough,—now I see it,—this is the sixteenth, and I am fiftytwo years today;—the age which John Hay has discovered, on the authority of Balzac, to be that when the man's charms are most fascinating.[1] Mrs Lodge is greatly pleased by this discovery, as she has numerous admirers of that period; but I think Mr Blaine, her truest adorer, would like to have the time extended, as he passed sixty a few days ago. You need not be surprised to see me yet in the closest intimacy with Mr Blaine, for my only intimate friends—Hay, Mrs Cameron and Mrs Lodge—are also Blaine's nearest intimates, and he is liable at any moment to be brought in very close contact with me. Naturally I don't mind, if he can stand it, but it is droll. The terrific shocks society has had here this winter have pretty well stopped gaiety, so that only intimacies remain, and as my society is nothing if not intimate, I am about as gay as anyone, especially as I knew neither the Blaines nor the Tracys, whose troubles have been the chief cause of gloom.[2] The breakfast table is barren of beauties, but only because the beauties are as scarce as snow and ice this winter.

Dwight worries me a good deal. His depression is as bad as last summer, and is accompanied by symptoms that alarm him as well as me. I ought to make him take advice and adopt a regimen, but when people fall into that state they are unmanageable; and I prefer to reserve for emergencies such influence as I have. He will probably go off to Auburn soon, and thence to

Boston. The journey will do him good, and then he will relapse unless he makes a sensible effort. Probably his trouble will be chronic. I am at a loss to prevent it.

Mrs Hay and the children have at length come, and add to our numbers. My nieces are numerous. Constance Lodge, Helen Hay and a Potter girl breakfasted with me yesterday, and chattered about school and playmates as naturally as their elders about Congress and Cabinet. The small boys are all in love with the small girls, and very funny to us elders, who conspire with them against their parents. My own attachment remains Martha, who is very gracious, and good fun. Did I tell you her definition of a Dobbit, "some one who amuses little girls when their mothers are busy"? She comes almost every day to see Dobbit, and Dobbit goes every day to take tea with her. This is my regular society. For the first time, I have been able to ride regularly through this winter; so my days are uniform and occupied.

The Luce's dined with me last Friday. I had Rockhill, the Thibetan traveller, to meet them, and we talked a little Gobi.[3] Was not La Farge's first paper charmingly done? Such a compliment as he pays me towards the end, is worth all the newspaper compliments I ever hungered for in days when newspapers represented immortality.[4] I wrote him that I thought it the most charming thing I could conceive as a compliment, except that I could see no relation between it and its object. I am really pleased that you liked,—or at least thought my present to Brooks characteristic of La Farge. I feared it would seem "frivolous and insufficient," as the jurors of a salon once declared his pictures.

The last concert disappointed and bored me. I hope you still enjoy them. I shall send you Vols. iii & iv when the binder gets them done. You should come to visit me, and enjoy this divine winter when the sky is cloudless with a rim of purple mist.

Ever Yrs   Henry Adams.

MS: ScU

1. Balzac was 51 when he finally persuaded the Countess Hanska to marry him; he died a few months later.

2. The Blaines' son Walker died Jan. 15, and their daughter Alice Blaine Coppinger died Feb. 2. Navy Secretary Benjamin Franklin Tracy's wife and daughter died in a fire in their house Feb. 3.

3. William Woodville Rockhill (1854–1914), with the U.S. legation in Peking 1884–1888, headed an exploring mission to Mongolia and Tibet for the Smithsonian Institution 1888–1889.

4. La Farge attributed his impulse to write about the architectural monuments of Japan to "the talk of my companion . . . for A——'s historic sense amounts to poetry, and his deductions and remarks always set my mind sailing into new channels" ("An Artist's Letters from Japan," *Century* 39 [Feb.], 491).

To Theodore F. Dwight

1603 H Street. 28 Feb. 1890

Dear Dwight

The enclosed is all that has come for you.

Things move smoothly and rapidly here. Friends drop in every evening, and last night I had Slidell Rodgers to dinner and began our match by beating him three straight games.[1]

I am very anxious to hear that you are feeling right. I cannot believe that the trouble is beyond easy and quick treatment. These clouds vanish as quickly as they come, and some day you will wake up right. Most men and women have had the experience.

I am treating Possum as well as I can for his maladies; but he too rebels against it, and causes needless delays. The doctor has restored his meat diet.

Ever Yrs   Henry Adams.

Theodore F. Dwight Esq.

MS: MHi

1. Thomas Slidell Rodgers (1858–1931), naval officer.

To Henry Holt

1603 H Street. 5 March, 1890

Dear Holt

Thanks! I am concerned only in the larger volume called "Chapters of Erie," but I guess my brother Charles feels as I do about it, so you might as well melt up the plates of both. Credit me with whatever is proper, and send me a bill of sale. I will pay the balance by check.

Perhaps I would do well to take a few of the "Chapters of Erie" myself. I have now no copy of my own essays in that volume. You might send me half a dozen copies in place of royalty.

With the year 1890 I shall retire from authorship. As an occupation I can recommend it to the rich. It has cost me about a hundred thousand dollars, I calculate, in twenty years, and has given me that amount of amusement. In July I sail from San Francisco for new scenes and adventures, leaving to younger and better men whatever promotion my vacancy may cause in the service. I hope they will enjoy it as much as I have done.

Ever Yrs   Henry Adams.

Henry Holt Esq.

MS: NjP

To Frederic Bancroft

1603 H Street. Thursday. [6 March 1890]

Dear Sir[1]

I return Broke and all the other books I have from the library.[2]

Can you oblige me by trusting the bearer with the following volumes if the library contains them:

The volume of Maps and Plans belonging to the Memoirs of James Wilkinson. (Phila. 1816.)

Vol. ii of "Guerres Maritimes" by Jurien de la Gravière.

Yrs truly   Henry Adams.

Mr Bancroft.

MS: NNC

1. Frederic Bancroft (1860–1945), historian and economist, chief of the bureau of rolls and library in the State Department 1888–1892.

2. *Admiral Sir P.B.V. Broke* (1866), a memoir including his journal and letters compiled by Rev. J. G. Brighton. Broke (1776–1841) was famous for his capture of the American frigate *Chesapeake* on June 1, 1813.

To Theodore F. Dwight

1603 H Street. 6 March, 1890

Dear Dwight

Yours of March 3 finds me in full winter. We are all frost and snow. I hope you find it does you good.

My friends rally faithfully to amuse me. Cabot Lodge took us to see Henrietta last night:—the Hays, Mrs Cameron and me, and of course sister Anne.[1] Constance comes this evening to play cribbage. Ward Thoron is again on duty, and cannot come here much. I sat an hour with Mr Ward the other day, and found him a good deal broken, but less so than I feared. Unfortunately one knows too well the stages of that decline.

Archy,—or probably Lotty—Hopkins left the Sun notices here, and I glanced over them. The first paragraphs delighted me. I breathed free. If you want to see solid butter laid on with a shovel, read the "Tribune" notice of Sunday, February 23, which Lotty enclosed with Hazeltine's.[2] I must speak more civilly of newspapers if they insist on treating me in that style. Mr Ward chaffed me about something Howells has said. I wish he (H.) would stop his style of complacency.[3]

Ever Yrs   Henry Adams.

MS: MHi

1. *The Henrietta* (1887), a comedy by Bronson Howard. "Sister Anne" is Anna Cabot Mills Davis Lodge (Mrs. Henry Cabot Lodge), sister-in-law as a result of BA's marriage to her sister Evelyn Davis.

2. Mayo Williamson Hazeltine (1841–1909) of Boston, literary editor of the New York *Sun,* dwelt on HA's impartiality. The treatment of Jefferson had in it "no trace of controversial purpose, no vestige of eulogistic legend or of traditional detraction" (Feb. 23). The New York *Tribune:* "The volumes here reviewed are, if possible, still more interesting than the former ones, and it would be difficult to speak too highly of the work as a whole" (Feb. 23).

3. Howells, in "The Editor's Study," *Harper's* 80 (March 1890), 646, wrote: "Mr. Henry Adams has just given us two volumes of American history which are not less important than any ever written."

To Charles Scribner

1603 H Street. 6 March, 1890

Dear Sir

Will you be so kind as to direct the proper person to return to me the volume of maps known as Aitkinson's, and intended for copying for the battle of Lundy's Lane. I am not satisfied with them, and will furnish better, but I want them for comparison.

Yrs truly   Henry Adams.

Charles Scribner Esq.

MS: ViU

To Charles Scribner

1603 H Street. 7 March, 1890

Dear Sir

Wilson reports that Chap. xvi will end on the p. 415. If that is the case the whole narrative will fill 1053 printed pages. The Index will certainly exceed one hundred pages. The plans and charts will bring the whole work to twelve hundred pages.

This seems to settle the matter. Volumes of six hundred pages would be a mistake. I have therefore written to Wilson to begin Volume ii with Chapter xvii.

Yrs truly   Henry Adams.

MS: ViU

To Lucy Baxter

1603 H Street. 10 March, 1890.

My dear Friend

I should have written yesterday, but La Farge was here, and my draughtsman came, and Martha and her mother followed, and I was taken for my Sunday walk to the garden, and in the afternoon to see a bric-à-brac gallery in Georgetown, so that I had not a moment's time; and now scribble a line only to say that I send you today the two last volumes, iii & iv, not so gorgeous as the other two, but still better dressed than their deserts warrant. I consider these four volumes as containing all I have to say. The remaining four or five are mere pandering to popularity and love of empty sound. When they appear, I shall be very far away, and shall not be able to send you the rest; so you will not have an edition all to yourself as now. Instead, I will send you sonnets from Tahiti.

Has Dwight been to see you? I hope he will recover his spirits in the coldness and rawness of the north, but this winter has been very discouraging. As for me, I am the lark, and sing and sing and sing,—you know how gaily. This is my primrose time. My breakfast table is the haunt of all the most charming women going, among whom I sit, a solitary man, and smile like the God Pasht. Today Rebecca Rae, Mrs Teddy Roosevelt, Mary Leiter, and I hope Mrs Cameron and Mrs Lodge will come to cheer me with their stores of wisdom and learning. I go to New York tomorrow with Hay for two days. We have a big Bohemian dinner at the Knickerbocker.

With love ever Yrs   Henry Adams.

I wish you could come on here with the children in April.

MS: ScU

To William W. Rockhill

1603 H Street. 11 March, 1890

My dear Sir

I received the book which interested me much, and the accidental presence of H. Shugio helped me to understand a little of it.[1] I am anxious to understand more, and to have your help. I go to New York today, but return tomorrow. Could you and Mrs Rockhill dine quietly here on Friday, and give me a Chinese education?[2]

Yrs truly   Henry Adams.

W. W. Rockhill Esq.

229

MS: MH
1. W. W. Rockhill, *Life of Buddha* (1884).
2. Mrs. Rockhill (d. 1898) was the former Caroline Adams of Philadelphia.

To Sir Robert Cunliffe

1603 H Street. 16 March, 1890.

Dear Robert

Thanks for the "Avon" report. You are a duck. The fool who comes after me will find small gleanings.[1]

I have not sent my book to England for reasons obvious enough. Frankness of speech is doubtless a good thing, but I cannot think better of any man for going out of his way to call his friends' attention to what cannot be pleasant to them. So the book, as far as I control it, remains on this side the water. Four volumes are now out, about equal to four volumes of Froude. Five volumes more are to come. Hay and I are racing, and carry about the same weight. Between us we have pretty well disposed of the History of the United States. Another generation will have other methods and objects, but I hear of no one among our contemporaries who proposes to jostle us from our seats.

I am anxious to hear about Neville.[2] Drop me a line when you receive this. Here in this warm latitude, the grippe has been common, but not serious except to a few delicate persons. I have escaped anything beyond ordinary colds. A day or two in bed has been the usual penalty.

The Morpeth youth has not yet appeared. When he does, I will offer him whatever Aladdin can get here.[3]

Yrs ever   Henry Adams.

MS: MHi
1. The British sloop-of-war *Avon* was sunk by the American *Wasp,* Sept. 1, 1814; the report of Capt. James Arbuthnot is cited in HA, *History,* VIII, 189–190.
2. Robert Neville Cunliffe (1884–1949), Cunliffe's second son and later 7th baronet.
3. Charles James Stanley Howard (1867–1912), Viscount Morpeth, later 10th earl of Carlisle.

To Theodore F. Dwight

1603 H Street. Sunday, 16 March 1890.

Dear Dwight

I have consulted Mrs Hay on the quartette scheme, and she approves; so you can inquire of Adamowski the terms, and if they do not exceed a hundred dollars, engage him and his quartette for Saturday night next. He will prefer Hay's house, I suppose, though he can use mine if he likes; but in any case the audience will not exceed a dozen or two.

Charles is here. I have a Schnupfen[1] and feel very spongy. The day is cold, windy and the worst of March. I have not even energy to index. I hope the month suits you better than me.

Ever Yrs   Henry Adams.

Please pay this little bill for me and set it down.

MS: MHi
1. *Schnupfen:* Ger., head cold.

To Theodore F. Dwight

1603 H Street. Friday, 21st [March 1890]

Dear Dwight

The enclosed has just come in.

Stoddard brought the Bishop to breakfast today.[1] We had a most edifying talk, calculated to upset the intellectual vibrations of the breakfast table.

Tonight we concert. Mendelssohn, Wagner and Beethoven are to be our resources.

Tomorrow I expect to go to Quantico with Willy Phillips.[2]

I hear of no news, except that McNutt goes to Constantinople as Sec. Leg. Already wild rumor says that Miss Tuckerman goes with him, but I have no trust in rumors.

Ever Yrs   Henry Adams.

MS: MHi
1. Charles Warren Stoddard (1843–1909), lecturer at Catholic University of America 1889–1902, wrote several travel books, including *South-Sea Idyls* (1873). John Joseph Keane (1839–1918), previously Roman Catholic bishop of Richmond, was rector of the university.
2. The Quantico Club (hunting and fishing) on Chapawamsic Island off Quantico, Va.

To Lucy Baxter

1603 H Street. Tuesday, 25 March 1890

My dear Miss Baxter

I went down the river for Sunday to inspect a new club I have joined, which stopped my usual Sunday letter-writing. Before I forget it, I wish you would look at the backs of the volumes I sent you, and see if Vol. i matches

Vol. ii precisely; and if Vol. iii matches Vol. iv. If not, please send them all back to me, and I will try to get them straight. I find I have mixed the sets, and those that remain are not matches.

Spring comes on apace, and all one's families and friends are coming here at once. The first half of April seems to be the time for everyone to descend on us. The Washingtonians are skurrying about, trying to make up parties for the amusement of visitors, and in consternation because all their friends write to announce immediate arrival. Daisy comes next Saturday to the Lodges. The children come the next week to me. Mrs Cameron's house is packed to the attic. Society consists in hunting for people to amuse guests.

One cannot complain of solitude at this season, for even I, who go nowhere and know nobody, found myself last week unable to escape engagements. They were chiefly concert and theatre parties with my only partners, Mrs Cameron and Mrs Lodge; but the principle is the same.

Your niece's fate seemed to me last summer an impending one; but marriage was so obviously the outcome of her position that you need hardly worry about her chances of happiness. The charm of women is the Hegelian charm of the identity of opposites. You can assume nothing regarding them, without assuming the contrary to be equally true. You all abominate second marriages, yet you all conspire to bring them about. I receive admonitions constantly on the subject, and am aware that my friends take an active interest in selecting a victim to sacrifice to my selfishness. I do not care to interfere with their search. My only precaution is to show a pronounced attachment to married women, so as to preclude any attachment that could cause a rumor of other ties. It would be useless and impossible to argue the matter, or to give reasons for preferring solitude seul to solitude à deux; but the reasons are sufficiently strong, and if I ever should act in a contrary sense, it would be because I should have begun to lose my will, and was in the first stages of imbecility. Just now my only wish is to escape from the dangers that remain in life with the least possible noise and suffering. I have had all I want, and the best. What folly you would think it for a man who had once been a King, to go on trying to be King after he had been deposed and lost his energies and illusions. The best he can do is, like Charles the Fifth, to make clocks.[1]

All the same, no amount of Stoicism can prevent one from hankering, not for the future but for the past; and even Faust, after his famous curse,—"Werd' ich zum Augenblicke sagen"—became so imbecile as to find satisfaction in building a Dutch dyke. I dread the decline of powers, and wish the moment were past when I could still say to the passing moment—Verweile doch, du bist so schön![2] I will try it on Fiji and Gobi.

Ever Ys   Henry Adams

MS: ScU

1. As recounted in W. Stirling Maxwell, *The Cloister Life of the Emperor Charles the Fifth* (1852).

2. "Werd ich zum Augenblicke sagen: / Verweile doch! Du bist so schön! / Dann

magst du mich in Fesseln schlagen, / Dann will ich gern Zugrunde gehn!" (Should I to the passing moment say Stay! You are so fair! Then you may in fetters bind me, Then will I gladly go to destruction.) Faust to Mephistopheles; Goethe, *Faust,* Part I.

To Theodore F. Dwight

1603 H Street. 27 March, 1890

Dear Dwight

A small package addressed to F. A. Burlingame, Morristown, N.J., with the Morristown struck out, and Washington written in, has been left here by post, with your card loose on the outside, and an inscription "For my dear Fred," &c. What shall I do with it? I presume the bringing it here is a stupidity of the Post Office.

I can't say that I have any new excitement to offer here. I index industriously, and wait for proof sheets that rarely come. Index-making is work really fitted for me. I find it much more satisfying than composition, and see a future open for usefulness there. I will help you to index the whole Quincy library at the rate of thirty pages per diem.

I went with Phillips to Quantico last Saturday, and took possession of my new club. It is quite a fascinating spot somewhere in the last century.

The Fergusons are expected today.[1] I am to dine with them at the Roosevelts Saturday,—my solitary feast, though I rarely dine alone.

Ever Yrs   Henry Adams.

MS: MHi
1. Emma Mandeville Munro-Ferguson (d. 1918), widow of Col. Robert Munro-Ferguson of Raith, Fife. Her son Robert (d. 1922) was a friend of the Roosevelts, as was his elder brother Ronald Craufurd Munro-Ferguson, who had not come with them.

To Charles Scribner

1603 H Street. 27 March, 1890

Dear Sir

I enclose drawings for the battle of the "Thames," "Chippawa," "Lundy's Lane" (2) and the "Chesapeake and Shannon." These are intended to be ready for immediate transfer to the plates.

I presume the "Chesapeake and Shannon,"—which is not to be reduced, but is to fill precisely the same space in the text—should be done at once, and the plate inserted by Wilson, in its place.

I shall be glad to finish the other plates, and above all to know what are now in hand. If I recollect right, besides the material now sent, or previously forwarded, I shall have about six more plates to provide.

Yrs truly   Henry Adams.

Charles Scribner Esq.

MS: ViU

To Lucy Baxter

1603 H Street. Sunday 13 April 1890.

My dear Miss Baxter

At this time of the year Washington is always overrun by visitors, and has hardly time to think. The children have been with me this last week, and are still here. Daisy made a flying visit. I expect W. A. Butler, the portrait painter, tomorrow, to paint Martha.[1] All my friends are equally busy. Two English boys, a young Lord Morpeth and his friend Jones have brought letters; and a family of Scotch Fergusons have lived for a fortnight at the Cameron's. Of course time has been rather a race, and my letters have remained unanswered.

The volumes were sent back to you at once. Thanks for your trouble in sending them to me. I think I told you that the rest of the History will make five volumes,—nine in all—and will not appear till autumn, when I expect to be away. So I shall not be able to print a ladies' edition of these. Dwight will see that you have the regular trade set.

Time runs on, horribly fast, though it carries with it pretty much all the rubbish that needs floating. The next six weeks ought to clear away the last objects of concern to me, and by June I expect to see the universe open like an umbrella to cover my steps. As luck will have it, Washington is peculiarly pleasant and sympathetic as I quit it. Our little set of Hays, Camerons, Lodges and Roosevelts, never were so intimate or friendly as now, and for the first time in my life I find myself among a set of friends so closely connected as to see each other every day, and even two or three times a day, yet surrounded by so many outside influences and pressures that they are never stagnant or dull. I am glad to close up my literary existence so cheerily. In Washington nothing lasts; and one should, like a man-of-the-world, bid good-night before the other guests are gone and the hosts are tired.

You tell me nothing of your own circumstances. On the whole, has your winter's experience been worse or better than you expected? I have been trying to get Edward Hooper to take his children abroad for three months this summer; and to overcome his resistance I have intrigued with Looly and Polly to get him to ask you to go with them, on the idea that Miss Hovey would be glad to give you a chance for a little run abroad. As yet I can't overcome Edward's reluctance to face the possibilities of sickness or accident, especially for Ellen. I think the journey more likely to do Ellen good, but of course the risks are great. Edward must have some lady to look after the girls, and see that they are properly protected; and I know no one whom I should so much like them to associate with as you. But I fear it is a failure, at least for this summer. You see I don't hesitate to expect you to undertake the burden, if called upon. As a matter of duty it is much more compulsory than any of your recent undertakings, and as an occupation it would be infinitely more amusing, at least for a summer vacation.

Things never go as I like unless I drive alone.

Ever Yrs   Henry Adams.

MS: ScU
1. HA meant George Bernard Butler (1838–1907), a New York artist recommended by La Farge.

To Charles Milnes Gaskell

1603 H Street. 13 April, 1890.

Dear Carlo

A letter just received from Robert tells me of your sister's death.[1] So long a time has passed since I last wrote to Frank Palgrave that I hesitate to write now and reopen relations which he, in his larger society, must have forgotten; but at your first opportunity I wish you would mention to Palgrave that I sympathize earnestly with him, and that I am as grateful as ever both to him and to her for all the kindness they showed me in old days.

To you I need say little, for I can easily conceive that your sister's death should be not only a severe loss, but possibly an increase of care and anxieties. I have lived so much in an atmosphere of constant loss and distress for some years past, that I understand better than I once did what is meant by trouble, and I feel less and less inclined to dwell upon it or palliate it. You will have to take it as it comes, and if there is any means of alleviating it, I have not discovered the prescription.

Robert too is evidently in trouble about his wife. I have watched her complaint with anxiety for some time. He has also written to me, from time to time, about Mrs Gerald.[2] I am afraid you have both had a hard year thus far.

In anticipation of a long absence, I have gone through all my papers lately, and destroyed everything that I should have wished an executor to destroy. Among the rest I have saved a large bundle of your letters, going back five-and-twenty years. I have not had the courage to read them over, but I thought you might like to have them, either to preserve or to destroy, and I shall give them to some traveller, perhaps to my brother Brooks, to take to you.[3]

I have not sent you my history for the reason that I do not think it a pleasant book for English reading, and do not care to send my old friends anything that could annoy them. In case you should hear it spoken ill of, you can always plead ignorance, and if you hear it spoken well of, you can smile acquiescence. Half of it is now out. The rest will follow in the autumn.

By that time I expect to be a pirate in the South Seas. In thus imitating Robert Louis Stephenson I am inspired by no wish for fame or future literary or political notoriety, or even by motives of health, but merely by a longing to try something new and different.[4] Civilisation becomes an intolerable bore at moments, and I never could abide an eternity of hares and rabbits, Ireland, or protective duties. As the English-speaking world seems content to busy itself with these practical pursuits, I mean to take a vacation; but I know not where or how long. Anything may happen,—even my reappearance in Europe. So keep up your spirits,—unless you will join me at Kashgar.

Ever Yrs   Henry Adams.

MS: MHi
1. Cecil Gaskell Palgrave died March 27.
2. Anna Baldwin Gaskell, wife of Gaskell's younger brother.
3. Gaskell replied on May 8: "I shall feel deeply the sight of all my old letters, the record of old times, and past pleasures. I have as you know all yours, and value them deeply."
4. Robert Louis Stevenson (1850–1894) settled in Samoa in 1889.

To Theodore F. Dwight

1603 H Street. Friday, 18th

Dear Dwight

You can close with Adamowski for the programme as offered, and fix the day to suit him. If he plays with the Choral Society, May 1 or any other day, I think he had chose that day. If he plays for us on April 30, and afterwards at the concert, we shall have rather too much of it for one pull. We should not go to the Choral Society, but we should to the concert.

I rather prefer an early hour, say two or half past two, when we are fresh; but I leave it to better judgment.

I presume of course Hay's house is the best.

You can tell Adamowski that there are only six people in Washington who listen to music. We will try and have them all to hear him.

Yrs ever   Henry Adams.

Please pay the enclosed for me.

MS: MHi

To Joseph Wheeler

1603 H Street. April 24, 1890

Dear Sir[1]

I have to thank you for your obliging communication of yesterday.

The volume containing the subject of Hull's Surrender has been already for some time finished and stereotyped, and waits only the publisher's convenience in making its appearance. As it is beyond my reach I can only hope that it may not differ essentially from your views. Persons who undertake the impossible task of writing history know how far from satisfactory their stories are, even to themselves, and in such a matter as the allotment of responsibility for a campaign they ought to be particularly cautious; but in Hull's case one can hardly escape the conviction that the Court Martial should have censured others as well as him.

I have to apologise for not seeing you when you called. Owing to peculiar circumstances I am at present much secluded.

I am yours truly   Henry Adams.

Hon. Joseph Wheeler.

MS: A-Ar
1. Joseph Wheeler (1836–1906) of Alabama, Confederate major general, military historian, Democratic representative except for intervals 1881–1890. General Hull's grandchildren, wishing HA not to accept the court-martial verdict that the surrender of Detroit was an act of cowardice, asked Wheeler to find out on their behalf what HA intended.

To Charles Scribner

1603 H Street. 3 May, 1890.

Dear Sir

I have already made the necessary corrections in Vols. i & ii.

A few small corrections should be made in iii & iv before another impression is taken. I presume you do not require more of Vols. iii & iv at present. I intend to send Wilson all my final corrections and changes on June 1, when printing (except the General Index) will be finished.

As time is becoming short, and after July 1 no communications will probably reach me for an indefinite time, I think the plans and charts should be hurried. I write separately on this subject.

Do you wish me to send you proofs of the volume of "Historical Essays"?[1] I have not yet received Wilson's bill for the composition, and you are at liberty to print the volume as your own or as mine, as you may decide.

Yrs truly   Henry Adams.

Charles Scribner's Sons.

MS: ViU

1. *Historical Essays* (1891) consists of nine essays, of which two were previously unpublished: "The Declaration of Paris, 1861"; and "Primitive Rights of Women," the revised text of a lecture at the Lowell Institute in Boston, Dec. 9, 1876.

To Charles Scribner

1603 H Street. 3 May, 1890

Dear Sir

I return one sheet of the Lundy's Lane maps for your consideration.

In supplying the maps in the form I did, I saved myself a little expense by causing only a fly-sketch to be drawn of the second battle, which was to be superimposed on the first, in the engraving. The engravers have sent me an engraving of the flysketch as a separate work. I intended two complete plans of the whole ground.

To me the separate small "10 o'clock plan" looks a little as though our money had given out, and we were economising on margins. I should rather prefer to make the eighth volume, in which these plans occur, an object of special expense. Fifteen or twenty maps are a moderate number, and I think you probably intended them to be as complete as possible. Indeed they are so nice and attractive as they stand, that I take it for granted you mean them to be an ornament, as well as an aid to the reader.

I intend to furnish also two similar maps of the Battle of Plattsburg and two of the Bladensburg campaign; probably one of Baltimore and one of Norfolk, these two last, single page maps.

I wish therefore to withdraw from the engraver the plan No. 10 (according to your list) of Gen. Ross's route or March of the British army. I will shortly send a better one.

There will then remain, I think, ten maps or plans in your office, to be completed. As these are my last care, I should be very glad to get them in shape. Would it be possible to provide the proofs by June 1?

If you wish to lessen the number of maps, I will do so. Two or three might be omitted without serious loss; but as they are historical maps, as essential as the text, I think on the whole the book would be the better if the maps were retained and the text omitted.

In regard to the battle of New Orleans I have been profuse of maps. This course is not due to the importance of the battle, which was really of little importance, military or political; but for some reason, probably sectional, the Battle of New Orleans has always held an undue place in popular interest. I regard any concession to popular illusions as a blemish; but just as I abandoned so large a space to Burr—a mere Jeremy Diddler[1]—because the public felt an undue interest in him, so I think it best to give the public a full dose of General Jackson.

On all these points I will defer to your opinion, but in any case I must manage to finish everything before July.

Very truly Yrs Henry Adams.

MS: ViU
 1. The character in James Kenney's farce *Raising the Wind* (1803) whose sponging and swindling gave the verb "to diddle" a new meaning.

To Charles Scribner

1603 H Street. 7 May, 1890.

My dear Sir

Of course in regard to rejected plates, wherever the extra expense is due to me, it should be charged to me. This rule should be followed if only to leave me free from *gêne* on that score. I may wish to reject any number, if I can do better; and as my only object is to obtain the utmost degree of interest and value for the book, without regard to cost, I should hardly feel at ease if I were restrained by the idea of imposing on you.

I will send the sheets of the "Historical Essays."

The printers have reached Vol. ix. The two last volumes, viii and ix, will not vary greatly from four hundred pages each, unless the general index should prove longer or shorter than I anticipate.

Yrs truly Henry Adams.

Messrs Charles Scribner's Sons.

MS: ViU

To Lucy Baxter

1603 H Street. 11 May, 1890.

My dear Miss Baxter

Since you wrote, Dwight has returned. We have had our Adamowski quartette at Hay's, and summer has fairly begun. All but the last half dozen chapters of the history are in type. Within six weeks, Scribner will have on his hands six unpublished volumes of mine, besides the four that are out. After such scandalous and profligate prodigality as that, nothing remains for me to do, but to fly the country. Better the cannibals should eat me than die of contempt at home.

Also, on June 7, the Hooper children sail for Europe. This sudden determination was announced to me only yesterday, and seems due to the Thornton Lothrops who are really taking Edward Hooper over in spite of himself.[1] I am glad for the children's sake, and a little for my own that I am not responsible; although I would have taken any responsibility necessary for the purpose.

I am glad that you are at last resigned to letting your niece be happy if she wants to be. True, marriage is a very dreadful sacrifice, and women must resign themselves to be neglected, despised, nagged, beaten with sticks, and at times tortured with thumbscrews and hot pepper. We all know that every woman repents marriage, and that they mostly wish their husbands and children were dead, or suffering life-sentences in the state's-prison for their cruelty to Women with a capital W. Still, with all this notorious, there is probably some temporary and fitful pleasure, as in alcohol and cream-soda, in the vice of marriage; and you show true philosophy in treating your niece mildly. Don't beat her, as Punch says: Sit on her head!

My young women here are now all married and settled. I have no longer one left to my breakfast-table, except Mary Victoria Leiter, and she has gone to Europe, like all other vertebrates. The Lodges and Hays have been in New York. Mrs Cameron has fallen and hurt herself so as to have been on her back the last ten days; and Martha has become a big, obstreperous girl, beyond my powers of amusing or being amused. Children are an illusion of the senses. They last in their perfection only a few months, and then, like roses, run to shoots and briars.

Dwight seems well again, and will, I hope, know how to manage himself the next time, although the liver is an awkward vice to manage. I suppose Brooks and Daisy are now established in my house at Beverly. As Brooks will of course think himself maltreated by me, because the house is not built of barley-sugar and ginger-bread, or some such sufficient ground of offense, I prefer to ask no questions and show no interest. About you I can be allowed to express the wish to know how you are coming forward. Gloucester may not be gay at this season; but before autumn I expect you to be much attached to it. In a hot summer no better place exists in America; only you must drive yourself in a phaeton, and row yourself in a boat. Tell Miss Hovey this, with my regards.

Ever Yrs   Henry Adams.

MS: ScU
1. MHA's cousin Anne Hooper Lothrop (1835–1930), daughter of Samuel Hooper, and her husband, Thornton Kirkland Lothrop (1830–1913), Boston lawyer.

To Joseph Wheeler

1603 H Street. 13 May, 1890

Dear Sir

In obedience to your request I send you herewith all the sheets I can recall to mind, which contain allusions to William Hull.

As this happens to be my only copy, and the sheets are apt to be required for reference in constructing the index which is now in hand, I shall be glad if you find that long detention is unnecessary.

I am very truly Yrs   Henry Adams.

Hon. Joseph Wheeler

MS: A-Ar

To Lucy Baxter

1603 H Street. 26 May, 1890.

My dear Miss Baxter

I expect to be in Boston from the 5th to the 7th of June to see the children off. Shall you be there, or shall you have flitted to some seaside spot? My own time has been much devoted to quartering my friends for the summer. Daisy and Brooks were quickly tucked away; but the children were a longer job. Now that they are settled, I am trying to get the British minister into Jeff. Coolidge's house at Manchester.[1] I made also an effort to get Mrs Hay and her children to pass the summer at the Glades, and let John go off with me; but she has other views. Finally I am much exercised about Mrs Cameron whom Brooks has turned out of her house. Hooper has lent the Gurney house, and so for the first time in history I have no house to lend. I feel bound to look out for Mrs Cameron more than anyone else, and am puzzled to provide more houses, especially as she declined Coolidge's.

As soon as all these things are settled, I shall take the train to San Francisco, say about July 8th or 10th to sail for the Sandwich Islands July 18, and there take, on August 2, the steamer to Samoa. I expect to reach Fiji in September, and shall pause there to consider further movements. Having no plans beyond these, I ask myself no questions.

As I hope to see you next week, I will cut off here. You had better go over with me to see the children off, if you should be still in town.

Ever Yrs   Henry Adams.

MS: ScU
1. Thomas Jefferson Coolidge (1831–1920), Boston merchant and diplomat.

To Lucy Baxter

1603 H Street. Thursday 29 May 1890

My dear Miss Baxter

I take Constance Lodge to Boston next week, arriving Tuesday night. The children sail, I believe, on Saturday, in the steamer that leaves East Boston at 12.30 P.M. If you can slip away for a morning, and come up to the office at about eleven, we will drive over, and see them off.

I shall return to New York by the next train Saturday afternoon.

I shall still try to get Mrs Cameron to take the Gurney house. I hope the quarters you have chosen will suit, for they are certainly for you the pleasantest possible. Please be civil to Lady Jane Gray who will be in Dr Hooper's old house below you. I have never called on her, which is of course fatal; but you need not speak of me.[1]

A line sent to me at the family office 23 Court Street (Room No. I forget what 621 Dwight thinks) will always catch me sooner or later.

La Farge is with me. I've half an idea that he means to suggest going to Fiji with me. He and I might wander far and get nowhere.

Ever affectionately   Henry Adams.

MS: ScU
1. Jane Matthews Gray, wife of Justice Horace Gray.

To William W. Rockhill

1603 H Street. Thursday. [29 May 1890]

My dear Mr Rockhill

A rumor reaches me that you and Mrs Rockhill are going abroad for years. I hope before you go, you will come to discuss your plans.[1] I sail for Samoa, July 18, from San Francisco. My movements are uncertain, and I know only so far ahead. In time I expect to get round to Pekin, but I know not when or how.

Could not you and Mrs Rockhill dine with me Saturday or Sunday? La Farge is here. Perhaps you would like to meet him.

I return you the books, with many thanks. I think they are all I have of your property.

Yrs truly   Henry Adams.

W. W. Rockhill Esq.

MS: MH
1. Rockhill was planning his expedition of 1890–91 to Tibet and Mongolia.

To W. C. Brownell

1603 H Street. 15 June, 1890.

Dear Mr Brownell[1]

I return more map-proofs, and the three last maps (including the cancelled one of the Bladensburg campaign) to be reproduced.

I hope you will be able to send proofs of these by July 1, for I shall be getting then short of time.

Can you send me a list of all the maps at last, so that I may mark where they are to be inserted.

Yrs truly   Henry Adams.

MS: ViU
1. William Crary Brownell (1851–1928), editor at Scribner's and literary critic.

To W. C. Brownell

1603 H Street. 17 June, 1890.

My dear Mr. Brownell

The Bladensburg map seems to me hardly up to our standard. Finding that the engravers did not mechanically repeat the lines, I allowed my draughtsman to draw his details roughly. Just as I did this, the engraver began a mechanical process. The consequence is that what I meant for the best map is the worst. Can't the engraver make the maps match, at least in this case?

Yrs truly   Henry Adams.

MS: ViU

To Lucy Baxter

1603 H Street. 22 June, 1890.

Dear Miss Baxter

Time wanes fast, and I feel the stress of the coming change in many ways, but in none so much as in parting from the group of friends who have so coddled and spoiled me for the last five years. If the subtlest forms of flattery could stir the embers of a defunct self-love, I should become as fatuous as an owl; but I can imagine that a man about to commit suicide should be passably indifferent to the whispers of his vanity; and I who am about to put an end to what is left of all the life I ever cared for, am in no immediate danger of overweening self-esteem, no matter what amount of kindness I receive. So I take your words in the same spirit with which I take poor Dwight's and Hay's and King's protests of opinion about my poor old book, grateful for the affection they show, but sympathising deeply in the sad intellectual wreck they indicate in the minds of the kindly but deluded beings whom I call friends. I wish when Browning wrote "Waring," he had gone on to tell Waring's side of the story; then I might have been spared the impossibility of explaining how a man feels who knows that he can give nothing—that he is bankrupt and a fugitive—when his friends imagine him to be rich. All I am rich in is your and the others' goodwill, and I am far more interested in knowing that you in time are to reach some pleasant harbor where all the tangled navigation of life will end in port and peace, than I am in knowing whether my own destiny will lead me to delegate my own indigestion of life to the cannibal that eats me. Please steer straight.

The little cottage on the road below your hill, where the road forks towards the beach, was where I passed the two happiest summers of my life, the constant and haunting memory of which is now driving me to the ends of the earth in the hope of somehow escaping it. I wanted Mrs Cameron to take the cottage this summer, because I am fond of her, and would like to imagine her and Martha giving a sort of life to the rooms in which my imagination still lives so much; but Mrs Cameron will probably, if she goes to Beverly, take the Eliot Cabot's house next you on the hill. Whether she will go at all is matter of much doubt.

Our little group here still hangs on, and has been joined by Adéle Grant—the beauty—who has come here with her mother to break up their former house before going to live in London. We are all together more or less every day, in country parties or expeditions down the river, or at lunches or dinners at my house or elsewhere. Mrs Hay and the children are gone, but Hay stays, and he and I are petted and patted as though we were Dresden figurines of shepherds with blue ribbons and crooks. The life, in this hot, intense atmosphere, seems, with its transient flashes of lightning and its daily thunder-gusts, to be about as unreal as that of Tahiti could be, and is probably in fact far more entertaining; but it must end in a few days, and, like everything in Washington, it must then end for ever. Washington never repeats itself.

Dwight is tolerably well and the dogs are hot. I think all will go north this week. I remain till about July 10 either here or in New York.

Ever affly Yrs   Henry Adams.

MS: ScU

To Theodore F. Dwight

[Late June 1890]

Regular Payments
for H.A.

———

On the first day of every month
send to William Gray $50.
    ” ” Maggy Wade   33.
    ” ” John Brent   40.
N.B. Their wages are $35 and $18 respectively, and each receives $15 for board. Brent gets only $5.00 a month for board, and in November will go wholly into Hay's service.
On the 27th day of every month, (after Brooks goes on Sept. 1) send check to W. H. Blanchard, Beverly Farms, for $35.

November 1, send for Washington Tax-bill (perhaps the Collector of Taxes, (Washington, D.C.) will send it to you by mail if you write to him) and pay it by check. Last year it was $827.78
July 1, Water Rents, this year paid $24.00

Every few months, I suppose, a bill will come from C. Powell Noland, Shenandoah, Va. for the horses; $2.50 each per month.

Freeman's bill for taking care of the palms at $10 a month comes in January.

———

Clubs due January 1:
    Knickerbocker $100.
    Metropolitan   50.
    Cosmos   35.
    Philosophical Society   5.
    Quantico   12.
    Anthropological   3.
July 1: Quantico   12.

The American Academy of Arts and Sciences sends bills when it pleases. For a year or two dues have not been collected. Pay as applied for.

———

Twice a year, say Jan. 1 and July 1, send a check for $50 to L. S. Emery, Office of Associated Charities, 707 G. St. Washington, D.C.

———

At all times bills will drop in for repairs or expenses incurred in the Washington and Beverly houses or grounds.

MS: MHi

To W. C. Brownell

1603 H Street. [Late June 1890]

Dear Sir

I fear I shall be obliged to cancel the last map—"Sketch of the Positions,"—as it was meant for a double map, and the scale is too small for the eye. I will write further about it, in a few days. Meanwhile let the matter remain where it is, and no more work be done on that particular map.

Yrs truly   Henry Adams.

MS: ViU

To W. C. Brownell

1603 H Street. 27 June, 1890.

Dear Mr Brownell

I enclose you a List of Maps, &c, to consider whether it should be inserted at the end of Volume IX as a supplement to the General Index. I am not sure whether such a list is needed, or where it should be placed. Perhaps you will take the responsibility of giving Wilson his directions if you decide to insert it. In that case please send it to him with orders to print it, or rather to put it in type in the proper place.

You will notice that my previous list was incomplete, wanting I think the Craney Island.

Yrs truly   Henry Adams.

MS: ViU

To Joseph Wheeler

1603 H Street. 29 June, 1890.

Dear Sir

I have received your's of the 2d and shall give most careful consideration to your suggestions. As yet I cannot be certain of adopting them literally, but I will in any case make some such changes as will tend to soften, if not to remove, the objectionable language.[1]

Unfortunately I cannot find the sheets. Without them I can do nothing, and if they are still in your possession, I should be glad to have them returned, especially as my time is growing short.

Yrs truly   Henry Adams.

MS: A-Ar
1. HA revised "His army became mutinous from disgust at his vacillation and at their own idleness" to "His army lost respect for him in consequence of his failure to attack Malden" (VI, 314). Nevertheless, his statement that Hull "had once been a brave soldier" (VI, 327) conveyed what the general had become by 1812.

To Charles Francis Adams, Jr.

1603 H Street. 3 July, 1890.

Dear Charles

My will was made long ago, and had better remain as it stands. I could add a codicil, but am perplexed to know how to do so without creating a trust which, according to my Law Dictionary is "a right of property held by one party for the benefit of another." In this case there is no other,—no cestui que trust,—and I know not how to create a trust without a beneficiary. If Balch can do it, all right! I am proud to say I am humble, and prepared to accept anything I am told; but the law in that case is holy nonsense—as in others.

Mind! I don't want to learn what the law is. I want only to get the thing straight. If Balch or anyone else will draw up a reciprocal codicil disposing of the income of so much money for so many years after our deaths, with a certainty of the income going to the library, I will sign it.

He must be in a hurry. Owing to an unexpected entreaty from La Farge to take him with me, I shall be delayed two or three weeks, and perhaps a month; but should La Farge write again,—as he will,—abandoning the idea, I shall be off like a shot. In that case you would hear from me next in the South Seas. My return is wholly indefinite.

If George or Charley weren't dormice, one of them would go with me; but I am just as well pleased to go alone; especially as I need consult no one and can dispense with plans. I remember in my youth reading some remarks of Mr Tennyson personally offensive to Time, whom he treated as a maniac scattering dust or slinging stones, or some such disreputable occupation.[1] Time is quite a gentleman, on the contrary, and my society is ample as long as I have him with me to an unlimited extent.

I presume you will also, in company with that companion, some day before long bolt for other worlds. You and I have had our minds fairly soaked with the kerosene of American ideas and interests, until we can neither absorb more, nor even retain what we have. Nausea has set in, and we might as well wash the nasty stuff out of us now, as let it make us sick. Perhaps we may meet in travel. As I know not where I am going, I am as likely to turn up in Europe as in Asia; but whenever the nausea leaves me, I shall come straight home. Between ourselves I should be mighty glad to be certain that one form of nausea would drive away another, and that in six months I should come back fit and good for ten years more work.

Ever Yrs   Henry Adams.

MS: MHi
  1. "And Time, a maniac scattering dust, / And Life, a Fury slinging flame"; *In Memoriam*, Canto L.

To Theodore F. Dwight

1603 H Street. 4 July, 1890

Dear Dwight

I enclose what appear to be bills. Nothing else has arrived.

Apparently I am not to get away on the 10th. La Farge writes me an appeal to wait for him—God knows how long. Time is no object to me, but I am wretched at having nothing to do. At any rate the delay will allow me to finish the Index.

If ever cool weather comes, I will send you the dogs. At present we are so steadily warm that I prefer their staying quiet.

Ever Yrs   Henry Adams.

MS: MHi

To Charles Milnes Gaskell

1603 H Street. 4 July, 1890.

Mr dear Carlo

As my brother Brooks does not mean to stop in England, and as no one else of my intimacy is going there, I have given the bundle of letters to Spring Rice to send through the Foreign Office to Thornes, where I hope they will arrive within a week after you receive this letter.

I had a letter from Robert yesterday saying that you had been laid up. This seemed to be all the news, and I hope your health is by this time sternly strong.

The summer waxes and still I hang on here, detained by the last sheets of Index, and by hopes of taking John La Farge with me again—this time to the South Seas. Hay also remains here, held by the last sheets of his great work, and we bask in the tropical heat of this empty city, alone in our houses. Hay goes north next week. My own movements are uncertain, but I am liable any day to start for San Francisco and Samoa. I shall need no preparation, for every last order is given; my trunks are ready for packing, and my wardrobe is ready also. I have fitted myself out for two years in the South Seas; but the length of my absence will depend wholly on my feelings. I may return in two months, if I find myself more bored there than here. I may be gone for twenty years if I find myself more bored here than there. I may turn up in England for a change, and you need not be surprised any fine day in April or May to see me walk into your breakfast room. Time is nothing to me, and health is the only unknown element of travel. Barring illness or accident I may go anywhere and do anything.

My disease is ennui, probably the result of prolonged labor on one work, and of nervous strain. The reaction of having nothing to do after steady labor without change for so many years, is severe. Probably it will rapidly disappear with travel. It has hitherto always done so.

Meanwhile I shall amuse myself with the thought of lighting on England by way of Polynesia, and telling you the joys of cannibalism. I expect to reach Samoa at latest by September 1, and for some time afterwards I expect that my safest address will be to the care of the United States Consul at Samoa. From Fiji to Tahiti is my range for next winter.

As far as you are concerned I shall really be nearer there than here, so it is not a matter to regret. My love to all yours.

Ever affely   Henry Adams.

MS: MHi

To John T. Morse, Jr.

1603 H Street. 5 July, 1890.

My dear John

You ask me a pretty tough question. I know slightly the man you mention.[1] My friend Dwight, whom he succeeded at the State Department, knows him better, and as Dwight is at Quincy, you can consult him. I have never seen his literary work, and can only say that he belongs to a class of minds good enough to produce results above the average, but whose papers I should not, as an editor, accept without reading. He is a mugwump doctrinaire; but so are most University men. He has a high opinion of his own qualificatons; but perhaps it is a correct one. I am told that he is not popular at the Department; but that is not necessarily his fault. On the whole, I should prefer to try him on something less serious than Seward.

If I might make a private suggestion, I think if I were you I would try to make John Hay do Seward. Just now Hay is weary and nauseated with his subject, and would refuse. He and Nicolay have fairly exhausted themselves, but they have done a work the equal of which I know not in any literature. If Harvard College had any literary (or other) sense, it would have crowned that work by giving every possible distinction to its authors, instead of doing—what it does.[2] Literary sense is extinct, but editors remain, and must do their best to feed a thoroughly inartistic audience. To an editor in your situation a volume by Hay would be a God-send.

Hay is now weary and must have rest; but, after I go away, he will next winter be much alone here, and will feel the want of some light work. He knew Seward and admired him. Above all he knew Seward's relations with Lincoln. He would write a charming biography, and would do it with ease. Probably it would be a real contribution to history, and I am sure it would be a great addition to your series.

If you incline to the idea, don't touch Hay, but go to Mrs Cabot Lodge and get her to attempt it. Mrs Lodge *fait la pluie et le beautemps* here, and if you want anything done by anyone you must always get some woman to do it. I would send you to Mrs Hay, but you don't know her, and can't get at her. Enlist Mrs Lodge, and you're all right. Read her this letter, if you like.

This is my literary bequest to you. In a few days I expect to be on my way to Fiji.

Ever Yrs   Henry Adams.

By the bye, if you have any opportunity to do a kindness to Miss Baxter who is living with your sister-in-law, do it for my sake if not for your own. Miss Baxter is a sort of sister in my family, and one of the half dozen very fine women I have ever known.

MS: MHi
1. Frederic Bancroft.
2. Harvard had just awarded honorary degrees to Lyman Abbott, Richard Watson Gilder, Henry Charles Lea, Seth Low, Charles Follen McKim, Charles Herbert Moore, Henry Codman Potter, Leslie Stephen, and Alfred Tredway White.

To W. C. Brownell

1603 H Street. 8 July, 1890

My dear Mr Brownell

I send the title-page to Wilson today. I think I omitted it because I was not sure when you meant to publish, and so left the year undecided.

Apparently I shall not get away this week as I expected. I am hanging by the claws, but may drag through the month.

Yrs truly   Henry Adams.

W. C. Brownell Esq.

MS: ViU

To John Hay

1603 H Street. 9 July, 1890.

Dear Departed

As I sat last night with Ward Thoron and Springy on the Cameron verandah, fanning myself with the mercury at 85 and no breeze, I thought much of you in your cheerful sleeping car, surrounded by all the luxuries of civilisation, and enjoying the cool air of your northern home. Yesterday my thermometer registered 96° by day and 84° by night. Everyone was cross and profane except myself, who sat all day on my stair-landing, under the back windows, and read Borrow's Wild Wales, borrowed from you.[1]

Molly writes me her engagement—but I told you that.[2]

Not a word from La Farge nor a line of proof. After a fearful wrastle I finished the letter to Molly, but have done nothing else since you left, except drink mint juleps at the club at one o'clock at night, with Seaton Monroe and Appleby.

I consider your taking Brent off my hands as ample rent for the stable; but you can also keep it in repair for me. You will find these two items quite rent enough.

Brent has not yet reported his return from Noland's. I fear he and Prince are melted down into axle grease.

I was so glad to see by the weather report yesterday that the weather about Cleveland and New York was not inclement. So far north one must enjoy an occasional summer day.

Alack, I am but melancholy, after all, and life seems strangely unreal and weird on this ill-balanced perch. One can so easily drop out. I suppose you will all go along just as straight, whether I drop or not; yet the flop of a winged bird always did jar my nerves.

Ever Yrs   Henry Adams.

Much love to Mrs Hay and the babes. Polly writes me that they have seen Whistler who is painting Mrs Jack.[3]

MS: RPB
1. *Wild Wales* (1862), by George Borrow (1803–1881), English travel writer.
2. Mary Ogden Adams married Grafton St. Loe Abbott on Sept. 30.
3. The only known portrait of Mrs. Gardner by James Abbott McNeill Whistler (1834–1903) is a pastel of 1886.

To Lucy Baxter

1603 H Street. Sunday, 13 July, 1890.

My dear Miss Baxter

I expected to have written you a letter on my way westward, but here I still am, and here or hereabouts I am likely to remain for some time yet. The printers have been provokingly slow, and have a full fortnight's work still to do on my index. Nothing is done that I intended to see finished. I have agreed to wait till August 8 for La Farge, and he wants me to wait till August 23. Time is of no concern to me, but I know not how to do nothing as a gentleman should, and I feel no confidence in anyone's promises. Altogether I am badly broken up, and have not much will or intelligence left. My own house seems the least disagreeable spot to stay in, for here I have books, horses, kitchen and comfort; but the devil is incessantly prompting me to fly somewhere else, and the devil generally has his way. I shall soon go, but the devil seems my only resource to go to.

Meanwhile Dwight is at Quincy, which is a relief, and Molly is engaged to her Grafton, which is Kismet. I know nothing of the man, but his classmates and contemporaries express no cheerful views as to Molly's future happiness. He is described as depressed in temperament, morose, solitary or unsocial and of not more than average abilities. For once even I, who as you know, regard marriage as the only real satisfaction in life, hesitate to approve.[1]

My last two or three months here, as I have often told you, have been particularly pleasant. Our little family of Hays, Lodges, Camerons and Roosevelts, has been absolutely devoted to each other, and as I was the one to be lost, I came in for most of the baa-lamb treatment. Now all are gone except the Camerons, and I expect Mrs Cameron to take wings at any moment, as she would have done long ago, had she known where to go. Even Spring Rice has gone and is on a visit to the Endicotts at Salem. You can suggest to Daisy or Brooks the propriety of inviting him to stay, as he would doubtless much like to be asked, and he is a very pleasant white rabbit in a house. As he has got for me letters of introduction to all the British government officials in the east, and as Sir Julian has taken much trouble to write a stack of them, I feel as though I were in their debt. No one else disturbs my repose. I owe no debts of civility to anyone except Sir Julian.

Polly writes me regularly from London long letters describing their enjoyment of everything. Whistler has come to call, and is painting Mrs Jack Gardner. Think of being the victim of Whistler after being clubbed by Sargent![2] The children are seeing sights and have their time and minds well occupied.

I trust you find Beverly tolerable, and make a little effort to strengthen your ties with people you like. I am about the last person in the world to criticise others, especially for unsocial habits, but I do make such clumsy efforts as I know how, to attach to me those whose friendship I value. Do try!

Ever Yrs   Henry Adams.

MS: ScU
1. Grafton St. Loe Abbott (1856–1915), Harvard '77, Boston lawyer and financier.
2. An obscene witticism making the rounds about Sargent's portrait of Mrs. Gardner in a black décolleté gown caused her husband to withdraw the painting from Sargent's exhibition at the St. Botolph Club in Boston and to decree that it not be publicly exhibited again. See Louise Hall Tharp, *Mrs. Jack* (1965), pp. 134–135.

To John Hay

1603 H Street. 14 July, 1890.

Dear Breadwinner

I hasten to acknowledge yours of Saturday to catch you before you get a new address which you won't send me for a month.

I ride your mare every other day. She is certainly quiet. Speck may have taught her a gait, but it isn't much faster than Speck's own.

Did you ever see Solitude? Classically speaking, she was a nymph—nicht wahr? She has now turned into Lachesis or the other old woman who cuts threads; and haunts me of evenings under the aspect of Evarts, depriving me of my julep, and driving me to wild impulses to cut threads myself. Lowndes is Fate No. 2. They always appear together: Nimmer, das glaubt mir, erscheinen die Götter, nimmer allein.[1] If they did, life would be impossible.

Ecco! a letter from La Farge dated July 11. It begins: "I can go with you August 8. I should prefer waiting for the steamer which sails August 23 . . . I can stay away longer if I go later." Did you ever see such a man? I shall wait till December and then go alone. Still, the delay gives me hope. Mrs Hay may by that time be tired of Sunapee, and will be ready to come with us. Helen will have her pirate isle, and La Farge and you and I will establish an ideal republic of which Mrs Hay shall be President, and in which representative government shall be the only cruel form of criminal punishment permitted among the cannibals. Perhaps Mrs Hay will be tired of you by the middle of August, and will send you ahead with us to select her empire.

To show her the ease of the undertaking, I will just mention that last evening the occupation of Lachesis and Atropos was suddenly disturbed by the arrival of my classmate Hartwell from the Sandwich Islands.[2] He had performed a feat of travel. Leaving Lake Champlain June 14 he had been to Honolulu, returned to Westport, and come thence to Washington, July 13.

To be sure he stayed only a day at Honolulu, but the month covered both journeys. If you sailed with us from San Francisco, August 23, you could pass aeons with Polly Nesia, and be back by Christmas.

Absolutely no proofs come. My index bids fair to take a year.

Martha is peaked. I fear she will have to go. Then where shall I be, without juleps? The idea is terrible—nay, impossible! Where she goes, I will go, and if necessary will telegraph sister Anne to come and matronize me.

Love to all yours.　Ever　Henry Adams.

MS: RPB

1. *"Nimmer . . . allein"*: "Never, it is my belief, never do the gods appear alone"; Johann C. F. Schiller, *Dithyrambe* (1796).

2. Alfred Stedman Hartwell (1836–1912), lawyer in Hawaii, previously supreme court justice and attorney general there.

To Theodore F. Dwight

1603 H Street. July 16, 1890

Dear Dwight

I am heartily glad to hear that the dogs had a quick journey, and are set loose again. At the hour they started, the weather turned hot again, and they just escaped a most oppressive heat wave. My registering thermometer yesterday did not rise above 93, but the saturation of the air made it feel quite 100. Today it is worse. Now, at 10 A.M. the mercury is at 88, and unless a change occurs we shall touch 98 by two o'clock.

Curiously enough I don't dislike it. At first the heat produced some little congestion and nervous excitement. At present I am very cheerful, well and contented, and last night slept as well as usual with the room at 85 all night.

Ward Thoron does not stand it so well. His head troubles him. Willy Phillips expands under it. Martha and her mother are all right. Only poor Sala wilts on his surgical bed. No one else is here except my classmate Hartwell whom I have taken in. He will probably sail with La Farge and me and Tom Lee for the Sandwich Islands, by the steamer of Aug. 23.

Ever Ys　Henry Adams.

MS: MHi

To W. C. Brownell

Washington. 22 July, 1890.

Dear Mr Brownell

About the Niagara River Maps I have no particular wish to separate them if they are meant to go together;—you can arrange them as you please. Since they were made I have discovered that, though printed by James, they are really Wilkinson's, and accordingly I recommend altering the lettering as noted in the margin of the map returned.

I note also for the first time an error of date in the "Attack on Fort Bowyer of Sept. 15." The date should be 1814, not 1815. The error is La-tour's, and not our's.

I enclose the missing map of the "British and American positions at New Orleans," viii, 359.

I have lost the last map (viii, 383) of the capture of Fort Bowyer, but I enclose the original sketch from which the engravers worked. They will recognise it.

In regard to the titles, I was myself in doubt, and am so still. If you think best, they can all be given verbatim. I regarded it rather as an index than as a table of contents, especially as in one or two cases titles were wanting. The diffuseness of the titles seemed to me also an objection, especially as the authorship would properly be included. This is a matter about which your judgment is better than mine, and if you prefer a full list of titles, pray substitute it. I cannot do it because I have not all the maps.

I will return the discarded plates. I supposed they were sent to me as being considered my property and charged to my account.

Yrs truly   Henry Adams

W. C. Brownell Esq.

MS: ViU

To Elizabeth Cameron

Tuesday. 1.30 P.M. [22 July 1890]

Dear Mrs Cameron

I have just returned from Berkeley Springs, very dirty and much disgusted at the dust and desolation of Washington. I shall try to see Mr Cameron this evening, but if I do not succeed, he being hard to find, I shall take the risk of going to Blue Mountain tomorrow anyway. I can't stand staying here, and must go to New York rather than face this trial. I am heartily glad you are out of it, and trust you will not think of returning at least till we get some rain. Martha ought not to return at all.

You are better off where you are than at Berkeley Springs which is certainly a hole. Rebecca's little cottage outside the town is tolerable, but there is no place at the Springs that would be suitable for you. The bath is the only Christian part of it.

Hasta mañana. Adios.

Ever Yrs   Henry Adams.

MS: MHi

To Marie Thoron Endicott

Washington. 27 July, 1890.

My dear Mrs Endicott

Thanks for your kind note of farewell. I wish I were answering it from the ocean, where my intended ship now is, but I have been obliged to postpone my departure till August 16, and must linger in a disconsolate way till then, wishing that Washington were a civilised capital where one could pass a summer without asphyxia.

If you have any commissions for Polynesia, or indeed for Melanesia, I shall be pleased to undertake them. Native costumes are probably cheap and becoming, and I imagine less dutiable than European. Unless perhaps Speaker Reed and Cabot Lodge can succeed in their ambition by putting a prohibitive duty on nothing at all.[1]

Mrs Cameron and Martha are on the Blue Mountain, near Hagerstown, a summer hotel, prettily situated, and looking towards the Shenandoah Valley. I passed two days with them last week. We have all grown thin. Martha has lost four pounds. I have lost fourteen. Mrs Cameron too shows the effect of wilting. The unfortunate Sala is said to be very much pulled down. I see no one here, and can give no news that deserves writing.

Please give my best regards to all your household and believe me

Ever Yrs   Henry Adams.

MS: MHi

1. In May, Lodge voted with the party regulars for the McKinley tariff; HA remained a free-trader.

To John Hay

Washington. July 27, 1890.

Dear Hay

I have been wandering a week, and therefore have not written to beguile your over-gaiety. I have been to Berkeley Springs visiting Rebecca Rae in her $700 cottage. Then I soared into the Blue Mountains where Mrs

Cameron and Martha are nesting in a summer hotel, high over the valley that stretches from the Potomac to Chambersburg, where Lee's army once disported itself. I passed two days on the Blue Mountain, making it many shades bluer, and it did me good. At last we were rained upon, and I returned to Washington yesterday to find the deserts of dust turned into morasses of mud, through which I made your little mare flounder. She is not so bad, and has an excellent trot, which can be developed, by judicious urging, into a sustained and fairly rapid gait. This is all. The gigantic index, which bids fair to reach two hundred pages, is near its end; but the revises have still to come.

La Farge is eviscerating his clients to get away on the 16th; Tom Lee is writing letters to say that he wants another month. Hartwell thinks he can't start till September. Whatever befalls, unless my destiny is strangely perverse or you promise to go with the other fellows, *I* start from New York or Boston on August 16. I am au bout de mes forces. The cock-crow is not more solid on ghosts than the 16th of August on me.[1]

Washington seems quiet as spring lamb, but Congress is busy enough, and Blaine too. I am anxious about the unfortunate Sala, who is in a more critical state than is known,—but don't repeat this to *anyone*. He does not yet know it himself. Hartwell is still with me. I have seen no one else.

Love to all yours.   Henry Adams.

MS: RPB
 1. An allusion to the superstition that ghosts vanish at cock crow, as in *Hamlet,* I, i.

To Cecil Arthur Spring Rice

Washington 27 July, 1890.

Dear S.P.Q.R.[1]

A thousand thanks for your letter, and will you be so obliging as to convey to Ronald Ferguson my most highly colored acknowledgments for his? If miladi Hopetown but turns her angelic smile on me, I shall be the fitter for the cannibals afterwards.[2]

I am rejoiced that you find your summer haunts for once tolerably pleasant.[3] Just at this season the rocks have a certain advantage over the asphalt. We did the Shadrach, Meshech, &c, rather too thoroughly for several days,[4] and it affected my nerves more than it oppressed my appetite; but we have now had rain, and feel better. I shall start for San Francisco August 16,—La Farge or no,—and by that time you will all be beginning to think of returning to work. When you reappear in these haunts, and are facing a bitter winter, think of me tumbling over cataracts with old-gold naiads in Nukuheva. With a straw hat for costume, I will rule my pirate isle. Then you will forget the harsh charms of northern seas, and pine away for envy.

As you are in correspondence with Mrs Cameron I can give you no news of her. I hope, though vaguely and without foundation, that she may return tomorrow. Give my love to all who deserve it, and my respects to Sir Julian and Lady Pauncefote.

Ever Yrs   Henry Adams.

MS: MHi

1. The initials SPQR were officially used for the name of the Roman commonwealth (*Senatus Populusque Romanus*); a play on "CASR," the customary signature used by Spring Rice.

2. Spring Rice, supplying HA with letters of introduction, wrote July 24 that Lady Hopetoun, wife of the governor of Victoria, Australia, was a beauty "with an angelic smile."

3. Spring Rice was staying at East Point, Nahant, Mass., the summer home of the Cabot Lodges.

4. Daniel 3: 8–25.

To Charles Warren Stoddard

29 July, 1890.

My dear Stoddard

Thanks for yours of the 26th which has just arrived. I hope you like the old family shebang, and am glad to hear that you are in it.

I knew that Stevenson had a relapse, and was about to resume his cruising. The south seas are large, and I am but small, so that he will scarcely see me on that scale, and I shall not hope to meet him. Peace go with him!

Washington is luridly solitary. I find something oppressive and weird in the absence of motive and activity in a place where I have always been busy and social. The prelude to the South Seas should be more cocoa-nutty.

My volumes are at your service; at least they would be, if I had some; but they were published so many—many ages ago, and so long a time has passed since I have thought of them, that I know not what idle curiosity can lead anyone to unearth them. Better let them repose under their six feet of dust at the publishers', and wait for a new incarnation. I fear that Dwight will have to gratify your wishes after I am gone, when I suppose the first pair of volumes will some day be printed with a few lies altered in form.

Ever truly Yrs   Henry Adams.

MS: MH

To John Hay

Washington 4 August, 1890.

Muy Señor mio

I start northwards next Thursday. Your mare is this moment starting with Daisy for their villegiatura in Loudon County. I have been at Blue Mountain again during the heat, and returned this morning bringing the senator and Mrs Cameron, with their accomplished daughter, back to their home. Mrs Cameron goes north also, and I hope will end the summer at Beverly. But this is still in doubt.

I expect to be in Boston by Sunday. If possible I shall run down to Nahant for a day. If you feel like a little jaunt, come down, and we will see the world. I must start for San Francisco on the 16th. Choose a day, Tuesday, Wednesday or Thursday; and drop me a line to 23 Court Street, care of J. Q. Adams.

Naturally I have no information to impart. The Blue Mountain is remote from haunts of gossip. There I lay most of the time on my bed, and read rubbish till sunset, after which I went to bed and lay awake all night.

Give my love to Mrs Hay and the young ones. By the bye, I have now a house at Honolulu, and know everyone. We shall be there a month.

I expect the King and Court to breakfast.

Ever Yrs   Henry Adams.

MS: RPB

To Cecil Arthur Spring Rice

Washington 4 August, 1890.

My dear Spring Rice

Please convey my warm thanks to Sir Julian for his kindness. I shall make a point of presenting his letter.[1]

My stay in these parts is drawing to a close. Next Thursday I start northwards, and expect to reach Boston Sunday at latest. For the last fortnight I have divided my time between Berkeley Springs, Washington and Blue Mountain, whence I returned this morning with the Senator and his agreeable wife and daughter. Up there the air was fresh, but the prospect of crossing the desert in this heat is not positively reposeful.

I feel much relieved to hear that Magnolia is a success.[2] This season suits it. Make the most of it, and don't regret lost opportunities. As for your fears of missing me next winter, you have yet to learn that the charm of Washington is variety.

If possible I shall try to get down to Nahant for a day, but am not sure enough to write to ask whether I should be received.

With my best regards to Sir Julian and his family.

Ever Yrs   Henry Adams

MS: MHi
1. To Victor Child-Villiers, 7th earl of Jersey, governor of New South Wales 1890–1893, and Lady Jersey.
2. Magnolia, a summer resort on the North Shore of Massachusetts Bay, across Kettle Cove from Manchester.

To Elizabeth Cameron

East Point, Nahant. Friday, 2.35 [15 Aug. 1890]

Dear Mrs Cameron

I ordered your serge, and also your bath-tub (I chose my own style which I want you to try. If you don't like it, you can exchange it) and your life-preserver, but could find no long boots light enough for Martha.

I took the telegram to the station at 7.30 this morning, but I felt that it would not reach you. The mere hope of seeing you again made me try the experiment, but it was foolish, for the disappointment is worse than the regret.

I start in twenty minutes, and go straight away to New York, leaving Hay here. Tomorrow evening, at six o'clock, we start for San Francisco. I feel that the devil has got me, for I have said to the passing moment "Stay,"[1] but the devil gave a splendid price for a very poor article.

Ever Ys   H.A.

MS: MHi
1. Goethe's *Faust* (see note 2 to letter of March 25, 1890).

To Elizabeth Cameron

Knickerbocker Club
Saturday. noon 16th Aug. [1890]

Dear Mrs Cameron

I arrived here at half past twelve last night, and now that I have finished packing, paid for my tickets and stateroom, bought my last little pair of shoes (I have now a dozen, I think,) and nothing more to do but look after La Farge who is struggling with the whole Inferno, I find your note of yesterday, and take a rest in answering it, or at least in acknowledging it. As I wrote you a line from the Lodge's, your's is already answered.

I never felt the sensation before of hurrying about with a hundred things on my mind, and only one thing in it. The prepossession made me forget even my last proof-sheets, which must now go to Dwight. I am also a stranger of late years to the choking sensation of departure, and hardly know whether to be glad or sorry at feeling it once more. Until now I never fairly realised that life has become mainly a series of farewells.

So be it, since it can be nothing else. Thanks to Eagle Head, my own eagle-headedness still lasts and makes me take everything gaily.[1] Of all kinds of intoxication, the most delightful and the most lasting must be that of the eagles.

I have a notion of mailing this at Albany, and adding a line in the train to let you know that we are really on our way. (Here I am interrupted by being called down to the telephone, where after fifteen minutes desperate struggle I learn that some unknown lunatic wants my brother Charles.) La Farge I saw at nine o'clock. He had then three pictures to paint, two windows to lead, and his packing to do, but promised to be ready at four o'clock. He was very gay and impecunious as ever, and is going to take his Japanese boy with him. To my constant amusement he always adds with the same grave serenity that he shall do this at his own expense. Austin Wadsworth left a note asking me to go with him this evening to Newport and tomorrow to Tuckanuck, Sturgis Bigelow's island, and there make Sturgis happy, but what would the old-gold girls say if I went back on them at the last moment?[2]

6.45. Here we are en route, without delay, running along the Hudson. La Farge is in high spirits, and already flattering himself with the appointment of court painter to the King of the Sandwich Islands. We have our state-room, so that I can at least get a sponging in the morning. The evening is pretty, and the sun is just setting beyond the river.

I do not lay claim to exuberant spirits for myself. I have a slight cold, and at best am given to thinking of other things than the Sandwich Islands; but at least it is motion, and motion is a form of vivacity.

Tomorrow night we should pass through Chicago, and when you receive this we should be well on towards Omaha. We are due at San Francisco on Thursday morning. Between now and then I shall write again, and tell you that I am a butterfly.

Just now I admit to being a trifle homesick. I should like to be going to get my julep, or to watch the moon at Blue Mountain, or to stroll on the beach at Manchester. My only reserve is to hope that my friends are thinking of me as I of them.

Ever Yrs   H.A.

MS: MHi
1. Eagle Head, a rocky point on the coast at Manchester, Mass. Mrs. Cameron was staying nearby at Masconomo House when HA visited her there the week before.
2. William Austin Wadsworth (1847–1918), of Geneseo, N.Y., and his brother Herbert had belonged to the Adamses' Washington set in the 1880s. Tuckernuck, a five-mile-long island off the western tip of Nantucket.

To Elizabeth Cameron

Monday, 2.30 P.M. [18 Aug. 1890]
Council Bluffs.

So far, all right! We passed through Chicago on time last night, and have arrived here also on time today. We have a gorgeous stateroom, and lots of dust, but the night was cold, and I actually slept quite as well as in my more luxurious couch at Washington. My little cold has vanished, and I eat breakfast like a dynamo. La Farge complains that he had a chill in the night, but he is none the worse today, and has beguiled our hours by discussing lights and shadows, greens and reds, and the tones of clouds and cornfields. He has also written a ream or two of letters, to the despair of his work-people, as his son confided to me.[1] I have beguiled a part of my leisure in the construction of another sonnet, which I will perhaps confide to you when it is sufficiently bad for prompt destruction. Thus far my chief enjoyment in travel has been to wash myself as often as possible, a pleasure the more constant because no result of cleanliness can be reasonably expected. Next week, however, I will cease to wash, and will take to seasickness for variety. Travel brings no end of these enjoyments.

Did I tell you clearly when and where to write? A letter sent Sept. 5 will catch the steamer "Australia" of Sept. 12, to Honolulu; and a letter mailed Sept. 14 will catch the next steamer that leaves San Francisco Sept. 20. Both letters may be directed to *poste restante, Honolulu, Sandwich Islands.* I expect to go on to Samoa by the same steamer that will bring the second mail, but La Farge is quite equal to wanting to remain indefinitely at the Sandwiches, and in that case I shall be much at a loss whether to stay or leave him. This matters little as regards letters, for I shall write by the return steamer of Sept. 20, and the letter should reach you by Oct. 4, in time for your next mail, which leaves Boston October 12.

So you have three mail-days: Sept. 5 and 14, and Oct. 12. There is another of October 4 by the Honolulu steamer of Oct. 10, but as I shall probably be gone to Samoa, it is a chance whether a letter to Honolulu would reach me.

Once beyond Honolulu, I can receive letters only four weeks apart, measuring from the steamer of Saturday, Oct. 18. Perhaps you had best allow a week for the mail, and always mail on Saturdays to avoid risk of losing steamers.

Tuesday noon. Just passed Laramie. We had a cold storm in the night which laid the dust, and left streaks of snow on the mountains of the North Park, but I feel as if my toes were iced, and my back was a glacier. The summit of the Rockies was covered with clouds, and we saw only mist till we got down to Laramie where a winter sun cheered us. The transition between seasons is a trifle too sharp for summer clothes. I wish I had some furs, and my mind wonders whether you are shivering over a seaside fire. Even the sage-brush looks wintry, and the flowers out of season.

Wednesday. 8 A.M. We are now on the Central Pacific, meandering through that marvelous region of color and light which our fellow travellers call the most God-forsaken country on earth. To me it has always seemed pure purple joy, and La Farge fairly dances about trying to catch the shadows and colors. Yesterday he gave me my first watercolor lesson, and I dabbled all day in cobalt, indigo and chrome. The result was what you may imagine, but I learned a deal of my ignorance,—as usual. We had more storm and cold; but today is my old sage-brush sunshine, and I have sat an hour on the platform drinking air.

Thursday, 8.30. Oh, but yesterday was a squealer. Up there in the Humboldt basin the heat was gay, and the dust was rich. I have seldom indulged in a much more hilarious railway experience but the landscape and the colors were superb, and La Farge and I dabbled in watercolors all day, while he tried to teach me that the color of everything on earth was purple, and of everything in heaven ultramarine. Luckily the night was very pleasant and dirty. We shall reach San Francisco in half-an-hour, and already I feel the awful coast-wind that is to send me to bed on Saturday; but as I have eaten nothing but grapes for twentyfour hours, I feel that the Palace Hotel has attractions not wholly despicable. On the whole, the journey has been quick and easy. The shortening it by a whole day is a prodigious relief.

I shall mail this dispatch at once, and begin another tomorrow morning which will follow in two days. I wish I could hope to get a letter before sailing, but I beat the mail by a day; and so good-morning.

Ever Yrs H.A.

MS: MHi
 1. Bancel La Farge (1865–1938), besides being a painter, was his father's business assistant in New York.

To Anne Palmer Fell

Sleeping Car "Pocatello."
Laramie Plains, 19 Aug. [1890]

My dear Princess Barbara

My servants told me of your visit to my house, and your letter came into my hands in some moment of confusion as I was hurrying through my last hours in Boston. At present I have leisure in abundance, and if this car were only a little less athletic in its motions, I should wish nothing better than to write to you.

At last I am fairly started on the long-planned journey. I do not know where I am going, or how long I shall be absent. My first stage is the South

Seas, where I expect to pass my winter. In about ten days I hope to be turned into a Sandwich islander, and after a month of Sandwiches I expect to become a Fijian or a resident among the Typees, or a cannibal of Borneo. If I find a stray island, I will make myself its king, and will invite you to take a court office. When Polynesia becomes a bore, Australia and Asia loom beyond; but if nothing amuses, I can always at any moment return to the vices of civilisation. My house at Washington remains open, and I should like nothing better than to feel that it was the pleasantest spot on earth.

Meanwhile the sense of motion has a certain charm, and as I take La Farge with me, I have society enough to fill the ambition of a common man. He and I have already crossed the Pacific twice in company, and I have no doubt we shall find new worlds again. He will return in a few months, but by that time I expect to feel at home among the cannibals, even if I have not already become one, and married a reigning princess, old-gold in tone, and archaic in personal beauty.

So I cannot have the satisfaction of visiting you at Nantucket, or of renewing my relations with Marian who must now be older than her mother, and a suitable companion for me. Give her my warmest love, and ask her to think kindly of cannibals for my sake. I wish I had seen her once more, not wholly for cannibalistic reasons. Should you pass through Washington next year, I wish you would drive out to Rock Creek Church, behind the Soldier's Home, to see the grave of her namesake, where I trust that a work will then be finished which I must leave unseen.

Good-bye for the present. If you ever write, enclose letters to Theodore F. Dwight, Quincy, Mass.

Ever Yrs   Henry Adams

MS: MHi

To Elizabeth Cameron

Palace Hotel. 22 Aug. 1890.

I wonder whether I ever told you how delighted I was last year at getting a farewell note from you from shipboard. It seemed to tell me more than a volume on land. My own attempts can have no such success, since you know in advance all that I have to say; but I will send this letter all the same from shipboard. It is now eight o'clock in the morning, and we have a day of preparation before us. Yesterday I accomplished little except to settle on staterooms and get put up at the club.[1] I never feel respectable at San Francisco until I have scrubbed my head with soap and received a card to the club. Yesterday I did both by stages, resulting at last in partial recovery of my color and in a very satisfactory recovery of appetite. Beyond these two qualified successes I accomplished nothing of permanent value to the divine plan, and felt as though I were a tramp begging for a seat on a car-truck rather than like a gentleman with a credit on the Barings and letters of introduction to all the nobility and gentry of Polynesia in my pocket. Well! I hope you are now on the beach with Martha, and I would desperately like to be with you. Now for John Spreckels![2]

Saturday. 6.30 A.M. At seven o'clock last night I was the tiredest historian in California but I had interviewed all the leading citizens of San Francisco, and had provided for all my expected wants for the winter, including a schooner if I require it. When I am tired I am homesick, and a sudden spasm came over me, just at the foot of the hotel stairs, that I *must* see Martha. I got over it with the help of a bottle of Champagne and a marvelous dinner at the Club, but I am at best homesick enough for Beverly. You have not seen my sonnet on Eagle Head. I will write it out for you on the opposite page. The octave is faulty in too much similarity of rhyme, but I think I like it notwithstanding its defects. By the bye, look into Clough's poems if you can find them, and read a short one beginning *Come back, Come back!* Poor Clough was another wanderer who could not make his world run on four wheels.[3] Here goes, then, for Polynesia! It is seven o'clock, and I must pack and do a thousand things to get on board the "Zealandia" at eleven. I will add a postscript there, and should feel happier if I knew where to address the letter.

Eagle Head

Here was the eagles' nest! The flashing sea,
    Sunny and blue, fades in the distant gray,
    Or flickers green on reefs, or throws white spray
On granite cliffs, as a heart restlessly
Beats against fate, and sobs unceasingly,
    Most beautiful flinging itself away,
    Clasping the rock by which it must not stay,
Sublimest in revolt at destiny.
Here where of old the eagles soared and screamed
    Answering the ocean's restless, longing roar,
While in their nest the hungry eaglets dreamed,
    —Here let us lie and watch the wave-vexed shore,
      Repeating, heart to heart, the eagles' strain,
      The ocean's cry of passion and of pain.

1 P.M. On board ship. We should have sailed an hour ago, but the mail is late, and we must lie in the baking sun till two o'clock. Our ship is crowded with English, mostly mild in type, but our staterooms are on deck, in the extreme bow where we should have as much isolation as falls to the lot of cannibals. A small child, rather pretty, howls like Martha in the next stateroom, and serves to remind me of anything you please. San Francisco bay is full of smoke, and the dock is deficient in interest. Awoki, La Farge's Jap., is

our only acquaintance, and he seems as little amused as ourselves; but La Farge is always unexpectedly humorous and sustaining. By his aid I keep quite chirpy at times.

2 P.M. Off, and running out of the bay. The ship is largely filled with cowboys and Indians of the Buffalo Bill persuasion, going somewhere to do something. The usual sprinkling of Jews and Jewesses; the irascible old gentleman, denouncing the company's officials; a few quiet young men, and the conventional British big-nosed female, seem to fill our crew. We are underway, and I am very shortly going to bed, the weather being too fine for confidence in my seamanship. I have done this thing before. So goodbye all! I daren't let myself think. Hasta luego.

MS: MHi
   1. The Union Club.
   2. John Diedrich Spreckels (1853–1926), president of the Oceanic Steamship Co. (San Francisco and Hawaii), was associated with his father in Hawaiian sugar cane plantations.
   3. In Clough's "Songs in Absence" (1852).

4.

Hawaii and Samoa

1890–1891

Henry Adams' first serial letter to Elizabeth Cameron was written in May 1889, when she was bound for England and shipping schedules made it pointless to mail installments separately. Because Pacific mail ships would be even less frequent, he planned on such letters in 1890 as a matter of course. He regarded them as a travel diary, and he took with him for that purpose the folio-size sheets (twice the size of his regular stationery) which he had hitherto used for his private journal. The shared privacy of these letters became his tacit premise: when he felt depressed, he did not note his state in the clinical way of his journal, but expressed it literarily as dejection.

As it turned out, Adams soon could report relief from nervous troubles, renewed savor of the senses, and engaged curiosity. In Hawaii he found few surprises. In Samoa his interest in custom, belief, legend, and especially the Siva dance led him to a new perspective on European culture. Yet, two months before leaving for Tahiti, he claimed to have "exhausted" the islands. Devouring news of financial disaster in Europe, reading the Odyssey and comparing the archaic cultures of Homeric Greece and present Samoa, and bemoaning (not always convincingly) his ennui, Adams described a pattern of moods that was to become habitual.

To Elizabeth Cameron

"Zealandia." Tuesday, 26 Aug. [1890]

When I gave my letter to the purser as we were running out of San Francisco, he told me that he had just sent to my stateroom a letter for me. I did not then find it, but when, towards evening I was drenched by spray on deck, and lay down in my berth, my steward hunted up the letter, which proved to be yours, and gave it to me as I was succumbing to my fate. All night I lay on my face in my clothes, clasping your letter between my hands, and only after twentyfour hours did I indulge in the pleasure of opening it. You are phenomenally clever at shooting-letters. I need not tell you how much pleasure this gave me.

As usual, the sea off California was up-and-down, swash and roll, trying as possible to a landsman, but it moderated a little yesterday, and we got on our legs again. We do not go to meals, but this is chiefly because the boat is full, and our seats offer no attractions. Our staterooms are pleasant, on deck, airy and private, and there we live, reading, sleeping, and now writing. Presently I shall get out my watercolors, and try to set La Farge to painting. The sky is thick and we have had little sun, but occasionally the sea is intensely blue. On the whole I see nothing peculiar about it. In fact I am disappointed. I thought that half way to the Islands I should feel the charm of tropical seas; but it is very like the Atlantic at the same season, and just now the sky is gray and the water almost muddy in color.

I feel quite proud to have really got so far, and to think that I am really here—wherever it is; but in the long watches of these nights,[1] as the ship flops slowly from side to side, and the waves pass under with a regular, rhythmic rush, not conducive to laughter, I think and think, and go on thinking a great deal, and for my life I can see no way out of it.

Thursday, 28th. If one must go to sea, these are certainly the seas to go to. Day after day we roll lazily along, the north-east trades blowing us gently ahead and never a change in their force or direction. The air is exquisitely soft; the sky always cloudy with broken masses of warm grey water-clouds, and now and then the sun comes out on a patch of blue sky, and shows us an ocean so intensely blue that the eye wonders whether the color is not really black. The ship is well enough if not good; of the passengers I know nothing. La Farge remains as always the pleasantest of companions. It is now seven o'clock in the morning, and I am taking my cup of early tea. Then I will read an hour on deck. I shall pass several hours trying to sketch the water and sky, with queer results, and I shall swear at my own stupidity for an hour or two more. The evening will be given to indolence and drowsiness over cigars on deck in the dusk, watching the water and struggling moon. Then bed at ten, and so in fortyeight hours we sight Molokai.

Friday, 29th. The flying-fish are usually my only variety of sight, and they amuse me perpetually, for they really fly long distances—fifty or a hundred yards—and look like exaggerated dragon-flies, sometimes as large as a mackerel; but yesterday we had a sunset that roused us all. Such softness of grays, violets, purples, reds and blues you will never see, for you will never venture into these deserts. Afterwards came a full moon, with light clouds, and it seemed to set everyone to singing and spooning. When I went to bed, I undressed by light of the moon's reflection on an intensely blue sea—at ten o'clock at night—a strange, tropical effect.

Saturday, 30th. 7 A.M. Molokai is in sight on our left, a dim bank in fog, and Oahu ahead, a higher range of hills behind which is our port, Honolulu. The air is still soft as the clouds, which are always a delicate violet that makes sunset and moonrise equally refined. At ten o'clock we shall arrive, and already the Sandwiches seem companions of one's youth, familiar as La Fayette Square.

Honolulu. Sunday, Aug. 31. We arrived yesterday morning at ten o'clock, and having established ourselves at the hotel, breakfasted, and got up our enormous baggage-train, we started out at two to find Mr W. O. Smith, my friend Hartwell's brother-in-law, to whom I brought a letter.[2] We discovered him at his office, expecting us, and, after a very short preamble, he drove us up to Hartwell's house. The drive of about two miles was amusing as a comedy, and full of "Look at that!" and "What is that?" and "What good eyes she has!" and so on, but I can't stop to speak of Kanakas or palms or banyans or reds or purples or flowers or night-gown costumes or old-gold women with splashes of color, but must hurry to our house which we reached at last over a turf avenue between rows of palms. We were half an hour in getting into it, for it was closed, and John, the keeper, was missing; but we had enough to do in looking about. The place is at the mouth of a broad mountain-valley opening out behind Honolulu, and overlooking the town and harbor, to the long line of white surf some three miles away, and then over the purple ocean indefinitely southward. The sense of space, light and color, in front, is superb, and the greater from the contrast behind, where the eye rests on a Scotch mountain-valley, ending in clouds and mist, and green mountain-sides absolutely velvety with the liquid softness of its lights and shadows. Showers and mist perpetually swept down the valley and moistened the grass, but about us, and to the southward, the sky was always blue and the sun shining. The day was hot in the town, and the air like a greenhouse, but up here the north-east trade-wind blew deliciously. As for the grounds, they were a mass of palms, ferns, roses, many-colored flowers, creepers, interspersed with the yellow fruit of the limes, and unknown trees and shrubs of vaguely tropical suggestions, all a little neglected, and as though waiting for us. The house when we got into it, was large, for Hartwell has seven or eight children, and there was an ample supply of all ordinary things. Both La Farge and I were eager to move in at once. Mr Smith drove us back to the town at five o'clock, and helped us to order our house-keeping necessaries; and I never but once saw La Farge so much amused and delighted with everything he saw, as in this afternoon's excitement where all was new and full of life and color.[3] We dined at the hotel, and at eight o'clock reached our house again, and installed ourselves. While our rooms were made ready we sat on the verandah and smoked. The full moon rose behind us and threw a wonderful light as far as the ocean-horizon. On the terrace were twin palm trees, about fifty feet high, glistening in the moonlight, and their long leaves waving, and, as Stoddard says, "beckoning" and rustling in the strong gusts, with the human suggestion of distress which the palm alone among trees conveys to me. La Farge never understood or felt the palm-tree, and I am a bit conceited at thinking that last night I brought him to a true way of thinking. Then we took some supper, and I eat my first mango, which, rather to my surprise, I found delicious, a little acid, and smooth as oil to the tongue. Therewith, after a sleepy, palmy, moon-light, tropical pipe, we went to bed, with doubts of centipedes and quadrupeds, but with the consciousness of a day full of boyish fun and frolic.

This morning we settled down. Now at noon we are fairly at home, all except a cook, for whom the city is being searched. So I sit on the verandah, looking occasionally off over the garden with its flowers, the town with its ships, and the long white surf-line; to a line of blue water, beyond which the ocean stretches distinctly purple to the horizon. The mino-bird chatters, the palms rustle, the breeze sweeps by, the thermometer stands at $83°$, and I hope you will not be bored by this long screed.

Tuesday, Sept. 2. 6.30 A.M. Mr Smith tells me that a mail is to go off tomorrow in a sailing vessel, and is likely to reach San Francisco a week before the next regular steamer, so I will close this letter, and try to give you a week's start on Honolulu advices. My other letters I shall reserve till steamer-day, so that you will have a monopoly of our news, and can keep it to yourself or make it common as you like. I have no more to tell. We are established as quietly as we should be at Beverly. As yet we have not even taken a drive, and our only visit to the town was last evening at sunset, to buy Apollinaris and soap. Our cook is expected today. We have not even left our letters of introduction or made a call, and not a word has been said about going off to the other islands, or our trip to the volcano. Nothing could be quieter than our house, where my one terror is the telephone and the butcher who calls me from dinner every day to tell him what I want for tomorrow. Although this is only our third day of Kanaka paradise, we are as lazy as though it were our third year. Yet La Farge has been out with his paint-box every day, and brings home, or rather brings in, wild daubs of brown and purple which faintly suggest hills and our great storm-cloud that we keep, so to speak, in our stable-yard, for it seems always to hang there. My own water-color diversions are not so amusing, but look like young ladies' embroidery of the last generation. If I could learn to paint like Martha, I should do wonders, but I cannot reach so far into high art, and only try to do like Turner or Rembrandt, or something easy and simple, which ends in my drawing a very bad copy of my own ignorance; but it has the charm that I felt as a boy about going fishing: I recognise that I am catching no fish on this particular day, but I feel always as though I might get a bite tomorrow. As far as I can see, La Farge gets no more, and is equally disappointed with every new attempt. I mean to photograph everything so that you may see it all, but photography is no longer an amusement now that it is all mechanical, and you have fifty pictures in half an hour.[4]

Here we are then, and you can imagine me, as though the verandah at Beverly looked over palms and tube-roses to the south seas, and I were seated on it, in a Japanese kimono, writing to you in the early morning, while La Farge still sleeps within. Our Kanaka boy is watering the garden, and our trade-wind is beginning to rustle the palm leaves. By noon the thermometer will rise to 83° and there stay till about five o'clock. I mean to explore our Nualuu valley (if that is its name) on horseback today, if I feel energy. Everything seems natural and easy except that you and Martha should be five thousand miles away.

Ever Yrs   Henry Adams.

Sept. 5. On taking my letter to the office I find that an intermediate steamer is to sail on the 9th which will bring letters quicker than any sailing-vessel could, so I kept the despatch for a postscript. Our first week here is at an end, but I am still sitting on Hartwell's porch at eight o'clock in the morning, dressed in the simply elegant costume of the kimono, and looking southward over a purple ocean. I have half a mind to send you my first little sketch, but it gives no idea of the thing, and might as well be from your bed-room at Beverly. We are lazy and dread more ocean, but we have been to breakfast with Judge Dole and to dinner with Mrs Dillingham, and Mr Bishop has shown me his kihalis, and his new Museum,[5] and I have ridden on the ambling rocking-horse of the island, and I have driven La Farge up the Nuuanu valley, where we live, to the great divide or pass, Pali, five or six miles up, where the lava cliff suddenly drops down to the sea-level, and one looks northward over green valleys and brown headlands to where the ocean, two or three miles distant, is breaking in curves and curls along the coast. The view is one of the finest I ever saw, and quite smashed La Farge. Yet I am amused to think what my original idea was of what the island would be like. I conceived it as a forest-clad cluster of volcanoes, with fringing beaches where natives were always swimming, and I imagined that when I should leave the beach I should be led by steep paths through dense forests to green glades where native girls said *Aloha* and threw garlands round your neck, and where you would find straw huts of unparalleled cleanliness always on terraces looking over a distant ocean a thousand feet below. The reality, though beautiful, is quite different. The mountains are like Scotch moors, without woods, presenting an appearance of total bareness. One drives everywhere over hard roads, and can go to most places about Honolulu by horse-car or railroad.[6] On the other islands, travel is more on horseback, but the stories of cockroaches and centipedes, not to mention scorpions, make one's teeth chatter; and the mosquitoes, at night, are as bad as at Beverly. The absence of tropical sensation is curious. One would come here to escape summer. The weather is divine, but the heat never rises above 84°, and at night the thermometer always stands at 75° with a strong breeze—too strong to sit in. After our July in Washington I feel as though I had run away to a cool climate, although the sense of a constant temperature is a constant surprise. I never get used to sitting regularly in a kimono out doors at seven o'clock in the morning.

Sept. 8. We have been away all day on an expedition to the Pali where La Farge wanted to sketch. The day passed rapidly, and as far as I am concerned, pleasantly, in the usual easy task of learning what I already knew, that I am a blooming idiot; but on returning with a sketch which would amuse Martha, and is nearly as good as she might make, I suddenly find that the steamer sails tomorrow morning, and if I don't hurry, I shall lose the mail. So La Farge and I are sitting on our verandah at night, writing by lamp-light, having driven away some of the mosquitoes by burning fly-powder, a lovely discovery.

Big as this despatch is, it seems to tell very little. Now that we are here, the islands seem a quiet spot, and furnish little excitement. I am not enthusiastic about the old-gold girl. Long residence in Washington has accustomed us to the color, and as far as I can see, Maggy would be rather a belle here. If there is any society here, it has shown no consciousness of our charms, and even the King, who is the most amusing inhabitant, has not invited us to the palace.[7] On the other hand, the weather is divine, the scenery, exquisite, and we are as comfortable as we should be at Washington. I cannot say that the place is particularly economical. Everything costs rather more than in New York, even fruit; but one must pay for being shut up in tropical islands. If you see Dwight or Stoddard, you can reassure their minds on the point of chief interest: I eat *poi* every day, and have to pretend to like it. All the island fruits and vegetables are a variation on soap. Even the mango is redolent of turpentine. They agree with me, but I sometimes rush for an orange to get something acid. We are particularly well. La Farge tells me that I was looking very poorly in Washington, and he was quite troubled to see me aging so fast. I can believe it, for I have not often felt as though I were more broken up in nerves; but so was Martha, and I only hope that she is now as placid as I. We go to bed at ten o'clock, and I generally stay there till eight. Sleep has come back, and I manage to catch six or seven hours without trouble. Unfortunately we must soon move again. This week we must go to Hawai to see the volcano, Kilauea, an expedition which will probably consume ten days. On the 28th we expect to sail for Samoa, and then our hardships will begin.

I have talked only about myself, and write to no one else by this mail. Perhaps you can imagine how much I want to know.

Ever Yrs   Henry Adams.

MS: MHi

1. A possible echo of "In the long, sleepless watches of the night," from Longfellow's "The Cross of Snow," written in memory of his wife and first published in *Life,* ed. Samuel Longfellow (1886).

2. William Owen Smith (1848–1929), a lawyer.

3. La Farge's account of this day and of the rest of the trip appeared posthumously as *Reminiscences of the South Seas* (1912), with color reproductions of 32 of his paintings.

4. HA brought with him one of George Eastman's first Kodaks, a box camera introduced in 1888, using 100-exposure roll film.

5. Sanford Ballard Dole (1844–1926), Hawaii supreme court justice 1887–1893; Emma Louise Smith Dillingham, wife of Benjamin Franklin Dillingham; Charles Reed Bishop (1821–1915), planter and banker, married into the Hawaiian royal family, founded the Bernice Pauahi Bishop Museum in 1889 to preserve native culture. The *kahili* is "the beautiful plumed stick of honour . . . which was the attribute of power, and which is still carried about royalty, or stands at their coffin or place of burial" (La Farge, *Reminiscences,* p. 23).

6. The first railroad on Oahu had opened only a month earlier, a 72-mile network built by Dillingham mainly to serve the sugar plantations.

7. David Kalakaua (1836–1891), reigned 1874–1891.

To Mabel Hooper

Honolulu. Sept. 10. 1890

My dear Polly

I wonder when I shall hear from you again, and know that you are at home. I wish you could make us a little visit here. You never saw anything more charming than our house, with its palm-trees and rose-garden, looking over the town to the ocean southward where we shall soon go. The house belongs to my classmate Hartwell, whose family is now living in Newbury Street, a very different place. Hartwell lent it to me. We took his Japanese cook, and here we have been nearly a fortnight, leading very lazy lives, and only energetic in scolding at the occasional necessity of going down to the town to buy something or make a call. Honolulu covers a great deal of ground, and one drives three or four miles through villas and parks, but it is a small place really, and about as thoroughly Americanised as Newport. Excepting the beautiful flowers and palms and the wonderful climate, with its sky and sea, the natives are the only novelty. They are not unlike our mulattoes, but they are very fond of flowers and colors. The women wear a sort of loose night-gown of all sorts of bright colors, and ride astride of their horses, as many of the foreign women do. Both the women and the men often wear garlands of flowers, mostly yellow, and look like the chorus of an opera. Indeed the whole thing is more like a wonderfully got-up stage scene than like reality, but the outside is the best part of it. We are never tired of looking at the scenery and the people; even the Chinamen are droll, but I don't care for the centipedes or cockroaches or mosquitoes, and I positively object to scorpions. The centipedes are numerous and the mosquitoes are a nuisance, but we have discovered that the fumes of burning fly-powder will clean out any number of night-mosquitoes, whereas the centipede, which is six inches long, goes where he will, especially in sugar-plantations.

As yet we have stuck close to our comfortable house, and have seen only the few persons to whom we brought letters, and whose society has been confined mostly to reciprocal calls when both parties were sure to be out. If there is any pleasant society here, we have not been much appreciated by it; but as I never go into society without being sorry for it, I don't much object to being alone with La Farge who is much better company than I can meet abroad. So he and I live always together, sleeping in adjoining rooms with the doors always open; breakfasting at about nine, and then usually sketching till afternoon, dressed in Japanese kimonoes, and never disturbed. My sketches are very funny, but I think he will take home a good deal of new work, for he enjoys it and has nothing else to do. Sometimes we drive off to some great view, and work all day. The only trouble is that no painter that ever lived could begin to catch the lights and colors of this island. I have learned enough to understand a little about what can't be done, but La Farge makes wonderful purple attempts to do it, though he knows how absurd it is. We have a good cook, who serves us the native *poi* and *taro* every day; but the *poi* is poor apple-sauce, and the *taro* is tasteless sweet potato, so we mostly live on melons, pine-apples, mangoes, bananas and oranges, with an occasional fish and chicken. The weather is divine. Almost always a strong northeast wind draws down the valley, from the ocean only ten miles across the island. The thermometer rises every noon to 83° and falls every night to 75°. I often get up at six o'clock in the morning and sit on our verandah till eight, with only my cotton kimono on, and am always surprised to find that I am perfectly comfortable. In November the rainy season begins, but till then the weather is always what we see it, and I do not know whether the mornings or the evenings are most beautiful.

The only person I have wanted to see is the King, who is a very droll character and the only amusing one I have heard of; but though we brought a letter of introduction to him, we have not been energetic enough to deliver it, and so we shall probably miss his Majesty, for we go off, day after tomorrow to another island to see the volcano, and shall be ten days gone, leaving only five days before we sail for Samoa. We expect to remain at Samoa till October and then sail for Tahiti. Perhaps you had better direct letters to the care of the U.S. Consul at Samoa, though I've no idea when I shall get them. If I stay about Tahiti till December, it would be better to write by a mail steamer which goes direct there from San Francisco every month, the post-office advertises the day. Anyway you might try a letter that way, to the care of the U.S. Consul at Tahiti. It is my only chance of hearing from you before January.

Love to you all.

Ever affectionately   Henry Adams.

MS: MH

To Elizabeth Cameron

Steamer "W. G. Hall." 13 Sept. 1890.

At sea again, or rather in port, for just now, at seven o'clock in the morning, we are leaving the little village of Kailua, and running along the south coast of the island of Hawaii. We tore ourselves yesterday morning from our comforts at Honolulu, and after a day and night of seasick discomfort on a local steamer, filled with natives, we are now in sight of Mauna Loa, and at evening shall land at Punalu on the extreme southeastern end of the island. As I detest mountains, abominate volcanoes, and execrate the sea, the effort is a tremendous one; but I make it from a sense of duty to the savages who killed Captain Cook just about here a century ago.[1] One good turn deserves another. Perhaps they will kill me. I never saw a place where killing was less like murder. The ocean is calm and blue; the air so warm that I turned out of my sleepless berth at the first light of dawn, and sat in my pyjamas in the cool air with only a sense of refreshment; the huge flat bulk of Mauna Loa stretches down an interminable slope ahead of us, with the strange voluptuous charm peculiar to volcanic slopes, which always seem to invite you to lie down on them and caress them; the shores are rocky and lined with palms; the mountain sides are green, and patched with dark tufts of forest; the place is—an island paradise, made of lava; and the native boats—queer long coffins with an outrigger on one side resting in the water—are now coming out at some new landing-place, bringing mangoes, pine-apples, melons and alligator-pears, all which I am somewhat too nauseated to eat. Our steamer is filled with plaintive-looking native women—the old-gold variety—who vary in expression between the ferocious look of the warriors who worshipped Captain Cook and then killed him, and the melancholy of a generation obliged to be educated by missionaries. They have a charm in this extraordinary scope of expressions which run from tenderness to ferocity in a single play of feature, but I prefer the children, who are plaintive and sea-sick in stacks about the decks, and lie perfectly still, with their pathetic dark eyes expressing all sorts of vague sensations evidently more or less out of gear with the cosmos. The least sympathetic character is the occasional whiteman. Third-rate places seldom attract even third-rate men, but rather ninth-rate samples, and these are commonly the white men of tropical islands. I prefer the savages who were—at least the high chiefs—great swells and very much gentlemen, and killed Captain Cook.

Awoki, our Jap, has brought me a pineapple and orange, on which I have breakfasted, with a headache for outlook. We are off again, and on the sunny side of our steamer the heat is too great for comfort. We have to sit on the shady side, and mostly lose the view.

10 o'clock. We have been ashore to see where Captain Cook was killed, a hot little lava oven where the cliffs rise sharp over deep water,—some old crater-hole—of all sorts of intense blue. Only a hut was there, donkeys and mules, a few natives and a swarm of crabs jumping over the red rocks by the black-blue water. Mauna Loa slopes back for forty miles or so, behind. So now I shall try to take a nap, having done my duty, and will wonder, for amusement, whether you are at Beverly, and how you look there.

Kilauea Volcano House. Monday, Sept. 15. 7 A.M. Our pilgrimage is effected at last. I am looking, from the porch of the inn, down on the black floor of the crater, and its steaming and smoking lake, now chilled over, some two or three miles away, at the crater's further end. More impressive to my fancy is the broad sloping mass of Mauna Loa which rises beyond, ten thousand feet above us, a mass of rugged red lava, scored by deeper red or black streaks down its side, but looking softer than babies' flesh in this lovely morning sunlight, and tinged above its red with the faintest violet vapor. I adore mountains—from below. Like other deities, they should not be trodden upon. As La Farge remarked yesterday when I said that the ocean *looked* quiet enough: "It *is* quiet if you don't fool with it. How would *you* like to be sailed upon?" The natives still come up here and sit on the crater's edge to look down at the residence of their great Goddess, but they never go down into it. They say they're not rich enough. The presents cost too much. Mrs Dominis, the King's sister, and queen-expectant,[2] came up here in the year 1885, and brought a black pig, two roosters, champagne, red handkerchiefs, and a whole basket of presents, which were all thrown on the lava lake. The pig, having his legs tied, squealed half an hour before he was thoroughly roasted, and one of the roosters escaped to an adjoining rock, but was recaught and immersed. Only princesses are rich enough to do the thing suitably, and as Mrs Dominis is a Sunday-school Christian, she knows how to treat true deities. As for me, I prefer the bigger and handsomer Mauna Loa, and I routed La Farge out at six o'clock—or was it five?—to sketch it with its top red with the first rays of sun. Had La Farge not waited to put his trowsers on, he might have caught the rosy-fingered dawn in perfection, but he lost five minutes howling to Awoki for slippers alone. As the clouds cover the mountain by nine o'clock, and rain commonly sets in by noon in floods, one must be economical on dawns. Just now, all is serene and lovely, but one suffers to be beautiful. I am still seasick, reeling with nausea, from the horrible two hours of our landing from the steamer in the surf, and La Farge was not much better. I have not been so violently sick and faint for years, as when tossing up and down, six feet at a jump, in the boat by the steamer's side, waiting for fat native women to tumble into it. I wished I was dead and hadn't come, and wondered how I was going through five years misery like that. I am still wondering, for all my suffering is before me, and I think nothing but dreams of Typee sustains us,[3] for La Farge recovers from his sea-sickness slower than I, though he suffers less acutely. The demon of travel sandwiches in a day or two of enjoyment with a day of misery, and lures us on. After the horror of Saturday evening we had a lovely day's drive yesterday up here, over grassy mountain sides, and through lava beds sprinkled with hot-house shrubs and ferns. The air is delicious, and the temperature, when the clouds veil the sun, is perfect either for driving or walking. If we can only escape the steamer on the windward side! but that implies sixty miles of horseback, partly in deluges of rain.

Hilo. Sept. 18. If you do not know where Hilo is, don't look for it on the map. One's imagination is the best map for travellers. You may remember Hilo best because it is the place where Clarence King's waterfall of old-gold girls was situated.[4] The waterfall is still here, just behind the Severance house where we are staying. Mrs Severance took us down there half an hour ago.[5] She said nothing about the girls, but she did say that the boys used habitually to go over the fall as their after-school amusement; but of late they have given it up, and must be paid for doing it. The last man who jumped off the neighboring high rock required fifteen dollars. Mrs Severance told this sadly, mourning over the decline of the arts and of surf-bathing. A Bostonian named Brigham took a clever photograph of a boy, just half way down, the fall being perhaps twelve or fifteen feet. So passes the glory of Hawaii, and of the old-gold girl,—woe is me!

As La Farge aptly quoted yesterday from some wise traveller's advice to another, à propos of volcanoes: "You will be sorry if you go there, and you will be sorry if you don't go there, so I advise you to go." We went. The evening before last we tramped for two hours across rough blocks and layers of black glass; then tumbled down more broken blocks sixty or eighty feet into another hole; then scrambled half way down another crater— three in succession, one inside the other—and sat down to look at a steaming black floor below us, which ought to have been red-hot and liquid, spouting fountains of fire, but was more like an engine house at night with two or three engines letting off steam and showing head-lights. The scene had a certain vague grandeur as night came on, and the spots of fire glowed below while the new moon looked over the cliff above; but I do not care to go there again, nor did I care even to go down the odd thirty or forty feet to the surface of the famous "lake of liquid fire." It was more effective, I am sure, the less hard one hit one's nose on it. We tramped back in the dark; our lanterns went out, and we were more than three hours to the hotel.

Yesterday morning we had to mount horses at eight o'clock and we rode till half past two,—more than six hours—to get over only fifteen miles of rough lava. Then we struck a road and a wagon, and drove fifteen miles more, to Hilo, in an hour and a half. During the drive we passed through our first tropical forest, and I felt a sensation. You who are comfortably at home cannot conceive the hardship of us poor travellers in trying to imagine we are anywhere else. I pass my time chiefly in trying to explain how Kilauea and Hilo happen to be within driving distance of Beverly. I was bothered to distraction in pitching into the middle of a jungle of tropical trees, creepers, ferns and flowers, when I felt sure that no such thing existed near Salem or Manchester. Perhaps I can show you where it is, but just now I feel constantly puzzled to account for all I see.

Tomorrow we start, through mud and gulches of torrents, on a five day's ride to Kawaihae, eighty miles to the westward, where we take steamer again. If you will believe it, I do this to avoid a day's seasickness.

Steamer "Kinau," Tuesday, 23 Sept. I take it all back. Hawaii is fascinating, and I could dream away months here. Yet dreaming has not been my standard amusement of late. Never have I done such hard and continuous travelling as during the last ten days, since leaving Honolulu. I have told you how we reached Hilo. Friday morning early we left Hilo, according to our plan, with a circus of horses, to ride eighty miles, divided into four days. Rain was falling as we drove out the first eight miles to take horse at the end of the road, but we started off like Pantagruel, and in an hour arrived at a lovely cove or ravine called Onomea where La Farge sketched till noon; one of the sweetest spots on earth where the land and ocean meet like lovers, and the natives still look almost natural. That afternoon we rode eight miles further. The sky cleared; the sun shone; the breeze blew; the road was awful, in deep holes of mud, with rocky cañons to climb down and up at every half mile; but I never enjoyed anything in travel more thoroughly than I did this. Every ravine was more beautiful than the last, and each was a true Paul and Virginia idyll, wildly lovely in ways that made one forget life.[6] The intensely blue ocean foamed into the mouths of still inlets, saturated with the tropical green of ferns and dense woods, and a waterfall always made a back ground, with its sound of running water above the surf. The afternoon repaid all my five thousand miles of weariness, even though we had to pass the night at one of Spreckels' sugar plantations where saturnine Scotchmen and a gentle-spoken Gloucestershire house-keeper entertained us till seven o'clock Saturday morning when we started off again over the same mud-holes and through more cañons, which disturbed La Farge because the horses were not noble animals and warranted little confidence; but to me the enjoyment was perfect. At noon we lunched at another plantation where a rather pretty little German-American woman, of the bride class, entertained us very sweetly, and closed our enjoyment by playing to us Weber's last waltz, while we looked out under vines to the deep blue ocean as one does from the Newport cottages. That was at Laupahoehoe plantation, and that afternoon we passed Laupahoehoe and rode hard till half-past five, when I dismounted before a country-house, and, before I realised it, tumbled up steps into an open hall where three ladies in white dresses were seated. I had to explain that we had invited ourselves to pass the night, and they had to acquiesce. The family was named Horner, and were Americans running several plantations and ranches on the island. We passed the night of Sunday at the plantation of another son, or brother, of the same family, at Kukuihaele, and strolled down to see the Waipio valley, which is one of the Hawaiian sights. Yesterday we rode twelve miles up the hills, stopping to lunch at the house of one Jarrett who manages a great cattle ranch.[7] Jarrett was not there, but two young women were, and though they were in language and manners as much like other young women as might be, they had enough of the old-gold quality and blood to make them very amusing to me. They made me eat raw fish and squid, as well as of course the eternal poi to which I am now accustomed; then after lunch, while La Farge and I smoked or dozed and looked across the grass plains to the wonderful slopes of Mauna Loa and Mauna Kea, the two girls sat on mats under the trees and made garlands of roses and geranium which they fastened round our necks,—or rather round my neck and La Farge's hat. I was tremendously pleased by this, my first *lei*,—I believe they spell the word so, pronouncing it *lay*—and wore it down the long, dusty ride to Kawaihae where we were to meet the steamer, and where we arrived just at dark in an afterglow like Egypt. The girls also drove down, one of them returning to Honolulu by the same steamer. Kawaihae seemed a terrible spot, baked by the southern sun against a mountain of brown lava without a drop of fresh water for miles. When I dismounted and entered the dirty little restaurant, I found our two young ladies eating supper at a dusky table. They had ordered for me a perfectly raw fresh fish, and the old-goldest of the two showed me how to eat it, looking delightfully savage as she held the dripping fish in her hands and tore its flesh with her teeth. Jarrett was there, and took us under his care, so that an evening which threatened to be awful in heat and dirt, turned out delightful. They took us to a native house near by, where a large platform thatched with palm-leaves looked under scrubby trees across the moonlit ocean which just lapped and purred on the beach a few yards away. Then they made the mistress of the house—an old schoolmate, but a native and speaking little English—bring her guitar and sing the Hawaian songs. They were curiously plaintive, perhaps owing to the way of singing, but only one—Kamehameha's war-dance—was really interesting and sounded as though it were real. A large mat was brought out, and those of us who liked lay down and listened or slept. The moon was half-full, and shone exquisitely and Venus sank with a trail like the sun's.

From this queer little episode, the only touch of half-native life we have felt, we were roused by the appearance of the steamer at ten o'clock, and in due time were taken into the boat and set on board. I dropped my faded and tattered *lay* into the water as we were rowed out, and now while the "Kinau" lies at Mahukana, doing nothing, I write to tell you that our journey has been fascinating, in spite of prosaic sugar-plantations, and that I am yearning to get back to Waimea, where I might stay a month at Samuel Parker's great ranch, and ride his horses about the slopes of Mauna Kea, while indefinite girls of the old-gold variety should hang indefinite garlands round my bronzed neck.[8]

Sept. 24. Honolulu again. We arrived, seasick as usual, at five o'clock this morning, and returned to our house with a sense of recovering one childhood's home, only worried by the thought of starting again in three days, "sailing, sailing, over the seasick sea." My girl of the Waimea rose-wreath, who came by the steamer with us, was also desperately sea-sick, and I fed her brown eyes with pine-apple, the only refreshment she could take. The distant line of purple ocean still lies to the southward, and the sun still lightens the white surf outside the harbor of Honolulu, as it did when I must have sported here as a child, among the roses and centipedes; but the refuge of our infancy must know us no longer, and I shall be obliged to perpetrate my lurid water-color sketches henceforward somewhere else. Now that I look back on our Hawaian journey of the last ten days, it seems really a considerable experience, and one new to common travellers in gaiters. If you feel enough curiosity to know what others think of the same scenes, read Miss Bird's travels in the Sandwich Islands.[9] I have carefully avoided looking at her remarks, for I know that she always dilates with a correct emotion, and I yearn only for the incorrect ones; but you will surely see Islands of the soundest principles—travellers' principles, I mean,—if you read Miss Bird, who will tell you all that I ought to have seen and felt, and for whom the volcano behaved so well, and performed its correct motions so properly that it becomes a joy to follow her. To us the volcano was positively flat, and I sympathised actively with an Englishman, who, we were told, after a single glance at it, turned away and gazed only at the planets and the Southern Cross. To irritate me still more, we are now assured that the lake of fire by which we sat unmoved, became very active within four-and-twenty hours afterwards. These are our lucks. I never see the world as the world ought to be.

In revenge I have enjoyed much that is not to be set down in literary composition, unless by a writer like Fromentin or a spectacled and animated prism like La Farge.[10] He has taught me to feel the subtleness and endless variety of charm in the color and light of every hour in the tropical island's day and night. I get gently intoxicated on the soft violets and strong blues, the masses of purple and the broad bands of orange and green in the sunsets, as I used to *griser* myself on absynthe on the summer evenings in the Palais Royal before dining at Véfour's, thirty years ago. The outlines of the great mountains, their reddish purple glow, the infinite variety of greens and the perfectly intemperate shifting blues of the ocean, are a new world to me. To be sure, man is pretty vile, but perhaps woman might partly compensate for him, if one only knew where to find her.[11] As she canters about the roads, a-straddle on horseback, with wreaths of faded yellow flowers, and clothed in a blue or red or yellow night-gown, she is rather a riddle than a satisfaction.

I expected a letter by the steamer of the 12th, but nothing comes from the post-office. Only Dwight encloses an exquisite little note, written after you bade me good-bye, which should have reached me before I left Boston, but is even more welcome here. As the mail goes tomorrow I will cut off this piece of island-yarn today, and send it off, hoping to get a real letter on Saturday before I sail. Otherwise I shall be uneasy for fear you or Martha are in trouble.

Ever Yrs   Henry Adams.

MS: MHi

1. Captain James Cook (1728–1779), who discovered the Hawaiian Islands in 1778, was killed in Kealakekua Bay in 1779.

2. Lydia Kamakacha Paki (1838–1917), wife of John Owen Dominis, reigned as Queen Liliuokalani 1891–1893.

3. Herman Melville's idyllic narrative of his stay in the Marquesas, *Typee* (1846), had to sustain HA over some 2,500 miles of open sea before he would reach Samoa, his first destination in Polynesia.

4. Clarence King had visited Hawaii in 1872.

5. The wife of Henry W. Severance of California, U.S. consul general 1889–1893.

6. Bernardin de Saint-Pierre, *Paul et Virginie* (1787).

7. Paul Jarrett was the manager of the 227,000-acre cattle ranch that John Palmer Parker (1790–1868) of Boston had begun to buy and develop in 1847.

8. "Indefinite girls" refers to the intermarriage between Hawaiians and Caucasians in the dynasty founded by John Palmer Parker. He married the Hawaiian chiefess Kipikane, granddaughter of King Kamehameha I. Samuel K. Parker (b. 1853) was their grandson and one of his main heirs.

9. Isabella Bird Bishop (1831–1904), *The Hawaiian Archipelago: Six Months Among the Palm Groves, Coral Reefs, and Volcanoes of the Sandwich Islands* (1875).

10. Eugène Fromentin (1820–1876), painter, novelist, travel writer, *A Summer in the Sahara* (1857), *A Year in the Sahel* (1859).

11. Reginald Heber, "From Greenland's Icy Mountains" (the "Missionary Hymn," 1819): "What though the spicy breezes / Blow soft o'er Ceylon's isle, / Though every prospect pleases, / And only man is vile."

To John Hay

Kilauea Volcano. Sept. 15. 1890.

My dear Hay

Behold us arrived! I will not ask you to envy us, for I am not so much anyone's friend as to hate him to the degree of making a pleasure of ocean travel to annoy him; but, *enfin,* here we are! Only a month has passed, and I write this for our first regular mail; but I imagine myself to have been geological epochs wandering over a gigantic planet covered with a tropical ocean and spotted with volcanoes. Just now we are on top of the biggest volcano in the world, looking down on some miles square of black lava, with a smoking crater at the end, but it is in a state of lamb-like quiet, and

La Farge and I have sat on its rim all the morning making impossible sketches that were enough to drive it into convulsions. Its only revenge has been to cover itself with mist, and leave us to repent.

As usual, our journey has been an experience of great amusement varied by hideous discomfort. We are never on shore long enough to throw off nausea, but the nausea makes us the more conscious of land-pleasures. We had a dream-like establishment at Honolulu, a house that left us nothing to desire except to stay in it; but after a fortnight's content, we must needs go to sea again and suffer agonies to come here. We shall return to it, after more and worse agonies only to sail again in three days for Samoa.

I hardly know how much you would have enjoyed the trip, or how much we ourselves have enjoyed it. You are a better sailor than we, I fancy, and would not be punished as we are by sea-sickness which is my worst annoyance. You would enjoy the air, the sea and sky, the tropical change, and all that, at least as much as we do, and as we have had no adventures, accidents or events, and neither seen anyone nor done anything, you would have got real pleasure in that too. The old-gold girl, and all King's illusions of 1872, belong to a region of youth and poetry which no longer exists in 1890. The native is rather sympathetic and rather pathetic, but is no longer archaic and as yet affects me little. What is more to the point, I notice that La Farge, in spite of excellent intentions, evidently fails to feel a yearn towards them. We have met many, of course, and our hostess up here at this mountain farm-house, is a very nice and pleasing specimen of the sex; but I miss the true archaic charm, and feel only as though I were becoming a mulatto at home. Besides that they are much more Americanised, they have become much less friendly, and much fewer in number. They wear flower-garlands still, but do not throw them round your neck. Absolutely no chiefs or members of the old high families remain, and the common people are very common, with local attachments to cockroaches and centipedes. It is a case of Japan aggravated to final dissolution.

Sept. 23. Perhaps I have pitched the key of these previous remarks an octave or so too low. Now that I am returning to Honolulu after riding round the whole windward side of Hawaii from Punalu to the Waipio valley and across by way of Waimea to Kawaihae—near a hundred and fifty miles—stopping except at the Volcano only in private houses—I am much more inclined to be enthusiastic. The travelling is hard physically, but I have stood it well, and so, I think, has La Farge. The scenery, the sky and ocean, the mountains, the valleys and ravines, the lights, and the constant pleasure of breathing, are enjoyments such as I hardly expected ever again to feel. The only element I dislike is the sugar-plantations which give you comfortable quarters at night at the cost of destroying all that interests a traveller. Since King's time the entire coast on the windward or northern side of Hawaii has been turned over to sugar. Twentyfour huge plantations, each employing from two hundred to four hundred laborers of the lowest class of Japanese, Chinese or Portuguese, occupy all the cultivable land, ruining the beauty of the finest cañons and absolutely extinguishing the natives. With this exception I found everything fascinating. Even the old-gold girl has at moments shown signs of continued existence. The line between the natives and the sugar-planters has become sharp, but the native still exists, though rapidly disappearing except in half breed.

I could now begin and really enjoy myself among these people, if I chose to give a few months up to it; but after all is said and done, it is not what I want. I think Cuba probably would pay better even in local color. The Spaniard is better fun than the Yankee, and the Cuban women are as amusing, I think, as the old-gold variety. Our ride round the island has given me an unexpected amount of enjoyment, but unless we are detained by amusements to be revealed within three days, we shall still sail on the 27th for Samoa.

I have told you little or nothing except generalities. The episodes have not been startling; only just steady and varied enough to keep us alive. I have intruded into lots of houses where we were evidently not wanted, and into some where we were evidently welcome. We know half our steamer-list coming back, where we knew no one, going up. My greatest triumph is to have worn all yesterday afternoon a *lay* or garland of roses, made for me by semi-old-gold-girls whom I never had seen till luncheon, but who eat raw fish as naturally as they talked perfect English with a slight intonation. I too swallowed my raw fish and squid and *poi* to their amusement, and La Farge beamed through his spectacles, a sort of stained-glass cowboy, with a rose-garland round his helmet.

Sept. 24. Back in Honolulu early this morning. The mail goes at once, so I close short. Love to yours.

Ever   Henry Adams.

MS: RPB

To Lucy Baxter

Honolulu, 27 Sept. [1890]

My dear Miss Baxter

We go on board our steamer for Samoa at nine o'clock, and the hour is now a quarter past eight. Your letter of Sept. 12, reached me this afternoon. I have not much time for answering it, but I can at least let you know that it has arrived.

Please write to me, on a chance, to Tahiti, care of the U.S. Consul. I hope to get there in about six weeks, but may be months in getting away. A mail leaves San Francisco direct for Tahiti at the end of October.

Thus far we have had a very successful journey—hard work, and loathsome seasickness, but great enjoyment at times. As one enters the tropics the charm of atmosphere, color, sky, water and landscape, by day and night, quite take one out of oneself.

We have been four weeks on these islands. Ten days were devoted to a journey on Hawaii, a day to the eastward, to see the volcano. We saw it, and also rode on horseback over abominable roads, from one end of the island to the other, about one hundred miles. The volcano was just what I expected, and happened to be nearly at rest. If you will get Professor Dana's new book on volcanoes from the Athenaeum and look over it, you will understand exactly what it is.[1] The charm of Hawaii to us was not the volcano but the scenery, which is as varied as the whole coast of America from Oregon to Mexico, with Mexico thrown in. I never had a harder journey or enjoyed one more. We passed the nights with the sugar-planters, and the days on horseback in scenery that made me feel like a boy.

Here in Honolulu we have kept house. My old friend Hartwell, who lives at 259 Newbury Street in Boston, has a house here, beautifully situated above the town, which is a mile away. Sitting on his verandah we look out over the harbor, over the ocean, towards the South Seas; and here we pass our time. To amuse my idleness I have been trying to learn, under La Farge's instruction, to sketch in water-colors, and as I never studied drawing and cannot tell one color from another, the result is often more amusing to others than to me; but you can hardly believe how absorbing the work is, and how much entertainment one can get from creating what one is to throw away in an hour. After all, La Farge's work is about as inadequate as mine to represent the real color of these skies and seas.

The natives are interesting too, in a way, but they are now few in number, and not easy to meet in their old simplicity. Japanese, Chinese and Portuguese have taken their place. One must hunt in very out-of-the-way places for natives of the old simplicity. I have seen none. Indeed, though I have met many people, and yesterday had an interview with His Majesty King Kalekaua, I know almost nothing of society in Honolulu, and my only experience of the way in which people live, has been in travelling, when we forced ourselves into their houses, and, willing or not, they had to entertain us. All were Americans or Scotch, and none were peculiarly interesting.

Rough and trying as our long journey has been, I think it has done La Farge good. He is quite as pleasant a companion as ever, and now that we are used to each other, and I know his ways, I find him more companionable than ever. He sees things so differently that it is like having another set of senses. As for me, I am certainly the better for the journey. I sleep better, eat better, and am wholly free from depression, or care, or nervousness. If this animal and physical comfort lasts, I fear I shall never again be contented at home.

Your letter was but half-reassuring about yourself, but I still believe that you will some day hit it right and get your ideal, more or less; for ideals vary with years. I hear nothing from the family except a short letter from

Dwight. As this letter of mine will be slow in reaching you, I address it to Boston, and shall go on writing from time to time without waiting to hear from you, as your letters may be many months in reaching me. Don't stop writing every month. You are the only correspondent I have in the family.

Ever truly Yrs Henry Adams.

MS: MH
1. James Dwight Dana (1813–1895) of Yale, *Characteristics of Volcanoes* (1890). HA had the book with him.

To Elizabeth Cameron

Honolulu. Sat. Sept. 27, 1890

Our steamer is lying at the wharf; our trunks are on board; four o'clock in the afternoon has come; we have yet to dine, before driving down in the moonlight to take possession of our staterooms. At midnight, or soon afterwards, the "Alameda" sails, carrying us two thousand miles further. She has already earned my gratitude by bringing me your two letters; that of the 5th which lost its steamer; and that of the 12th. I write now only to acknowledge them. My letter will wait some three weeks for a conveyance from here, but it will still reach you earlier than any I can write from Samoa.

In the first place, I believe I can now say with confidence that your letters have all reached me. They have reversed the order of writing, but I have received all you mention. I hope that mine have reached you, but you can always tell with some certainty from the continuousness of the dates. They are a sort of diary, and should run together.

Then I must say—what you must understand without saying—that I am something more than dependent on your writing. Now that I am here I find what I expected to find when I came away—that you are my only strong tie to what I suppose I ought to call home. If you should go back on me, I should wholly disappear. Already the charm of tropical life has wiped out the nervous excitement and anxious sleeplessness of Washington. I feel no more worries except seasickness. I enjoy myself, and the sense of living, more than I had done in five years. I am glad to be dead to the old existence which was a torture, and to forget it, in a change as complete as that of another planet. You are the only remaining tie, but I still cling to you; although I shall be wholly white-haired when you next see me, and, if you throw me over, I shall not struggle. After all I have had more than my share.

All this egoism is only to vary the form. Your letters are so much to me that I cannot help dreading lest you should think them less than they are. So you think me a poet? I have had another high compliment today. I finished at last a drawing of a ridiculous, quite infantile palm-tree, growing out of red tufa-rock, with a violent yellow supposed sand-beach beyond, and a blue-green surf, backed by a purple ocean. To my surprise, and naturally to my huge flattery, La Farge struck on it at once, called it a success, and said it was remarkable. I would fold and enclose it to you, just to gratify your innocent curiosity, if I had not packed up all my large envelopes and sent them on shipboard; but you can take my word that it is the kind of thing Martha might aspire to do, as ill-drawn and childlike as Lear's Nonsense.[1] In my belief this is why it pleases La Farge. The lights and colors, the shadows and variations of this atmosphere are impossible to paint. You can give an idea of a Scotch mountain, but you cannot begin to render in art a suggestion of Mauna Loa or Mauna Kea or Haleakala. Air and ocean, sun and sky, combine to defy paint. La Farge feels this, and yet is fascinated by the wonderful beauties which he knows he can't catch, and is always catching at. So when he sees a childlike daub in purple and yellow masses, with a blue sky, whose very childishness gives a sort of light and distance to it, he thinks it good. He knows that if it were really good, it *must* be bad.

He and I had our audience of the King yesterday. We went to the little palace at half-past nine in the morning, and Kalekaua received us informally in his ugly drawing-room. His Majesty is half Hawaian, half negro; talks quite admirable English in a charming voice; has admirable manners; and—forgive me just this once more—seems to me a somewhat superior Chester A. Arthur; a type surprisingly common among the natives. To be sure His Majesty is not wise, and he has—or is said to have—vices, such as whiskey and—others; but he is the only interesting figure in the government, and is really what the Japs call omusuroi,—amushroi—amusing. I have listened by the hour to the accounts of his varied weaknesses and especially to his sympathies with ancient Hawaii and archaic faiths, such as black pigs and necromancy; but yesterday he sat up straight and talked of Hawaiian archeology and arts as well as though he had been a professor. He was quite agreeable, though not, like our own chief magistrate, an example of the Christian virtues. I would not be thought to prefer Kalekaua to Benjamin Harrison, but I own to finding him a more amusing object.

Socially this seems a queer place. I cheerfully forgive society for ignoring us, for I have caught glimpses enough of it to imagine worse than Washingtonian horrors; but I find it strange that no one ever suggests our doing anything social, or tells us of anything to be done, or desirable to do. I make my own inferences, but without much real knowledge. After a month, I know little or nothing of Honolulu. We know everybody of much account, but we have not even been put up at the club. Almost no one has called on us. As for dinners or parties, we have as yet cost Honolulu not a bottle of wine. Apparently in order to see the interior of a white man's house here, one must invite oneself into it, as we did on our journey last week. I should suppose we had given offence, except that no one seems to do more than we do, or to have more social vogue.

Now for one request before another long departure. Please, some day, drive out to Rock Creek Cemetery and see if my work is done or doing. Take Rebecca to see it.[2]

Hasta luego.

MS: MHi
1. Edward Lear (1812–1888), traveler and artist-author of *The Book of Nonsense* (1846) and other "Nonsense" works.
2. Rebecca Dodge Rae.

To Elizabeth Cameron

The Equator. Oct. 2, 1890.

I believe it was Charles Lamb who created the new crime of speaking ill of the Equator.[1] For my own protection I can say that I know no harm of it. The temperature was a little cool at five o'clock when I took my usual shower-bath on deck, and now, at eight, when I sit down on the venerable sea-chair which I never quit, to write a few lines of record for this momentous occasion, I am quite comfortable in my white suit, without a hat, in the draught of the foresail. I wish I could speak as well of my comfort in other respects, without regard to the equator; but this voyage has shaken my confidence more than any other experience. I am more persistently and inexcusably seasick than ever, and the annoyance becomes more and more intolerable. I think of asking the ship's doctor whether in his opinion I am going to have a baby, for my sensations seem more nearly to resemble that feminine stage of life than any masculine experience; but to endure it all, and have no baby, seems to take the fun out of life. I begin to dread every new movement, and look forward with terror to retracing my thousands of miles. In three more days we are to be dropped overboard into a native cutter, filled with cockroaches, off Tutuila, and must sail sixty miles to Apia. I dread it like a nightmare, not on account of the cockroaches, but because of the new and acute variety of seasickness which I must suffer. If I were a good sailor I could find constant pleasure in this travel, but my pleasure is terribly streaked, as it stands.

October 3. The Equator behaved like a gentleman yesterday, and for a few hours I almost forgot to be seasick, and dabbled in water-colors. La Farge actually put on a light overcoat in the evening. This morning, before dawn, when in a moment of wakefulness, I stept out on the solitary deck, the moon seemed gone wrong. She had got to the north of me, and today, I am told, we pass the sun. I am not so familiar with these great celestial dignitaries—Equators, Moons, Suns, and King Kalakauas—as to know precisely how to behave in treating them with such familiarity as to pass by without saluting them. To be under the Sun and south of the Moon, sounds like a fairy story for Martha.[2] Yet except for indescribable sunsets and sunrises, all is commonplace enough, and our steamer is filled with the usual run of colonial people, differing from Atlantic travellers only in talking of Australia and New Zealand rather than of New York and London. I am a morose traveller, and being now fairly dead I have no more prickings of conscience, and never speak to anyone unless I am spoken to. Apparently my face tells this story, for no one ever speaks to me, and La Farge is little more favored than I. So we sit together in our usual solitude *à deux,* and laugh at our own little jests, while the passengers collect every evening in a Congress and debate the relative merits of their colonies with obvious jealousy of the United States.

The purser tells me that the "Zealandia" picks up the mail at Tutuila on the 10th. Shall I reach Apia in time to send this letter from there to announce our arrival? Probably I shall have a day to spare, and will risk it.

Apia. October 9. Well! we are here, and I am sitting in the early morning on the verandah of a rough cottage, in a grove of cocoa-nut palms, with native huts all about me, and across the grass, fifty yards away, I can see and hear the sea with its distant line of surf on the coral reef beyond. Natives, clothed mostly in a waist-cloth, but sometimes their toilet completed by a hybiscus or other flower in their hair, pass every moment or two before my cabin, often handsome as Greek gods. I am the guest of Consul Sewell, whose consulate is within the same grove, near the beach.[3] In short, we are here, and for once I feel a little as though I had really got where I expected; but one pays for such luxuries. I still feel seasick, though more than twenty-four hours ashore; and my worst fears of the cutter were more than realised. Sunday morning at nine o'clock or thereabouts the "Alameda" turned a corner of Tutuila, and I saw the little schooner knocking about in the open sea beyond. The day was overcast, threatening rain. From the shore, half a dozen large boats, filled with naked savages, were paddling down with the wind, singing a curiously wild chant to their paddles. La Farge and I felt that we were to be captured and probably eaten, but the cruise of sixty miles in a forty-ton schooner, beating to windward in tropical squalls, was worse than being eaten. We dropt into the boat among scores of naked Samoans, half of them swimming, or clambering over our backs, with war-clubs to sell, and when we reached our schooner, we stood in the rain and watched the "Alameda" steam away. That was our first joy. Whatever fate was in store, we had escaped from the steamer, and might die before another could come.

The cutter was commanded by Captain Peter, a huge captain, but little skilled in the languages with which I am more or less acquainted. His six sailors were as little fluent in English as though they had studied at Harvard. Captain Peter talked what he supposed to be English with excessive energy, but we could catch only the three words "now and again," repeated with frequency but in no apparent connection. "Now and again" something was to happen; meanwhile he beat up under the shore into quieter water, and presently, in a downpour of rain, we cast anchor in a bay, with mountains above, but a sand beach within the coral reef, and native huts half hidden among the cocoanut palms. I insisted on going ashore straightway without respect for H.M.'s mail; and Captain Peter seemed not unwilling. A splendid naked savage carried La Farge, in an india-rubber waterproof, mildly kicking, from the boat to the shore, and returned for me. I embraced his neck with effusive gratitude, and so landed on the island of Tutuila which does not resemble the picture on the Oceanic Steamship Company's colored advertisement. I found it densely covered with tropical mountains and vegetation, but glad as I was to set foot on mountains and see vegetation, I was soon more interested in the refined hospitality of the cultured inhabitants. We entered the nearest hut, and put on our best manners, which were none too good, for the natives had manners that made me feel withered prematurely in association with the occupants of pig-sties. Grave, courteous, with quiet voices and a sort of benevolence beyond the utmost expressiveness of Benjamin Franklin, they received us and made us at home. The cabin was charming when one looked about it. Nearly circular, with a diameter of some forty feet, its thatched roof, beautifully built up, came within about five feet of the ground, ending there on posts, and leaving the whole house open to the air. Within, mats covered a floor of white corals, smooth and almost soft like coarse sand. Fire was made in the middle of the hut. Only women and children were there. One was staining a tapa-cloth; another was lying down unwell; others were sitting about, and one or two naked children, wonderfully silent and well-behaved, sat and stared at us. We dropped our umbrellas and water-proofs and sat down on the mats to wait for Captain Peter to sail; but presently a proud young woman entered and seated herself in silence after shaking hands. Captain Peter succeeded in making us understand that this was the chief's daughter. Other young women dropped in, shook hands and sat down. Soon we seemed to have a *matinée*. As no one could say more than a word or two in the other's language, communication was as hard as at a Washington party, but it was more successful. In a very short time we were all intimate. La Farge began to draw the Princess, as we called her, and Wakea—for that was her name,—was pleased to drop her dress-shirt, and sit for him in her native undress, with a dignity and gravity quite indescribable.[4] The other girls were less imposing, but very amusing. One, Sivà, a younger sister of the Princess, was fascinating. Of course I soon devoted my attention to talking, and, as I could understand nothing, talk was moderately easy; but through Captain Peter we learned a little, and some of the touches of savagery were perfect. I asked Sivà her name—mine was Henli,—and her age. She did not know her age; even her father, an old man, could not say how many years old she was. I guessed fourteen, equivalent to our eighteen. All her motions were splendid, and she threw a plate on the floor, as Martha Braggiotti would say, like a race-horse. Her lines were all antique, and in face she recalled a little my niece Lulu, Molly's sister.[5] Presently she brought a curious pan-shaped wooden dish, standing on eight legs, all of one block; and sitting down behind it, began to grate a dry root, like flag-root but larger, on a grater, over the dish. This was rather hard work, and took some time. Then another girl brought some cocoa-nuts full of water, and she poured the water on the grated root. Then she took a bundle of clean cocoa-nut fibre, and seemed to wash her hands in the water which was already muddy and dirty with the grated root. We divined that she really strained out the grated particles, which were caught on the fibre, and wrung out by another girl. When all the grains were strained off, the drink was ready, and we realised that we had got to swallow it, for this was the *kawa,* and we were grateful that in our first experience the root was grated, not chewed, as it ought to be, by the girls. Please read Kingsley's account of it, in the "Earl and the Doctor," a book you will probably be able to borrow from Herbert, as it was done for or by his brother Pembroke.[6] A cocoa-nut half full of it was handed to us, and as usual La Farge, who had kicked at the idea more than I did, took to it at once, and drank it rather freely. I found it "not nice, papa, but funny"; a queer, lingering, varying, aromatic, arumatic, Polynesian, old-gold flavor, that clings to the palate like creosote or coal-oil. I drank the milk of a green cocoanut to wash it off, but all the green cocoa-nuts in the ocean could not wash out that little taste. After the *kawa* we became still more intimate. Besides Wakea and her sister Sivà, we made the acquaintance of Tuvale, Amerika, Sitoa, and Faaiwu, which is no other than Fayaway, I imagine.[7] We showed them our writing, and found that they could all write very well, as they proved by writing us letters on the spot, in choice Samoan, which we tried to translate, with the usual result. So evening came on; we had some supper; a kerosene lamp was lit; and La Farge and I began to cry out for the *Siva.*

The *Siva,* we had learned to know at Hawaii, is the Samoan dance, and the girl, Sivà, had already been unable to resist giving us snatches of the songs and motions. Sivà was fascinating. She danced all over, and seemed more Greek in every new motion. I could not understand what orders were given by the elders, but, once they were assured that we were not missionaries, all seemed right. The girls disappeared; and after some delay, while I was rather discouraged, thinking that the Siva was not to be, suddenly, out of the dark, five girls came into the light, with a dramatic effect that really I never felt before. Naked to the waist, their rich skins glistened with cocoanut oil. Around their heads and necks they wore garlands of green leaves in strips, like seaweeds, and these too glistened with oil, as though the girls had come out of the sea. Around their waists, to the knee, they wore leaf-cloths, or *lavalavas,* also of fresh leaves, green and red. Their faces and figures varied in looks, some shading the negro too closely; but Sivà was divine, and you can imagine that we found our attention absorbed in watching her. The mysterious depths of darkness behind, against which the skins and dresses of the dancers mingled rather than contrasted; the sense of remoteness and of genuineness in the stage-management; the conviction that at last the kingdom of old-gold was ours, and that we were as good Polynesiacs as our neighbors,—the whole scene and association gave so much freshness to our fancy that no future experience, short of being eaten, will ever make us feel so new again. La Farge's spectacles quivered with emotion and gasped for sheer inability to note everything at once. To me the dominant idea was that the girls, with their dripping grasses and leaves, and their glistening breasts and arms, had actually come out of the sea a few steps away. They entered in file, and sat down opposite us. Then the so-called Siva dance began. The girls sat cross-legged, and the dance was as much song as motion, although the motion was incessant. As the song or chant, a rhythmical and rather pleasant, quick movement, began, the dancers swayed about; clapped their hands, shoulders, legs; stretched out their arms in every direction and with every possible action, always in harmony, and seldom repeating the same figure. We had dozens of these different motives until I thought the poor girls would be exhausted, for they made so much muscular effort, feet, thighs, hips and even ribs working as energetically as the arms, that they panted at the close of each figure; but they were evidently enjoying it as much as we, and kept it up with glances at us and laughter among themselves. All through this part of the performance, our Princess did not dance but sat before us on the mats, and beat time with a stick. At last she too got up, and after ten minute's absence, reappeared, costumed like the rest, but taller and more splendid. La Farge exploded with enthusiasm for her, and expressed boundless contempt for Carmencita.[8] You can imagine the best female figure you ever saw, on about a six foot scale, neck, breast, back, arms and legs, all absolutely Greek in modelling and action, with such freedom of muscle and motion as the Greeks themselves hardly knew, and you can appreciate La Farge's excitement. When she came in the other dancers rose, and then began what I supposed to be a war or sword-dance, the Princess brandishing a stick and evidently destroying her enemies, one of whom was a comic character and expressed abject cowardice. With this performance the dance ended; Sivà got out the *kawa* dish; Wakea and the others went for our tobacco, and soon we were all sprawling over the mats, smoking, laughing, trying to talk, with a sense of shoulders, arms, legs, cocoa-nut oil, and general nudeness most strangely mixed with a sense of propriety. Anyone would naturally suppose such a scene to be an orgy of savage license. I don't pretend to know what it was, but I give you my affidavit that we could see nothing in the songs or dances that suggested impropriety, and that not a word or a sign during our whole stay could have brought a blush to the cheek of Senator Hale himself. Unusual as the experience is of half-dressed or undressed women lying about the floor, in all sorts of attitudes, and as likely as not throwing their arms or their shoulders across one as one lies or sits near them, as far as we could see the girls were perfectly good, and except occasionally for hinting that they would like a present of a handkerchief, or for giving us perhaps a ring, there was no approach to familiarity with us. Indeed at last we were extinguished by dropping a big mosquito netting over us, so that we were enclosed in a private room; the girls went off to their houses; our household sank into perfect quiet, and we slept in our clothes on the floor as comfortably as we knew how, while the kerosene lamp burned all night in the centre of the floor.

The next morning we very unwillingly tumbled into our boat, after a surf-bath, and then, for the next four or five hours, we were pitching about, in a head wind and sea, trying to round the western point of Tutuila. Nothing could be more lovely than the day, the blue sea, and the green island stretching away in different planes of color, till lost in the distance; but I could only lie flat on deck, and fight seasickness. At two o'clock that afternoon we rounded our point, and our boat went ashore to fetch off Consul Sewall and Lieut. Parker on their return from Pango Pango, where they had gone to settle on the new naval station.[9] They came instantly on board, and we four Americans then lay on the deck of that cutter from two o'clock Monday afternoon, till two o'clock Wednesday morning, thirtysix hours, going sixty miles, in a calm, with a vertical sun overhead, and three of the four seasick. You can conceive that we were glad to reach Apia on any terms, and tumbled ashore, in a leaky boat, in the dead of night, only too glad to get shelter about the consulate. Our only excitement at sea was a huge shark that looked like a whale. Once ashore, supper and bed were paradise; but my brain and stomach went on turning somersaults, and I was not wholly happy.

October 12. Sunday here, when it should be Saturday, but Samoa is above astronomy. Time has already made us familiar with our surroundings. I find myself now and then regaining consciousness that I was once an American supposing himself real. The Samoan is so different from all my preconceived ideas, that my own identity becomes hazy, and yours alone remains tolerably clear. I took one day of entire rest, after arriving, and passed it in looking at the sea, and rejoicing to have escaped it. The second day we performed our visits of ceremony. First, we called on King Malietoa, and I assure you that I was not in the least inclined to joke about him. He is not *opera bouffe,* or Kalakaua. The ceremony was simple as though we were in a democratic republic. We began by keeping His Majesty waiting half an hour while we lounged over our cigars after breakfast. When we arrived at the audience-house, we found Malietoa gone, but he was sent for, and came to receive us. The house was the ordinary native house, such as we were in at Tutuila. We sat on the floor. Malietoa was alone, without officers or attendants, and was dressed as usual with chiefs on state occasions, in an ordinary white linen jacket and trowsers. He is an elderly man, with the usual rather pathetic expression of these islanders, and with the charming voice and manner which seem to belong to high chiefs. He talked slowly, with a little effort, but with a dignity and seriousness that quite overawed me. As the interpreter translated, I caught only the drift of his words, which were at first formal; then became warm in expressions of regard for Americans; and at last turned to an interesting and rather important discussion of the political dangers and uneasiness in these islands. He said nothing of his own sufferings or troubles, but seemed anxious for fear of disturbance here, and evidently dreads some outbreak against his own authority unless the three foreign powers execute their treaty promptly, which the three foreign powers seem, for reasons of their own, determined not to do. If you want a lecture on Samoan politics, I am in a fair way to be able to give you one; for though I loathe the very word, and of all kinds of politics detest most those of islands, I am just soaked with the stuff here, where the natives are children, full of little jealousies and intrigues, and the foreigners are rather worse than the natives. The three foreign powers have made a mess, and the natives are in it.[10] Even in case they fight, I do not much expect to be massacred, as Americans are very popular indeed; but I am a great *alí*,—nobleman—because all the natives knew the frigate "Adams," and I am the first American who has ever visited the country merely for pleasure;[11] so I feel bound to look grave and let Sewall do the talking. Malietoa was sad and despondent; Mataafa, the intermediary king, who led the fighting after Maliatoa's deportation, and was deposed by the treaty of Berlin, seemed also depressed, but was even more earnest in his expressions of gratitude to America. We made also a ceremonial call on Mataafa, after we had seen Malietoa, and while we were going through the unavoidable *kawa*, which becomes a serious swallow after many repetitions, Mataafa talked of his gratitude to America. I won't bore you by explaining why he is grateful. I don't much care myself; and was much more interested in watching the dignity of his face, the modulation of his voice, the extraordinary restraint and refinement of his rhetoric, and the exquisite art of the slight choking in his voice as he told us that his only hope was in Christ and in America,—I felt more interest, in the art of his civilisation, you understand, than I did in the detail that Bayard and Sewall had saved the islanders from being killed or enslaved. As rhetoricians and men of manners, the great Samoan chiefs, and, for that matter, the little ones too, make me feel as though I were the son of a camel driver degraded to the position of stable-boy in Spokane West Centre. Aristocracy can go no further, and any ordinary aristocracy is vulgar by the side of the Samoan. For centuries these people have thought of nothing else. They have no other arts worth mentioning. Some day I will tell you of their straw mats, their chief artistic pride; their houses, too, are artistic in their way, and their taste in colors is splendidly bold; but their real art is social, and they have done what in theory every scientific society would like to do,—they have bred themselves systematically. Love-marriages are unknown. The old chiefs select the wives for the young chiefs, and choose for strength and form rather than beauty of face. Each village elects a girl to be the village maiden, a sort of candidate for ambitious marriage, and she is the tallest and best made girl of the good society of the place. She is bound to behave herself, and marry a handsome young chief. The consequence is that the chiefs are the handsomest men you can imagine, physically Apollos, and the women can all carry me in their arms as though I were a baby.

The chief of Apia is Seumano, the hero of the hurricane, who took his boat through the surf and saved the shipwrecked crews.[12] Our government sent him a present of a fancy whaleboat, very handsome though a little like a man-of-war, requiring fifty men to move it. Seumano is a giant in strength; his wife, Fatolea, is quite a *grande dame,* and their adopted daughter, Fanua, is the village maiden, or Taupo, of Apia. Sewall got Seumano, who is as warmly American as all the rest, to give us a big Siva dance that we might see the thing properly, and the occasion was evidently one of general interest. In general the scene was the same as at Nua in Tutuila, but instead of an improvised affair, Seumano gave us a regular party, with the whole village taking part or looking on. Fanua was the centre girl, and had nine or ten companions. Fanua wore an immensely high and heavy head-dress that belongs to the village maiden. The others were dressed in the Siva costume, but spoiled their effect by wearing banana leaves round their breasts, in deference to missionary prejudices. The figure is everything in the native dance, and the color counts almost as much as dress with you creatures of civilisation. The banana leaves were as little objectionable as such symbols of a corrupt taste could be, but they reminded one of the world and the devil. Our impromptu at Nua was better, for though some of the girls were more or less grotesque, the handsome ones, with fine figures, were tremendously effective. You can imagine what would be the effect of applying such a test to a New York ball-room, and how unpopular the banana-leaf would be with girls whose figures were better than their faces. Nevertheless the Siva was a good one, especially in the singing and the drill. The older women sat in the dark behind the girls, and acted as chorus. Sewall, his vice Consul Blacklock, La Farge and I sat in front, opposite the dancers. Towards the end, when the dancers got up and began their last figure, which grows more and more vivacious to the end, Fanua, who had mischief in her eyes, pranced up before me, and bending over, put her arms round my neck and kissed me. The kissing felt quite natural and was loudly applauded with much laughter, but I have been redolent of cocoa-nut oil ever since, and the more because Fanua afterwards gave me her wreaths, and put one over my neck, the other round my waist, dripping with cocoa-nut oil.

October 14. I am hazy on dates. This may be any day of the week or month. I only know time by its passage. The weather has been warm, about 88° at noon-day, though cool enough except from eleven till four. Yesterday morning I took my boat out fishing on the reef. By-the-bye, I have set up a boat, as one sets up a carriage. The Consulate had none, and I thought I could repay Sewall's civility no better than by giving him a boat; so we have a swell man-of-war's boat with five fine natives to row us, and an awning and a consular flag, fine as Fiji. These luxuries are not inexpensive. A boat here costs as much or more than a carriage at home; but here I must be a great alí or bust. So, as I had nothing for my boat to do, I took it out to see how the natives fished. My stroke oar, or coxswain, did the fishing, and succeeded in catching a squid, or octopus, about twelve or eighteen inches span in the tentacles. The process was curious, and I shall write about it to Willy Phillips; but the fun came afterwards. Sewall sent the squid to Mele Samsoni—in English, Mary Hamilton—a native woman, married to an elderly American, who lives near by,—and asked her to make some squid soup for us. So at noon we had a lunch in Samsoni's hut in the banana grove hard by. There was old Hamilton—once a whaleman and pilot,—his wife Mele or Mary, three girls who live with them, Sewall, Blacklock, La Farge and I, sitting on the mats with the lunch spread on banana leaves before us. The squid soup was first distributed, and I found it delicious; rather rich, but not so strong as either clams or oysters. The squid is cut up and boiled in cocoa-nut milk. I am certain that in French hands it could be made a great success. To my horror I was then given a large dish of the squid itself. I had seen it for sale, dried, as an article of food in Japan, and had even tried to eat it in Honolulu where our American friends regarded it as they do oysters or truffles; but this was my first meeting with it face to face, and I attacked it with the shudder of desperate courage. In the end I eat nearly the whole beast, refused to eat anything else, and afterwards sucked half a dozen oranges, drank a green cocoa-nut, smoked a cigar and dropped off asleep, while Mele Samsoni fanned the flies from me with a banana leaf.

October 16. Yesterday I moved into my native house. We sleep and eat at the Consulate, but I have set up a native house as a studio and reception-room. It is a large, handsome hut, commonly used as the guest-house of the village. The native church stands between it and the sea which is fifty yards away. Mataafa's house is a few rods to the right, across the village green. Native houses are scattered round the green. Bread-fruit trees and cocoanut palms surround us. Just now half a dozen girls in costumes varying between the ordinary missionary nightgowns and the native waist-cloth, are chattering about the place, doing so-called work for us. Yesterday Mataafa sent us a chief with a big green-turtle as a gift, which is a present only made to great people. We are engaged for no end of feasts and dances, and I fear that the missionaries are deeply disgusted because we have caused their best parishioners to violate church discipline by our grand Siva at Seumano's, which turns out to have been a political event and demonstration of Samoan nationality. As we avow without disguise our preference for old Samoan customs over the European innovations, we must expect to give offence; but a just fear of ridicule restrains me from the only truly comfortable step of adopting the native want of costume. Possibly the mosquitoes and flies have something to do with the ridicule too.

Yesterday afternoon we took the boat to town, which is a mile or more away, and a heavy rain drove us to shelter in Seumano's where we were entertained with a pineapple and the infernal *kawa* which I swallow only by compulsion. I asked Seumano to show us his fine mats, so the women took down the bundle from the cross-beams where their valuables are stored, and untied it, producing half a dozen mats, about the texture of the finest Panama straw, some five or six feet square. These are the Samoan jewels and heirlooms, which give distinction and power to their owner, and are the dowry of the women. The gift of a fine mat will pay for a life, and the last war was caused by an attempt to confiscate mats. If possible I will buy one and send it to you, but you can do nothing with it, for it is too rare for use, and not showy enough for ornament. You will have to put it into a coarser mat, tie it with cords in a bundle, and put it up in the attic, if you wish to be appreciative and Samoan. Fine mats are rarely made now; the whole number of them in existence is small and diminishing; they are more highly prized than ever by the chiefs, and I am almost ashamed to take any out of the country. Just as I am writing, a woman has come in from a neighboring village with four fine mats for sale, and I have bought the oldest and most worn, but the best, for a little more than thirty dollars. If I send it to you, it must go to Martha as a dowry to secure her a handsome young chief for a husband. Three or four such would secure her the swellest match in Samoa.

October 17. Yesterday afternoon Sewall took La Farge and me to call on Robert Louis Stevenson. We mounted some gawky horses and rode up the hills about an hour on the native road or path which leads across the island. The forest is not specially exciting; not nearly so beautiful as that above Hilo in Hawaii, but every now and again, as Captain Peter, or Pito, used to say, we came on some little touch of tropical effect that had charm, especially a party of three girls in their dress of green leaves, or *titi*, which La Farge became glowing about. The afternoon was lowering, with drops of rain, and misty in the distance. At last we came out on a clearing dotted with burned stumps exactly like a clearing in our backwoods. In the middle stood a two-story Irish shanty with steps outside to the upper floor, and a galvanized iron roof. A pervasive atmosphere of dirt seemed to hang around it; and squalor like a railroad navvy's board hut. As we reached the steps a figure came out that I cannot do justice to. Imagine a man so thin and emaciated that he looked like a bundle of sticks in a bag, with a head and eyes morbidly intelligent and restless. He was costumed in very dirty striped cotton pyjamas, the baggy legs tucked into coarse knit woollen stockings, one of which was bright brown in color, the other a purplish dark tone. With him was a woman who retired for a moment into the house to reappear a moment afterwards, probably in some change of costume, but, as far as I could see, the change could have consisted only in putting shoes on her bare feet. She wore the usual missionary nightgown which was no cleaner than her husband's shirt and drawers, but she omitted the stockings. Her complexion and eyes were dark and strong, like a half-breed Mexican.[13] They received us cordially enough, and as soon as Stevenson heard La Farge's name and learned who he was, they became very friendly, while I sat by, nervously conscious that my eyes could not help glaring at Stevenson's stockings, and wondering, as La Farge said, which color he would have chosen if he had been obliged to wear a pair that matched. We sat an hour or more, perched on his verandah, looking down over his field of black stumps, and the forest beyond, to the misty line of distant ocean to the northward. He has bought a hundred acres or more of mountain and forest so dense that he says it costs him a dollar for every foot he walks in it. To me the place seemed oppressively shut in by forest and mountain, but the weather may have caused that impression. When conversation fairly began, though I could not forget the dirt and discomfort, I found Stevenson extremely entertaining. He has the nervous restlessness of his disease, and, although he said he was unusually well, I half expected to see him drop with a hemorage at any moment, for he cannot be quiet, but sits down, jumps up, darts off and flies back, at every sentence he utters, and his eyes and features gleam with a hectic glow.[14] He seems weak, and complains that the ride of an hour up to his place costs him a day's work; but, as he describes his travels and life in the South Seas, he has been through what would have broken me into a miserable rag. For months he has sailed about the islands in wretched trading schooners and stray steamers almost worse than sailing vessels, with such food as he could get, or lived on coral atolls eating bread-fruit and yams, all the time working hard with his pen, and of course always dirty, uncomfortable and poorly served, not to speak of being ill-clothed, which matters little in these parts. He has seen more of the islands than any literary or scientific man ever did before, and knows all he has seen. His talk is most entertaining, and of course interested us peculiarly. He says that the Tahitians are by far finer men than the Samoans, and that he does not regard the Samoans as an especially fine race, or the islands here as specially beautiful. I am not surprised at the last opinion, for I do not think this island of Upolo very beautiful as these islands go; certainly not so beautiful as the Hilo district of Hawaii; but I shall wait for our own judgment about the men and women. Tahiti and Nukuheva are his ideals, which encourages us with something to look forward to. He had much to say about his experiences, and about atolls, French *gens d'armes*, beach-combers, natives and Chinamen; about the island of Flatterers where the natives surrounded him and stroked him down, saying "Alofa," "Love," and "You handsome man," "You all same as my father"; and about islands where the girls took away all his plug tobacco and picked his pocket of his matchbox, and then with the utmost dignity gave him one match to light his cigarette. But the natives, he says, are always respectable, while some of the whites are degraded beyond description. Pembroke, in his "South Sea Bubbles" has scandalised all Polynesia by libelling the chieftainess of one island where he was very hospitably treated, and is said to have behaved very ill. I can easily understand getting very much mixed up about Polynesian morals, for I feel that the subject is a deep one, and the best informed whites seem perplexed about it; but I remember how much poor Okakura was perplexed by the same subject in America, and how frankly La Farge and I avowed our own ignorance even among our own people. Stevenson is about to build a house, and says he shall never leave the island again, and cannot understand how any man who is able to live in the South Seas, should consent to live elsewhere.[15]

October 22. Time runs on, bringing no great variety, but every day a little novelty to amuse us. I have taken to my water-colors again, because I find that La Farge will not paint unless I make believe to do so. We sit in our native house, receiving visits; watching what goes on among the natives of the village; firing off our Kodaks at everything worth taking; and sketching the most commonplace object we can find, because the objects worth sketching are unsketchable. Every day I pick up more queer knowledge of the people about me,—knowledge that would have made a great Professor of me twenty years ago, but now has no other value than to amuse me for the moment, and perhaps to amuse you some day when my wanderings end. Our great neighbor Mataafa comes over to see us often, and sends us many fruits and eatables; but the most entertaining of his attentions is the *tafolo* which he sends every day. Usually at eleven o'clock we hear shouts from the further side of the village green, and instantly two splendid young men, dressed only in their waistcloths—lavalavas—of green leaves, with garlands of green leaves round their heads, come running and jumping and shouting across the green towards our house. As they come near we see that their faces are blackened; sometimes one whole side is black, sometimes only a square or wedge-shaped patch at the corner of the mouth; and their look is ferocity itself; but they arrive in a broad laugh, and one of them carries a wooden trough, full of baked breadfruit kneaded with cocoa-nut milk and generally a little salt-water, which he sets on the ground under our eaves, and then ladles out with his hands into large breadfruit leaves, after which they bound away again. I can do no more than taste it, for it is a rich, pasty stuff, like corn-starch or batter; but the natives consider it a great treat; and yesterday Mele Samsoni and Fangalo and various other guests came to share Mataafa's generosity. La Farge and I photographed the two men as they ladled out their *tafolo;* but I fear it will be a long time before I know how my photograph succeeded. By the coming mail I shall send letters to all the "family," and shall enclose a few photographs; but to give an external appearance of equality to the letters, I shall enclose them all to Mrs Lodge and John Hay. You can borrow or seize them, if you care enough about my story to want a sort of prosaic idea how it looks to me; but remember that the photograph takes all the color, life and charm out of the tropics, and leaves nothing but a conventional hardness that might as well be Scotch or Yankee for all the truth it has. The women especially suffer, for they pose stiffly, and lose the freedom of movement and the play of feature that most attact us. The bare back of a Samoan woman, when she is in motion, is a joy forever. I never tire of watching the swing of their arms, and the play of light over the great round curves of their bodies. At this moment two of them are sitting on the mats by my side. One of the two, Tagata—or Kanaka, as she calls it,—is a giantess who lives with Mataafa, either as his daughter or niece or wife, I cannot decide which; for Mataafa is believed to have had so many wives that the world never knows which is the last. Tagata is as jolly as she is big, and talks a little English. Today her hair is powdered with lime to give it a proper red tone for a picnic we all attend tomorrow; she looks like a *marquise,* but instead of jewels in her hair, she has tied round her head a single reddish-purple ti-leaf, as classical as any Greek coin. Her face is not classic, but broad, good-natured and in its way rather fine. I have photographed her half a dozen times. On the whole the jolliest girl is Fangalo whose photograph I send to Hay. Fangalo and the two other girls at Samsoni's supply our house with flowers every morning, and generally the whole foreign population—English or American—is to be seen lounging on Samsoni's porch, or sprawling on mats in his enclosure, laughing with Mrs Samsoni or Fangalo or the others. I send also a photograph of Fanua, the *taupo* of Apia, who led the Siva in our honor, and kissed me. Fanua is not handsome, but the photograph is peculiarly hard on her. When excited she is not without effectiveness, witness her Siva. I send also to Hay the likeness of a lot of other girls whom I do not know, or who are now married or dead. You can judge of the variety of feminine styles from them.

Day after tomorrow we start on a boat-journey along the coast to visit the chief towns. Seumano, our chief at Apia, escorts us in his boat, and is certain to make a great affair of it. He has already written ahead to prepare for our reception. We shall have *kawa,* roast pig, *tafolo,* Sivas and gifts wherever we go. Consul general Sewall goes with us. Tonight we dine with the German Consul Stuebel. Tomorrow a big feast *chez* Papalii, the Samoan native chief-justice.

October 23, 1890. I seal and send this long diary, all about myself when I want to write only about you. The rest you must fill in, as you would like to have it, and you cannot make it too strong. As the winter approaches I seem to think more and more about you and Martha, and long more to see you. The contrast between my actual life and my thoughts is fantastic. The double life is almost like one's idea of the next world. Meanwhile I flourish and am not only well in health as possible, but well in spirits, greatly amused, and constantly occupied. If your report is equally good, I shall go ahead without anxiety; but I dare not think about next summer, if you go to Europe, for I cannot foresee whether it will be possible for me to get there, and, if I did get there, I cannot help foreseeing that I should have done better not to go. Please tell me what to think, for I am distracted in mind, and being naturally as near a fool as is manufactured, I feel too much or too little when I ought to see as a matter of course what is the correct and proper conventionality. Anyway remember that I belong to you, and am ever yours.

MS: MHi
1. An allusion to an anecdote in which Lord Jeffrey was said to have damned the North Pole, and Sydney Smith (*not* Charles Lamb) added that he had also spoken "disrespectfully of the Equator" (in Lady Holland's 1855 *Memoir* of her father, Sydney Smith).

2. "East of the Sun & West of the Moon," *The Blue Fairy Book* (1889), ed. Andrew Lang.

3. Harold Marsh Sewall.

4. After first asking whether HA was "misonari" (La Farge, *Reminiscences,* p. 74).

5. Louisa Catherine Adams (1871–1958), second of CFA2's five children.

6. George R. C. Herbert (1850–1895), 13th earl of Pembroke, and his physician and companion George Henry Kingsley published *South Sea Bubbles* "by the Earl and the Doctor." Lord Pembroke's brother was Michael Henry Herbert.

7. Fayaway is the romanticized native companion of the American sailor-protagonist in *Typee.*

8. A Spanish dancer, then a New York celebrity.

9. By the American-Samoan treaty of 1878, the United States gained exclusive rights over Pago-Pago Harbor. Congress made appropriations for a new coaling station there in 1889. Lt. Charles F. Parker.

10. Although supported by most of the Samoan chiefs, as well as by the British and American consuls, King Malietoa Laupepa (d. 1898) was deposed and exiled in 1887 by the Germans. In the ensuing civil war, the German puppet ruler was overthrown by the Malietoa party under Mataafa Josefo's leadership. The General Act adopted at the Berlin Conference of the three powers restored Malietoa as king and recognized Samoan independence, but provisions such as placing a newly established supreme court under a foreign chief justice gave actual control of the government to the foreigners. The treaty was still not in effect because of delays in the appointment and arrival of the foreign officials.

11. The *Adams,* a U.S. warship in Apia Harbor for several months in 1887, provided medical care to the Mataafa-Malietoa faction.

12. Despite the rescue work of the Samoans, the Americans lost 51 men in the hurricane of March 15, 1889, which destroyed or disabled the seven warships (American, British, and German) in Apia Harbor.

13. Frances Van de Grift Stevenson (1840–1917) was an American of Swedish and Dutch extraction. She was divorced from Samuel Osbourne in 1880.

14. Symptoms of tuberculosis, from which Stevenson had suffered since the 1870s and which he hoped the South Seas climate would cure.

15. "Vailima," the house that Stevenson eventually built on his 300 acres, had a banquet hall, Oriental rugs, a piano, a fireplace, and other European amenities.

To John Hay

Vaiale, 16 October, 1890.

My dear John

In pity for your probable ignorance I will explain that I date this letter from my native house in the village adjoining Apia. The consulate is here and for many reasons I have found my convenience to require constant support from our authority. As you know I have always maintained that there was some use in our government, and Consul General Sewall has been worth to us several Presidents and at least one Senate.

If I had doubts whether the journey to Oahu and Hawaii would have been worth your while, I have none about Tutuila and Upolo, the two Samoan islands we have thus far visited. They are what Hawaii was a hundred years ago, except for a tinge of missionary, disagreeable but not so bad as elsewhere. Poor King may subside into peace on the old-gold business. La Farge and I are up to our necks in old-gold, and are hand-in-hand with all the handsome women of Polynesia. Hawaii is nowhere. We are the first Americans who ever came to these islands as great chiefs travelling for pleasure, and the natives regard Americans as their saviors and dearest friends. Nothing is too good for them. From Maliatoa and Mataafa downwards we are received with open arms. We have drunk *kava* in the houses of all the chiefs. We have had a great Siva dance at the house of Seumano in defiance of missionary remonstrance and even of the women's opposition. Seumano's daughter, Fanua, kicked like a cassiowary at being obliged to lead the Siva in the Samoan undress, which is somewhat like that of our ballet-dancers, without waist; but the Samoan society made her do it, and I must say I thought she enjoyed it as much as the other girls did who were less Europeanised. I do not yet know whether she went through the ceremony of her own accord, or was put up to it; but in the last Siva figure she pranced about, approaching and retreating, till at last she came close up to me as I sat cross-legged on the ground, and then bending over, put her arms round my neck and kissed me, amid shouts of applause and laughter from the whole village. As far as I know or can learn, the women of rank here are in their own way perfectly respectable. Nothing would be easier than for us to settle down in any native village and take temporary wives; but of course both we and the women would lose caste to a certain degree unless we assumed a Samoan character and conformed to their ideas of marriage. Of open license I have seen no sign. Neither man nor woman has said a word to me, or made even a sign suggesting indecency or immorality. We have associated only with the first society—the families of the powerful chiefs—and I know nothing of the common people except as I see them pass by; but even in the remote village of Nua in Tutuila, where a white man must be an extreme rarity, we passed the day and night in the chief's family, and all the girls of the village—mighty handsome too—kicked about on the mats, sprawling over us to look at our drawing or writing, or to see whatever struck them as curious, until we seemed all mixed up with naked arms, breasts and legs, yet apparently as innocently as little children. The sensation of seeing extremely fine women, with superb forms, perfectly unconscious of undress, and yet evidently aware of their beauty and dignity, is worth a week's seasickness to experience. La Farge was knocked out by it. His first Siva dance, improvised on the evening of our landing at Nua through stress of weather, was a corker. Greece was nowhere. I imagine he never approached such an artistic sensation before. For my own part, I gasped with the effect of color, form and motion, and leave description to the fellow that thinks he can do it. To me the effect was that of a dozen Rembrandts intensified into the most glowing beauty of life and motion. Of course the contrasts are great. Some of the women have a dash of Melanesian or negro blood. Some of them have stocky figures, or their breasts are not firm, or they have blemishes in the eyes, or their legs are thick. They grow old early, and a naked old woman is not pretty. But a handsome girl, unmarried, of sixteen years old, tall and strong, is as superb a creature here as the world has to offer, unless the young giant of a chief is still handsomer. Crowned with their usual garland of green leaves, they are Greek fauns and Apollos to a man.

For once, the reality has surpassed all expectation. The Samoans are not only interesting, but personally the most attractive race I ever met. They are not yet vulgarised at all. Their manners, at least as I see them in state, are as dignified and gracious as possible, and their rhetoric is Greek, like all the rest. The quiet restraint of their voice and manner in speaking is a study of art. King Maliatoa spoke well, but Mataafa's address was even more perfect. Both talked chiefly of their gratitude to America, who had saved their liberties and lives; but Maliatoa seemed depressed and anxious for fear of outbreaks unless the treaty of Berlin could be instantly acted upon; and indeed we have every day fresh rumors of danger from local disturbances consequent on the unintelligible neglect by the three powers to settle this business. You can tell Walter Phelps, if you like, with my compliments, that his recent newspaper remarks on that subject are calculated to give us an accurate idea of his diplomatic usefulness. They have done about as much harm as he could do; but W. W's success in giving offence is probably his happiest social experience, so I would not flatter him too much, but confide it to the breast of Mrs Hitt.[1]

How I hate politics! even this allusion to Samoan politics makes me seasick again. Please take note that what we have enjoyed here has been the beauty and the art, not the utility. I would like to hang to the consular flag-staff one politician, one political economist and one female traveller who writes books, as well as one or more missionaries,—merely *in terrorem*, to preserve these islands from notice. The natives, like all orientals, are children, and have the charms of childhood as well as the faults of the small boy. They are not so bad as most small boys. The oldest white resident here tells me he has never seen two natives quarreling to the point of blows, and I can swear that they laugh as much as the Japanese. They show no fancy for gratuitous cruelty, but they have plenty of wars, and the chiefs are great athletes and fighters. They work little, and show their superiority over our idiotic cant about work, by proving how much happier an idle community can be, than any community of laborers ever was; but my boat's crew rows as hard as man-of-war's-men, and when any exertion has to be made, the men take pride in making it. I am inclined to profanity when I think that religion, political economy and civilisation so-called, will certainly work their atrocities here within another generation so that these islands will be as melancholy a spectacle as Hawaii is, and the dignity of [contract][2] labor will be asserted as God's own lesson to Polynesia.

La Farge and Sewall are like me, but each of us sticks at some native taste. My *crux* is the *kava* which I am obliged to drink at every visit I make; but I like squid, to my astonishment, and rather enjoy banana-soup. Bread-fruit is not bad; better than taro in Hawaii and nearly as good as sweet-potato. In fact I can live well enough on native food here, when I famish on native food in Japan and Alabama. The pineapples are delicious, but as yet few foreign fruits have been introduced. Even the mango is rare, and the mangosteen and durian unknown. When you consider that even now there are not three hundred white people in all the Samoan islands, among thirty thousand natives, and no industry except three or four cocoa-nut plantations belonging to a German Company, and that no one but the missionaries have ever introduced anything, you can imagine that Samoa is really fresh and unpolluted by white influence. The only white influence I would like to see is fruits. Curiously enough we get delicious mutton from New Zealand, but bananas, oranges and pineapples are almost our only fruits. The fish is good when we can get it, but the natives prefer to eat their own fish when they catch any, and we seldom get it. Apia has no market whatever, and we live from hand to mouth, but if one could live on green turtle we should do well. Of late we have averaged one green turtle a day in gifts, and as the turtle is almost confined to royalty, or to very high chiefs, we are rather bothered to eat up to our average supply. Mataafa has just sent over a dish of *tafolo*, or baked bread-fruit pounded in cocoa-nut milk; we eat it at his house the other day, and saw it made. Unlike the *kava*, the *tafolo* is always made by the men, and the process is a sight which La Farge is eager to paint; but I am not so eager to eat the dish again.

I wish you had been with us on our visit to Stevenson today. King and you, with La Farge and me, calling on Stevenson in the forests of Samoa, would have been a spectacle to cause a smile on the face of a native missionary. In the absence of King and you, we could only get half our rightful amusement. We rode about four or five miles up the hills and struck a clearing covered with burned stumps with a very improvised house in the middle and a distant sea-view over the forest below. There Stevenson and his wife were perched—like queer birds—mighty queer ones too. Stevenson has cut some of his hair; if he had not, I think he would have been positively alarming. He seems never to rest, but perches like a parrot on every available projection, jumping from one to another, and talking incessantly. The parrot was very dirty and ill-clothed as we saw him, being perhaps caught unawares, and the female was in rather worse trim than the male. I was not prepared for so much eccentricity in this particular, and could see no obvious excuse for it. Stevenson has bought, I am told, four hundred acres of land at ten dollars an acre, and is about to begin building. As his land is largely mountain, and wholly impenetrable forest, I think that two hundred acres would have been enough, and the balance might have been profitably invested in soap. Apart from this lapse, he was extremely amusing and agreeable. He had evidently not the faintest associations with my name, but he knew all about La Farge and became at once very chummy with him. He talked incessantly for more than an hour, and became affectionate—to La Farge—at the close, but his wife would not let him invite us up there to a meal because they had nothing to eat, and I suspect nowhere to eat it, while he could not promise to return our call because it would cost him a day's work. Our visit was as full of queerities as any social experiment I can recall, and in contrast to our visits to the natives, with their ease and grace of manner, their cleanliness and generosity of housekeeping, and their physical beauty, it gave me an illuminating sense of the superiority of our civilisation. Stevenson claims to be very well, and has not the slightest intention of dying, but his emaciation is a marvel, and his weakness is such that, if not supplemented by a sufficient diet of self-esteem, I think he would drop, as it were, all standing. Meanwhile he goes through fatigues, deprivations and squalor enough to kill a dozen robust Samoan chiefs, not to mention his wife, who is a wild Apache.

I doubt our seeing them again, but in any case we could never receive another impression so weird and grimy as this, and to add to its local color, the evening was wet and gloomy. I shall never forget the dirty cotton bag with its sense of skeleton within, and the long, hectic face with its flashing dark eyes, flying about on its high verandah, and telling us of strange men and scenes in oceans and islands where no sane traveller would consent to be dragged unless to be eaten.

October 22. I enclose you a number of photographs of girls. Some of them, like Fanua and Fangalo, I know very well. Others, like the big Taupo at the head of the Manono warriors, are married, or like Patu's daughter Lengati, are dead. Of course the photographer has selected mostly the girls considered handsome, but Legati was also famous, having been daughter of a great warrior whom we know, and having been killed in action during the war. On the whole the types are fairly characteristic, but you must supply for yourself the color, the movement, the play of muscle and feature, and the whole tropical atmosphere, which photographs kill as dead as their own chemicals. Please show or send the photographs to Mrs Lodge and Mrs Cameron, as I refer to them in my letters. To your civilised eye they may appear a little nude; but here nudity is a dress, and one cannot conceive how fatal clothing is to feminine or masculine beauty until you see these same men and women in European dress, or for that matter in any dress at all. They are vulgarised in an instant.

I am closing up my letters now, a whole fortnight before the mail goes, because we are to start the day after tomorrow on a boat-excursion along the coast, and to the neighboring islands. Consul Sewall goes with us, and Seumano, the chief of Apia, escorts us in his great boat, the gift of the United States government. We do not know how many days we shall be absent, but I may not have time to write much after my return.

La Farge wants to stay here another month if his letters by the next steamer seem favorable. In that case we shall not reach Tahiti before January. Please write me a letter addressed there to the care of the U.S. Consul. My getting letters is rather a chance and I have not an idea what address to give after Tahiti, but I suppose it will be Fiji, if I can get there. Apparently the only way of reaching Fiji is by way of Sydney, which is a dreadful bore.

Meanwhile we are in the height of social activity. This evening we dine with the German Consul. Tomorrow is a great native function or picnic given by Chief Justice Papalii, at which we must appear in state. The Chief

Justice was very civil to us, and when we made our call, we received two large green-turtles which were duly hoisted on the backs of our men, and carried through the town to testify Papalii's magnificence, for a turtle is a gift of one noble to another. I caused careful inquiry to be made among my native friends, and I imagine that they consulted the Chief Justice himself, as to the most acceptable gift I could make in return; and was told that about five dollars was the correct thing. I insisted that he, being the richest native in Apia, would be insulted by a gift of money, but I was laughed at. Then I said that I really could not send five dollars; I could not offer even the Chief Justice of the United States less than ten. So yesterday I sent him, through Mrs Samsoni, a ten-dollar gold piece. This morning I receive two large pine-apples from him. He cannot be offended.

Love to Mrs Hay and the kids. I am longing to hear from you. My mind runs sadly on you all, and I dream of Washington.

Ever Yrs   Henry Adams.

MS: RPB
1. William Walter Phelps, U.S. minister to Germany 1889–1893 and commissioner to the Berlin Conference of 1889. Phelps's conciliatory remarks about Germany to reporters in New York, Sept. 24, must have reached Samoa out of context: he was referring to the U.S. hog-trade negotiations with Germany, not to the delayed Samoan appointments. Robert R. Hitt was chairman of the House Committee on Foreign Affairs.
2. HA's brackets.

To Anna Cabot Mills Lodge

Samoa, October 21, 1890.

My dear Sister Anne

Two months have passed since I left your door, and I have been at least two years absent, if I can measure the time from the long months I have passed in seasickness and repining. Occasionally I get on shore for a week or two, and then I am quite happy except for dreading more sea. We arrived here a fortnight ago, and a fortnight hence we leave for Tahiti. Then we sail for the Marquesas. By that time I expect to be finished, and I shall probably decline to sail again anywhere; so you had better arrange to visit me in the Typee valley next summer, and bring Constance and the boys.[1] I have discovered that the equator is the only place for cool summer weather, and I am unable to contemplate the terrors of returning to a warm climate.

Just now we have settled into a haven of rest under the wing of Consul General Sewall, at whose table we make a joint household, while for our studio and state apartment we have a native house, shaped like a turtle, nearly forty feet long, and open all round, unless we choose to drop the mats. The floor is of coral stones covered with mats. We have introduced

tables covered with tapa-cloth, and even the barbarous chair of your civilisation. Bananas and oranges hang on the centre-posts, cocoa-nut bottles
and cups decorate our shelves. We are surrounded by other native houses
and the native church; the sea laps the shore a few rods away, and the green
is shaded by large bread-fruit trees and cocoa-nut palms. Banana groves
extend outside our village, and beyond the bananas is a forest more or less
dense to the mountains. La Farge is sketching the sea; just behind him a big
native woman, who has just walked in, adorned with a brilliant purple
shirt and tapa waist-cloth, has seated herself and is watching him. We have
just had a long morning visit from Mataafa, the king whom the Germans
set aside, and who lives in the house opposite us, about twenty yards off, in
the middle of the village green. Natives in groups, usually without other
clothes than their blue or red or yellow waist-cloths, pass continually along
the path or road which skirts the beach, and their chocolate skins glow in
the sun, against the surf-line of the coral reef outside. The whole thing is
obviously a stage-decoration, and I constantly expect to see the prima-
donna, in green garlands and a girdle of ti-leaves, step out of Mataafa's
house, and begin to invoke the cuttle-fish or the shark, with a Wagnerian
chorus of native maidens.

La Farge and I are school-boys on a lark. We have been as amused as
though we were supernumeraries at the opera. Every day brings us some
new variety of childhood's fables. Samoa is very little changed from what it
was in pagan times. The Christianity is native, and differs little from the
native paganism except that more customs are kept secret. I am not sure
but that if we stayed here a few months anywhere except in Apia, we
should be obliged, in order to maintain our dignity as chiefs of America, to
take wives and contract alliances with neighboring chiefs. The relation
need not be permanent, and our partners at our departure would be regarded with great respect and would probably marry native missionaries
instead of pining for us. As far as the women are concerned I am confident
the alliance would be eagerly welcomed, and, as far as I am concerned, I
admit that I have seen a fair number of women who would by no means
discredit the situation. Of course our high standard of morals and the approaching arrival of our steamer will prevent us from entering into arrangements justly repugnant to the habits of American society; but as high
chiefs, and guests of chiefs, we ought to do it, according to Samoan standards, if only as a testimony of sympathy with the people. Every married
woman here, after a few years residence with her husband, returns to her
father with half the children, and lives as she likes. I think the custom will
commend itself at once to New York society, not to mention that of Washington.

We have plunged deep into Polynesian customs, in conversation at least.
Once a day I pump all the information out of at least one Samoan chief;
and it is great fun. Owing to their familiarity with our frigate, the
"Adams," the natives caught on to me at once as a great man, and Sewall
has cultivated the illusion. We are the first Americans who ever travelled

here for pleasure, without a business object; and this singularity confirms the simple native in his view of us. I am rejoiced to find, for the first time in my life, that my name is worth something to me; but the natives are solid aristocrats to a man, and they evidently know a swell when they see one. The credit is theirs, not that of my respectable ancestors, who would think me a worse savage than the Polynesian.

Our European rival, Robert Louis Stevenson, lives in the hills and forest, where he cannot rival us in social gaiety. We have been to see him, and found him, as he declared, very well. I should need to be extremely well to live the life he has led and is still leading, but a Scotchman with consumption can defy every fatigue and danger. His place is, as he says, "full of Rousseaus," meaning picturesque landscapes.[2] I saw no Rousseaus, the day being unfavorable, but I saw a very dirty board cabin, with a still dirtier man and woman in it, in the middle of several hundred burned tree-stumps. Both the man and woman were lively, and in their respective ways, amusing; but they did not seem passionately eager for constant association with us, and poor Stevenson cant talk and write too. He naturally prefers writing.

Please do not let my remarks get beyond the family. The Polynesiacs are like all other maniacs. Every remark made about them comes back and makes trouble. In these vast ocean spaces a whisper echoes like W. W. Phelps's voice, and causes earthquakes. As we have already offended every white man within sight of our track since leaving New York, we would not further rouse a spirit of revenge. Let it be enough that we have become Samoans in spirit and only abstain from adopting their dress and habits out of pure moral conviction that the Congregational church is the only safe guide in those matters. I do not doubt that Stevenson is like ourselves, only more Presbyterian.

I mean to enclose some photographs if I can get them, to show what is the matter with us; but remember that the photograph takes all the fun out of the tropics. Especially it vulgarises the women, whose charm is chiefly in their size and proportions, their lines, the freedom of their movements, the color of their skin, and their good-natured smile. Sometimes though rarely they have also straight noses and fine faces, but generally the face is thought of less consequence than the form and scale. The young men are superb, and in their leaf garlands look like fauns. The scenery is also spoiled by photographing. The softness of lights and colors, the motion of the palms, the delicacy and tenderness of the mornings and evenings, the moisture of the atmosphere, and all the other qualities which charm one here, are not to be put into a photograph, which simply gives one conventional character to New England and Samoa alike. Now New England is not alike.

I am not quite so sure about Tahiti after all. La Farge threatens to stay here if his letters permit. I ask no better. In that case we shall not reach Tahiti much before January. Still, you had better write to me to the care of the American Consul at Tahiti. You will not get this letter before December, and your reply cannot reach Tahiti before February. I cannot at the earliest, leave Tahiti before that time. Probably I may be there or at the Marquesas an indefinite time, for the seasick mariner does not easily find conveyances in those regions, and time is the most common of all commodities there. I do not yet allow myself to look ahead; but the further I go, the more I am appalled by the horrors of the journey back, and its increasing length.

We start in three days on a *malanga,* or coasting trip along the islands. Seumanu, the chief of Apia, escorts us with his swell boat, the gift of our government. We are to have feasts and dances at all the chief villages, and shall receive gifts.

My love to Constance and all yours. Tell Constance that the native girls here are rather in her style.

Ever Yrs   Henry Adams

MS: MHi
  1. George Cabot ("Bay") Lodge (1873–1909) and his younger brother John Ellerton Lodge.
  2. Such as Théodore Rousseau's paintings of Fontainebleau forest.

To Elizabeth Cameron

Iva in Savaii. 26 Oct. 1890

If you consult my Stieler's atlas, you may—or may not—find the island of Savaii at the west end of the Samoan group. Iva can hardly be more than twenty miles in a direct line from Apia; but it is, or should be, about five hundred in time. Our adventures have not been startling, but varied.

We left Apia at two o'clock Friday afternoon, October 24. Do not be bothered by Friday not being the 24th; it's a way we have here. Our outfit was royal. We took our own boat with five men for our traps and extraordinary needs, while Sewall, La Farge and I, with Awoki and our boy-interpreter Charley, a half-white, embarked with Seumano on his beautiful American boat, the gift of our government, and rowed out with a crew of ten men, and the flag of Samoa. When we caught the trade wind, we hoisted our sails, and for the next three hours, ran along the shore of Upolo, the middle island, in smooth water, the fringing coral reef on our right, half a mile away, and on our left the beautiful mountains of Upolo. The afternoon was exquisite, and the colors divine; we had no cares, except that La Farge complains much of feeling seasick and weak; and Seamano reclined his huge bulk in the stern of the boat, with an inimitable air of unconsciousness that time, space or thought exist. Devoutly as I hate the sea, I could not help recalling your quotations about my soul today being far away, and happy crew, my heart with you, &c;[1] for the crew sings all kinds

of songs, chiefly historical and local, and I am becoming quite attached to
Samoan songs. They have sometimes a certain amount of melody and lilt
which, except at two o'clock in the morning, I can hear with some enjoyment.

At about four o'clock we landed, supposing we were to pass the night,
but we had only a banana-leaf spread, after the somewhat cocoanut-oily
cooking of the natives. I make frightful efforts to eat the food, and do rather
better at it than either Sewall or La Farge, for the food itself is excellent;
but Papalii's big feast of Thursday rather upset me, especially two hundred
and fortyseven cold roast pigs of every possible size, which were brought in,
greasy and black, in the arms, or on the shoulders, of half-naked natives,
and piled in a huge mass on the grass in the rain. After that, my appetite
for native cooking was slow to recover, but I made heroic efforts to play-
pretend, and tried one thing after another to please our hosts. We broke up
the feast early to call on the Père Gavet, a French missionary priest, whose
church, or what remains of it after the hurricane, stood hard by. The Père
received us with evident pleasure, and La Farge did the talking. Then we
took boat again, and rowed three miles further, to a town called Satapuala.
Just at dusk we drew up to the long white beach, and as we landed our
baggage the darkness came on, and the moon began to glow. We bathed in
the warm ocean, with its floor of white sand, as charmingly as though we
were not afraid of all sorts of sharp animals supposed to be hastening to
seize our toes. Then we stepped across a fringe of palms and creepers, and
found ourselves on a sandy green, or greeny sand, with several native
houses, of the usual turtle-back shape, scattered about. One of these was
brightly lighted, and as we entered it, we found that it had been charmingly decorated with palm leaves and flowers, for our reception. A gigantic
young chief received us. An equally gigantic young woman, the chief's sister, also received us, she being the *taupo*, or village maiden. They were of
very high family, children of a former king. His name was Saipaia; hers was
Leolofi. They received us with the same grave dignity which we meet
everywhere, and immediately the long banana leaves were spread on the
floor, and the invariable breadfruit, taro, chickens, pigeons and combinations of cocoanut, with mullet and smaller fish, all cold, and cooked, I believe, in oil, when roasted in their furnaces of hot stones, were set before us,
with the usual apology for poverty, and excuses about "befo' the war." We
sat down, cross-legged if possible, and eat, or pretended to eat; and when
eating was decently performed, we chiefs drew back and smoked, while the
village dignitaries took their turn, and the lower people with the children
looked in from outside.

Oct. 27. Having just finished dressing, in the presence of six young dam-
sels who are decorating our house with green vines, and who, to do them
justice, are even less clothed, and certainly much better worth looking at,
than I, my narrative shall be resumed till breakfast is announced.—Seven
chiefs have come in, and sat down while the *kava* is getting ready. I have

had to sit with them an hour, to hear speeches and drink *kava,* but now I will start fresh.

The feast at Satapuala having been disposed of, the floor was cleared, and the Siva began. It differed little from Seamanu's Siva in Apia, as far as the scene was concerned, but in other ways the difference was great. Except Leolofi, no women danced. All the dancers were men, and, among them, Saipaia took the chief's part. I tried hard to admire his performances, but without much success. Some of the figures were interesting, and in some cases the dance became actual acting, and in its way amusing, but it is hard to keep up a mere historical interest in jumping and making faces. Leolofi was splendid,—something like a Titanic cow, such as Zeus had a fancy for—but her style was rather that of calm indifference than that of action, and as a dancer her motions and poses were rather languid, a bar or so behind time. They kept it up till midnight, and we might have gone on all night, in which case we should have had the wilder and more undress performances that are no longer commonly given in missionary circles; but we were tired, and so were the dancers, and we broke it up at twelve o'clock. The moon was superb, and La Farge and I strolled on the beach, watching the wonderful combination of clouds, calm sea, and white beach, all running into each other, as though a water-color artist of unlimited capacity had painted the scene with careful exclusion of all apparent difficulties. La Farge is fond of describing the peculiarity of the Polynesian 'world' in this way. Sky, sea and land are all judicious water-colors, toned with one general purplish wash with the most exquisitely delicate gradations, but never running into violent contrasts. Even the whites have an infinite gradation of violets, when contrasted with the dead white of a ship or a house.

Saturday morning, after a swim in the ocean, we bade farewell to our host and hostess, to whom I made my usual present of ten dollars; and then, taking boat, we rowed along passing the end of our Upolo island, and crossing a strait a mile wide to the little island of Manono where we landed at a village called Faleu, on the southernmost point. The spot was so picturesque that, as soon as we were established in our house, we got our water-colors out to paint the opposite shore of Upolo with its extinct crater-mountain, and the marvelous green water of the strait between. A heavy rain soon wiped out our greens, and we tried to paint the greys. The village gathered about and watched us, and I tried to draw the children. Naturally all my painting was childish, but I hope I induced La Farge to catch something worth keeping. Suddenly we were interrupted by a delegation from the neighboring villages, bringing food in palm baskets. At their head came two huge young men, with clubs, crowned with garlands, and girt with green leaves. At about twenty paces distance they stopped and performed a fantastic comic dance to the great amusement of the village, throwing their clubs in the air, and catching them, and acting a mock fight. When they finished, the orator, or *tulafale,* came forward: an old man leaning on a staff, who looked bewilderingly Homeric, and made a long speech, enumerating a number of things unintelligible to us. All this little scene was classic to a point quite beyond belief. I could imagine Seamanu to be Ajax, and we his companions. He sat lazily, with his huge bulk, by my side, repeating in a low voice what the orator was going to say, and at the end merely thanking them in one word. Then they all disappeared and the day went on, with intervals of *kava*, food, and a walk half way round the island. In the evening the villagers gave us a Siva which I thought extremely good. The island is very remote from white men, and is famous for its success in war. The dance-songs were all local and mostly warlike. The girls were good-looking, well-made, and extremely well-dressed in leaves and flowers; they wore only their old, native, Siva dress, bare to the waist, with strings of red, coral-like berries hanging to their necks and half covering their breasts. The *taupo*, or village maiden, was a very young girl, quite small, who was evidently not up to her position, and her married sister, the ex-taupo, did the real work. When the girls were tired, they came over and sat among us, and the young men danced. They did it extremely well, but we were exhausted with want of sleep, and could not keep our eyes open. At ten o'clock we stopped the dance, I fear rather discourteously. La Farge and I strolled in the wonderful moonlight along the sandy road, in the black shadow of the palms, with the native houses glimmering in the moonlight, and the surf rolling over the coral reef half a mile away. The natives passed us with an *alofa* or a *tofà*, or stopped to try to say a word of English; and a splendid young chief, who had danced for us as grotesquely as a village clown, came by, with a silver-headed cane marking rank I suppose, and stopped to receive our thanks with the same grave and rather sad dignity which seems to mark most the greatest chiefs. In all this I was most struck by the absence of anything suggesting impropriety. I rather expected drunken orgies. I find that kava is about as intoxicating as lager-beer, and as for the women, I might marry any of them, and divorce them as easily as in America; but they are the most valuable of the village possessions; I must have a long courtship through third-parties; I must pay two or three hundred dollars; and I must be the prey of all my wife's family as long as I live. As for common women, I do not doubt that a common man could have as many of them as he wanted; but we are great chiefs, and we can't even approach a common woman. We must sustain our rank. We could marry and send away a dozen wives in succession, if we liked, without loss of character to them or to us, and any *taupo* in Samoa would be glad to marry us on these terms; but we could not possibly get such a girl on any other terms without committing what is regarded as the worst possible theft on the whole village and clan. We should be obliged to make reparation, not to the girl but to the village. So far from the girls being loose livers, all the best are not only well behaved but are carefully watched and guarded. You may imagine that our respectability is safer here than anywhere in civilised lands.

Apart from this sad disappointment, and La Farge's dyspepsia which causes him to assert about once a day that he must return to Apia, we find no serious difficulties. Our severest day thus far was yesterday. We left

Manono at seven o'clock in a native boat, paddled by a native crew, while our own boats escorted us. We were to visit the little island of Apollima, which is nothing but a volcano's crater, sticking up in the ocean a mile west of Manono. The volcano was long since extinct, but one side of the crater is open to the sea through a narrow break in the coral, and the heavy ocean swell rushes and foams in and out of the little harbor through this passage just broad enough to admit a boat with paddles. To get there, we had to leave the protection of the great coral reef within which we had sailed till then all the way from Apia, and to trust ourselves in a light whaleboat to the full sweep of the trade wind. Luckily a mile is not more than infinity. Just as I was becoming uncomfortable with the tossing of the boat on the big waves, we reached the dark cliffs of lava and turned into the channel. For two minutes I forgot to be seasick. We were swept on the foaming and roaring surf directly on the coral rock till we fended off with poles, and then, paddling hard, the crew forced the boat round a corner and into a cove where we were soon dragged and swept into quiet water. The men carried us ashore on their backs, and I felt as though I would like to get away faster than I came, for the idea of being shut up there a week or two by a sudden storm, was dispiriting. The old crater was occupied by a dozen native houses of the poorer class, whose only wealth seemed to be a few co-coanut trees. Sewall climbed to the top of the island. As I have seen ocean enough, I sat in the missionary's hut and drank a cocoanut till I was tired, and returned to the beach. We stayed only an hour or so, and then put out again. The exit looked more difficult than the entrance, but I was surprised to find that after a moment of rush through foaming surf, we were again tossing outside without sign of violent exertion. We had far more trouble in getting on board Seumano's boat, but we tumbled in at last, without tum-bling overboard, and spread our sails for Iva in Savaii, four miles to the westward. We were three quarters of an hour only before getting within the fringing reef into calm water, and we were comparatively free from sick-ness, but I do not like open boats in the middle of the Pacific, with the trade wind blowing fresh, and a good deal of sea. We escaped with a drenching and some amusement. Drenching in warm water and warm air matters lit-tle; but we were glad to land at last, among friends, and I sat all day cross-legged, receiving village chiefs, making speeches and drinking *kava,* glad to watch dreamily the children playing, the old men talking, and the palms rustling above.

October 28. Yesterday was a great day for the American *alí;* especially for the *alí* Atamu, who is not a little surprised to find that Seumano has at-tributed to him the distinction of this great *malanga* or boat-excursion. We seized the morning to rest, for we were all used up, dyspeptic and sleepy. La Farge made a sketch and I wrote to you, as you have read. Our repose was broken after lunch. At about two o'clock our host, the *ali* Selu, who is a rather European or missionary Samoan and talks English, took us to a house on the village green, and seated us there, cross-legged, to receive the chiefs. The day was fine; all the women and children, and some men, were scattered about, to see the show, which was like the reception of the Prince of Wales when I was young and serious. Such affairs are rare here, and the people enjoy the fun. There we sat for two or three hours, till my back and legs ached as much as my head did. Whatever we came to Samoa for, we got it this time. Everything was shown us. First, we had a military review and sham fight. The whole military strength of the village, about two hundred men, dressed in their most barbaric leaves, feathers, and flowers, led by their *taupo,* or village maiden, and all armed with clubs, big bush-knives, and Snyder rifles which they fired at frequent intervals, showed us a battle in which the shouting, leaping, running, and confusion proved how incompetent the Parisian stage-managers must be. For a fantastic exhibition of Polynesian savagery or barbaric fun, I want to see nothing better. Then all sat down, and the *tulafale,* or orator, rising in the centre, about sixty yards from us, made a speech, leaning on his long staff, with arms crossed. Our chief, Selu, then replied for us. Then the gifts were collected, which had been thrown; yams, *taro,* and several small pigs which squeaked and kicked Homerically. Then the dance began: first, the girls, then the men, and lastly four very small girls, who went through it all with the precocity commonly attributed to American children. Neither men, women nor children showed the smallest idea of a distinction between what was beautiful and what was not. Like the Japanese they gave exquisite charm of posture, song and movement alternately with clownish grimacing and jumping, and the one seemed as natural to them as the other. I saw very little grossness and no indecency, though the costumes were simple enough; and neither men nor women were likely to be shocked. Probably the missionaries are responsible for the propriety, for Iva is rather a missionary stronghold, and I never saw a more curious contrast than at suppertime, when each hut was brightly lighted by its fire, and from every hut came the singing of an evening hymn, which sounded to me very like a Siva song. During the show, I toiled over my Kodak, and took thirty or forty views, none of which I expect to find successful, but which, even if only one turns out well, may help La Farge to paint a Siva picture. After two or three hours of this display we had an interval for supper. The sun set with an afterglow like extravagant painting; the moon rose with a full flood of violet light; and we started in for a new Siva at eight o'clock with only the light of the fire, fed by dry palm-leaves, to show the dancers. The firelight is most picturesque, but a bit warm for the tropics. My head ached, and my back ached worse. I was sleepy and weary of savagery for the moment. Yet the sitting dance of the girls charmed me as much as ever, and I think I find it more beautiful now than I did when I first saw it with such delight at our little haven in Tutuila. La Farge still avers that Sivà was more charming than any other girl we have met, but we have met so many that a law is risky that excludes competition so much at large. We had four *taupo,* past and present, sitting with us last night, and they gave us rings and *tapa* mats. We were all kissed, or had our noses rubbed in the afternoon dance. Mine was a good square kiss, squarely returned by me; and a sweet little girl too, who fled panic-stricken into the distance, her leafy covering swaying as she ran. At the night dance, La Farge avers that he had no other support for his helpless back than the shoulder of his neighboring *taupo,* who embraced him like a mother and tenderly soothed his slumbers. Fortunately we were released before ten o'clock, and could stretch out on the floor and look at the moon in peace.

October 29. The next morning, as soon as the wind rose, we bade good-bye to Iva, and walked about three miles, along the shore, to Papalii, the home of the Malietoas. We were received with the usual form by eight or ten chiefs who were mere imitations of Ajax and Odysseus, and who sat round the guest-house exchanging solemn speeches with us, until my eyes could not keep open. Luckily Malietoa's niece, Aenga, "the first lady of the land," was there, and, as was her duty, devoted herself to entertain us. Aenga is a big, good-natured girl, a little too negresque, but bright in her way and extremely sympathetic. Nothing could be more touching than the way in which she rolls up her cigarettes and smokes them, occasionally spitting with great neatness and accuracy; but she does not care for my pipe. On this occasion she sat in the chief's place and presided, while another girl made the *kava,* and a third, by hereditary right, passed round the cup. We went through our speeches, and a rather palatable cup of sago, I think, and swallowed our *kava,* but cut the feast, and stretched ourselves on the floor of our house where Aenga entertained us while we napped. In the afternoon we had another *talolo,* or military reception, with Malietoa's black assassins in the place of distinction. I snapped a lot more photographs, and then La Farge and I tried to sketch the lovely view over the coral-reef to Upolo. Failing, as usual, to get any result worth our trouble, we had a modest tea of brown bread and roast pig, with Aenga, and then began the interminable Siva.

The Siva at Papalii was not a good one; the dancers were not handsome and did not dance well; while I was tired to extinction, and lay down at full length at the extreme end of the house during the last and most interesting part of the affair, towards midnight, a witness with a headache and deep disgust at inability to sleep. As I say, the Siva was not a good one, but it was nevertheless a dance to be remembered, for it can hardly fail to make a good deal of scandal in native Samoan society. Poor Aenga, being a church member, is positively forbidden to dance, even one of our foreign dances. Expulsion from communion is the punishment, and Aenga's position as Malietoa's niece, the most conspicuous young woman in society, gives no end of interest to her expulsion. She is in fact *the* Princess of royal blood now unmarried. She ought not to have been present at the dance, but she was our hostess, and being there, like the good-natured child she is, she could not resist the temptation, and our entreaties. She gave us three or four figures, and then would do no more, and was evidently overcome, as far as a Samoan ever is overcome, by remorse, or fear of the scandal. This was not all. We had turned out the public early so as to have a private exhibition, and the dancers gave us some of the scandalous dances, of which so much is said in the books and in conversation. At my age, or to my eyes, indecency in itself has no merits. To the savage or boor, indecency is a form of humor. Like the Japanese, the Samoans seem to be unconscious of a vicious object in anything they do. If one could conceive it, in our American society, both dancers and spectators were as unaffected by the dancing as they would be in Paris by the ballet at the Grand Opera. Yet one of these two or three wicked figures struck me as exquisitely beautiful, and I would give a deal of money to see it again with better dancers. It is called the *paipai*, a name which I do not venture to translate, any more than I should translate the title of Calypyge—if that is the spelling—given to a famous statue of Aphrodite.[2] The girls stand, as usual, with their waist-cloths but no other article of dress. The dance, as far as I had time to notice, differed little in its movement from a number of the other dances; but as the girls kept on, turning or gesticulating, one was conscious that their cloth, which is merely twisted about the waist, was becoming looser and looser till the hips began to show. Again and again the dancers caught at the dress, as they always do when the cloth gets loose, and seemed to pull it together, but each time one saw that it was more loose, until at last the chief dancer lets her's go, and as it dropped to her feet, she turned about in one complete movement of the dance; then suddenly snatching up her covering she bounded off into the dark with a laugh.

October 30. Aenga was very low in mind and body, with a severe cold and deep contrition when she came to our house the next morning to bid us goodbye. We consoled her as well as we could, and the simple savage feels nothing so deeply as to darken life long. Life to them is play. The serious is a foreign annoyance like the mosquito, which drove me mad all the night at Papalii between the tombs of the Malietoas! They fear death and the devil, but meet both carelessly when they come. Their tolerance towards children and other nuisances, like foreigners and lunatics, is a constant wonder. We left Aenga on her hillside, looking over a stage-blue sea, and drinking cocoanuts or sucking oranges or smoking cigarettes, to reflect on the fortune which had caused her grandmother to be noosed by one of the old Malietoas who had hidden himself in the top of a tree to waylay beautiful *taupo* passing along the path beneath;—whence came Aenga as well as Malietoa Laupepa, the king now recognised by our various governments. Our path was equally strewn with *taupo*. After another walk of an hour through a long succession of native houses scattered under the cocoanut trees close by the waterside, we came to Safotulafai, the town of the great chief Lauati. Here we had another grand reception, a dozen chiefs sitting about the large guest-house, which was charmingly decorated with green vines and hybiscus flowers. Two stout, good-natured *taupo* were present, and sat with us on chairs at one end of the house, and led us to the feast afterwards, spread out on banana leaves under an awning outside. Lauati himself looks like Herbert Wadsworth.[3] He is a great orator and a man of the highest social and political influence. Evidently he laid himself out to make our reception impressive, although I do not think the afternoon military display, big as it was, quite equalled that at Iva. I have exhausted my roll of Kodak film on these reviews, and can take no more pictures, but the barbaric extravagance of each display seems to leave nothing more within possibility. Of course the *talolo* included a Siva in the open air, and piles of *taro,* yams and pigs as presents to Seumano and us. We had time for a stroll after the *talolo,* and then took some supper as darkness came on. Seumano then brought us back to the guesthouse where we found the *taupo* Fa-auli, Lauati's daughter, and while she prepared sugar-cane for us to chew, we lay about her on the mats and babbled. Suddenly someone remarked that Fa-auli was going to make an evening prayer, and she began with a long impromptu missionary address, very prettily delivered, alluding, as I could make out, to us and our *malanga,* and closing by the Lord's prayer and a long hymn. The next moment the dancers, in full barbaric nakedness, came in,—four men—and sat down on the mats. The evening Siva then began by the light of the burning palmleaves, which, in the strong breeze, threw out flames and flying embers across the house, and made my sleepy eyes smart with smoke. I was too drowsy to care much for the dancing until Fa-auli appeared, but I really wish you could have seen her. She danced for some two hours, more or less, and I came gradually to the opinion that she lay a good bit over any dancer I had seen. She wore a dress rather more scanty than usual; indeed she had only a black cloth about ten inches wide, ornamented, I think, with beads or color of some kind, and showing the outline of the hip on one side, like a Parisian opera-dancer except that this was the real thing, and made our ballets seem preposterous. Fa-auli's figure was splendidly full, round and firm, though her legs were large. Glistening with cocoa-nut oil, she stood out against the rich brown of the background like an ivory image of Benvenuto's.[4] Her movements were large and free, full of strength; sometimes agile as a cat's, as when she imitated a rat and swung on the cross-beam; sometimes divinely graceful, as when she imitated ball-playing, or splashed imitation water over companions in bathing, or waved her hands about in the thousand movements of the regular sitting-Siva. I never had fully understood how little mere beauty of face had to do with beauty itself until I saw what a houri Fa-auli became the moment she showed her form; and the contrast was all the more startling when presently she and her companion-*taupo,* tired, came over, and sitting down by us, said quietly that they were no longer in the church. To amuse us, they, like Aenga, had sacrificed themselves.

October 31. Still at Safotulafai under Lauati's protection. I am a little vague as to the day of the week or month, but Clarence King would go wild with envy if he could see me lying on the floor watching Fa-auli peeling sugar-cane for me to eat, and then going through a whole cane on her own account. When she rolls over and lies on her stomach, with her head sup-

"Interior of native house. This is either the house we live in or that of
Mataafa next to us."
Inscription by Henry Adams, Samoa, 1890

"Fa-a-uli and her father Lauati"

ported on her hands, she reminds me of a baby hippopotamus, and would draw crowds at the Zoo. Her goodnatured smile is half a yard square, and when I suggest that she should marry me, she is convulsed with mountainous laughter and hastens to tell her next friend. She tells me that she went to the war as *taupo* of the village warriors, and was afraid of the bullets. She could hold a cask of bullets without fatal results. She has none of her father, Lauati's, fineness of face, but is grand as a grenadier, and, what is curious, as she strides across the village green, she does not look broad or heavy, but has a masculine figure with little breadth of hip and only a broad acre or two of brown back, on which the sunlight plays in oceanic planes of light and shade. I never tire of watching her, especially when she lies stretched at full length on the mats in the dusk, and rolls from one position to another, while La Farge furtively dashes rapid sketches of her on his sketch-book. By the bye, today I did a little water-color of a view from our windows—if window is the proper word for what are open spaces. Lauati saw it and I found he wished to have it, so my first picture will remain here.

This afternoon I took Fa-auli's measurements. Here they are. To begin with, she is shorter than I am, by about two inches. She stands in bare feet about five feet three inches high. Taking her round the chest, including the arms, she measures fortyfive inches; round the upper waist, thirtytwo and a half inches; round the hips fortytwo inches; round the calf of the leg, seventeen inches; round the ankle, ten and three quarters; round the arm, next the shoulder, fourteen, ½ inches; round the wrist, eight inches; round the neck, fifteen inches; length of foot, 9½ to 10 inches. Lastly,—and to me the most curious,—round the head, as one measures for a hat, compressing the hair close, and crossing the forehead just above the eyes, twenty three inches, which is precisely the measurement of my own head.

As we are to sail in the early morning for Apia, we all walked back to Sa-papalii this afternoon to bid Aenga goodbye, and we took Fa-auli and the other taupo of this place with us. Somehow this addition to the party proved to be a mistake. Aenga was more than usually embarrassed and silent. She had sent me a present of a *tapa* cloth and a comb such as women wear in their hair, with an affectionate *Alofa,* this morning, which I took for a sort of acknowledgement of the ten dollars I had given her. Though I spell her name Aenga, it is written Aiga. La Farge declares that she is different from other girls, and that her high birth and breeding have made her conscious of emotions unknown to the usual Polynesian. I do not feel sure that he is right, but her shyness is actually painful. She could neither talk, nor get the two other girls to talk. Both Sewall and La Farge said that she was jealous of them, and considered them as rivals who had come to exult over possessing us, as though we had left her for them. I half thought she might have a fancy for Sewall, though he has treated her very roughly as well as tenderly, and flirts with every girl he meets. In a moment of moving about, when she could say a word to me without being overheard, she leaned towards me and muttered a little speech in broken English, evidently prepared beforehand, of which I could catch only the usual Samoan expression, "me love you," and lost the rest. I would like much to know what it was, but I am not so fatuous as to think that I am the object of her trouble, though I have taken some pains to show sympathy for her, as we have all done. After about an hour of an awkward visit, I broke it up at sunset; we bade good-bye, and started for home. La Farge was then sketching by the seashore, and as we picked him up, he had to go back to bid Aenga good-bye. He tells me that he found her lying on the floor, in tears, and actually wringing her hands. I leave you to find an answer to this little riddle of old-gold romance.

Apia. November 3. We returned from Savaii on Saturday, starting at six in the morning and arriving at eight in the evening, the crew rowing the whole distance. The American mail should arrive tomorrow, but as the outward mail starts tomorrow evening, I shall end my Savaii story here. I enclose some photographs to illustrate our adventures. They will give you, I know, a false impression of everything, but they are fairly good of the two girls, Aenga and Faauli, who figure in the narrative so largely. As I expected, our Siva affairs have already made a scandal. We have swept all the *taupo* from Apia to Safotulafai out of the church, poor Aenga among them, and the church will hardly forgive us; but I think the chiefs are all right, and we certainly made liberal presents in return for the civilities shown us. On the other hand we have been given three fine mats, a quantity of *tapa* cloth, several combs, and no end of food. Our *malanga* will be long remembered among these simple people, and Lauati's cabin will be decorated by my little water-color, for the aesthetic education of the Savaiians.

I cannot have my own photographs developed here, so I must wait indefinitely, or send the roll home for the purpose. Meanwhile the enclosed professional pictures will answer. La Farge is at last working fairly hard, and if his health remains tolerable,—he complains much,—will carry back a large mass of material. I expect to see the Siva figure without end, in his future painting. I wish I could do a water-color too, for you, but the more I labor, the worse I paint, and now I try only to match cloud tints and discover the proper washes to produce old-gold flesh tints. Drawing is beyond me. Yet the amusement is constant, and I am only too happy to have discovered something that takes the place of books.

MS: MHi
1. From "Drifting" (1860) by the American poetaster and minor painter Thomas Buchanan Read, the first and penultimate stanzas: "My soul to-day / Is far away, / Sailing the Vesuvian Bay. . . . / O happy ship, / To rise and dip, / With the blue crystal at your lip! / O happy crew, / My heart with you / Sails, and sails, and sings anew!"
2. Callipygian Venus, so called for her courtesan's pose of uncovering her shapely buttocks, Roman copy of a Hellenistic statue in the National Museum, Naples.
3. Herbert Wadsworth (d. 1927), of Geneseo, N.Y. HA meant the comparison to indicate Lauati's refinement of features.
4. Benvenuto Cellini (1500–1571), Italian sculptor.

To Mabel Hooper

My dear Polly

My last letter to you was written as we were leaving Honolulu, and since then we have had no steamer to take or bring letters. We expect our next mail in three days, when I hope to hear from you. Our plans cannot be decided until La Farge gets his letters, so that I do not know how long we shall be here; but unless something arrives to hurry us, I fancy we shall stay here another month. You had better write to me to the care of the consul at Tahiti, for we shall probably be there when your letter in reply to this, arrives. We have been immensely amused here, and returned only last night from a week's excursion in boats to Savaii, the western island of this group, about twentyfive miles off, where we had a splendid reception. The Consul went with us, and we were very great people, I can tell you.

Whenever we came to a large village where our coming had been announced in advance, we were met by the chiefs, generally six or eight in number, at the guesthouse of the village. We always sat down cross-legged on the mats in the place of honor, at the right hand of the principal chief, or *ali;* and the other chiefs sat down round the room in the order of their rank. Then the orator addressed us in a complimentary speech, which was translated to us; and we made a reply which was translated to them. The Samoans are splendid men and look like Homer's heroes. They generally wear no clothes except a *siapa* or cloth round their waist, sometimes of blue cotton; sometimes of the native bark-cloth called *tapa;* sometimes a fine mat like Panama straw. They are beautiful orators, speak in rather a low voice, without noise or gestures, and their manners are as dignified as possible. After the speeches, a young woman made *kava* in a wooden bowl which stands on eight legs and is polished like porcelain inside. *Kava* or *ava* is a root, something like flagroot, of a bush that is common here. It is queer tasting, rather aromatic, not intoxicating unless one drinks tubs of it, and even then it only paralyses one's legs, but does not affect one's head. I have had to drink it several times a day, but have never been able to see that it had more effect on me than root-beer. The way of making it is not pretty. Formerly girls chewed the root, and then soaked it. Now the root is usually grated, the grated stuff put in the wooden dish, and the girl, after washing her hands, takes a lot of cocoa-nut fibre, and carefully strains out all the particles of the grated root, leaving what looks like dirty water. Then they all clap their hands, and a man announces that the *kava* is ready. Someone then solemnly says that the first drink is to be given to Suasey, which means Consul Sewall, or to Atamu or Akamu, which means me, and a girl or young chief brings a cup of it, in half a cocoa-nut polished black, and with a long sweep of his arm, presents it to one of us. I usually drink a little and return the cup, but I can, if I like, merely touch it and return it. The same ceremony is gone through with each person. Afterwards we are led out to a feast spread on banana leaves on the ground. Baked fish and pig, a sort of pounded root called *taro*, bread-fruit, yams, chickens, cocoa-nut in various forms, and green cocoa-nuts to drink, and sometimes very unpleasant big worms raw, are piled on the banana-leaves, and the girls or men tear up the pig or chicken or fish with their fingers, and give one great chunks to eat. I pretend to eat voraciously, but it is hard work, for the food, though good, is not nice to look at, and is cooked without salt. After the feast is over, we are left in peace to stretch out on the floor, and take a nap or do what we like.

Luckily the Samoans have one habit which makes their society very amusing. Every village chooses one girl, or if there are two *ali* in a particularly large place, one girl is appointed by each chief, to entertain strangers. She is called the *Taupo* or village maiden, and is always accompanied by a married woman or duenna. She is often the chief's daughter or niece, and the handsomest girl in the place. When a young chief or distinguished man, wants a wife, he generally selects one, or rather is given one, of the *taupo*. Marriages in good society are always arranged by the elders. Love marriages are unknown except as elopements. The *taupo* is generally very dignified and imposing, but often she is as jolly as possible when she knows one better. We found the *taupo* charming. I know at least a dozen, perhaps twenty, and am tenderly attached to several. They are often twice my size, and have arms and legs like giantesses. They dress in all sorts of ways, sometimes in a sort of night-gown which the missionaries introduced; sometimes in a shirt and waist-cloth of cotton; but usually, when they are not on their dignity, they wear only the waist-cloth, reaching to their knees, and a sort of bib round their necks. None wear shoes, but their feet are hard as hoofs. They generally lead the dances, and then wear round their waists a fascinating opera-dancer's short skirt made of long green and purple leaves of the *ti* plant, and are rubbed all over with cocoa-nut oil so that their skins and garlands glisten. Almost every evening, and often after big shows, in the daytime, we were entertained with dances, or Siva, and though I was often tired to death, I found the Siva fascinating. There are many kinds of Siva, but the great distinction is between the sitting and the standing dance. In the sitting Siva six or eight girls or men sit on the ground and go through all sorts of movements to an accompaniment of unearthly singing. In the standing Siva, several men and women imitate all sorts of acts; they pretend to play ball; to fight with spears and swords; to be birds, like owls, or beasts, like cats or rats; and to climb cocoa-nut trees, and get the nuts; or to splash water over each other in bathing, or to hammer on anvils, or to do anything that they think of in daily life. Sometimes they are wonderfully graceful, and the music is almost fine; sometimes they are grotesque and repulsive; but when a set of fine young men and women dance these dances in the evening by the red light of a palm-leave flame, in one of the open native houses, it is a scene to remember. When the *taupo* is tired, she comes over and sits by us. Occasionally they amuse themselves, in one dance, by kissing one of us, a surprise that took my breath away at first; but this is a figure of the dance. Except there, I have never seen the *taupo* show the least disposition to kiss me. They are wonderfully well behaved, and I have never dared to kiss one of them, though they are as familiar in their manners as my nieces would be, and sprawl over the mats, or lean on our shoulders watching us write or paint, as freely as though they were little children. Their native mark of affection is not kissing, but rubbing noses, which is apt to leave a persistent smell of cocoa-nut oil that drives one mad. They always make us presents of some small thing, like a *tapa*-cloth, or a curious comb they wear, or their leaf-dresses which reek with cocoa-nut oil, or they put their garlands round our heads or necks. La Farge with a crown of green leaves looks like Dante or Virgil. Their faces are not often handsome, though I know some pretty ones. The prettiest type here, in the lively way, is a little like my niece Lulu Adams. Generally they are round-faced, very coppery, and good-natured looking. Some of the very highest have heavy features, too much like negroes. The Samoans care little for beauty of face, but ask only for beauty of figure and size. They prefer the lighter colored skin to the darker, which does not surprise me, for a fine girl's back is like that of a big man, and I feel as though I were looking at whole acres of brown skin on which the light plays as though it were a cornfield.

The Samoans are tremendous aristocrats. Family is everything, and a great chief is a feudal lord who owns his village. Their king, Malietoa, is an elderly man, who looks as though he had suffered a great deal, and his manners are perfect. The second man in Samoa, who was himself king in the war with the Germans, is Mata-afa, who lives in a native house about a hundred feet from our native house, across a part of a village-green. We see Mataafa often. He comes in and takes a cigar, and talks through an interpreter, and sends us food almost every day, sometimes fruit, but generally a dish called *tafolo,* which is baked bread-fruit, kneaded in cocoanut milk, and served hot. The form is rather startling. Almost every morning at about eleven o'clock we hear a sort of warrior's shout from behind the huts at the further end of the green, and we know the *tafolo* is coming. Instantly two splendid young men, with their faces partly blackened, dressed in waist-cloths of green leaves, with leaf garlands round their heads, run at the top of their speed across the green towards our house. One of them leaps and prances; the other carries a wooden trencher of stuff like dough, or thick blancmange, in milk made by straining the old cocoa-nut meat. The bearer sets the trencher down under our eaves, and with his hands ladles out a quantity of the *tafolo* into big green leaves on the pebble-floor. Then with more shouts, both dash away, and I have to swallow a mouthful of the paste, which is not bad, but is very cloying.

Our greatest shows were the military reviews in Savaii. At every large town—three of them—the whole population turned out to these displays, which are called *talolo.* Each town could produce from one to two hundred warriors. We swells sat in a native hut or house, and waited for the review. I took lots of photographs, and if they turn out well, I can give you an idea of the fantastic and unbounded barbarism of the show. The warriors acted the whole business of a fight. First came running skirmishers wildly dressed. Then always followed six men, their bodies blackened, who crept up, pretending to hide themselves in the grass, till at one place, one of them, as I happened to be sitting out on the green, reached out and seized the toe of my boot. These were Malietoa's black assassins, who, before the missionaries came, used to creep into the houses of hostile chiefs at night, and stick the sleeping enemy with the small poisonous barbed bone of the sting-ray. Next came the *taupo* in full warlike undress, with a high structure of hair and feathers on her head—or their heads, for sometimes several marched before their warriors;—and finally the warriors themselves in their war-costumes, brandishing big war-clubs, or bush-knives, or firing their guns. They rushed up, with howls and jumps, till they came close to us, and then turned, throwing at our feet as they went away a hail-storm of gifts; yams, *taro* and even pigs.

My friends Fa-a-uli—Black Cloud,—and Lilia—meaning Fear-of-falling-from-a-treetop-when-the-wind-blows,—led their warriors at the last place we were in. They were the two *taupo* of the chief Lauati at Safotulafai. Faauli, who may be seventeen years old, was great fun and danced superbly. She looked ten feet high and four feet broad; but a curiosity seized me to know her exact measurements, so I took them. She is only five feet two inches high. Round the chest, over the arms, she was fortyfive inches; round the upper waist, thirtytwo and a half inches; round the hips, forty-two inches; but round the thick upper part of the arm she was fourteen and a half inches; round the wrist, eight inches; round the calf of the leg, seventeen inches; and round the ankle, ten and three quarters. Her hands and feet were well shaped and not large for her size. The foot was nine and a half inches long. She let me take all these measurements carefully, only saying with a laugh that I measured her as they did with pigs.

Of course we have not all the refinements of civilisation when travelling so among the natives. Generally they gave us a house to ourselves, but at the last place we could count ten men and women sleeping on the floor of our house. As the house was at least thirtyfive feet in diameter, nearly circular, and open at the sides, there was room enough; but at first I felt rather awkward in putting on all my clothes with at least six women, young and old, looking on, and very curious about the process. I soon lost all shyness, for at worst I was never so little clothed as they were; and I was never bothered except by the small boys and fear of centipedes. We had mosquito nettings which make little rooms to sleep in, and though transparent enough, prevent animals like rats, dogs and pigs, from walking over us. The native house otherwise is charming, and I prefer it for the daytime. We have a nice one here, which we use for a studio and reception room.

The weather is pleasant; never very hot, and always cool at night. Thus far I am very well. Please send me as good a report, and write long letters.

Ever affectionately   Henry Adams.

MS: MH

To Lucy Baxter

Apia (Samoa) Nov. 4, 1890.

My dear Miss Baxter

Your letter of October 9 arrived here last evening. You must have received mine of Sept. 26 immediately afterwards. I am very grateful to you. Your letter gives me all the domestic news I have. If Dwight wrote, his letter missed the steamer, and my only account of the Quincy wedding is from you.[1] From you too I learn that Edward Hooper and the children have got back, which is very satisfactory, as I take it for granted they must be all right. As for my own letters, you must remember that this is the first opportunity I have had to send one since we left Honolulu. We crossed two steamers, I think; but could write by neither.

My only difficulty now is an excess of material. I have seen and done so much, and have made acquaintance with a world so unlike anything I imagined, that I can write a book more easily than a letter. A month ago we were dropped over the side of the "Alameda" into an open boat off the coast of Tutuila, sixty miles from here; and since that moment I have had every day as much novelty as would fill half a volume. New ideas of history, society, science and art have crowded on me so fast that I could not even note them down, much less arrange them; and as I have no thought of trying to instruct the world any more, but want only to become Polynesian, and forget today what happened yesterday, I cannot undertake to be literary and accurate. You can imagine me living in a model archaic world such as I studied in books, and lectured about as Professor; where everything is thousands of years old, yet to me new; and where Christianity is a mere veil which covers a paganism almost as fascinating as that of Greece.

Homer is constantly before me. If you never read the Odyssey, read it now. Get Bryant's translation, and imagine me a companion of Ulysses instead of La Farge.[2] You can see the whole picture. I enclose some photographs to help your imagination. Two of them represent the exterior and interior of a native house, such as I am now writing from. The floor is covered with mats of cocoa-nut or some other fibre. The roof is heavily thatched, and the sides are all open. Within, the light is delightfully soft, and the thatch is the coolest of covering. The heat is never intense—87 ° is the highest yet,—and when the trade-wind blows, after ten o'clock usually, the temperature is perfect. We sleep in a board house near the consulate, a few rods away, but we have slept also in many native houses with no other discomfort, as far as concerned the house, than that the floor of coral pebbles, covered by mats is somewhat hard.

We have seen the Samoan islands from Tutuila to Savaii, coasting along the shores, either within the fringing coral reef or out at sea, in small cutters or in open boats, a distance of near a hundred miles; and we have lived with the natives on four islands as though they were our dearest friends.

They are children in most ways, but, unlike the Japanese, they are personally and physically attractive. I find myself in Greek society. We are ourselves great chiefs from America—*alí*,—and almost the first question we were asked was as to our relative rank: was La Farge or I the greater *alí?* We associate only with good society, the chief's families, and could not well do otherwise. The chiefs own their villages and do all entertaining. They give and receive the presents. They are high born, and are physically the finest men I have yet met in the world. They are warriors and politicians. Their manners are astonishingly fine, and their rhetoric, either in conversation or oratory, makes me ashamed of my own race. If we enter or land at a village, we must be received by the chief, in the presence of the other village chiefs all seated cross-legged round the guest-house; and after an hour or so of speech-making while the *kava* is being made, we must drink a bowl of *kava*, and then sit down to a feast of fish, pig, chicken, *taro*, yam, breadfruit, with green cocoanuts to drink. The natives never have anything intoxicating to offer except *kava*, which is about as intoxicating as lager beer, I am told, although I am inclined to think lager beer the stronger; and I ought to be a judge, for I have had to drink the *kava* constantly.

I enclose for your better eyes a photograph of a great chief who entertained us for two days at his town of Safotulafai in Savaii. Lauati is not physically a very big man, as men go here, though tall and finely made, handsome, and the most renowned orator in Savaii; but he is a man of natural abilities who has acquired great influence without the advantage of great hereditary position. Properly, I believe, he is the *tulafale*, or orator, of his town; but in fact he is both orator and chief, and his daughter Fa-a-uli, who sits by his side, is the *taupo*, or village-maiden, an office which needs a book to tell about.

The position of women—or Woman, if you prefer,—in an archaic society, has always interested me, and I have lectured and talked about it until I am tired. I have caught it here all alive, and find it just what I did not expect,—the queerest jumble of professor's books rolled together into a practical system, that no one could guess at;—the strangest compound of laxity and strictness, of absolute freedom and rigorous restraint, of charm and repulsion. Of vice, such as one sees in our cities, there is little or none. As Robert Louis Stevenson said the other day when we climbed to his dreary clearing: "The natives are always respectable." Their vice is mere absence of morals, not deliberate violation of decency—except so far as the missionaries have given them the apple to eat. I could marry the first and noblest young woman in Samoa,—some splendid creature, six feet tall, who would carry me in her arms like a child;—and could send her home in a year or two, and marry another, and so on, without loss of character or social position either to me or to them, if I only made the proper gifts and paid the value of the girls to their villages, a matter of one or two hundred dollars. Probably every *taupo* in Samoa would be glad to marry me on these terms, for a great American alí is their ideal of a husband; but if one refused obstinately, she would be driven out of the village. Yet if I eloped with one, or had clandestine relations with her, or did not take her into my own house, at least for a day, as a recognised wife, both of us would lose caste; I should be regarded as a thief, and our children would be illegitimate.

Such a code is amusing, and I am greatly amused to find the woman as socially conspicuous here as in America,—perhaps more so, for she is as prominent in war as in peace. Every town chooses a village maiden—taupo—for its social representative and candidate for high connection in marriage. The taupo should be high born; if possible the chief's daughter, sister, or niece. She should be well made and strong, but mere beauty of face is not much regarded. You see what sort of a face my friend Fa-a-uli, the taupo of her father Lauati, has. She is the jolliest girl you can imagine, and as her garments are not troublesome, I took measurements of her. She is only five feet, three inches,—63 inches—high; round the head, above the eyes, 23 inches; round the neck, 15 inches; round the chest, including the arms, 45 inches; round the upper arm, 14½ inches; round the wrist 8 inches; round the upper waist, 32½ inches; round the hips, 42 inches; round the calf of the leg, 17 inches; round the ankle, 10¾ inches. Notice the enormous relative size of arms and legs. The same thing can be seen in the photograph of Sau-sau's daughter, a celebrated taupo, now married. Sau-sau is the largest chief on the islands, and his daughter was very tall. I know her only by photograph; but I have taken measurements of another girl, Fang-alo, who is one of our intimates here at Apia, though not high-born or a taupo. Fang-alo is 63½ inches tall; 14 inches round the neck; 43 inches round the chest and arms; 12½ round the upper arm; 7¾ round the wrist, 31, round the upper waist; 40, round the hips; 16, round the calf of the leg; 10 round the ankle. The length of her foot was 10½ inches; that of Fa-a-uli's was about 10 inches.

These must be the true and normal proportions for women. As far as women depart from them, they depart from the ideal animal, for the animal here exists under the most favorable conditions for its development. They are bred for size and figure, too, almost as systematically as we breed cattle.

The taupo is not merely for ornament. When we reach a village, the taupo is obliged to come to the guest-house, if the chief is not there; she sits in the highest place, and we seat ourselves on her right; she orders the kava and scolds the servants, or rather the other girls; she supplies food; she stays till we go to bed, to see that our beds and mosquito-nets are properly arranged; she is on hand in the morning to see that our beds are removed, and our breakfast supplied; to her we give the usual gift, and she gives some object of interest to us. She is always accompanied by a duenna of certain age, who has had children. She is watched with care, and any misbehavior is fatal to her character.

The taupo, in war-times, leads the warriors even to battle. She wears a showy war-costume, but Fa-a-uli candidly told me that, in the German war, she was afraid of the bullets. In the three great military receptions given to us by the three towns we visited in Savaii, the taupo all appeared, bare-breasted and bare-legged, at the head of their men, and one of them wanted me to photograph her with her revolver. Of course the effect is immense. One's eye instinctively watches the outline of the feminine figure.

From all this you can understand how large a share the woman plays in this archaic society; but this is not all. Of course in a few hours one becomes extremely intimate with the *taupo*, who much resembles women of other countries, only more so. You would laugh to see us sprawling over the mats, chattering with the *taupo* as we best can, while she smokes our tobacco, or peels sugar-cane for us with her teeth, or sits up to be sketched or photographed, or writes letters to us with our pens on our paper. Generally other girls come in, and if we drop off to sleep they fan us; or exchange small gifts, or levy freely on our tobacco, or give us rings and take handkerchiefs, or lean over us while we sketch or write, their bare shoulders rubbing cocoanut oil freely into our clothes. This is great fun to them, and they are as free as children in attitudes and little declarations of regard. "Alofa," their commonest word, means everything: "Love," "Good-day"; "Howdye"; "Best wishes," and a whole dictionary of customary phrases; but the very generality of it shows that "love" is not a deep emotion. They have no deep emotions or strong passions. They have sympathies and little jealousies, but their hearts are not breakable. Any show of emotion is so rare as to rouse notice at once. I have witnessed none.

I have left to the last the greatest social accomplishment of the *taupo* and her girls. This is the *Siva*, or dance. Samoans dance by instinct, and every Samoan, man or woman, knows all the complicated Siva figures from babyhood. The first evening of one's arrival in a village, one is sure to have a Siva. La Farge and I were driven by bad weather, on leaving our steamer, to seek shelter in a little village in Tutuila where foreigners must be a great rarity. Everything was new, strange and delightful to us; but I never shall forget the feeling of fascination to me, when, after dark, as we sat in the dimly lighted house, the girls, five of them, came in, costumed for the Siva. They wore only waist-dresses of long green and red leaves—the *ti* leaf, and the dress is the *ti-ti*,—with necklaces of red berries, and leaf-crowns on their heads. Their rich skins glistened with cocoanut oil as if they had just come out of the sea, as I thought at first they had done. The effect of color and form was rich beyond description. Of course the girls vary much in beauty, but one or more of them is sure to have a statuesque figure, and naturally is proud of it. Nakedness is her natural dress, and she is never so much at ease as in the *titi* dancing. They sit in a row on the floor, and begin to sing, clap their hands, wave them about, and go through a thousand movements, some exquisitely graceful, but with no meaning except their supposed appropriateness to their notions of beauty. This is the sitting-Siva, and lasts till they have enough of it. Then they rise and dance on their feet. The standing Siva has always, I think, a meaning, but the number of figures is apparently infinite. They imitate all the ordinary acts of their life: Gathering and stripping cocoanuts; hammering; ball-playing; fighting; the motions of birds, cats and rats; bathing; sometimes with infinite grace; often with clownish grimaces and comic acting of the boorish kind. Sometimes men dance with the women; sometimes the men dance alone. All these dances are, as far as I could see, perfectly proper; but there are other figures, decidedly otherwise, which the missionaries have driven out, at least in ordinary dancing.

The missionaries forbid the Siva altogether under penalty of exclusion from church-membership. Our visit has caused no end of scandal for this reason. All the *taupo* have had to dance, and all have lost their church-membership. From poor Ainga, the king, Malietoa's, niece, who entertained us at Sa-papalii on Savaii, and Fa-nua, the *taupo* of Apia, to Lauati's daughter Fa-a-uli at Safotulafai, the havoc of *taupo* has been sweeping. The Samoans insist on preserving their native customs; the *taupo* must dance as one of their chief duties; they like it themselves; every human being dances as a matter of course; the dance is their one means of displaying their beauty or grace at its best, and of attracting husbands or admiration; and the church can fulminate till doomsday before stopping it. My sympathies are all Samoan, and I like the Siva, though often I am tired to desperation by the long strain of sitting through it.

I have now made a sketch of Samoan society as an entertainment. You must imagine us living in it. We feed at the Consulate and sleep in beds near by it; but our interest is wholly with the natives. La Farge works hard at his sketching or writing, and is very nervous about his health. Under his instruction I am trying to sketch, and, as I think I wrote you from Honolulu, the work amuses me, though my sketching is utterly childish. We have made a great journey through the western islands, with Consul Sewall, and had a reception such as was seldom known. The Samoans are just now extremely grateful to the United States, and lavished kindness on us. I found myself instantly recognised as a nobleman because the frigate "Adams" was formerly well known here, and my name, "Atamu," was Biblical. My grandfathers have been dragged out as kings, and my gold has had to be lavished accordingly. Luckily a gift of ten dollars is princely here, and twenty profuse. The Chief Justice gave us two turtle, and I sent him ten dollars. To Lauati I gave twenty. To the *taupo*, I always give ten. All have accepted the gifts with thanks, and I am assured by the oldest inhabitants that they like money best of all gifts.

In the photographs you will notice that the girls all wear different dresses. Ainga has a *titi* or *lava-lava* of native *tapa* cloth, torn in strips to show the legs. Faauli has a fine mat, like Panama straw, the most precious of native possessions, worth thirty or forty dollars. She wore four at our state-reception by her father. Sau-sau's daughter has a *titi*, I think, of green and purple *ti*-leaves. Fang-alo has a *tapa*, or *siapa*, of the native cloth. All these are regular toilets, but here in Apia the girls commonly wear either loose night-gown dresses, or shirts with their *lava-lavas*, or at least a sort of tippet in front.

You had better write to me, care of the Consul at Tahiti. I may not get it, but I know no better address.

Ever truly Yrs   Henry Adams.

MS: MH

1. HA refers to the wedding of Mary Ogden Adams and Grafton St. Loe Abbott.
2. *The Odyssey of Homer* (1871–1872), translated by William Cullen Bryant.

To Elizabeth Cameron

Apia (Vaiale) Nov. 4, 1890

My dear Friend

Your letter from Harrisburg, October 8–11, arrived last evening. In return I send you two huge despatches; one through the State Department, which should be read first; the other enclosed here. They are books rather than letters, and they are written only on the chance that they may give you half an hour's amusement. If they bore you, burn them. They are for you, and not meant to be preserved.

I am depressed by the thought that this letter will find you in Washington, while I shall be still looking out on my village-green at Vaiale, and confusing my brain with a queer medley of pictures, among which your house will pirouette with Mata-afa's; and as I sit here in the dusk of the evening, poor Taele, about whom I will write some day, will crouch on the mats by my chair and think I am ill because I seem so troubled. Taele is a pretty woman too, and pathetic in her way, and the *convenances* do not forbid her to walk through the side of my house when she pleases. She is charged with the care of it, being our nearest neighbor, and she is certainly a curious contrast to what I have been accustomed to in the way of feminine sympathy.

La Farge does not feel well enough to undertake the Tahiti voyage yet. We shall wait here six weeks more, I imagine. Could you not write me a line or lines both to Samoa and Tahiti to say you are well.

Ever Yrs   Henry Adams.

MS: MHi

To Elizabeth Cameron

Vaiale (Samoa) 8 Nov. [1890]

My two long despatches of October should start for you today from Tutuila, and should reach you before Dec. 1. Although nothing has happened since they left here on the 5th, another letter will do no harm, seeing that it cannot reach you till Christmas. Only odds and ends remain to be said, and a letter written now can hardly be gay, for we are all dyspeptic. I am almost as much upset as I used to be in the London season; La Farge thinks his sufferings worse than in Japan, and I dispute in vain only the relative demerits of his ailments; Sewall is doubled-up with pine-apple and

Dover's powders;[1] and poor little, delicate Mrs Parker, who is here with Lieutenant Parker on the naval station business, has been nearly dead for three days with sick headache, from which all the authority of her uncle, the President, cannot relieve her. In these relaxing climates, one's whole system relaxes, and one's repugnance to physical effort stimulates profanity at the indolence of the liver. One lives in the open air, which would satisfy any Christian liver, in any dry climate; but the Polynesian pagan is exacting, and requires Dover's powders besides. The idea of walking or riding two hours a day seems monstrous here, where the temperature is usually $85°$, and where the air is like a hot-house involved in orchids and delicate ferns. Not that I dislike the air, though it is oily in its clinging softness; but I do dislike effort. La Farge dislikes both. What is worse is that the steamer "Richmond," our only means of reaching Tahiti, passed through here this week, and we went on board to see what our fate was to be. Nothing so wretched has yet visited us. She is only 800 tons, with no deck-room except what is occupied by sheep for Tahiti. All the staterooms are below, and flush with the water-line. We must pass a week in this pen, butting into the heavy trade-wind, with the prospect of returning in her, *via* Auckland, to tranship in another of the same class, for Fiji; a voyage of about three weeks. I hope La Farge will not attempt it. As for me,—*nada*, as the Spaniards or some other dialect has it! Yet this is luxury compared with what Stevenson has done for two years past.

Stevenson returned our call the other day, and passed several hours with us. He was cleaner, and his wife was not with him, for which reasons perhaps he seemed less like William Everett. He talked very well, as usual, but said nothing that stuck very hard. He will tell his experiences in the form of Travels,[2] and I was rather surprised to find that his range of study included pretty much everything: geology, sociology, laws, politics and ethnology. We like him, but he would be, I think, an impossible companion. His face has a certain beauty, especially the eyes, but it is the beauty of disease. He is a strange compound of callousness and susceptibility, and his susceptibility is sometimes more amusing than his callousness. We were highly delighted with one trait which he showed in absolute unconsciousness of its simplicity. The standard of domestic morality here is not what is commonly regarded as rigid. Most of the traders and residents have native wives, to whom they are married after the native custom: that is, during pleasure. A clerk in the employ of an American trader named Moors was discovered in too close relations with the native wife of a lawyer named Carruthers. The offence was condoned once, and this lenity seemed very proper to Stevenson, who declared that he had no difficulty in forgiving his wife once, but not a second time. Recently the scandal was renewed, and caused great tribulation. Stevenson was deeply outraged, and declared that he could no longer dine with Moors for fear of meeting the clerk. Moors, who has had various wives to say nothing of incidental feminine resources, was also scandalized, and dismissed the clerk, though the clerk was indispensable to his business. Carruthers was painfully saddened. The woman's father, an old native, was worst of all. I have not yet learned the views of Mrs Stevenson; but we are curious to know why, in the light of their own experience, they could not have suggested the easy device of advising Carruthers to let his wife go, and allowing the clerk to marry her. The unfortunate clerk is the victim of outraged Samoan morality, and is to be sent back to San Francisco where the standard is, I presume, less exalted. This part of Stevenson's talk was altogether the most humorous, and as grotesque as the New Arabian Nights; but Stevenson was not in the least conscious of our entertainment.[3]

Samoa becomes more curious, in this sort of grotesqueness, the more one sees of it. The sexual arrangements are queer enough, and the stories of old Samasoni, or Hamilton, formerly pilot, harbor-master, American Vice Consul, and what not, amuse me beyond description, though they are rarely capable of record. In my last letter, somewhere, I may have mentioned Taele, a native woman who keeps a supervision of our native house. Taele is still young; hardly more than twenty; and unusually pretty. Her prettiness so much attracted a recent British Consul named Churchward, that Churchward married her, after Samoan custom, and she was known as his wife. They had a child, a handsome boy, now five or six years old, who lives with our old village chief To-fai, close by our sleeping-quarters, and is inseparable from the old man. A couple of years ago or thereabouts, Churchward was ordered elsewhere, and went, leaving Taele with a small pension and the hope of his return.[4] Taele waited for him dutifully until she despaired of his return, and then she married a native carpenter who had been a missionary teacher. Very recently I learned from Mele Samasoni that the second husband had gone off to another province and had taken another wife. Taele quietly remains here, much respected and very interesting in the melancholy style of some Samoan beauty; but she is scared into the forest because I want her to serve as a model to draw from. She cannot endure the idea of being painted, even in full dress, covered up to the ears, and is in deadly terror because I wanted her to wear the *lava-lava,* or waistcloth, which every native habitually carries. Yet I have no doubt that Taele will have another husband soon.

In other ways the natives are more inscrutable. Chiefly for want of something to talk about during the interminable visits of native chiefs, I ask questions about the old customs, families and religion. Three times out of four, when I reach any interesting point, I am blocked by the reply that what I ask is a secret. At first I thought that this was only a way of disguising ignorance, but was assured that it was not so. I am pretty well convinced that all matters involving their old superstitions, priesthood, and family history, are really secret, and that their Christianity covers a pretty complete paganism with priests and superstitions as strong as ever. Indeed, To-fai made no bones of telling me, at great length, the whole story, and on his information I have in several cases surprised other chiefs into admissions that they did not intend to make; but I am still convinced that the Samoans have an entire intellectual world of their own, and never admit outsiders into it. I feel sure that they have a secret priesthood more powerful than the political chiefs, with supernatural powers, invocations, prophecy, charms, and the whole paraphernalia of paganism. I care too little about these matters to make any searching inquiry, so they may keep their secrets for anything I shall do; but I never imagined a race so docile and gentle, yet so obstinately secret. They never killed a missionary, but they are just masters in playing the missionaries off. The chiefs especially detest the missionary teachers, who are all common people of no social rank, and who have mostly chosen to become teachers in order to get a position of any kind, which can be done only by undermining the power of the chiefs.

November 13. I write the date at a venture; it cannot be more than two or three days wrong. This is Friday, I am almost sure. Since our return from Savaii a fortnight ago, the weather has been persistently bad. Every day has been rainy, and we have seen little of the sun. Luckily we are all well again, or at least we are all about, eating well, sleeping well and doing whatever we please, though La Farge, who always can and does accomplish, in every way, twice what I can, persists in thinking himself an invalid. Men who think so, as they certainly know best, commonly have grounds for thinking it; but La Farge looks twenty years younger than I, and, in everything, except legs, I think he is so. Consequently he gives the impression of being a *malade imaginaire,* and nothing is more irritating than to see one's troubles treated as imaginary, even if they are pure invention. Long and intimately as I have known La Farge, I have not the least idea whether he is really delicate in health or not; but for a man of fiftyseven he seems to me to have surprising elasticity, and as he always rebounds easily from the depths of illness to the energy of apparent health, I know no reason why he may not go on so, for twenty years, and break his neck at last. At all events, he has worked hard and made several sketches better than anything I could get him to do in Japan; and yesterday he found no difficulty about getting up at six o'clock in the morning to go with me on a picnic, although we had every reason to expect bad weather. I had arranged the picnic with Fatuleia, Seumano's wife, the head of society in Apia. I never get used to the idea of a Duchess asking for my washing; and Fatuleia is my ideal of a nurse for Martha rather than of a *grande dame;* but in Samoa they keep the two functions in harmony, and Fatuleia's women do up my underclothes while Fatuleia entertains me in the same room. So the Duchess of Apia arranged my picnic, and took our friend Mele Samasoni as her associate. I wanted to see a real cataract of old-gold girls, in order to satisfy Clarence King, whose story of the Hilo cataract was received with such incredulity by sceptics at home. In the hills, five or six miles from Apia, is a little waterfall called the Papaseea, or Sliding Rock, because it is a favorite place for the natives to go over. It is a lonely spot in the forest, and one must take one's girls with one, if any sliding is to be done. Fatuleia and Mele drummed up half a dozen girls: Fanua, the *taupo* of Apia, about whom I have told you before; Fang-alo and Otaota, whose photographs I have sent you; a pretty little missionary girl named Nelly; a girl named Suey, of the Samasoni household; and one or two others. We started at eight o'clock, we elders on horseback, the girls mostly on foot, and two or three of my boat-crew carrying luncheon and our traps. Awoki and Charley accompanied us, also mounted, Awoki's suspenders prominent as usual from afar. The natives seem to delight in the little Jap who is regarded as the funny man of our set, and they like fun. So we started in a long procession, and soon, leaving the road, plunged into the forest by a narrow path, ducking under wet trees and fallen tree-trunks, and splashing through mud. The day was overcast with light showers, but the light was soft in the woods, and although the forest here is nothing startling but might almost be a forest in Pennsylvania, at first sight, yet there are fine trees of curious forms and rich foliage, ferns hanging high over one's head, from the tree-trunks, beautiful hanging vines and creepers, and occasionally strange notes of birds more like the cry of some animal than the song of our mocking-bird or thrush. We rode an hour through these woods, till we rose several hundred feet to a spot where, through a clearing, we looked down over the distant bay of Apia and the surf breaking on the coral reefs along the coast. There we dismounted, fastened our horses, and clambered down a steep ravine. At the bottom, a small stream leaped over the lava rocks, in successive falls, coming from thick forest above, and lost from sight among the branching trees below. Above us the the ravine walls rose one or two hundred feet, topped by lofty trees. The sides of the ravine were green with shrubs and creepers, ferns and the beautiful green of the wild banana, the most tropical in look of all the forest growth. You may imagine that the place is a picture, and perhaps some day you may get a better idea of it from La Farge's sketch, if he makes one. The Sliding Rock is rather more than twenty feet high. The water, running over it, causes a growth of thin grass or some slippery stuff, and makes the surface smooth. I clambered down to the pool below, which is some ten feet deep, and placed my Kodak on a fallen tree-trunk opposite the fall. Before I had prepared it, down flopped Fang-alo, as though coasting, and plunged into the pool with a splash that sent spray half way up the rock. By the time her head appeared above water, Otaota shot down after her. Fang-alo wore only her *lava-lava*, or waist-cloth, but hung a garland of green leaves round her neck, as a sort of covering, and she looked like a true naiad as she came dripping out of the pool, and wrung the water from her hair. The other girls wore what they liked, either the long, night-gown, missionary dress of colored calico, or a shirt, or jacket, with the *lava-lava*; but of course the cotton, when wet, clung so closely as to show the whole figure, while the colors rather increased the effect of the picture. I snapped a dozen photographs, but the velocity of the girls' fall was so great that the Kodak can give only a blur. La Farge drew as quickly as he could, making rough outlines for memoranda. The sun came out, and the girls kept up the fun, coming over two at a time, with shouts of laughter and constant babble of unintelligible Samoan. Then the men joined them, looking like fauns. They had no occasion to undress, but slid down as they were, and let their lava-lavas dry or remain wet; it matters little to them. Below the higher rock is another smaller fall and pool, and there the girls made another picture, lying in the rushing water as though they lived there. Only Fa-nua was timid, and waited till the very last; indeed she made the jump but once, and then paddled about with Nelly, hunting for shrimps under the stones, and eating them alive like berries. The funniest was Awoki, who, after long tremors on the verge, clinging to the rock, in a *lava-lava,* at last let himself go, amid great applause. At noon we had lunch and a respite. You know by this time pretty well what we eat here, and as no ice can be had for love or money, we must eat everything quick. Our lunch today was only remarkable for my having at last tasted *pollolo,* a Samoan delicacy of the repulsive order. The *pollolo* is a curious salt-water worm, or long thin creature like a very slim earthworm; it appears only once a year, just at dawn, at a certain place on the coral reef opposite our Consulate. As the day happened about ten days ago, we all went out to see the show, starting at four o'clock with the first light of dawn. As we bumped and hauled over the coral, we could gradually see a dozen or more boats, mostly the narrow, native dug-outs, about a distant spot near the outer, or barrier reef. When we came up, we joined them, and, peering into the water, with the growing light, we could at last see one or two long, thin, thread-like creatures swimming near the surface. They had some sense akin to sight, for when I tried to catch them with my hand, they swam away. At last I caught one, and as I looked at him in the hollow of my hand, the little wretch kicked himself in pieces, and I had half a dozen little kicking earwigs in my hand. The same thing happened in the water. As the day dawned, the creatures became thicker, but each soon divided into inch- or half-inch sections, and the top of the water soon swarmed with things, which the boat-people caught with fine hand-nets, or sieves, and turned into pails. Nothing seems to be known of the creature, or why he should come on one particular day of the year, at certain, far-distant spots, for an hour before dawn, and should disappear at sunrise. The water was but two or three feet deep on the coral rock, and the creature has ample motive power to come out or go in as he likes, but he comes and goes only by the calender. The natives eat them raw; but to keep the luxury longer, they cook it with cocoa-nut meat, pounded; and Fatuleia brought some of it for lunch; a greenish, pasty stuff, like fine spinach. I tried it on bread, and thought it rather like *foie-gras.* As usual our lunch was spread on banana-leaves, close by the water, and when it was over we smoked our cigars under umbrellas, in a shower, sitting on the Sliding Rock. Then came more bathing,—very pretty indeed from above, as the girls rambled about, half under water or half hidden by trailing vines or foliage, or sitting in picturesque attitudes in the bubbling water. We started for home at two o'clock, and not till we were well on our way did the rain at last come down in its usual torrents. The women were simply drenched, but perhaps they are used to it. La Farge and I had umbrellas and water-proofs, but were glad to change all our clothes on reaching home.

November 17. We are now told that the rainy season has begun, and I hope it has, for I should be sorry to know a rainier season than this. Since we arrived, the fall of rain can hardly have averaged less than an inch a day. It comes in tremendous showers which might as well measure solid sheets as raindrops; and as the weeks go on, the showers become continuous. We have had but one sunny day in seven, of late. At night the deluge on our sheet-iron roof keeps us awake by hours. The sun and moon have disappeared, and we mildew to the tips of our close-shaven hair. Summer rains are among the smallest annoyances of life, and I should not mind them much, if they were not accompanied by violent squalls of wind which make sea-going a discomfort if not a danger. We want to make another boat-excursion,—this time, to the eastward,—but we must go outside to get anywhere, as the barrier-reef stops about two miles to the eastward of Vaiale. I do not fancy being blown against the cliffs, or swamped in the surf; and there is no land-path. Consequently we sit all day in our native house, and sketch. I find this an interesting, but a hopeless amusement, for the more I work, the more I learn of the desperate difficulties of painting. I found the ocean bad enough, but the forest is worse. I am struggling now to paint a banana grove,—green on green—and despair fills my soul. The detail is infinite, and the greens of one's paint-box are nothing like the greens of a tropical vegetation. The lights and shadows, even in the rain, are infinite. There are no unbroken masses, no distances, and no deep shadows. I labor all day on three square inches.

November 21. Our rain became a storm. The wind blew violently and the flood fell in a deluge. The little bridge across a stream that separates us in Vaiale from Apia, was washed away by the freshet, towards evening. The German war-vessel, the *Sperber,* which has been here since our arrival, got up steam and ran out to sea. A barque lying in the harbor was in imminent danger of driving on the reef, and escaped by a few feet only. Towards night I walked down to the little river to see how things looked, and I never felt rain and wind together so heavy. I came back soaked. The cocoanut palms writhed, and their great leaves twisted up in the sky like snakes, a hundred feet above us. La Farge made a little sketch of one. He caught the expression of torture very well, and I wish only that he had had time to paint more. At nine o'clock in the evening the wind and rain suddenly stopped and the next morning was calm and blue again. La Farge and I took the boat and went fishing with our village. The day was lovely, and we sketched the fishing. I have half a mind to enclose you my rough sketch, taken in the boat, but, if I do, you must remember that it gives no idea of the fishing, but only of the sea and color. Put it in the full sunlight, as it was painted, and perhaps it may give you a sort of notion of the scene; but do not show it to outsiders. Yesterday Seumano had his great feast for his little daughter, "The Bush sheltering from the Wind." The crowd was immense, some two thousand people, mostly a mass of brown backs, and garlanded heads. Three hundred and fifteen pigs were immolated on the occasion, and Seu's house was like a shop, full of gifts of *tapa*, bottles of beer and drink of various kinds hung from the roof, umbrellas, fine mats, and what not. My present was my usual ten dollars in gold, which I would have made twenty except from the fear of being ostentatious. About a dozen or fifteen *taupo* were there, some from Savaii, some from the opposite end of this island,—Upolo,—all in a house by themselves, dressed in the *taupo* style, some *fa Samoa* without other covering than their *siapas* or fine mats round their waists, others horribly *fagottées* in paper-tinsel and silk or cheap satin bodies. Of course they were dripping with cocoa-nut oil, and my right hand became saturated from handshaking. Some of them were prettily decorated. One had powdered her hair with the small purple and white petals of a flower, which stuck on, either with cocoanut oil or gum. They commonly wore necklaces of the red pepper, like coral. Some wore bodies of braided purple *ti*-leaves, looking like armored fish. Some were quite handsome, and had fine figures, but none of them seemed to me equal to Leolofi or Faauli, though I saw them only sitting on the floor, and could not well judge. The crowd was so great that I did not try to see the Siva which followed, and I was so tired with the noise and movement that I escaped early, and returned to the peace and repose of my native house, where the girls come to chatter with us, and save us the trouble of hunting for models and making conversation.

November 22. While I was writing, Fatuleia sent an invite for the afternoon to another dance. She had been disgusted by the crowd of the day before, and wanted us to be better treated. After lunch we went in our boat to Seumano's, and were asked to come into his house. This was a distinction, for, at the time, a curious family meeting was going on there, which we were glad to see. Seumano's relations sat on one side of the house, and Fatuleia's on the other. Between them, a woman was spreading one fine mat after another, yesterday's gifts to Vao, "The Bush &c." One or two of the mats were very old, and quite in tatters; one or two were very fine; all were jewels, in Samoan eyes; and after each was shown, murmurs of "good" rose among the audience. The woman showed all, and announced at the close that thirty fine mats and two thousand *tapa* had been given. Then we were politely dismissed and the family turned to the task of redistributing the fine mats among each other, for a gift in Samoa has always to be returned in equivalent, and the task is one of great delicacy. Naturally every one expects to receive something more than he gave, and, as this is impossible, the less favored betray their displeasure in open complaints. I should have liked to see this part of the affair, but old John Adams, in the most high-bred, aristocratic English, sent us off to see the dances; and we went.[5]

The open-air dance is never particularly pleasant to me, but we went patiently through it, and La Farge and I were distinguished by sitting on either side of the Queen, Malietoa's wife, whom we had not seen before. She is a big, good-natured, plain Raratonga woman, whom Malietoa insisted on marrying a year or two ago, to the disgust of the Samoans who wanted him to marry some highbred Samoan woman. Malietoa lost position by this marriage, and his queen has never gained any hold on society. She made no attempt at conversation, but smiled graciously, smoked cigarettes, and spit accurately and fluently. We applauded the dancers, shook hands with the *taupo,* and tried to make ourselves agreeable for an hour or two. The rain held off, and we had benches with backs to sit on,—a luxury. When the dancers were all tired, we were allowed to go, and on our way home we went with Mele Samasoni to call on the *taupo* of Fangaloa, a town at the east end of this island, where we mean to go next week, on another boat-excursion. Our call was duly formal. We carried two tins of canned salmon and five loaves of bread, as the regular gift of the occasion. We found the handsome *taupo* receiving. Three good-looking girls were making *kava,* and for the first time in my experience the *kava* was chewed, not grated, which is supposed to improve it. Our present was graciously received, and immediately divided, more than half of it being given, rather to my disgust, to a chief from Savaii who was also making a call. I gave the *taupo* a cigar, which she lighted, and five minutes afterwards I saw my cigar in the mouth of another man, while my girl returned to her cigarette. This is the fate of every gift, except money, and for that reason I prefer to give money, for I do not like seeing my umbrellas, silk-scarfs, gowns, cigars, &c, parading about town on strangers; and they are sure to pass through a score of hands, in this communistic society, before they are lost from sight. In return for our present, we received some of the usual eatables in a basket, which Mele Samasoni received for us, and presently politely returned, much to my relief at learning that I was at liberty to disembarrass myself of these troublesome gifts. Then we asked the *taupo* to dance, and I invited her to use my own native house that evening, for the purpose. She smilingly consented, and in the evening, at about nine o'clock, in the interval between rains, we all assembled at the house, which was also occupied or surrounded by our native neighbors, who flock to a Siva like flies. Consul Sewall and our neighbor the British Consul, a youth named Cusack-Smith; Lieutenant Parker and his delicate, gentle little wife; the Samasoni's; ourselves; three photographic cameras, and a crowd of natives, were in attendance. Parker flashed lights, and Mrs Parker and I took pictures as hard as we could, while the dance went on for a couple of hours. This morning the girls came here again, and I took their measurements,—two of them. The *taupo,* whose name is Faasei, was not so large as her companion, or *tulafale,* Pui-pui; but both are very good specimens of Samoan girls, seventeen or eighteen years old; and you can, if you feel any interest in the matter, compare their measurements with those of Fa-a-uli which I sent you last month.

Height	Fa-a-uli, 63½, Faa-sei, 65½, Pui-pui, 68,		
Round chest and arms	45	45	49
" upper waist	32½	34	35¾
" hips	42	42	41
" head	23	24	23½
" upper arm	14½	13½	13½
" wrist	8	8	7½
" calf of leg	17	16¾	16
" ankle	10¾	10	10
" neck	15	14½	16
Length of foot	9½	10½	10

Though Pui-pui is much the tallest, she seems to me the best made, but they run very even, as the men do. One never, or almost never, sees a tall figure which is thin or weak, or a short figure disproportionately stout. All are evenly developed, and differ chiefly in the tendency to be thick and heavy in details. After sixteen they coarsen rapidly, and lose their firmness of figure. Both Faasei and Puipui were taken by me for married women who had children, till I was assured to the contrary. By-the-bye, Samasoni reassures me as to the probable first cost of a taupo-wife. In pigs and mats, she would come higher, in apparent price, than in coin. Cash-down, in Chilian silver dollars, Samasoni thinks that a hundred dollars would be sufficient. This is about seventy dollars in gold. Dog-cheap, as far as the gift is concerned; but unfortunately the family expects further to share all one's possessions, and the wife often runs away to her father in order to extort a double-dowry for her connections. Indeed the tie between father and daughter is stronger, through life, than that between husband and wife. As I expect to sail for Tahiti in three weeks, I will wait and see whether I cannot do better there.

Are you fairly tired of old-gold girls, or can you stand a few more statistics? Within five-and-twenty years, all the lingering remnants of archaic society, in its higher forms, will probably have disappeared. A civilisation so hopelessly self-conscious, and so radically diseased, as ours in Europe and America, will never approach, or even understand, the physical standard from which it started on its downward course, or the intellectual standard from which it started on what we hope is its upward development. Only unlucky men, with a sceptical turn of mind, who have unwillingly betaken themselves to the study of history, for want of having had an education to fit them for better employment, are likely to treasure the facts of an ideal archaic Arcadia, and to feel their meaning. Our ancestors were once certainly like these people. Not so very many generations ago,—say thirty,—our grandmothers were proportioned at four feet round the chest, three feet round the waist, and three-and-a-half feet round the hips, like Pui-pui, to a height of 5 ft. 8 inches. If you think these dimensions too heavy for grace, you may prefer those of Aotoa and Aolele, daughters of the powerful chief Tangaloa, of Savaii; or, if not his daughters, esteemed so highly by him that he makes them both *taupo* of his village of Tufu. They came to Seumano's feast, and we seized on them to photograph.

	Aotoa	Aolele
Height	66	65½
Round chest and arms	41¾	43½
″ upper waist	33½	32
″ hips	39	38
″ head	23½	22½
″ upper arm	13	12
″ wrist	8	7½
″ calf of leg	16	15
″ ankle	9½	10¼
″ neck	14	15
Length of foot	10	10½

These are two pretty girls, not so heavily built as is the apparent rule among Samoans. They average about three-feet-and-a-half round the chest, and 33 inches round the waist, against 38 inches round the hips, with a height of five-feet-six. All the measurements, except round the hips, are taken on the bare body; but a little allowance must be made for the thickness of the *siapa* on the hips. Notice the size of the wrists and ankles, and the strength it implies. Neither women nor men show much muscle. Their flesh covers the muscle smoothly, and takes the light in planes, even on their arms and legs; but the play of their limbs and bodies in the light is beautiful. They differ greatly in color, but at a distance, in the sunlight, they are a decided red. I have seen a few with hair naturally reddish, but as a rule they give an artificial red color to their hair by powdering it once a week for a few hours with lime. When my boat-crew go out powdered, I feel as though I were rowed by half-a-dozen French *marquis* of the *ancien régime*. Now and then a man or woman has crinkly hair, but usually the hair is straight, and cut short, with an artificial curl produced by combing and brushing.

November 25,—or thereabouts. We are waiting to hear from Seumano that he is ready to start, and as soon as he notifies us, we shall begin our active preparations for the cruise about the island. I feel as though I were Robinson Crusoe, and I have no idea how long we shall stay away. The weather is once more fine. La Farge likes to linger. He is not yet ready to sail for Tahiti, and has decided in favor of another month here. To me it is all the same. I dread a little the necessary knocking about in an open boat, outside the reef; but it will not be worse than at Apollima, and a few hours in a boat is nothing compared with a week in a steamer. We are already old Polynesians. Probably every chief on the islands knows all about us, and would be glad to have us for guests. Hereabouts we are adopted acquaintances with every man and child. As I stroll to my dinner at seven o'clock, in the dusk, I am greeted by half the dim figures that pass me, with a *Tofà Akamou*, though I can reply only *Tofà*, for I cannot even see them, much less call them by name. *Tofà* is Good-night; Good-bye, Sleep-well, or whatever you please at parting, as *Alófa* is a similar greeting. *Akámou*, or *Akamu*, is *Atámu*, Adam, for the natives interchange *k* with *t* in all their words, spelling with *t*, but pronouncing *k*. It is regarded as a vulgarism, but is nearly universal, and very ancient. *Akamu* is my native name, and is becoming more familiar to me than my own. La Farge's native name is *La-fa-el-e*, which he likes because it happens to be identical with Rafaele, the *l* and *r* being also interchangeable, or rather, the *r* being almost unpronounceable with Samoans. Our house is a favorite place for the girls to visit. They all want to see La Farge's sketches. Hardly a day passes that some *taupo* does not come to be photographed and measured. Otaota comes every afternoon to be painted, and brings half a dozen chattering boys and girls, who drive La Farge wild by announcing from under the table, or between his legs, every touch he gives to the nose or the mouth or the hair. The old women and the young chiefs rarely come near us. They dislike white men because the girls like them and prefer to marry them. The old chiefs are on the girls' side, and dislike only missionary influence. Even there, they are hostile chiefly to the native teachers, and because native missionaries are hostile to them. The few white missionaries are becoming liberal, and there is almost a breach between them and the mass of native teachers. Seumano's great feast the other day was an aera in this matter, for the leading white missionaries, for the first time, publicly looked on at the *Siva*, which was a formal abandonment of their old attitude. I am relieved at this concession, for it prevents an open quarrel between us white laymen and the white clergy; but it forbodes a desperate struggle with the native teachers, who are a low caste, struggling to retain power.

If we could get rid of the native teachers and substitute trained sanitary inspectors, Samoa would be vastly benefitted. The Samoans suffer chiefly from sores, which are very slow to heal in this climate, and their own medical practice is that of the old women. They take cold as we do, and their colds are about as severe. I am rather surprised to find them complain of head-aches, for they live chiefly on fruits and vegetables or fish. My chief, To-fai, an elderly man of the highest rank, and a redoubtable warrior, has had a very severe cold and head-ache for several days. Yesterday I dosed him with quinine. He was well enough to let me ask him questions for two hours, which implies strength at least, for the Samoans easily weary of any effort, especially intellectual; but I was asking about subjects which are *saa* to the common people, and *vavao*, or forbidden, except among the highest and most courageous chiefs, who can afford to disregard their own rules. I asked much, too, about their *a-iku* or spirits, ghosts and devils, of which they have a plenty, though commonplace enough. To-fai is an *esprit-fort*, but my coxswain, *Sa-mao*, who is himself a chief of good rank, was charmingly childlike in his good-faith. There is a devil that haunts the road at a river-ford about a mile beyond us, and howls at night, or appears as a large beast of various characters, and I tried hard to get *Sa-mao* to take me to see him, but *Sa-mao* admitted he had himself never seen an *a-iku*. Samasoni has a pretty good ghost story of his own, but chiefly for his queer, abrupt way of telling it; and it was evidently a case of native terrorism to drive him out of some property.

I shall cut off this despatch here, as it is already extravagantly bulky; and shall send it, with my other Washington letters, under enclosure to Wharton. Probably I shall not be able to write from my *malanga* by this mail, which closes a week from today. So I shall not be able to acknowledge letters that arrive, but I expect none, for you must suppose me at Tahiti.

Tofà   Akamu.

Apia. November 25, 1890. 4 o'clock, A.M.

> The slow dawn comes at last upon my waking;
>   The palms stand clear against the growing light;
> And where long hours I heard the ocean breaking,
>   I see at last the broken line of white.
>
> All night the palms and ocean have been gleaming
>   Beneath the softness of the tropic moon,
> And lit a marble terrace in my dreaming,
>   And leafless trees that were so green in June.
>
> I know that, where you are, the noon is falling;
>   I look once more down the familiar street;
> Below is Martha for her Dobbitt calling;
>   I hear the patter of her eager feet.
>
> John Hay is hurrying from his house to meet us;
>   My sister Anne is coming up the stair;
> But still I strain to see the street beneath us,
>   To catch the whiteness of the dress you wear.
>
> It is the surf upon the coral streaming,
>   The white light glimmering on the village lawn;
> The broad banana-leaf reflects the gleaming;
>   The shadowy native glides across the dawn.
>
> Death is not hard when once you feel its measure;
>   One learns to know that Paradise is gain;
> One bids farewell to all that gave one pleasure;
>   One bids farewell to all that gave one pain.

MS: MHi
1. Dover's powder, named for the eighteenth-century English physician Thomas Dover, is a mixture containing opium and ipecac.
2. *In the South Seas* (1896).
3. Stevenson, *The New Arabian Nights* (1882).
4. William Brown Churchward (1845–1920), *My Consulate in Samoa* (1887).
5. Lima, a Samoan known as John Adams, whose accent "brought back indefinable associations . . . some old officer of the navy . . . some far-back Englishman or antique Southerner?" (La Farge, *Reminiscences*, p. 218).

To John Hay

Vaiale (Apia) 16 Nov. 1890.

My dear John

By this time I had expected to be in Tahiti, but we have found more in Samoa than we expected. Our nasty little pigstye of a steamer sailed for Tahiti a week ago or so, and will not return for a month. Then perhaps we shall sail, and when this reaches you on Christmas Day I hope we shall be established at Papeete. I doubt whether it will have much novelty after Samoa, but it will give a chance for you to join us. By taking the mail sailing-ship from San Francisco, you can reach Tahiti in about a month; perhaps less, for what I know.

Your letter of October 10 arrived by the last mail. All my letters were very satisfactory, yours highly so, except for Sombrerete, which is sombrereteer than ever.[1] I am brewing a letter to King which I shall write some day, and it will be a volume, for I have seen heaps of things that I can tell him what I don't know about; but the chiefest thing is that a man can still live on these islands of the South Seas for pure fun. The Consuls themselves, the greatest men within a thousand miles, may spend four or five thousand a year. The richest trader can hardly have more. King Malietoa has not a Chilian quarter-dollar to his back. My neighbor and friend Mata-afa, ex-king, goes every morning to work in his *taro*-patch, or to fish on the reef with the villagers. I have had no little difficulty in obtaining a thousand dollars to spend here, and I am regarded as fabulously rich. When I staid in Savaii with Aiga, Malietoa's adopted daughter, my gift at parting was ten dollars; to Lauati, the great orator and chief of Safotulafai, where we staid three days, I gave twenty, which was equivalent to a fine mat, the costliest of possessions; and as a token of regard for Anai, chief of Iva, I am going—God forgive me—to supply his little daughter with a year's schooling at the missionary college at Malua. You see that a dollar still goes a long way in Samoa, and when I tell you that I pay the extravagant rent of ten dollars a month for my native house, and that a horse costs thirty dollars and is not worth riding when he is bought, you can safely assure King that the South Seas can always shelter him though Sombreretes fall. Indeed, for that matter, a great reputation can be made here with mighty small capital. Darwin and Dana and Wallace have only scratched the ocean's surface. The geologist who can explain these islands, and the artist who can express them, will have got a sure hold on the shirt-tail of fame. If I were twenty years younger, and knew anything to start with, I would try it on. King, who is always young and bloomful, can do it at any time.[2]

The curse of money has touched here, but is not yet deep, though mountain forests, covered with dense and almost impenetrable vegetation, are held at ten dollars an acre, and the poor chiefs, whose only possession is a cocoa-nut grove, have mortgaged it to the eyes. By the Berlin treaty, the whites are not permitted to buy more land from natives, but the whites already claim under one title or another, more land than exists in the whole group of islands. If the sugar cultivation is introduced, the people are lost. Nothing can stand against the frantic barbarism of the sugar-planter. As yet, the only plantations are cocoa-nut, and these are not so mischievous, especially as they are badly managed by German companies which spend more money than the copra brings. Yet the social changes are steady, and another generation will leave behind it the finest part of the old Samoan world. The young chiefs are inferior to the old ones. Gunpowder and missionaries have destroyed the life of the nobles. In former times a great chief went into battle with no thought of the common warrior. He passed through a herd of them, and none presumed to attack him. Chiefs fought only with chiefs. The idea of being killed by a common man was sacrilege. The introduction of fire-arms has changed all this, and now, as one of the chiefs said with a voice of horror, any hunchback, behind a tree, can kill the greatest chief in Samoa.

Since I wrote to you last, I have made a journey along the coast as far as Savaii, the westernmost and largest island of the group. We were an imposing party. The Consul General Sewall, whose guests we are, was the head of it, and Sewall is extremely popular among the Malietoa and Mataafa chiefs who consider him to have saved their lives and liberties. Their expressions of gratitude to him and to the United States are unbounded, and they certainly showed that they felt it, for in their strongholds we were received like kings. Our escort was Seumano-tafa, the chief of Apia, Malietoa's right-hand man. You may remember that, in the great hurricane at Apia, Seumano took his boat through the surf, and saved many lives. For this act, our government sent him some costly presents, among others a beautiful boat, perfectly fitted out for oars and sails. On our *malanga*, or boat-excursion, we went with Seu in his boat, and our own boat followed with our baggage and stores. We carried on Seu's boat the Samoan flag; on our own, the American; and our entire party, including servants and crews, was more than twenty men. We were absent some ten days, with fine weather, and visited the most interesting parts of the islands. I felt as though I had got back to Homer's time, and were cruising about the Aegean with Ajax. Of all the classic spots I ever imagined, the little island of Manono was the most ideal. Ithaca was, even in the reign of Ulysses, absolutely modern by the side of it. As the *mise-en-scène* of an opera, it would be perfection. If I could note music, I would compose an opera, on the musical motives of the Samoan dances and boat-songs, gutturals, grunts and all. You may bet your biggest margin it would be a tremendous success, if the police would only keep their hands off. The ballet alone would put New York on its head with excitement. You would rush for the next steamer if you could realise the beauty of some parts of the Siva. There are figures stupid and grotesque as you please; but there are others which would make you gasp with delight, and movements which I do not exaggerate in calling unsurpassable. Then, if I could close the spectacle with the climax of the *pai-pai,* I should just clean out the bottom dollar of W. W. Astor. The *pai-pai* is a figure taboo by the missionaries, as indeed the Lancers and Virginia Reel are; but it is still danced in the late hours of the night, though we have seen it only once. Two or three women are the dancers, and they should be the best, especially in figure. They dance at first with the same movements, as far as I could see, that they used in many other figures, and as I did not know what they were dancing I paid no special attention. Presently I noticed that the chief dancer's waist-cloth seemed getting loose. This is their only dress, and it is nothing but a strip of cotton or *tapa* about eighteen inches wide, wrapped round the waist, with the end or corner tucked inside to hold it. Of course it constantly works loose, but the natives are so well used to it that they always tighten it, and I never yet have seen either man, woman or child let it fall by accident. In the *pai-pai,* the women let their *lava-lavas,* as they are called, or *siapas,* seem about to fall. The dancer pretends to tighten it, but only opens it so as to show a little more thigh, and fastens it again so low as to show a little more hip. Always turning about and moving with the chorus, she repeats this process again and again, showing more legs and hips every time, until the *siapa* barely hangs on her, and would fall except that she holds it. At last it falls; she turns once or twice more, in full view; then snatches up the *siapa* and runs away.

You must imagine these dances in a native house, lighted by the ruddy flame of a palm-leaf fire in the centre, and filled, except where the dancing is done, by old-gold men and women applauding, laughing, smoking, and smelling of cocoa-nut oil. You are sitting or lying, with your back against an outer-post. Behind you, outside, the moon is lighting a swarm of children, or women, who are also looking eagerly at the dancers. The night air is soft, and the palms rustle above the house. Your legs are cramped by long sitting cross-legged; your back aches; your eyes droop with fatigue; your head aches with the noise; you would give a fortune to be allowed to go to bed, but you can't till the dance is over and the house is cleared. You are half mad with the taste of cocoa-nut oil. You are a little feverish, for this thing has gone on, day and night, for a week, and it is more exhausting than a Pan-American railway jaunt. You are weary of travel and tired of the South Seas. You want to be at home, in your own bed, with clean sheets and a pillow, and quiet. Well! I give you my word, founded on experience, that, with all this, when you see the *pai-pai,* you are glad you came.

Of course the Siva, and especially the figure of the *pai-pai*—beautiful thighs—is made to display the form and not the face. To the Samoan, nine tenths of beauty consists in form; the other tenth in feature, coloring and such details. The Samoan Siva, like the Japanese bath, is evidently connected with natural selection; the young men and young women learn there to know who are the finest marriageable articles. Probably the girl who could make the best show in the *pai-pai* would rise in value to the village by the difference of two or three fine mats and a dozen pigs. In such a case the *pai-pai*, danced by a chief's daughter or *taupo*, does not prove license but virtue. The audience is far less moved by it than a French audience is by a good ballet. Any European suddenly taken to such a show would assume that the girl was licentious, and if he were a Frenchman he would probably ask for her. The chief would be scandalised at European want of decency. He keeps his *taupo* as carefully watched and guarded as though he were a Spaniard. The girl herself knows her own value and is not likely to throw herself away. She has no passions, though she is good-natured enough, and might perhaps elope with a handsome young fellow who made long siege of her. The Frenchman would be politely given some middle-aged woman, more or less repulsive in person, and the mother of several illegitimate children, who would have to be his only consolation for losing the object of his desire. The natives would fully appreciate the joke, and probably nickname the victim by some word preserving its memory.

I have not changed my ideas on the point of morality here. As elsewhere, vice follows vice. We have not sought it, and consequently have not found it. Thus far, no one, either man or woman, has made so much as a suggestion, by word or sign, of any licentious idea. My boatmen probably have license enough, but, as the German Consul warned me, I have none. I might as well be living in a nursery for all the vice that is shown to me, and if I did see it, I should only be amused at its simplicity beside the elaborated viciousness of Paris or even of Naples. I never have lived in so unselfconscious a place. Yesterday La Farge and I snorted with laughter because our boy Charley, a half-caste who acts as our interpreter, informed us that "a girl had just been caught running away with a man." On cross-examination, La Farge drew out the further facts that the pair were literally running, in full sight of half the town, along the main road by the seashore, where they might have dodged into a trackless forest within fifty yards; that the girl was then in a neighboring house getting a scolding from her mother; and that after the scolding she would get a beating. La Farge was so much delighted that he wanted to start off at once to see the girl, with a view, I think, to some possible picture to be called "The Elopement," but he was hard at work painting a sketch of Fang-alo sliding down the waterfall, for Clarence King's satisfaction no doubt, and he could not leave his sketch.

Apropos to cataracts of girls, they are common as any other cataracts here. Any waterfall with a ten-foot pool at its base, and a suitable drop, is sure to be used both by girls and boys, and by men as well. The difficulty is that the coast is mostly flat; the waterfalls are far off, and few of them are suited to the purpose. The only one near Apia is fully five miles away, in the hills, far from any village; and one must make up a party of girls from here, and devote a day to a regular picnic, in order to see the show. For King's sake I did this last week. My friend Fatuleia, Seumano's wife, the chiefess of Apia, took charge of the affair, and summoned half a dozen of the belles of Apia:—Fanua, the *taupo;* Otaota, whose photograph I must have sent you, a pretty girl standing before the grave-monument of a chief; Fang-alo, whose photograph you also have; Nelly, a pretty missionary girl; and two or three others. We rode two hours through the forest, and clambered down a ravine to the spot, a deep valley, with cliffs overgrown with verdure, and topped by high trees far above us. To my surprise I found that the waterfall was little more than a brook, as far as the water had to do with it, though the fall was steep enough; full twenty feet into a deep pool. For this reason the place is called the Sliding Rock, for the water has smoothed the hard stone, and covered it with a slippery grass or fine slimy growth. The girls sit in the running water, and slide or coast down, with a plunge of ten or twelve feet below. They go like a shot, and the sight is very pretty. La Farge and I were immensely amused by it, and so were the girls, who went in as though they were naiads. They wore whatever suited their ideas of propriety, from a waist-cloth to a night-gown dress; but the variety rather added to the effect, and the water took charge of the proprieties.

The most curious part of our experience here is to find that the natives are so totally different from what I imagined, and yet so like what I ought to have expected. They are a finer race than I supposed, and seem uncontaminated by outside influence. They have not suffered from diseases introduced from abroad. They have their own diseases,—elephantiasis is the worst, but skin-troubles and sores are common, and eyes are apt to be affected by blemish,—but they are otherwise strong and would shame any white race I ever saw, for the uniform vigor of their bodies. One never sees a tall man who is thin or feeble. Their standard of beauty varies between six feet, and six-feet-six, in height, but is always broad and muscular in proportion. The women are very nearly as strong as the men. Often in walking behind them I puzzle myself to decide from their backs whether they are men or women, and I am never sure. La Farge detects a certain widening towards the hips which I am too little trained to see; and no wonder, for I have taken enough measurements of typical specimens to be certain that a girl of my height, or say five-feet-six, will have a waist measuring at least thirty-three-and-a-half inches, and hips measuring not more than fortytwo. Her upper-arm will be 14½ inches in circumference; her wrist, eight; the calf of her leg at least sixteen; her ankle near eleven; and yet her foot is but 10½ inches long, and both foot and hands are well shaped. These are masculine proportions, and the men assure me that the women have nearly the strength of men. Child-birth is an easy affair of twentyfour hours. Every motion and gesture is free and masculine. They go into battle with the men, and, as one of the most famous fighting chiefs, Pa-tu, my neighbor, told me of his own daughter who fell in battle by his side, "she was killed fighting like a man."

Now comes the quality which to me is most curious. Here are these superb men and women,—creatures of this soft climate and voluptuous nature, living under a tropical sun, and skies of divine purple and blue,—who ought, on my notions, to be chock-full of languid longings and passionate emotions, but they are pure Greek fauns. Their intellectual existence is made up of concrete facts. As La Farge says, they have no thoughts. They are not in the least voluptuous; they have no longings and very brief passions; they live a matter-of-fact existence that would scare a New England spinster. Even their dances—proper or improper,—always represent facts, and never even attempt to reproduce an emotion. The dancers play at ball, or at bathing, or at cocoa-nut gathering, or hammer, or row, or represent cats, rats, birds or devils, but never an abstraction. They do not know how to be voluptuous. Old Samasoni, the American pilot here for many years, and twice married to high-class native women, tells us that the worst dance he ever saw here was a literal reproduction of the marriage ceremony, and that the man went through the entire form, which is long and highly peculiar, and ended with the consummation,—openly, before the whole village, delighted with the fun,—but that neither actors nor spectators showed a sign of emotion or passion, but went through it as practically as though it had been a cricket-match. Their only idea was that it was funny,—as, in a sense, it certainly was; that is, it was not nice. Sentiment or sentimentality is unknown to them. They are astonishingly kind to their children, and their children are very well-behaved; but there is no sentiment, only good-nature, about it. They are the happiest, easiest, smilingest people I ever saw, and the most delightfully archaic. They fight bravely, but are not morally brave. They have the virtues of healthy children,—and the weaknesses of Agamemnon and Ulysses.

I could babble on indefinitely about them and their ways, but I think you care less about the Archaic than King or I do, and I might only bore you. For myself, I am not bored. I go to bed soon after nine o'clock, and sleep well till half past five. I eat bananas, mangoes, oranges, pineapples and mummy-apples by the peck. I smoke like a lobster. I write, or study water-color drawing all day. The rainy season has begun. Our gay colors and warm lights have washed out into a uniform grey and faint violet. Expeditions are too risky, for one is sure to be drenched, and the rain falls here solid. But we are well, cheerful and dread moving. I ought to take more exercise, but I don't, and time slides as though it were Fang-alo on the Sliding Rock.

Nov. 25. Fine weather again. We are starting on a boat-tour of the island.

                              Alofa   Atamu

MS: RPB
1. The Sombrerete Mining Co., founded in 1881, one of King's most promising Mexican mining schemes, was being liquidated.
2. Darwin's theory of the development of coral reefs and islands, advanced as early as 1839 in *The Voyage of the Beagle* and elaborated in 1842 in *The Structure and Distribution of Coral Reefs,* was developed and confirmed by James D. Dana in *Corals and Coral Islands* (1872) and by Alfred Russel Wallace (1823–1913) in *Island Life* (1880). HA's friend Alexander Agassiz challenged the theory and was answered by Dana in the 1890 edition of his book.

To Theodore F. Dwight

Apia. November 24, 1890.

Dear Dwight

The last mail brought no letter from you, and I expect none by the next, as you probably think us in Tahiti. We expect to start off, in two or three days, on a boat-excursion round this island,—Upolo,—which will probably consume ten days, if the weather does not stop us. On our return here we must decide whether to take the steamer for Tahiti on December 13, or to hang on at Samoa. Our decision will depend on La Farge's health and energy. He feels now fairly well, and is doing first-rate work. If you go to New York, stop at his studio and ask to see what sketches he has sent home. A batch should go by this mail. We are comfortable and contented. I feel some doubt whether Tahiti and the Marquesas will furnish as good artistic material as Samoa. Here we are already well-known, and our social position is accepted by the natives as entitling us to the highest consideration. We have only to express a wish, and the whole group of islands is at our disposal. Time is nothing to me, and sea-voyages in bad steamers are my worst terror. So I cannot say whether we shall sail soon for Tahiti or not; and as the next mail will go about a week hence—during our absence,—I cannot wait to tell our decision. You had better direct letters to Tahiti for the present.

Our worst annoyance is the weather, which is unnecessarily rainy and windy. The rainy season seems to have begun early. We have had one violent storm. The trade-wind blows with less and less regularity, and the sun shines less frequently. As a slight compensation, the temperature is lower, and the mercury stands more constantly at about 80°. The mosquitoes annoy us more, the flies less, than at first. The ocean is greener and less blue, the skies less purple, and the mildew on leather and cloth is more abundant, than I like. When the rain falls in these regions, which is several times a day, it is apt to fall in sections, six inches, or so, of it solid, and the air is saturated for days.

One strong motive for delay is that we are still far from having exhausted the Samoan territory. In some respects, Samoa combines many advantages, and no group in the western Pacific equals it. Fiji is inhabited by a darker race, more kin to the negro. Tonga is flat and the people are tyrannised by missionary rule. One must sail a thousand miles to the eastward to find islands combining equal advantages. Stevenson chose Samoa as a residence chiefly for these reasons. He says that Tahiti would have suited him equally well except for the French *gens-d'armerie;* but I suspect that he also feels himself here a more important and useful personage than at Tahiti, and looks on himself as a sort of protector of the natives. We have seen little of Stevenson, partly because he lives five miles back in the forest, and has only a very dirty shanty, with nothing to eat in it; but chiefly because he discourages visitors, who consume his time and strength. He has been extremely friendly whenever we have met, and has offered me letters of introduction to native chiefs in Tahiti, which I accepted of course with much gratitude. At his own suggestion, I am going up some day to breakfast with him, taking the precaution to send my breakfast in advance, as he warned me to do. He is an eccentric creature, a sort of cross between a Scotch presbyterian and a French pirate; and his wife is more piratic and less French than himself; but they are an amusing pair, and have gone through, and still invite, fatigues and deprivations enough to kill a Samoan warrior.

Our way of life, quiet and lazy enough as our preference, is broken by constant efforts of energy. We made one long boat-voyage to Savaii, and were ten days absent, living among the natives, and almost killed by receptions and dances. The three towns which we visited in Savaii gave us great war-like displays such as our Indians tribes might get up for the visit of a President. Nothing could be more beautiful or more interesting to an ex-Professor of archaic history; but sitting cross-legged from early day till midnight, saturated with noise, cocoanut oil and movement, requires a constitution of steel-wire. In our native house here, a mile from the town of Apia, with the coral-reef to look at, and native chiefs to protect us from annoyance, we recover strength, and grow fat on bananas, mangoes, oranges and idleness. I write letters or try to learn to sketch. La Farge paints. Every few days we wander abroad. This last week we passed one day at a distant waterfall in the hills, watching our favorite girls go over the rock, twenty feet down into the pool beneath, and paddle about, catching shrimps under the stones, and eating them alive, like chestnuts. Another day, we went out with our village to net mullet on the reef, and passed long hours sketching the men and women, in their canoes or in the water, a pretty sight when the sun is out, and the water is brilliant with shades of blue, green and purple. Two other days have been given to Seumano's great feast, and one evening I gave a quiet Siva in my own house, for the *taupo* or village maiden of Fangaloa, whom we photographed by flash lights. I have taken at least a hundred and fifty photographs, but do not know with what success, as no one here can develop them. One roll of a hundred has been sent to Sydney for developement, but will not return for six weeks. I take measurements of all the *taupo* I can catch, and of any other typical girls I choose to send for. Our lives are strictly virtuous withal, for we find that even a Samoan wife is a serious responsibility for a European of any social position, and we have no place for women in our housekeeping; but our house has no lack of them in the way of society; only the old women rarely come, except as duennas.

On the whole, we have found what we came for. The outside world very rarely intrudes. I tried to read the last files of the "Herald" and "Sun," but they bored me beyond patience. Give my regards to my brothers, and believe me,

Ever Yrs   Henry Adams.

MS: MHi

To Mabel Hooper

Apia, 24 November, 1890

My dear Polly

You will get this letter at Christmas, I hope. I wish it were a better Christmas present, but you girls must all remember that, if you want anything, you are to get it, and call it a present from me. If your wicked father objects, you must let me know. All he has to do with the matter is to pay any bills you may bring him, and charge it to me. I don't mean this merely for Christmas, but for always; so don't let him bully you out of it. I have had no letters from you since you were in Switzerland, but Miss Baxter mentioned your return, so I hope you are all right.

La Farge still favors staying at Samoa, and I am quite unable to guess when we shall go. He fears fatigue and dyspepsia, sea-voyages and a variety of ills, which I suppose are real, since he fears them; and I am indifferent whether we stay or go. So we hang on contentedly, and I think with wonder that you are beginning winter. Here we have been and are deluged with rain, and once had a violent gale, but the temperature never varies much between 75° and 87°. Whether we are in winter or summer I do not know, but as I write I look at the shadow of my thatch eaves, and notice that the sun is precisely vertical, or an inch or two to the south of us. The morning is hot, perhaps 87°, for there is very little wind. The strong trade-wind of last month now blows less steadily. Today is the only brilliant day we have had for weeks.

I have become very Polynesian. If it were not for the abominable mosquitoes and flies, I should drop European clothes, and wear only a bath towel round my waist; but the insects are troublesome enough when only one's face and hands are exposed; they would murder me if I wore no clothes. The natives are annoyed by them, but bear it, though the flies are sometimes as bad as in Egypt. The natives are pretty tough, especially in the soles of their feet; but they suffer too, as their scars show. The children have the best fun. They live out doors, for there are no doors to live *in*; they wear nothing but a cotton cloth wrapped round their waist, and always loose; they seem to have no school or work; they play or sleep all the time, and on moonlight nights the whole place is a play-ground; they are very well-behaved and gently treated, so that I feel quite happy when I hear one getting whipped, for I know he deserved it. The strangest thing is that they have no toys, and even the little girls never saw a doll. They play on the beach, or about the village green, and peep in at us sometimes, and seem to have a perfectly happy life; but they have none of the playthings that our children use. Instead they tumble into the water, and swim on boards in the surf, or make little boats and sail them, or throw imitation spears, or have imitation dances. The church stands about fifty feet from our house. Today is Sunday, and we have had the benefit of Sunday school. As the church windows are all open, and no building in Samoa is more than one floor, on the ground, we can hear all that is said and done in church; and as far as I can understand, the children have a regular lark. They go to church besides, and we hear the sermon. Sometimes La Farge gets our boy Charley to translate it for us. Generally two or three small babies, just able to walk, are toddling in and out of the church door, without a rag of clothing, and make faces at me, while their mothers are watching them from inside, and the preacher is denouncing their sins.

The old chiefs and the girls are our principal society. The chiefs sit cross-legged and smoke; the girls, if strangers, look stern, and, if intimate, do nothing but laugh. They wear all sorts of clothes, from a colored night-gown to a waist-cloth of native bark-cloth, according to their tastes, but they are otherwise much alike. The other day, at my request, my friend Fatuleia, wife of the chief of Apia, and a royal princess, got up a picnic for me, to the waterfall called Papa-sea, or Sliding Rock. She summoned half a dozen of the prettiest girls in Apia, and we went about five miles into the hills. There, in a deep ravine, lined with verdure a hundred or two feet above us, we found a pretty little waterfall over a slippery cliff about five-and-twenty feet high. The girls sat down in the babbling water, and slid down, with a sheer drop of about fifteen feet, into a pool of deep water below. They screamed and laughed like any other girls, and chattered Samoan; and swam about, or lay at full length, or in any attitude, in the water, and evidently enjoyed it immensely. None of them seemed cold, though Charley, who is a half-breed, shivered till his teeth seemed to chatter. The girls wore just what they had on, as far as I could see; or put on a garland of leaves round their necks, for propriety, if they took off their jackets. They looked wonderfully pretty, like Greek naiads, among the rocks; but they like to eat their fish and shrimps raw, like oysters, and they catch them in the water for fun. They cook fish mostly to keep them a few days longer than fish keep when raw. We have no ice at all, in Samoa, not even at the Consulate where we have our meals; and we have to eat fast. A few days ago, La Farge and I went out with our village to seine mullet in the shallow water within the reef. It was a pretty sight; a whole village, including the chiefs, and King Mataafa, in canoes, or in water to their waists, or swimming, and all busy with the nets. La Farge made a sketch of it. By the way, he will probably send half a dozen sketches home by this mail, and if your papa should be in New York he had better go to the studio, and see them. I think them amusing.

I try hard to sketch too, but it is desperate work and I seem to go backwards. Still, it absorbs one's soul, and seems always on the point of success.

Love to all.

Ever affecly   Henry Adams.

MS: MH

To Elizabeth Cameron

Voyage round Upolo.

5.30 A.M. November 27, 1890.

Pretty pretty this early cool morning, on the water in my whale-boat, my five men rowing and singing, and much disturbing my handwriting, while the green mountains loom ahead, on my right, and the surf on the reef divides me from the ocean on the left. The sky is blue, the sun is bright, and the waves are not dancing; at least, not enough to disturb me. Shelley may have liked waves; I like them but moderately.[1] I have left La Farge behind, to follow with Seumano in his boat, and catch me up, while I should take the morning's freshness on the water. La Farge threatened to be late, but as usual was in fact ready, and is probably now fretting to be off. Hightytighty, how pretty it is, and how the mountains take the morning shadows! I am Robinson Crusoe voyaging round my island. Happy Robinson was not bothered with a Kodak or a complete artist's outfit, and probably had taken breakfast. I have breakfasted on two bananas and a cigar. I have four bananas, two mangoes, three pineapples, and a plug of Virginia tobacco in reserve. We are coming abreast of Vailele, the German cocoanut plantation. I wish you could see it. It lies under mountains; but the reef stops not far beyond, and I must go out to sea, more's the pity.

We have seen much of Stevenson these last few days, and I must say no more in ridicule, for he has been extremely obliging, and given me very valuable letters of introduction to Tahiti and the Marquesas. He has amused and interested us, too, and greatly, by his conversation. Last evening he came at five o'clock, and brought his wife to dine with us. Their arrival was characteristic. He appeared first, looking like an insane stork, very warm and very restless. I was not present, and the reception fell on little Mrs Parker, who is as delicate and fragile as Stevenson, but as quiet and gentle as a flower. Presently Mrs Stevenson in a reddish cotton nightgown, staggered up the steps, and sank into a chair, gasping, and unable to speak. Stevenson hurried to explain that she was overcome by the heat and the walk. Might she lie down? Mrs Parker sacrificed her own bed, and gave her some cognac. Stevenson says that his wife has some disease, I know not what, of a paralytic nature, and suffers greatly from its attacks. I know only that when I arrived soon afterwards, I found her on the piazza chatting with Mrs Parker, and apparently as well and stalwart as any other Apache squaw. Stevenson then devoted an hour to me, very kindly, and was astonishingly agreeable, dancing about, brandishing his long arms above his head, and looking so attenuated in the thin flannel shirt which is his constant wear, that I expected to see him break in sections, like the *pollolo.*— Confound the swell! We are now outside the reef, and I have to balance myself on my pen.—He has an infinite experience to draw upon, and to my great relief is not a Presbyterian, but is as little missionary as I am. His sufferings here as a farmer are his latest fund for humor, and he described, with bounds of gesticulation, how he had just bought two huge farmhorses, and stabled them in a native house near his; and how at midnight, in a deluge of rain and a gale of wind, he had heard unearthly howls from the stable, and had ventured out with a lantern. As he approached, by the glimmer of the light, he became aware of two phantom excrescences protruding from the stable-roof. These were his horses' heads, which, after eating off the roof of the house, were wildly tossing in the storm, while the legs and bodies were inconceivably mixed up, inside.—I have stopped to eat a mango, which Stevenson says is a stimulant almost as strong as fluid extract of coco. I hope it is, for I have then a reason for liking them. By the bye, we have passed *Laulí*, in a green chasm, and are approaching *Fale-fà*, where is a waterfall, and where my boat will stop till Seumano comes along. I just wish you *could* see this mountain shore of green velvet with a white surf binding. Luckily the sea is very quiet, for I am still outside the reef, and the surf is on the beach. A queer rock projects into the sea ahead, with two cocoa-nut palms on top. It would make a pretty sketch. Thereabouts is Falefà.

Enough of Stevenson! His stories are not for me to tell, and towards eleven o'clock, we summoned our boatcrew, and sent him back by water, in the moonlight to Apia. We may never see him again, for he talks of going to Auckland next week, and some day I suppose we too shall go away somewhere. Our parting last night, on the beach, in the Samoan moonlight, was appropriate, and my last distinct vision of his wife was her archaic figure in the arms of my coxswain, trying to get her legs—or feet—over the side of my boat.

Fangaloa, 29 November. We stopped at Falefà from half past nine till four. It was a lovely fraud. All waterfalls are. I passed two hours or more, devoured by mosquitoes, which tried to prevent my making a water-color libel of their waterfall. They did not succeed. I made a horrid daub, and then found out that the fall was not worth painting. We all lay for an hour or two, after lunch, about the floor of our hut. The lights were lovely, like our most perfect June days, and the air was cool. Then I walked a couple of miles up the little river, into the interior. I was surrounded by mountains, wooded to the tops, and pretty as the Alleghanies. Except for the palms, I might have thought myself in western Virginia. I met no one, and saw not even a house. On returning, I found all ready to start again. I changed into Seumano's boat, and we set off, with a crew of twelve men rowing. We had to face the open sea again, but it was in its best temper, the wind off shore, and not a cloud in the sky. The coast is bold at this point. The green mountains fall abruptly into the water, and the trees grow down to the water's edge. Where the rocks jut out, the surf is heavy, and we ran close into it, barely keeping outside the breakers; but there are no cliffs worth mentioning. All seems old, covered with green, and stained by time. You can imagine how pretty it is, but the prettiest was the last, when we rounded a jutting reef in the surf, and an immense fiord opened before us, as though it was Scotland or Norway, mountains all about it, and not a trace of human life. We rowed far into it, and ran ashore on a sand beach behind a small coral reef, where the village of Fangaloa stands, visible only as one comes near. Two or three waterfalls, several hundred feet high, tumble down the perpendicular mountains behind it, losing themselves in the dense foliage. As usual, the scene is preposterously like a stage-decoration; but in this case the scale is quite grand; the bay is miles in stretch, and the mountains are thousands of feet high. Altogether it is the finest scenery I have seen in these islands, and impressed us the more because it was unexpected. Our friend Fasaei, the *taupo*, had expected us two days ago, and the big guesthouse had been decorated, three pigs and various hens had been slaughtered, and every other preparation had been made, for our reception. We arrived before sunset, and we stayed on the beach to watch the afterglow, which seems to me as fine here as in Egypt. Then we had our supper,—canned soup, curried rice, broiled chicken, and pine-apple,—and lay down to smoke and wait for the Siva. We were dog-tired, for we had slept little the night before; my eyelids closed in spite of myself; and the Siva, good as it was, has no longer the excitement of novelty. Fasaei is an excellent dancer, and here we are beyond the prudery of Apia, where women think it good style to wear ugly waists of cloth or silk. Faasaei wore a short *tapa* skirt, with a leaf *titi* over it; but she soon took off the titi, and threw it across the floor to me; and then went through the ball-dance,—which represents an extremely active game of cricket, with hard running and jumping,—clad in her *tapa*-skirt, which is not calculated to hide much of the action of the legs. On the central post of our house, a paper is pasted, containing the written rules of the establishment. One of them forbids indecent dances. There was nothing indecent about Fasaei's dances, but I noticed that the audience always laughed when she showed an excessive portion of her muscular thighs. They are very particular about the slight amount of clothing they wear, and even the men, when bathing, keep their waist-cloth carefully on. The dancers constantly tuck their *siapas* in, between their legs, and seem quite nervous about it. Stevenson tells me that the standard of morality has been maintained here against white influence, much higher than elsewhere; and it is a fact that I have never yet seen or heard anything, to my address, which I could consider as immoral. To be sure, when we were tired, we had our mosquito-nets put up, and under them we undressed, put on our pyjamas, and went to bed, while the dance continued; and I heard the girls long whispering near my head, after the dance ended; but a house here is really out-doors, and forty people may be in it without one's disturbing one's sleep. Now, as I write, at eleven o'clock Sunday (Saturday) morning, I count eight figures sleeping before me, and La Farge is asleep behind a tapa. Fasaei is lying on her back, with a *tapa* up to her neck. Some one else lies by her side, resting his or her head on the same bamboo pillow. Awoki and I are alone awake; and I am sitting cross-legged, writing, with Fasaei's garland round my neck, its cocoa-nut oil soaking into my white coat, not to mention my nose. Outside the sun is lighting up the ocean to the northern horizon, and the green hill-side that rises, a mile away, above the breakers and the purple-blue of the bay. It is a tropical picnic. I have had my morning bath round a distant point in the bay; we have taken our coffee and eggs, and chattered an hour; a cool breeze blows through the house, and all is still except the surf.

Alepata. December 2. (Dec. 1, with you.) We passed two days at Fangaloa, and left it three hours ago. I have enjoyed nothing in my travels so much as these last days. Fangaloa is an exquisite spot. The people were friendly and devoted to us. Faasaei and Pui-pui and Atua and two or three other girls, were always lying about the floor, making garlands, or sleeping, or ready for the Siva. La Farge had a good day yesterday, and sketched. I tried, too, to paint the view, but my poor little attempts make me blush at my own commonplaceness when I see it fairly set down in blue and green. In the night, the mosquitoes got inside my net, and drove me out into the moon-light where I stayed a couple of hours; but Seumano came out and made half a dozen men act as a sort of guard for me, so that, to spare them, I turned in again, and covered myself, clothes, shoes and all, including my head, with a sheet, and so managed to get some sleep. The mosquitoes and flies are the chief nuisance of the Pacific, and worry the natives in spite of cocoanut oil, though they suffer less from the bites than we do. Luckily the day makes up for the night, and yesterday was a lovely one. In the after-noon, the natives got up a little *talolo,* or reception, for us. The procession of girls, as they came out from among the trees, was perfect. I could think only of the opera. It was Norma, but the background of sea, mountain and sky, was lovelier than the best scene-painter in Europe commonly furnishes.[2] I snapped some Kodaks, almost hoping they would fail, for without color such scenes are caricatures. The *tulafale* made a speech, but went off with-out waiting for my beautiful reply which remained an unsung poem. Then I made Faasaei take me out in a canoe. My indolence has till now made me neglect the native canoe, or I had been scared by stories of its difficulties. It is a long, very narrow dug-out, with an outrigger resting on a parallel bar which supports it on one side, in the water. One sits on the outrigger where it crosses the boat, and one uses a paddle. I found it perfectly steady and fast. The bay was lovelier than ever, from the water. I can imagine nothing more beautiful, and the view beneath was as fascinating as that above, for the colors of the water, the variety of the living coral, and the flashing blue and green of the little fishes, beat our friend's "duplicated golden glow" flat.[3] I pushed out at once for the deep water, and wanted to cross the bay, but was surprised to find that Faasaei became nervous, and said she was afraid of our being upset and having to swim back among the sharks. I chaffed her about her timidity, but when I asked how she led her village to battle if she was afraid of sharks, she said very simply that she was afraid of battle too. So we turned to the reef again, and at last went ashore and sat under the shade of the trees, and decorated ourselves with ferns. My boy interpreter, Charley, was with us, and the proprieties were strictly observed; but we became very intimate, and Clarence King's heart would have been in Heaven under the genial laziness of Faasaei's acres of brown flesh and her broad, goodnatured smile of content as she said that entertaining strangers was easier work than cutting copra, the ripe cocoa-nut. When we returned, I strolled along the shore to see the sunset. One of the girls met me, and took me to her house where they were gathering orange-flowers to make garlands for the Siva. I sat down and tried to imitate their Siva movements. My ignorance amused them, but I am not much worse than some of their own men and women, who dance badly, though they have seen, and done it, ever since they were born. We saw them playing their favorite game in the evening, which owes its humor to this ignorance. The men on one side match hands with the women on the other, and whichever side loses, has to dance. A splendid young fellow, Lauati's adopted son, who is one of our crew, amused the audience greatly by his bad dancing.

This morning at nine o'clock we bade good-bye to Fangaloa. We brought away various presents of *tapa* and such things, and I gave the *taupo* three five-dollar gold-pieces besides various gifts of a smaller kind. I thought the place lovelier than ever as we rowed away, with three of the girls sitting on the grass, waving farewell to us. All our grandeur was no compensation for the charm of what we should never see again. I am already an old Samoan, and have seen a great deal of the islands, but nothing so near the conventional ideal of the South Seas as the bay of Fangaloa. Our cruise from there to this place, at the extreme southeastern end of Upolo, was also beautiful. The shore was mountainous, and the mountains were covered with forest. The sea broke on the lava cliffs, which were lambs of cliffs considering that they have been exposed forever to the full force of the ocean and the trade-wind. The sky was exquisite, and shaded with strong violet on the horizon and the clouds. Although we were at sea, without protection from the swell, for once I was unconscious of sea-sickness. We ran along the outer edge of the breakers, and enjoyed them. As we turned the end of the island, we ran through a narrow passage, in foaming surf, inside another reef, and presently landed opposite the house of the old chief Sangapolutele. The *taupo* here is named Mauniu o Fataua, or Mauniu for short, meaning "Lost cocoanuts," also for short. Literally it means "Fa-taua where there are many cocoanuts but they drop into the sea, and you get none." Mauniu is another Faasaei, not so handsome in face, but the same type of somewhat too round and indolent splendor in person. I mean to take her measurements to increase my gallery.

Lé-pà, December 4. We left Aleipata at half past nine o'clock this morning, after passing two days there. The most interesting part of our experience at Aleipata was the old chief who entertained us royally, and made us rich gifts. As usual I felt like Odysseus, and had to diminish my supply of gifts considerably, and double my usual present at parting. The old man gave me a fine mat, the first I have ever received in the character of guest, although I now possess half a dozen from one source or another. Sagapolutele looks like an old Arab sheik such as pilots one's boat down the Nile cataract. He talked very freely about old Samoan customs, and said he had Fiji blood. He has turned to the church in his old age, and with Arab simplicity explained that he was once the best dancer in Samoa, but since he has grown weak he had become missionary, or preacher, and could no longer dance, nor was there anyone left who knew how to dance. Our boatman, Maua, who talks English, explained to us that the chief had been "the baddest man in all Samoa," but Seumano denies it, and says he only had "plenty wives." Sagapolutele talked freely of Samoan superstitions. He is a sweet pagan, and has an *aïtu* or spirit of his own,—the ghost of his son, killed in the last war,—who is always about the place, and came, in likeness of an owl, to announce our arrival, or *malanga*, before it was known otherwise. His village *aïtu* is the cuttle-fish; the spirit of the kingdom is the rainbow,—Aatua is the province or kingdom, and the spirit is Atúa. We talked long about spirits and local customs; but his brother, the Tulafale developed a real historical genius; wrote out for me their oldest poem about Pili and Siga, a new thing to me; and promised me a quantity of poems or songs, and traditions.[4] I shall hand them over to Stevenson.

Yesterday we sailed a mile or two out to sea, and visited an island,—Nuutele,—an old crater, like Apollima, with one side open to the north-east or east. I wanted to geologise, for I am growing amused by the geological problems hereabouts. You know from Darwin's Voyage of the Beagle about the amount of geology yet settled or unsettled in regard to the South Seas. Most of the islands,—thousands in number,—have the wonderful peculiarity of being just flush with the surface of a very deep ocean. Of course this precise level must be due to some equalising cause, acting at the surface. Darwin made a great reputation by suggesting that the Pacific ocean was a field of exhausted or expiring volcanoes, and that as volcanic activity ceased, the volcanic islands subsided; as the tops went slowly under water, the coral polyps took possession, and built as the volcanoes sank. The theory is lovely, and I adore it. After visiting Hawaii, I can believe anything, and deny nothing; but just for fun I like to make theories of my own, and have manufactured six or eight that delighted me. All are equally reasonable and untenable. So I stick to Darwin and subsidence; and I visited Nuutele today to satisfy myself that it was the top of a lava crater that had subsided ten thousand feet, and, with five hundred feet more subsidence, would become a coral atoll. What I found was a mud volcano, absolutely without lava, except that its *stratified,* sandstone cliffs, were full of sharp-edged pieces of lava, as well as of fine-grained sand and shell. To prove something or other, I knocked a small piece of shell out of the cliff at sea-level. I suspect it to be a recent shell, and if so I have proved that Nuutele, and probably all Samoa was no lower than it now is, when the crater-sides were raised. That is to say, the only thing I have proved is that one Pacific island was first a sea-beach, and then was elevated about five hundred feet, and since very ancient times—say ten thousand years perhaps—has not subsided at all. Indeed a very recent coral bed shows eight or ten feet of elevation. Naturally I feel rather floored about subsidence, but will go at it again with sublime defiance of facts. Darwin must be sustained or the Pacific will never be calm.

We came this morning some ten miles along the shore. Still out at sea beyond the reef, through shower and shine, looking at a bold, cocoa-nut-lined coast and an indigo sea; landing before noon at another village, received by another chief and another taupo, in another garlanded house, on the beach. I must now break off to eat the feast and taro, and, if I am lucky, bananas.

At this village of Lépà I find a young chief, and two stout taupo of the commonplace kind, except that one of them, whose name is Siatu-fiti,—"the Fiji Islands,"—begs for everything she sees. This is not good form, and is the first case I have met among taupos. We have had another lot of pigs, chickens and sugar-cane. I have walked a couple of miles along the shore geologising, only to find evidence of upheaval,—only about eight feet, but uniform over the whole island, at least at the east end. I stopped in a big village where the children surrounded me and followed me, very goodnatured and well-behaved, but rather troublesome, as I was alone. So I retired into a missionary house, and drank *cava.* The people were cutting up a shark.

December 5. (1 P.M.) After two hours at sea in a burning sun, with a calm air, we have landed at another village. To instruct you precisely, let me add that we are in the house of the chief Tui-loma (literally King of Rome). How such a coincidence happens as to find here a king of Rome, history says not; but here he is, and has probably been, from times sufficiently classic. His house is "Le aga o le lulu"; "the House of the Owl," and has a wooden owl as protecting spirit on the house-beam above us. Of course the chief is very missionary, for he has a branch of the missionary college here, with sixty pupils; but the Christianity of Samoa is a bit mixed, and the old aïtu, or spirits, are still very much alive. The village is called Fale-ulu, or Bread-fruit house; in the District of Fale-a-lili, which is in the ancient province or kingdom of Atua; which is the eastern portion of the island of Upolo. You will hardly find the place on any map, but it stands on the south side of Upolo, nearly opposite Fagaloa bay which is on the north side. We have had the usual talk with the village dignitaries, and are now waiting for Awoki to bring us some lunch.

To go back to last evening:—we had another long Siva with relays of dancers. The taupo—"Fiji islands"—after appropriating two handkerchiefs, my eye-glasses, some pounds of tobacco, and threatening everything I had, took a strong fancy to appropriate me too, and wanted me to marry her, then and there, and take her to America. The Lord knows whether she would have done it; but she had to dance in the Siva in the evening, till midnight, and this morning I sat in solitary grandeur as far as possible away from her, while her brother, the chief, made me gifts. There was marked offence in her bearing when at last I shook hands and took leave; but the gift-business is a severer burden than the taupo-duty. My boat is half-filled with mats, *tapa*, wooden bowls and other presents, which become a bigger load every day, and require rather large returns. I am now giving some twenty dollars a day in return-gifts, and this is on a very moderate estimate of the money-value of their presents. I want to check them, and can do it only by adopting a rule, and letting them know beforehand that my present is fixed. The chiefs bring, or give me, commonly, several pigs,—sometimes half a dozen,—a dozen or more chickens, large fish, any quantity of taro, and all the supplies for twenty men; and besides this, they think it right to give me mats, bowls, and other things precious to them, and now becoming costly in Apia. If I increase my presents, they double theirs. They are ruinously extravagant in such matters, and of course expect the same style from me. I give gold, because they commonly get much of that, but would have to divide all other presents, like canned provisions, biscuits, or clothing, on the spot, with their village who bring the eatables for us. In short, traveling *en prince* has almost as many difficulties here as in other places, and costs even in this primitive world, about fifty dollars a day, yet it is necessarily harder on the host than on the guest. Pretty much every chief is a poor man because he is obliged to share all he has in the world. They sell land, or mortgage it, and are always hard up. Communism always victimises the strong. Property victimises the weak. I am no philanthropist, and care not a *réal* (the coin used here) whether communism or property is the sounder system; but La Farge is conservative and insists on preserving what is established. I defer to La Farge's sound views, especially as last night he sat out a Siva till midnight, and fairly used up dancers, crews, taupos and me, always threatening to be strong when he gets well.

December 6. Vao-vai (Between Rivers) Another short advance this morning; but we are now on a flat coast, uninteresting and comparatively uniform. The mountains rise behind us, but between us and them is a swamp with suggestions of doubtful sanitary chances. We left the Owl House at noon without special regret. The people were kind, but not interesting. We are now at a small village which seems to be also the usual thing. I slept little last night and am not positively hilarious. I rarely am so on this day; but if five years can pass, I suppose I can stand ten.[5] I am weary and indifferent, but have had to sit through two sets of speeches and two *kava*-drink-ings. The form is perfectly mechanical. We know word for word all that is to be said. I have taught Seumano a little speech for Akamu and Lafaele, which he repeats every day. We know the cava-names of our chiefs, and can often catch what the chiefs are talking about, only that a very slight change of a vowel-sound converts meanings into wonderful eccentricities. *Maalié* means *good;* and *malié* means a shark; an awkward change in the meaning of King Malietoa's family names; but for my life I cannot detect the differ-ence in sound. I talk commonly about old songs, customs, and *aïku*, or spir-its. Just at this point is great spirit territory; for the chief *aïku* of Atua has his residence in or about a lava-reef a mile or two away, and the rocks are his human victims. About two months ago, the *aïku* of Savaii announced war against the *aïku* of Upolo. The central kingdom of Upolo—Tua-masanga—has an *aïku* of its own, who sent off to this Atua *aïku* for help. The Atua *aïku* replied that he could not leave Atua on a warlike expedition, *because he had become missionary* (joined the church), and the church permit-ted only defensive war; but if the Savaii *aïku* came to Atua, he would fight. The Savaii *aïku* did come, and drove the Tua-masanga *aïku* into Atua. Then our Atua *aïku* came out, and a big battle took place off this village. The guns were heard by a veracious young woman whose intimacy with the spirits enabled her to supply this accurate report. The Savaii *aïku* were beaten, and retired in their war-canoes to Savaii; but at Molifanua, the ex-treme western end of this island, they stopped to land one of their wounded. A chief of Molifanua who happened to be at the beach in the night, saw the spirit canoe, a mile long, and heard the directions to land the wounded. My men assure me that the people believe the whole story, and I suspect it is mixed up with the uneasy condition of the islands, and the idea that another war is imminent. The missionaries denounce *aïku*, but are all natives, and as superstitious as pagans. The touch about the Atua *aïku* hav-ing become missionary, is just tender.

To cheer me, I have just received, in the midst of heavy rain, my mail from home. Not a letter, except one of October 18, from Constance Lodge. All must have gone to Tahiti. An Auckland newspaper is also sent me an-nouncing a financial panic of the worst kind, and the practical failure of the Barings.[6] Gay news! I get no letters and can probably get no money. No one knows where I am, to send me a few dollars to save us from beggary. I must turn Samoan; live on taro and yams, beg for breadfruit, and wear a *titi* of ti-leaves. Come! Worse things have happened, and if I must starve, this is the place. My fisherman's hut is a palace; the rain will stop; the *taupo* will still be kind; and I can always catch shrimp in the ocean at my feet, even if I eat them raw, *fa Samoa.*

I see also news of the elections, and wish—wish—wish I knew more.[7]

Saangapu, December 8. 3 P.M. A long stride today. Fifteen miles, mostly out at sea, running past an abrupt lava-flow which exposes a long, honey-combed cliff to the ocean, and spouts foam-fountains high in air. I was glad to get well past this awkward stretch,—Pupu-i-siuma, "Siuma holes"—and to find that I was proof against two hours of the long Pacific swell, on a bad coast. We ran by, with a fair wind, watching the black rain-clouds and waterspouts on the mountains, while all was pleasant seawards. Tomorrow we hope to round the western point, and run for Apia. My misfortunes culminated yesterday in a toothache of the old-fashioned kind, which never leaves me, and is torture of an ingenuity deserving admiration. I keep it to myself, for I will bore no one except you with my troubles; but last night I had to draw on my medicine chest for anti-pyrine, which got me some sleep. Tonight I must try morphine. A few days of such pleasures would use me up; so I shall press for Apia, and get Dr Funk to pull out my teeth. La Farge is glad to return, and we have now seen the whole island except a patch of ten miles or so. As there are no towns or people,—nothing but mountains and forest,—in the interior, we have in fact seen everything.

Satapuala, Dec. 9. (5 P.M.) Things are ridiculous. After I had written the remarks of yesterday, I had to shut up, and listen to the usual *cava*-speeches. The air was sultry and very lifeless. Heavy clouds and a dead calm shut me in. Swarms of naked little children played about, or gazed in on us. My tooth-ache steadily increased till it became intolerable. I writhed with pain, and my eyes streamed with tears. As a last chance of a stimulant, I seized a cup of hot tea that Awoki had set by my side, and took a sip of it. The heat seemed to go instantly to the tooth, and with a last wrench of devilish passion, something broke. Almost instantly the pain subsided, and I felt such calm happiness as only angels know. I could have hugged the tedious chiefs, and drunk a whole bowl of cava at a draught. Of course the tooth is lost and must come out; it will pain me more or less constantly; and it probably marks the first happy effects of the climate in lowering my condition; but I can eat and sleep, and I sat out a Siva till ten o'clock, with two or three relays of dancers. They danced well, too. This morning we were off, before eight o'clock and pushed straight out to sea. As we passed through the opening in the reef, a strong wind and rather heavy sea pitched us about in an unduly familiar spirit; but we set all sail, and ran swiftly westward, up and down the long waves, which seemed twenty feet high, but, to the best of my measurement, were not more than six. Once more I escaped sickness, to my increasing surprise; for indeed the sea was pretty trying. We were four hours in reaching the Manono entrance. Once there we slipped for the last time inside the reef, and finished our circumnavigation. The day was exquisite. I was able to confirm my belief of a month ago that the view from Manono over the reef towards the crater-mountain To-fua is one of the most astonishing for color that can be invented. The greens are like glass-greens, so brilliant that they look wrong, like bad painting. This view and the bay of Fangaloa are the best things we have seen.

At the German cocoanut plantation Molifanua—"Land's End,"—we took lunch, and came on our old Savaii track. Here I got more and better news from the Consulate, which relieved my mind from fear of poverty, at least for a time. Then we rowed on an hour to our old stopping-place Satapuala to see Leolofi again. A simple little spot it seems, on a second visit, but the palm-leaf decoration of the house, which was repeated, is still the prettiest piece of decoration we have seen in all Samoa. Our big chief is away—like us—on a *malanga* to Atua; but we are promised the society of Leolofi, whom I shall photograph and measure. Tomorrow afternoon we reach Apia.

Apia. Dec. 11. We arrived safely at home—or our Consulate—at four o'clock yesterday afternoon, with the usual effect of picnics fresh on our minds. In short, I was glad to get back. As the devil arranges these matters, there is always some flatness in one's second glass of Champagne. I am getting to know my Polynesian too well, and to feel the Opera bouffe side of him. When I know him better, I shall get back on the serious side, but La Farge is a terrible creature to see fine comedy, and, about a week after he has caught a new point of view, I am sure to catch on to it. He is now filled with delight at the moralities of the simple savage, and with disgust at his somewhat vague ideas of cleanliness. Yet, to my vast relief, our twelve days of rather trying travel, which has cost me a hard strain, has done him good, and he has come back in better health, he says, than at any time since we started. This is illogical enough to please us both, and as he found little to sketch on our travels, he is the more ready to work now. We have exhausted the islands, and know more about them than any other pleasure-traveller has ever learned. We shall attempt no more long expeditions, but shall stay quiet until the time comes to clear out for new cocoanut groves.

MS: MHi
    1. "The sun is warm, the sky is clear, / The waves are dancing fast and bright"; "Stanzas Written in Dejection, Near Naples" (1818).
    2. Vincenzo Bellini, *Norma* (1831).
    3. Thomas Buchanan Read, in "Drifting," describes "Blue inlets and their crystal creeks, / Where high rocks throw, / Through deeps below, / A duplicated golden glow."
    4. La Farge noted of HA: "he is patient beyond belief; he asks over and over again the same questions in different shapes and ways of different and many people, and keeps all wired on some string of previous study in similar lines. . . . Web after web I have seen him weave around interpreter and explainer, to get to some point looked for, which may connect with something we have already acquired. As many times as the spider is brushed away, so many times he returns" (*Reminiscences*, pp. 242-243).
    5. Marian Adams had died five years ago on this day.
    6. The Barings' crisis was precipitated by Argentine repudiation of a large loan. The Bank of England saved the firm's credit, but the near-failure led to a drastic general decline in security prices.
    7. The Democrats overwhelmingly defeated the Republicans in the congressional elections on Nov. 4.

To John Hay

Falealili, 7 December, 1890.

Dear Hay

This is Sunday in Samoa. I am circumnavigating the island, with the same outfit I took to Savaii, but without Consul Sewall. My crews have chosen to rest for Sunday at a village—Vaovai—in the province of Falealili on the south coast, about half way round. It is afternoon. I have wobbled over the coral reef in a native canoe with a native hunchback, named Japhet, and a native youth to paddle me. We have inspected an island scented with sweet-smelling trees, and happily uninhabited. I have a bad tooth-ache, though my teeth were carefully put in order before leaving home; but my toothache is no harder to bear than my wish for statistics from home. My last mail reached me here at dusk last evening. No letters at all! I expected none, knowing that they would go to Tahiti; but the Consulate made up for the deficiency by sending me two newspapers. One contained news of the elections; the other, of the London panic and the Barings' troubles by telegraph from Auckland. You may imagine my emotions. At best it is hard to negotiate a draft here, but now I apprehend flat refusal. I have not a dollar, and owe several hundreds, and cannot leave Samoa without money. No one at home knows where I am, to send aid. As far as I can foresee, I am destined to three months of poverty and imprisonment.

Well! If La Farge can stand it, I can. I shall write to Tahiti for my letters, which will arrive in five weeks. I shall cut down my expenses, and wait for rescue. Samoa has amused me for two months; I will marry a *taupo*, (on credit), and see if she can amuse me for two months more. I doubt it, but will give her the benefit of the doubt. My acquaintance with *taupo* is now very considerable, and if all of them came to breakfast at once, even you could hardly entertain them; but it is not likely that they can all visit Washington together. My hostess at this village tells us that most of her neighbor *taupo* have run off with young men, or in other words, have made love-matches, rather less permanent than the ordinary marriage. At our last stopping-place the muscular maiden announced her strong desire to run off with me. As yet, their raiment of cocoanut oil has proved an impassable barrier between them and me; for I cannot take a bath every time my beloved touches me; but bankruptcy is a powerful motive for a marriage of inconvenience, and I know not what number of pigs and fine mats might save me from starvation. Everyone has his price.

I have been a week absent from Apia, cruising in open boats along the shore of Upolo eastward until we turned the corner and came westward. What I don't know about Samoa is hardly worth the bite of a mosquito. Of its thirtythousand inhabitants, fully half must have seen us, if I have not seen them. I have flirted with girls in a score of villages, and talked of ancient law with chiefs of hoary antiquity. I have been amused and have been bored. The amusement has been great; the boredom has not been small. When I come to figure up the balance, I will tell you how it stands; as yet the account is very current. I admit to a great liking for old-gold, but perhaps what I really like most is the limitations, and yet its limitations are a bore. One delights to see splendid men and women, all well made with rich color, and no clothes; but one grows tired of finding them even more alike than the less romantic inhabitants of Saugus West Centre.[1] Their contrasts, on the other hand, redeem them. Their theory of religion and morality is in constant and enlivening contrast with their practice. They supply the most unexpected and humorous contradictions which keep one's mind from stagnation. They are all as like each other as two casts from the same mould, but they are quite unlike us, and the perpetual cross-purposes at which we all labor, make life very unexpected. Within their limitations, they are a marvelous success, complete all round, and physically a joy to look at. Their social system is communism so aristocratic as to make our communists turn green with horror. Their aristocracy is so democratic as to carry a chill to the bones of William Waldorf Astor. Their social, political and religious system is preposterous to a degree quite incredible, but it has worked well enough to make them the happiest people on earth for an indefinite past. They are sweet tempered, gay, full of humor, and astonishingly gentle. Their frequent wars have kept up a high standard of courage, at least among the chiefs, though I think them really a timid race. They have a keen sense for grace, strength and beauty, as you can see in their dances.

Now for the limitations! They are, as far as I can see, the least imaginative people I ever met. They have almost no arts or literature or legends. Their songs are mere catches; unmeaning lines repeated over and over. Even their superstitions are practical. They live in an atmosphere of spirits and devils that would satisfy the greediest spirit-medium in the United States; but they have no good ghost-stories and no mischievous devils. The best spirit I have found is in Fangaloa Bay where a woman comes down from the mountain and goes fishing at night with the villagers. She walks on the water, and carries a light. The villagers see her as she passes down the bay, and when she returns they can watch her light as far as the top of the mountain. She is the sister of a devil who lives on the mountain, but who was absent in Savaii when I passed. This is all. Fangaloa Bay is one of the loveliest spots in creation, and should have a first-rate article in legendary ghosts, but no legend has grown there. Further away, in Aleipata, at the eastern end of this island, I stayed with an old chief who had a spirit always with him; but it was only that of his son who was killed in war about two years ago. The whole village recognised the fact, and knew the spirit perfectly; but though it was so obliging as to come, in the form of an owl, to announce our intended visit before the news arrived by letter, I could not learn that it did anything unusual for the most commonplace American spirits. Every family, every village, every district and every kingdom, has its spirit; and only two months ago the spirits of Savaii came over in canoes and fought the spirits or *aitu* of Upolo, but were perfectly practical about it, and went quietly home when beaten. The only pretty superstition that I found was that of the old kingdom of Atua, at the eastward. There, when going to war, they are guided by the rainbow. If it crosses their path, either before or behind them, they stop. If it appears to the right or left, in a line with their march, they go on, confident of success. You could make a pretty war-song of this. "When Israel, of the Lord beloved."[2]

In the quality of imagination as in physical qualities, they are, as Stevenson assures me, inferior to the Tahitians. Their moralities are another matter, and interest me greatly, because they certainly have moral standards though the most elusive, not to say delusive, I can conceive. As far as I can see, they are very honest. I have been here two months, and during all that time my things,—sometimes money, but always articles valuable to them,—have been scattered about, in native houses, boats, and people's hands,—without caution on my part; but nothing has been taken. Yet they are so communistic that any present one gives them, even a cigar, will probably pass through a dozen hands—or mouths—before it is used up. The chiefs complain much of Samoan thievery, but this is because they are themselves the police. A fortnight ago the halyards of the consular flag-staff were stolen. The next day, Mata-afa came, as he often does, to our native house, for a talk. You may remember that Mata-afa was king, while the Germans held Malietoa, and still Mata-afa is probably the first man in Samoa as far as reputation goes. We live within a stone's throw of him, and he regards us as under his protection, as well as under that of To-fai, the chief of the village. I mentioned to Mata-afa the loss of the halyards as a joke, without a thought that he would take it seriously, but it seemed to shock him, and he did not recover from it. During the whole visit he was absent-minded, and repeatedly returned to the subject. Whenever a Samoan is put out, he has a way of clucking—Tut-tut-tut,—and one always knows what he is thinking of. I found his sensibility rather a bore, for I did not care a cent whether our government lost its halyards or not; but a few days afterwards, early in the morning Sewall heard a lively chattering outside his door, and on getting out of bed, and going out, he tumbled over a man lying regularly trussed and ironed, at his threshhold. To-fai had found the thief somehow, and the native judge promptly sentenced him to sixty lashes and six months labor. The fun is that, of course, at Sewall's intercession the sentence was mitigated to three months' labor; and now the convict, perfectly unguarded and always smiling, is usually sitting in front of the consulate, supposed to be keeping the weeds down, but really chattering and smoking cigarettes with his friends in the coolest and pleasantest spot near Apia.

With this exception of Mata-afa, I have never seen a Samoan shocked, and often wonder whether they know the feeling. Nothing that we regard as indecent shocks them; yet they observe conventional proprieties with strange strictness. One seldom or never sees a grown Samoan naked, except for some rare reason. The women are never indecent in the way of solicitation. I have not once been annoyed by advances such as I should certainly meet, within ten minutes, by night, in the streets of any large city. They do not always know me, so that the reason cannot always be their respect for the American *alí*, and indeed the girls show familiarity enough in other ways. Yet, for indecency—*Cré Dieu!* as some Frenchman may have observed. Indecency is a European fiction strange to a Polynesian, to whom all facts are equally practical. Some of their dances have turned my few remaining dark hairs gray with horror, and are quite beyond description; yet even these are so simply and humorously expressive that I cannot help laughing at them. Other dances are indecent without intent. At one of the last towns we have visited, when I was dozing off, overcome by sleep, in the drowsiness of the unavoidable Siva, I was suddenly and completely roused by the funny-man of the dance, who began on an unmistakeable imitation of the process of child-birth. It was excessively laughable too. For twenty minutes or more, the man went through a sort of pantomime, accompanied by monologue; representing the pains of child-birth, the birth of the child, and the suckling of it, by an incompetent mother who committed all sorts of extravagances; and we laughed as heartily as anyone, to the delight of the audience. I own that I laughed till the tears came, though the acting was realistic in the extreme. I laughed almost as much at another dance by girls, called "Digging yams in the famine," of which La Farge was to a slight degree the victim. The regular or sitting Siva, is always perfectly proper, as far as I can see or understand it; but the standing dances are regular pieces of acting, and one never knows what may be the subject of the funny-man's humor.

So, too, in the relations of the sexes. I cannot comprehend their notions of morality, but apparently they have some, rudimentary perhaps, but tolerably clear to them. La Farge was much delighted by the prattle of one of our crew, named Maua, who understands and speaks English, and who explained to him that as ours was a European *malanga,* or picnic, the crew did not insist on having women; but that on a native *malanga,* every man who did not have a woman with him would be laughed at. Every native *malanga* commonly ends in the running away of half a dozen women with the departing boats; and at one village we were gratified by an illustration of the principle. As we were making ready to leave, we heard a great noise of children laughing and running about outside; and on inquiry we learned that they were making fun of a girl who had been persuaded by one of our crew to run away into the bush, on the idea that our boats would pick her up, on the shore, and take her off. Apparently he had, at last, undeceived her, and she had returned, to be laughed at by the village, as Maua explained, "to make her ashamed." I do not think she was much ashamed, and I was assured that her moral character was not essentially affected by the escapade; but if ours had been a native *malanga,* she would have been taken off as a matter of course. As it was, she probably got a whipping from her father, or mother, or elder sister. Whipping is the only corrective for violations of conventional rules. When a man sends away his wife, and takes another, it is apt to end in promiscuous whipping. The family of the injured wife takes it out on any member of the new wife's family, or on the new wife herself, if they happen to lay hands on her, and in such a case the victim gets an unmerciful thrashing. Only in case the new wife belongs to a higher social rank is the revenge not inflicted.

Apia, December 13. We returned here three days ago, after successfully circumnavigating our island. Luckily we had good weather and no mishaps. Little as I like the ocean, I think I enjoyed most the sailing, especially where the coast was bold. On the greater part of this northern side, the coast is lined by a barrier reef, and one sails or rows within it as on a pond; but there are long stretches of bold lava-cliffs to the eastward and on the south coast, where there is no reef, and where one must take the whole force of the ocean swell. I had been in a nightmare of dread, expecting constant sea-sickness, and was so much surprised at finding myself perfectly well, that I got double enjoyment. Of course the island is very pretty from the ocean, with its fringe of palms, and its mountains covered with dense forest, but the sea and sky were fine too, with many lights and colors, and dense rain-clouds hanging about like stage scenery. The whole island is but fortyfive miles long, yet I think few or no foreign pleasure-travellers have sailed round it before. I did some geology, only to find that the subsidence theory would not work, at least within my means of investigation. The coral-reef business, too, is far beyond solution by any simple theorem. You can tell King that I am just as wise as ever, and know less. So with the origin of this people, I understand even less now than before how the devil they got here, or how they got further eastward. A vague idea haunts my mind, founded on my observation of the people themselves, that they may have been origi-nally far better endowed with civilisation than they now are; that they are in fact a deteriorated branch of some highly energetic stock, and that a thousand years ago, the race may have had larger vessels and more knowl-edge; but even in that case the difficulty of populating Tahiti and Hawaii, against the trade-winds, seems insuperable. Certainly no Samoan now ven-tures to suggest that any of his people would dream of a canoe voyage even to Tonga or Fiji, and I can find no tradition of the sort, nor any old song alluding to ocean voyages. The Tongans came here in canoes, but they came with the wind, and got back as they could. Hawaii, Tahiti and the Marquesas were beyond their reach or apparent knowledge.

I amuse myself too with archaic law which is in full remembrance here, and the *patria potestas* which is in full activity. I am still trying to sketch, and make daubs as abominable as any impressionist can show.[3] La Farge thrives on hardships, and seems better in health and energy than at any time since we started. Should you go to New York, stop at his studio and ask to see what he has sent home. We are now so thoroughly domesticated here that I read the New York newspapers without intolerable nausea. I have read all about the elections, and find them to fit so exactly into my grooves of political imbecility that you can imagine all my comments without reading them. An entire evening passed over the New York Tri-bune evolved only the item that Miss Leiter had returned home. The cli-mate is having its effect in making me more indifferent than ever. I find no special enjoyment in sitting here, in my native house, and looking through the palms to the ocean, or wondering what I shall do next, when there is no possible object in doing anything; but in the South Seas such a mental condition seems natural, and I think with terror what it would seem at home. The other day I suddenly bethought myself that we had been here two months. For a moment I was quite startled but La Farge gently ob-served—Why not?,—and I sank in sleep again.

December 30. 10 P.M. The mail is just in, with news to the 15th but no letter from you. I shall get it by way of Tahiti, doubtless. Much news, more or less surprising, but I have not time to study the Tribune, which has become my only literature, as I have devoured all else on the island. I must close this letter tonight in order to catch the cutter which sails for Tutuila tomorrow morning. Imagine me struggling to catch a cutter to take a letter to a savage island to catch a passing steamer. Our Swedish Chief Justice has arrived at last, God have mercy on the poor man.[4] Even Samoa is not different from our world:—it would be tolerable except for its amusements and its politics. We sail for Tahiti in four weeks, or I will inquire the reason why not. I am becoming restless to move on. Love to all yours.

Ever truly   Henry Adams.

MS: RPB
  1. Saugus, north of Boston, was a small town HA passed en route to Beverly Farms.
  2. "When Israel, of the Lord belov'd, / Out of the land of bondage came, / Her fathers' God before her mov'd / An awful guide, in smoke and flame"; Sir Walter Scott, "Rebecca's Hymn," *Ivanhoe* (1819).
  3. A decade and a half after the Impressionists' famous exhibition of 1874, HA's attitude was still not unusual, even among the educated art audience.
  4. Otto Conrad Cedercrantz (1854–1932), a Swedish judge, selected by the king of Sweden according to the terms of the Berlin Act.

To William Hallett Phillips

Apia, 13 December, 1890.

My dear Phillips

I am going to send a box of rubbish to Washington, and in order to give you all the trouble I can, I shall invoice it to you through the Georgetown custom-house. You will have to swear all sorts of things, and to pay the duties. As you have little or no chance of salvation anyway, the swearing does not matter; but the freight and duties you can recover from Dwight.

In the box are some stone stuff for you. The best is an egg-shaped stone, the only stone implement still in use here. Though you guessed forever, you could not guess how it is used, and unless you have some special means of information, you would remain ignorant unless I told you, for few except old residents in these parts ever saw one in use. Soon after I arrived here, I set up a boat, as I would a carriage; and in the effort to find something to do with it, I told Samao, my coxswain, that I wanted to go fishing. He seemed bothered, and asked, in chief's Samoan, what sort of fish I wanted to catch. I replied, in less elegant English, that I wanted to catch the same fish that I saw the Samoans fishing for. He said something about *fe'e,* which he pronounced *fay.* I knew nothing about *fe'e,* so I went to dinner.

At six o'clock the next morning I got up, and walked out to my boat, which lies moored in front of the Consulate. Samao and his men appeared, and having carried me aboard on their shoulders, started to row off towards the reef. Then I noticed that Samao had this queer stone with him, which I took for a sinker. When we had got well out, Samao took his apparatus, and dropping the stone over, in about four feet of water, began bobbing it gently up and down, while the boat moved slightly along. As I watched the stone, with its shell, in the water, it looked like some curious and novel animal, swimming rapidly. As nothing happened, I turned away to look at the purple coral, and the green and blue fishes, when presently I heard a jerk and a splash, and, looking round, saw Samao grabbing an ugly squid or cuttle-fish, which had its tentacles round his hand, and which he held towards me, saying *o le fe'e*, whereby I learned that *fe'e*, meant *squid*, and that I had gone squid-fishing without knowing it. Then I became interested, not because of the sport but because of the stone. Samao called my attention to the next squid that jumped at the stone, and he declared that the squid took it for a rat, and that since ancient times there had been a feud between the squid and the rat, because the rat had once bitten a squid in the back when the squid was kindly carrying him ashore. I found that this peculiar stone was used only for squid-fishing; that it was not made in Samoa where no such stone as onyx exists, but came from Tonga or Fiji; and that it was among the costliest articles of a Samoan outfit. In fact I had to give five dollars for it, from which you may estimate my regard for you. I bought it, to show you how little you know about the use of stone implements.

I eat the squid, which was delicious, both as soup and as stew, but I have not been squid-fishing again, for the creature has a scattering way with him, and is always crawling about one's legs. Satisfied that the Samoans use no other stone in fishing, I asked what they do use, and bought a hook and line. You will observe that the hook, though of mother-of-pearl, is baited with a feather. The authorities here—even Europeans—consider it more effective than a barbed iron hook.

Further inquiry into the stone-implement business ended in the constant reply that Samoans never had any stone weapons; they used hard wood. They never had arrows or arrowheads. They had no stone quirts such as the Hawaiians made. They used water-worn pebbles for net-sinkers. Their only stone instrument was an adze, with which they cut down trees, built houses and canoes, and did very neat joining work. To show me the instrument, one of the most renowned warriors here, old Pa-tu, labored for some four days to make a stone axe such as his father had made in his youth. I send you the axe with its handle, as Pa-tu brought it to me. You will observe that, like all these Polynesian axes, it is an adze, and made of a very compact, heavy lava, found here in the beds of streams. I send also two genuine old stone adzes, obtained in my travels round these islands. All I have seen are like these, and I am assured that all were of the same material, and differed only in size. At Molifanua, the extreme western end of this island, I saw their former workshop where instruments were made. A good-sized stone, with a smoothly polished concave surface, was shown me as the grindstone on which the adzes were sharpened.

The most remarkable result of all my inquiries is the smallness of the result. The Samoans were far behind the Hawaiians in the stone business, as generally in the arts. They depended on their woods, and had no good stone in the islands. Sometimes they sharpened a large shell for an adze, but they never finished their axes nicely. I suspect that in very old days they may have done better; but no one has ever seen a very old stone-implement to know it as such. I have made no end of inquiries, all over the islands, without discovering a trace of older civilisation. Even their traditions hardly go back of their Tongan war, some three hundred years ago.

Besides these stone things, I pack up a quantity of mats and *tapa*, or native cloth, which is still made here in large quantities. The finest mats are used for dress, on state occasions, and are the chief articles of Samoan wealth. They are pretty costly, according to their age and historical interest; for mats have histories. I gave thirty dollars for my best one. Others have been gifts. Between Samoans they serve as money, and are given in return for services, such as house-building, or for the dowry of girls, or at funerals, or other great occasions. I send a few home as curiosities, but it is a pity, for few are now made here, and they are too valuable for common use, and not fine enough for hanging up.

Of the coarser mats, used here as bedding, some are Tongan, and these are the best. The Samoan are hardly worth sending home. I don't suppose you want any; but I have marked a few for presents to my breakfast-table ladies. They will serve in hot weather for floor-mats.

I have filled up the box with *tapa*, which is cheap enough, and is a kind of bark-paper. You can take any piece you want, unless it is marked for some one else. In Hawaii, tapa has become rare and expensive, but here it is still a common manufacture, cheaper than cotton. The chiefs have given it to me by the acre.

The fly-switches are a sign of rank here, but I have not bought them to show my wealth. They are the best fly-switches I ever saw, and I meant to lay in a supply for my old age. Some are gifts; some are purchases, but they are not specially valuable.

I think this is all, except perhaps a few small articles like girls' combs, also gifts from the chief beauties of Samoan society. My acquaintance is large and affectionate, but a pervasive atmosphere of cocoanut oil obliges me to keep at a certain distance from my friends, and until the oil has evaporated I cannot advise you to wear the combs.

La Farge and I have now been two months in Samoa, and expect to remain another. You may perhaps infer from the length of our visit that we have found something to interest us. I will not wholly deny it. At all events the perpetual summer here is somewhat more pronounced than in North Carolina.

One thing I can do here which I cannot do in North Carolina. I have lived for weeks in native houses, and at a pinch can eat native food. As they can only bake their food, and have no salt, and use cocoa-nut with everything, and have only banana leaves for dishes, and the floor for a table, this is fair evidence that they must have good eating. Yet the things are not especially good; the fish is rather insipid; the crabs are fair; the only meats are pig and chicken; and the staple is breadfruit, *taro* and yams, and co-coanut. Even the banana is scarce in remote villages. Nevertheless I can find more to eat in a Samoan hut than in a Carolina town.

By way of becoming Polynesian I have made excursions. With two big boats and twenty men, we have visited the neighboring island of Savaii, and have made the circuit of this island, Upolo. These trips consumed three weeks. There are so very few whites on the islands that during our ab-sence we might say we saw none, but lived wholly with the natives when on shore, passing the nights as guests of chiefs. The natives are very little changed from what they were before being Christianised. They wear their tapa or leaf waist-cloths very commonly, or change it only for a cotton one. They live in their old huts, which are well suited to the climate. They sit on the floor. They keep their superstitions. They dance their old dances, and in every village one has to go through all the forms of a reception, ending at night with a Siva or dance, whether one wants it or not. The *taupo* or village maiden has to see that the visitor is properly entertained, and in a manner she tucks him in bed at night, and dresses him in the morning. After a fair consideration of the subject, I have not cared to press my relations with the female sex to any further intimacy, though the women are splendid crea-tures; and on their side the utmost delicacy has been shown in avoiding anything in the shape of over-cordiality. The fact is that if I wanted any woman worth having, I must either marry her, for a time, or run away with her, and I don't care to do either. I do not like cocoanut oil, and want no encumbrances.

I am already so much accustomed to the South Seas that I have learned to remember La Fayette Square as filled with palms and bread-fruit at this season. How do you live without it? I am told your village is cooler than mine. Yesterday was warm—87°, and no breeze, and the sun just about overhead. I suppose your thermometer did not rise above 80°. How is that owl, Tom Lee? I will drink a green cocoa-nut to your health, or a bowl of kava if you prefer it.

Ever yours   Kakamu.

P.S. Jan. 24. The box starts tomorrow via Auckland.

MS: MH

To Elizabeth Cameron

Vaiale, 15 December, 1890.

We find Stevenson still here. He has not gone to Auckland. Apparently we are to see much more of him, for the steamer "Richmond," which is our only conveyance to Tahiti, will not return here for six weeks. La Farge is not yet ready to go; so we have sent for our letters, which cannot arrive till near February, and then only in time for us to acknowledge them before sailing. By that time we shall be well in arrears, for our last letters from home were written early in October. We are to leave Samoa about February 1, and by that time should have three months' arrears of letters to answer on reaching Tahiti.

Having now pretty much exhausted the possibilities of travel in Samoa, I am casting about for amusements during the next six weeks. We are not without distinguished society. Saturday afternoon Mata-afa came over to see us, as he often does; but this time he brought some presents of *tapa* and baskets, explaining that he is now poor and has little to give. The formula is almost a matter of course, but in this case it is probably more than a form, for Mata-afa is an abdicated king, and is struggling with difficulties. I think he would be a marked man anywhere, but he is a long way the most distinguished chief in these islands, and the only one we have met who carries his superiority about him so decidedly as to set him at once apart. He brought me, on Saturday, some old songs I had asked for, and which he had good-naturedly caused to be written out. Two of his oldest followers were with him, and sat at the end of our native house, while Mata-afa himself, in the regulation official white jacket, sat on a chair between us. I had much to ask him about the legendary songs, and he, with a deprecatory smile as though I were a spoiled child, told me at great length the story, or a part of the mass of stories, about Pili, "the Lizard," which seems to be the principal material of Samoan verse. It was not very amusing, and he was aware of it, but I asked him to go on, and he must have toiled an hour, giving sentence after sentence for translation by our boy Charley. I shall not bore you with the doings of Pili, either the father or the son. You can read volumes of such childlike stuff by getting from the Congressional library either Fornandez' great book about Hawaii or Sir George Grey's Maori Legend's about New Zealand, or Turner's volume on Samoa, or half a dozen other books on the South Seas.[1] Polynesians are not imaginative, but eminently practical, with childish ideas as to what is humorous or imposing. My object is only to find out what they have done; so I listened with gravity to Mata-afa, who labored on, until at length Stevenson dropped in, and we turned to discussing the latest appearance of a certain interesting spirit or female enchantress who recently killed a young chief, in whose father's house we stayed at Vao-vai. I thought then that we were rather an interesting company, as the world goes. Mata-afa may fairly rank as one of the heroic figures of our time. Stevenson is a person sufficiently known to fame; and La Farge will probably not be less well known a hundred years hence than now. The group struck me as rather a peculiar one, considering that we were a good many thousand miles from places where people usually hunt lions, and I felt encouraged to think that even here I was not in an atmosphere of hopeless mental stagnation. Stevenson stayed to dine with us, and was quite on his manners, but as usual had to borrow Sewall's clothes. La Farge and I promised to come up to his place the next morning

(Sunday), and to send our breakfast before us. I cannot conceive why they should ever be without food in the house, but apparently their normal condition is foodless, and they not only consented but advised my making sure of my own breakfast.[2] Stevenson himself seems to eat little or nothing, and lives on cheap French *vin ordinaire* when he can get it. I do not know how this régime affects his complaint, for I do not know what his complaint is. I supposed it to be *phthisis,* or tubercular consumption; but am assured here that his lungs are not affected. The German physician here says that the complaint is asthma; but I am too weak in knowledge to explain how asthma should get relief from a saturated climate like this, where constant exposure leads also to severe colds, not easily thrown off. Asthma or whatever you please, he and his wife, according to their own account, rarely have enough to eat in the house, so I sent off a native, at seven o'clock in the morning, with a basket of food, while I started on foot at half past ten, and La Farge followed at eleven on horseback. This was my first experiment at walking hereabouts. The climate is not stimulating to legs. Since we arrived, the season has changed; the blessed trade-wind has died out, and the apparent heat is much greater. I walked very slowly, under an umbrella, but was soon in a state of saturation, and, as the path is not interesting, I found pedestrianism a bore, but arrived just at noon, letting La Farge precede me a few minutes. We found Stevenson and his wife just as they had appeared at our first call, except that Mrs Stevenson did not now think herself obliged to put on slippers, and her night-gown costume had apparently not been washed since our visit. Stevenson himself wore still a brown knit woollen sock on one foot, and a greyish purple sock on the other, much wanting in heels, so that I speculated half my time whether it was the same old socks, or the corresponding alternates, and concluded that he must have worn them ever since we first saw him. They were evidently his slippers for home wear. He wore also, doubtless out of deference to us, a pair of trousers, and a thin flannel shirt; but, by way of protest, he rolled up the sleeves above his shoulders, displaying a pair of the thinnest white arms I ever beheld, which he brandished in the air habitually as though he wanted to throw them away. To La Farge and me, this attitude expressed incredible strength, and heroic defiance of destiny, for his house swarmed with mosquitoes which drove us wild, though only our heads and hands were exposed. Of course it was none of our business, and both Stevenson and his wife were very friendly, and gave us a good breakfast,—or got it themselves,—and kept up a rapid talk for four hours, at the end of which I was very tired, but Stevenson seemed only refreshed. Both La Farge and I came round to a sort of liking for Mrs Stevenson, who is more human than her husband. Stevenson is an *aïtu,*—uncanny. His fragility passes description, but his endurance passes his fragility. I cannot conceive how such a bundle of bones, unable to work on his writing without often taking to his bed as his working-place, should have gone through the months of exposure, confinement and bad nourishment which he has enjoyed. Their travels have broken his wife up; she is a victim to rheumatism which is becoming paralysis, and, I suspect, to dyspepsia; she says that their voyages have caused it; but Stevenson gloats over discomforts and thinks that every traveller should sail for months in small cutters rancid with cocoanut oil and mouldy with constant rain, and should live on coral atolls with nothing but cocoanuts and poisonous fish to eat. Their mode of existence here is far less human than that of the natives, and compared with their shanty a native house is a palace; but this squalor must be somehow due to his education. All through him, the education shows. His early associates were all second-rate; he never seems by any chance to have come in contact with first-rate people, either men, women or artists. He does not know the difference between people, and mixes them up in a fashion as grotesque as if they were characters in his new Arabian Nights. Of course he must have found me out at once, for my Bostonianism, and finikin clinging to what I think the best, must rub him raw all over, all the more because I try not to express it; but I suspect he does not know quite enough even to hate me for it; and I am sure that he would never have the fineness to penetrate La Farge, though, compared with La Farge, I am a sort of Stevenson for coarseness. He is extremely civil, and gives me things of his own to read, which have not been published, and he would not trust to strangers;[3] he gives us letters to Tahiti, and shows a strong wish for our society; but I dare not see him often for fear of his hating me as a Philistine and a disgrace to humanity, because I care not a copper for what interests him. On the other hand he is perfectly safe with La Farge, and La Farge is still safer with him. After all the extreme intimacy of my long acquaintance with La Farge, I am always more and more astonished at the accuracy of his judgment. I knew how fine it was, and how keen, but the infernal triumph of the man is his correctness. I have never managed to catch him in an error. His judgment of men and women is as unfailing as his judgment of a picture, and he understands a Polynesian quite as well as he does a New Yorker. He sees all round a character like Stevenson's, and comments on it as if it were a painting, while Stevenson could never get within reach of him if they were alone on an atoll. The two characters in contact are rather amusing as contrasts; the oriental delicacy of La Farge seems to be doubled by the Scotch eccentricities and barbarisms of Stevenson who is as one-sided as a crab, and flies off at angles, no matter what rocks stand in his way.

December 18. The "Richmond" sailed for Tahiti yesterday and I was sorry not to sail in her. La Farge wishes to remain here, and I care so little whether I go or stay, that I assent to any decided wish of his; but we have now been here nearly three months, and I am beginning to find time drag. The wet and hot season has come, and the trade-wind has ceased blowing. Sir John Thurston writes to me not to visit Fiji till the dry weather returns.[4] On becoming acquainted with the South Seas, I find that the island-groups of interest are very few. I could not stand the flat, coral islands more than a day or two, and the high islands, with scenery and Polynesian natives, are limited to this group, the Marquesas and Tahiti. Our long stay here, among the least changed natives, has made us comparatively indifferent to the natives of Tahiti, who may be superior in every way, but are very few in number, and have abandoned native customs and costumes. I think a month at Tahiti would probably more than satisfy me, and if I give another month to a cruise among the Marquesas, nothing will remain in Polynesia to amuse me. Then I shall turn to New Zealand and Fiji, which are not likely to occupy me long, especially if La Farge leaves for home. Should he leave me, I should certainly become very restless. I shall then hurry to eat my *durian* in the Malay archipelago, and turn off to Ceylon and India. Naturally, China would be the next stage, but I do not look forward so far, though, if health and endurance last, I ought to pass next winter at Pekin. I do not venture to think of what I might do if I knew what is going on at home. At Tahiti I shall be quite as near home as here, and can change my movements to suit. Meanwhile we are to pass six weeks more in Samoa, where we are comfortable enough, and have plenty of acquaintances, but, as far as I am concerned, nothing to do. The Polynesians are a singularly superficial people, and, except to sketch, have nothing but their mysterious origin to occupy one's mind. I try to study their old customs and laws, but the *patria potestas* and the system of female descent are dry food. I find that the only result of trying to sketch is disgust at the results, and constant bucking against my own limitations, not merely in technique, though the inability to draw is bad enough, but still more in artistic sense both of color and mass. Even La Farge's work does not satisfy me any more than it does him, though he has all that I lack. My only consolation is that I should be far more at a loss for occupation at home.

Two more personages of interest to us have come to dinner. One is named Atwater; he was formerly our consul at Tahiti; a Yankee who married into the chief native family, and, through his wife, got large interests in cocoa-nut plantations and pearl islands.[5] He suffers from asthma and cannot live in Tahiti now, but is on his way there, to attend to some business. For taking the fun out of anything, a Yankee matches a Scotchman, and Mr Atwater has perhaps been long enough in the south seas to reach the universal lava-foundation of commonplace. Even the natives are not exempt, and I found, on our last tour round the island, that the happy and indolent islander is extremely bored by his ideal existence. I was slow to believe it, but the *taupo* were frank on the subject, and the young men were devoured by the wish for something new. I believe that ennui is the chief cause of their wars; but at a large village called Saangápu, in the district of Safata, I met an example of restlessness that beat even my own or Atwater's. In the dusk of evening, as I returned to our hut after a stroll along the beach, I was surprised to find a native talking English with La Farge. He turned out to be our host, Angápu, the chief of the village, and a nephew of our chief, Seumano-tafa, our companion and escort. Angápu is a dignified, middle-aged man, and speaks English with the same high-bred beauty of tone and accent that struck us so much in old John Adams at Apia. He has been a great traveller as a common Kanaka-seaman, and has been to San Francisco, New Orleans, New York, Liverpool, Glasgow, Hamburg, as well as to Australia, China, Japan, and all over the Pacific. I asked him whether he was satisfied to stay at home now, and he replied that he would like to go off again; but Seumano, who, as head of the family, can control his movements, would not consent. Angápu was bored by the smallness of Samoan interests and the restrictions of society, yet he is a considerable chief, belonging to a powerful family; his position is one of power and his duties and responsibilities must be constant enough to give him steady occupation. His village was one of the largest and richest we saw. With all this, he was unhappy because he could not go off as a common sailor before the mast, to knock about the ocean in cold climates which were his horror. In his presence I felt myself an ideal representative of stay-at-home, immoveable fixity and repose. Atwater is another example of restlessness. Evidently Tahiti bores him, and he finds San Francisco a relief. He calls himself a bad sailor, yet he wanders from San Francisco to Sydney, and back again, as though the ocean were a French play. He told us much about his pearl-fishing, which seems to have amused him most, but he says that in New York or Paris he can buy pearls cheaper than he can fish them, and in infinitely larger quantities and of better quality. He says that he can buy pearls at San Francisco and sell them at a profit in Tahiti, and that the pearl industry is but an adjunct to that of mother-of-pearl; a sort of accidental margin for the business.

Atwater was very friendly and promised to prepare the way for us at Tahiti, especially with his brother-in-law, Tati Salmon, the head of the greatest native family on the island, to whom Stevenson had already given us a letter. Tati Salmon is half London Jew; half hereditary high chief of the Tevas or Tefas; and looks down on the Pomares with lofty contempt, as parvenus. We shall probably put ourselves at once under his protection, and fly from Papeete where Pomare and Frenchmen have sway.[6]

Our other distinguished visitor is named Shirley Baker, and dined with us last evening. In these parts of the world, three persons seem to be preeminent among the English. One is old Sir George Grey of New Zealand, about whom you can read much in Mr Froude's dull book called Oceanica.[7] I shall probably never meet Sir George Grey, for I have no letters to Auckland. The second is Sir John Thurston at Fiji, whose guest I expect to be. The third is Shirley Baker, who ruled despotically the Tonga group of islands, called Friendly on the maps, several hundred miles south of Samoa. Thurston at Fiji did not approve of Baker's doings at Tonga, and at last, just before we left home, took the strong step of sending a war-vessel to deport Baker, and practically to annex Tonga to his own government. I have taken care not to know anything about the subject, that I might have no prejudices about the men, but the affair has made a great noise in these hollow oceans. Baker was naturally angry, and I imagine that he wants revenge and reinstatement. He has lately come here from Auckland, perhaps with the idea of going to Washington and seeking aid from you and sister Anne. Last evening he dined with us, a London-aldermanic looking person, doubtful on his aspirates, but singularly quiet, restrained and intelligent. His talk was very interesting to us, for he is a converted missionary who has been thirty years at Tonga, and knows more than anyone else of Tongan history and affairs. You are happily ignorant that Tonga was the missionary stronghold where they played pranks such as uncontrolled priesthoods commonly indulge in. Tonga too is or was a stronghold of the Polynesian race, and a central point of its distribution. Probably New Zealand got its Maoris from Tonga, for the Tongans were great navigators, while the Samoans never ventured far to sea, or attempted foreign conquests. Baker had a great deal to say on these subjects, and said it well; but I suspect he is writing a book, for he seemed cautious about telling all he thought; and on the Polynesian battle-ground where everyone has an exclusive and extravagant theory to argue,—the source of the Polynesian race,—he would go no further than suggest that the race and the pig came together, and must be traced back to Asia together. This strikes me as inadequate treatment, but perhaps I do not sufficiently respect the pig; and I have an opposite hobby, that the race came necessarily with the trade-winds,—not against them,— which Baker rejects, riding too confidently on his pigs against the wind. I refer the dispute to you for arbitration, as Baker would certainly reject your only rival, Sir John Thurston.[8]

December 24. (23). Another storm yesterday. The wind and rain were strident, and, with the surf, made us feel at sea again. In this open-air existence, where we never close doors, but take our meals on the verandah, and sit till bed-time, reading, talking and smoking as though it were La Fayette Square in July, we are amusingly badgered about by a storm, and have to hunt for a spot where the wind will let a lamp burn, and the rain will not splash directly on one's head. The interior of the Consulate is untenable, for the wind blows through the open eaves and extinguishes the lamps. Another annoyance is the result of wind. Swarms of very minute winged insects gather round our lamp, blown to leeward, and end by driving us to bed. Last night, in spite of difficulties, I hung on to my book—Stanley's big Africa—till half past nine o'clock, and then had to give it up.[9] Thousands of the little flies were lying on the table, burned, or on the lamp, caught in the kerosene oil that adheres to its inequalities of surface. This morning Awoki reports that the ants have carried away all the flies. Of course we mildew apace, but not so much as I should have expected, considering how little dry weather we get. My ideas of the south seas have changed not a little under the influence of closer acquaintance, but we are now, I suppose, in the rainy season, and can expect worse and worse until April. Our life is perfectly uniform. We sleep a great deal. I go to bed at ten o'clock and get up at about seven, which for me is immense; and La Farge sleeps still more. The first act of the day is to take a shower-bath, and dress. Then I take my breakfast, usually alone;—two mangoes, an orange, two boiled eggs, and coffee. Then I come to my native house, and write or try to paint. Natives come with mats or *tapa* or other things to sell; or visitors drop in, usually chiefs, to chat with us. The chiefs are always welcome to me, but I make them useful by cross-questioning them on every subject I can think of. Especially old To-fai, who is a very high chief, has to earn his entertainment. I have pumped him about history and institutions until he gets too deep even for his own dignity. My last effort was to drag out the whole of his family-organisation, and the nature of his authority as its head. You are properly indifferent to Roman law, and know little in theory of the *patria potestas,* but To-fai tells me that he has nearly two hundred persons under his authority as head of the family, and none of them can do any important act without his assent, under penalty of being beaten more or less severely, or expelled from the family with the consequent loss of protection and rights. The chief has another authority over his village or district, but this seems to be political or military, and interests me less. Every chief has an official name which carries with it the authority. For instance, To-fai is really a title, like an English peerage, but not strictly hereditary, for the persons who elect him may prefer a younger son or a nephew, to a less competent eldest son. Then the elder brothers as well as the uncles and older relations are equally subject to the authority of the younger man. Does this bore you too much? Even to me it is not passionately exciting, but it is more than I have got out of books. The chiefs interest me much more than the common-people do, for they are true aristocrats and have the virtues of their class, while the common people would sink to the level of the Hawaiians if the chiefs were to become extinct. Sometimes I am confounded by an exhibition of feeling which upsets my theories. Certainly the Polynesian is as superficial as you like, but every now and then, here as elsewhere, one is a good deal startled to find that there is no dependence on apparent superficiality. One of our village-chiefs is Pa-tu, an older half-brother of To-fai. Pa-tu, as I have somewhere told you, was the great warrior of the late wars. La Farge says he suggests your uncle Tecumph in look and manner, and it is true.[10] In the war, some two years ago, Pa-tu's daughter was killed in battle, fighting by her father's side, and Pa-tu felt her death deeply. La Farge was struck by the character of her face, as he saw it in a photograph at the photographer's; and with the idea of using the type, had an enlargement made. He thought that he would take two impressions, one for himself, one for Pa-tu, as a present; so the other day, when Pa-tu happened to come in, La Farge gave him the enlargement. Apparently Pa-tu had no idea what to expect, and was quite unprepared, so that I, who was sitting above him, in a chair, while he sat on the mat, watched curiously to see what effect the picture would have on him. He took it as though he supposed it to be what he was familiar with; then he looked at it some time without a word, but I could see his face growing more and more fixed as though he were trying to control himself; then he slowly bent his head down nearly to his knees, still holding the photograph as a sort of veil before him. Naturally La Farge and I were almost as much disturbed as he was, and felt very uncomfortable, but he quite finished us at last by sitting up again, his eyes streaming with tears, and saying, quite simply, a few words which were interpreted to us to mean: "Thank God, I have this day once more seen my daughter as she lived." There was no pretence at thanks or forms. The old man was thinking only of his daughter.

Fanua's wedding invitations are out, for the 31st. She marries an English trader named Gurr, and this time the marriage is English, not Samoan. I like Fanua, who resembles Aenga a little, in being shy and sensitive, though not handsome either in face or figure. As the adopted daughter of Seumano and Fatuleia, and the *taupo* of Apia, we must give her a wedding-present, and go to the feast. Meanwhile another German war-vessel has arrived. The "Sperber" has long been here, and Captain Foss who commands her, has been a very agreeable acquaintance. We must now pay a visit to the Admiral on the "Leipzig." Our own tub, the "Iroquois" is at Pango-pango, and is to come over for the arrival of our Swedish Chief-justice who is to arrive by the next mail-steamer. Then we shall have awful festivities, which I would gladly escape.

December 30. The obstinately wicked get their reward. Here is an outcast who fled from his own country to escape the interminable bore of its nickel-plated politics and politicians; yet when he seeks refuge in an inaccessible island of the South Seas, ten thousand miles from an Irishman, he finds politics running round like roosters without heads. Politics are commonly more or less *bouffe,* but here the whole thing is pure Offenbach. The bloody villain is Stuebel, the German Consul. If Stuebel says it rains, he means mischief. If he says it doesn't rain, he lies. If he says nothing, he is deep in conspiracy. War is to break out in Savaii at once; Manono is coming to seize Malietoa; Stuebel has written to Tamasese to be ready;[11] the "Sperber" is going to Tutuila; the "Leipzig" is going to fetch the new Chief Justice; Malietoa is to be deposed, and the Germans are to seize the island. Stuebel is at the bottom of it all. Every day these stories come to us. Old Samasoni waddles up, almost insane with native rumors, and predicts civil war within twentyfour hours. Mata-afa always has some absurd native story which he tells us with his grave, quiet smile, as though he were sorry to amuse us with his people's folly. You can imagine me in this poultry-yard. After several times expressing myself in my usual offensive and dogmatic manner on the character of this small beer, I have sunk into silence more or less sullen, and let the talk go on as it will. As far as I can see, it is all the play of these brown-skinned children, who are bored for want of excitement, and are quite capable of getting up a fight about nothing, but meanwhile we are standing along the shore, glasses in hand, watching for the smoke of the "Iroquois" which is supposed to be bringing our Swedish Chief Justice from Tutuila. The Chief Justice is to settle everything, it appears; but what is to happen if the unfortunate man should prove to be a tool of the wicked Stuebel? I give it up, and the mail goes out immediately, so I hand over the problem to your superior wisdom. Anyone who can understand Pennsylvania politics, can grapple with Samoa.

Luckily the weather is again fine, and of late I have been able to go out towards sunset in my native canoe and paddle far and wide along the shore and over the reef. Of course it is ideally pretty. The water is shallow, and one sees the fish and coral almost as clearly as the clouds and mountains. The sunsets are miraculous. They are too evanescent and soft to allow one even to think of catching their tones in paint, and although La Farge has

less pounding of the surf on the barrier-reef, half a mile to sea, is almost muffled. It is nine o'clock; I have just finished my breakfast of coffee and mangoes at the Consulate, where Lieutenant Parker and his wife are packing, to go on board the "Iroquois"; my letters went off by the sailing cutter two days ago, but the Parkers will catch up with them at Tutuila. Ought I to send letters—two days later news from Samoa—to you by the Parkers? I think not. Surely you could stand the load of another letter, even with two days' later. Besides, I want time to think. If these fearful monthly mails are to continue, they will break me up. You would laugh to see me read the New York Tribune with interest positively intense; but apparently, just as soon as I leave a place, the fun begins. Certainly in twenty years nothing has occurred in the United States so revolutionary and startling as the events of October and November, 1890;[1] and when one takes in England, the drama meloes; it becomes tragi-farcical in Ireland, as usual. I have laughed, like a ten-year-old child, over Parnell and the dear Grand Old Man; the Thackeray Irishman O'Shea; the adorable Kitty; and the Kilkenny row, the solemn faces, the cracked heads, and the Charley O'Malley, Lever-esque, buffoonery of the whole affair, which is as much more entertaining than a novel as you are than Benjamin Harrison.[2] Then the long financial drama has had a manysided personal interest still stronger than the purely artistic perfection of Parnell and Grandpapa Gladstone. I have read through it from October to December 16 with more excitement than I ever expected to feel again in such subjects. The first mysterious squeezing of the market; the slow yielding of stocks; the howls and groans of the unfortunates whom the bears hugged; the awful crash of the Barings, and my own narrow escape from being stranded penniless here; the collapse day by day, and the gradual taking-form of the mysterious power that was to profit by it all; the looming-up of Jay Gould in the background, and his gentle, innocent-minded comments day-by-day on the situation; the seizure of Pacific Mail; the seizure of Union Pacific; and the unrelaxing severity of the grip that is to restore order by creating chaos;—all this would be a delight if I were twenty years younger, for, if you happen on my new volume of Essays which ought soon to be published, you will see that I wrote the first chapter of this story in an article called the "Gold Conspiracy." The second chapter has been my brother's administration of Union Pacific, and its foredoomed failure. The last chapter—in my lifetime—has still to come, but is close at hand. I do not know the climax, but am devoured by curiosity. According to my diagnosis, Jay Gould too is foredoomed to failure; his scheme is still more impracticable than my brother's, and he has personal and political enmities infinitely more serious. If I am right, and if Gould must fail, I see the most splendid possibilities of a climax. Will he subside quietly? Will he break down? Will he be hung on a lamp-post? Will government and society stand under the shock?

My brother Charles will doubtless live to write the story and the epitaph of Jay Gould, who is certainly a great man, worth writing about. If I thought I should be alive twentyfive years hence, with my full powers of mind and body, I should prepare to continue my history, and show where American democracy was coming out. We shall know all about it by that time. As yet we can but guess, and Jay Gould has much to tell us. Unfortunately I am cursed with the misfortune of thinking that I know beforehand what the result must be, and of feeling sure that it is one which I do not care to pursue; one with which I have little or no sympathy, except in a coldly scientific way; and a man cannot with decency or chance of success take a part in a stage-play when he cannot help showing the audience that he thinks the whole thing a devilish poor piece of work.

You find my last two volumes more critical—deliberately fault-finding?—than the earlier ones. They were written chiefly within the last five or six years, and in a very different frame of mind from that in which the work was begun. I found it hard to pretend either sympathy or interest in my subject. If you compare the tone of my first volume—even toned down, as it is, from the original—with that of the ninth, when it appears, you will feel that the light has gone out. I am not to blame. As long as I could make life work, I stood by it, and swore by it as though it were my God, as indeed it was.

Meanwhile I read your letters over and over—they are all the letters I have to read,—and look at your photographs; and my spirits sink deeper and deeper as I seem to feel that, like the unfortunate Robinson, I cannot get back to land. My only hope is to keep knocking about till I am tired beyond endurance. The chance is a small one, for I was tired before I started, and am much more tired now; but so was Robinson. Who knows? I am surely in a healthier mental condition than at any time in the past five years. Perhaps you may cure me after all, and I shall come back contented and in repose of mind, to be your tame cat, after the manner of Chateaubriand, and various elderly English gentlemen, once my amusement to watch.[3] Is it worth your while? Please say yes.

Apia. 1891. Jan. 9; after a week of slow recovery from the agitation of mail-day. In the interval La Farge has been unwell and has only just recovered; I have been much bored and out of spirits, and have also stiffened up. I have read every book in Samoa, and have no more to read except your letters, which I know by heart already. I dread sitting down without something in my hands, if only Homer to annotate with Samoan knowledge. The horrors of thinking are intolerable. I feel at times as though I must just run home to have an hour's conversation with you, and that, without it, the world would run off the trestle; but I reflect that I can equally well have the conversation here, as I know it, like your letters by heart, and Martha has doubtless grown up to be a young lady, with little lovers whose battles she prefers to my petting. By the way, apropos to Martha, I am interested to find that even the Samoan child, which should have no nerves, living in a climate like a hot-house, and always in the open air, still has tantrums of hysterics, and yells like a demon, half an hour at a time, rolling on the ground and kicking, apparently without cause, and at any hour of the day or night, greatly to the disturbance of my sleep as they can be heard half a mile away. One of the English missionary-ladies informs me that their parents are too indulgent, which sounds like New England.

Great events have occurred here during the last ten days. Our Swedish Chief Justice has arrived, and the islands have begun their new career as an independent power under the Berlin treaty. The Chief Justice is a young man named Cederkranz, who looks honest and fairly intelligent, but has one eye that seems to be fixed, and glares perversely into space. He arrived in the midst of our confusion caused by the Parkers' departure, Fanua's wedding, and the departure or arrival of various war-vessels and mail-steamers. Fanua was married at the British Consulate, her husband, Gurr, being a British colonial here, and taking her as a wife after our law. We breakfasted that day with Stuebel, the German Consul, and after breakfast took the Chief Justice to Fanua's wedding reception. You will observe that since our travels have ceased, you hear no more of the old-gold girl. The *taupo* stays at home, and so do we. Poor Aenga, it seems, is in a manner banished at Sa-papalii in Savaii, where we saw her. I learned that she incurred displeasure by a *tendresse* for Seu-mano's son, probably because he has a wife already, and Malietoa or Seu-mano or he himself thought divorce unadvisable. At all events we have heard nothing from her or from Faa-uli or Faasaei or any of our other *taupo* loves, and have had no more Sivas or cocoanut oil. Fanua was married without assistance from *taupo* colleagues, though she wore a very becoming wedding-dress of fine mats. She had a ball, too, but La Farge and I do not go to balls; not even to that in honor of the Chief Justice. To atone for this want of respect, I stimulated Consul Sewall to give the Chief Justice a dinner, regardless of expense, to throw all previous Samoan entertainments into outer darkness. For four days Sewall has devoted all his energies and thoughts to this dinner. We are very short of ladies here, but the wife of the British Consul, Cusack-Smith, arrived just in time. She is a young blonde of the modern British type, rather pretty and painted-silky in costume. Mrs Clarke and Mrs Claxton, the British missionary wives, filled up. Mrs Claxton is pretty, and not over-missionaried. The native wife of Blacklock, a consular official, made a fourth; and Sewall asked Mrs Stevenson, who sent a letter in reply, so characteristic that I begged it of Sewall, and intend to inclose it to you as the most amusing product of Samoa I have met. Stevenson himself has sailed for Sydney after an affectionate parting with us; and Mrs. Stevenson did not appear at the dinner. Please do not show her letter, except under caution. I should be very sorry to have any remarks of mine come back here. These were all the ladies eligible. The men were Cederkrantz himself; Cusack-Smith, an idiot of the good-natured polo type; Stuebel; Captain Bishop and a small ships-crew of lieutenants and doctors from the "Iroquois"; and half a dozen subordinate German, Swedish and American consular, official or missionary parties. Twenty persons sat down at table under a forest of palms and ferns. You know too well my weaknesses to need my giving you a detailed account of my sufferings. Sewall kept his word, and the dinner was three hours long. I was placed next to Stuebel as the only intelligent person in the company, and managed to have some pleasant talk. On my left was one Ulfsparre, a young and interestingly muddle-headed Swede. La Farge sat between Clarke, the missionary, and Henne-berger, the doctor of the "Iroquois," who was supposed to be the social charmer of the navy and devoted his powers of fascination to ungrateful Mrs Cusack-Smith on his left. Of Cederkranz I could see and hear nothing, as he sat three places from me on my right. I earnestly hope that this great entertainment strengthened and extended Secretary Blaine's purposes and influence in the South Seas; but I admit to having felt prodigious comfort when the ladies and their husbands departed under umbrellas at eleven o'clock, and I slipped off to finish my cigar in the soothing darkness of the verandah of my own sleeping-cabin, whence I heard a louder and louder uproar of conviviality at the Consulate long after I was in bed, and needed not the later information of La Farge to acquaint me that most of the young men were drunk, and that Captain Bishop, who, like ourselves, drank nothing, being a reformed inebriate, was waving a lantern patiently for an hour or two, on the verandah, as a signal to his lambs in the dining-room to collect about him and go aboard ship.

We learn today that, after all, Mrs Stevenson came down last evening, arriving late; that her horse refused to ford the stream between Apia and here; that she could not get a boat, and was not strong enough to walk; so she had to pass her evening at the missionary house, the missionaries being here. More traits! What with her shoes, her horse, and herself, she is charming.

Apia. January 14, 1891. Unless I have lost the little memory I once thought belonged to me, five months have passed since the day I bade you good-bye. Statistically speaking, this fact belongs to the commonplace. In other points of view, it is anything but commonplace. I spare you any com-ments on it, for the present, especially because I have nothing to say that has not been said again and again, until you must be thoroughly tired of my want of novelty or variety of ideas. You can imagine it all, much better than I could write it; yet I admit to feeling surprised at finding myself, after five months, still in Samoa, my true travels having not yet fairly begun. To be sure, the Hawaiian journey was one of the most wonderful I ever made, and Samoa has been most interesting, and entertaining; but still the slow-ness of my movements suggests eternity. Since our voyage round Upolo, I have done nothing whatever but kill time, waiting for the Tahiti steamer. Another fortnight must be given up to the same occupation. So indolent have I become that I no longer move from my chair, except to paddle for an hour or two in my canoe towards evening. I have even refused to go with Consul Sewall, on the "Iroquois" to Pango-pango, though he urged me strongly and wanted me much; for he was going on a job that I had in a manner driven him into. A murder of a very curious kind was committed at Pango-pango on the night of December 20. The victim was one of the

"Iroquois" crew; a seaman named Power, coxswain of the Captain's gig; a good fellow, popular with everyone on board, and without a known enemy on shore. Captain Bishop and the officers of the "Iroquois" showed incompetence or indifference, or both, in investigating the crime; and in the want of amusement, I took it up, and induced Sewall to begin an investigation. The first result was a quarrel with Captain Bishop, in which he showed himself an ass, and quickly backed down. The second result was that Sewall had to go to Pango-pango, and I refused to go with him. My true reason is that I will not consent to appear, without official authority, as a meddler in official business; but my interest in the case is great, and I am sorry not to be at hand to help Sewall as amateur detective.

How would the story do for a Samoan melodrama? The murdered man, Power, had been in Samoa before, as one of the crew of the "Adams," two or three years ago. He came back in the "Iroquois" which arrived about December 1, or soon afterwards, while I was circumnavigating this island. When I got back to Apia, December 10, the "Iroquois" was in the harbor, and my boat passed under her stern as I steered across to the Consulate. The next day she sailed to Pango-pango, our coaling station in Tutuila. Power did not go ashore till Sunday, December 20, when he, with his closest intimate and chum, a seaman named Brennan, and three or four other men, went ashore on leave, and passed the day playing poker inside the bar of a drinking-saloon, kept by an American named Pike. Power won a few dollars, coming out a little ahead. He left the card-table four or five times, for two or three minutes at a time, but never went further than the immediate front of the house, and was not seen to speak with anyone but his party. At sunset,—six o'clock,—all returned to the ship. Very soon afterwards, towards eight o'clock, he suggested to Brennan to swim ashore, and have some more poker. Brennan agreed, and understood that they were to send out a canoe from shore, to the ship, secretly, in the dark, to fetch off two or three other men, who could not, or would not swim. These men, when cross-questioned by Sewall, say that Power did ask them to swim ashore, but the weather was threatening, the swim was long, and they not only refused to go, but thought it strange that Power, who, as Captain's coxswain could always get leave, should want to do it. This took place between eight and half past eight, and ten or fifteen minutes later, Power and Brennan crawled out through an open space in the bow, and dropped from the chains into the water. They had agreed to swim to a point, some four hundred yards away, but the wind rose, with rain, the current was strong, they wore their clothes as they stood, and Brennan, being the weaker swimmer, could make no headway to the point, and at last, nearly exhausted, turned on his back to rest. He heard Power hail "Hallo, Shortie!"—Brennan's nickname—and the voice came from the direction they had intended to go, as though Power were well on his way to the point. Brennan was carried further into the harbor, and made out to reach the pier, near Pike's saloon. As soon as he got ashore, he walked along the beach to the point, expecting to meet Power. Failing to find him, Brennan called out: "Power, Power!" so loud that he was heard on the ship. Still Power did not answer, and Brennan walked back to Pike's, meeting natives who spoke to him. As the saloon was closed, he paid a native a dollar to take him to Pike's house, some distance beyond. He found Pike; they returned to the saloon; drank one bottle of whiskey; and Brennan, taking another, went on board ship in a canoe at twelve o'clock. He waked two of his mates and took them up to the forecastle where they drank the whiskey, and discussed what had become of Power.

The next morning, at quarters, Power's absence was reported. The same afternoon one of the ship's boats, between the pier and the anchorage, about a hundred yards from the ship, came on a body, floating in the water. The head was gone, both arms were cut off at the shoulder; one leg was gone; the other was cut to the bone; and the body was recognised by its tattooing, a part of a trouser leg, and a shoe. The autopsy showed no sign of drowning, but clear evidence of hacking with a knife or cleaver.

Brannan gave himself up at once, and was put in irons as charged with murder. Sewall sent for him, the "Iroquois" having returned here, and I heard Brannan tell his story, which was perfectly straight. He is, I believe, as ignorant as I am. Who, then, committed the murder, and why? You will probably say, offhand: "He met some native, as he came out of the water, and the native knocked him on the head to rob him." That would be the natural European explanation, but it is the last to occur to us. Natives never commit European murders. They very rarely indeed commit murder at all, and when they do so they kill each other, not for money but for revenge. No common Samoan would dare to murder a white man, for he is naturally timid, and dislikes violence, and knows he would certainly be hung. We put the probability of such an explanation last of all possible clues, and yet we have literally no evidence to warrant another, except the speaking fact that Power should have wanted to go ashore at all, that night; should have deceived Brannan into accompanying him; and should have behaved throughout in the way one would expect if he had some secret inducement powerful enough to overcome every obstacle. Who was she? This is the conundrum that interests us, and you see what a sweet melodrama it suggests. Had Power old relations with some woman? Had he made an agreement to meet her? The point of this suspicion is very Samoan. The woman must be an unusual person if her husband—or anyone else—commits murder out of jealousy. Few Samoan women are murdered, yet not many are Penelopes. Very few Samoan men would dare murder a white for such a cause,—perhaps no one would dare it, unless he were a half-caste or a chief. Even then he must be a conspicuous personage. Who is he?

January 18. The last few days a great surf has been rolling over the reef and into the harbor, sign of a heavy storm to the northward. The air was calm and oppressive; a flood of rain fell; and the effect of a tremendous sea in such an atmosphere was uncanny. I strolled at evening towards Apia to see what the surf was doing with the wrecks,—for to Apians the sight never

out of their eyes is the hulks of the Trenton and Adler, the most conspicuous objects in the harbor.[4] I met Stuebel, and we stood half an hour on the
shingle, watching the surf roll in, and the small boys ducking under it, and
playing with it. At times the whole shore was froth, and the hulk of the
Trenton stood out black against a sea of foam. In the way of a sea-scape I
never saw anything so remarkable as the effect of some very big waves
striking the Trenton and not only dashing a cloud of spray high over her,
but bursting through her, and spouting masses of foam out of her portholes
on the landward side till she was like an enormous whale spouting foam
from everywhere. Stuebel said the surf was the heaviest since the cyclone,
but we had no storm, and the barometer was higher than usual. Meanwhile
I am becoming utterly apathetic and torpid. I sit in our native house, and
when I cannot force myself to draw or paint, I read the Odyssey and annotate it after Samoan experience. La Farge is again working hard, and is
quite gay, but I am sinfully bored, for I have nothing to do. Do you care to
see how I throw away time? If I were quite sure you would burn these letters I should enclose more of my efforts at painting, but I shudder at the
idea of their continuing to exist. I paint only to give a mechanical occupation to my mind, and the results are as mechanical as the process. You can
see them in this miniature attempt to make a likeness of Faasaei of Fangaloa, from a photograph, which I think I sent you. The likeness is poor
enough, but I did hope for a moment that I had put a certain effect of color
and flesh into it, and that, at a certain distance, it had warmth, until I put
it alongside of La Farge's work, and saw how thin and hard it was. Your
photographs are far more satisfactory, yet this scratchy miniature is a
week's work.

Yesterday a great *talolo,* or costume review, was given at Apia to the new
Chief Justice, but we did not go to it. I was too lazy, and do not care for
Apian crowds or surroundings or for daylight Sivas. I am told that both
Aenga and Faa-uli were there, leading their Savaii contingents, and dancing, but they sent us no notice, and unless they come to see us, we shall not
see them. In the evening, Consul Sewall arrived from Pango-pango, after a
week of discomfort, heat, seasickness and vexation, and total failure to discover his murderer. He has gone over the whole place with a comb, so to
speak, and put everyone through the teeth of it, only to find that no clue
leads to a result. The mystery remains mysterious and more melodramatic
than ever. I am rather glad, for the sake of art. The *mise-en-scène* becomes
the more effective, and the instantaneous disappearance of a strong man, at
a spot within call of several hundred people, on shipboard and ashore,
without trace of struggle or suggestion of cause, is a lovely motive for a
South Sea drama, while the surroundings are among the most beautiful in
all Polynesia. My prosaic mind is now paralysed by the commonplace idea
of sharks; for the astonishing incompetence of the ship's officers in their
original investigation leads me to doubt whether the beautiful Dr Henne-
berger took the trouble to make certain that sharks could not cut heads and
legs off, as well as tear arms from the shoulders; but I struggle against this

suggestion as fatal to my drama, which needs a dusky savage with a cleaver and some strange archaic motive. Luckily the mystery abides, and leaves one free to imagine whatever one prefers. The fact is that the man is dead, and one can comfort oneself with that.

You cannot fill up the background of my existence here without imagining me every evening towards sunset, paddling my canoe far out on the reef, or floating on the long ocean-swell in the harbor, waiting for the sunset, and thinking of you and Martha and all that may or may not be happening at Washington. The contrast is almost laughable between this velvety, oily, half-dead or half-vegetable atmosphere, intellectual and physical, where even the ocean-water is warm to the touch, and even the stormiest sunsets are soft violet in tone, and the heaviest rainy horizons are strong purple over a purple ocean, and your winter in La Fayette Square which comes before my mind as the more real of the two. Do you ever read Rosetti's Blessed Damozel? The world, from where she stood, spun like a fretful midge.[5] From here it does not even seem to spin.

Apia. January 24. The canoe behaves very well with me in it alone, but shows a fiendish temper when I take anyone else; and last Sunday, when I took La Farge out for the first time, it coolly upset us both headfirst into the water. Martha would have been delighted with the fun, for the water was only six inches, or so, deep, and a flock of native children ran out and picked us up. Since then, for elegance and comfort, I have adopted the native lava-lava, with a shirt, as my boating-costume; and the village applauds me every afternoon as I stalk across the green in a flaming red waist-cloth, and legs as bare as a Scotch Highlander's. Out on the reef I am happy, and there I seem to feel the south seas as nowhere else. The longer I stay here the more I begin to understand the grace of the island. A sunset is a set of pictures, varying every instant, but more delicate and coquette than the toilet of the loveliest girl in Parisian outfit. The refinements of tone and tint, the exquisiteness of the flesh-color and blushes, the studied elegance of the lights and shades, the defiance of apparent difficulties, and the laughing superiority to rules which regulate ordinary feminine beauty, are enough to make even a dull lover infatuated. As for an artist, he gets a whole Madrid picture gallery passing before his eyes in an hour, from Cimabue to Titian, and every picture is perfect. The after-glow is the richest and most beautiful of all. In despair of giving even an idea of the refinement that is the soul of the island, I have thrown aside my Kodak and my water-colors, and trust to memory. The photograph is a coarse fraud, and seems to delight only in taking the whole beauty out of the picture. As for my photographs, I could not get them developed here, so I sent my first roll,—a hundred,—down to Sydney, more than two months ago, to be developed, and they have not been returned. I doubt they're ever turning up. Many thanks for your offer to send more films, but I still have several hundred to spare. La Farge has taken the local photographer into his employment, and in that way takes all the studies he wants. He is now working desperately to get ready for our departure on the 29th.

Another murder! Samoan existence is pleasantly diversified. This time it is a Samoan chief, Fatuleia's brother, who disappeared from Manono, the little island where we passed a day on our trip to Savaii. He was supposed to be drowned. This was about Christmas, only a week after the mysterious Pango-pango murder. After he had been missing a month, his mutilated remains, or a part of them, were discovered buried at Molifanua, the co-coanut plantation at the end of the island, only a mile or two from Manono. We stopped to lunch there with the German overseer on our return from our last trip. The plantations are all worked by black men imported under contract from the Solomon islands and other like barbarous regions. Inquiry showed that the Samoan chief had been blown out to sea in his canoe, and at last had got to shore again at Molifanua, where he went to the hut of one of the black laborers whom he knew. He slept a whole day or more, and was ill. Two or three of the black men then told his host that the sick man would die in his house, which could not be permitted, so they were going to kill him, to which the host, after some coy reluctance, seems to have assented. Thereupon the negroes went to the hut, killed the sleeping chief with an axe, chopped him up, and, as is supposed, eat him.

This is worth while. We begin to feel that we are really here. Cannibalism is supposed to exist still in the Marquesas, and is not wholly forgotten in Fiji, but no case of it has been known in Samoa since the memory of man. Nothing troubles a Samoan more than to be chopped up and eaten, and in this case the victim was a chief of a very high family. I should not wonder if the Samoans ended by killing the whole lot of black laborers unless the authorities act energetically, but we are as yet ignorant who is to act, or how. Meanwhile our Pango-pango murderer is free, and no blacks are known to be in Tutuila to suspect. We have our own suspicions, amounting to conviction, but the object of them is neither black nor Samoan, but an American or English half-breed.

January 27. My steamer, the "Richmond," is in sight, Charley says, and will be quickly in the harbor. I must go out to her at once to see about my quarters. Rain is falling in occasional buckets, and the morning is black with clouds. I am really glad to be moving again, but La Farge seems decided to remain another month to carry on his work, and then follow me to Tahiti. Our monthly mail from San Francisco is due, but has not arrived. The outward mail, which takes this letter, closes today or tomorrow, and I must finish and send off this despatch. It is a very dull one, as you have seen, but I can do no better. If you want to follow my course, get Miss Gordon Cummings' book on the South Seas, and look over it, remembering that I see things in a light as nearly as possible opposite to her's, and that, as I see them, her impressions are as flat and dry as my own painting.[6] Now I must start off in the boat, and inspect the "Richmond," make farewell visits, pack up, and arrange my finances. I must also set out farewell presents, and write notes. I hope to get a bundle of letters by the "Richmond," forwarded from Tahiti but luckily your's came direct, and I have had the pleasure of them without distraction from others. I have sent home a case of Samoan stuff, which is consigned to Willy Phillips. In it is a fine mat marked for you. Seumano gave it to me at Christmas, and, as Seumano is a rather famous chief, his mat has a certain interest, and may properly go to you as an heirloom. If you want any of the *tapa,* except La Farge's two big pieces, take it. I do not see how it can be utilised, but I send the things home because they were presents. There are combs, too, and fans and fly-switches.

Goodbye, once more! I wish I could be at home for a day or two—you may imagine how much. In fact, you must imagine pretty nearly everything. Letters are the feeblest of human feeblenesses.

Henry Adams.

MS: MHi
    1. The McKinley Tariff Act, passed by the Republican Congress in October, raised tariffs to an unprecedented level. In the November elections the Democrats gained control of Congress with a greater majority than any they had had since Andrew Jackson's time.
    2. Ending in November, Captain Willie O'Shea's successful divorce suit against Katherine ("Kitty") O'Shea shattered the political career of Charles Stewart Parnell (1846–1891), who had been named as corespondent. Gladstone, the "Grand Old Man," withdrew the support of the Liberals, and Parnell's own Irish Home Rule party deposed him from leadership. When he electioneered in Kilkenny in December to reinstate himself, he was attacked by angry crowds. Escapades of brawling Irishmen are the staple of Charles Lever's novels, as exemplified by *Charles O'Malley* (1840).
    3. François René de Chateaubriand (1768–1848), nicknamed the "Cat." His passionate love for Mme Récamier was transformed in their later years into devoted friendship.
    4. Ships wrecked by the 1889 hurricane.
    5. On the "rampart of God's house," the blessed damozel looks down on "The void . . . where this earth / Spins like a fretful midge"; Dante Gabriel Rossetti (1828–1882), "The Blessed Damozel."
    6. Constance Frederica Gordon Cumming (1837–1924), *A Lady's Cruise in a French Man-of-War* (1882).

To John Hay

Samoa, January 4, 1891

My dear John

Here we are still, lingering in Samoa when we should be in the Marquesas. The weather is very fine, though too hot for effort or energy. We are comfortable enough. The Consulate is at our disposal. The amiable and solemn Ah Su, our cook, or rather Sewall's cook, is obliging. We have servants and a whole village at our orders. Two of the greatest chiefs in Samoa, not to say half a dozen of them, are our devoted friends, ready to carry out all our wishes. The German Consul, Stuebel, is equally friendly. The new Swedish Chief Justice, Cederkranz, has arrived, and thus far has satisfied our hopes. I cannot say that a single thing has gone wrong, but rather everything has turned out more agreeable than we could have expected; yet we have suddenly gone to pieces. La Farge's digestion has broken down, and he has ceased to do anything but lie on the Consulate verandah and doze over newspapers and novels. I have come to the end of my resources, and am desperately bored for want of occupation. Stevenson, whom we have kept for an occasional excitement, came to lunch Sunday, to say that he was about to sail for Sydney to meet his mother, and I suppose he starts today. Lieutenant Parker and his wife, who have been at the Consulate since we arrived, sailed for San Francisco last week. The Consul himself, Sewall, means to go off this week in the "Iroquois" on a trip to Tonga and Fiji. He has invited me to go with him, but I have no energy, and dread unnecessary oceans. Sir John Thurston does not want me till the rainy season is over, and has written me to come then. So La Farge and I are likely to doze here alone, until the 26th when our wretched little steamer will arrive for Tahiti. I do nothing but sit in my native hut, and look out on the ocean. Towards evening I take a native canoe or dug-out, and paddle out to the edge of the reef to enjoy the sunset. I begin to understand why Melville wanted to escape from Typee, and to enjoy the beauties of Lynn,—or was it Salem? He did not passionately yearn for Salem, but he was bored by himself. The true wanderer cannot stop.

I have read through the complete file of the New York Tribune from October 1 to December 14 with interest I never expected to feel in that or any other daily journal; but certainly such a series of astonishing and amusing events has not occurred for twenty years. Why do you start the fun just as I am driven off by the tedium? The elections were startling enough, and Parnell is sufficiently amusing for one geological epoch, but when you throw in a financial convulsion; the earthquake of the Barings; the appearance of Jay Gould as savior of society; the overthrow and suppression of my brother in the same character; and the immediate prospect of silver monometallism, with the wiping-out of indebtedness to follow it,—you pile up your climaxes beyond the demands of art. As in Macbeth, battle and murder are not enough, but you must stuff in the witches too.

I am rather glad not to have the difficult task of meeting the Lodges just now. Cabot has all the self-confidence that politicians should be endowed with, yet the Lord has granted to few men to lead their party into such a defeat as he and Reed have challenged. Some future remarks of my own on John Randolph persistently hang on my lips when Cabot is in my mind; all the more because to some extent I sympathised in the general course of Lodge's and Reed's ideas. If I remember right, you and I, being sceptics and political cynics, looked with little confidence on their struggle to make Congress efficient, though we admitted that, unless Congress could be made efficient, the value of our government was likely to be small. If the elections settled anything, I imagine they settled this.[1] The more efficient you make Congress, the more dangerous you make it, and the more unpopular. The people do not want heroic treatment, and like nothing better than to sit on their blooming heroes. This has been the law of American politics from the beginning—No heroes except soldiers!

To the twin-brethren, Reed and Lodge, I can suggest no consolation. Personally they may recover authority, become senators, cabinet ministers, or what not; but their bottom, as sea-going craft, is knocked out; their ship, as a matter of pilotage, is stranded. I am willing to keep out of the way till they find some raft to drift on, or drown. For this reason I have not written to my sister Anne of late, waiting until the elections should be forgotten, or at least for-spoken. Silence seems harsh, but it is my solitary recipe for the universe. It is the only thing that defies the Arabic motto, and will not pass away.[2]

These words of wisdom are not in the lotos-eating dialect. I have already observed that the lotos, as a diet, is dyspeptic and bilious and bores me; but the dyspepsia is not of the same kind as that of politics. My dyspepsia here is greatly modified by a counter-diet of mangoes. Anyway it is due to the hot-house atmosphere of the tropics, where the slightest physical effort wastes itself in perspiration. Stevenson is the only man whose energy resists the atmosphere, and Stevenson owes it to his want of flesh to perspire with. La Farge usually announces his arrival in one of the happy phrases which are La Farge's exclusive property: "Here comes the *aïku!*" An aïku is a Samoan ghost, spirit, or demon in the Greek sense. The islands swarm with aïku, sometimes friendly, as of dead parents or children; sometimes hostile, as of tempters; occasionally verging on fetishes or symbols like the rainbow, or certain rocks; but at bottom simply uncanny. This is the note of Stevenson, although to us he has been human, not to say genial. He comes to pass half the day with us. He gives us letters to Tahiti and the Marquesas. His talk is lively, agreeable, and almost quiet. Yet in spite of this, he is an aïku, and whenever we catch him unprepared, we feel that he has no real body, but only eyes, hair and bones. His strength or energy is phenomenal; he has done in these seas ten times what would have done me for life; he enjoys hardships that none but an aïku could face, and he is killing his poor wife, who, though another aïku of great promise, is yet unable to keep him from sucking her blood. These are the true reasons why Stevenson is so much superior to us in energy. Perhaps we too may become aïku with time, but I dread it, because I feel that La Farge is the more powerful spirit, and that he and Stevenson together would reduce me to abject servitude. La Farge, like Stevenson, finds strength in weakness, but labors under the delusion that he is weak; while Stevenson knows himself to be strong; a difference that places La Farge at a certain disadvantage, at least in aïku-dom.

Now that the Chief Justice and the New Year have come, and the German frigates have gone, the natives have apparently ceased to fear being relegated to slavery by the Germans, and I hope to escape before they can inflict more of their political imbecilities on me. Excitement in Samoa always seems to come and go with the mail-steamer from San Francisco. For a week we are convulsed by agitation; then the reaction comes, and we are bored. I catch the tide with the rest, and am left even worse stranded. Sewall is getting up a dinner for the Chief Justice, to exceed in splendor any dinner ever given in Samoa. Unfortunately we have neither meats nor game, nor vegetables, nor cooks, nor ice, nor even much choice of fruits, nor a market, nor guests, except our few selves. Sewall is devoting all his energies to it, but except New Zealand mutton, one day killed, and indifferent champagne, I do not know what he can provide. Money for once is powerless. I have offered to help him with any amount of money he can spend, knowing that I am perfectly safe except on the single article of Champagne, and they can't ruin us on that, even if they all get dead drunk. A Samoan feast, where I should have to provide three hundred pigs, would be different, for pigs are held nominally at five dollars a head, and Samoan guests have a touching way of surreptitiously filling baskets with the food provided for themselves, and passing the baskets over the fence, if there is one, to their families and friends outside, until not a pig's-foot or a piece of *taro* remains within; but our guests are foreigners and their families are small or absent. So I look forward with confidence to the great occasion, and trust it may strengthen our just influence in the Pacific. Immersed in this affair of state, Sewall has even laid aside a lovely murder at Pango-pango— Goward's favorite Pango-pango,[3]—where the coxswain of the "Iroquois' " gig was found floating headless, armless, and partially legless, within a hundred yards of the ship. Of course the Captain—one Bishop, commonly known as the reformed drunkard—attributes this *jeu d'esprit* to the natives. My own suspicions point emphatically to the crew, and I opine that Sewall, whose powers of life and death are absolute in these waters, will have the pleasure of hanging two or three sailors, if he is not murdered by them in advance.

Among the other ways in which lassitude affects me is the loss of interest in sketching. Having carried it to a point where real labor comes in, I find the labor oppressive. I can already see that my way of seeing is just the way I do not want to see. Instead of catching a poem by the tail, and feeling that though I lost the poem I caught the poetry, I spread my net with infinite labor, and catch only my own fingers in the mesh. La Farge once in a while, apparently by accident, succeeds in pinning some momentary light or movement, which is quite untrue as statistics, but suggests poetry. His hard work over studied compositions is interesting, but it does not much interest me because I have seen the original subjects, and know how little of them can be put on paper or panel; but now and then he gives me a light or a movement that I could not see, or could not see as he did; and these I envy him. I cannot get expression for the South Seas. Languor that is not languid; voluptuousness that is not voluptuous; a poem without poetry.

January 20. If you can imagine such a conundrum, perhaps you can answer it. Possibly when I get far enough away, so as to be out of sight, I can see it. Just now I feel as though I were badly treated because the Samoans are so blamed amiable and handsome. They've no business to exist unless they mean something, and they wont let me know what they mean. One cannot live permanently on purple mist and *soufflé*. One does not want to be an angel in an earthy Paradise, if one is to live on flavorless spiritual breadfruit and *taro*.

We shall have passed four months here, if we go away next week. Four months is a long time even in London or Paris, when one supposes oneself to be travelling, yet La Farge is only beginning to get into the spirit of work. He has done a good deal, but it has come hard. At last he is going at it with real enjoyment. I hesitate to drag him away, and shall offer to leave him behind to follow me, or go home at his leisure; but I know that if I go, he will go, even if he prefers to stay. He is, in certain ways, feminine. By this time, if anyone knows him I think I must; and certainly I do not know half a dozen persons in the world whom I could have lived with so long and so intimately without their tiring on me. He is one of the most agreeable companions in the world, but the greatest surprise to me is not his *agréments,* but the dependence I have learned to feel on his practical sense. I thought I was the practical partner of this firm, but I know better now. I am only the positive partner; he is everything else. When he has an opinion, it is in ninetynine cases out of a hundred just what I want to find expression for; and the hundredth case is at most only the personal error of the best mathematicians. Even on that, I have learned not to back my own personal error against his. I have never known a surer instinct either about men or things. The only weakness he has, if it be weakness, is the artistic one of instinctive imitativeness. If his next neighbor drinks coffee, he takes coffee. If anyone suggests mangoes, mangoes are his preference. The hypnotic law of suggestion is excessively strong with him; so strong that he has sometimes spoiled careful drawings because, on his showing them to me, I have asked some question about the probable effect of putting in some other light or shade or balance. So about going to Tahiti. I know that if I insist on going, he will go. If I were to insist on staying here, he would be glad to stay, but I have already waited two months, and am really bored to death. I should grow morbid again if I condemned myself to drag on here indefinitely; and—who knows—I might prefer to go home.

You will recognise the extravagance of morbid imagination which could lead to such an idea. Go to Tahiti I must, and yet if you knew the disgust we have for another ocean voyage, you would feel our heroic qualities. Stevenson absolutely loves dirty vessels and suffocating cabins filled with mildew and cockroaches; he has gone off to Sydney chiefly, I think, to get some more sea dirt on, the land-dirt having become monotonous. By the bye, for our eternal souls' sake, don't repeat what I say of the Stevensons, for he has been extremely and voluntarily obliging to us. I have none but the friendliest feelings for him, and would not for the world annoy him by ill-natured remarks; yet he is dirty. On that Samoan soil I feel no fear of contradiction, though some of contact. A man who likes cruising on steamers and copra-schooners in the South Seas, must be able to stand more than becomes a clean man. La Farge and I have no such endurance. The voyage will sicken us for a month. We shall curse Tahiti, and find it a bore, for we have already taken the cream off Polynesia in Samoa. Yet we shall go ahead, as we have gone a dozen times before when we dreaded it, because travellers must travel, or go home.

You should have seen La Farge and me, last Sunday, upset our canoe and go flop into the water. Our bewilderment was the drollest part of the scene. We could not understand what upset us, as one never can. I suppose even wiser men, like Tom Reed and Cabot Lodge, feel much the same astonishment and irritation at the canoe. I hope only that they fell like us, into the ocean where it was but six inches deep, and comfortably warm. Some little girls picked us up, cleared the canoe of water, and started us off again. They laughed at us too. I hope Reed and Lodge may have little girls to laugh at them, and start them off once more.

Sewall has come back from Pango-pango, but without finding his murderer. I want to make an opera of the plot, with Samoan music, ballet and scenery; but I fear it would be *bouffe*. To travesty Polynesia is fatally easy, and the "Iroquois" is absolutely *bouffe* pure and simple as she steams. Ship, officers and captain are out of Offenbach or Gilbert and Sullivan. The whole opera is there, scene, plot, characters, music, dance and all, worth a hundred thousand dollars to Gilbert and Sullivan but I would rather see them drowned than let them have it.[4] So vile is envy.

Give my love to Mrs Hay and the infants, if the infants are not already grown. Some day I expect to get your letters.

Tofà   Henry Adams.

MS: RPB

1. HA had at best an equivocal sympathy with Lodge and Reed. During the summer of 1890 the House passed a Federal Elections bill providing for federal supervision of congressional elections upon request of 500 voters, a "Force Bill" such as HA had opposed since the 1870s. Lodge, as elections committee chairman, managed the bill in the House with help from Speaker Reed, who prevented a stalemate by ruling that a quorum include members present but not voting. In the *History* HA observed that such rules tended to make the House "rather a court of registration than a deliberative body," but conceded "a sufficient cause behind them, even though they led to worse evils" (V, 354).

2. "This too will pass away," a maxim often quoted in nineteenth-century verse, supposedly derived from an Indian tale told by Warren Hastings.

3. Gustavus Goward (d. 1908) was the commissioner sent to Samoa by the State Department to put into effect the Treaty of 1878 by which the United States gained sole rights to establish a naval station at Pago Pago.

4. The collaborators of the comic operas, William Schwenck Gilbert (1836–1911) and Sir Arthur Seymour Sullivan (1842–1900).

To Lucy Baxter

Apia, January 18, 1891.

My dear Miss Baxter

I have little or nothing to tell you this month. My Samoan interests ceased on our return from our voyage round the island when I felt that I had exhausted my energies and had seen enough. Had a steamer offered itself, I should have sailed for the next place, but the steamer comes only at intervals of a month, and I have ten days still to wait. La Farge is unwilling to go, for, like me, he dreads the ocean and is comfortable here; but if comfort were my object I should have stayed at home, and if I were a painter I should probably feel as he does. If we do not take the next steamer, we should wait till April, for March is the cyclone season, and even February is a bad month for weather. We ought to have made the voyage in December at latest. So I intend to go by the next trip of the "Richmond," and miserable I shall be for a week on board that wretched cattle-steamer. At worst I shall leave La Farge here, and go on alone, for although I should be very sorry indeed to lose La Farge, who is as agreeable a companion as ever, yet I might as well bore myself at home as bore myself here, and at this rate I shall pass more years in the South Seas than I have to spare; for I want to pass next winter in Pekin.

Nothing could be more regular or indolent than life here of late. The weather has been fair, with little rain for the season, and never a wholly rainy day. I resolutely lie in bed till eight o'clock, whether awake or not. La Farge and I sleep in a small house with two rooms; a hundred yards behind the Consulate, where Consul Sewall, a young Maine man and Harvard graduate, lives alone, and shares housekeeping with us. At eight o'clock every morning I get up and stroll over to the consular shower-bath. Having dressed, I take my coffee. Then comes the struggle for occupation. I can write a letter, or can study Homer, or can try to draw or paint; but it is hard work. The days are too oppressive for physical exertion. The moist warmth of these tropical seas saturates one in ten minutes of walking. If I could strip like the natives, I could do it, but the mosquitoes and flies would drive me wild. So I sit in my native house, and do whatever I can force myself to do. Such a life, always in the open air, and air as pure as five thousand miles of surrounding ocean can make it, ought to be healthy, and apparently is so. We are thin and well. At one o'clock we have breakfast, or lunch, as you may choose to call it. Then come more hours of difficult occupation till five o'clock, when I get into my native canoe, a rough dug-out, and paddle over the reef, which is a sheet of water, perhaps averaging half-a-mile broad, and, for my purposes, endless. I can go to the left, and turn into Apia harbor where I am in deep water and have the long Pacific swell to ride on; or I can skirt the edge of the reef and watch the surf that tumbles on it, in breakers six feet high, but washes across only in small waves of foam that make the canoe dance, but can do no great harm even if they upset it, for the water at half tide is hardly eighteen inches deep, and at low tide will not even float the canoe. Or I can paddle to the right, as far as the bay of Matafangatele, or as much further as I like, if time is of no account. After sunset I come in, wet, for I wear only shirt and drawers on the water, and rather enjoy wetting in the warm ocean temperature. I have just time to dress, always in white cotton or linen clothes, and then we dine—Sewall, La Farge and I,—at seven, in the open air, on the verandah of the Consulate. After dinner we sit on the verandah, smoke and read. I keep a supply of novels—any rubbish I can get—and look over one every evening. We rarely have an evening when the wind is so strong as to blow out our lamps; the surf is always grinding like a coffee-mill in the distance; and on a moonlit night, the sea is very beautiful, coming within fifty yards of our verandah. Usually the native boys and girls keep up no end of a noise, playing, singing and chattering, on the road which skirts the beach; but a road here is only a grass-path under cocoa-nut palms, for a wheeled vehicle is so rare a thing in Samoa as to be practically wanting. Once or twice I have seen carts coming or going, but only as far as a German cocoa-nut plantation a few miles beyond us. There the mountains come sharp to the shore, and no cart or horse can go further. Our only passers are picturesque natives on foot, or still more picturesque riders, racing half-fed horses along the beach at low tide. In the evening we hear endless laughing and singing, and, if I stroll down the path, I am greeted by scores of semi-visible, garlanded figures, in male or female voices, with "Alofa, Akamu!," which means then, "How are you, Adams"; to which I reply "Alofa," for I know them only to know that they must be villagers of our town, since they all know me.

Such a life seems pleasant enough, especially in comparison with Beacon Street in winter, but a true traveller should be restless, and I am qualified in that particular to be high in the profession. Today is a peaceful Samoan Sunday. The sky has been clear and the sea blue. The thermometer, when I last looked at it, was 86°. The natives are all asleep in their houses. Sewall, La Farge and I have lunched, and after lunch sat an hour, smoking, and watching the blue ocean pile masses of dazzling white surf on the barrier reef. As a Samoan Sunday afternoon, it was quite perfect. It might have been Beverly in July, except for an indefinable softness in sky and sea, not like English summer, but probably due to the same moisture in the air. Now comes a gust of wind and a shower, which I have watched coming for an hour, from the eastward, for showers here come, with the lower wind, from all quarters, while the upper clouds drift steadily from the west. The rain falls briskly, but such showers come and go without our noticing them, except perhaps to drop a blind, or shade, of palm-mat, to keep the rain from blowing in on our paper. La Farge goes on painting. In a moment, the rain is over, and the sea is blue again.

We have had great political events in Samoa since Christmas. Our long-expected Chief Justice has arrived, who, under the guaranty of the three powers parties to the Berlin treaty, is to act as a sort of Lord Protector to the islands. He is a Swede, about thirtyfive years old, and looks like a well-meaning and fairly intelligent man. He has had various big native entertainments which I was too indolent to attend, and we have given him a big dinner, which I had to sit through. I made up my mind to endure, and endured. La Farge also went through it, even more heroically, for at least I had the German Consul, Stuebel, to talk with, who is the only intelligent man—or woman—in Apia, and, as there was no other, La Farge had a hard time. Most of our guests were officers of our war-ship "Iroquois," and did not add to the interest of the occasion. As everyone has been occupied with politics, and as I am particularly daft in my antipathy to politics, the time has been unusually quiet. Even the arrival of the British Consul's wife—Mrs Cusack Smith—from England, did not cause a ripple, for more than one evening, although she is a young woman of some pretensions to feminine charm, as far as I can judge from her appearance and manners. My native girls have all abandoned us, or we them. La Farge and I speculate as to the causes of our indifference. When I try to remember that I did think the old-gold girl a possible emotion in life, I am puzzled to explain why she is not. She is certainly much what I expected her to be, and even a good deal more than I imagined. Physically she is superb. Sometimes she is handsome in face, but always in figure. She is good-natured, affectionate, and companionable. La Farge says that the impassable barrier is cocoanut oil. Yet we wash ourselves every day with cocoanut oil in the form of soap, and are not troubled by it. I am in the dark about it, and vary between the reflection that La Farge and I are both well past fifty years old, and the counter-thought that the girls really can't get near us; cocoanut-oil, language, habits of thought and occupations, are all as far from us as though they were our great aunts four thousand years old. If you will read your Odyssey, and look again at the account of Nausicaa in the sixth book and the following, you will appreciate better what I mean in saying that the daughter of a high Samoan chief is many generations more archaic than Nausicaa. All that the best Samoan *taupo* has, Nausicaa had, and much social and artistic sense beside, such as the Greeks even in Homer's time were already steeped in. I might conceivably have taken a fancy for Nausicaa, as Odysseus clearly did, in spite of Penelope at home, but I cannot manage a *tendresse* for Nausicaa's indefinitely-great-grandmother, oiled or otherwise. Old as she is, she is not enough *grande-dame*.

My painting drags heavily, for I have taken to figure-work, and have tried to paint from photographs to learn drawing. The attempt is not serious, but merely to pass time, and the drawing is mechanical. I force myself to begin, and, once begun, the difficulties absorb my mind and lure me on. The result is of course worthless, and, like my history, seems to me, when finished, precisely what I wanted not to do. I know what I want, and yet invariably accomplish something quite different and absolutely without interest to me. The trouble is not in the technique, but in the mind. Some infernal old ancestor does the actual work, and some other ancestor, who detests the workman, is always taking pleasure in telling him how bad it is.

I don't count at all. Five or ten different ancestors are mixed up inside of me, and they all fight.

January 25. I expect to sail for Tahiti on Thursday, 29th. La Farge is still in doubt. A solitary journey and stay in Tahiti is not wildly to my taste, but adventure is the soul of travel, and if I can stand the *longueurs,* I shall probably enjoy the excitements. Nothing has happened here. I have passed the week chiefly in trying to paint an enlargement of a photograph of a Polynesian woman, with the usual result. La Farge gives me instruction, which at least teaches me why painters do not satisfy me. We just slip up because we don't know how.

Ever truly Yrs   Henry Adams.

MS: MH

Tahitian watercolors painted by Henry Adams in 1891

"From Tati's back porch, looking under the burau tree
seaward"

"The island of Moorea seen from Papeete"

"Papeete Harbor, May 1891"

"Tautira in Tahiti"

"Memorandum from memory of afterglow in the Tautira valley.
From canoe on the reef"

"Attempt at green on green, from our porch at Tautira.
Unfinished"

5.

Tahiti

1891

The four months Henry Adams spent in Tahiti—from February 4 to June 5, 1891—constitute a major episode of his life. Robert Louis Stevenson, who had been "given a name" and adopted in Tahiti, had furnished such glowing descriptions of what to expect that Adams was at first disappointed. He found there a prevailing old-gold decay—no more beauties, no more undress, no more dance or song except for the *himene,* whose very name gave away the missionary effect on the old way of life. Also, contact with European culture had reduced the population catastrophically.

Stevenson had given him an introduction to the old royal family, and presently Adams developed cordial friendship with Tati Salmon and his sister Marau, the deposed queen. He became closest of all with their old mother, Ariitaimai. With her his ethnographic inquisitiveness tapped into a fund of historic memories of which she was the last custodian. In him she found a listener— though she spoke no English—whose romantic interest in "dead aristocracy" turned into a sustained effort to share and preserve her lost world. The love that grew between them testified to Adams' renewed power of sympathy. His restored emotional vigor showed itself also in his anxiety about Marian Adams' monument and his undefined relation with Elizabeth Cameron. Immersed in recapturing a Tahitian past, he did not escape consciousness of his own lost world.

To Elizabeth Cameron

Papeiti, 6 February, 1891.

Tahiti! does the word mean anything to you? To me it has a perfume of its own, made up of utterly inconsequent associations; essence of the South Seas mixed with imaginations of at least forty years ago; Herman Melville and Captain Cook head and heels with the French opera and Pierre Loti.[1] Of course I expected something different from what I find, yet the reality fits in, after a fashion. Here is what I find, or at least here is where I am. A cottage of three or four rooms and a verandah. In front, a little garden twenty feet deep, with flowers and vines. Then a paling; then the road; then the sea, or rather the harbor, with small waves flopping on the beach, twenty yards from me as I write on the verandah; then a broad stretch of blue water until, ten miles away, the horizon ends with the soft outline of the mountains of Moorea, another island, which reminds me of Capri, as the water does of the Bay of Naples. La Farge and I have just finished our first breakfast in our new establishment, and I feel highly pleased because it was quite Parisian. Our new cook is a Frenchman, bearing the name of Peraudot. I pay him fifty dollars a month in Chilian money, or about thirty-five dollars in gold; and if you were only here, you would find my new breakfast-table better than at Washington. In an hour we are to go to see the King. Till then, I shall stay here, with you.

We have been here but two days. Of the voyage, the less said, the better. For six days and a half I lay on the sofa of the upper cabin, or so-called Social Hall, of the little steamer Richmond, dressed in nothing but a Japanese kimono, and reading trashy novels. Night and day I lay there, eating nothing, wretchedly miserable as the steamer butted into the trade-wind, and jumped up and down the never-ending swell. We had the ship to ourselves, and no women were there to restrain my extreme insufficiency of costume, but we were far from happy, and I am still nearly as seasick as I was on board. At last, early one morning we entered the harbor of Papeete, and hauled up close to the shore. Atwater, our former Consul, and young Doty, a Georgetown youth, our actual Consul, came on board to receive us, and I asked to what hotel I had best send our trunks.[2] "Well! there is no hotel in Papeete," the two gentlemen rather awkwardly replied. I was a bit staggered, and asked where then I could go. They suggested that I had better take a cottage.—Could I find one furnished?—"Well! no! probably not. But there were one or two to be had, and I might soon buy or hire furniture." Then and there we stepped on shore and went house-hunting. We shortly learned that there was but one available cottage, and that we must vacate it on the 15th. I wish you could have seen its condition. Fortunately we had no choice, so Doty took us to breakfast, and by miraculous efforts of Awoki we slept in our cottage that night.

So here we are. J'y suis, mais je n'y reste pas.[3] Next week we must put our new cooking-stove and our pots and pans in a whale-boat, and move elsewhere. As we never meant to remain in Papeete, we are not annoyed, but rather pleased, and meanwhile have begun a vigorous social campaign, necessarily short, since society is phenominally small, but still to us formidable. Papeete is the strangest little corner of earth you ever invented to amuse Martha. Here is a native king, Pomare, with no functions whatever except to drink. His divorced Queen is of course a Teva, since the Tevas are the true princes of Tahiti, and equally of course she is a Brander by connection. Please consult Miss Gordon-Cumming's book on these family matters. Then comes the French Governor who is a Martinique negro.[4] I am gratified to learn that some governments are stupider than our own. The French actually send here a full corps of West India negroes to govern a people almost as high-blooded as Greeks. Society now consists, as far as I can learn, of the Branders and their connection. These are four or five sisters, daughters of a deceased London Jew named Salmon, who married the Teva heiress and created a princely house of Salmon.[5] As my letters are likely to be filled with Salmons or Salmonidae, please grapple at the outset with the following consanguinity:

One of Salmon's daughters married King Pomare, and a few years ago got a divorce. She now lives in a house behind the consulate.[6]

Another daughter married Atwater, our Consul, and lives a little way behind the town.

Another daughter married Brander, a Scotchman of good family, and had nine children. Brander died of softening of the brain, and some years later she married another Scotchman named Darsie, and has had three more children. She now lives in the country, two or three miles behind here.[7]

I won't bother you with the other sisters, who can wait. So can the brothers, Taati and Narii Salmon, gentlemen of the first importance here, of whom I shall probably have much to say hereafter.[8] As yet we have called only on the Queen that was; Mrs Darsie, and Mrs Atwater; and found only Mrs Darsie and Mrs Atwater at home. They are both women of a certain age, decidedly Polynesian, rather handsome, with ways and manners that a little suggested Mrs John Hay. We liked them. They talk excellent English, and are familiar with America and Europe.

If there were a Court, these would be it. Pomare's sale of his royal rights to the French, and his pleasant vice of royal drunkenness, have left Tahiti courtless. The nicest royalty was said to be the Princess Moe, wife of Tamatua, another Pomare brother, once king of the neighboring island of Raiotea, but expelled for potting his subjects with a rifle when drunk. You have read of the Princess Moe in the Earl and the Doctor, where "that unutterable cad, Pembroke," according to Stevenson, gave an account of her that exasperated everybody in these regions, and quite broke up poor Moe, who, in consequence, never would visit Europe. Miss Gordon Cumming, too, had much to say of her. Stevenson adored her, and gave us a letter of introduction to her; but our first news on arrival was of Moe's death, which happened a month ago. Her husband Tamatua died before her. So that chapter we found closed.

Now then! Of all the female Salmonidae, Mrs Brander-Darsie and her twelve children are naturally the most pervasive. Everything social in Papeete is Brander. The nine Brander children are now grown. Five of them are handsome young men; and they are chiefly to be found about our Consulate, where we tumbled headlong among them, howling for houses, beds, cooks, laundresses, social instruction and general advice. The howls were very obligingly responded to; and from Doty we learned much of the private history of these youths. It is rather interesting. Their father, Brander, was the great merchant of these seas. His plantations produced cocoa-nuts by the million; his pearl-fisheries sent tons of shell to Europe; his ships carried all the trade of the islands; his income was very great, and his wealth estimated by millions. He sent all his sons to Europe to be educated as royalties, and the boys duly coronetted their handkerchiefs and their Gladstone bags, and bore themselves so as to do credit to their uncle-cousin, the King of Tahiti. They were English subjects, and were Scotch gentlemen, so they went to Universities, and I've no doubt were howling swells, as all bloods-royal should be. Then their father died, and his estate, when settled, shrank to the modest amount of a million dollars. The widow took half, leaving half a million to be divided among nine children equally. The boys who were educated on the scale of a million a piece, were reduced practically to nothing, or just enough for a modest bachelor's establishment in Papeete. Here they are, very gentlemanly young Englishmen, rather such looking men as William Endicott, but handsomer and brighter. They want careers, and they find our Consulate convenient.

Socially speaking, I have now described Papeete. No one else exists here except the occasional French naval officer, who is not specially at home among the Salmonidae. The Martinique governor and his adjuncts are still less favored. Apparently La Farge and I are welcomed, but you can judge of the number of travelers from the fact that literally Papeete has no hotel. Even Apia, small as it is, had more than one tolerable hotel, but Papeete has no accommodation of any kind for travelers. Yet the shops are fairly good—much better than in Apia, and European customs are very long fixed. I get an excellent French cuisinier at European wages, but I cannot get a cottage with a sitting-room. The same queer contradictions run through the whole place. The little town, with its suspicion of French provincial queerness, and its street running under shade-trees along the water-wall, is sweetly pretty. Neat schooners, in twos or threes, are hauled up, stem-and-stern, against the sea-wall. There is no perceptible tide. Occasionally a man walks by. Sometimes he drives a pony in a chaise or a cart. Quiet reigns except when broken by the frigate's regular calls. The air is like that of Naples. In the evening nothing stirs; by ten o'clock the silence is tremendous. There is a little club, and my first act was to sit down on the verandah and play dominoes; it seemed so obviously the correct thing to do; and at other tables half a dozen Frenchmen also played dominoes. To me the atmosphere is more than tinged by a South Sea melancholy, a little sense of hopelessness and premature decay. The natives are not the gay, big, animal creatures of Samoa who sang and danced because their whole natures were overstocked with life; they are still, silent, rather sad in expression, like the Hawaiians, and they are fearfully few in number. I catch myself always wondering what their towns will be like; but their towns, at least hereabouts are thin and uncared for, and their houses seem never to belong where they stand. Even within ten years, life has fast drained away. There is far less sense of activity, less society and less gaiety, than ten years ago. Probably I like it better, but then it is not what I expected. Melancholy in such air and with blues so very ultramarine, has charm, and if La Farge could catch it in color, he would do something uncommon delicate; but behind the melancholy there is disease, and the old Hawaiian horror crops up here to make one sick with disgust. Except in the remoter places, the poor natives are all more or less diseased. They are allowed all the rum they want, and they drink wildly. They are forbidden to dance or to keep any of their old warlike habits. They have no amusements, and they have gens-d'armes.

These are my first impressions of Tahiti, or Taiti as the natives call it. They are very delicately mixed. I hardly know which to call the dominant flavor. This morning Atwater drove us nine miles to Point Venus to look up Admiral Wilkes's coral observations.[9] The early morning drive was lovely; the air fresh and dry; the scenery occasionally very fine. We are glad to get back to crisper air and more daring landscapes than Samoa gave us; and here we feel half way back to the first revelation of Mauna Loa and Mauna Kea. Tahiti is very–very old; seamed and scarred by deep valleys, with mountain ridges sharp as knife-edges, and not forest-covered, like Samoa, but showing great stretches of red earth or jungle-like grass-land. It is bordered by the same broad coral reef as in Samoa, with a broad edge of surf. As in Samoa, the low shores are covered with cocoa nut palms, but the phyloxera has been introduced, and has turned its attention so vigorously to the palms that they are all yellow, diseased and dying. Mango trees grow everywhere, and we are revelling again in their turpentiny lusciousness. You can see from all this that we have found nothing very new or startling to us; only a sort of half-way house between Hawaii and Samoa. Yet the change is pleasant to me, for I was very tired of Samoa, and I can pass the two next months here, which are the months of rain and wind, more agreeably than I could anywhere else. At the same time I astonish myself by looking at the map and seeing how little distance we have apparently come. Thirteen hundred seasick miles, which would have carried us from Boston to Texas, or the Lord knows where, seem to have brought us only a step. By some trick of geography, we are still much nearer to San Francisco than we are to Valparaiso.

On arriving here I found a whole cargo of letters, including two from you, the last at Christmas. They were as grateful as land to the seasick traveler. You must imagine what I cant write, and be sure you imagine it strong as it is. Thanks and thanks for your visit to Rock Creek Church. Formerly, in Hawaii, whenever a new house or temple was built, a human victim had to be killed to be put under its first post. If I could, I should club St Gaudens and Stanford White, and put them under their own structure. Nothing has distressed me like their outrageous disregard of my feelings in this matter. Never spare an architect or artist hereafter. Make their lives intolerable, and have no pity, for they will have none on you.[10] I need not tell you how much I wish I could have been with you at Christmas, or how much I want to see Martha. You can have no doubts on that subject, or, if you have, they must be queer ones. I get no sort of satisfaction from the consciousness that you are much better off to be rid of me. That is an aggravation of my vapours, and I can see no possible ground for contentment in the thought that one's friends are to be congratulated because one is ten thousand miles away. I should really like to know your philosophical views on this abstruse point.

Tuesday, Feb. 12. I forgot to explain that La Farge decided at last to come with me rather than remain at Samoa. He thinks me dreadfully restless, and he is right. I never care to stay three days in the same place. The effort of passing four months in a place like Samoa, absolutely without occupation or resources, was too great, and I am much afraid that Tahiti will be worse. I do not think that, outside of London and Paris, I could find a spot even in Europe where I should want to pass more than three days at a time,—unless you were there. By-the-bye, you have said no more about Europe, and I am almost glad of it, for evidently I cannot get there next summer, however much I might wish it. I had expected to finish the South Seas in six months, and to reach Australia by May; but apparently I shall not get down to Sydney much before autumn. So I hope you will go to Beverly for the summer, and postpone Europe for another year, when I shall move more rapidly. La Farge's painting is now my chief object, and I consent to sit still for months at a time to give him a chance. His society alone enables me to do it. Whenever I lose him, I shall probably find myself intolerably bored by stationary solitude, and shall run over thousands of miles at a jump, like Martha's giants. For next winter I still have Pekin in my eye, but how to get there by November, I cannot explain. If I could only cure my seasickness, I should feel equal to any amount of distance, but the misery of ocean travel is indescribable.

Already we are settled down to indolence in Papeete. So far I have had my letters to write, and as these are rather numerous this month, I have had something to do. When they are finished, I shall be in despair, for I can see no possible resource. I never saw a people that seemed so hopelessly bored as the Tahitians. The foreign residents here avow it with unnecessary energy, and the natives express it in every look and attitude. Rum is the only amusement which civilisation and religion have left them, and they drink–drink–drink, more and more every year, while cultivation declines, the plantations go to ruin, and disease undermines the race. The melancholy of it quite oppresses me, though La Farge, being at last very well, seems unconscious of it. Last Sunday afternoon at five o'clock we strolled up to hear the native band play, in the little square before the unfinished building meant for a royal palace. All the books talk of this band-playing, from Charley Stoddard's to the last newspaper correspondent's letters in the New Zealand Daily Polynesian, if there is one. I expected a gay little crowd with some French vivacity, but I found only a dozen men walking up and down by threes and fours, and about twice as many native or half-caste women in the usual cotton night-gowns, sitting on benches or on the wet ground, and appearing as little amused as myself. A few vehicles were drawn up by the side of the street, and the ex-Queen Marao with her sister Manihini, drove up and down the road in a somewhat dilapidated poney-wagon. I enclose for your benefit a photograph of Marao and her sister. The other sister, in the family group, which I also enclose,—the handsome woman next to the old lady,—is Mrs Atwater. Mrs Brander, the elder sister, is not there. The Atwaters have quarreled with the Branders, and don't speak to them. The fat old lady sitting on the right, is the hereditary chiefess of the Tevas, the grandest dame in Tahiti. She is the widow of Salmon, the London Jew. Behind her stands her eldest son, Taati Salmon, the representative of his mother as chief, and a sort of king in his way, especially since Pomare abdicated. Taati and his mother do not live in Papeete, but at Papara, one of the Teva districts about thirty miles from here, on the west coast. Perhaps you can make out the place on the little map which I enclose. Next week I hope to drive round there with one of the Brander boys, and visit Taati, to whom I bring a letter of introduction from Stevenson. From Papara I propose driving on, across the isthmus of Taravao, as far as the district of Tautira. Perhaps you can make out the name, running along the eastern side of the Peninsula. There Stevenson staid, as the guest of the chiefs Ori and Arié, and was adopted as a brother by Ori, and "given a name," as you can see in the dedication of his new South Sea poem: "The Song of Rahéro."[11] "Giving a name" is a serious matter here, like giving a title of nobility in Europe, only more so, because a real name, or title, is here a fixed thing, and goes with certain lands. In fact, to "give a name" is a regular feudal enfeofment; and Mrs Salmon, as head chiefess, was by no means pleased with Ori for giving Stevenson a serious distinction of the kind. La Farge and I hope to establish ourselves at Tautira for a month or perhaps more, as it is said to be the most beautiful part of the island. We shall take our cook, and send our outfit round by water. When we return, we shall probably cross over to Moorea, another island some ten miles from here. It is not on the map, but you can see its outline on the horizon in the photograph of the coast which I enclose. I also enclose two photographs intended to be joined so as to give a panoramic view into the harbor of Papeete, and up to the mountains behind. Our cottage is in the shadow on the extreme right.

I wonder whether all this writing and photograph-stuff will convey to you any clear idea of our existence. The rest is much what it was in Hawaii and Samoa. Rise at seven; dip in the sea; mangoes and coffee; letters; breakfast at noon, usually in heavy rain; cigar and more writing or guests; walk at five, poking at rocks to geologise, and enjoying the sunset; dinner; a novel; and bed at ten. I have not yet resumed painting or canoeing, and may yet take to riding; but there seems to be only one road for horseback. One cannot go over the open hills. The native band plays twice a week; bad enough but still a diversion. If I could paint, like La Farge, or knew enough to pursue a scientific fad, I should be very happy; as it is, the longueurs are somewhat in excess of my share.

February 13. The "Tropic Bird" sails tomorrow, and should bring you this letter about April 1st. When you answer it, by the May mail, please direct once more to the Consulate at Samoa. By that course your letter will probably reach me here as quickly as by the sailing-vessel, and if I am in Fiji it will reach me quicker. Yet if you could drop just one line to go by the packet for Tahiti, only to say you are all right, I should feel safer. I may then be in the Marquesas, or here, or in Auckland, or in Fiji. I have no idea of my movements.

We are doing nothing industriously. My seasickness is now almost wholly gone; only a trace left in the morning, or when fatigued. My letters, all but this, are finished and mailed. La Farge has settled down to painting, varied by his usual mania for collecting photographs. I call it a mania because with me it has become a phobia; and he is almost afraid of telling me about his photographs because I detest them so much. Not that I blame him; for in my own line of manuscripts I did the same thing, and had to collect ten times what I could ever make useful; but I hate photographs abstractly, because they have given me more ideas perversely and immoveably wrong, than I ever should get by imagination. They are almost as bad as an ordinary book of travels. By the way, if you want to be kind to poor wanderers, mail us your old Centuries, Scribner's, or Harper's, when you are tired of seeing them about; or stuff the Sunday Sun, with Stevenson's letters, into the post-office, or anything that might interest us in the newspapers.[12] We are now beyond such things, and value them. I would tell Dwight to do it, but should enjoy them more if they came from you. I am afraid, too, that Dwight might do it too literally. I was delighted to see that some one was attacking my Vols. V & VI, in the Tribune, not that I wanted to know what he had to say in the way of attack, for I like abuse as little as other men do; but that I felt sure at last that I had one unknown reader.[13] Till then I doubted greatly whether a hundred copies of the book had been sold. I still doubt, but am a little more hopeful. Really I think I do not much care, for I feel that the history is not what I care now to write, or want to say, if I say anything. It belongs to the *me* of 1870; a strangely different being from the *me* of 1890. There are not nine pages in the nine volumes that now express anything of my interests or feelings; unless perhaps some of my disillusionments. So you must not blame me if I feel, or seem to feel, morbid on the subject of the history. I care more for one chapter, or any dozen pages of Esther than for the whole history, including maps and indexes; so much more, indeed, that I would not let anyone read the story for fear the reader should profane it.

Lord, Lord! how egoistic you have made me, and what a responsibility a woman assumes in being a female, as Anne Palmer says! There is no one else in the world to whom I should dream of making such an ass of myself. Now then! Let me pull myself together and close up. We have done nothing of late except eat. Wait!—we did pass an hour calling on Marao, the ex-Queen, and her sister Manini. They are the same type as their sisters Mrs Darsie and Mrs Atwater; talk English well, and have the same Mrs-John-Hay-effect. Darsie has called on us, and this afternoon I may walk out there to call again. The British Consul, Hawes, has also returned our call. I find that I am always pompous and affectedly patronising to British Consuls, who ruffle me in spite of myself, and so I devolve on La Farge the task of coping with them. He has more tact than I, and a much more delicate as well as more effective way of taking the hide off a man without his knowing it. All this Papeete life does not count. We are only resting after our voyage. Our real experience in Taiti will begin only when we start out again, and come in contact with the natives. I have talked much on the subject of pearls and pearl-fishing. Everyone assures me that pearls are fifteen or twenty per cent cheaper in Paris and London than here. I shall try to see what there may be, but generally the traders here send them off as fast as they come in, and never offer them for sale. The fisheries are falling off, and few pearls are now found. Nothing else is produced except cocoanuts and oranges—not even fine mats.

Does Martha remember me? I am almost glad to think that you will soon leave Washington, and that I might as well be here as there, for all that I should see of you or her.

MS: MHi
1. Melville, who visited Tahiti in 1842 after his escape from Taipi, used the island as setting for his romance *Omoo* (1847). Capt. James Cook, whose Pacific explorations took him three times to Tahiti, left extensive accounts in his *Voyages* (1773–1782). Pierre Loti (1850–1923) reworked his Tahiti diary of 1872 in the widely read *Le Mariage de Loti* (1880). Delibes' *Lakmé* (1883), though set in India, is based on *Le Mariage de Loti*.
2. Jacob Lamb Doty, U.S. consul at Tahiti since 1888.
3. When Marshal McMahon, after storming the Malakoff Tower at the Siege of Sevastopol in the Crimean War, was urged to withdraw, he replied: "J'y suis, j'y reste" (Here I am, here I stay).
4. Tahiti became a French colony in 1880; the governor from 1886 to 1893 was Dr. E. Theodore M. Lacascade (1841–1906), former French navy surgeon and colonial official.
5. Alexandre Salmon arrived in Tahiti in 1841. In 1842 he married Princess Arii Oehau, or Ariitaimai (1821–1897), daughter of the chief of the Teva family. They had ten children.
6. Marau Salmon Pomare (1861–1935); King Pomare V (1837–1891).
7. Titua Salmon (1842–1898) married John Brander (1814–1877) in 1858 and George Darsie in 1878.

8. Nariivaihoa (shortened to Narii) Salmon (1856–1906), captain of a small coaster.

9. Adm. Charles Wilkes (1798–1877) led a U.S. scientific expedition to the South Seas 1838–1842 that touched at Tahiti. James Dwight Dana was among the scientific staff that produced 27 volumes of reports.

10. After visiting the MHA memorial site, Elizabeth Cameron wrote: "The work is again delayed. The foundation is there, also great blocks of granite, and two sections of the bench, all more or less enclosed in boxes. They now promise for January . . . but I do not think they can work here at that season" (Dec. 2).

11. Manihinihi was one of the names of Alexandrina ("Chica") Salmon (1866–1919). Ori a Ori (1838–1916) gave the name Teriitera to Stevenson.

12. The New York *Sun* published in its Sunday magazine section, February to December 1891, thirty-four of Stevenson's travel letters, reprinted in part as *In the South Seas* (1896).

13. The first of two article-length letters entitled "A Case of Hereditary Bias," signed by "Housatonic," appeared in the New York *Tribune* Sept. 10. The second, to which HA refers here, appeared Dec. 15. The letters attacked the *History* for hostility toward the Federalists. HA presently began to speculate on the identity of "Housatonic" (see HA to T. F. Dwight, Feb. 10, note 1).

To John Hay

Papeete, 8 February, 1891.

Dear John

Once more be so obliging as to knock three blows with a club on something—say Del's head,—and haul up your portière curtain.[1] Another comedy is about to begin, of which I know neither plot nor plan, but which I shall doubtless have the amusement of reporting in the usual number of acts. The first scene opens on the harbor of Papeete;—pretty stage, and absolutely correct in make-up. A cottage with vine-covered verandah; a shady road crossing the stage; blue harbor beyond, with French man-of-war; hazy mountains on the horizon, after the bay-of-Naples formula. Nothing passes on the road. On the verandah, two men, silent; one sketching; the other writing letters. Sound of surf in the distance. Attitude of expectation.

As yet, this is about all. We arrived last Wednesday morning; this is Sunday afternoon. We have set up our establishment and set down our cooking-stove. Our cook is a French chef. Our cottage is, I suppose, a French cottage; at least it is small, very dirty, and not in the least comfortable, but is rather superior to the other houses of the place. We have been introduced into society, and with the assistance of the youthful Mr Doty, who supports here the honor of our government, we have left cards on various kings, queens, governors and persons of distinction, as required by Pierre Loti and Miss Gordon-Cumming, whose works please consult. Papeete is a veritable stage-ideal, and just large enough, topographically and socially, for a three-act comedy. It might be socially quite a fascinating little capital, but I can give you the best idea of what it actually is, by describing a festivity which we attended last night at the club; a sort of annual meeting, ladies excluded. Our party consisted of Doty, three young

Branders,—Norman, Arthur and Winfred,[2]—and ourselves. Arthur Brander had dined with us; the others joined us. The Branders—remark in passing—are the swells of Tahiti; princes, if you like; about half native; quarter Salmon, or London Jew; and the rest, Scotch gentleman; Brander the father having married one of the Salmon girls, and Salmon the grandfather having married one of three Teva girls, daughters of the greatest chief of the island. The Salmon-Teva family look down on the Pomare family, who, by help of missionary muskets, got the throne; but the two families are all mixed up; the Pomares are usually married to Tevas; Arthur Brander is the present Pomare's adopted son; Norman Brander's wife is a Pomare, and their child is presumably next in succession to the royal title. As the title is all the King has,—the present Pomare having sold out his royal rights to the French for $12,000 a year,—the succession is not a speculative success.

With this party we strolled into the little club, which consists chiefly of a broad verandah, with card-tables and many paper lanterns. A rather noisy crowd was gathered there, chattering chiefly French. The men were dressed as they pleased, mostly in white coats and black trousers, but also in any sort of clothes. A majority were officials, a minority were traders, a few were military, but the navy did not seem to be represented. Of course the mixture of types and classes was startling. Second-rate French and provincials predominated, but we were introduced, right and left, to all conditions of men. Perhaps the two tallest were the native Prince of Bora-Bora,—sweet title for the proposed play,—and a full-blooded negro, a chief from Senegal,—with an under-lip of portentous size,—who is a department clerk. Seated at a card-table in the middle was his majesty, King Pomare, already royally drunk and very noisy. He knew us, for we had duly called on him, and presently he came up and insisted on our drinking Champagne with him. During the ceremony he talked volubly in very broken English, informing us affectionately that he liked the Americans, but that the French were b——, in short, his majesty's epithets are apt to be drawn from sailor's dialect and wont bear strict literary tests. He apologised for his deficiencies, but to do him justice, I think he understood the true force of his meaning. As I was not on the drink, so to speak, I shirked my Champagne, and dodged behind the écarté table, where a dozen people were eagerly betting Chilian dollars on the game. Tired of écarté, and delighted to find that the king had dragged Doty to his card-table, so that I was temporarily safe, I emerged to rejoin La Farge who was discussing Polynesia with a French notary-public. I would have sought solace in the conversation of the Prince of Bora-bora, but the Prince seemed to me deficient in lightness of humor; he made no remarks. Finally La Farge and I sought refuge on a sofa, and with the aid of the Brander youths, in their lucid intervals of écarté, passed half an hour more in increasing sleepiness, until at last we silently vanished away. This morning at ten o'clock, as we were working, Winfred Brander walked in, suavely and affectionately drunk, having kept up the festivities all night.

This is Papeete. The miserable Pomare has wrecked everything. His wife, one of the five Salmon daughters, was obliged to leave him and get a divorce. Society has no head or centre; and Pomare is decidedly a poorer sort of animal than even Kalakaua. The natives, from Pomare downwards, drink for their only amusement, and run after women for their only profession. The French administration is portentously stupid and imbecile. The islands are an expense to the French government, and whatever commerce they have must necessarily profit only San Francisco or Sydney. Year by year Tahiti loses activity and character. The natives become more and more diseased and weak. The society becomes less and less polished. Presently, in twenty or thirty years, the Americans will swoop down, and Tahiti will become another Hawaii, populated by sugar-canes and Japanese laborers.

Well! At least I shall catch the tail of it. In a week or so, we shall leave Papeete, and go to stay among the native chiefs in the remote districts where we shall see a life more like what we saw in Samoa. As for Pierre Loti,—well! Our young friends the Branders find his version of Tahitian society poetic, but do not encourage our hopes of discovering any young woman of the kind he so happily invented. My knowledge of the old-gold girl will be extended here, but I am struck to see that she plays no such role in Tahiti as in Samoa. Neither do the young men speak of beautiful women, either native or half-caste. The dances that in Samoa gave them the chance to show their physical beauty, are here prohibited and lost. I am curious to see whether women count at all here. Certainly the photographers have no portraits to show except of half-castes and low-castes. I have seen most of the Salmon and Brander women, and recognise the type as very Hawaiian rather than Samoan. The distinction is one of greater delicacy and less stamina; more beauty, and less strength. Morally speaking, the Tahitians stand lower than the Samoans; but in matters of the sexes Polynesian morality is a vague phrase anyhow, and I set little by it. What I want to know is whether the Tahitian woman has any standing left her, or any social faculty to amuse a jaded voyager not a Loti. I notice one barrier removed. The Tahitians seem not to use cocoanut oil; or to use it with great discretion. One can shake hands without smelling of it for two days. Perhaps this seems a trivial detail, but to us it is vital. Love's torch does not burn cocoanut-oil crude.

Meanwhile I have your letter of December 12, for which, as for all your honored communications, I am greatly grateful. You can tell King that I am still at work on the South Sea problem, and that my letter to him is growing. If it grows much more, he will never read it, which will excuse me from writing it. The more it grows, the more I adore the naïveté of dear old Darwin who invented such nice explanations of everything he didn't see. How I wish I could ever invent a theory without throwing rocks at its windows afterwards. Two scientific facts take long precedence of all others here. These are the mosquitoes and the mangoes. Darwin did not explain them, and I cannot; but La Farge and I can no longer endure the thought of a mango-less existence, while we burn tons of Brihac and other powder to protect ourselves from the mosquitoes. Perhaps you don't know that the gay skeeter which laughs at 12-inch Gatling dynamite bombs, just keels over and quits at the smell of a little burned insect-powder. So wherever we are, there is the incense, and we are getting to be Josses in the eyes of true Confucians.

By the time this letter reaches you, April will have begun, and another winter will have dropped its tail-feathers and moulted. I have carefully studied the New York Tribune down to Jan. 1st. Apparently excitements were exhausted. The world could not keep up its pace of October and November. You should have told me whether your big book is fairly out.[3] Your flattery of mine is both graceful and gracious, the more so that I have heard of it nothing else except the less appreciative comments of the gentleman—or lady—named Housatonic, in the Tribune. I know not Housatonic, but apparently I have trodden on his—or her—corns. I can only hope—though with little confidence—that Housatonic paid for the volumes he finds so worthless; for then I should know that Scribner had sold one copy at any rate. At present I suffer under the conviction that Scribner is cursing the day I was born. I gave him fair warning, and made him every possible offer of protection; but these publishers are fatuous, and never will learn that the author knows the public best.

Ask Mrs Hay to give a glance now and then into my deserted house, and keep up the spirits of the gentle William and Maggy whom I have so basely deserted. Encourage them to bear the sad burden of my absence. Give my love to my sister Anne and my niece Constance. Thank Mrs Roosevelt for a kind little note I have found here from her. La Farge sends his love, but seems even less disposed than I to recross the dreadful sea. Mrs Hay and the children know my love without a message.

Every faithfully Yrs   Henry Adams.

MS: RPB
 1. Del was the Hays' son, Adelbert Stone Hay.
 2. Aged 26, 27, and 22.
 3. Nicolay and Hay, *Abraham Lincoln, A History* (10 vols.), was published in December 1890.

To Ward Thoron

Papeete, 8 February, 1891.

My dear Thoron

Your letter of November 12 reached me February 4, on my arrival in Tahiti, which will perhaps serve to excuse my want of activity as a correspondent. I had not calculated on so slow a motion; yet I am now sorry for having moved so fast. Had I given three months to Hawaii instead of one;

and three to Samoa, instead of four; I should have done better. I expect to give three months here; perhaps more, if the adjoining groups are to be done. La Farge requires time, and plenty of it, for painting; and, except for being bored, I am indifferent how much time we take.

Thanks for your family news. Your grandfather and grandmother have evidently struck a bonanza in you, and small blame to them if they exploited it. I wish I could also do something, or anything, to give them even a moment's amusement, but our kaleidescope is rather too far off for effect. If your grandfather should pass through New York, he might look in at La Farge's studio, 51 West 10th Street, and look at his sketches, mentioning that I invited him to do so. Perhaps, however, he may still retain a sufficiently strong antipathy to artistic habits of business to make him indifferent to La Farge's work. You must exercise your discretion on the subject. Of course La Farge's sketches are not in the least panoramic or topographical or complete as a record of travel. They are rather a set of more or less rapid and arbitrary impressions of moments, often less worth recording than a crowd of moments left unrecorded; but they strike me as being probably the best work ever done in these regions where artists so seldom come; and some of them are true in a sense much higher than ordinary painting ever reaches. The first artistic pons asinorum that one crosses here is the general theorem that the square of the hypotheneuse is the devil. These skies and seas and mountains are not to be caught by throwing paint on their tails with ever so accurate an aim. The painter is only maddened by their evanescence when he tries to fix them. One might better paint flying birds of Paradise. The best one can do is to surprise a light or a movement and even to do that, one must render it by an equivalent or arrangement which is quite untrue as a reproduction of the actual light, but suggests an emotion like what one feels in seeing it. The peculiarity of the tropics is that every object, even in shadow, is flooded with light, and here the light is not only a flood, but it is also softened into infinitely delicate gradations of tone and color which make the charm of the atmosphere. The light never remains the same for an hour at a time. Even the colors shift incessantly. A coral reef which at ten o'clock is green with the intense lustre that only glass can represent, is deep purple at noon, blue at two o'clock, and may be brown or grey or violet or rose or orange or red before dark. The prevailing tone is probably violet, but I have often disputed with La Farge whether the violet was not really a blue or even a green. All these colors are saturated with light. The clouds, the water, the surf on the barrier reef, the figures standing in the sun, all reflect light so strongly as to change the relations of their color. A native whose skin is strong brown in shadow, is strong red in sunlight. The white of the surf is far stronger than the white of paper, no matter what blue or purple you may put against it. As for the blues and greens, no forcing of color is of the smallest use. All pigment is opaque compared with them, and their gradations are past expression. The attempt to be true to nature, in the sense of matching colors, is more preposterous here than anywhere else, and nowhere is it very feasible.

So much for La Farge's painting. As for my own occupations, I have very little worth telling. We have been in Papeete too short a time to get any occupations. I am writing letters chiefly. La Farge is trying to sketch the harbor. Papeete is a pretty little piece of Opéra Comique, with paste-board cottages of three and four rooms, in small gardens, opening on a practicable road along a well-painted sea-terrace with real salt-water at the bottom of the stage. Though we have been here only three or four days, we know all the society, or at least have left cards on them. Apparently society is satisfied to accept us; but, so far as I can see, Papeete can not do much for us in the way of entertainment; and as we have the only good cook in the town, I suspect that as usual the breakfast-table of H Street will figure in Papeete more frequently than the dinner-table of its neighbors. Our only dining-room is a narrow verandah shaded by a hybiscus and vine. The sea, charmingly colored in French blue, laps the sand twenty yards in front. This is Sunday morning, half past eleven, and I regret that you are unable to stroll in for breakfast at twelve. I would give you a mango as big as your head, and an excellent French déjeuner à trois, with delicious coffee, fair Bordeaux and tolerable cigars. I would take you to walk to hear the native band at five, or out into the country which is singularly pretty, or you should go to call with me on young ladies of the native aristocracy who speak as good or better French and English than ourselves. You cannot come? Bien! some other day then.

A revoir   Henry Adams.

MS: Faith Thoron Knapp

To Theodore F. Dwight

Papeete, 10 February, 1891.

Dear Dwight

On arriving here a week ago, I found a bundle of letters from you, all very satisfactory except in regard to St Gaudens. Your previous letter had prepared me for that disappointment, so that it was less trying than it would otherwise have been. Apparently both St Gaudens and White are afraid to write to me, and perhaps it is best they should not. I should either have to leave their letters unanswered, or express myself in a way that would do no good. White knows already my feelings on the subject, and I think St Gaudens must suspect them, if no more. So I will continue my silence, as far as concerns them, and will wait to see where they are coming out. At times I begin to doubt whether St Gaudens will ever let the work be finished. I half suspect that my refusal to take the responsibility of formally approving it, in the clay, frightened him. Had I cared less about it, I should have gone to see it, as he wished, and should have admired it as much as he liked; but I had many misgivings that I should not be wholly satisfied with his rendering of the idea; and that I might not be able to conceal my disappointment. So I devolved the duty on La Farge, and I know not what qualifications La Farge may have conveyed to St Gaudens' mind. I knew well that I should only injure St Gaudens's work without obtaining my own ideal by suggesting changes, for the artist is usually right in regarding changes, not his own, as blemishes. From the first I told St Gaudens that he should be absolutely free from interference. The result is that after nearly five years I am not certain that his work will ever be delivered, although contract after contract, one more binding than another, has been signed without question or discussion on my part.

I tell you all this that you may be able to explain my situation in case of difficulty. I still trust that by the time this letter arrives, St Gaudens will have delivered the bronze, and Norcross may be able to go on. If not, I suppose some explanation will be voluntarily given. I shall be very sorry indeed to have to demand one; but if May should arrive—a whole year after the contract time—without producing the work, I shall have to call for some serious decision.

I am relieved to hear that Scribner reported, on October 7, a sale of two thousand copies of Vols. I & II, but I cannot quite understand how he made it out, or feel entire confidence in his figures; for the first edition of fifteen hundred copies had not been wholly sold out when I came away in the middle of August, and I can hardly believe that five hundred copies should have been sold in the six weeks of summer when no one buys such books.

The ways of publishers are past finding out, and I have no special interest in the affair except that of wishing to cause Scribner no loss. As you know, I never expected that the book would produce anything for the author, and regarded fifteen hundred copies as the probable limit of sale for the first year. Thus far I have heard nothing to alter my opinion. In the Tribune I stumbled on a diatribe against me by one Housatonic of Washington. I was well enough satisfied with the line of objection taken by Housatonic, who is welcome to his views as far as I understand them; but I felt some curiosity as to the writer. Who is Housatonic? Except Moncure Conway I could think of no one likely to criticise at all, and the letter did not sound like him.[1]

La Farge and I arrived in Papeete on the 4th, after a quiet but very seasick week at sea. Papeete is a spot where quiet runs to extravagance. We have taken a cottage on the harbor; set up a cook, and called on all the nobility and gentry. The task does not consume much time. We are going next week round the island. Our mail by the "Tropic Bird" sails on the 14th. You should get this letter about the 1st of April. I think that your answer had better be addressed to the care of the Consul General at Samoa. If anything important has to be sent you might address two letters, one to Samoa and one here. Wherever I may be in June, when these letters arrive, the Consuls will forward them to me. Samoa is the best distributing place for Fiji, and even for Tahiti the time would perhaps be less than by the schooner.

We are well and carrying out our program by regular stages. I have literally no idea how long we shall remain in these French regions. Alone I should be off by the regular conveyances, for one can do everything here in a few days. As we travel I am as likely to stay three months, or six, as I am to stay so many weeks. There being nothing whatever to do, we are not obliged to hurry in doing it. La Farge paints, and I lounge. The weather is fine like our July; the scenery pretty; the people friendly; the island for the time being belongs to us; and we shall take possession of it by stages. Next week we intend to establish ourselves in the extreme south for a month.

My regards to my brothers and sisters. Tell them I am all right.

Ever Yrs   Henry Adams.

MS: MHi

1. Moncure Daniel Conway (1832–1907), Unitarian minister and second-generation Transcendentalist, wrote lives of Emerson, Carlyle, Thomas Paine, and, in 1888, of Edmund Randolph. "Housatonic" was William Henry Smith (1833–1896), an Ohio newspaperman and historian, general manager of the Associated Press; his identity remained unknown to HA, who later expressed irritation at the anonymity (June 2, 1893).

To Elizabeth Cameron

Papeete, Feb. 23, 1891.

At last we are about to leave Papeete where we shall have staid near three weeks instead of one, as I had expected. The only result of staying the extra time is to make us more glad to go. Papeete is one of those ideal spots which have no fault except that of being insupportable. Stevenson warned us of its character, yet I am not sure but that, at some future day, when the halo of its distance again surrounds it, we may look back on our stay here with wonder that it bored us. The sun and moon leave nothing to desire. The mountains and the sea are fit for all the Gods of a Deological Cyclopaedia. The town is different from anything I ever saw in the long catalogue of towns I have met, and has an expression of lost beatitude quite symbolic of Paradise, apart from its inhabitants. As for the inhabitants, I cannot imagine why I should be worried by them, but I am; and yet they are more amusing than we had a right to expect. My chief trouble is the pervasive half-castitude that permeates everything; a sickly whitey-brown, or dirty-white complexion that suggests weakness, disease, and a combination of the least respectable qualities, both white and red. To be cooped up among two or three thousand such people, in a dirty shanty, with similar so-called cottages within ten feet on either side, makes one forget how exquisitely the morning sun filters through our vines and lights up our breakfast-table, and how blue the sea is, before our gate, to say nothing of the tones of the mountains of Moorea in the distance. Yet even when I forget the half-breeds and the cottages, and go swimming, so to speak, in the blue and purple light, I never lose consciousness of a sort of restless melancholy that will not explain why it should want to haunt a spot that by rights ought to be as gay as a comic opera. If Samoa were not a proof to the contrary, I should think that the fault was mine, but Samoa was never melancholy, though it was sometimes tiresome. Taïti, or at least Papeete is distinctly sad. Towards evening, when the thermometer begins to climb down from 88°, and the heat becomes less oppressive, La Farge and I commonly drive or walk out of town. Sometimes he catches an outline or a figure for a sketch, while I stroll along the shore or round the hills, poking the ground with my umbrella in the vain chance of finding a stone implement, or any sort of object, geological or unexpected, to diversify the charms of undiluted nature. My favorite stroll is back to the saluting battery, which stands on a shoulder of the central mountains, several hundred feet above the town. After Taïtian fashion, the battery is there, with the paraphernalia of a fort, but without other sign of life. I can lie down on the decaying parapet, and watch the sunset without society; and what strikes me more and more, with every visit, is the invariable tone of pathos in the scenery. Upon my word, even the French tricolor looks softly purplish and shockingly out of place. Lovely as it is, it gets on my nerves at last—this eternal charm of middle-aged melancholy. If I could only paint it, or express it in poetry or prose, or do anything with it, or even shake it out of its exasperating repose, the feeling would be a pleasant one, and I should fall in love with the very wrinkles of my venerable and spiritual Taitian grandmother; but when one has nothing else to look at, one rebels at being forever smiled upon by a grandmother whose complexion is absolutely divine, and whose attitude indicates the highest breeding, while she suggests no end of charm of conversation, yet refuses to do anything but smile in a sort of sad way that may mean much or mean nothing. Either she or I come near to being a fool.

One other result our stay at Papeete has had, for it has brought us into rather friendly relations with the Salmonidae, of whom I told you in my last letter. We have dined with the Darsies, who, by the bye, are to sail for San Francisco by the "City of Papeete" which departs on March 15, carrying also our Consul Doty, and this despatch. Taati Salmon, the head, or representative chief of the Tevas, has come here, and proves to be a very pleasant acquaintance. La Farge says he suggests Richardson, our old friend the architect; and he has the effect of bigness and good-nature that was poor Rich's charm. The whole family have the same effect. Not only Tati, but Mrs Darsie, Mrs Atwater, and Marao the ex-Queen, look as large and genial as whales. Tomorrow we start off at seven o'clock in the morning, and drive to Papara, about three hours, to stay with Tati, and pay our respects to his mother, the Chiefess of the Tevas, who, though only sixty-something years old, is regarded as the only person left on the island who belongs to the old times and retains the old royal tradition. We shall stay awhile at Papara and then go on to Tautira, as I warned you in my last letter. Our household goes to Tautira in advance, and carries our cooking-stove, our china and glass, and all our outfit for a month or so. We are to live on oysters, shrimps and bananas, to be served with French sauces and such other additions as M. Peraudot will kindly devise. M. Peraudot has already caused me one sharp attack of dyspepsia, and with such resources he can hardly fail of great success in causing more. At Tautira we shall be formally out of the world. Not even in our journeys round Samoa have we ever been so very far from your blessedness as there; but even Tautira is an industrial and social centre compared with the Marquesas, our coming destiny. Nukaheva is so remote that we seriously doubt our getting there. Nothing short of a fortnight on a schooner, beating against the trade-winds, will carry us to the Typee valley. We doubt whether we can do it, for these voyages seriously impair our health, and we do not want to be nervous dyspeptics for the short rest of life. Even you would give me up if dyspepsia supervened.

Pápara, 26 February. We escaped from Papeete two days ago. At eight o'clock in the morning La Farge and I, leaving Awoki and Peraudot to take charge of our household movement, mounted into a wagon, and were driven off for fresh wanderings. Unlike Samoa, Taïti has a road. The French built it, and it is not bad, at least on this side of the island. If you can stand another dose of geology, you will understand better why the road is good; why the drive was pretty, and why Mr Darwin and Mr Dana are the eyes and lungs and liver of science and geology, for they have made an immortal name by discovering that all this part of the Pacific has sunk, is sinking, and is morally bound to sink, in order to explain how the coral polyp can, at the rate of an inch a year, more or less, keep the eighty coral atolls of the neighboring Paumotu archipelago just flush with the surface of the ocean. This is clear as the sun, isn't it? You see the whole mystery as plain as you see me, sitting here on Tati Salmon's broad porch, at seven o'clock, in the morning, with the velvet-green mountains, streaked by long white threads of waterfalls, looking down on me as though they wanted to know when they are to sink and disappear under water, to leave only a coral atoll above them, as I can certify that they are morally obliged to do, in order to be scientific. Bear me out now, and never let on that I question the truth of the universe. If Darwin and Dana choose to sing this song of McGinty, and insist that Taïti must have sunk to the bottom of the sea,[1] I, who swear by them, have no scruple in adopting and believing their faith;—only the road from Papeete here runs the whole distance along the foot of an old line of sea-cliffs, carved and modelled in charming variety by water-action, and evidently extremely ancient. At the foot of these old sea-cliffs is a strip of flat ground, evidently the old coral reef, sometimes a few yards wide, sometimes half a mile or more, and elevated barely ten feet above the sea-level. Out at sea, sometimes near, but never very far away, is the more modern barrier reef with its surf as usual. So, here as in Samoa, instead of subsiding, the wretched island has certainly—at least on this side—risen ten feet in its last geological movement, after having remained stationary for many ages; and neither above nor below, in the water or out of it, can I see the faintest trace of a sign that anything ever was different; which is the reason why the road is level and good; the scenery charming, and Darwin always right.

At eleven o'clock we arrived at Papara, and were set down at Tati's door. Door is not the right word, for one is not very conscious of doors hereabouts; but Tati's house is an old French affair, and though not very different from a Mexican adobe house, is planned with some regard to exits and entrances. From the first moment, I felt contented—and I assure you, the sensation was both pleasant and unaccustomed, for some months have passed since I have felt disposed to say to the passing moment,—Stay![2] The house stands flat on the sea-shore, and as I shook hands with Tati, and his old mother, and his sister, I caught glimpses of an intense blue sea, through the open doors and windows behind; a sea that came close up to the grass, and had three lines of surf rolling in, through an opening in the reef, and rolling close up till they sent small waves into the entrance of the little river that flows close by the house. We sat down to breakfast on the inner verandah, that looks up to the hills, and we had at last the delight of feeling the cool mountain air again, coming down just to oblige us. Tati is charming as a host, and his resemblance to Richardson is more and more striking. He is intelligent, well-informed, full of interest especially in all matters that concern his tribe and island, and a grand seigneur such as can seldom be seen in these days; for the eight Teva districts of the island have no will but his, and his influence is greater than that of the French government, the Pomares and the church together. Tati is a young man still, thirty-eight years old, and his wife is not here. I never like to ask about wives, in the South Seas, so I have not yet disturbed this part of the family. The present lady of the house, ad interim, is Tati's sister, a young lady lately returned from Hamburg, with health affected by a German climate, and with no small amount both of intelligence and beauty of the Miriam type, which, you remember, I like more than you do.[3] In her, Miriam is stronger than the old mother, who is pure native, and delightful; almost as untouched by Europe as my Samoan matrons were. Old Mrs Salmon will not sit at table with us; she sits on the floor, like a lady, and takes her food when she wants it. When she is inclined to talk, she tells us about pagan Taïti; old songs, superstitions and customs. We know almost all of it, for we have been over the ground in Samoa, and we recognise here the wreck of what was alive there; but here the women wear clothes and no longer dance or swim on the reef. Long ago, each district had its professional beauties who were carried about on *malangas* and matched with the professional beauties of other districts. The great swells made songs for themselves, to be sung when they went out to show their figures by riding their planks on the surf. No more beauties exist. Neither Tati nor any other chief can show me a handsome woman of pure blood. Instead of fifty or sixty thousand natives, five or six thousand are scattered in straggling houses round the island, without social

The Salmon family, Papeete, Tahiti, about 1883.
Left to right: brothers Narii, Ariipaea, Tati; sisters Manihinihi, Marau, Moetia; mother Ariitaimai

Queen Marau
in her youth

Tati Salmon

Ariitaimai

"A Himene at Papara"
February 26, 1891, watercolor by John La Farge. Below
the painting in his handwriting: "Moonlight. In front of Tati
Salmon's—the chief's house. The two children were in front of the
lamp which is apparently obligatory. The man at the left standing
delivered the opening and closing prayer—Tati's mother, the old
chiefess, called Aritamai, or Hinarli, repeated legends and stories
suggested by the songs—memories of ancestors—praises of the
beauties who unveiled themselves at the bath—all now sung by
these quiet sad people in straw hats, gowns and scarfes with an
occasional umbrella—as the woman at the left"

life except in the church. Tati summoned his people to give us a *himene,* all that is left of the old song and dance. The very name—hymn—shows why this fragment has survived. The singing was almost identical with the Samoan, but more finished and elaborate. Some of the songs were old, and some were Teva warsongs; but the life was gone.

Early yesterday morning, our consul Doty, the British Consul Hawes, and two of the Brander boys, dropped on us, having walked by night most of the way from Papeete, twentyfour miles. All went away in the evening, and Tati also, except Winfred Brander who stayed to go with us tomorrow to Tautira, and introduce us to our new hosts, Ori and Arie. These last three days have been charming. Taïti begins to be worth while.

Tautira, March 1. The old chiefess kept us till twelve o'clock of Thursday night telling the legend of a young chief of marvelous power, whose process of selecting a wife involved such difficulties of translation as kept Miss Pree and Master Winny much wider awake than I was. We all lay on mats on the verandah, in the moonlight, while the surf roared softly near by. Only La Farge and I had remained. Tati had gone to Papeete; a place he hates, and calls a nasty hole. Winny Brander stayed to take us to Tautira. We were quite happy so. The old chiefess was fascinating; and her daughter whose nickname is Pree, short for Beretania,—Britain,—has great charm, both of face and manner. I think you would enjoy the manner if not the face, but you will never see her. She is about twentyfour, I believe. At Hamburg, while studying music, she broke down; her lungs were affected, and the doctors ordered her home. She came,—by way of Cape Horn, Valparaiso and Easter Island,—but she saved only her life, not her lungs. She coughs incessantly, and is bored besides. One may survive either of these afflictions, but not both. I tried to photograph the old lady, but I had not the heart to risk spoiling Pree's Syrian beauty by distorting it in my camera.

Friday morning we bade goodbye to Papara. For once I was heartily sorry to leave a place, and would gladly have lingered; but no solid excuse seemed to offer itself, and as both our hostesses were soon to go to Papeete to bid Mrs Darsie goodbye, we felt a little in the way. So off we went, taking Winny Brander with us, and sending our luggage on, in another wagon. The drive this day was enchanting. Certainly Taiti is lovely beyond common words. I seemed almost to feel again the freshness of my first travels, when the sun had not grown so stupid and prosaic as it is now. Of course Taiti is not so grand in scale, or so varied in landscape as Hawaii, but it is exquisitely graceful in outline, and radiant in light and color. I have seen more brilliant blues and greens in Samoa, but never so enchanting a variety of light and shade, or of vegetation. We drove always on the level strip at the foot of old sea-bluffs, but, as we advanced, the vegetation became richer; the orange trees and bread-fruit gave a deeper green to the roadside; the ferns grew thick on the dripping banks, and the sea actually glowed blue through a lace-work of the long pandanus and cocoanut leaves. I wondered what sort of a landscape you were looking at, in your February, and whether you would really enjoy being with us for this one day which has to stand as the traveller's only compensation for months of ennui and discomfort. We stopped for two hours at a very dirty Chinaman's eating-place to lunch. This was on the isthmus of Taravao, as you can see on the map I enclosed in my last letter. There the road crosses from the west to the east side of the island; and from there we entered the peninsula of Taiárapu. Plunging through mountain streams which were luckily low, we rattled along till about five o'clock when we performed what resembled a double-somerset into the river at Tautira. The view here is what you can see in the photograph I mean to enclose; but we struggled through the stream and beyond the valley, half a mile further, till we came to our house in the village of Tautira, looking out over the reef, for all the world exactly like our quarters at Apia. Awoki and Peraudot had everything ready for us. Our host, Ori, Stevenson's friend and brother, beamed on us. We called at once on Arié, the chief, a conventional official, with a round face, who speaks French, and has been to Paris. You can judge of our remoteness by two details. Here we are at the end of the inhabited island; the road stops, and there are no villages beyond. Here, too, we can find no interpreter. Except Arié and the French priest; a Scotchman, deaf as a block, and bearing, if you please, the name of Donald Cameron, boat-maker; and a waif long ago wafted from England, named Parker, who lives on the road to Taravao, no one here speaks or understands a foreign language. Winny Brander stayed a day to start us, but could find no interpreter for us. I sent at once for Donald Cameron, who was an old man at whom I howled wildly orders to make tables and stands. With Ori we try to hold converse by dictionary. Stevenson stayed here two months in the same situation, but we do not willingly put up with deprivations that Stevenson thrives on. In other ways we are better off. The house is comparatively large and has a good big room in the centre, for living in. We can get neither milk nor meat, but Peraudot manages to feed us in one way or another. My only grievance is that they wont let me swim in the sea, for fear of some poisonous fish or coral, I know not what; while the river is full half a mile away. Then, too, as in Apia, one's walking ground is confined by streams that cross the road at short intervals and have no bridges. Still I think I can manage to hold on for some weeks, or even a month, if La Farge wants to paint; and as the natives all wear clothes of some kind, the temptation to paint is less than in Samoa. I will try to paint too, for I find that the occupation absorbs me, miserable as the result must always be. Indeed, if I painted as well or as ill as the best painter alive, I should feel no better satisfied with the result than with my school-boy daubs. Perhaps I should feel less so, for the sense of disappointment would be added to that of incapacity.

Anyway here we are! Taiti offers no more, unless I take to the mountains; and even these would not take time enough to occupy one very long. Perhaps canoeing will prove a resource, though the reef here is not so good for canoeing as at Samoa. You have nearly finished your winter. Congress will rise in three days. I shall have the occupation of wondering where you are, and what you are doing. I suppose no woman can have the heart to object to being made love to, if the offender remains ten thousand miles away. Even Miss Grundy can say very little that is ill-natured on such a theme. I take for granted that the most exacting husband would take it as a good marital joke; and so I will let myself have full swing in that amusement if in no other.

Tautira, March 4. Your letter of Jan. 10–24 arrived here yesterday afternoon, with others. Long as it is, I think I know it by heart already, or at least can repeat everything in it. The general formula that you are an angel has become so monotonous that I hate to bore you with it. Love is more trite, if possible, than angels. I know no new combination of love and angel to offer you, and am reduced to sheer bêtise, which, at a seven thousand mile dilution, is exasperatingly stupid; but you can at least to some degree imagine what sort of emotion I might be likely to feel at having you take me by the hand and carry me on with your daily life till I feel as though I had been with you all the month. This sort of flattery is even more seductive than what you say of myself, for although I suck in, with the delight of a famished castaway, the flattery which you and Hay are alone in feeding me with, I know myself and my work too well to be changed in my estimate of either; but the other sort of flattery raises my love both for myself and for you. To be sure I want to talk over everything with you, and object strenuously to having to listen without comment or reply. When you say that you wish I would come back, I want to break in with observations on that subject which would soon tire you out. Yet what is the use? How can I come back? Matthew Arnold asked what it boots now that Byron bore, with scorn that half concealed his smart, from Europe to the Aetolian shore, the pageant of a bleeding heart.[4] I am not Byron, and bear no pageant, nor, for that matter, a bleeding heart,—any more than he did,— but I wish you would tell me how I can come home and be contented there.

You will say that I am not contented here. True! but I am not in mischief; I am doing no harm to anyone; I am able to bore myself in many innocent ways; and in some slight degree I am even able to be of use to others. Do you really think I should improve matters by going home? Certainly I often wish I were there, and with quite as much energy as is good for me. I have repeatedly offered La Farge to take the next steamer to Auckland, and go straight to Paris to pass the summer. I am ready to go anywhere or do anything, except go to sea in a copra schooner, or pass a month in Berlin. If you think I ought to come home,—I am willing to accept you as judge,—I will agree to come. Can I say more than that?

This is by way of being disputatious, and because Tautira offers little or nothing to write about. We are comfortable enough, but the thermometer is at 88 ° every day, and although the wind tempers the heat, we do not feel much like making physical exertion. Stevenson to the contrary notwithstanding, the people are not specially interesting. I have, since arriving here, passed my time in writing letters so as to have them ready in case, as is possible, we should suddenly be offered passage to the Marquesas in a French war-vessel which is soon to take the Governor on his tour of inspection. We cannot afford to throw away such an opportunity, and we might have only a day or two of notice. So I have not resumed my efforts at painting, though your pleasure in my poor little attempt is a strong motive for doing so. I wish I could give you even a faint idea of the beauty of the coloring in these skies and seas. Every evening La Farge and I stroll to about the point from which the enclosed photograph is taken, and there we wait for the after-glow, which lasts about half an hour, and gives a succession of lights that defy imitation or description. La Farge is trying to suggest them in water-color, and some day you may see what he makes of it; but glass is the only possible medium for such tones, and even glass could not render all. Should you go to New York, you might stop at his studio, and ask to see the sketches he has sent home. They would certainly amuse you, after reading my letters about the same things. Only I fear you would be ashamed of me for venturing to touch a brush when he was near. He has a wonderful faculty for getting light into his color. I study in vain to find out how he does it, though I see all his processes. I mix my colors by dozens, and lay one deep wash over another; but the result is always feeble and timid. He splashes in deep purples on deep greens till the paper is soaked with a shapeless daub, yet the next day, with a few touches it comes out a brilliant mass of color and light. Of course it is not an exact rendering of the actual things he paints, though often it is near enough to surprise me by its faithfulness; but whether exact or not, it always suggests the emotion of the moment.

Our days are quiet beyond anything you ever knew. As the chief Ariié told us at our arrival, nothing ever happens here. The people have but one social amusement. Nearly every evening they sing in a sort of concert which they call a *himene,* and which is in fact a curious survival of the old dance-music such as we knew so well at Samoa, but appropriated as hymn-music for church-purposes. It is pretty and well-done; better than the Samoan, and more developed; but it is monotonous and to me it wants the accompaniment of the dance-movements for which it was made. The dance degenerated here so low that it had to be abolished. La Farge hopes to find means of seeing it, but I cannot believe that the women I see here could possibly dance well, or that the men are well enough trained to make an effective show. The people have lost the habit, as they have lost that of kava-drinking, human sacrifices, and other harmless and simple pagan practices. People who wear clothes can't dance. So they sit on the ground and sing.

You think that the "Earl and Doctor" give a low impression of morality in these parts. The immorality is mostly a foreign importation. Polynesians belonged to a stage of society earlier than modern morals, and when sex was a simpler affair than now. Apparently La Farge and I are hopelessly respectable, for in these immoral communities we have been so absolutely neglected that we might as well have been in our nurseries. No Fayaway has come near us. No Princess has made love to us. Except old Mrs Salmon, the chiefess, no woman has shown a disposition to encourage our attentions. Naturally I am much disgusted, for I expected to be quite besieged by splendid young female savages. They are a fraud.

March 8. The Governor has sent word that perhaps he will take us to the Marquesas in the ship-of-war "Champlain," probably next month. In that case I may miss writing by the next mail. Please address yours to care of our Consul at Samoa, as of old. More and more, Samoa tends to become the distributing centre for the South Pacific. Our island mail goes on the 12th, so I must close up, and send this letter to Papeete, with a bundle of others. By the way, is sister Anne offended? She has never acknowledged my letter, written ages ago. Don't put her up to answering it, for I don't care to split my letters, and give you only half; but if Cabot has forbidden her to communicate with me, I shall feel very pleased and proud.

You will find another water-color enclosed; surely not to show you that I "can do anything I choose"; for the drawing shows plainly, to anyone who ever tried to draw, that I "chose" to do something very much better than I succeeded in doing. It is childish enough, but perhaps for once its childishness is almost what is least *manqué*. It is meant to show the morning light, and is taken from our breakfast-table at Papeete. I should not send it as a drawing; I am not bête to that point; but I tried to make it a literal reproduction of light and color, and it is really so near that my eye calls it correct;—though my eye is not La Farge's. It is meant to show you our Taïti weather; since our arrival, it has been the same, varying only in intensity. Yesterday the thermometer touched 90°. We are so remote from Europeans here, and the mosquitoes are so merciful, that I have reduced my costume to the native scale,—shirt and table-handkerchief. At Apia I wore this undress only in my canoe. Here I can wear it all day, and its only objection is that Stevenson did the same. Apparently we are destined to play seconds to Stevenson. For myself I don't care, and am willing to play second to anyone who goes first,—Stevenson or Goward or even James G. Blaine or Benjamin Harrison,—but it is hard on the immortal Scotchman. If you have read his ballad of Rahero just out, you will see it is dedicated to Ori, and the dedication is rather the prettiest part of it. Ori exchanged names "in the island mode" with Stevenson, giving him the name Teriitera, and Stevenson takes it *au serieux,* as the ballads show. Much was said on the subject, and Stevenson's native name here is always Teriitera. I dreaded a repetition of this baptism, and tried to show total indifference to the native custom; but last evening when we were taking our absynthe before dinner, Ori informed me that I was to take his name, Ori, and then and there, I became—and had to become,—Ori, and he Atamu. La Farge also had to go through the same process. Although Ori is, I think, only a nickname, and probably not an island title like Teriitera, it happens to be the name used by Stevenson in dedicating his poem. I presume that Stevenson—or Teretera—and I, are brothers of the Teva clan, and that his poem bears my name. The situation is just a half-tone too yellow-green. I fear that Stevenson will fail to enjoy the jest, and I am myself not altogether clear about it, for without the express approval of Tati and his mother, I do not care for such adoption. Ori seems intimate with Marau,—Marao,—the divorced Queen, and I wonder a little whether she put him up to it. I have seen Marau less than any of her sisters,—Mrs Darsie, Mrs Atwater and Pree,—though she is really the most interesting; for it was Marao who made, in her divorce suit, an answer that I consider sublime. The King in giving evidence, said that the last child was not his. "None were his!," broke out Marao. For an exchange of insults, I know nothing finer. As for the justice of either charge, that is an insular detail hardly worth attention; but public opinion rather tends to the idea that the oldest daughter of Marao may have been a Pomare, as the King thought; which makes Marao's insult the more murderous. I liked Marau, or what I saw and heard of her; for she seemed a little more Polynesian and possible-savage, than the rest; she had a certain external indifference that might be assumed or occasional. She is, too, with Mrs Atwater, engaged in a fearful family feud with their sister, Mrs Darsie. The depths of this, where I have caught glimpses into it, seem to me grandly black, like old Taïtian mysteries. There is my Polynesian romance all made; and it is not Pierre Loti, *par exemple!* One could make pure Balzac of it, with red-hot Chili pepper added; but the story is too well-known, and the family too respectable to maltreat in such a way; and Pomare is almost too vile for art. Marau writes often to Ori, and perhaps Ori may have consulted her about naming us. If possible, I hope to escape talk about it, for Stevenson's sake. Meanwhile I am quite contented here at Tautira. The retreat is a hermitage, pure and simple; we see no one, and the days are too hot to do anything but write or paint. I try to do both, and find occupation in it. The weather is divine beyond imagination; the scenery, a sort of Paradise for lost souls, the beauty of archangels fallen. Every evening at five I paddle out over the reef and care not if my rippling skiff move swift or slow from cliff to cliff; with dreamful eyes I watch the—flies, according to rhyme,[5] but really the fish, and the strange, positively wierd forms of coral, with patches of color, and sudden sinking, from coral rocks that scrape my canoe, down to dark green depths to a bottom which the sun barely reaches, two or three hundred feet below. I ought to write a canoe-song to native music, but all the native music has the lilt of a quick march—like Kamehameha's march at Hawaii,—and is not fitted for the purple peace of the coral polyp. Even for you, I cannot make the verse or the motive suit the music. The coral will not dance. So I can only watch the sea beneath, and the less rich sky above; and on calm evenings paddle out, from behind the protection of the reef, upon the great bay, where the ocean swell swings me up and down its long sweep of bottomless and endless waves. When the afterglow dies out, at half past six, I come ashore, for my absynthe and my baptism. As for La Farge, he paints,—but oh! how he does paint!

"Farewell! thou art too dear, &c."[6]   H.

MS: MHi

1. In the song "Down Went McGinty," the hero's imprudence ends with him at "the bottom of the sea."
2. Goethe, *Faust;* see March 25, 1890, note 2.
3. Loïs ("Pree") Salmon (1863–1894). HA is saying that she is Jewish in appearance, like Miriam in Hawthorne's *The Marble Faun.*
4. "What helps it now, that Byron bore, / With haughty scorn which mock'd the smart, / Through Europe to the Aetolian shore / The pageant of his bleeding heart?"; "Stanzas from the Grande Chartreuse" (1855).
5. "I heed not, if / My rippling skiff / Float swift or slow from cliff to cliff;— / With dreamful eyes / My spirit lies / Under the walls of Paradise"; T. B. Read, "Drifting."
6. "Farewell! thou art too dear for my possessing"; Shakespeare, Sonnet 87.

To Charles Milnes Gaskell

Tautira. March 1, 1891.

My dear Carlo

My letters are becoming rare. I've not written to you since last June or July. I've had no news from England in all that time, and am likely to have none for as much longer. Indeed, any letter must take at least two months to reach me, and probably a great deal more, for, with each move, I get further and further away. I am now in Taïti, after passing four months in Samoa. Your notion of Taïti, or, as the old travellers called it, Otaheite, may be a trifle mixed between Captain Cook and Pierre Loti; but a terrible old maid from Scotland named Gordon Cumming wrote letters from the South Seas some fourteen years ago which give a certain idea of Taïti; and if you feel interest enough in my whereabouts to want information, you can bore yourself an hour or two over the volume. Or you can take Robert Louis Stevenson's volume of South Sea ballads, which is advertised in the magazines as out, and you will find much about Taiarapu and the Tevas, and perhaps something about Tautira where Stevenson passed two months in the house belonging to his adopted brother Ori, where I am now established, with my companion John La Farge; our French cook Peraudot, and our Japanese boy Awoki. We are out of Europe, in a degree. Tautira is the extreme end of the solar system, and even of Taïti. We are alone among the natives, and helpless to make ourselves understood; but we have lived much among natives for six months past, and we feel rather more at home here than in London, though we have been in this particular village only two days. Our friend Ori will not eat us. On our arrival he brought a black pig with a sucking pig, slung squeaking on a pole; a basket of green co-coanuts, and a bunch of plantains; and, laying them at our feet, he told us that the house and the land, and all that was his, was ours, and that he himself was at our service. He meant it too, and I should not dare offer him a dollar in payment. I must only exchange presents.

We are almost alone in the South Seas. Except Stevenson, whom we met intimately in Samoa, I know of no other traveller within the whole range of the southeast tradewind, from Valparaiso to Auckland. Only a few Europeans, Americans or half-castes, are scattered on islands at least a thousand miles apart. We have naturally been received everywhere with distinction. In Samoa, we were great swells, for the native chiefs there adore the Americans, for saving them, as they think, from the Germans. Here we are in French territory, and the French officials are by no means inclined to affection for Americans, but the natives have views of their own, and the chiefs are as cordial here as in Samoa. We have just come from a visit to the Teriitere Ito-oarai, the hereditary chiefess of the great Teva clan which forms the larger part of the kingdom. She married a London Jew named Salmon, who is long since dead, and she lives at her capital, Pápara, with her eldest son Tati, who talks English and French, and knows his Paris, and is grand seigneur comme le grand Turc, and an uncommon good fellow besides. The old Chiefess talks nothing but Taïtian, and old Taïtian at that. She will sit at none of your vulgar tables, on chairs, but on mats on the ground, like a true princess; and I, who like lying on mats, was glad to sit by her side and ask her about her ancestors and race. The Polynesian chiefs are aristocrats such as one reads about in books; aristocrats with a backing of endless tradition and war. Only one generation separates the old chiefess—who is only sixtyeight—from her pagan temple on the neighboring point, and from human sacrifices to your choice. I was taken to see the remains of the family temple, which were about as extensive as Wenlock Abbey, and I told the old lady that the only unusual part of the visit was the not going as victim. She laughed, but denied that chiefs were ever sacrificed at her temple;—only commoners.

We stayed three days at Papara, and I enjoyed it the more because it came after a stay of three weeks at Papeete, a place which merits the title of hole, though it is pretty as painting. The best of these trading towns in the Pacific are bad enough, but when they have no trade, they are worse, if possible, than at other times. I mean their amusements, not their morals, for they have no morals, and I am not exacting on that point. Of course, everyone knows that the women of Taïti are quite free from ideas of chastity, and have from the earliest times had great charms for the foreigner of the sailor class. For men of our time of life, and tastes, the danger is not terrifying. My morality has as yet been not in the least endangered in the South Seas; not even in Samoa where we were intimate with crowds of girls who were splendid in figure, and wore no clothes but a waist-cloth and garlands. No doubt our fifty-odd years had something to do with our indifference, but even at twenty I think I should have wanted something more or less than the Polynesian women have to give. They are goodnatured, jolly, laughing animals, and there is a sort of companionship in lying on mats in their native cabins, and letting them feed us or dance for us, or look on at our occupations, but we should be fearfully bored by taking them in to live with us. All their habits and ideas are so different from ours that no sort of common life could be devised. The woman would always be in the way, and as the man who lives with a woman must always accept her family too, in this communistic society, he must either become Polynesian, or turn his woman out. Of course, lots of foreigners do still live with native women, either as wives in Samoa, or as mistresses here; but the habit does not smile on me, and I have found no difficulty in keeping absolutely clear of it. At Samoa, marriage is apparently as simple as sleeping. The highest chief in the island would be glad to let his daughter marry a high American *alí*,—chief;—I should have had to make presents, say twenty pounds in gold; the girl would have been delighted to come; unless she got homesick and ran away to her village, as often happens, she would have stayed with me till I went away; and then she would go back to her father, with gifts, and would have been an object of envy to every woman of her district as the wife of a rich American chief. In a few months she would take another husband, and stay with him till he too left her, but she never would lose caste. In Taïti, foreign influence has corrupted the women more, and they are shameless, which is not the case in Samoa. The corruption does not increase their attractiveness to men of our kind; and the Taïtians are now so few in number that fine women of chief's rank are very few. The difference between chiefs and common people is great, and there is always, in spite of the want of morals, a distinct loss of respect for a man who takes up with common women. So, you see, the thing is not so simple as it seems. Very early in my stay at Samoa, Stuebel, the German Consul, a man of really superior character and long experience, warned me that while a gentleman's servant or his cook might have all the women he wanted, the gentleman himself had not half the freedom here that he has in Europe.

So much for the woman question, which seems to affect the imagination of all foreigners so much whenever the South Seas are touched upon. I give you the middle-aged gentleman's view of it. You can get the other *passim* in the books. As far as I am concerned, I can only say that the women have been as kind as possible to me, and have never once made advances or bothered me by offering or asking anything whatever, except presents of the most innocent kind, like handkerchiefs or perfumes. I have lived for weeks in their houses on terms of intimacy such as would be inconceivable in Europe, but I never yet had to snub one.

Of my plans, I can say nothing. I may linger on here indefinitely. I may make a sudden bolt, and turn up in India, in China or even in England, without notice. One is often bored in travelling, and does absurd things from the hope of changing the form of ennui. Whenever La Farge has to return home, I shall probably find the solitude of travel more difficult to bear, and shall move faster. As long as La Farge wants to sketch, I shall hang about and wait. Of course I have little to do. I can write a letter occasionally, or paddle a native canoe over the coral reef, or ask questions through an interpreter about legends and ghosts. As I have no idea of writing a book, I have not the resource of collecting materials. The climate is of course ideal. For six months we have never known such an infliction as a closed house. The days are hot. The thermometer mounts to 88°, but the trade-wind is cooling, and the nights fresh. As far as Paradise consists in landscape and atmosphere, it is here. The entire population keeps me company in doing nothing. The surf pounds industriously day and night on the barrier reef, and the cocoanut leaves rustle in the trade-wind; but with these exceptions nature is as indolent as man. I look out to sea, but never see a sail. I am reduced to reading the Odyssey, and annotating it from my own experience among a similar people.

Should you write me, address to the care of my brother John Q. Adams, 23 Court Street, Boston, Massachusetts. From there, it will be forwarded to me, and in time I shall probably receive it. I am living in the hope that I may find some means of going from here to Fiji, but nothing is more difficult than to get from one place to another on the Pacific. Unless I go to Auckland in midwinter, I can get nowhere. No ships come here; still less steamers. One small steamer of about 700 tons comes monthly from Auckland. A sailing packet comes monthly from San Francisco. Otherwise we are isolated as the stars. As I want to go neither to Auckland nor to San Francisco, but to the Marquesas or Fiji, I am in a mess. Being a very bad sailor, I dread voyages, especially unnecessary ones; and having at least twenty thousand more miles of ocean to cover, I object emphatically to covering twenty-five thousand. A thousand miles in these vessels are worse than three thousand on Atlantic steamers; and even they are intolerable.

I can ask nothing about news, for I am far behind its current. My latest letters were of Christmas. I can only hope that all goes well, and that the cold did not harm you. My kindest regards to all yours. Ever truly

Henry Adams.

MS: MHi

To John Hay

Address Care of U.S. Consul. Samoa.
Tautira. March 2, 1891.

My dear Hay

Of all the Scotch lunatics who have helped to distort and mislead my mind since the reign of Lady Macbeth, I believe Robert Louis Stevenson to be the daftest. The only symptom of sanity I have yet observed in him is that he takes himself for *un homme sérieux;* yet this is, in fact, the wildest effort his grotesque fancy has made. Every hour of the day, since my arrival in Taïti, I have sworn at him, and wished to defile his grave. He gave us an idea of Taïti that Paradise could not satisfy. All the men were Apollos; all the women were, if not chaste, at least in other respects divine. He detested Samoa and the Samoans, but adored Taïti and Taïtians; though, to do him justice, he always excepted Papeete which he recognised as a hole. I have now seen all of Taïti that he ever saw. From Point Venus, at one end, to this district of Tautira at the other, we have scoured the whole inhabited part of the island. We have been here nearly a month. We have seen and talked with everyone of any special interest, and have been treated with the greatest kindness by the natives. The result has been one consecutive disappointment which would have been quite unnecessary had Stevenson been only idiotic.

Compared with Samoa, Taïti offers only a moderate interest, for it is a complete wreck, and if we had not been at Samoa we could not even have put together the fragments of Taïti so as to make them intelligible. In habitable territory, Taïti and Upolo are about equal, but while Upolo seems to swarm with life, Taïti seems a mournful succession of deserted village-sites. The whole native population is hardly nine thousand. When you parcel this number out among old people, middle-aged people, marriageable people, and children, you see how few of each class can exist. Of marriageable girls, for instance, the island contains about twelve hundred. Of these we must have passed among the larger number, and seen a fair share. Yet we are still unable to say what the typical Taïti girl is like. They are all carefully swathed in night-gown dresses which give no suggestion of figure. A large proportion have white blood, or are tainted by foreign disease. Nowhere have we met a full-blooded girl, of chief's rank, to talk with her, or even to know her as such. I worried old Teriitere Ito-oarai,—Mrs Salmon—the hereditary chiefess of the Tevas, and the only real, native, pure-blooded, great lady of the island, to tell me where I could find a beautiful girl or woman, of high, or even of low, rank; but she positively asserted that none existed any longer. For the handsomest unmarried woman we have met was the old lady's daughter Pree, or Beretania; but she is more Jewess than Taïtian, and her charm comes chiefly from Palestine, through old Salmon, her father. I have seen enough of the common women, and of the prostitutes who hang about the streets of Taïti, to be sure that the Taïtian women have been very fine, and that perhaps the type is higher than the Samoan; but I can only piece it together, and, as for the figure, I can only take it for granted. Even here in the remotest district of the island, where we are the guests of the chiefs, and objects of curiosity, not a young woman has shown herself or seems to exist. At Papeete the photographers knew nothing of native beauties, unless you care for rather second-rate women of the streets.

Taïtian native society has gone to pieces like everything else. Foreign influence corrupted the dance till it had to be entirely abolished. Even Tati Salmon, the son and representative of the old chiefess, and not only the most important chief on the island but also the most actively interested in preserving native history and customs, could not show us a dance. The natives, he said, had forgotten all their dances except the indecency, and could no longer perform the movements. The only relic of the dance that remains is the singing, and on this the natives concentrate their social energies. The *himene,*—hymn-singing—has taken the place of the Siva. To us, the *himene* seems a pretty colorless affair, for the women and children sit still in a circle, or on benches, and rattle off song after song, without more variation than if they were in church. Only last night we sat for two hours in the long town-house here, so dark that we could not see distinctly even the front bench of the singers, while they went through no end of songs. Having heard the Samoans so much, we could appreciate in a moment that the same style of singing must have been carried to a much higher point here, for the music and execution are more complicated and better understood, which made us regret the more that the dance was lost. As it is, the *himene* like everything else in Taïti, is a wreck, not quite so awful as in Hawaii, but painful and melancholy enough.

The men are often fine, but not distinguishable to me from Samoans, unless their skins may be a shade darker. For dignity and character no one here compares with Mata-afa or even with Malietoa, or Lauati or Seumano or half a dozen other Samoan chiefs we met.

On all these points Stevenson misled me in a way so wildly wrong that I feel it a moral duty to hold him responsible, especially as I cannot forget him, because we are now occupying the house he had for two months, and, from the walls, the portraits—done in black silhouettes by Mrs Stevenson—of R.L.S. and his wife, mother and step-son Osborne, glare about, impossible to forget or ignore.[1] Had Stevenson known what he was talking about, and had he told us what was the commonplace truth, we should have been saved a succession of disappointments and should have looked only for the things we could honestly enjoy. Taïti is full of charm, but the charm is almost wholly one of sentiment and association. The landscape is lovelier than any well-regulated soaker of Absynthe could require to dream in; but it is the loveliness of an *âme perdue.* In Taïti, the sense of the real always shocks me; but the unreal is divine. I can see nothing here but what is tinged with violet or purple, always faintly or positively melancholy; yet the melancholy glows like sapphires and opals.

Our pleasantest experience was the drive from Papeete here, including a visit of three days at Papara, Tati's place. Tati is a jovial host. La Farge said he recalled Richardson. Tati is quite as big, and has the same large, rolling way, and cheery manner. His sister, Pree, is delicate, and has the beauty of the Jewess with the sympathetic quality of the Polynesian women. Both are quite English, and talk English habitually; but the old lady, their mother, whose names or titles are so many that she herself does not know them all, was far the most interesting member of the household. She is pure Taïti of the old source. I could understand from her what old Queen Pomare was. Evidently she was pleased by our attentions, and developed into a sort of coquetry that reminded me of our Samoan taupo.

Every evening at sunset, the mats were laid on the grass by the sea-shore, where the heavy surf rolled in through an opening in the reef; and when I lay down at her side; she told me to ask questions. So I asked all the questions I could imagine, especially about the women of pagan times, and she talked by the hour, bothering her daughter and grandson terribly because they did not understand her old-fashioned Taïtian words, and scolding them because they did not know their own language. Tired of asking questions, I begged her on our last evening, to tell us legends; and she started in on a sort of fairy story that held on till twelve o'clock. As she crooned along, I would drop off into a doze, and wake up when the translating began.

Nowadays the Pomares are nowhere. They were never a very great connection, and owed the crown to the missionaries; but this wretched King has quite broken up the family, and the death of the Princess Moe, just before our arrival, has taken away the last social prop of the concern. Properly the Tevas should have reigned, but they accepted and supported the Pomares quite loyally, and now the crown is only a name, so that our old chiefess of the Tevas, and her eldest son Tati are the principal people in the island. Our acquaintances are all of this family. The eldest daughter, Mrs Brander that was, Mrs Darsie as is, sails for San Francisco by this mail, with her husband and younger children. Perhaps you may some day meet her somewhere; and if so, please be civil to her for my sake. The second daughter married our Consul, Atwater, and lives in Papeete commonly. The third is Marao, the divorced Queen. A fourth, Mrs Schlöter—or some such name,—lives in Hamburg.[2] A fifth, Pree, we met at Papara. A sixth, Chica, or Cheecky, lives with Marao. Besides these, four Brander children, or even five, are about in Papeete, as old as their younger aunts. With the British and American Consuls, this Teva connection practically makes society.

Here at Tautira we are quite alone in a remote native village. We cannot even find an interpreter to make conversation possible. Ori, Stevenson's adopted brother, a big native and properly the chief here, can speak no word of a foreign language. Arié, the actual chief, speaks French, but is not interesting. We have not yet seen the priest, who is French. With these exceptions, we are shut off from native society; but I think we lose little. The natives here seem to have no great fun in them. There are about six hundred, but they seem shy, at least the young ones, and they leave us much alone. The only attraction of the place is the scenery of the river-valley near by; the house, which is habitable and has five rooms; and the fact that Tautira is not Papeete. We hoped that La Farge could paint here.

On the whole, Taïti seems hardly to have enough interest to detain us long. For my own part I am already satisfied with it; but how are we to get away? I wish I may become a cannibal if I know. Unless we go to Auckland in midwinter, no resource seems left. I am greatly bothered by this difficulty. Being a very bad sailor, I will not rough it in copra schooners, and nothing else sails these seas. What are we to do?

March 4. Your letters of Dec. 30 and Jan. 10–20 arrived yesterday afternoon. I assure you that whatever amusement my poor adventures may have given to you is amply returned by the amusement your letters have given me. That of Dec. 30 I handed to La Farge who enjoyed it as much as I did. I offered to start with him at once for London to meet you in May, but he was cold; yet we are really doing nothing here except that he turns out a clever—very clever water-color every few days. Tautira has one great charm of being as near as possible absolutely devoid of possible occupation. So completely am I stranded that your idea of Polynesian romance has become an *idée fixe;* but I assure you that I am not of that force. A Polynesian novel must be some totally new creation of the human mind. Stevenson has tried poetry in Rahero, and, prose in the Wreckers.[3] I have not seen the Wreckers, but I feel that Rahero does not count for all the labor it must have cost. Yet the motive is good, and the situation strong. I cannot see any serious fault in his narrative. Where then is the failure?

I am not the man to write Polynesian. My methods are all intellectual, analytic and modern. George Sand might have made something out of these islands by treating them *à l'ingénue,* like the Petite Fadette, the Mare au Diable, &c;[4] and Balzac could have worked up a horrible tragedy by his cumulative process of adding black to black in heavy washes of shadow; but I should laboriously fail in any conceivable form of work. Yet to the enfeebled mind, the background is so charming as to haunt one's thoughts. If I could only paint! What fun to paint a beautiful naked figure, standing on her swimming board, with the surf around her, and one of these divine sunsets of rose and violet, in the sky! I hope La Farge will do it.

I have just finished a very long scientific letter to King, which will exasperate him because it says not a word about old-gold. Meanwhile I am losing a tooth every month, and shall certainly be obliged to travel all the rest of my life in order not to return home in a toothless and mumbling idiocy. What business has such as I with old-gold or girls of any color? I only know that the temperature is 88° every day, and that the south-east trade blows here with a gentleness which I wish it would emulate at sea. If there is any old-gold girl in Taïti worth our looking at, why does she not show herself? Am I to rake all Taïti with a comb in order to catch one girl? Not so, my brother. I am but a worthless limb, yet I am excessively lazy.

Ever Yrs   Henry Adams.

MS: MHi
1. Stevenson's mother, Margaret Balfour Stevenson (d. 1897), had cruised the South Pacific with him and his wife in 1888, returning to Scotland in 1889. Lloyd Osbourne (1868–1947) was a writer and his stepfather's collaborator on several books.
2. HA mistook the generation here. "Mrs. Schlöter" was Mrs. Henri Schlubach (1856–1937), the former Margaret Brander, eldest daughter of John Brander and Titua Salmon Brander.
3. *The Wrecker* (1892), a South Seas adventure story written with Lloyd Osbourne.
4. George Sand (1804–1876), *La Mare au diable* (1846), *La Petite Fadette* (1848).

To Clarence King

Taïti, March 3, 1891.

My dear King

You have, no doubt, had from our letters to others a sufficient amount of gossip about us. If not, you can easily get it; and as I am tired of writing about adventures which never happen, and excitements that never occur, I shall write you on subjects calculated to display better my very extensive knowledge of what I don't know. Here goes for a little science,—corals and volcanoes; upheaval and subsidence; but no viscosity, until I come to the old-gold girl, which shall close the book.

You know I brought with me Dana's two recent volumes:—Corals and Volcanoes. At sea I read and reread them. Being a full-blooded Darwinian, I made ready to watch what I should see, with the usual secret thought that perhaps I might see something new, and even convert the Darwin hypothesis into a scientific certainty. That the coral reef marks subsidence was obvious. My great curiosity was to know the amount of subsidence. I hoped even that I might be able to get a shaft sunk on some atoll. After six months' experience, I wonder now that I was so modest. The materials for building great reputations lie here as thick as cocoanuts. I see the means for making half a dozen. If I were twentythree instead of fiftythree, and if great reputation seemed to me any longer worth getting, or likely to teach me music, or painting, or make me a poet or a Polynesian, or anything worth the trouble, I would go seriously to work, and begin by learning some science. As I am only rather bored by tropical islands, coral reefs and extinct volcanoes, and have nothing to do in this do-nothing world of tiresome ocean swell, except to kick the stones at my feet, I mean to inflict my possibilities on you.

Hawaii was great, and grows greater with every new group of islands I see or hear about. I regret that I did not pass at least three months there; but at least I did see the island of Hawaii itself fairly well, and rode or walked over it for a hundred miles. It is stupendous, both in its perfectly original style of beauty and in its scientific interest. I could hardly tell whether I took more delight in the marvelously noble lines of Mauna Loa and Kea, which express such repose and dignity as I never realised before in nature, or whether I took more interest in the conundrum of the force by which a big column of molten stone could be raised through a shaft thirty or forty thousand feet high, and ejected, still fluid, at vents which seem to have no superficial connection. Everything at Hawaii confirmed Darwin. One saw the process of elevation still going on at Kilauea. One recognised that the normal height of volcanic islands might be at least fourteen thousand feet above sea-level, and that the possibilities of subsequent subsidence and erosion were indefinite. At Honolulu the artesian wells proved that subsidence had already taken place to a depth of more than a thousand feet, as shown by coral brought up by the borings. If Oahu had already subsided more than a thousand feet, nothing but a continuance of the movement was needed to reduce Mauna Loa to a coral-atoll.

At the same time, I was bothered by some small details that did not seem to fit into a neat demonstration. The island of Hawaii itself is a compound problem. If Mauna Loa was growing, the mountains at the western end were certainly very much older, and the Waipio valley was a wholly different affair. That such a valley could have been caused by the erosion of fresh water, seemed a preposterous idea. No island of that size contains, or can contain, rivers large enough to dig out valleys a mile wide and several miles deep. In northern latitudes, one jumps at once onto a glacier, and digs out thousands of feet in a jiffy. What a lovely idea that the Waipio valley had been once elevated fifteen or twenty thousand feet into glacial conditions, and had been eroded by ice! Why not? If the Darwinian hypothesis was not good to that extent, to what extent was it good?

In want of ice, one must fall back, to explain the Waipio valley, on the crater theory, or on ocean action, or on both combined. I saw no objection to this, except that it obliged me to accept the more or less recent elevation of the island by ten or twelve or twenty or fifty feet, to account for its present condition. A fresh-water lake ought somehow to be smuggled in as a narcotic. On the whole, I found the Waipio valley less simple than Mauna Loa. Time has that way of mixing things; but anyway subsidence was clearly more complicated than elevation.

This point was further stuck into me by the borings at Honolulu. At first sight nothing was simpler. Subsidence is subsidence. Yet this subsidence was in a wrong and wholly impossible place. If a coral reef of any extent had formed, it must have formed on a gentle incline to seaward. That is to say, the island under water must have had this general incline.

Obviously if Honolulu stands at H with an actual coral reef at present sea-level, any previous coral reef, now subsided to a level a thousand feet below, must be at B, far out at sea, a thousand feet below the water. On the theory of subsidence, borings at Honolulu ought to strike solid lava or bed rock almost immediately. If they strike coral, the coral must have subsided vertically from a point above. Anyway one coral reef ought not to have another coral reef below it, except on an atoll, which is assumed to be over the apex of the mountain or crater. I could not see how such subsidence was possible except by pouring intermediate beds of lava, or mud and tufa, over old coral formations. In that case I must assume subsidence coordinate, or keeping pace with the superficial elevation, and apparently stopping with it; which was not the subsidence I wanted. Such seemed in fact to be the evidence of the borings, and I could not feel certain that the whole of the Honolulu lesson had any application to the law of subsidence in general. It might indicate only local disturbance, and the settling of a honeycombed mud-volcano. Dana agreed that the latest movement was elevation.

Apart from this perplexity I came on to Samoa with a mind calmly confident. If Samoa were a well-regulated island, I ought to find that it had subsided about ten thousand feet, assuming Mauna Loa and Haleakala to be the standard measure of volcanic force. At Samoa volcanic energy ceased within the century by a last eruption on Savaii, and if Upolo and Tutuila are not sinking, coral reefs are frauds. Accordingly I went all round Upolo hunting for proofs of subsidence. I did not find them; but I did find clear evidence that both the ultimate and penultimate movements were elevation, not exceeding twenty or thirty feet. Above that level I could see no trace of sea action or of coral. The whole movement up or down, apart from the lava or mud-flows, seemed limited to a few yards.

Then I took to the coral reef, and studied that. For months I sailed and paddled over that Samoan reef, in and out, until I had actually been over most of it, and the whole extent of the Upolo and Manono reef. The result was nothing. I could easily see that the coral polyp was at work, but I could see no more. I could see only coral living in water, and dying when exposed by a very low tide. At Samoa the tides are about three feet, which keeps the level down. Nothing showed that the limestone rock extended to great depths. Where it had been elevated, as it was in an old sea-beach at Lepà, it seemed only a few feet deep. At the edge of the barrier reef, averaging perhaps a quarter of a mile away, it might—or might not—be deeper. Further out, I do not doubt that the combined effect of land-erosion and coral-building extends downward several hundred feet. In fact, on visiting a small island a mile from the extreme southern end of Upolo, I found it to be a recent mud-volcano with one side open to the ocean. No lava was visible, but the sides of the crater, and the sea-cliffs, were a consolidated sand and debris of shell and lava-blocks, evidently deposited in the sea, for they were stratified. The height of the cliffs might be five hundred feet. I could see no coral beds in it. Such elevations of island-shores are not uncommon. One occurred at Tonga only ten years ago, and was described by Baker, the premier, who is now in America. They show what became of the eroded materials of the main islands, but I could not see proof of subsided coral reefs.

Disappointed at Samoa, I felt that Taïti would recompense me. Of late, geologists have decided that the western Pacific is undergoing elevation. Some of the atolls themselves have been raised till they show two or three terraces of old coral reefs. On the other hand, the Society Islands[1] and the Paumotu Archipelago are a great region of supposed subsidence, and the last remnants of a submerged continent. This was the peculiar property of Darwin and Dana. The extreme age of Taïti was proved by excessive erosion, and this extreme age gives ample field for slow subsidence, necessary to account for the scores of atolls in the Paumotus. Of course, rapid subsidence would destroy the coral-polyp and the theory.

My first glimpse of Taïti, as we passed by the neighboring island of Moorea, was quite exciting. The mountains of Moorea rise in needles, so sharp as to seem perpendicular for at least a thousand feet. As I watched them through the glass, I could not believe that mere rain could give such forms. Bear in mind that Moorea is a small island; a nearly right-angled triangle with sides only ten or twelve miles long. No great rivers can exist there. All erosion must be the work of rain or small streams, and the annual rainfall at Taïti, according to the official Year Book, seldom exceeds one metre. Water gives rounded shapes. How could so small a rainfall, flowing so short a distance, raise needle-like peaks with sheer sides a thousand or two thousand feet high? Once more I said that such forms were ice-forms, and that Moorea must once have been ten thousand feet higher, in a glacial age.

On seeing Taïti, the same impression grew stronger. The mountain-ridges of Taïti are knife-edges of lava, so sharp that you can straddle them. They rise more than seven thousand feet. Read Dana's account of climbing Aorai, and believe, if you can, in his explanation of the erosion that produced it! For my own part, I was dead-bent on ice, and came ashore, as it were, on a cake of it.

That Taïti had subsided, was subsiding and was morally obliged to subside, could not be doubted. Ten thousand feet was the least I could admit, to account for the ice-action, and the number of coral atolls in the Paumotus, five hundred miles away. With that idea firm in my mind, I took my first stroll along the road out of Papeete.

This is what I saw! Towards the sea, the usual coral reef, varying in breadth but certainly not wider than the Samoan. This troubled me, for if Taïti had subsided ten thousand feet, with great slowness and regularity, the coral reef ought surely, at least in some places, to be many miles from shore, as is the case with the Australian reef. I could not off-hand account for this pestilent short-coming.

The next thing I saw, fretted me more than the first. I had not fairly cleared the town when I observed that the road ran along a flat strip of ground, perhaps two feet above sea-level, and of varying width, but always abutting against a hill-side not far away. At this, I swore a great oath. Here was Oahu and Upolo over again;—an elevated coral reef, by the great God Tangaloa! Not a doubt could exist. There it was, as plain as Mount Aorai; and it meant that the last movement here was one of elevation.

Then I said that if this flat terrace was in truth an old reef, the abutting hill-side must be an old sea-cliff. The idea fairly paralysed me, for the hill-side was not a matter of a few feet, but of scores, and I could see in the distance signs that the old sea-bluffs might have been a hundred,—two hundred,—three hundred feet high, even here on the leeward side of the island. That is to say, not only was the last movement, and that an ancient one, a movement of elevation; but, anterior to that, I could see back for thousands on thousands of years, when the sea had remained at one level, eating back into the hills as slowly as the mind could conceive; for the hills were protected by the coral reef on which I walked.

I walked back, a saddened man. The world, instead of giving way beneath me, actually seemed to get up behind and kick me. My ice vanished very much faster than it came. The old sea-cliffs ran behind any ordinary glacial age. I turned to my Dana for comfort, and to my utter astonishment I found that he went back on me, and even admitted that, anterior to my sea-cliff, there was no subsidence. "The valleys," he says (p. 376), "terminate for the most part near the sea-level instead of extending deeply beneath it; as is proved by the fact that the outline of the island is nearly even, instead of being indented with deep bays." This let me out. The game was up. If the erosion never extended below the present sea-level, there can have been no subsidence at all. There is no sign of any elevation beyond a few feet. Then the island must have remained perfectly stationary; which is equivalent also to saying that the bed of the ocean has remained exactly at its present depth since the island has existed.

What say you to this? Sudden subsidence being excluded by the nature or conditions of the problem, and slow subsidence being negatived by the evidence, what remains but to admit absolute equilibrium and permanence? Yet I was not wholly convinced. I had then seen only one side of the island. A week ago I started from Papeete and drove round, still to leeward, till I crossed at the isthmus of Taravao, and came to Tautira, on the windward side. All the way, the road ran on the raised coral reef I first noticed, and the elevation did not change. The official Year Book bears me out: "Tahiti présente sur les bords de la mer, en certain points, surtout à l'ouest et au sud de la grande presqu'île, (where I am now at Tautira), une bande de terre fertile, reposant sur les coraux, dont la largeur, souvent très faible, atteint cependant quelquefois trois kilomètres." The whole population lives on this "bande de terre fertile, reposant sur les coraux." Everywhere it abuts on old cliffs of varying height.

Taïti, then, has not subsided. If so, what becomes of the Paumotu continent and Darwin's theory? I do not need to go to the atolls to answer this question. One can study it much better on the large islands where the lava core is visible, and the coral lies directly against it. If I could bore into an atoll, I would do it; but there is not a boring apparatus nearer than Hawaii. Even if the boring showed a thousand feet of coral, it would prove nothing except for that particular island. The Pacific swarms with paradoxes as numerous as the islands. No general rule will hold, not even Darwin's.

Still I cannot help bothering with the subsidence, for want of other things to think of. The atolls are queer things. I passed one, on which I was told that Beechey struck a ledge or dyke of quartz running straight across it?[2] You can tell me what that means. Not subsidence, I should suppose. Even in the Paumotus there are several coral atolls elevated bodily above water, sea-wall and all. On one, at least, the coral branches are still standing erect, and had to be levelled to make a road. I have heard of no case where an atoll has subsided perceptibly, but there are many instances of evident elevation.

The coral reef, now under my eyes, runs along this shore hardly a quarter of a mile wide. About a mile beyond here, the cliff abuts directly on the water, and there the road ends. The barrier reef still runs outside. Mark the topography. All these volcanic islands, Hawaii, Savaii, Upolo, Taïti, whatever the erosion, still show the original slope at which their lavas flowed. You know that of Mauna Loa. It is extremely gentle, and looks like the segment of an immense circle. The outline of Savaii is much the same, and so is that of the western crater of Upolo. Here, in the peninsula of Taiarapu, the mountains show a similar gentle curve from the centre to the sea. This is a rough suggestion of it:

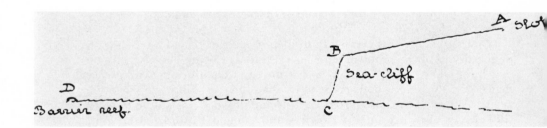

Everywhere the same rule seems to me to hold. Whatever the height of the sea-cliff, B.C., the slope AB, when prolonged, strikes very near the barrier reef at D. Obviously the whole mass of lava or tufa from B to D has been washed away, and is deposited along the shore. Little or none goes far away, except in chemical solution. Yet in spite of the immense erosion at Taïti, both in the mountain valleys and on the sea-coast, the barrier reef at D remains always at or near the original shore-line indicated by extending the slope AB. That is to say, the coral polyp seems to have worked only on the ground eroded by the waves. If my observation is correct, you can see that its consequences are alarming. In fact, it restricts the polyp within a very narrow field of usefulness. This is not all. The sea-cliff AB seems to be here at least three hundred feet high. I cannot say what is the extreme height to which sea-erosion has reached, but obviously every island not exceeding three hundred feet high, and half a mile in diameter must have been washed away,—not *"may"* but *"must,"* since that is the amount of necessary erosion shown by this coast. God knows how many such islands existed in the Paumotus; but be the number large or small, every such island would become an atoll as readily in that way as by subsidence from the bottom. The lagoon in the centre need not be due to subsidence, and in fact has never been attributed to it. Some islands must, on the mere doctrine of chances, have been washed away, and these certainly are now atolls, for no other low islands exist. If every atoll only half a mile wide represents an eroded island, we dispose of a certain number, and perhaps of more than we think.

Add to this that every summit that came within a hundred and fifty feet of the surface would be built on by the polyp; and you account for a number more, without requiring subsidence.

Yet the occurrence of scores of atolls in archipelagoes implies something more. If I am forced to abandon subsidence except as an exception not more frequent than upheaval,—which is rare and not great in amount,—I must have some excuse for so many islands, all near the same level. This is a matter for physicists. For my own part, if you tell me that the dynamic energy of the central machine which supplies these deep-sea volcanoes, is or tends to be equivalent to raising the liquid column just about to sea-level, I should accept the statement as readily as any other theory; leaving you to account for exceptions like Hawaii. Much as I detest mathematics and mathematical methods, I do not think I should have much trouble to prove that a column of liquid lava, rising from the bottom of an ocean, would enormously increase in pressure as it approached the surface, and in still more rapid ratio as it emerged into the air. The mathematical consequence must be a greater proportion of volcanic islands nearby flush with the sea-level. My only reason for doubting this conclusion is its apparent mathematical certainty. Another curious incident, which is less mathematical and therefore in my eyes more reasonable, is the tendency of the high and low islands to arrange themselves in groups. The Paumotus are eighty in number, and all low.

As I must compress into a letter a subject which requires a volume, I omit a lot of details that properly belong to it, and illustrate if they do not prove the character of these volcanic islands. The sum of the whole is simple. I do not mean to deny that the subsidence theory may be correct. All I say is that as yet I have been unable to see a single piece of evidence to prove it. The theory is nothing but theory. Taïti, which ought to prove it, proves the contrary as far as its evidence goes. As for the idea that this region of the Pacific was ever a continent, I can see nothing to support it. Neither the fauna nor the flora shows evidence of such diversity or completeness as should mark continental evolution. Nowhere can one find the sedimentary rocks or strata that should be found on a continent. One island alone—Rapa—is said to contain a seam of coal, but even that hardly proves a continent, and Rapa is a solitary island, some seven hundred miles to the southward, with a very deep ocean intervening. The high islands— the Sandwich, Samoan and Taïtian, for example,—have all the same insular characteristics; they are all built up in the same way; and they all tend to prove the perfect stability of the ocean bed at its actual level, for many thousands of years.

So I have been obliged to surrender my dear Darwin and my own Dana, very unwillingly too, for their view was much more entertaining than mine. I do not love uniformity to the extent of abandoning diversity and accepting a mathematical world in the midst of Polynesian mysteries. I came here with very different thoughts, and find loss of interest with every fresh concession.

This letter has grown so long that I can't make it decently longer, and yet the whole subject of the Polynesian people remains untouched. I must make another letter of it some day. The subject is too big for a single sheet. The old-gold girl alone needs more dressing than that. Besides, I want, if possible, to visit the Paumotus and the Marquesas before closing the anthropological chapter. So I will shut up. In another month or two, I will start fresh.

My letters tell me of your sister's marriage.[3] I am sorry not to have been at home to offer my congratulations and services. They also speak of George at Washington.[4] Hay says that you are going to Newport, and he to England. I would meet him there if there were not so much ocean between; and in spite of your Halcyonic promises, I find the Pacific a very seasick and weary waste. When one is obliged to go a thousand miles to windward in small vessels, one's liver becomes a fiend. The long swell then becomes a short one; the trade-wind becomes a half-gale, and instead of a "dark-blue sky vaulted o'er a dark-blue sea,"—a line which proves how little Tennyson can have known of the sea,[5]—one has a tiresome light-grey sky, diversified by rain-clouds and showers. The extreme rarity of communication between these distant groups of islands adds to the labor of the deep-blue ocean. I would I were a flying-fish or a shark.

Things seem to have run along at home in a wobbly kind of way, uncomfortable enough but apparently not particularly concerning me. If nothing happens to my health, I shall probably get through the Pacific this summer, and begin on Asia. Except that I am losing all my teeth, and every new voyage costs me a month of sea-sickness and subsequent dyspepsia, I am all right, and so is La Farge. We have really seen a good deal, and I hope that the journey, even from an artistic point of view, has been worth his while. Whenever he returns home, I shall be in a bad way. Probably Hay has told you about our relations with Stevenson. I am curious to see his letters in the Sun. I never met a man with less judgment, and on a venture I would damn in advance any opinion he should express, but he is excessively intelligent, amusing, and, to us, friendly, not to say more. Don't abuse him.

Iorana,[6] for the present.   Henry Adams.

MS: MHi

1. The island group which includes Tahiti was named for the Royal Society, sponsor of Cook's expedition.

2. Frederick William Beechey (1796–1856), English rear admiral and geographer. His *Narrative of a Voyage to the Pacific and Bering Straits* (1831) contains a section on Tahiti, but makes no mention of a dike of quartz.

3. King's half-sister, Marian Howland, had married Clarence Page Townsley, an army officer, on Jan. 7.

4. George Snowden Howland (1865–1928), King's half-brother, an art student in Paris. Mrs. Cameron reported that he had turned up in Washington and was "very good looking" (Elizabeth Cameron to HA, Jan. 1, 1891).

5. "The Lotos-Eaters."

6. *Iorana:* Tahitian for "goodbye."

To Lucy Baxter

Dear Miss Baxter

Your letter of January 4 arrived here yesterday. Your informant at the Post Office must have been a particularly imbecile official. The Taïti mail always leaves San Francisco on the first day of every month. I am greatly bothered to know what address to give next. Your reply to this letter cannot be written till May, and could not reach here, by the sailing-packet, before July. I ought then to be in Fiji; but you had better direct once more to the Consulate at Samoa. Probably it will go quicker if forwarded to me from there.

Your account of yourself and of Boston and the family is very important for me, as I have no other correspondent except Dwight to tell me of such matters. Charles used to be my source of information, but after he became an over-worked man, we ceased corresponding, and have not resumed it. The truth is, I am not fond of family lectures, and prefer to take mine diluted. Having fairly made up my mind that the world is much too complicated a machine for me to run it, I object to its running me. So I depend on your letters rather than on family disquisitions.

We are now quietly waiting for something to turn up. Having got to Taïti, the next step is to get away from it. Taïti itself offers little of human interest; it is lovely and comfortable enough, but easily exhausted. Pretty much the whole population is on the western side, and we have passed through it in driving from Papeete to this point. The French have made a road, which was not a difficult task, but they have pretty much destroyed the people and obliterated all that was remarkable in them. Originally they were probably a finer race than the Samoans, but at present they are to me far less interesting and hardly more than one fourth as numerous.

The drive from Papeete to this point was exquisitely beautiful; always close to the sea, and for the last twenty miles running through rich vegetation, where the cocoanut palm was less conspicuous, and where the orange grew wild in forests. As for the ferns, they were forests too. I have never seen a drive more enchanting, though of course I have seen many where the scenery was grander. The mountains of the island lie in the centre. No one lives there and there are no roads. Within a mile or two of the coast, the valleys narrow into gorges and the paths become climbs. The natives go up to get plantains which grow wild there in great quantities; but I am not tempted to penetrate such a region, which is wonderfully cut up in gorges, but somehow is still monotonous for want of an occasional monotony. Here at Tautira is a prettier Apia. The same coral reef and purple ocean; the same cocoanut strip of raised coral beach, backed by swamp; the same big bay round the same corner, but without town or shipping; the same mountains behind, only more beautiful. Last evening I paddled out for the first time over the coral reef. The same little blue fishes, and striped ones, were playing among the same purple corals. Yet there were differences. The corals looked bigger and older, and grew in crowds of large mushrooms of stone at the bottom, or in round masses which came so near the surface that my canoe touched on them. The afterglow in the sky was richer in tone, and the western light rose up into a hazy blush over the sky above me. A turtle stuck his head up to look at me. The mountains of the main island rose in more aristocratic outlines than those of Samoa.

Aristocracy was and is the mark of Taïti. Dead aristocracy is always romantic, and so is Taïti; but it is still dead. We stopped for three days at Papara, on our way here, to stay with Tati Salmon, the most considerable chief in the island, and with his old mother, hereditary chiefess of the Teva clan. The old mother is a pure native, and delighted me, but she married a London Jew named Salmon, and Tati is half English. The mixture is not a bad one. Tati is a first-rate fellow, thirty-eight years old, big as a good-sized hill, and very intelligent; good-natured, active and respectable; as different from the miserable animal Pomare, his ex-brother-in-law, as possible. Tati ought to be King or Governor, but is too shrewd to want such honors, and duties. He is powerful enough as he is. Yet, much as I enjoyed my visit, and liked him, I felt that the old Taïti was in the mother, not in the son, and that I might as well go and stay with the Duke of Argyll as with Tati Salmon, as far as the old Polynesia was concerned.

Are we, or are we not, going to the Marquesas? I wish I knew, though I dread more ocean. If we do, we shall have old Polynesia crude. We are waiting for a vessel.

Ever Yrs   Henry Adams.

MS: MH

To Elizabeth Cameron

Tautira. Sunday, March 16, '91.

A week ago today we made up a large bundle of letters, and a box of La Farge's water-colors. As the "City of Papeete" was to sail for San Francisco on the 12th, we made Ori hunt up a wagon for us, and at two o'clock on Sunday afternoon we started for Taravao, to hand our letters and box to the gens d'arme or resident or mailagent or Chinaman or whoever might be the proper person. Our first adventure was one which occurs here with much regularity. In plunging into the river, at its deepest part, which is luckily only a hole of about three feet just now, the horses balked, and left us planted. To get us out of the water, and up the opposite bank, was a matter of half an hour, for the horses had to be taken out and La Farge and I had to be taken out too; and then the wagon had to be hauled out by hand. After this delay we rattled along over green grass and under foliage of Paradise, and through small streams that set traps for us in the road, until our harness broke and we nearly upset. Another half hour started us off again over more grass, under more huge wild-orangetrees, breadfruits, cocoanuts, mangoes, and wonderful big-leaved, glossy trees that look like the magnolia grandiflora run mad; and all the way the blue sea—theatrically blue and arranged in harmonies—gave little love-slaps on the sand a few yards away, where the trees leaned over the water to keep it cool. Two hours of this jaunt brought us to the Chinaman's at Taravao, where we found the *gen d'arme,* and the *résident,* and the mailagent, sitting under the palm-leaf shed or rain-shelter, playing dominoes—of course—, and drinking vermouth. After all, we are not so far from the Bois de Vincennes and the Barrière de—Taïti; coelum non dominum, or dominos;[1] we too sat down and shared the vermouth, while La Farge in his very best French explained our object. Then we drove back to Tautira successfully; and after a week we learn that our last Sunday's effort was perfectly unnecessary; that the "City of Papeete" has not yet sailed, and that our drive was the only advantage of our otherwise wasted energy. I sit down now to tell you this, because I have nothing else to tell.

I am bored—oh great Taaroa, known in Samoa as Tangaloa, how I am bored! Never have I known what it was to be so bored before, even in the worst wilds of Beacon Street or at the dreariest dinner-tables of Belgravia. My mind has given way. I have horrors. No human being ever saw life more lovely than here, and I actually sit, hour after hour, doing nothing but look out at the sky and sea, because it is exquisitely lovely and makes me so desperately homesick; and I cannot understand either why it is so beautiful or why it makes me so frantic to escape. We have seen not a human being except villagers whom we cannot talk with. In desperation at sitting still, I try to paint, and the painting seems more futile than the sitting-still. We have read all the books in Taïti, and as for me I am so tired of reading about the virtues and vices of the Taïtians that I wish I could see some. As for the Taïtians that have come within my acquaintance, except when they happened to be Jews, they have been the most commonplace, dreary, spiritless people I have yet seen. If they have amusements or pleasures, they conceal them. Neither dance nor game have I seen or heard of; nor surf-swimming nor ball-playing or anything but the stupid mechanical *himene.* They do not even move with spirit. If I were not afraid of extravagance I should say that they were more melancholy than Hawaiians.

As the devil will always have it, the governor sent word that neither of the French war-vessels could go to the Marquesas, at the very moment when I was becoming eager to go. As I am honestly too miserable at sea to risk a month in a small schooner, I saw myself obliged to abandon the Marquesas at the same time when I realised the true inwardness of Taïti. Add to these causes of seriousness that our cook Peraudot broke down with headache, and went back to Papeete, and that La Farge and I were reduced by some mysterious article of diet to the decided opinion that life was not worth living when it depended on the liver. On the whole, the past week on this crumpety-tree has been far from gay to this pair of kwangle-wangle-kwee. As the poet truly said, very few people come this way.[2]

My only comfort is that somehow we have already passed more than a fortnight in this solitary little hiding-place! If a fortnight can slip away, a month can go. We shall some day escape, and then Taïti will seem a Paradise. After all, one sees so many beautiful women and beautiful islands that are fit only *à dormir debout,* as Hay would say; life is full of such experiences; why should one feel always freshly surprised at realising them! When I think that, as far as I can see, we must, on or about May 1, go to Auckland in the "Richmond" at a season corresponding to a home November, and from there face an undeterminate future; that if La Farge goes to San Francisco, I shall go to Fiji; but if he decides to take the European route, I shall be strongly tempted to go with him, and vary Polynesia by a little Paris and London;—when I reflect on this eternity of seasick discomfort so near at hand, I ought surely to enjoy a month of quiet beauty here. Alack, it is disease! I had a vague hope that somewhere in the round world, merely on the chances of the cards, I should sooner or later happen on some spot where a combination of attractions or amusements would detain me and give me interest or occupation; but the hope has almost vanished. The Polynesian is thin. The Melanesian is thick. The Mongolian irritates me with his invariable air of cheeky superiority,—just, but ungenerous. Motion alone amuses, and I see only the desert of Gobi that offers room for even a moderate exercise of the horse.

Sunday, March 23. The last week has gone better, thanks to an improvement in the conditions of Mr Mallet's (is that his name) problem,[3] and to a visit from Tati, who came here to load the Richmond with oranges, and brought with him a Los Angeles man named Meserve who is getting orange trees for California. Tati is like a northwest wind at home; he brings freshness and gaiety wherever he goes. He not only made things lively here, and started the people off in schemes to amuse us, but he laid out our own plans, arranging that we should go back to Papara on or about April 5th to stay a few days more with him and his mother, and then should cross over to the neighboring island Moorea or Eimea, and stay a few weeks in his house there. Moorea is said to be the most romantic spot among these islands, and I can believe it from what I saw in passing. We have now been three weeks in Tautira, and although La Farge has not at all exhausted its artistic resources, I shall be well satisfied to make a change, especially as I want to sail for Auckland or Fiji in the Richmond on her next trip about May 1. Tati wants us to stay another month to see a great festival at Moorea, but this will depend on many things. Meanwhile La Farge goes on painting, nothing very important, but always interesting, at least to me, though I am curious to know how his drawings look in a New York studio light. I too worry on laboriously trying to learn the secrets of my paint-box, and under La Farge's guidance study tones and values as solemnly as though I were at an art-school learning a profession. All this week I have been toiling on two sketches which absorb me, if they do not closely resemble Turner or Cotman. La Farge has even condescended to praise one of them. He is always very good about my childlike attempts, and never laughs at them as he must want to do; but, on the other hand, my struggles do much to make me a greater admirer of his, so that they have a sort of retroactive value for him. The friendly villagers seem to take about an equal interest in both, and come by dozens, men, women and children, to see our progress day by day. Ori acts as showman, and, being over six feet tall, can choose his own sights. Unluckily we have no interpreter, and conversation is slow when worked out in a dictionary, especially in a language like this, made up of vowels, with a few l, m, n, r, and other soft consonants thrown in anywhere, and varied at will.

With Tati and Meserve, we went on the reef one afternoon. Although I paddle every day along the reef, touching it, my first attempt to land on it had been only a partial success. I live now almost entirely in native costume—shirt and *pareu*, or *lava-lava* in Samoan, a blue cotton cloth wrapped round the waist, with the end tucked in,—and in my canoe I go both barelegged and bare-footed, as one is apt to get wet. The reef looks smooth as glass, but when I stepped on it, I found that the smoothness was only the water which always washes over it, and that in fact the coral rock was pretty sharp and full of irregularities. The natives don't mind it, but I do. So I took canvass shoes, when we went with Tati, and managed to do better. The reef is an excessively curious coral wall, standing some two feet above the level of the lagoon, and averaging forty or fifty feet wide, like a superb boulevard, with a shining surface, absolutely unbroken by the smallest stone or inequality for miles. The outside surf constantly washes over it, and the surges of boiling foam every few minutes swamp one up to the knees, and often take one unexpectedly in a way that disturbs one's scientific reflections. I will not disturb you with the afterthoughts raised either by the reef or its waves, but to me the corals growing and building their wall two feet above sea-level, were a very astonishing sort of pyrotechnics in water. These reefs extend round every island hereabouts, and to my ardent want of imagination they knock Mr Darwin cold. I surrender. A coral island is not necessarily a subsidence. The reasoning is a little matter of several volumes which I will omit for a more convenient occasion when you are busier; but you will understand the core of it perfectly by simply following my train of thought, which is, in brief, that I can make neither head nor tail of the matter either above water or under it, polyp or Darwin. La Farge was luckier. He was delighted with the picturesqueness of the reef, with the water always rushing in little cataracts over its inner walls, and dashing in blue and green masses, dissolving into what Shelley calls star-showers, on the outer plane.[4] Apart from a little nervousness as to the particular kind of poisonous coral, or slimy mass of tentacles, or purple or red animated bladders with indefinite worm-like arms, on which one walks, one is not reasonably nervous, for a big wave would knock one clear into the lagoon where one would be perfectly safe in three feet of water. The natives who go outside in canoes to fish, are sometimes, in heavy weather, obliged to jump the reef on a big wave, and do it generally all right. Tati told us of one native who was chased by a shark, and had just time to drop himself, canoe and all, on the reef. He split up his boat on the spot, threw his fishing-tackle into the surf, and bade good-bye to the ocean then and there, scared out of his life. A big shark, twenty or thirty or forty feet long, is an appeal to our finest instincts as I know, for one gave us his society on our sail from Tutuila to Apia. The shark is a great family God among the natives. Our chief Arié has him. One of them carefully escorted the body of the member of the family who was last brought here by boat to be buried.

By-the-way, I must tell you about our Marae here, the great religious grove of the Taïtian God Oro; but the subject is too gay for this serious sheet.

Tautira, March 29. This morning over our tea and mangoes, we have read the San Francisco newspaper of March 1. Think of it! When will the progress of our marvelous age end? Our excitement was not so great as it would have been last Sunday, for we have had a surfeit of California newspapers this week,—six weeks of them, from Jan. 1 to Feb. 14,—and they have made La Farge quite ill, and cured me very effectually. They are a wonderful invention—newspapers—quite wonderful. No happy home should be without one. Six weeks of them gave me Stevenson's first letter from the Marquesas and Ingall's defeat in Kansas; the two items that alone interested me in all this mass.[5] Two such items! Have I not cause to be contented with my modest lot. I do not include the account of your uncle's death, for I knew it already by telegraph and steamer from Auckland.[6] I fear that your uncle John will feel the blow hard, but I wait a letter from you, which ought to have arrived with the newspaper, to tell me about it. I am uneasy, too, about Martha, whose health you speak of; and the more so because one of my fads is disbelief in malaria in winter, and distrust in any and every doctor who covers his ignorance or incompetence by that sort of medical cant, quite as futile as any Polynesian incantation. I wish the idea of malaria would go into the pigs and quit the devils of doctors.[7] We might then have a chance to be seriously diagnosed. My own calm has not been much disturbed of late, and I go on, trying every day to make pictures, and every day learning, as one does in a new language, a word or two more, just to show that the thing is laughable. Still, I have learned enough, from La Farge's instruction, to make me look at painting rather from the inside, and see a good many things about a picture that I only felt before. Perhaps this is worth while. Perhaps it isn't. I don't know, and think I don't care. La Farge is not much better off, for although he knows and cares intensely, he satisfies himself rather less than I do, and has been for a week as blue as his own ultramarine, the favorite subject of despondency being dissatisfaction with his work. I really think that at times his impressionable nature tries to turn itself out of its shell like a crab. Still, when we come to blues, I tell him truthfully that I can go him better every time, and beat his head off on color in that line of art if in no other; which seems rather to encourage him.

Meanwhile Tati has come back, and proposes to take us to Papara for a function on the 3d. From there we should go over to Moorea to wait the Richmond, due about April 28. I propose to pay the Richmond any necessary amount to take us direct to Fiji, where we should arrive about May 10. I imagine that we shall not want more than a month there, and then—who knows? The world is round.

Tuesday, March 31. Your letter arrived this afternoon,—the February letter, with its account of poor Tom Lee's attack,[8] of Martha's trouble, of your uncle's funeral, and all the rest, including Stevenson's Marquesas letters, the last of which La Farge is now reading, opposite me, with growls of criticism. Your's is the only letter that has come to me, and I read it with eagerness that rather upsets my idea that I have lost the faculty of being interested. Somehow, I seem already to have replied to it in the pages I have written here. I am sure at least of one thing—that you never wrote letters before which could have had a reader who was half as absorbed in them as I am. After devouring it, I went out in my canoe and paddled round the reef, without seeing anything, only thinking about what you wrote. I shall take the letter to bed with me to read again when the dawn wakes me as usual a couple of hours before I want to get up. Unluckily I fear your next will get here after we have gone, and I must submit to go perhaps for months without hearing again. Indeed, I have not an idea when I shall get more letters, for even if I get to Fiji next month I may not stay long enough to receive letters through Samoa. Still, Samoa is the best place to direct to, and I shall have a better chance of receiving the letters sooner or later if you direct to the Consulate there. I have already told you our plans as far as I know them,—that is, as far as Fiji. From there I expect to go to Sydney, and thence Heaven knows where. Tati, who is an angel, some three hundred pounds of angelic material, has not only arranged for our transport to Papara next Friday, and provided us with a house at Moorea, and another at Papeete, when we have to stop there, but got up a dance for us here yesterday. The dance was not very beautiful, to be sure, for a dozen men in a row, in shirts and trousers, kicking and jumping, are neither savage nor instructive; but the scene was pretty in the sunset with the whole village gathered about, the women mostly in red dresses, and the children in pathetic brown eyes. We enjoyed that part of it more than we did the dance. Indeed, quiet as Tautira is, and bored as I have at times been, I feel no such intense relief at the thought of getting away, as I have felt after confinement in other places. The charm of the scenery, the exquisite air, and the divine perfection of the climate, are beyond ordinary boredom. Then, too, I must own to having enjoyed my mornings under the cocoanut trees by the sea-shore sketching the distant Taïti mountains. I have actually painted two pictures—I mean goodsized watercolors, a foot or more long—that are near enough to the truth to be worth keeping. I would send them to you if they were not too elaborate to fold. One of them, I think, does really almost catch a thought of the delicate melancholy which is my haunting impression of Taïti wherever I see it. La Farge approves it, else I should not dare to think so.

Papara, April 4. Back again at Tati's. The festivity is on account of the opening of a bridge, which took place yesterday. We came from Tautira the day before, by an elaborate composite movement, I coming as far as Tarauao by boat, and La Farge by carriage. Our parting with Tautira was touching. Haapi-vaine,—that is, or, perhaps, it is not, the name of Ori's wife, for I pride myself on absolute contempt for accuracy when I write letters—wept all the morning, and hung about, patting us surreptitiously on the shoulders, as though she could not resist the temptation of touching us now and then. I was conscience-stricken at her grief, for I had been a little troubled that neither La Farge nor I had shown decent sympathy with Haapi in her archaic devotion to us. She was good, and matronly, and charmingly grateful for small attentions, but she could do so little for us; and here she was, crying silently all day because we were going off, while we, hardened to the iniquities of constant change, scarcely gave to our departure a thought, or to her a regret. One has parted from so much, in this preposterous life; and poor Haapi is so very small an incident in it. She was a mother to me, though certainly not forty years old. At that age, women here are elderly. I had an idea that she, rather than her husband, gave me my name of Ori, and adopted us into the Teva clan; a tenderness which has really some meaning here, and puts us on a different footing. Partly owing to our acquired relationship, we felt ourselves quite at home when we finished our journey that evening, and after a drive of three hours or so from Taravao, through the same dream of ferns and palms and gleaming seas by which we came, were dropped at Tati's in the midst of a big family party. There was Hinari, our old grandmother, sitting on her mats surrounded by small grandchildren; her daughter Marau,—the Queen, you remember; Miss Pree, more handsome, and I thought more delicate than a month ago; Manahini, or Chica, or familiarly Cheeky, a handsome girl of twenty or so; the three Brander boys, Norman, Arthur and Winny; a big daughter of Tati's and another of Marau's that look like pictures from Gulliver's travels; no end of smaller children, dogs, chickens, occasional pigs, horses and domestics; and beyond, hardly a stone's-throw away, the surf rolling in miles of foam straight up to our hands. Tati, surrounded by all his duties and household cares, seemed to take us in at a gulp, as easily as if we had been more children. Hinari, Marau and the two sisters were cordial as possible, and we sat down to dinner feeling a little as though we had returned to the world.

In its way, which is a queer enough little way, Taïti does represent a sort of world. The fête of the bridge-opening was the sort of thing that one naturally puts in a novel. At nine o'clock, the Governor punctually appeared at Tati's, the *chéferie;* and of course we were all in white suits to meet him. Monsieur de la Cascade was, I believe, a banker at Martinique or Guade-

loupe, and I should say he was a quadroon, but à mourir de rire. La Farge
and I, on comparing notes, found that he was a wonderful combination of
August Belmont and the typical stock-broker of the Gymnase and vaudeville, who will turn out either to be the victim or the villain, but villain
twice out of three times. He was very affable, and gave us all sorts of invitations which we could not accept, jerking out his conversation with a sort
of Japanese mixture of deference, patronage and suspiciousness. His staff
was modest, and hardly worth describing. We had to be formal for near
two hours with this little man in a tall silk hat, frock coat, and tri-color
sash, until I sighed for our old Samoan receptions and the speeches of the
tulafales. Then we went ahead to the bridge, Marau and Manihini and the
Branders in charge of us; but the bridge was dull. One or two hundred natives in bright dresses, and faces sometimes pleasant and sometimes plain
but never beautiful, lined the road, but did not sing or dance or show more
animation than so many European peasantry would have done. The actual
formalities were stupid beyond the proper limits of French officialdom.
Then we had a lunch which was better, and to my mind quite prettily
done. The Governor was host, and sat on one side of a long table with a big
bouquet of leaves in front of him as though he wished to blot out his majesty King Pomare who sat opposite in his goggles. At that hour in the
morning, Pomare was not obviously drunk, and made no noise. Almost
back to back with him, at a parallel table, was Marau with her sister Manihini. Tati and I sat opposite to the Governor again, looking at the King's
back. The rest of the company, mostly French officials or trades-people, did
not interest me to the extent of their numbers, which was perhaps a hundred. We eat our dishes, drank our Bordeaux, had a toast to the ladies, and
there an end.

In the afternoon we had an entertainment of a different sort, which Tati
and I witnessed alone, for the others were all scattered elsewhere. A division
of the district, say a hundred or more people, came to Tati's for the division
of a present of salt pork and other food, made by the government to the
laborers on the bridge. Tati was asked to see to the division to prevent a
row, and he had an idea that perhaps they might get dancing and be
amusing. Once more I was disappointed. The natives were, as Tati said, far
too drunk for making a dance. I do not understand the thing. They could
have drunk very little, yet indubitably drunk they were, Tati said with excitement chiefly. They were sober enough not to permit actual fighting,
and the women and children were apparently not at all worried by the
drinking or drunkards, but they seemed to me a rather more drunken
crowd than I ever saw abroad. They were noisy but not funny. Tati, used to
his own people as he is, had to stand over them all the time to prevent a
row, and was evidently much pleased to get it over.

A ball was going on all the afternoon and night at a neighbor's a few
miles away, and Pree and Cheeky went to it, with Marao to matronise.
They are pathetically eager about dancing. Tati too had to go. La Farge
and I begged off, and I had a quiet evening reading Stevenson's Donkey in

the Cevennes, after which, at ten oclock I went to bed and lay awake thinking of you, and other matters.[9] Suppose I should return next winter— what then? Things are not changed in a year. How long could I stay? I suppose the crows still fly over Washington,[10] and scandal does not stop.

Papara, 8 April. Very unwillingly we shall probably leave Tati's hospitality tomorrow. Our visit here has been one of the bright spots of our travels. If I struck such episodes often, I think I should travel indefinitely, yet I hardly know what it is that we find so pleasant. As long as the women were here, we had society, for they would be interesting persons in any country-house. The old lady, Hinari or Grandmother, is a very fine type indeed; quite a royal person in her island way. Naturally I have treated her for what she is; that is, next to Mataafa, altogether the most interesting native figure in the whole Pacific. Apparently she felt that I meant what I said, for she was very goodnatured and open with us. She told us freely her oldest legends and traditions, and took a motherly interest in us. My adoption into the Teva clan by Ori was rather a joke. Indeed I had sent word to the old Chiefess through Tati, a month ago, that I should not think of accepting such a relationship without her formal and express approval. I supposed she would have given it on our arrival here, but she did not; nor did she ever call me Ori, as she should naturally have done if she approved, so that I rather inferred that she did not like the adoption, as she was said to have been displeased by that of Stevenson. I was quite upset, last Monday morning, just before they all went away, when the old lady with a certain dignity of manner, drawing a chair near mine, sat down and made me a little formal speech in native words, which of course I did not understand, and which Marao, who was in the secret, instantly translated. The speech was, I believe, the proper, traditional and formal act of investiture, and conferred on me the hereditary family name of Taura-atua, with the lands, rights and privileges attached to it. The compliment from such a source was so great as to be awkward. To be sure, the lands attached to the name of Taura-atua are only about a hundred feet square, a few miles from here; but the name is a very real thing, and was borne by Tati's ancestors, and is actually borne now by his second son. To give it to me was a sort of adoption. Of course, I expressed my sense of the honor, and got Marao to speak for me; after which she turned to La Farge and repeated the same form to him, conferring on him another name, also real and hereditary. The whole thing was done simply but quite royally, with a certain condescension as well as kindness of manner. For once, my repose of manner was disturbed beyond concealment. So I am now Taura-atua and Ori-a-ori; a member of both outer and inner Tevas, and a close relation of Tati himself. La Farge also is Teva by double adoption, and I suppose we are both brothers of Mrs Stevenson.

The adoption was the more formal because it was done in the presence of Tati, Marao, and all the family then here, and they had been consulted beforehand. I was glad of this, because I like them all, and especially took interest in Marao, the queen, who is a woman very much out of the common. You have her photograph. She is, I imagine, somewhere in the thirties, and her face and figure have grown heavy and somewhat Indian, as is rather the rule with the women here. If she was once handsome, certainly her beauty is not what attracts men now. What she has is a face strongly marked and decidedly intelligent, with a sub-expression of recklessness, or true old-goldishness, that always charms me and Clarence King when it is real. One feels the hundred generations of chiefs who are in her, without one commoner except the late Salmon, her deceased parent. Hebrew and Polynesian mix rather well, when the Hebrew does not get the better; and Marao, like her brother Tati, is more Taïti than Syria. At all events she is greatly interested in Taïti history, poetry, legends and traditions, and as for ghost-stories, she tells them by the hour with evident belief in them, and entire confidence in the independent evolution of native ghosts and ghost-seers. As everyone here does in his heart believe in all the old native spiritual faiths; and Christianity is just one more, only successful because Jehovah is biggest and has licked Taaroa and Oro, there is nothing really strange in Marao's frank outspokenness; but it is entertaining all the same. Marao has the same big, Richardsonian, ways that her brother Tati has. She always seems to me to be quite capable of doing anything strange, out of abstraction; as she might mistake me for her small child, and sling me on her arm without noticing the difference, such as it is, in size. She is good-natured, I should say; easy, indolent, and yet, like her race, capable of committing any kind of folly, and of going to the devil like a true Polynesian for sentiment or for appetite, for love, jealousy or ennui. Luckily she is now pretty well past her jeunesse outrageuse. The next generation is the one now in trouble, and of that I hear much, but see little. Even here I am sometimes reminded of my fifty years, and the young women in their teens do not seem to expect me. Poor Pree has had to go to Papeete to see her doctor again, and I fear her cough is worse. La Farge has made a little drawing for her album, and I have written in it a metrical translation of a dozen lines from the Odyssey. Manini is a true girl, with no formed character. All of them went away on Monday, leaving us alone with Tati and his wife. Tati's wife is shy and avoids us, probably because she speaks none of our languages, and is neither a Pomare nor a chiefess in her own right. Tati does everything. This afternoon he drove us in the farm-wagon a mile or two through the woods to see my duchy, Taura atua. Apart from the personal interest in my estate of six orange trees and a mango or pandanus, I was interested in the glimpse of history. Some fifteen generations ago, old Taura was a great warrior. I imagine him like Pa-tu in Samoa. He was military chief of the two districts here, and must have led several thousand men, but never owned any land except the hundred feet square on which his house stood. There Tati showed us the stones which limited the low platform or terrace on which the house stood. As Taura atua I had also a private Marao and the right to order human sacrifices. St Gaudens and Stanford White had better avoid Taïti. I took investiture of my duchy in the shape of an orange. On our way back we spied sharply for the cave in the cliff where the heads of Tati's ancestors are hidden, and which Tati himself does not know. The old man, whose hereditary duty was to take up the heads and keep them oiled and fresh, can no longer climb up there, and has no son to succeed him, and is bound by oath to tell the secret to no one else. The family must lose its heads. Tomorrow we bid Tati good-bye. He is a dear fellow, and if ever he comes to America, you must love him.

The mail goes in three days, and probably I shall write no more by this packet. Burn these little water-color follies.

MS: MHi
1. HA's own version of Horace, *Epistles,* III, 12: "Coelum, non animum mutant . . ." (They who cross the sea change the sky, not their minds).
2. " 'The longer I live on this Crumpetty Tree / The plainer than ever it seems to me / That very few people come this way / And that life on the whole is far from gay!' / Said the Quangle Wangle Quee"; Edward Lear, "The Quangle Wangle's Hat" (1877).
3. William Hurrell Mallock (1849–1923), *Is Life Worth Living?* (1879).
4. "I see the waves upon the shore, / Like light dissolved in star-showers, thrown"; "Stanzas Written in Dejection, Near Naples."
5. Stevenson's account of the Marquesas, where he had stopped on his Pacific cruise of 1888–1889, had begun to appear in the New York *Sun* in February 1891. The Republican senator from Kansas John James Ingalls had lost his seat to the Populist leader William Peffer.
6. Gen. W. T. Sherman died Feb. 14 at the age of 71.
7. Jesus cast out evil spirits from the possessed into a herd of swine; Matthew 8, Mark 5, Luke 8.
8. Thomas Lee suffered a stroke on Jan. 31.
9. *Travels with a Donkey in the Cevennes* (1879).
10. An allusion to Hay's poem "The Crows at Washington."

To Lucy Baxter

Tautira, 2 April, 1891.

My dear Miss Baxter

No letter from you by this mail, as yet, though the packet arrived at Papeete a week ago. None from the Hoopers or from Dwight, and I have not an idea when I shall get another letter, if we leave Tahiti, as we expect, at the end of this month. Direct still to Samoa, care of the Consulate.

Our stay at Tautira ends tomorrow. We have been here a month, and in all my travels I have never before found a place where the month of March was tolerable. Certainly the climate of Tahiti is divine. At midday the heat is sometimes oppressive, but not unbearable. The place where we are is extremely pretty, and the people are kind. Otherwise we have little to tell. Nothing on earth could be quieter. One cannot walk far, on account of water or dense woods and abrupt mountains, so I take my exercise wholly in canoe, paddling every evening for an hour or two about the shores. Of course I have been more or less bored for want of occupation; but that is the case everywhere, and by a rigorous arrangement of small tasks, hour by hour, I manage to pass the time fairly. The people here are much too civilised for us. You can imagine what a wreck they are when you think that a little more than a century ago they numbered two or three hundred thousand, and that barely ten thousand are left, including a large proportion of half-breeds. They were once the gayest people in the world, and now are as quiet and silent as Americans. They have very little poetry or legend, and very few interesting customs. To me Taïti seems always a very beautiful grave-yard, but one learns to be fond of it, and perhaps Heaven may be the same sort of thing if I understand the clerical idea of it. Certainly the angels cannot easily sing more hymns, for the eternal *himene* is the last surviving local and social habit of the Taïtians.

Tautira is rather an interesting spot in some ways. Beyond, to the southward, is nothing but a bold coast, without population or path. A few people always have lived there, but the world practically ended here, and here in old days was the Maräe or sacred ground of the chief Taïtian God, Oro, to whom the human sacrifices were chiefly made. No one but the priests lived then at Tautira; and the path, along the coast, ran behind, over the hills. Any intruder was killed. Oro had it all to himself; and his grounds must have been wonderfully impressive. They were filled with very large, old, ceder-like trees, curiously funereal in effect, though all but two are gone. The dead were brought here, often, for so-called burial; that is, the bodies were placed on platforms and left. This manner of populating the plain must have had inconveniences, but was only a part of the show. All the human victims sacrificed for any reason, and at times they were sacrificed pretty freely, were killed at home, their bodies, in wicker or palm-leaf baskets, were brought here in boats, and at night were silently brought ashore, and laid before the priest's house. In the morning, the priests hung the bodies to the trees. I have tried in vain to imagine what the effect of such ornaments must have been. No one saw it. Even the fishermen paddled by, far off, without impertinent curiosity.

I suppose Stevenson, who spent two months here, will give a properly ghastly account of the old Marae, which is now the village cemetery and innocent enough. My story may serve to prepare you for his. I have read his two Marquesas letters, and feel sure he will warm up as he gets to the human sacrifices. Our friend Tati, the greatest chief in Taïti, tells me that only head-chiefs had the right to order a human sacrifice, and that his father, or grandfather, who was head chief of the Tevas—that is to say, of more than half the people—in two years that his chiefery lasted, somewhere about 1820, ordered two. This does not seem to show as many human sacrifices as one would wish.

Tomorrow we go to Papara for another visit to Tati and his old mother and pretty sister. Thence to Papeete for a day, to cross some twenty miles of sea to the island of Moorea or Eimea. Did you ever read Herman Melville's Omoo? He has more or less to say about these haunts. So has Miss Gordon Cumming. We shall stay in Moorea, in Tati's empty house there, until the Richmond returns about April 25, when we may probably try to get to Fiji.

House-keeping is not easy in these parts. We live entirely on chickens for meat, as we do not eat pig, and no other meat is to be had. The fish are not much to boast of as food; but the crayfish are not bad, and we get a nice little oyster from Taravao, a few miles away. I do not recommend Tautira for rich diet, unless one like cocoanuts and cuttle-fish. I do like them, but La Farge does not, and I do not inflict them on him.

La Farge sketches away, and we hope his work will please somebody, though we cannot at all judge of it ourselves. I go on sketching in my childlike way, and have been driven by sheer vacuity to do some rather large ones here. I go even so far as to think that they are not so bad as some of the worst that amateurs are ashamed to show. One gets a sort of fatal facility in mixing colors.

Ever affectionately   Henry Adams.

MS: MH

To Elizabeth Cameron

Oponuhu, 13 April, 1891.

They call it Opouno, and I do not care how they spell it. You can find the spot—perhaps—if you happen to know where to look for it, in the travels of a few great people like Captain Cook, the Pembroke youth, Miss Gordon Cumming, and J. La Farge, a painter, better known in Taïti as Teraitua of the inner Tevas, who visited the South Seas towards the end of the nineteenth century, and could never be induced to return to New York.

First, I will go back to Papara where my last sheet was written. We stayed there until last Thursday, the 9th, and then were driven to Papeete by Johnny and Taura. Taura is Tati's second son, "that fat boy whom Tati spoils," as the stern aunt Beretania always describes him. Taura and I have the same name, Taura-atua—God-perch; Japanese Toro; lighting-place or resting-perch of a God, I am told. Taura was going back to school, and being twelve years old, had the sentiments of his age on the subject; while Johnny, another boy, who was charged with the equipage, bore the assurance of a thrashing if Taura should escape. The adventures of Taura and Johnny diverted us greatly, for Johnny succeeded only by the aid of two aunts and several cousins in at last penning Taura in the Frères' prison, and so avoiding his thrashing; but these adventures do not directly concern ours except so far as that they ran parallel in the wagon; and, after all, we did get to Papeete, without wreck, just at dark, so Johnny and Taura have not our lives on their presumed consciences. We liked both the boys the more for their dusty Polynesiacity. As I detest Papeete almost as much as Taura my junior detests school, I was not pleased when we found ourselves, at dusk, dropped at Tati's empty and rat-haunted cottage, but we were glad to have any refuge in the unhostelried Papeete, and we were allowed by monsieur Peraudot, our cook, to take our meals at his house, in the want of a kitchen at Tati's.

We passed two days at Papeete, mailing our various despatches by the "Galilee" packet. La Farge sent another lot of drawings, and I sent my heavy letter to you; but after disposing of all my mail, and arranging with our Opouno boatman to take us to Moorea on Sunday, I had naught to do, and was a little bored. Only a little bored, this time, I own, for Taïti, and especially Tati, have done me good, and I am glad to feel that for the last six years I have never been so healthy in mind as now. Much as I dislike Papeete, it certainly was in its way amusing, even when I sat for hours on the porch of the little consulate, doing nothing at all, and even thinking nothing. The light is so exquisite here, the air so perfect, and the indolence so complete, that even my nerves soften in time. Then one learns at last the humor of Papeete existence. An afternoon has its drolleries. For instance, Saturday afternoon, La Farge and I dawdled an hour at the family house—Hinarii's; grandmother's,—with our two sisters Beretania and Manihini, Pree and Cheekey; then we called on the governor, M. La Cascade, whose hair curled as closely as ever, and who talked as much like a Vaudeville actor as usual, furnishing us constant innocent amusement. Then as we strolled towards dinner, we found Pree and Cheekey and Norman or Arthur Brander sitting on an old wooden packing case by the Consulate, looking at the sunset. Then Marau drove in, from Faaa, where they usually live, some five miles towards Papara. I do not know whether Marau and the old lady were brought up by a sharp attack of bronchitis which has alarmed them about Pree, or whether they came up to struggle with a quarrel which the Atwaters are forcing on the poor old lady, who is driven to despair by constant quarreling in her large family; at all events, Marau appeared at sunset, and she too came out, and sat on the old box, till the wonderful gold and orange light faded about the mountains of Moorea. I know few other places in the world where one can sit, as it were, on the boulevard, looking at such a landscape, and chatting with the Queen—*divorcée*,—leaning on a wood fence. That evening we went again to the house to bid good-bye to Hinarii and Marau, whose adoption of us has surprised society. When we talked about it with Mrs Atwater,—Moétie, the other daughter, who was not at Papara owing to the new quarrel,—Mrs Atwater declared her astonishment. Only once before, to Prince Oscar of Sweden, had her mother given a name, and to us she had given two of the best names in the family.[1] Clearly we are appreciated at last, though we had to travel far for it.

All the same, I was glad when our boatman appeared at our house at seven o'clock the next morning—yesterday, Sunday,—and we prepared to sail. The "Galilee" was to sail at the same hour, nine o'clock, when the trade-wind should begin to blow; but the trade-wind quite emphatically refused to blow. La Farge and I sat on the ground in the shade till ten o'clock watching the brig till all the passengers and the mail were on board, and nothing stirred. Then we had to start in our whale-boat, with five oars, and at quarter before eleven we were outside the reef, rising and falling on the long swell, which made great waves of surf against the coral, but was hardly noticeable in the boat. The day was splendid; the ocean was like ultramarine oil; the mountains, the sky and the sea were all bathed in a flood of indescribable light; and we sheltered ourselves as well as we could, under our umbrellas, while the men toiled at the oars, and the skipper slept with his arm round the rudder. Awoki and Peraudot were with us, and served us from time to time with oranges, a watermelon, and iced selzer-water with limes. Very slowly we drew across the ten miles of open water, and not till three o'clock did we run through the Moorea reef, and land. By way of a change we walked a mile or two, along a shore-road just like our Samoan paths. Then we got into the boat again, and as the sun set, and the after-glow followed, we turned into the long bay of Oponou, where the mountains, in peaks and with outlines as unreasonable as a theatre drop-scene, rose round us, more like the Lake of Como than like a respectable Polynesian island. The scene was impressive; the finest we have yet struck. The mountains were two or three thousand feet high, with fine masses and peaks as sharp as needles and knives; but it was dark when we reached our solitary big house at the bottom of the bay, and a young moon lighted us ashore. We had a long delay in getting into our house, and Awoki and Peraudot had to work in an unpolynesian activity to get us some dinner at nine o'clock, and to put up our beds and mosquito-nets by eleven; but here we are, and very beautiful it is. For once, no village is near. We have the universe to ourselves, and a dozen pictures to paint from our porch without turning round. Why could we not have found the place at first?

Oponohu, 19 April. If I had written at all, in the course of the last week, I am afraid I should have told you of nothing but ailments, and fears of the effect of climate. Nothing in special is the matter, but one does not know oneself under tropical conditions, and we have had an unbroken year of tropical temperature since the April and May of youthful breakfasts at the Country Club. Much I would like to be there, this soft Sunday morning, but I console myself by thinking that you and the family are in Europe or somewhere. If you remain till September, I will almost promise to see you in Paris. What think you? I have told La Farge that if he would stop with me a month in Fiji, say the month of May, I would go with him to Sydney in June, and take the next steamer to Ceylon, where we would pass a month, and go on to France in August. I have no special reason for going one way rather than another, but I think a little winter will be an unpleasant change worth trying. I could employ a winter profitably in Europe, and perhaps, while so near, I might drop in at Washington for a spring. This is looking a whole year ahead, which is rash; but a casual brig sails for San Francisco on the 26th and I want to utilise it to tell you where to write. Address to the care of our Consul at Sydney. Probably the letter will not reach me, for it can hardly get to Sydney till July, when I should properly have passed through, on my way to Ceylon; but the chance is something. If you are in England, you might telegraph the fact to Sydney—just your address—and I could telegraph mine, in return. If you are at Beverly, you can also telegraph the fact to Sydney, care of the Consul, and the telegram should reach me on my arrival there. Then I could telegraph my address. Does this seem to you to be asking too much? I own it seems rather outrageous, but I am in despair at the idea that between now and August I shall otherwise hear not a word from anyone. From the Western Union office in State Street (the central office) you can send a telegram without the least trouble, and I think at only a dollar a word. One word would be enough,—just *Beverly,* or *Morgan,* or any address that I should understand. I will send an answer immediately on receiving it. If you are anywhere in Europe, the process is even easier, and any village telegraph-office will do.

I do not yet know whether we are to be compelled to go to Auckland or not. I have offered the owner of the Richmond a thousand dollars to take us directly to Fiji, and am waiting an answer which I hope to receive before closing this letter. As the Richmond earns not many thousands, and would be put only to an expense of two or three days voyage out of her course, the merchants at Papeete think I shall find no difficulty. If the Richmond refuses, we must go in her to Auckland, and then I doubt whether I shall have the courage to face the long voyage back to Fiji. We should probably go on to Sydney.

Perhaps we are foolish to go anywhere. Taïti is lovely; the climate is perfect; we have made a sort of home here; and I never shall meet another spot so suitable to die in. The world actually vanishes here. Papeete was silent and sleepy; Tautira was so remote that existence became a dream; but Opunohu is solitude such as neither poetry nor mathematics can express. Now that I have seen this little island—Moorea or Eimea—I see that it was once a big volcano, enormously long ages ago. The crater was on the level of the sea, but its walls rose, like those of Kilauea and Haleakala in the Sandwich Islands, several thousand feet above the floor of the crater. Peaks, sharp as knives and toothpicks, still remain three or four thousand feet high. We are in the old crater, and need imagination to know it, for it is two or three miles long, and instead of being a great pit, like Kilauea, it broke its sides out in two places into the sea. So it now makes an irregular amphitheatre, looking out on the ocean through our Opunohu bay, and the neighboring Cook's bay, each some two miles long, while the valley behind us, which was the crater, extends back still greater distances till it abuts against walls of lava-rock worn and colored by time. Geology breaks down in measuring time here. Nothing has ever changed. The seasons are all summer; the trade-wind has always blown; the ocean has always been infinite about it. Moorea is the oldest spot of earth I ever saw. Compared with it, Taïti is a younger brother. I believe it has stood here since time began, and oceans cooled. At all events, I defy geology to prove the contrary; and have my private opinion of Darwin and Dana, as by this time you know. If Taïti was sad, Moorea is sadder. Man somehow got here, I think about a thousand years ago, and made a society which was on the whole the most successful the world ever saw, because it rested on the solidest possible foundation of no morals at all. As far as I can learn, the Taïtians were in one particular more successful than the Samoans, Tongans or Hawaians, for they numbered some two hundred thousand physically perfect and even noble people, remarkably healthy and happy, and as depraved as possible; not merely without morals, but with elaborate refinement of immorality. I found myself obliged to accept the universal evidence that Taïti was probably the most triumphant example on earth, of total wickedness. The people knew better, and carried licentiousness as far as they could, not because they were ignorant, but because they liked it. I see no use in talking about morals here. Morals must be a European invention, for no sooner were they introduced here by three English and French ships only about a century ago, than they swept away the entire population in fifteen or twenty years. Where vicious people swarmed, the virtuous scarcely exist. A quarter of a million depraved and splendid people throve here a century ago; today, some ten thousand delicate and carefully conducted natives, half-breeds and Europeans, lead a melancholy existence, the prey to consumption, rheumatism and ennui.

Do not impart this historical observation to Martha. I admit to astonishment at the fact, and I know the miasma of European commonplace which would overwhelm me if I announced it publicly. I too can talk commonplace explanations by the measure, when I want to hide anything. Here I am outside of Europe and commonplace. I am in a rich valley, which once supported easily thousands of people as vicious as they knew how to make themselves, and which is now waste, without an occupant or a cultivated field, when the people are comparatively moral and decent as well as Christian; and the situation grows constantly more moral and more sad. The paradox is worth a little sea-sickness to witness, but it is properly adapted only to middle-age, and is not to be recommended to young and pretty women. As for the men, I presume they have no morals anywhere. So women say.

Papeete, 24 April. Last night, at Opunohu, just at dusk, a boat arrived from Papeete bringing us notice that the Richmond had come, and its owner positively refused under any circumstances, to take us to Fiji. He was bound to go straight to Auckland, but was going first to Papara for a cargo of oranges, and was to sail from Papara for Auckland on the 26th. Here was a pretty complication. We had to decide instantly whether to remain indefinitely in Taïti, or to sail for Auckland. After a struggle of mind, we decided to return at once to Papeete, and sail for Auckland, since we could sail nowhere else. We packed up; went to bed for a few hours; rose at three o'clock, and set out, in beautiful moonlight, from our solitary home in the mountain seas. Our men rowed till dawn within the reef, along the moon-lit shore; and just as the east grew red, we passed out on the ocean which tossed us about like a jumping cat. The passage was long. The Richmond passed us, running down the coast, while we were still far from port; but at eleven o'clock, after roasting well in the hot sun, and taking our last panorama of these exquisite sceneries, we reached Papeete.

There we found ourselves in worse confusion than ever. We had no place to sleep in, but that was a trifle. The worst was that the Richmond had fifteen cabin passengers, and we could not be sure of getting a stateroom, of which there are only eight. We decided to send a messenger to Papara to ask what accommodations we could have. The advantage of a family connection then became apparent. We found that Tati was in town, just starting for Papara. He took our letter, and is to send an answer tonight. Till then we shall not know whether we are going or not.

The rest of the day has passed in repacking our trunks; getting out thick clothing; and closing up our affairs. Five o'clock has come. I am at the empty Consulate, and seize an hour to tell you our difficulties. If we go to Auckland, my next letter will reach you possibly before this one. If we do not go, we shall pass another five weeks here. Apparently we shall not go; but I shall tell you the result before this letter is closed. The "Courtney Ford" sails also on the 26th and carries an extra mail to San Francisco.

Hateful as the Richmond is to me, it has done me one good service by bringing at last my set of Kodak photographs, which has been printed and mounted at Melbourne. They are very queer things, and of course very bad photographs, but they delight La Farge, and give him almost endless material for work. I shall give him one set, and shall number the other set, with a memorandum on the back of each. As soon as may be, I will send it—or bring it, to you. The series is extremely curious, but needs very intelligent eyes to understand the mysteries of the action. Of late I have seen little that was worth photographing.

25 April, 1891. Our answer from the steamer is that we cannot have a stateroom. So we are obliged to remain here another six weeks, and all our trouble is thrown away; all our plans are set back, and really I am excessively bothered to know what is to come next. La Farge does not seem to mind. My annoyance always comes first, and his comes over the consequences. Anyway, we cannot carry out our plan. I cannot tell you where to write, but think I would try Fiji, for the next letter, if it is sent early in June. Probably it will reach me if I am still in Fiji in August. This is unlikely but possible. On the other hand, I may be able to get some sailing vessel to take us direct to Fiji, or we may go down to Auckland and there find ourselves so worn out by sea-travel that we shall go to Europe direct, without further attempt to see more islands. In almost any case we must pass through Sydney, at latest by the end of August, and possibly by the end of June. You had better *write to Sydney,* therefore, *care of our consulate there,* and I shall probably pick up your letter in passing. The letter to Fiji would be only a shot; and a flying shot at this distance is not easy.

You would not naturally suppose that, in these days, one could have so much trouble in getting over the regular tracks of travel; but the Pacific ocean is still a very far-away place, and this steamer Richmond, a miserable little craft such as you never would put your foot in, and so small that she looks underwater, is the only means of getting from Taïti anywhere. There is no commerce. No ships ever seem to stop here; and every vessel that happens to come, is sure to be bound to San Francisco. I am not sure that we may not be obliged to go by sail to San Francisco at last, even to get to Fiji. Miss Gordon Cumming did it in order to get to Honolulu.

Well! I will mail this fragment of a disappointing letter, just to show that I meant well. Perhaps my next, by the regular packet, a fortnight hence, may be more coherent. I wish I dared direct my next to Beverly or to London; but perhaps the packet, due in a week or less, may bring a letter to tell me what your plans are. Not that I expect any letter. You can judge how much the subject is on my mind, since I have written of nothing else; and you can rest assured that this autumn will see us arrive in Europe if we are to arrive anywhere. Once there, I shall be able to take whatever course seems best. I can return to India and China, or cross directly to America in the spring; or even pass a year in Europe. Between now and then, you must reflect deeply on the subject, and give me your well-considered professional opinion and advice. You have three months to consider it, and in September you should be prepared to write me to Paris or London your matured views as to what I had best do. I will come home if wanted; but shall I come home to stay, or shall I come home for no other object than to get myself miserable again, and be forced to come back here because I cannot make life suit?

MS: MHi
1. Oscar Carl August Bernadotte (1859–1946), second son of Oscar II of Sweden, had gone on a worldwide naval expedition, 1883–1885, that touched at Tahiti.

To Clarence King

Address:
wait till I know one.

Opunohu, Moorea. (Taïti)
22 April, 1891

My dear King

I wonder whether my big letter written six weeks ago, has reached you yet. On sound principles, I should wait to hear, before writing again, but we expect to leave Taïti and Polynesia in a few days. If possible we are to go direct to Fiji, and in any case we shall lose sight of the old-gold problem forever. My letter was only half a one. Even on the geology, I said only part of what is lying about loose here. When we come to ethnology, I want to swear a little before forgetting what I am swearing about. We have now lived more or less among old-gold since last August. We have read the literature; discussed the subject with scores of intelligent people with opposite views; seen the conditions, and frequented the happy homes of the recent savage. I suppose we know something about the man and woman. If not, I will take no offense. We—that is, La Farge and I—detest paradox because it is always conventional, and we love conventionality because it is at bottom a paradox. I pass my time trying to upset other people's paradox, and to reestablish solid conventional sense. The Polynesians and their islands are as far from paradox as I am. They are as conventional as their own cocoa-nuts. I tried to explain this law, when I wrote about their geology, and offered you my tearful protest against the really outrageous paradoxes of Dana and Darwin, which are now, after fifty years, seen to be evidently conventional commonplaces. The simple commonplace, which they rejected, is the true science for me, being particularly paradoxical when prayerfully considered.

The Polynesians are not so much of a paradox, when closely approached, as they seemed to be when I saw them from Washington. As usual, the commonplace explanation of them is the most natural. They must have branched off from the main pre-Aryan stock not so very far back;—since our Indians, but before the Greeks. As a separate race, if they deserve the name, they are the youngest of all; the spoiled youngest child of the human family. I should be perfectly willing to accept any tolerable evidence that they were an offshoot of the Aryan migration to India. Their astonishing resemblance to the Greeks; their system of law and society; even their language and religious traditions, and their want of relations to the races about them, suggest such an origin so distinctly that I should not care to dispute it. The question how they got here, is another point that seems to me not worth disputing. They came by way of Java almost necessarily, and they called every island of any size by that name: Savaii, Hapaii, Hawaii; even Taïti was called so; you find the name in every group. They were certainly never numerous. If there were a thousand, the number was ample for all they did. They may have stopped here and there, but they could not expand among the inhabited islands where even the whites have not found expansion easy. They consisted of families, each led by a chief, and the chief was the state. When the chief said: I go,—the state went. The chief still remains, and still does the same thing. Today a chief who had reasons for doing it, would start in the same way, and possibly in the same craft.

On coming among them, I am surprised to reflect that so much difficulty should have been made about their sailing so far. The Greeks were good sailors. The Norsemen discovered and populated Iceland a thousand years ago. The Iceland ocean is enormously worse for navigation than these tropical seas, and the Norse vessel was nothing like so convenient as the Polynesian. If we did not know the story of Iceland, it would be ten times as mysterious as that of Easter Island. In fact, granting the sea-habit, and a race of bold chiefs, and the whole story is told. Both in Hawaii and in New Zealand the actual history of their voyages is authentically preserved. Their vessels were huge. They built canoes of great length, and partly decked them. Two of these were lashed together, and a regular house was built across them. They carried masts and sails, and had ample room for stores.

Fifty people could easily go in them, and if my experience in these oceans counts, they would easily keep up a supply of rain-water for months. They knew the seasons and the winds. They could sail to windward, but they always watched carefully for fair winds; and the regular trade is very far from regular, as I can witness. History is quite clear on the subject. The Tongans habitually went and came between Tonga, Fiji and Samoa. A whole army of Tongan warriors, certainly five thousand in number, came to Samoa and conquered it, four hundred years ago; and the story is perfectly well preserved in both groups. Mariner's Travels or residence in Tonga in 1805,[1] a book quite classically good, though unknown to me till I read it in Samoa, tells all about the nautical ventures of the Tongans, who were very possibly the main reservoir of colonisation for New Zealand, Taïti and Hawaii; for they were apparently more enterprising than the Samoans, and between those two groups the current most likely flowed. From Tonga to Raratonga, and from Raratonga to Taïti, was an expedition natural enough to men whose business for many generations had been the discovery of islands. The Hawaiian group, and Easter Island were the two furthest points they can be proved to have reached; but I am very much inclined to believe that they could not have stopped there, and that our central American civilisation was Polynesian. I will not argue this point now. Easter Island and Hawaii will do.

They brought with them their favorite means of subsistence. The cocoanut seems to me to have been everywhere introduced by them, for it never grows wild, and is always proof of cultivation and human life. The breadfruit was another. Probably the plantain and banana, as well as the *taro* were all introduced. They brought the pig and hen, clear proof where they came from. They brought bits of jade. I suspect they brought even certain birds of bright plumage, for ornament. They came in small numbers; perhaps only one canoe company for a whole group like Taïti or Hawaii, and certainly only two or three for New Zealand; but they repeated their voyages, and loved conquest. Within record, they have been still doing the same thing in a small way. They had little commerce but much adventure; and of course two canoes out of three might be lost without affecting the movement. How could they know that the distances between archipelagoes were great? They started to find out.

They could work stone, though they were lazy. Their stone implements, especially in Hawaii, were sometimes beautifully made. They built stone platforms, terraces and foundations for their houses, and shaped the stones. They built occasionally fortifications of stone, and frequently built walls. My own house at Papara—by adoption, I am Taura-atua, a great ancestor of the Tevas, and I own the ancestral place by gift of the old hereditary chiefess, Hinarii, who gave me the name and estate in presence of her son Tati, the representative chief, and Marau her daughter, the divorced Queen, wife of King Pomare,—my own house, I say, shows now only its platform of cut or rounded stones. My family temple or Maraë at Papara was, and still is, a huge stone structure, and was described by Captain

Cook, as you may read in the history of his voyage. The famous carved stone deities at Easter Island are also examples of stone-work, and, as you may read in Moerenhout's Travels, are not peculiar to Easter Island, but are found in several others quite near Taïti.[2] Had the first adventurers found here a race of docile workmen who could have been made to labor for nothing, I do not doubt that these islands would have been covered with stone-work quite as curious as that of Central America. As the adventurers, like all noble races, were extremely averse to all labor that required steady compulsion, they built little; though what they did was good. Even in the hopelessly barbarous and cannibalistic Marquesas, stone was universally used in building, as Herman Melville describes, although he could not, as Stevenson justly complains, spell accurately a language as yet without spelling.

Doubtless the race has forgotten pretty much all that it knew when it left India. Not for nothing is a people shut up in islands five or six or seven thousand miles from its nearest equals in blood and genius. It has deteriorated. Yet the chiefs are still true nobles,—a distinctly higher type than the common people; and in many respects, the race has preserved a sort of pre-Homeric quality which tells the story of its origin. Its physical beauty goes with its refinements and especially its order of intelligence.

In calling them the spoiled youngest children of the human race, I am as serious as if I were listening to a Samoan Siva. They are just that,—no more, no less. They came here quite recently. Forty generations is the utmost, if every ancestor is assumed to be born on his own island. He may have been born on some other fellow's island, or in India, for all that is certain about him; but I rather incline to take forty or fifty generations as the limit,—say twelve or fifteen hundred years. I prefer this limit because it happens to coincide with a period of great nautical activity in Asia, as I learned in Japanese and Chinese history; and also because it probably includes the bloom of our central American civilisation. These events ought—à priori—to hang together. Between the fifth and eighth centuries of our era, India was in bloom, doing wonders; and Polynesia is but a trifle for India to produce by way of a passing fancy, when India chose to set really to work. Before the fifth century, navigation hardly took such big flights, at least to the eastward of India. I don't insist on this view; but I think it runs with the record.

Thoroughly spoiled as any children ever were, these Polynesians are, even now that four fifths of them have perished from mere contact with the European. Children! No American child is so childish. All, except the greatest chiefs, are cast in one mould, physically and mentally; and all are made only to wreathe garlands and dance and kill each other,—the true objects of true life. Here in Taïti they carried life to a degree of refinement that they seem not to have known elsewhere. I cannot quite make out how numerous they were, but no doubt they numbered at least fifty or sixty thousand. The smaller islands show better the rate of depopulation, which often has left hardly one man in ten. Taïti is a small group; smaller than

Samoa or Tonga, and of course very much smaller than the Hawaiian. The amount of habitable land is rather less than in the outer high islands. The mountains come close to the water, generally, and were never thickly inhabited. I do not see how a very great number of people could have been crowded in; but certainly they carried their refinement to a degree of depravity that implied considerable crowding. They were really depraved, measured on a Polynesian standard. Elsewhere the Polynesians show ignorance of what we call morals; here they showed abundant consciousness that they revelled in violating their own notions of morality. Especially their voluptuousness was studied, and they had regular organisations for carrying it to the furthest possible extent. Taïti beat anything recorded of the Greeks and Syrians, except that the Taïtians knew little of Greek arts. Samoa was a gross democratic innocence compared with this place.

Now as to the old-gold woman! I cannot say I know her, and this is telling the whole story. I have seen her, and somewhat intimately, but, simple as she looks, she is still a woman, and even very much a woman. In Samoa I thought I caught her sometimes in her state of nature, and as far as clothes were concerned I did in fact have little to complain of; but a woman may be naked as a fish, and yet show mighty little of her character. Here she is, and always was, a more complicated creature than in Samoa. The woman of Taïti was pretty near the European standard of female faults. She was not nervously diseased, to be sure. She bore children easily, and liked the carnalities of sex. I think she was healthy and strong, though these races seem never long-lived. She was affectionate after a certain pattern. That she had strong or very lasting passions, I doubt. The record seems to show that she was peculiarly archaic in the rule of *semper mutabile*. That she had more mind than the men is unlikely; and the men had the minds of children. Properly speaking I have never found mind in Polynesian women, who are mechanisms capable of vices and nice impulses, but not of intellectual processes. The true difficulties of the civilised woman, apart from physical matters, are all existent, as far as I can see, in the old-gold woman, and some of them in an aggravated degree because she has few strong emotions and is bound to yield to the first she feels or inspires. She will run away *with* you, if you insist; but she will as easily run away *from* you. She will cry if you leave her, and laugh the next instant. Her capacity for quick change is marvelous. I prefer the old ones to the young ones, except for looks; but although I have seen many, and lived intimately with some, I have not yet met one who inspired me with improper desires. Fiftythree years are a decided check to sexual passion, but I do not think the years are alone to blame. Probably I should have behaved differently thirty years ago; yet as I look back at the long list of dusky beauties I have met, I cannot pick out one who seems to me likely, even thirty years ago, to have held me much more than five minutes even in her arms. They are jolly, obliging, and quite ready to attach themselves. No London girl in her fifth season is readier to snap at a rich elderly nobleman, than an old-gold maiden to jump at a foreign *ali* with a name for wealth and liberality. They require no life-contracts or settlements. They are willing to be sent home whenever they become superfluous. All they ask is that they should be recognised as a so-called wife for the time-being. In Taïti, I am told, even now they hardly ask so much. My young Telemachuses and Anacharses,[3] born and bred in these islands, tell me that one need only say—Come! I have not been tempted to say it, nor has La Farge; but I have seen plenty of women, and several handsome ones; not so intimately as in Samoa, but close enough to watch them; and I am still unable to select one I want.

The moral of this is whatever you please. To my mind the moral is that sex is altogether a mistake, and that no reversion to healthier conditions than ours, can remove the radical evils inherent in the division of the sexes. Yet as nature has made the blunder, it is irreparable, and we might as well look on at it, and see how nature is to get out of the scrape. She is hard at it, and evidently means business. As the matter is no longer one of much consequence to me, I can afford to sit still. Deadheads ought not to hiss the actresses.

Though I regard the old-gold woman as a failure almost as emphatic as the New York female, I have found much entertainment in making her acquaintance. Historically, the Samoan *taupo* is archaic. Homer's women— Penelope, Helen, Nausicaa,—are modern types compared with Faauli and Leolofi. My Samoan princesses knew only the bathing-pool and the naked castaway; they never dreamed of the fortified city, the bronze-doored palace, the silver and gold drinking bowls, the beds, the chairs, the dresses, the jewelry, or even the pottery of Homer's time. They were dead ages before Troy was built. Indeed I doubt whether Faauli and her friends were ever in southern Europe. They never left their woods. They were faraway great aunts of Helen and Penelope, many generations behind, and if they existed at all in Europe in that age, they existed somewhere else than on the Mediterranean. That they were ancestors of the Greeks, however remote, I firmly believe; and one of my favorite amusements in flirting with them was in the thought that I had so far mastered my Odyssey as to make love to Nausicaa's great-great-great-great-and-indefinitely-great-grand aunt, which poor Odysseus himself could not dream of doing. The idea struck me as far more poetic than Goethe's rather commonplace personification of Helen in Faust. I know Helen's grandmother, and could run off with her too if I liked, quite as if I were Paris's grandfather. My Helen is Greek too; she has the shape of a Greek Goddess before the artists refined her too much; she dances like a Greek statue; she wears wreathes and garlands like a Greek woodnymph; she oils her skin like a Greek wrestler; she leads her village to battle as Greek women had long forgotten how to do; and she is amphibious, as few Greek women ever were. Finally, she has no mind, which was also her granddaughter's characteristic. That was in Samoa, where I met her. In Taïti I am in what is left of Asiatic Greece, long before art began. Here I know where Venus rose and Cypria flowered. That is past, but the smell of the—cocoanut, hangs round the shores still.

We shall not go to the Marquesas. I am scared by the certainty of a fortnight's seasickness in a small schooner; and my interest in Nukuheva is dulled by the accounts I get of its melancholy desertion. The natives there were hardy and simple—not depraved as here—but they perished all the same, and keep on dying. Their dances are all gone. Melville's valley is deserted, at least by the tribe he knew. The whole island, according to Stevenson and other travellers whose stories I have asked, offers no inducement equal to the effort. Indeed everywhere else in Polynesia the missionary has worked his wicked will. The Paumotus alone retain here and there traces of the old dance and song and old interest; but even there I believe the men and women wear clothes and hats. I can hear of no island like Samoa, where the world is still young.

So we are trying to charter a steamer to take us to Fiji. I want to see one black island before closing the chapter. Fiji had great influence on Polynesia, chiefly in cannibalising my poor friends, who never took as much pleasure in eating their enemies as I should do in eating mine if I had any. In my time—as Taura-atua—I ordered a human sacrifice on any great occasion, and the eye was offered to the king, if he were at hand, but we did not generally eat the bodies; we hung them to the trees in the Maraë at Tautira. I never ordered very many sacrifices; one or two or three a year perhaps; but only a great head-chief like me had the right at all. What I did, when not fighting, was to drink very strong kava which acted like opium. Chiefs alone did that, and when we had kava, we dressed in full dress, and forbade the cocks to crow or the dogs to bark.

Don't mention to anyone that I have a Taïtian name. At home it is a joke, but in Polynesia it is serious. Stevenson would be furious if he knew it. He is quite proud because Ori, his host at Tautira, gave him a name, Teriitera. Ori also gave me his own name, Ori a Ori, but I don't want Stevenson to hear of it; still less that the old chiefess, the greatest woman in the whole of Polynesia, the pure native heir to all Taïti nobility, actually gave me the best name in the family. Prince Oscar of Sweden alone ever enjoyed the honor of being adopted by her, until she adopted La Farge and me. So don't tell of it, or I shall get abused for mimicking Stevenson.

Ever Yrs   Henry Adams.

MS: MHi
    1. *An Account of the Natives of the Tonga Islands* compiled from the communications of William Mariner, by John Martin (1817).
    2. J. A. Moerenhout, *Voyages aux îles du Grand Océan* (1837).
    3. Anacharsis (ca. 600 B.C.), a Scythian prince who traveled widely in quest of knowledge.

To Elizabeth Cameron

Papeete. Sunday, May 3, 1891.

The "Tropic Bird" has arrived. I have just finished your letter postmarked March 1, and have opened all the Magazines directed in your hand; but how curious! The Magazines include the April numbers, while all the letters are written in February and should have come a month ago.

You are the only one who knew enough to mail your letter in time for the March packet. Dwight, Mabel Hooper, Miss Baxter and Sturgis Hooper all wrote a day or two too late. You too have sent the magazines here, but must have mailed your March letter to Auckland. There in truth I ought to be, but I wrote you last week why I could not get away. The devil was wilder than usual last Sunday, for while my letter was going all the way to Tautira to be put on board the "Courtney Ford" which had shipped her cargo of oranges and was going to sea the next day, the "Courtney Ford" was dragging her anchors in a gale, and going ashore in the bay where I have so often paddled my canoe through the swell. She was got off the next day, apparently unhurt, and is shipping a new lot of oranges in place of four hundred thousand thrown overboard; but I imagine that my poor letter, if it goes in her, will not reach you sooner than this one, which will go back in the "Tropic Bird" ten days hence.

As usual, you are the one who does just the right thing. I wish one could say with cold white paper what one has to keep to oneself on this subject; but you must fill in the blanks and supply the colors. Do you see any picture in your mind of our situation here? For it is really queer, at least to me. Our paroxysm of energy in the night voyage from Oponuhu seems to have exhausted my last drop of vitality. We took possession of the little Consulate, and there I have sat every day, all day long, on the porch, sometimes reading Walter Scott and wondering at finding myself interested in Guy Mannering and Ivanhoe, which read better than ever; sometimes chatting and smoking; sometimes dozing, or looking over the blue sea for the "Tropic Bird"; but always feeling as though under the effect of a mild opiate. Effort has become impossible. I have not walked fifty yards for a week. I can no longer paint; the constant attempt to do what I can't do, has become too fatiguing, and I have thrown aside my brushes. The mind and body are torpid, and your letters are all that wakes them. I had been roused at half past four in the morning by Atwater to go to market, and had lingered till seven chatting with La Farge and Marau who was also attending to household affairs hard by; then I had gone to bed again and dozed, vaguely wondering whether you had not by this time grown tired of writing, and whether I had not best let the world drift where it would, without more fretting; when Captain Harte, the acting Consul, brought in the letters and enclosures. They seemed to brace me up like quinine; only, thank my luck this time, I can enjoy a sweet tonic which is just as healthy as a bitter one. In a day or two I shall drop back into my laziness, but now that I am galvanised into a few hours of life, let me tell you what I have been thinking about. Like Robinson Crusoe and Herman Melville, I have been able to turn my mind to nothing except escape from my island. I wanted so much to carry out my promise of reaching London by September, that, after the Richmond sailed without us, I persuaded myself to risk my precious health in a sailing vessel, and I instructed Captain Harte to charter for me the best schooner he could find to take us to Fiji. The best schooner he could find was the Nassau of thirtyfive tons, which means a little boat fifty feet long and twelve feet wide, in which we were to sail two thousand miles as best we could. With full consciousness of the misery I should certainly suffer, I authorised Harte to pay fifteen hundred dollars for this cockboat for the voyage to Fiji. No sooner had I made the offer than the German firm here took up the Nassau for a trading cruise, and the captain decided that his interests required him to do what the firm wished. Then I made the same offer general. I applied for any schooner properly built and commanded, and even offered to buy any of them if they could not be chartered. All my offers were refused. No one would either charter or sell, or enter on discussion of terms. Of the dozen schooners about these islands, not one could be had. I have passed a week in useless search, and am now obliged to give it up. As for a larger vessel, I have no hopes. No vessels bound westward come here. Indeed no vessel except the "Courtney Ford" and "Tropic Bird" are to be found within a thousand miles. The chance is very small that any ship will turn up which can go out of its course so far as Fiji for any money whatever. I thought seriously of returning to San Francisco in the Tropic Bird, and crossing to Europe by way of New York, if my letters offered any excuse for so wild a course; but our letters are all innocent of any such matter. So we must wait another month for the Richmond, and go down to Auckland in midwinter, in order to go on to either to Fiji or Sydney, with the certainty of stormy passages in small steamers that are worse than sailing-vessels. Meanwhile I have exhausted Tahiti which is a true Crusoe island. Luckily we are not unhappy here. I am not even in low spirits, as I was at Samoa in the last month of my stay there. La Farge is well and apparently happy, and busy painting. Our society is limited enough; but our sisters Beretania and Manihini are next door; Marau comes up and down from Faa, and is almost energetic. Our grandmother Hinarii comes to town occasionally. I tell the women that of all the straight-laced, puritanical, highly-moral communities I ever struck, Taïti is the strictest; for they will not even come to breakfast on our porch, or sit there to watch the sunset; and Marau discourses eloquently on the propensities of Papeete society for scandal, although she knows that I come from Boston and scandal cannot touch a Bostonian. I tell them that all the most highly moral young women in America come to breakfast and dine with me in Washington, but it produces no effect on them. For a woman of forty,—if that is her age,—who has been a Queen, and divorced, and has had experiences, Marau my sister is a study. She amuses La Farge even more than me, and we all bewail the ravages of civilisation; but evidently she still considers herself to be Queen, and means to give her good subjects in Papeete the example of a Godly and exemplary life. I wish you could know her. She would amuse you certainly; perhaps she could even instruct you.

Sunday, May 10. Another week of exasperated idleness. A schooner called the "Gironde" has come in. It belongs to the German firm, and I have been trying to charter it. The firm uses it to bring cocoanuts and such produce to freight ships with, and although the schooner barely pays its way, the owners refuse even to discuss letting us have her for six weeks. I have got so far as to suggest willingness to pay two thousand dollars net, besides another thousand for the expenses of the vessel, which is five times as much as they ever dreamed of getting for a six weeks use of the wretched craft; but still the old Dutchman will not listen. Naturally I am vexed, for I could get a good yacht for such a price in America; but here I am helpless. Still, I think by dint of perseverance and money, I can drive an idea even into a German head; or if not, I can make noise enough to attract some other vessel; for there are about fifteen such schooners plying from Papeete to the neighboring islands, though none but the Gironde are in port. Another week may settle it so that I can hope to reach Fiji by the middle of June; but meanwhile the "Tropic Bird" will be off with the mail, which closes on the 14th, and I may not be able to tell the result in this letter. Meanwhile, too, I do nothing whatever. I am positively unhappy at the thought that another man would be getting no end of amusement here, but that I, from mere want of energy and ideas, am wasting all my opportunities.

By way of excitement or something to talk about, I some time ago told Marau that she ought to write memoirs, and if she would narrate her life to me, I would take notes and write it out, chapter by chapter. To our surprise, she took up the idea seriously, and we are to begin work today, assisted by the old chiefess mother, who will have to start us from Captain Cook's time. If I had begun this job when we first arrived, I might have made something of it; but now at best I can do only a fragment. Do you think it dangerous for me to get into such relations with a young divorced Tahitian Queen? I should rather like to think myself in danger; but whether it is that I am not any longer in my twenties, or that I am naturally clammy, or that I am the property of some other woman, or that the Polynesian is not my ideal, I have been astonished and rather annoyed at finding myself so indifferent to the archaic woman with all her physical magnificence. There is something in Clarence King's remark that "after all, sex is such a modern thing." The Polynesian woman seems to me too much like the Polynesian man; the difference is not great enough to admit of sentiment, only of physical divergence. The old-gold woman has most of the drawbacks of modern women, except the extreme nervous sensitiveness. She is physically better adapted to her work, but intellectually she suffers the more. The old-gold woman is incapable of resisting any impulse. She yields easily to a stronger will, which is natural enough; but she yields also to any temptation, no matter how slight. She has no habit of resistance. She yields to a lover, which is not surprising, seeing the force of the passion; but, in her, I doubt whether there is a thought of resistance, unless it is fear of being killed by a husband; for jealousy is violent here. If another lover comes along, she yields just as easily to his will. The same weakness runs through every appetite she has, and makes her drink, for example, or do whatever comes into her head that is not absolutely *tabu*. This weakness is the cause of the fearful depopulation of the Pacific Islands, but the poor creatures have still gone gaily to destruction, and only of late years one begins to see the look of sadness which always goes with civilisation, and means that a race has opened its eyes to its cares. For this sort of woman, I am a very poor sort of man. To be sure, Marau and her sisters are not wholly of this kind. They are half Jewess, and though Beretania, in certain lights and attitudes, is a very beautiful Jewess, Marau, who is ten years older, has become rather coarse, as orientals, and occidentals also, sometimes do; but still Marau is very Polynesian and, what is more, she is high-caste Polynesian, which is very different from common Polynesian. If she would tell her whole story, it would certainly be amusing, but even a Polynesian will hardly tell everything in these days. Civilisation has made such ravages that truth can no longer be expected. Still, she understands the old-gold woman all through, as no writer of European blood ever has done; and perhaps I can manage to note a little of the local color.

Wednesday, May 13. Tomorrow I must mail this letter, though I am still unable to say what our next step is to be. I have formally, and to the astonishment of my friends, offered old Jorss three thousand dollars for the Gironde. He could hardly sell her for much more; but he has replied that she must go first to the Paumotus, and that on her return I can have her. This does not suit me, but both she and the smaller schooner Nassau, and perhaps Naarii Salmon's schooner will probably arrive within a fortnight, and I think I can get one of them in time to sail by June 1. In that case we should reach Fiji before July 1, and get down to Sydney in August. This is the utmost I can now hope, and you can imagine, not only from the amount of money it costs, but from my willingness to endure a long ocean voyage in a coprà schooner of sixty tons, the genuineness of my effort to get on. Yet, even if I reach Europe this autumn, my return to America will still depend on whether I am wanted there. For all that I know now, I should be doing a favor by staying where I am; for at least I harm nobody there or here, and I might plunge into no end of mischief in returning. By that time I suppose even my poor old history will have made me enemies and though criticism generally hurts little, it gives trouble. Do you think I can escape setting people by the ears? Or shall you tell me in a few months that I had better go back to the South Seas, which is such a safe place for people to talk scandal? Has Washington improved, and is my empty house sacred? I never feel quite sure that my letters are not read by his excellency the Governor La Cascade, or by any one else who happens on them in the course of their long wanderings, and as for your letters, I am confident they will fall into any hands rather than mine, for I am likely to go nowhere that they are likely to be; but if we ever do reach Europe, where something like neighborhood exists, I shall want to know all about myself, now that myself and I are two different persons; one a mere shadowy possibility in Washington; the other an almost equally thin shadow in unknown or uncertain night. You are the only person who can tell me what I want to know, and this letter will have to be answered to Paris, I suppose; for if it reaches you after the 24th of June, you can send no letter this way which can catch me, if I carry out my plan of passing through Australia in August. I gave in my last letter a means of catching the trail again by telegraph to care of our consulate at Sydney; but even that could not bring me a letter before I started for Europe. The only chance is that you could hit me at Ceylon, care of our Consul at Colombo in that island. I should be there in September if at all. A letter mailed from London would reach Ceylon in about three weeks, I imagine. From New York at least a month would be required. So a letter mailed from America on August 1 should certainly reach me if I ever get to Ceylon at all. Yet the chance of my missing it is so great that you must reserve all that Eugenia Mifflin used to call *vital*, for my arrival at Paris. A letter mailed to Fiji before June 24 would catch the San Francisco steamer to Auckland, and might catch me before I leave Fiji.

If you knew how much I wanted to see you and Martha again, you would not wonder at my tediousness in repeating over and over again the same story and trying to fix these very vague connections. To be in Europe seems to be next door to you. I feel as though I could run in at any time; and even if I do not cross the Atlantic, I can halloo across, every hour or two, and wish you good day.

My life here has ceased to be more than mere waiting for departure; yet I have actually begun on Marau's memoirs, and sketched the introductory chapter after taking a mass of memoranda from her dictation. The work is useful in distracting my thoughts from sheer vacuity, and it teaches me a little more, or at least a little more exact knowledge of the island than I should ever have got from books or conversation. The trouble is that Marau never stays here two days, but dashes off to Faaa, five miles out of town, to look after her children or her farm or whatever she has there; and unless I pursue her to Faaa, I must wait till she comes up again before I can go on. Next Saturday we are to have native breakfast at Faaa, after the style of our Samoan banana-leaf feasts; no plates or knives and forks; but plenty of breadfruit and pig. We are sure to find it amusing, and in my opinion quite as good as our own style of French cooking, which has become intolerable. Housekeeping is as much of a bore here as everywhere else, and the cook-problem quite as insoluble. Our cousins Pree and Cheeky are shocked at the way I let myself be robbed; and indeed I suppose the waste of my establishment would run theirs, though to me the whole expense seems small after the waste of your—I mean my household at Washington. Are you naturally a good economist? I suppose I am not, for I can economise only in scale, not in detail. Here no one spends more than two or three thousand dollars a year, I imagine, or has it to spend. The British Consul is paid £600, I think, with some allowances. Our Consul gets a thousand dollars and a sort of house. My friend Tati, who is the great man here in native estimation, told me all about his life, which has been a hard struggle to make a mere living, and to feed his children. He tells me that his sister Mrs Darsie, veuve Brander, after closing up all her affairs, can hardly be worth more than a hundred and fifty thousand dollars; yet Brander was much the richest merchant hereabouts. There are at least a dozen houses competing here for the business of these scattered islands under French rule,—Paumotus, Marquesas, Tahitian and what not, containing barely thirty thousand people, half of whom absolutely refuse to work for wages,—and the whole value of exports and imports combined, does not exceed $1,500,000 in gold. Naturally men can make no large fortunes on such a business, and if life were not a constant picnic, they could not live here at all.

As I shall not visit Nukuheva, where I hoped to sketch for you the scenes of Melville's book, I send you a photograph of a Marquesan house to paste into your copy of Typee. I suppose Stevenson must have described the valley, which is said to be now abandoned to a sand-fly worse than the mosquito;—and the mosquito is bad enough, especially when one has burned up all the Buhach in the island. We have heard so much and talked so much of the Marquesas and Paumotus that I seem almost at home there, and have the less curiosity to go. I am more curious now to see Borabora, Raratonga and Tonga, where we should touch on our voyage to Fiji; and one of my reasons for wishing to go in my own schooner is that we may visit these groups on our way.

Thursday, 14 May. The mail closes this afternoon, and is to start in the Tropic Bird tomorrow if the weather permits. I have no more to say. We are bound here for at least a fortnight more, and if we get away then, it will probably be by means of the "Nassau" which will have to stop a week or two at Raratonga in carrying us to Fiji. Meanwhile I must wait at least a couple of months before receiving any letters, lucky if I get them at all. I shall not know whether you are at home or abroad, or whether you are well or ill. I am afraid you will forget me, and cannot blame you if you do. A thousand thanks for your magazines and cuttings. We read everything we can lay hands on. La Farge sends home today another batch of sketches; and if you have not yet visited his studio, the next time you are in New York you had better go there. Tell Martha that when I come home I shall eat her à la Polynésienne.

MS: MHi

To Arthur G. Adams

Papeete. 9 May, 1891.

My dear Arthur[1]

Your letter of February 27 reached here just a week ago, so please don't think I've neglected to acknowledge it. The South Seas are a long way from Boston. If you ever come here, you had better bring your own boat, for you can't get away without it. I am waiting here for the "Gossoon" to come along, for I see no chance of any other craft to take us off.[2] I want to go two thousand miles westward to Fiji, and I can't find even a forty-footer to carry me. Tell Charley to hurry up. I am tired of waiting.

The Pacific Ocean is a great place for anyone who likes the sea more than I do. The best thing about it is the weather, which is better than our summer weather because it is not very hot or very cool, except in the middle of the day; and then everyone seems to be asleep. I think they stay asleep a good deal at all hours, for Tahiti is the sleepiest place ever I heard of. Tahiti is an island about fifty miles long, with mountains inside, and some eight or nine thousand red Indians living among cocoanut groves and breadfruit trees along the shores. Quincy has a much greater number of people than all Tahiti has got, but rather a different kind. The Taïti people are very kind and friendly, and live mostly in wooden cottages with jig-sawed porches and galvanised-iron roofs, and talk a little English or French sometimes, and are much too civilised for my taste. Still, they have some of their old habits, and are as lazy, almost, as I am myself.

You would have great fun here. Along the shore, about half a mile off, is the coral reef which runs round most of the island. The reef is a regular low wall of living coral, about forty or fifty feet wide, and projecting about a foot above high water. This regularity is caused by the tides, which are very queer, for they are always high at noon and midnight, and their rise and fall is only about a foot or eighteen inches. As the ocean-swell outside is always several feet high, the constant surf keeps the reef awash and the coral alive, but only at just this level, so that the reef looks as smooth as though it were levelled by measure. The surface is rather rough, and full of small holes, but good to walk on, though I prefer to wear shoes in doing it. Of course no end of creatures grow there. One can walk miles along it, and every few minutes the big surf swashes over it, up to your knees, and tumbles in a little cataract into the lagoon inside. My regular amusement has been to go out every evening on the lagoon in a native dug-out canoe, and paddle about. In quiet weather, one can paddle outside through the openings which make the harbors, and the long swell is rather pleasant, barring big sharks which are very rare so near shore, but out at sea run thirty feet long. Once off Samoa in a cutter, a shark followed us that must have been at least eight feet across the head, and looked like a whale, but all spotted and unpleasant. I often see the fins of small ones in the deep water of the harbors, but never in the lagoons, which are shallow, and vary from an inch to three feet in depth, with coral or sand bottoms. The water is very clear and about 80° in temperature. The corals at the bottom grow in queer shapes, sometimes like big mushrooms, sometimes like plants and shrubs, and sometimes only blotches of color, yellows, greens and purples. Little fish that flash like emeralds and sapphires, or are striped in violent colors and irregular patterns, fly about among the corals, and eels with black-and-white patterns. I don't think much of the fish to eat, though there is no end of them. The best water-eating is a very large cray-fish about a foot long, that looks like a centipede. The small cray-fish are good too, but have not the flavor of ours; and there are good small oysters. The best fish are freshwater; but the cuttle-fish I think excellent. There is a big cuttle-fish at Samoa supposed to be thirty feet span, which sleeps on the rocks off Fangaloa; but here the squids are small, only a foot or two span, and they are caught by hand, and stewed in cocoanut milk. In the hollows of the coral, on the outside the reef, are big eels, like boa constrictors, twelve feet or more in length, and thick as one's leg; but a stranger eel is found in a lake high up in the mountains; he is very large, with big ears, and how he ever got there is a mystery.

You would like the surf-swimming too, on boards. The surf shoots one up like a steamengine. The sailing of course is splendid. I have had to go in boats a good deal, and always in whale-boats when coasting, for the whale-boat stands any weather, sails well, and has oars which are very necessary among these narrow passages where a sailboat must either be blown off by the trades, or go ashore in the currents. I rather enjoy sailing, even in fairly rough water, but I hate steaming in small steamers against the trades. The chop is very trying, and never stops, even if you go for weeks. The trade blows from the southeast to northeast, and is often a strong wind with a good deal of sea, and decidedly uncomfortable unless you are running before it. In boats, I have been more bothered by calms, which come just when I don't want them; and to flop about at midday in a dead calm, with a vertical sun, in the middle of the Pacific ocean, is an amusement I never enjoy, though I've had lots of it.

I had meant to visit the Marquesas, about seven hundred miles northeast of here; but there is no steamer, and I should have to beat to windward in a small schooner for at least a fortnight. I can't stand that, so I have given up the Marquesas and am trying to reach Fiji, also a fortnight off, but two thousand miles to leeward. I have offered no end of money for any good schooner, even no larger than thirtyfive tons net, but as yet have failed to get one, and apparently must go to Auckland by steam next month.

After that, I don't at all know what I shall do. Perhaps I shall go to China. Perhaps to Europe, if La Farge wants to go there. Perhaps come home to see about my teeth which are in a dreadful state. I must get out of the tropics anyway by August or September, for I am growing too lazy to live here. But what a good time you would have here!

Give my love to your mother and all the family. Write again, but I can't tell where to.

Ever affely   Henry Adams.

MS: MHi

1. Arthur Adams, son of JQA2, was 14 years old.
2. Arthur's older brothers, George and Charles, had in 1890 commissioned their third and fastest racing yacht, the *Gossoon;* it was competitive with the best in its forty-foot class.

To Elizabeth Cameron

Papeete, Sunday, 17 May, 1891.

My letter by the Tropic Bird was mailed three days ago, but I doubt whether the Bird has flown yet. She has been taking in a cargo of oranges on the south side of the island, and yesterday was still there. I wish I could decide when and where this letter will be mailed. I should fix Tonga for the place, and June 10, at latest, for the date; but I fear it is hopeless. I have still no clue of escape.

Luckily I am rather amused and occupied. My "Memoirs of Marau, Queen of Tahiti" give me a sort of excuse for doing nothing. Whenever Marau comes to town, I get from her a lot of notes, which I understand very little, and she not much; then I write them out; then find they are all wrong; then dispute with her till she becomes energetic and goes as far as the next room to ask her mother. The dear old lady has been quite unwell. The other evening I was taken in to see her, and found her sitting on her mat on an inner verandah. When I sat down beside her, she drew me to her and kissed me so affectionately that the tears stood in my eyes. She was looking very badly, but is better now; all right, I hope. Marau gave us a feast yesterday at Faaa, and I was only sorry that the old lady could not be there. La Farge is not in love with her as I am; he takes more to Marau and the girls; but I think the Hinarii is worth them all.

Marau's feast was very pleasant and simple. The house is a rough sort of cottage in the midst of a great cocoanut plantation, four miles from here, on the sea-shore. The feast was spread on a low table under a palm-leaf trellis ornamented with yellow leaves, and we were all ornamented with wreathes like Greek Gods. We sat cross-legged on the mats, and eat all sorts of tasteless native dishes, much better to my mind than our own greasy French stuff, but rather funny than nice. I drank orange rum, which is only orange-juice slightly fermented, a sort of orange-ade, which, with ice, I rather like, and which seems harmless. Only Marau, Pree, Manini, Norman and Arthur Brander, two native ladies married to foreigners, and the French *médecin* were the party. After the long breakfast we had much singing, including a *himene,* till five o'clock when we drove in. Compared with the frank savagery of our Samoan feasts, this was highly civilised and almost Versailles; but the native customs were as much kept up as could be expected where savagery has been so long *tabu* as here. The only genuine native article was the nose-flute, which is rather a pretty accompaniment to their songs.

This morning Pree and Manini brought in two lovely straw hats which their mother sent us. They are so light and white, and so fascinating to look at, that La Farge and I are irresistible Cupids in them. I shall try to send mine home, but I know that you will take possession of it, and I should much like to see you wear it. These hats are made of the fibre of the arrowroot—I believe, or else I dreamed it. The people make hats, fans, lamp-shades and such things, of all sorts of fibre, and very pretty, but I think these are the finest I have seen.

Sunday, 24 May. Another struggle this week to get a schooner from the German Company, but its last behavior has been so bad, not to say Jewish, that I have sworn to deal with them no more. A German hog is really no worse than an English or French or American hog—perhaps even less noxious,—but he seems to the imagination, chiefly because of the intellectual swinishness expressed in his sauer-kohl habits of mind, to be a cruel infliction. Everyone tells me that I have been treated only as everyone else is treated, so I console myself by rejoicing or hoping that I am not like this publican;[1] but it saddens me to see how even these poor natives, contaminated by more than a century of contact with Europeans, still maintain their superiority. What can the European-Aryan race have done to become the low-bred wretches they are! Their manners are what they themselves call vulgar, and their minds are more vulgar than their manners. I have never seen a vulgar Polynesian, though some of them come dangerously near it, from associating with Europeans and Americans. Well! we shall sail on the Richmond a fortnight hence, and can only hope we may be dropped at Tonga. I would have paid any amount of money to go to Fiji by way of the islands, but it was not a question of money.

Meanwhile another week has passed in this lazy life, and here is another lovely Sunday morning with the women going to church in their red calico nightgowns, and the blue sea looking as gentle as a peacock. The longer I stay here, the less I am bored. Being now thoroughly adopted into the Teva family, I find myself provided with occupation, for I have at last got them into a condition of wild interest in history. My interest appears to have captured the old lady, who astonished her children by telling me things she would never tell them; and as they had to act as interpreters, they caught the disease one by one, till at length they have all got out their pens and paper, and are hard at work, making out the family genealogy for a thousand years back, and tracing their collateral connections in every direction. The difficulties and complications are very amusing; and as I am always asking questions and forgetting the answers, they never get their minds clear. The old lady's memory is prodigious, but even she often makes mistakes. Marau tells me a story; Moetie (Mrs Atwater) tells me a different one; the old lady laughs at both, and tells it in a way totally unlike either. Tati is coming from Papara today, and will doubtless join the dance. I have stopped writing the memoirs because I found that, without the genealogy to hang it on, the narrative was always wrong or unintelligible; but every day a crop of new stories, legends or songs, turn up, until a year's work would hardly be enough to put them in shape. If Alexander Dumas had ever struck this *trouvaille* he would have made a wonderfully amusing book of it. Stevenson could have done it, too, but he never got in with the old lady, and only touched the outside rim of Tahitian history. His legend of Rahero is extremely well done, and has only the fault of being done with more care than the importance of the legend deserves. In reading it, one is constantly worried by wondering that he should have worked so hard on so slight a subject. Rahero was a very subordinate figure in history, and connects with nothing. The legends and poetry of the island can be made interesting only by stringing them on a narrative, and Stevenson could have done it better than any one else, for he has a light hand, when he likes, and can write verse as well as prose. My hand is too heavy for such work, and here I am anyway only a passing traveller trying to find a moment of amusement to vary the wild monotony of island life. You cannot in your loftiest visions imagine the quiet of Tahiti. Even time does not seem to pass here; the seasons do not vary; the years run into one; and geological epochs are unknown. The sun comes and goes, as individuals are born and die, but the rest never changes, or changes too little for notice. Rain falls occasionally, but no storm worth the name comes near us. Generally eternal sunshine falls on eternal cocoanuts. The purple ocean looks vaster about us than it does from shipboard. I gaze over it by the hour, wondering what lies beyond. Sometimes I half feel as though I really were Taura-atua i Amo, and never should know more of the world than that the ocean is big and blue. Shall I really ever escape from here, and shall I see you again, and will you be the same, or am I the same, and is La Fayette Square really where I dreamed it? Only when the monthly packet arrives from San Francisco, I realise that my old life is still going on. At other times I am as dead as Adam, and hunger only for mangoes, which belie my own assertion about time, for they have passed and gone into the ewigkeit. Even La Farge is beginning to want occupation. Actually one day last week I read Harry Lorrequer from beginning to end. It was far duller than the surf pounding on the reef.[2]

Sunday, May 31. Positively I have worked. I am not quite so brazen-faced as to claim to have done real work; but I have been quite as busy as I should be at home. I have untangled two centuries of family history, and got it wound up nicely. I have rewritten two chapters, making a very learned disquisition on Tahitian genealogy, mixed up with legends and love-songs. The thing would be rather pretty if I only knew how to do it, or perhaps it might be better if I were writing it on my own account; but as it is for Marau in the first person, I have to leave out everything risky. All the family have labored in a most unusual spirit of interest, but they are now pretty well exhausted. Energy in Tahiti is a very brief affair. I shall not have time to carry the memoirs beyond an introduction, and shall leave it with Marau to finish if she chooses, and send it to me to put in shape for printing privately. If she does it, you shall see it; but I have no faith in the future of any undertaking left in Tahiti to the people. They finish nothing. My papers may perhaps be kept, but generally even papers are scattered and lost. Marau is the only one of the family who carries the interest to the point of enthusiasm, and she finds it hard to work alone.[3] When the old chiefess dies, no one will be left on the island who has any real accurate knowledge of the past. The Pomares never amounted to much, and Hinoi, the last male of the family, is an owl for stupidity.

The Richmond is expected now any day next week, and the instant she arrives, we must jump. She will take in her oranges at Hitiaa, on the east coast, and we shall drive there, to escape the sea as long as possible. Tati will be there, as he looks after the oranges, and we hope to have a day or two for La Farge to sketch. I have not touched my paints for a month, and feel helpless to return to them. All my courage is needed to face a voyage to Auckland. If it were not that I have left so many beautiful places without missing them, I might fear being homesick for Tahiti, which is, after all, a queer little place, with an existence so different from our American experience that it seems part of another world. I feel that it has done me good, though I kicked like a bucking broncho at it for a long time. I have been even amused, and the deadly sensation of disgust at everything has mostly passed off. The life here is not in the least ideal. I see nothing to keep me. The charm of climate palls. I am too old and too *exigeant* to care for these dusky women who are children in mind and deadly uninteresting. They are sometimes handsome, but I have never got so far as to feel any sense even of physical charm in them. The men—especially the young ones—have all a look of dissipation and dissoluteness. The old island aristocracy is gone, and only Hinarii, my dear old native chiefess, keeps its traditions.

So I am quite ready to start for new pastures, and perhaps somewhere I may come upon traces of home friends. My last home-letters were written in February, and tomorrow is June. I have not an idea where you are, or are to be, or where I should address to you, or where you should address to me; but my two last letters were very full on that subject, and my address is just what it was then. I mean to post this letter here, before sailing, so that, if we go to the bottom of the ocean, you may have the last news of me; but if we reach Tonga or Auckland I shall write by the next mail-steamer to San Francisco, and that letter should reach you before this. If the Richmond stops at Tonga, we shall stop there, and trust to finding a schooner to take us to Fiji, or go round by Samoa. Otherwise we go to Auckland. Yet La Farge always dreads getting letters calling him home, and until we are fairly off, we are not sure.

Monday, June 1. The Richmond suddenly arrived this morning, bringing your March and April letters from Samoa, with the photographs of St Gaudens's work. St Gaudens himself, and Dwight and Hay also wrote about it, but none of them gave me so much as you, though Hay's little description of it gave me a regular old-fashioned fit of tears, and I have not yet at all recovered from the effect of reading and re-reading what you have all said.[4] As for you, I can say nothing that I have not said so often as to be ashamed of not saying more. I am infinitely grateful. You make me feel as though my last anxiety was removed, and I had no more to worry about in life. If the statue is half what you describe it, I can be quite contented to lie down under it, and sleep quietly with her. At the end of all philosophy, silence is the only true God.

Meanwhile, your letter, instead of bringing silence, brings nervous activity. You are now in England, and are to remain there till November. The owner of the Richmond brought me information that he had obtained from the Auckland authorities permission to touch at Fiji, and would take me there for £400, besides our passage-money. I closed with him on the spot, and we sail for Fiji on the 5th. I hope to arrive on the 16th. If we stay a month in Fiji, and then go on to Sydney, we ought to be able to pass a certain time in Ceylon, and reach London in October. Of course this depends on catching steamers that fit our plans; but I feel strong hopes that we can do it. Perhaps you may want to fit out at Paris before going home, and in that case you can have the supreme advantage of my taste and judgment in selecting your gorgeous raiment. I could get a month to be with you at least, and beyond that, *nous verrons!* I will not look beyond that,—at least not now. We are plunged in all the mental confusion of a hurried departure, but I shall send this letter by the packet which leaves here on or about the 15th, in the hope that it will reach you before the Auckland mail can do it. Yet I shall send a few lines through Auckland too, to announce our arrival at Fiji. Write to Ceylon, care of our Consul at Colombo, as I said in my last. You should get this letter in August, and if I find a telegram from you at Sydney, you may hear from me by telegraph before this arrives.

Tahiti is as lovely as ever in bidding us good-bye. Our family is affectionate, and we shall be a little sad at ceasing to be Taura-atua and Terai-tua. Marau is to go on with her memoirs, and send them to Washington. So she says, with her ferocious air of determination, half Tahitian and half Hebrew; and if she keeps her word, I shall have a little occupation at Washington which will amuse you too, for I have begged her to put in all the scandal she can, and the devil knows she can put in plenty. She tells me today that her late lord, King Pomare, is very ill, and supposed to be dying. Apparently I am fatal to Kings. Kalakaua and Pomare march to the grave as I pass. I should be employed by the anarchists.

Your news of poor Tom Lee and Lowndes and the rest is enough to think about on my voyage.[5] We have a long–long journey before us; but I fear that La Farge will wonder at my eagerness to hasten it, after such long indifference.

———

Wednesday, June 3. 9 A.M. We breakfast at eleven with our grandmother and the family, and start at twelve for Hitiaa in carriages. There we shall have a day, while the Richmond loads oranges. Friday morning we shall come round to Papeete to take our mail, and then we are off. Of course I am fretted by lots of small closing matters, and feel as though I had been put through a mangle and squeezed out. Actually I wish I were at sea. My only source of energy is that I am actually starting on a ten-thousand-mile journey to see—you!

MS: MHi
1. Luke 18:11.
2. Charles Lever's first novel, *The Confessions of Harry Lorrequer* (1837), a series of military adventures in Ireland and France.
3. *Memoirs of Marau Taaroa, Last Queen of Tahiti* was privately printed by HA in 1893.
4. "The figure is something more than life size, and the bronze is most beautiful in color. . . . The whole pose is strong and calm, full of repose. I was disposed to criticize a little the background of the figure, but I think that no judgement would be fair until the grass, hedge, and general green background to it all is there. The stonework—the bench—is beautiful" (Elizabeth Cameron to HA, March 14, 1891). For Hay's judgment, see HA to Saint-Gaudens, June 23, 1891.
5. Thomas Lee was no better. James Lowndes was engaged to Laura Tuckerman, the daughter of Lucius and Elizabeth Gibbs Tuckerman.

6.

The End of the Circuit

1891

In Tahiti, Adams had dressed Tahitian and lovingly learned the world of his adoptive family. In Fiji, as the guest of Governor Sir John Thurston, he dressed for dinner European-style and observed the local culture with an outsider's eye. He found himself, in reflective moments, basically unsympathetic to European imperialist expansion over the Pacific world. As he traveled to Australia, Java, and Singapore and watched economic development extinguishing local cultures everywhere, he was so taken aback as to question, for the first time in his life, the market economy that lay behind it. He conceived that only China and the United States stood apart from the well-nigh universal imperialist system.

Adams could not choose his worlds at will. In Ceylon, he made a pilgrimage to the sacred bo-tree where Buddha had attained nirvana. As he wrote Elizabeth Cameron, she was a sufficient reason for his not keeping his thoughts fixed on Buddha. In less frivolous terms, he expressed his failure to find nirvana in the poem "Buddha and Brahma," which he wrote on shipboard on his passage back to Europe.

Adams' detachment from the world, like his recoil from society, depended on recourse to intimates, of whom Mrs. Cameron came to be preeminent. The long voyage across the Indian Ocean and the Red Sea was taking him back to her. She for her part crossed from England to Paris to meet him. But she was nevertheless very much of the world and society, and, to complicate matters further, she traveled with her daughter and grown stepdaughter. In Paris and then in London, during the next three and a half weeks, Adams had little time for anything besides attending Mrs. Cameron and her party, but he found that the intimacy of the diary-letters eluded him.

When Mrs. Cameron left for home and Adams became a letter-writer again, he faced at last his inability to come to terms with her "apocalyptic Never." The pain of baffled love had become central in his life—but not all-engulfing. His most anguished letter contained high-spirited passages on politics and art and, at last in his fifty-third year, riding to hounds.

To Theodore F. Dwight

Papeete, June 2, '91.

Dear Dwight

I start tomorrow for Fiji, and have only time to thank you for the March and April letters just arrived by way of Samoa. They are a great relief and pleasure to me. I will not make up my mind, from the photographs, whether I am entirely satisfied with the work. I cannot be quite sure of my own feeling, until I see it. At any rate the photographs make certain that I shall not *dis*-like it, which is a vast comfort for me, who have dreaded hating it. Of course I cannot hope that my own thoughts passing through another man's mind and hands, will come out in a shape familiar to me; my only anxiety is to know that the execution is better than the ideal.

In order to get from here to Fiji I have been obliged to charter a steamer, or rather to pay $2500 for one to go out of her way. I expect that my drafts will break my brother John and impoverish us all for life, as I have decided to go with La Farge from Fiji to Sydney; thence to Ceylon, and so up to Paris, where we hope to arrive in October. You can hardly hit me by letter on the way. Perhaps a telegram to Sydney in August, or Ceylon (Care of our Consul at Colombo) would reach me, if absolutely necessary; but you cannot get this letter before August, and a reply could but barely reach Ceylon by September. If I need news I will telegraph from Sydney about August 1.

By all means, accept the Librarian-ship if it is offered you.[1] I do not know how far you have got along with the Quincy library; but I suppose by this time that it is sufficiently in order; the papers arranged, and the indexes carried far enough to be finished in reasonable time. After these things are once organised, the work of carrying them on requires no great care or labor. A year of attention ought to exhaust the whole thing, as far as it requires your close labor. I take for granted that this is long ago done, and that you have really no more to do at Quincy, and rather need a bigger field and better position. If I were you, I should certainly take it, as I told you long ago, when we first discussed the subject of your leaving the Department.

I hope to reach Fiji on the 16th, and shall send on a letter or two by way of Auckland to announce our arrival.

Yrs ever   Henry Adams

MHi

1. Dwight was being considered to head the Boston Public Library; he became librarian in April 1892.

To Elizabeth Cameron

Hitiaa. Tahiti, 4 June, 1891.

Our last day in Tahiti. After mailing my letter to you, which may not arrive as soon as this, I breakfasted with my family. The old chiefess never sits at table; she hates such Europeanisms, and she had to go to church to pray for Pomare and the sick; a special prayer-day on account of the epidemic of fever and dysentery which has been ravaging the island ever since we arrived. So Marau presided, with her brother Nari, just from the Paumotus. By the bye, Nari, who is as charming as Tati in his way, showed us, at La Farge's request, a box of pearls which was the total result of fifty tons of pearl-shell. The shell is worth about a hundred dollars a ton, I think—or a thousand—or a hundred thousand,—I neither know nor care which, and my love of inaccuracy, and want of memory drive La Farge half mad. He is—don't laugh!—phenominally accurate and precise. No one will believe me, but I tell what I know, when I say that he is as systematic, exact and conventional as he thinks he is. The world altogether misunderstands us both. He is practical; I am loose-minded, and looser still in my management of affairs. He is to be implicitly believed wherever facts are in question; I am invariably mistaken. Revenons à nos perles! Nari's box contained half-a-dozen pearls,—or seven, or five, or, in short, a small number. He valued them at an average of about a hundred dollars, gold, apiece; his consignee, the animal Jorss, estimated them at less than half. None were worth buying for you. One alone was tolerably large and fine, in quality, but defective in shape. So we had better buy your pearls in London or Paris, where the fisheries will certainly be better and more productive, and I shall have the help of your knowledge and judgment.

Besides Marau and Pree and Nari, all the Brander boys were at table: Aleck, Norman, Arthur and Winny; and we had a gay breakfast; but I cared much less for the gaiety than I did for the parting with the dear old lady, who kissed me on both cheeks—after all, she is barely seventy, *va!*— and made us a little speech, with such dignity and feeling, that though it was in native, and I did not understand a word of it, I quite broke down. I shall never see her again, but I have learned from her what the archaic woman was. If Marau only completes the memoirs, you will see; and I left Marau dead bent on doing it.

So Taura-atua and Terai-tua y Amo drove away from the home of their nobility, and left forever the scenes where they had been great warriors and splendid lovers. I wrote poetry then. Marae-ura was her name, and she lived at the pae-pae, among the bushes. I had to leave her because *my* family objected; but I immortalised her in verse. That was a century—or two—or three—ago. Time goes so fast! Four months seem now an eternity,—just the time I have been here, and must take to get elsewhere, counting from one o'clock yesterday afternoon when we started from Papeete on our drive to Hitiaa. We need not have made the journey, but we wanted to see the east side of the island, which is almost prettier than the west. The road, much of it, is a narrow and rough wagon-way cut in the cliff, and not safer than it should be; but it always skirts the big ocean—such a big ocean!—and when it wanders a few rods away, it runs through a grassy avenue of forest,—not tropical, as one imagines it, but much as it might be in England, if England produced palms and breadfruit besides oaks and ash.

After rambling four hours or more along this somewhat bumpy but all the more beautiful road, we arrived towards sunset at an ideal Tahitian village—Hitiaa—where I am now writing, on the green turf, or at least grass, before the hut, with the surf close behind me, and the big trees above. It is almost the prettiest spot we have seen. To the southward, twenty miles or so across the bay, we see our old quarters at Tautira, and our little steamer lies three miles down the shore, loading with oranges. The season is mid-winter. The temperature has fallen several degrees, and is now about eighty. The ocean is rough with the trade-wind, and looks as blue as I feel at going again upon it. The people are as friendly and mild as ever, and, for the moment, are not drunk. Tati, who has the oranges to ship, received us with open arms, as big and handsome as ever. I wish you knew him, for he is to me quite fascinating, with the sort of overflow of life that made Richardson so irresistible. If he ever stays with me at Washington, you and I will have him to ourselves, and not let the natives misunderstand him. His wife, a sweet-presenced native woman who speaks no foreign jargon, and ripples out from time to time only with tiritaratauauteve, or something like it,—for these sounds mean everything,—bids us *iorana* which is good-morning, or good-day or good night, like the Samoan *alofa;* and then tells the small baby Tita, *haremai,* which means *come;* or, to pacify La Farge I will say, *go;* and that is all we know about it. Our native house is perfectly clean, and has a floor, and beds, and the host and hostess think it their duty to watch us undress, and dress in the morning. My bath in the river is a levee. Aue! 'twill all be over tomorrow.

Rarotonga, June 10. We ran out of Hitiaa into a rough sea which washed our low deck; but we stopped three hours at Papeete and got some dinner, and again bade good-bye to all our family, with tender parting from the old chiefess. At four o'clock on the afternoon of the 5th we were off again, bobbing about in the big swell, and going nine miles an hour southwestward. We have passengers aboard, who crowd me out of my old sleeping-corner in the "social hall," so I pass the nights on deck, with my sea-chair for a bed, and at six o'clock in the morning, before daylight, the men washing the deck wake me, and I take my bath by the simple means of letting them play the hose on me. We had a good day, the 6th, and I felt well enough on the 7th to dine at table, which pleased me, but the wind blew that night, and I dragged my bed all round the deck to dodge the rain, and I felt very qualmish, so that I felt joy at getting behind this island, and getting ashore on it, and staying there all last night, sleeping moins bien que mal on a sofa, among mosquitoes. Rarotonga is a small replica of Moorea, six hundred miles on our way. The British resident, Mr Moss, was friendly, and took us to see the Queen, Mokea, to whom Marau had given us a letter. Mokea is big, middle-aged, good-natured, with a certain breeding, but she is as Polynesianiacally untalkative as most of her race. These little islands are so small—so very small,—and so like each other, that they tell nothing. The natives all wear clothes, have stopped their old amusements, and are missionary ridden. Their morals and conversation are supposed to be at least liberal still, but they go to church five times a' Sunday.

In an hour we are off for Fiji, twelve hundred miles, or a trifle more than five days.

Sunday, 14 June. Long. 175° West. We have jumped a day, before crossing the 180° meridian; but we might have jumped a week and the reckoning would still seem to me too short. I have been a month on this wretched little ship, jumping and bumping over the waves; too miserable at last even to read, or to do anything but doze. I grow worse and worse at sea. Last night, lying on my chair on deck where I sleep every night, whatever the weather is, I began seriously to doubt whether my strength would hold out. Unable to eat; without space to move; groaning with nausea, and faint with sickness and exhaustion, I felt as though I must break down somehow. Today is quieter, and I am picking up; but the worst is that we have had no bad weather to warrant sickness. This is what seamen call Paradise. To me, the South Seas are vile. Three days out of four we have head-seas, or cross-seas, that knock us all about, and feel like the British channel. The trade-wind never blows steadily; but, like any other wind, hauls round ahead after a day or two; a heavy swell is always coming from the south or somewhere to roll one out of one's meals; the sea is dull in color; the sky is grey and almost cold; even the sunsets and sunrises are spiritless. I have now sailed over this ocean in pretty much all seasons, and ought to know it from end to end; so I look forward with abject horror to twelve or fourteen thousand more miles, when twelve or fourteen hundred have brought me so low. I read your magazines and newspapers till I could read no more, wondering at times whether this or that article or story were one that you had read and wanted me to read. Est-ce moi, le Normand? Probably not, but I was amused by the suspicion. As you sent the particular number of the Revue, I was bound to find something in it that might have struck you, and it was certainly not the Duc de Broglie.[1]

Well, we are now in sight of the first outlying islands of the Fiji group. Tonga already lies behind us, just out of sight; and in fortyeight hours we should be ashore at Suva, under Sir John Thurston's protection. Only eighteen hundred and fifty miles have we travelled when we get there, but the Richmond goes barely nine miles an hour, and will take ten days, with her stoppage at Rarotonga, to cover the distance. By schooner I should have taken more than three weeks, and how miserable I should have been! That at least is escaped. Of course the Richmond has no other advantage. Passengers enough, including a missionary and his wife, and four ramping children; Frenchmen three or four; stray mysteries a few; but no one whom I want to exchange a nod with. I prefer the captain and crew, who are plain English, very friendly and simple; and as for the crew, pretty seedy in spots. Ain't I glad it is nearly over? The voyage to Sydney will still remain a nightmare; but from there we get big steamers and some speed. These ocean voyages shake me up badly. I am more than a year older since I saw you last. I am almost quite gray, or white if you prefer it; and I have no teeth left, and not many eyes and ears, and still less memory and mind. A sad wreck, but you will have to be good to what is left, and Martha must make fun of my dotage with reasonable decorum. I mean to answer Martha's lovely letter, at Fiji, and my answer shall go in this, unless the mail-steamer should be actually starting for Sydney.

Government House, Suva, Fiji Islands. June 16, 1891. Bravo! Here we are at last, in Sir John Thurston's hands, and only a trace of inward rolling reminding us of the Richmond and the sea. Our last two days on board were not so bad, and we turned up well and smiling to enter Suva harbor yesterday morning. Sir John sent his private secretary to fetch us ashore, and brought us at once up to the Government House where he is alone, his wife and family being at Sydney. The house covers half an acre of ground on the hill overlooking the harbor and sea, with mountains stretching far away; an exquisite view; but the strangest sensation is the dropping suddenly into civilised life after a year's absence. Suva is a scrap of England dropped into space. We lounge in a big library among newspapers and magazines. We dress for dinner. The young men are nice-mannered and play cricket. The women wear dresses and play lawn-tennis. We talk of home and are taught botany and politics. Sir John is agreeable, very intelligent and educated, with very little that suggests British-English; rather the Australian or Australasian type, which is a kind of first cousin to the Harvard College American. As yet we have done nothing but unpack trunks and wash off sea-associations, and look at a game of cricket. We have not even been down to the little town. As for the Fijians, we have seen nothing of them except a few chocolate men, with huge mops of hair sticking out straight, reddened with lime as in Samoa. A lovely sentinel, with a waist-cloth and a hundred-weight of hair, and a gun on his shoulder, walks day and night before the house. Our attendants at meals are three gigantic Fijians in barbaric want of costume, and cannibalistic masses of hair, who smile kindly on us since they are deprived of their natural right of eating us. Curiously enough, I have always found the cannibal a most insinuating fellow, remarkable for his open and sympathetic expression. His impression of human nature is evidently favorable. He regards men as I regard snipe. Even the Solomon Islanders, who are still, when at home, cannibals of the most gormandising class, and black as night, look like the jolliest, cheeriest and friendliest of human kind. Once among cannibals, I feel that my heart is with them. They may eat me, but they will do it in pure good-fellowship. Sir John is to take us to the ancient haunts of Fijian civilisation, and I believe he is to begin tomorrow with some expedition. I am delighted to find that he has sound views on savages, and insists on their retaining all the savagery possible, consistent with a cuisine which excludes man-steaks from the *menu*. So we shall go through all the forms again, and I hope we shall have dances and songs worth our trouble. How I wish you were here for a few days. Generally the discomforts of island life make me feel that women would not enjoy it; but here one is as comfortable as you can be in England, and the amusement for a short time would be great. Of course we have talked much of Springy and Dwight, and I was glad to have your account of the boy, to give Sir John.

June 20. The Sydney steamer is just in the harbor, and this letter must be mailed to go by her return voyage three or four days hence. In case you should receive this letter before you get my last Tahiti letter,—both should reach you about August 1,—I ought to explain that we are straining every nerve to reach Paris by October 1. I expect to reach Sydney by August 1; to reach Singapore by August 15; Ceylon, September 1; and Paris Oct. 1. Of course the inevitable delays in such a big journey may at any point smash my hopes; but nothing short of necessity will prevent my seeing you in October. Count on my doing all I can. Stay as late as possible in the haunts of dressmakers and milliners. Perhaps La Farge will cross with you; at any rate we can have some pleasant weeks in Paris and London, and you shall dispose of my future movements. If you say so, I will return to Washington to try the old experiment of living; if you say not, I will return to finish in the east my interrupted wanderings. If you say nothing at all,—well, I shall be no worse off! I can always ramble on till I meet some one who will take the trouble of telling me what to do. My own will is much too feeble to make a decision, and the tropics enfeeble it daily still more. Otherwise I am almost my old self; morbidness gone; nervousness and nervous excitement subsided; depression vanished; sleep and appetite good; so that I feel only twenty years older than I felt twenty years ago. Indeed I sometimes forget how preposterous the cosmos is; and almost feel an old illusion of my being a part of it,—until the newspapers arrive and throw me out again. So if you refuse to take the responsibility of driving me in the highroads, after the habits of civilised animals, I can still roam off on the commons of Gobi, and trot with the Tartars and Kurds. Just now, we are trotting with the Fijians, who amuse me mildly, and I feel much as though I had returned to my long-lost archaic home, so familiar are their Samoan faces and songs. Sir John took us, two days ago, on our first excursion. With Captain Grenfell and several officers of the British corvette "Cordelia," we went twenty miles in Sir John's small steam-yacht, inside the reef, to the Rewa river, a stream about as large as the Thames at London, and stopped at the chief's place to have a reception. The whole affair was a sort of variation on our Savaii excursion last autumn, but so different in detail as to be rather new. The Rewa district, or province, or kingdom, or whatever it might be, is the delta of the Rewa river, and as like Holland as you please. I never saw a prettier, sunnier, cheerfuller scene than the sluggish stream with its thatched native houses, and its boats of natives coming and going to or from our show. We arrived at about three o'clock, and were taken to the chief's house which was given up to us. I was rather surprised to find the Fijian native house quite the finest I had yet seen. It is much like the Samoan in a way, but the decoration shows taste, and the dignity of it is really something pretty effective. The sides are thatched up to the eaves with leaves; for Fiji is quite a cold place, and the mercury goes as low as 64° at night now. When wind blows, one feels positively shivery. La Farge picked up some sciatica at Tahiti before sailing, and finds himself quite suffering from the inclemency of the tropics. Fiji houses are lighted by half a dozen doors, closed by a sort of mats if necessary. They are very large, so that when our mosquito nets were all hung up at night, they looked like a camp under a huge roof. We went through our old ceremony of the *kava* first, with much singing but no speeches; many men but no women; and the men differing immensely in type between black African negro and light Polynesian. Rewa is largely Tongan, which is Polynesian. The Tongans came here and conquered part of the island, and still show their blood; but the Rewa chiefs have none of the wonderful general uniformity of beauty which the Samoans had. They seemed to me rather ugly as an average, but more intelligent. They seem to have no fancy for oratory, and none of the love of posing which delighted us so much at Samoa. Nymph and naiad, orator and faun, have no place among the practical Fijians. The poetry has pretty much all gone. When we came to the dances, we saw this still more plainly. The dances were just what I have been unable to find in the other islands, and they were certainly very effective, but they were war-dances and nothing else. A phalanx of men, perhaps a hundred in number, with war-clubs, axes, spears and war-paint of black and vermilion, go through a regular war-dance, beginning with slow, and ending with quick movements. The effect was fine and very savage, and the warriors brandished their clubs and spears as though they still knew how to use them. The women and children and the non-dancers in general, sat about, on the grass, perhaps fifteen hundred of them, and I studied their looks carefully, but without much satisfaction. They run from black to red, but are coarser by far than the Samoans, and are a mere brutal mob compared with Tahitians. The brutality shows most in the women, who have evidently been treated as pretty poor creatures, with none of the eminent social advantages that were enjoyed by their neighbors to the eastward. I regret to say that the morals of Fijian society, where women were practically slaves, were very much better than in Samoa, Tahiti and Hawaii, where women were almost equals with men; and what is worse, the women are going to the bad rapidly since polygamy and clubs were prohibited by the missionaries. The children die, and the mothers prefer not to have them. The chiefs debate the causes of the decline in population, and when they are tired, refer it to the Governor General. In the native council, one very old chief who rarely spoke more than a grunt of approval, paralysed the audience by an address which, Sir John says, ran much like this:—I am an old man, and a fool, and know nothing, and what I say is not worth your hearing. When I was young, these things were not so; the children lived; the women took care of them. Now the children die; the women neglect them. I am an old man and a fool. You are young men and know everything. What I say is said by a fool; but I see no good in talking and sending to tell the governor that we leave it all to him and the Queen. When I was young, things were different, and though I am a fool, and you are wiser and young, I think, instead of leaving it all to the governor, you had better send to the governor to ask him to give us back the right of clubbing the women.—Painful as it is to admit such a possible moral *impasse,* the best judges here seem to think that the old man's advice was the only practical means of avoiding the destruction of the race. Polygamy and clubbing were the foundations of society, and when they were taken away, society began slowly to perish. I do not commit you to sympathy with views of this nature. Of course American women, not the men, do the necessary clubbing nowadays, and maintain society by their own energy; but the archaic world is very simple and humorous in its frank way of showing us the blessings of our virtues. Fiji, like Tahiti and Samoa and Hawaii, is a monument to our high moral standard. All is for the best in our best of possible worlds.[2] The virtuous woman flourished with the help of the club at Fiji. The excessively unvirtuous woman flourished like the breadfruit at Tahiti. Both perish in the presence of our enlightenment and religion.

June 23. Tomorrow the steamer starts for Sydney, and I must now close up. I wish we were going with our letters, but we must first tramp through the mountains with the Governor, and explore this island. We are to start in three days, and on our return shall take the next steamer to Australia. Meanwhile we are simply resting, and it is the last rest we shall get for many a week. I am still more or less seasick from my voyage, and sea-sickness will be my chronic condition till we reach you. Suva is naturally a perfectly dull little place, with no miseries in the way of amusements; but the devil has sent Her Britannic Majesty's Corvette "Cordelia" here, whose officers, being young, energetic and frivolous, do things. They have theatricals, to which we must go; and they have asked us to dinner, to which we must also go. I will make up for it in London by going nowhere. Fiji is a good place for rest. I do not think I should find much to interest me either in the island or the people, although the island is a big one, as Pacific islands go, and the people are still numerous, and fairly savage. I suspect they are a bit stupid and deadly practical, but I shall probably soon know more about them. As for the island, it is another of the usual volcanic rocks, but much more broken up than the Polynesian islands, and without central craters or peaks. I fancy it might be interesting if I were geologist enough to find out what is in it; but all I can see is that it is very old; its volcanoes long extinct; and that it contradicts with unnecessary violence all my dear Darwin's subsiding theories. As a geologist I am certainly a fool, like my native chief, the orator on the great Woman-question, for I can see nothing but what contradicts my own favorite hobbies. From Hawaii to Fiji I can see only proofs of permanence and uniformity which I hate. Sir John is a botanist, and gives us coaching on the botanical side. Il ne manquait que ça. I am left no excuse for any ignorance at all, though I have made every possible effort, and have even lived nearly a year in Polynesia without learning a single word of the language.

As we come to the end, my thoughts turn more on you than on Fiji, which is surprising considering the relative charms of the two subjects. I want much to know where you are and how you are, and how your summer is succeeding. I am on thorns for fear that after all I may fail to reach England in time to find you there, and I swear violently in advance because of perverse steamers that may not connect closely when I am in a hurry. My emotions are best expressed by the delightful grammar of a letter written by old King George Tubou of Tonga to Sir John Thurston only a fortnight ago; it runs thus:—"When the first man fell from the former state of good he received from God, there came upon our hearts pain, doubtings, strife and division among ourselves in regard to unforeseen things that may happen in the future. But it is with God alone to restore happiness." My heart too is come upon with doubtings as to steamers that may sail in the future, and I much fear that God troubles himself little about their time-schedules; but you will hear, by telegraph, of our progress, if you are in England, and will know long beforehand whether we shall succeed or not. If we were only beginning our travels I should gladly linger here, for Sir John is a charming host, very kind, intelligent and frank; an excellent talker, and full of experience in all matters connected with the Pacific; so that our stay would have been a first-rate education for travel; but now we know as much about the Pacific as most people can boast, and especially the romantic part of it, so that we have no more great experiences to desire except to eat the durian and mangosteen in the Malay archipelago. Next to missing you, my chief fear is to find them out of season, which would be an inexpressible disaster since they were my chief object in coming to the tropics at all. Surely I should be obliged sooner or later to return, and ten thousand miles of ocean are a high price for one durian.

Give Martha her letter with my love. I wish I could bring her something from here, but the only Fijian toy is a war-club.

MS: MHi

1. In Gyp's "Une Passionnette," concluded in the *Revue des Deux Mondes,* March 1, 1891, the "Normand" with whom HA identifies loves a married woman but is too circumspect to make her his mistress. He is a Breton, but she wonders if he may not have been born in Normandy—"the country of apples and of prudence" (104:39). The memoirs of the Duc de Broglie (1718–1804), on the War of the Spanish Succession, are in the same issue.

2. The maxim of Dr. Pangloss in Voltaire's *Candide* (1759).

To Martha Cameron

Government House, Fiji. [16? June 1891]

My dear Martha[1]

Your beautiful letter came to me at last, after traveling ever so many weeks over the ocean. I have lots of things to tell you. Do you remember that I asked you to come with me to see the people that eat little girls, and you said that you would not go to be eaten. I have just reached that country, and am living among the people. Ask your mamma to show you some day where it is. Tell her to show you a globe of the world. Then, if you are in England, on top, look directly down under your feet, and if you can only see through the ground far enough, you will see this island where I am. It is exactly under you, but we have to walk on our heads here, when you are on top. You wouldn't mind walking on your head, but it is sometimes rather hard for old people to get used to it, and it often makes me sick, especially at sea. Now that I have got here they tell me that the people dont eat little girls any more. Isn't it too bad. I have come all this long way to have girls to eat, because I like tender little girls, and now I cant have any, and must come home again without knowing how nice they are. You might have come with me after all, if you had known that. You would have seen the fishes flying like birds all over the sea, and you would have had lots of new fruits to eat, and you would have seen the bread growing on trees, and the loveliest blue and green and yellow and red fishes playing at the bottom of the water; and the water is so warm that you could play all day in it, and sail beautiful little boats that the little boys make, and go faster than any boats you ever saw. The children here go out on the water in big wooden bowls which they paddle with their hands, and when they upset, they laugh at each other. One day, I upset my canoe and tipped Mr La Farge with me into the water, and the little girls laughed at us, and ran in, and set the canoe up again, and pulled us along in it till we got home. I think you would have great fun here. The people are almost black, and wear very little clothes, but their hair is thick, and they comb it out straight so that their heads look as big as drums, and as though they were too heavy to carry. The hair is red at the ends, and dark underneath, and makes the men look as though they would eat us, but they are very nice men and kind to little children, and never cross.

Some day I will tell you all about them when I come home again. Remember to love me, and be very good to me when I come back; and come to play with me. I love you, and am always your only devoted

Dobbitt.

MS: MHi
1. This letter is inscribed in block capitals.

To John Hay

My dear John

Your letter of March 25 reached me through Samoa with great promptitude on or about June 1, just as we were leaving Tahiti. A thousand thanks! That you like St Gaudens' figure is a great relief to me; even greater than to know that at last the work is done. I cannot tell my own feeling about it until I see it, but the photographs relieve me of my worst fears. If it is not exactly my ideal, it is at least not hostile. St Gaudens is not in the least oriental, and is not even familiar with oriental conceptions. Stanford White is still less so. Between them, the risk of going painfully wrong was great. Of course White was pretty sure to go most astray, and he has done so; but probably the mistakes are not so serious as to overbalance the merits.[1] At any rate I hope and think it is so, and wait with a relieved mind till the day when I may have to make up my final opinion. I know of very few people whose judgment on such a work would carry much weight with me, so I am not greatly concerned about what is said or thought; but after having your approval, I am satisfied.

So you see we have at length reached Fiji, where I expected to arrive last October. As it was, I had to pay the wretched little steamer "Richmond" twentyfive hundred dollars, or rather £450, to bring us here; otherwise I know not when we should have succeeded. We left Tahiti, June 5, with real sorrow. Not that we wanted to stay, for we were very anxious to escape, but that the place has a peculiar and quite undescribable character of its own which seems to contradict all one's natural instincts, and slowly blanket one's emotions. Nothing so like another world has ever passed my experience, and I can hardly realise that such an unreal life could be real. The mixture of material and ideal is an annoyance to me, for the commonplace, after all, is the bottom-rock on which one bumps everywhere; but in Tahiti one is bored in a gently melancholy way, and bored so steadily, so persistently and so much as a matter of necessity, that one submits in the end. Our relation, too, with the old Chiefess who gave us names, and with her children and grandchildren—Tati, Marau, the Queen, and the others,— grew to be more than fraternal, and became affectionate. I love the old lady with all my heart, and quite admit King's estimate of the archaic woman, if she is the standard; but she is a long way the grandest female figure in all Polynesia. Her daughter Marau is half-blood and more archaic in temper, but nothing like her for true archaism.

We were eleven wretched days on the Richmond, made the acquaintance of another Queen—Makea—at Rarotonga, and arrived here on the 16th. Sir John Thurston brought us up to the Government House, which is empty, his family being at Sydney. Here we are in full English civilisation, and dress for dinner, but the town of Suva is hardly larger than Apia, and we are not bothered by society. Fiji is as different as possible from Tahiti. The natives here are much like the Samoans, without their charm. They are more Polynesian than I expected, but they show a good deal of black blood, and are more artistic and less civilised. The women want for very little. The men are everything. Suva is an English town with more Indian coolies than native Fijians, but Sir John has already taken us on one expedition to a large native town where we were received with official solemnities and presents, drank kava, had a big dance, and slept in the chief's house. The general idea of the thing was Samoan, so that we might have fancied ourselves back in Savaii; but the differences were decided. The dance was a big war-dance; one or two hundred men in column, painted black and vermillion, with barbaric costumes of tapa and leaves, armed with clubs and spears, going through a regular savage drill symbolic of fighting. It was very effective indeed, and just what I wanted to see, but the women took no part and only sat about on the grass looking on with the children and old men. Neither men nor women are so splendid as the pure Polynesians; they are uneven, half black, and with all sorts of faces; but on the whole they are not quite so black as they are painted, or quite so devil as they are black. The women, being ugly, are virtuous, or being virtuous are ugly,—I will not commit myself to the sequence,—and have been kept in order by free use of the club. In the South Seas no rules of morality, or, for that matter, of immorality, have universal application; but perhaps as a general law one may say that in old days a race was high in proportion to its sexual immorality, and that the Tahitians, being the most consciously and elaborately immoral of all, were the handsomest. Yet on the other hand it is true that the blacks of the Solomons and elsewhere combine vice with ugliness to an unreasonable degree. Their vices are but coarse and low brutalities, so that they are hardly exceptions to the rule. They eat each other; a habit which the Tahitiens regarded as vulgar. The Fijians also were cannibals, which proves their low breeding. What is more curious is that the artistic sense increases as breeding descends. The Fijians are more artistic than the Samoans or Tahitians, and the black islanders show more taste in decoration than any of them.

Sir John takes us off this week for a long tramp through the interior. As soon as we return, we shall sail for Sydney, and there take the next boat for Singapore. La Farge goes home by way of Europe, and I am so gone to pieces that I must get patched up. I fear we shall be too late to catch you in Paris or London, though I would give much to do it. We expect to reach Europe in October. My further plans are vague, but I may pass the winter, or part of it in Europe.

Ever Yrs   Henry Adams.

Address to Baring Brothers &Co. London.

MS: MHi

1. The photographs of the Adams monument in 1891 have not been found. The cornice of the architectural background was added in 1893.

To Augustus Saint-Gaudens

Siwa, Fiji, June 23, 1891.

My dear St.-Gaudens:[1]

. . . As far as the photographs go, they are satisfactory, but I trust much more to the impression produced on John Hay, who writes me that he has been to Rock Creek to see the figure. "The work is indescribably noble and imposing. It is to my mind St.-Gaudens' masterpiece. It is full of poetry and suggestion, infinite wisdom, a past without beginning, and a future without end, a repose after limitless experience, a peace to which nothing matters—all are embodied in this austere and beautiful face and form."[2]

Certainly I could not have expressed my own wishes so exactly, and, if your work approaches Hay's description, you cannot fear criticism from me.

Source: *The Reminiscences of Augustus Saint-Gaudens,* ed. Homer Saint-Gaudens (1913); MS not found.
  1. The opening and the ending of this letter are omitted in *Reminiscences.*
  2. Quoted from Hay to HA, March 25, 1891.

To Elizabeth Cameron

Fiji. Sunday, 28 June, 1891.

Of course you feel not the smallest curiosity to know what the interior of Fiji is like. I am sure you do not in the least care whether it is a desert or a Paradise; but as I can't help myself, being decidedly there, you shall have such useless information as I can give you, which is compressible into the single concrete fact that I am now passing Sunday at Joske's station, at the village of Vuni Ndawa some forty miles up the Rewa river. Mr Joske is a young Englishman, gentlemanly and well-educated, the magistrate of the district, and his station is beautifully situated, on a bluff or hill above the river, and looks south and west towards distant mountains. The day is exquisite.[1] The native house is cool and softly lighted; Sir John has gone to church with the two magistrates, Carew and Joske; Mr Berry, Sir John's brother-in-law, another official, is reading on the lounge; young Spence, the private secretary is reading in the reclining chair; La Farge is reading in another chair, and all will soon be dozing. Our party consists of these seven men, reckoning myself as one, and we are doing Sunday here, before starting tomorrow morning for the mountains.

We all dined on the "Cordelia" Thursday evening, as guests of Captain Grenfell. The dinner was good, the officers were nice fellows, and very civil indeed, and Captain Grenfell is a sea-dog of quite a new variety to me, with more of the hunting-squire than of the tarry mariner; but I had an unpleasant cold in my head, in consequence of the inclement tropical climate; and I barely scraped through the dinner without breaking down. Captain Grenfell's wine was good, and the Captain towards the close of dinner became quite as ripe as the wine, so that I was pretty well demolished by the time we got into our boat; but the next morning we were up bright and early, and before nine o'clock were away in boats dragged by a steam launch by the same way we travelled before, along the coast, inside the reef, until we reached the mouth of the Rewa; then up the river to the sugar-mills where we arrived soon after noon, but stopped only to get upon a stern-wheel, light-draught steamer of the sugar-company, and then pressed on. The day was very fine, and as we got higher up, the banks became very pretty, and the groups of people, sometimes Fijians and sometimes Indian coolies, exquisitely picturesque; but I imagined myself in India. The river-bank was lined with fields of sugar and bananas; comparatively few cocoanut palms and almost no breadfruit; the people very dark; the landscape flattish; hardly a trace left of our old Polynesian scenery and surroundings. With hundreds of acres of bananas ripening for the Sydney market, none were offered us to eat, or were eaten by the people except cooked green. Not an orange or a lemon or a lime, far less a cocoanut or custard-apple, was brought to the Governor; and as for the garlands of our youth and beauty, we are now far from Samoa and Tahiti, and never shall wear garlands any more, or see the flaming hybiscus in the hair of our fauns and naiads. Fiji is practical and unromantic. Now and then our steamer stopped either to pick up a local magistrate or to receive a native chief, who brought the usual gifts of big baskets of yams, taro, and a pig, which was immediately divided among our escort; but we got nothing, and saw only groups of elderly savages squatting on the bank.

Romance is gone, but prettiness remains, and we had enough to amuse us all day until towards five o'clock we reached the head of steam-navigation, and stopped for the night at the native village called Viria. Here as everywhere the houses are large and apparently clean, and the village is neat, but our receptions have none of the fun of Samoa. We sit down cross-legged on the mats, and we take our kava with the due forms, but the ceremony seems to me a little cold and perfunctory. After the kava we are left to ourselves. No *taupo*, in tinsel and cocoanut-oil, smiles on us, or dances for us; indeed we see no women young or old, and few children. Instead of the noisy, playing, singing swarms of young that bothered our lives at Samoa, Fijian villages are quiet and to me rather melancholy. The Tahitians are sad, but they do at least sing their *himenes* as though they were Siva songs. The Fijian evening hymn is a regular slow psalm-tune, more serious than Old Hundred, and when the night has fallen, this lugubrious music is heard all about, near and far, announced by the beating of the wooden drums which resound over the whole country, from every village, at prayer-time morning and evening.[2] We have our supper, and then smoke and chat awhile, and go to bed, having seen as nearly as possible nothing of the natives.

Saturday (yesterday), La Farge, Spence and I started again at nine o'clock, in a canoe, roofed over with thatch, so that we could see little and sleep a good deal. Sir John and the others rode or walked the fourteen miles to Joske's. Our canoe was poled by six natives, and we were nearly five hours on the way. The weather was beautiful, and the scenery was pretty. As we go up the river, the stream becomes rapid in places, and our canoe scrapes the gravel, so that one gets ahead slowly. I lay on my side and watched the bank or the boats that passed. The country was hilly and wooded, but no mountains. The prettiest thing is the tree-fern, which grows everywhere, but the trees are not very fine. The landscape is rich, but the richest thing about it is that for the first time since ten months ago, we are not in sight of the sea. We reached Joske's station towards two o'clock, and found ourselves in what I imagine to be like a hill station in India. The house is native, but the people in it, the books and reviews, the tastes and the conversation are English. Even the house-servant is an Indian who looks like a prince in disguise, and wears bangles and long oiled hair with a red silk skull-cap. The curry is divine, but nothing Fijian is even suggested to eat, unless it is the yam, which here takes the place of the cocoanut, the bread-fruit, the wild-plantain and the banana of Polynesia. The landscape is lovely, but it is more like a summer-day in the Alleghanies than like an island of the South Seas.

Tomorrow we start seriously into a wild country where no Europeans live, and among native tribes who were howling cannibals fifteen years ago, and are still fairly savage, at least in thought and superstition. I am in a blue funk—Fijian for nervousness—for fear my feet may get used up in walking twelve miles a day, for I have not walked five miles in a day for years, and my feet are as tender as my hands, to say the least; but I must get on somehow, through streams and over sharp mountains; and so must La Farge, for an indefinite time.

July 2. We have labored steadily up the water-channels of the Rewa till we are now in the centre of the island, shut in by mountains. Not a dozen white men have ever penetrated these regions, and, of these, nearly all were government officers. The journey is very amusing. Sir John travels like Stanley in Africa. We have certainly a hundred and fifty native carriers and attendants, who are strung out in a long line, winding across the river and round the gorges, as picturesque as if they were on the war-path. Our mode of travel has so far been easy. I turn out of bed at seven; put on a jacket, a *sulu,* or *pareu* or *lava-lava,* (as you like to call the waist-cloth, here, or in Taïti or in Samoa), and slippers, and tumble down to the bathing-pool, which is always in the river close by. The sun is just rising above the mountains, the mists lie over the valleys, and the thermometer ranges from 54° to 60° at daybreak. The water is cool and fresh like the air. I scramble out as soon as I can, and go back to our hut to dress and inspect my toes to see that they do not get rubbed by my shoes. The others are engaged more or less in the same occupations, and get to the breakfast-stage at about

"J.L.F. and H.A. sitting at the door of their palace" at Fiji in 1891

Fiji, July 1891: "Mr Berry's photograph. Sir John wigging the chiefs at Undu for heathenish practices. Sir John sitting in the centre under the tree. I am directly behind him. Joske and Carew on his right. Servant holds umbrella over him"

"Dance of War, Fiji"
Pencil and gray wash drawing by John La Farge

nine, at latest. Once, at Na Vuna Wai-wai Vula, I think it was, two days ago, Sir John was detained till afternoon to hold a big council, and give a wigging to an unfortunate chief, or Mboule, whom he threatened to hang and shoot and burn if he didn't make his people behave themselves. The chief defended himself with great dignity, and quite won my sympathies; but as a matter of fact the people are still savage, and would be back at their old practices in six months, with their incantations and wars and cannibal feasts, if the foreign government were taken away. All the older men about us have been glorious cannibals within twenty years. As it is, they are ornaments to human nature, especially when painted black and vermilion in stripes down their faces, or with black faces beautifully spotted with vermilion. Our day's journey once begun, we walk, if the path is dry; and, for the river-crossings, Mr Joske, who runs the party, has provided three chaises-à-porteurs, in which Sir John, La Farge and I are carried, while Joske, Carew and Berry bravely wade. Poor Spence sprained his ankle in wading, and has been sent back by boat. Our boats had to be left behind two days ago; our horses still earlier; and today our road was a river-gorge, perfectly wild, and a mere bed of round rocks. We make short days; four hours walking is the utmost I have had to do; but it satisfies me, and as the sun is hot, I am more than ready to get into quarters and plunge into the river; but sometimes when we arrive early, we have a big reception, and a *meke-meke,* or dance. The men march up, with spears and clubs, as they did at Rewa, and go through various movements symbolic of all sorts of mischief to their enemies. The women never appear. We bring too many men with us for the peace of the Fijian hearth. By the way, we are now in the land of hearths. The nights are cold, and the big native houses have often half a dozen hearths, with large logs smouldering in them. Our evenings are always quiet; no songs except hymns; no dances; no visitors. We get our dinner at seven; smoke and chat till nine; then go to bed and sleep peacefully in the big, dark houses, till some one stirs at dawn. I lie awake a good deal, but nothing seems to imitate me. Once in a while I hear some night-bird, more or less uncanny, but the silence of the night is rather strange. The whole forest seems to have nothing to say.

Today we have marched two hours through as wild and beautiful a ravine as I want to see, coming out at the mountain-village of Nasongo, which is different from all we have seen; and our house is growing conical until I begin to think myself in Africa, and about to buy a girl for a feast. Yet the scenery is very like the Virginian Alleghanies, if you would throw in a few tree-ferns and palms and long, pendent creepers. Occasionally a green parrot squawks about us, but I have seen no parroquets. We find no fruits but wild lemons of which we make lemonade. We get no food except chickens and yams, for the pigs and *taro* go to our army. The people are poor, very African, and yet sometimes not ill-looking; but the villages are extremely pretty, and Sir John Thurston has done more in a dozen years to make the country human than has been done by the French in fifty years at Tahiti. The natives are cutting roads, or paths, with energy that is miraculous, and very grateful to my tender feet. We are now beyond the farthest range of even the European trader; when the natives want anything, they must walk a day to the nearest trader's; these hill-tribes are set apart under the absolute authority of the governor, and no white or black nonsense is suffered to interfere with his will; but yesterday we tramped for some two hours along a new road cut through the forest on the sharp side of the mountain, and, except a few steep places, the path was perfect. In another ten years, I've no doubt the whole interior will be intersected by easy paths, which will doubtless make my next visit less alarming to my imagination. Just now I am lying awake o' nights because our next move is through a forest and over a mountain-range by a rough native track.

Besides the novelty of finding at last an unknown country where the simple savage is truly simple, and would gladly eat you if such were the Christian commandment, we have at last reached a region where science has got another tough job to settle with its conscience. For the last two days we have tramped between vast walls of conglomerate and breccia, the wreck of older mountains long ago broken into small bits and carried down probably below the sea to be compressed solid under heavy weights of wash or lava, and then lifted up again at least seven hundred feet. The torrent has cut deep through these beds, and the natives make use of caves in them for burial places. What interests me more is that we have reached a spot where coral rock is said to lie on or in the mountain-side. Tomorrow Sir John is to go for that coral, and will take me with him. If we find it, I shall not have the first gleam of an idiotic suspicion when or how it got there, or what it wanted there anyhow, but it will be rather fun. I have been hunting everywhere for a raised coral bank, not because a raised coral bank has the smallest personal interest to me; but because it is a kind of coralline conundrum which, as a serious Darwinian, I am morally bound to defy and repudiate. Darwin says that the coral islands have miraculous powers of sinking, while all the coral islands I have seen are perfectly stupid evidences of rising. Till now I have never seen or heard of a clear case of rise more than perhaps two or three hundred feet. Here they claim a thousand or more feet of it. If we can settle this, I give you all the advantages. The next time you meet a geologist you can hit him on the head with my specimens, like Abner Dean of Angel's.[3]

July 4. We duly went for the corals yesterday, but the bed of the stream being most evil walking, we went no further than was necessary to select specimens from the loose rocks and boulders in the dry part of the channel. These were quite enough to prove anything under the sun. In pity for you I will only say that all Viti Levu seems to be one big mass of broken volcanic stones in sand-beds, with shells and coral, all solidified into a coarse conglomerate, and proving elevation of at least three thousand feet, while vast amounts of mud, discharged from the volcanoes, made foot-hills and flat alluvial shores. I regret to say that my fourth coral group is still more disgustingly anti-Darwin than any of its predecessors. With this final blow, my battle for subsidence ends, leaving me knocked clean out of the ring at every round. You may breathe more easily, for you will probably hear no more geology from me. The day turned to rain and became melancholy. La Farge sketched and Sir John and Mr Berry photographed, in a dismal drizzle. We were driven early into our hut, and so to our dinner, our backy and our beds. The party is quite a cheerful one, and fond of fun in a quiet way. Five of the six are fifty or more years old, so we are not sky-larks, but we keep our dotage fairly green. Even the mornings are not hard. I was up at half past six today, and plunged into the pool in a morning mist which looked like a fair sample of rain. We breakfasted hastily, and started at ten minutes before eight. As the river-bed became here a mass of big boulders with constant wading, we left it, and struck straight up the spur of the mountain, by a native wood-path, slippery with mud, and often giving no foothold but roots. The creeks and ravines round Washington have sides much like these Fiji valleys, except that we rose a thousand feet in an hour. For about three hours and a half we climbed pretty steadily, until we stood at last twentythree hundred feet above sea-level, with a drizzling mist and a temperature of 62 °. La Farge gave in, but the Governor had provided for this well-understood probability, and La Farge was promptly reclined in his palanquin, and carried the last mile or two. The rest of us reached the top, with our army of carriers, or part of it; and there we lunched; and then and there, to my great disgust and to the lively amusement of the party, Sir John made me drink Ben Harrison's health, and our guard fired three rounds of shotted cartridges in honor of the day. I entreated them not to tell my friends that they had played so rough a practical joke on me as to harry me with Benjamin and the Fourth of July in the middle of the forests of Fiji where no white man had been before me; but they swore they would print it. I don't think they will quite descend to this; but La Farge is sure to tell it, so I might as well tell it myself. Then we began to descend again, by another breakneck trail. As I had two stalwart Fijians, with mop-heads, to pull me up-hill, and to tumble upon whenever I slipped going down, I got along very well. La Farge, by the grace of his Christian merits, escaped being capsized, and was a most picturesque sight as his bamboo boat was carried among the tangles of palms, ferns, creepers and tree-trunks, now standing apparently on one end, now on the other, and swaying above a noisy crowd of black wild-men. Sir John led our column, following close on the wood-choppers, and as a path had to be cleared for the palanquin, we came down slowly, which gave Sir John time to show me the botany of the forest, and especially the peculiar ferns. I had a fair taste of the tropical forest. Flowers were rare and not much worth noticing, but like a true Yankee I consoled myself by reflecting that at every step I trampled on plants worth at least five dollars apiece in New York or London, and that no emperor tossed so much possible wealth about, as I did. The forest had a charm of its own, not of color or of scent or of any of the qualities that we like most in our woods, but for depth of verdure, richness of parasitic growth, with lines and masses quite strange to our notions, and a certain waste and extravagance quite profligate and reprehensible, but not wicked. The missionaries would stop it if they could, but the rains fall, and the ferns and creepers still cling high on the tree trunks. The tree-fern is almost unnaturally graceful and delicate, rather too much like feminine art-decoration, but it is at least wild, as all the forest is. Neither cocoanut palm nor breadfruit intrudes here. We had an hour of this lounging among the ferns and orchids; then we reached our creek again, still the Na-songo, close to its head-waters, under an amphitheatre of mountain, and here we went into camp at half past one. We are now beyond even the native villages, and are in the least frequented parts of the forest, but we live as usual. Hundreds of people bring up yams and other food. Huts are built for us as we go. Above all, I drop down to the creek and get my dip morning and evening, while La Farge laughs at me for saying that the water has a pleasant chill. He suffers from cold. I expect to suffer also, when we reach three thousand feet tomorrow, and the temperature at night falls to the forties.

July 5. Camp-fires last night, and, later, rain, with thermometer at 62 °. I slept not at all, till morning, owing I guess to tea; and the outlook was dismally wet when I clambered down to my bath among the boulders. Our breakfast and meals grow painfully tinned; even a roast yam is a luxury. Today being Sunday, we had native prayers and left camp at nine. Another desperate, slippery, headlong climb up the mountain began our march. La Farge was lashed into his palanquin and dragged up somehow; I did not see him, being much too busy with dragging my own legs. Dense forest surrounded us everywhere, even when we walked along narrow spurs hardly six feet across, with an indefinite drop on either side, where a single big tree blocked the whole road. For three hours and something more we tramped through the soaked woods, slipping and sliding down ravines, and clambering up, until at last we turned the flank of the range, and came on an open grass spot, thirtyone hundred feet above sea-level, and looking far westward over the valley of the Singa-toka. I was heartily glad to escape from the wet Rewa country to the dry central and western region, where patches of grass are scattered about among patches of forest. We lunched at our grass-patch, and then tumbled down to the camp on the Singa-toka river, a little mountain stream, in which I seated myself with the utmost rapidity, weary though I was with five hours of heavy tramping. La Farge too walked the last half. Our camp is still far from villages. We carry a good-sized village with us, but see nothing except wild country. Last night we were sixteen hundred feet above sea-level; tonight we are twentythree hundred, but the clouds tonight lie on the mountain behind us. I hope our next march will at least have drier foothold, but my feet and legs hold out better than I feared.

July 7. Light rain fell all night, and when we broke up our camp the next morning, yesterday, the rain was still drizzling, and we began our march in a path slippery with trampled mud. As usual we had a narrow valley to cross, and then a steep hill, by a true Fijian trail, straight up, without curve or holding-ground for our boots. Powers alive, how we slipped and swore! A stalwart naked Fijian, whose toes clung to the mud, took me by the hand and lifted me up the hill-side. Two others supported La Farge. Sir John led the march, also drawn up by an aid. About two hundred natives in single file, carried boxes and bags, or followed for their own amusement, carrying nothing. We were happier than usual in having only a short range to climb, and were well over the worst in fifteen minutes, but Carew who is a heavy man, was badly blown and looked quite blue when we reached the top. Then we tramped on along another of the knife-edges which seem to form the crests of all these mountain-ranges. Slipping and sliding up and down the inequalities, of ground, we splashed on among masses of ferns and brush, with splendid *dakua* or kauri-gum trees here and there rising far above us; but our tramp was not long, and we soon tumbled down again into the next valley, coming out, in an hour, on the little village of Mata-kula, with a dozen conical huts, on the long spur of the mountains we had just crossed. This was Sir John's objective point. In this valley where the Singa-toka takes its rise, he hoped to establish a sanatarium, and our journey was for the purpose of exploring the ground, and planning a road. Here we are within fifteen miles of the sea to the westward, and twentytwo hundred feet above sea-level. The valley is the widest in all the mountain region; about two miles long by half a mile wide; but the mountains all round it are so cut up by ravines, and their sides so steep and stony that, if this valley does not answer, there seems to be no chance of getting suited, and Sir John had been sure that we should find here an elevation of three thousand feet. The discovery that we could get no more than twentytwo hundred feet out of it, quite upset his calculations. We went into quarters at once. As the only decent house in the village was the missionary's, which is a box for stowing at most half a dozen beds, Sir John, Mr Berry, La Farge and I are there, and there we have meals. The others are quartered all about, among the huts or under shelter of palm-ferns for tents. I was satisfied to rest yesterday, for my legs were draggy, so I lay on a fern-bed in front of our hut, and dried my clothes and boots as the clouds disappeared and the air became dry. We are now in a dry country, where I can no longer get my dip in the mountain streams. Water is brought up by the children in bamboos from half a mile away. Towards sunset I strolled down, across a reedy, rank meadow, to the little river which hardly trickles along its bed, deep under a bower of dense trees and ferns. Broad patches of coarse grass are interspersed among the masses of forest. Green parrots and parroquets fly out of the cover. We had a dinner of pigeon-curry which was uncommonly good, and today I have begged Joske to try a parrot-curry and baked bananas. We are still among the poorest mountain tribes, and our supplies are far from splendid; yams and taro are the staple food, and I hanker after neither. Ripe bananas are not to be had; we are beyond the region of fish, and we wont eat pig. Our village seems to be the only one in this valley, and between here and the coast is a rough and sharp descent of more than two thousand feet which cuts us off from luxuries. Today is lovely. We slept as usual on our mats, with ferns underneath, after an evening round a regular old-fashioned camp-fire. I can sleep on fern, but the ridges are still rough, and by seven o'clock I am quite ready to come out and watch the mists roll away, while I toast my legs before the fire and drink a cup of cocoa. One by one the party turns out and inquires the minimum temperature of the night. The range yesterday was from 73 ° at noon to 54 ° at dawn this morning. Now, at noon again, it is 80 ° or very near it, a lovely day, and I am sitting on the ground, under a shelter of ferns which the men have made for me, and trying to write on my knees without breaking my back. Tomorrow we begin our march to the coast, and I suppose, by the day after, we shall find the Governor's steam-yacht, the "Clyde" somewhere, and finish with Fijian mountains.

July 12. We left Mata-kula at half past nine o'clock and walked up the valley, through open meadows, into more forest, tramping along as usual, over a path more or less broken by gullies and streams, until in about two hours, we came to the great wall which lines the northern side of the island, and which must be the lip or edge of what was once an enormous crater, the other lip of which is the island of Vanua Levu, sixty or seventy miles, across the water. Out of this huge hole the vast mass of broken stone must have been thrown which now makes the mountains of both islands; a bed of pudding-stone or agglomerate at least three thousand feet deep, and tilted so as to incline southward to the coast some sixty or eighty miles away at Suva. So much my travels have taught me, but I doubt whether I can make money out of the investment. You are welcome to all the profits. I did not even make a landscape out of it, although we stood on the crest of a precipice like the Pali at Honolulu which is one of the finest views in the world. The whole valley beneath us was full of clouds and mist which eddied up to us, and looked like an active volcano, but cut off all outlook. I lay an hour on the grassy edge while Sir John climbed further up the hills to fix the site of his sanatarium, for we were all satisfied that this was the proper spot. We were twentyfour hundred feet above the sea, and an extra five hundred feet could easily be got by rising a bit to our right where a stream was tumbling into the mist. When we had lunched and finished prospecting, we began our descent, and slid or stumbled down the sharp hill-side in the clouds, until about five hundred feet below we got beneath them, and could see across a dozen miles of open hills and valleys the ocean to the northward. An hour's work, and a descent of twelve or fifteen hundred feet, brought us to the village of Wai-kumbo-kumbo, another hamlet of the mountain-tribes, where we halted for the night. As usual the villagers were gathered to receive us; the head-man presented the usual whale's tusks, and the people brought the pigs and yams to feed our carriers. Then we took a bath in the mountain-stream, and felt happy. The liveliest enjoyment of tramping is the getting to the end of the day's journey. A new village is always amusing and often charming. Wai-kumbo-kumbo was a poor little place, and our house was stuffy, with only one small entrance to creep through, and much suspicion of bugs, centipedes and mice; but the place was picturesque and lively with a swarm of half-naked blacks who looked as savage as ex-cannibals should. Under mosquito-nets one feels almost protected from wandering insects, and with a little more light I could have eaten my stewed parrot off my boots without difficulty, for appetite is not one of the missing virtues in mountain tramps. Sleep is harder. Before I have been half an hour asleep, some of our guard tumble in and go to bed, waking me of course. Then a mouse squeaks to her young one's in the thatch by my ear. Then a rat walks across the mats, pat-pat-pat. Then a pig sets up a terrible squealing as he is dragged down to be drowned or otherwise killed at the stream, while I see the light of the fire which is heating the stones in which, wrapped in banana leaves, he is to be baked for breakfast. The natives squat about the fires, drinking kava and smoking, till late at night, and they murmur distantly. A child in a near hut has whooping-cough. Still I do get to sleep at last, invariably, and wake at six by daylight or moving about me. Then I lie till seven, thinking of—England; and then I turn out for my toilet among the rocks in the stream. Breakfast comes in time; our carriers take our traps; and soon after nine we are off. This was the last march and went to the sea through a hilly, bare, brown country, under a hot sun, on a splendid day. After the first hour, La Farge was mounted on a horse belonging to the young magistrate of the district, Marriott, who sent him up for the purpose. The rest of us walked. Berry and Joske have left us, to explore the ranges to the east, and we shall not see them for three or four days. Sir John, Carew and I tramped along the road, which was a real road, grassy and springy, and we took it easy. At noon we stopped by a stream and had a cup of tea. Half an hour afterwards we met some men who brought us some green fresh cocoanuts to drink, and I assure you that the world offers few things more refreshing than a green cocoanut to a thirsty traveller. The last two hours of our march seemed hard, for my toes got rubbed and sore from two days successive tramp. We gradually left the hills, crossed a plain, and entered a mangrove swamp, walking an hour or so along a dyke just above the tides. We were probably not more than four hours and a half on foot, and ten miles at the utmost, but we were uncommonly glad to reach the village at last, where the "Clyde" was waiting us. The day was still young; we arrived at half past three, and we had a deal still to do. Everything was ready for our reception, and the town of Vanua-kula looked delightfully pretty and cool in the shade of its glossy-leaved *ifi* or chestnut trees. We had chairs on the grass, and received our whale's tusks and speech, and then looked on at a *meke-meke,* or war-dance like that we saw at Rewa and elsewhere. The dancers come in enveloped in fantastic mountains of white *tapa,* which is wound round them up to their necks; coils and puffs, making them look like walking bags, brandishing long spears and clubs. When the dance is over, they uncoil themselves, and leave the tapa in a big heap on the ground as a gift for the governor. Then the women, in a long procession, dressed or rather, fagottées, in violent purples, yellows, reds and every color to be bought in tinsel-paper or cheap cloth, marched in, carrying baskets of food, including fish and crabs. The girls, or virgins, wear no tunics, and have pretty figures. On one side of their heads, the hair is braided in queer little tails; a mark of their marriageable character. This was the first time I got a fair sight of the women, and on the whole they were not so bad as I expected; but these coast towns are as much Polynesian as Fijian. The whole affair was pretty and gay, all the more because we could rest, and take off our shoes, and drink cocoa-nuts. Then at sunset we bathed in the river Tavua, and had some dinner, after which the Governor sent us on board the "Clyde" for the night. The "Clyde" lay near three miles below, and we had to be rowed or poled or dragged an hour among the mangroves, which are weird at best, but by the dim light of a new moon, just setting, are an experience. Once on board, our day was not ended, for the captain made us a whiskey cocktail, and we were kept awake pretty much all night by noise, and were turned up at six by Sir John coming aboard with twenty or thirty followers. At seven we were off, a thoroughly weary and sleepy party, and I, for one, cross as a Yankee cannibal, but we watched the coast, had some crab-curry for breakfast, and soon after nine o'clock ran into the river Mba, or Ba, and landed at the first town. This is another large river which drains the northwestern coast, and has sugar-plantations, and a civil magistrate of the first class, a young Englishman named Marriott. We are comparatively civilised here. The native chief is a *Roko*, or Prince, who has Mboules (the B is always pronounced Mb) under him. He gave us a big, clean house, with pretty mats, chairs, a table and even a looking-glass, pleasing to one who had not seen a reflection of his beard for a fortnight. The reception was very correct and formal; the kava or angona as it is called here, was prepared and drunk with the exactly proper singing. The *meke-meke* or war-dance in the afternoon was particularly good, and the tapa made a big hill. The Roko looks like an Arab and is soft-spoken as such a high-born cannibal should be. The people are not beautiful—far from it—but the scene at the *meke-meke* was extremely pretty, with sitting groups and lively colors. We were very tired and slept much of the day, and the bath was by no means a clear mountain stream; but we are comfortable, which is lucky as we remain three days. Yesterday we were rowed up the river three miles to Marriott's station, where we lunched on real cooked things, and made the acquaintance of Mrs Marriott, a pretty, sweet, refined London girl, just married and only a few weeks buried in this ultra-remote cane-brake. As La Farge remarked, it was pathetic, and needed only a baby to be tragic; but the solitude, the flies, the mosquitoes and centipedes, and even the natives, are not much more of a bore than at an American or English watering-place. The climate is exquisite and healthy; the distant mountains are beautiful, and there is no want of work. On the whole, once over homesickness, the life is tolerably intolerable. After lunch we crossed the river to the sugar-plantation and were received by the manager's wife, another young woman, but from Sydney, and I was interested to watch the contrast. Mrs Fenner is as American as Mrs Marriott is English. I do not understand why Australia should be almost typically American, but all the Australians I meet might come from Chicago for any British peculiarities they show. They are quite as well acquainted with America, apparently, as with England, and have as many American faults as we have. Mrs Fenner received us with the same pie-crust fluency and thinness that we know so well in Washington congress-women, and united the same delicacy of appearance with the same perfect self-possession which make our own social aristocracy preeminent.

Today is Sunday and we are quiet. I have read five magazines three times over, and have struggled like a slowly agonizing lunatic over the last pages of George Meredith's last novel, which he doubtless understands.[4] Tomorrow we move on.

July 15. We left Nailanga and the Mba river Monday morning, and steamed back past the coast we had already seen, until we came off the small village of Tonga-vere, and in trying to approach it, ran aground. As we were inside the reef, and on a soft sand, the running aground was no special matter, and we were not troubled with fears of being eaten, as Pembroke and Doctor Kingsley were, who were wrecked a few score miles to windward of us, and cautiously sailed in open boats in full view of all the settled islands, including Tairuni, where Sir John Thurston was then living, and of course eating Earls and Doctors daily with his kava. The joke was too good to be put into South Sea Bubbles, but Pembroke did lose his yacht, while we had only to tramp half a mile through mud at low tide in order to land at Tonga-vere, and establish ourselves in the guest-house among the mud channels of a small stream with no chance of a bath. These little coast villages have nothing but mangrove swamps to recommend them, and our errand there was not calculated to recommend us. This part of the coast is apparently the oldest and classic ground of Fiji where the venerable primitive God Dengue had his residence, and where the old ancestor-worship still clings even to the elders and communicants of the Church. Sir John stopped here to give the backsliders a terrible wigging, and order a village to remove bodily to another residence where it should be made more civilised. Yesterday morning we walked a couple of miles back to see the wicked village, which was the usual score of huts with a mud ditch round it, and inspired no sympathy. In the mountains we inspected a house in which the old religion had lately been practised. Nothing about it was different from other houses except that from the centre of the roof hung eleven cords of sinnet with a basket at the end. The ancestors have been disgusted at their descendents for becoming Christians, and have left. The first object is to induce them to return, so the priest prays and makes offerings until at last the ancestors return and slide down their string into the basket. As far as this goes, the amusement is harmless, but the next step is to conspiracy, human victims, wars, and general confusion; so Sir John puts them all in prison and they go to Suva and work "in the government service," as they say, for prison is an easy residence, and the natives rather like it. We brought several prisoners with us as carriers. The term of one expired last Saturday, but he said he should go along with the Governor still, and so he has. Generally they are in prison for some woman-scrape, for human nature in that respect remains quite independent of civilisation; but sometimes a whole batch gets shut up for heathen practices which are a form of sedition. Everyone knows that the natives are all Christians only in form; they try any sort of God that comes handy, on the idea that it can't do harm and may do good. The officials have to carry on a constant struggle to keep the heathen practices within bounds, and to me the contest seems quite humorous, for the natives are excellent at lying, and have no fixed principles more than a six-year old child. Having settled that job, and passed a disagreeable night in a suspiciously dirty house, with little to eat and nothing to drink in the way of water, we left Tonga-vere yesterday at eleven with a mob of native Mboules, or chiefs, and their tails, on their return to their villages. We ran about twentyfive miles to the eastward as far as Viti-levu Bay. The coast looks bare, brown and mountainous, like Scotland. I cannot account for the difference between Fiji and the other South Sea Islands. Fiji is never soft or graceful. As La Farge says, it has insides. This northern shore is harsh, and at this season looks cold, for the trade-wind blows half a gale in our teeth, and our little steamer labors hard against it, while the men who are towed behind in open boats are nearly swamped and chattering with cold. We reached Viti Levu Bay at about half past four o'clock, and met there our companions Berry and Joske, who had tramped down through the mountains. We are all quartered in the big native house of Joni Mandraiarivi, John Sourbread, a nephew of old King Thackambau, who hung Joni's father, after the happy native prejudices of too near relationship; but Joni took to education and became a protégé of Sir John, who has raised him to the magistracy so that he is a sort of king. Here we pass a day; then on to Suva and Sydney.

July 18. I took a stroll to the top of a hill, Wednesday afternoon, and lost myself in the reeds till I thought I never could get out. Melville's account of going through them at Nukuheva has an amount of accuracy that I can now swear to. I got down only by tumbling into a dry water-course, and crawling along its bed, under the overbranching vegetation. Yet the hillside looked bare, only a short distance away. Thursday morning before dawn we were drummed out of bed, and at quarter past six were already aboard the Clyde. Sir John wanted to reach Suva in one day. We puffed along the coast with fair weather and nothing much to look at except a bold and rocky range of mountains with glimpses of the inner ranges we had crossed. We passed the island of Ovalau with the old capital Levuka some dozen miles on our left, and towards noon we neared the long flat delta of the Rewa river where we had already been twice before. As the Clyde had to go out to sea in order to pass round the mouth of the Rewa, and as Sir John was not eager to be pitched about in the swell, we all got into the gig, and entering one arm of the river, were rowed through the bayous and branches a long way till we came out at five o'clock on the other side, and found the Clyde waiting. At six we were at Suva, and I allow that a comfortable bed felt welcome after three weeks of sleeping on the ground. So we have fairly done Fiji, and know as much about it as anyone wants to know. On the 22d we are to sail for Sydney. Sir John expects Lady Thurston by the same steamer that is to carry us away, and so the chapter will close. I shall send you, I hope, some of the photographs taken as we went along.

July 25. Here we are at the New Hebrides Islands. I hardly expect to remain here many months, for our steamer has stopped only an hour, or two, or three, or four, to please the Hebrideans and me; seeing that it gives me time to get a meal,—the first since leaving Fiji, and probably the last till we reach Sydney. You must have heard enough of South Sea islands by this time, so I will spare you Aneityam, especially as I shall not go ashore. It looks like the west coast of Scotland, mist and all, with a howling south-east trade on top, and nothing to recommend it. We left Fiji two days ago in the steamer Rockton, which is a megatherium compared with the Richmond, and is really a comfortable, tolerably steady ship of some fifteen hundred tons. Our last week in Suva was uneventful. Sir John was always kind and attentive; we were always indolent and dyspeptic—"dull dogs," as President Hayes once correctly described my friend Godkin and me.[5] Lady Thurston did not arrive, as expected, but the day of our departure did, and we came on board the Rockton with little regret, for Fiji makes no appeal to sentiment. The Fijians are not sympathetic. They have been, till our time, about the most feelingless, ferocious brutes on earth, and Dahomey was a kind of Paradise compared with it. They look it. I send you lots of Grenfell's, Sir John's, and Berry's photographs, so you can judge for yourself. Alack! that, to leave them, I have to pass through more horrors than cannibalism, for, though the weather is fine and the ship steady, I have been more suddenly and violently seasick than I ever remember to have been since childhood, and am aching all over from the strain. Five days more of it, and then—begin again!

July 31. Sydney at last. We got on shore at noon, after eight days horribly tedious and nauseated journey, and my first act was to drive to the Consulate and get a big bundle of letters, way back to March. Two were yours,— and the telegram. I have devoured them with such an appetite as you can imagine, and with feelings mixed like a big boa-constrictors after devouring a whole ox, horns and hoofs. I must hurry now to send off this letter tomorrow, and my return telegram as soon as I know when my next steamer sails; for the one I should have taken, sailed today. Your last letter fills me with dismay. You sail in October. I have carried out my promise exactly; I am here by August 1, and shall press on as fast as I can get La Farge to go; but I have done only four thousand miles, and I have thirteen thousand still to do. I am desperately afraid of arriving too late, and I can't hear from you again. The situation is gay. I don't want to go all the way to Paris for nothing; yet apparently I shall. I have much to consult you about, and even a few hours talk would be everything. Give me all the margin you can. Hang on till the very end of October, if possible. I cannot go back to America with you, but my going back at all will depend much on my seeing you before you sail. If I can't do this, I am *planté*. I should do much better, then, to pass the autumn and winter here, and go up to England in the Spring. You cannot get this letter before September, but if it arrives before September 12th, please telegraph to me at the American Consulate, Colombo, Ceylon, what day you are to sail. If possible, I shall sail from Colombo for Europe by September 15, but as yet I don't know how best to get to Colombo. I daren't risk the awful sea-voyage direct, by the mail-route. Already I am *au bout de mes forces* with the sea. We must take the easier but longer route through Torres Straits and Batavia or Singapore. I don't know and can't possibly tell whether we shall go by way of Brindisi, Naples or Marseilles, for this will depend on the time-tables of the lines from Ceylon. So you see I am in a pretty considerable mess of hot broth, and have to be regulated by La Farge besides, who knows nothing of my motives, and is not easily hurried.

I am delighted at your enjoyment of London; and after all, Paris was not so bad—was it? Some day you will tell me about your visits and your conquests in worlds which I shall never enter and therefore shall want the more to be enlightened about.[6] As for your thinking of me through all the whirl of your social triumphs, I am more than touched by it. I am as grateful as though I were a ten-year old boy whom you had smiled at, and put in a rapture of joy at being noticed. The more you please others, the more you delight me, all the way out here under your feet, where my solitude in a howling Australian kangaroo of a city is made brilliant by the thought that you are enjoying all sorts of social electrifications, and still remember me. Fascinate John Hay by all means! How I wish I had been with him in his illness,—or he with me! Thus far I have kept La Farge pretty well; at least, we have not had *grippe*, as all of you have. We are thin, (122 lbs.)—aren't we, just!—and I am much out of repair, but quite cured of depression, and apparently never in better health, barring seasickness and dyspepsia, which is only travelling. My letters from home seem all cheerful and satisfactory. Some have gone lost,—Lowndes's, certainly, though Lodge's has turned up—but I think all yours have come to hand, as well as the magazines you have so liberally sent me. I have also a letter from Hay in London, mostly about you, as, indeed, my correspondents commonly write about you, knowing apparently my interest in the subject. Gaskell writes, too, mostly about *grippe*. Sturgis Bigelow, too, and even my brother Charles, sent long letters, and very kind ones. You must give my love to all my English friends. Tell them just as much or as little as you think best about my plans, always remembering that you are the only person who fully knows them, and that you take the risk of responsibility for me as for Martha and other like personal property of your own. Whatever you say or do is right, and, indeed, if it were not, it could hardly matter much to a Polynesian-Malay-ourang-outang who has only to take to his jungle to escape even the most dangerous weapons of men—and women: namely; to wit; videlicet; their tongues. Dusk is coming on, as I sit at my lofty window looking down a ridiculous British street, like Liverpool washed clean. Everything is English, and absurdly near you, yet so far. I might as well be in Bond Street,—but I'm not, more's the pity, and I have not yet fairly begun my journey. I wish only I could give you a little slice of the delight you have given me today. So, *à revoir!*

August 1. Will this letter never end! I have read it over, and pity you, but must add a postscript, if only to explain the telegram I sent you today: "Start Thursday via Batavia." I hope you will get it today, but at any rate on Monday. Our friend Consul Sewall turned up here yesterday, also anxious to get to Singapore, but having made every inquiry only to be assured that it could not be done. I was not convinced, and this morning dragged them to the steamer-office, where we learned to our great delight that, though the Jumna left here yesterday, we could still catch her at Townsville, and need not even leave here till Thursday night with the mail, going by rail to Brisbane, and from there by quick coaster to Townsville, while the Jumna has to wait to take cargo at various ports. This secures our arrival at Batavia about the 20th. From there we expect to take the weekly steamer to Singapore and thence to Ceylon by the first mail-steamer. I hope to reach Ceylon in the first week of September, and after a week's rest there, go on to Europe. With anything like luck in connections, we ought to reach Paris early in October, and I will cross at once to England if you are still there. Write me a line to the care of Hottinguer &Co unless I telegraph my hotel address at Paris. On arriving at our Mediterranean port I will certainly telegraph all I can of our movements so that you can instruct me. La Farge's letters press his return home in October. Perhaps he can sail with you. I must pass the winter in Europe, for objects I will explain when we meet, if I am to return at all. Towards Spring I may be ready, and of course shall then come back to go on the stump for Cleveland or Hill, or whatever noble democrat we are to elect for our next President. Please do not breathe a word of all this, for I want no one except you to know anything of my future plans. When the time comes, I want only to say that I am coming back temporarily, for personal reasons, and leave myself free from questions which would require lies. Above all, I want to return quietly and unexpected, so that I mayn't be bothered by Historical Societies and invitations which I should decline. Is this morbid? I don't care if it is. If I come back, it will be solely because you have said: Come! I can't give that reason to anyone but you, and any other would be a lie. As you know, I ask nothing even from those I love most. I have no more interest in the world than I had when I came away, and have given it all I have to give. If I return now, I must carry with me some means of filling my time and avoiding ennui, at least as far as that awful malady can be dodged or drugged; and if, after all, anything should happen to interfere with the experiment, I must be able to dart off at a moment's notice to the desert of Gobi.

MS: MHi
1. Adolph Brewster Joske (1855–1937), later Adolph Brewster Brewster, in the Fiji civil service 1884–1910, author of books on ethnography.
2. Old Hundredth is the hymn tune composed by Louis Bourgeois in 1551; it is used with such texts as "All people that on earth do dwell" and the doxology "Praise God from whom all blessings flow."
3. In Bret Harte's poem "The Society upon the Stanislaus" (1871), miners in a California gold camp who have formed a geological society argue a scientific point about fossils by hurling them at each other. Abner Dean of Angel's Camp is knocked out in the row.
4. *One of Our Conquerors,* which Meredith himself called "my most indigestible production," was serialized October 1890 through May 1891 in the New York *Sun.*
5. See HA to Parkman, Feb. 20, 1879.
6. Describing her arrival in London in mid-May, Mrs. Cameron wrote: "Some kind friend gave us an opera-box. Another asked us down to Sussex for Whit Sunday. Others to lunch, dinner &c. It was like being welcomed home" (Elizabeth Cameron to HA, May 21). The "triumphs" she enjoyed on returning to London, June 3, after an interval in Paris, included a dinner party given by the German diplomat Rücker Jenisch. At the table covered with orchids, she was seated next to a German prince; among the other fashionable guests were the reigning London beauties and two acquaintances of the Prince of Wales involved in a much publicized baccarat scandal.

To John Hay

Sydney, 2 August, 1891.

My dear John

La Farge and I turned up here two days ago, just as seasick as ever, and eight days from Fiji. On leaving the steamer we drove straight to the Consulate and got your letter from London of June 4. Although in this antipodean British-American city, I feel as though you must certainly be within a walk, I constrain myself to remember that I have not got back to America, and that you have. I wish only that you had been with us, and so escaped your grippe. No less than four of my letters hinted that the writers, on account of their recent influenzas, thought they might about as well submit at once to the inevitable, and, taking as it were, their grip-sacks in their hands, descend to the tomb that was yawning for them; but I think this condition of mind must be a part of the microbe, and that summer will put the monster to sleep. Certainly the new form of spring vegetable incident to this complaint, is getting to be a bore. I prefer the tropics and old-fashioned yellow-fever.

Your babble of green fields[1] in London and Paris is excellent good for one so far gone, and I wish that my knowledge of Australia were wide enough to repay it; but as Australia to me is only an unavoidable bore,—a stepping-stone to another tropical ramble—I shall just skip it, and let up on you. We have done our South Seas at last, clean cooked and eaten. The dream of hot youth has become the reality of what we will call mature and sober experience. I am almost sorry—and yet rather glad—to have accomplished the queer sensation of realising so old a vision, and one so fixed that the vision and the reality still manage to live peaceably together in my head—two South Seas, not in the least alike, and both in their ways charming. Anyway, it is done! *Cras*, as Horace used to say, et cetera, I may do what I can; all the same, I shall have seen Hawaii, Samoa and Tahiti. After all, a year might have been worse spent in America, being a useful member of society, and doing good to my fellow man. To have escaped a year of Congress and high-thinking, by bagging a year of solid Polynesian garlands and materialism, is as sweet a joy as to run away with another man's wife. The profit is a duplicated golden glow.[2]

Of Fiji, I can tell you only what is practical and commonplace. If you want to know what Fiji was when we were younger men, get the volume of Admiral Erskine's "voyage"; look into the Appendix, and read the narrative of a stray English seaman who lived among Fijians as almost a native for many years.[3] It is all true, or sufficiently so to be a true picture. The Fijians are not romantic. They have only two ideas, eating and women, therein being quite Parisian. The men are dull; the women are ugly; and being the most brutal of all known cannibal races, they were and are sexually very correct and respectable, and despise the immorality of my poor Samoans, who in their turn shudder at the Tahitians. No man can have a ghost of a dream how fantastic this world is till he lives in the different moralities of the South Seas. Every fresh island has been to me a fresh field of innocent joy in extending my museum of moral curiosities, and in enlightening me on the subject of my fellow men. Truly I care not to eat my neighbor; but—

Sir John Thurston took us a most interesting three weeks' journey through the remotest recesses of Viti-Levu, where no travellers have been before, and among tribes as little known as any in the South Seas, barring the Solomon Islands. All are now good churchmen, and say long grace at every possible occasion, but they are precious closely watched too, and about half of them are in prison at Suva for heathen practices. The Governor did little but give them tremendous wiggings for persisting in heathen ways. I enclose a photograph of one such scene, where you can detect me sitting behind Sir John who is giving fits to a poor chief whose people would pray to their grandfathers to come back; the grandfathers having cleared out to some more agreeable spirit-residence because they didn't like missionaries otherwise than boiled. We were guests of these mountain tribes for weeks, and I shook hands with more old cannibals and murderers than I could reckon. Lots of leprosy about, too, and skin-diseases and ringworm and such. I did not hanker to sleep in their houses or to hang on their necks, but I did it; and I was carried up rocky river-courses, and hauled up straight mountains only to slip in the mud down the other side. We were several days working through tropical forest; the real glass-conservatory tropical thing, with fifty-dollar ferns to walk on, and parasitic forests in the air. La Farge did the worst part in a litter, usually with his feet somewhere in the trees and his head in the mud; but he found the attitude uncongenial, and walked all he could. Luckily for us, five of our six white men were past fifty, and we took it very easy on the march, so that I really enjoyed the trip enormously, and mean to write King another geological lecture on upheaval and subsidence, illustrated by the angles of La Farge's litter. We went up about three thousand feet, and crossed straight through the island without regarding obstacles, and when necessary for the litters just widening the native trail with cleavers. We had more than a hundred natives to carry our traps, and I felt singularly as though it were Central Africa, and somehow we were to discover Stanley, or relieve him, or kill him.

So I say that we know our Fiji—we have learned to know it, so to speak, in its own way, namely by devouring it. The island of Viti Levu is quite a baby continent; it has an inside as well as an outside; two or three different races more or less mixed, and resources galore. Of all the Pacific Groups, Fiji and Hawaii are alone worth owning, for any profit to be made out of them. After inspecting Fiji thoroughly, I am glad that England has taken the contract, and am bound to say that Governor Thurston is a long way the most of a man in the Pacific; but the job hardly pays as an investment. There is little money in it;—none at all, I believe. South Sea islands are made for bubbles.[4]

As for the Fijians, I think that they, as well as all the Melanesians and Papuans, may with benefit to all parties, be put to death. Being ugly and black, and their women being virtuous, they are not fit to live. Either the Hindustanee or the Chinaman would then come in, who would at least grow me something to eat, besides yams which I despise, and pigs which are so near to being Fijians as to suggest unpleasant cannibalistic tastes. I could find nothing Fijian worth eating. They had not even songs or traditions or legends, and no satisfactory ghosts, to take the place of good food. Intellectually they are even more disappointing than the Samoan, who does like to sing.

Sir John was extremely kind, and took entire charge of us during our five weeks stay. Without him we could have seen little worth the trouble of our journey, for Suva is an uninteresting little British village, far from any native towns, and dull as Billerica Junction.[5] If I ever get home, my first duty must be to collect a set of our Agricultural Reports, as nearly complete as possible, and send them to him. He has that fad, and believes firmly that these Reports are invaluable. While there I read up South Sea literature in his library, and became posted on it. So I am now fitted to come away and forget it.

Our next cruise is round the world. At last Bancel La Farge begs his father to come home. His father is no more eager to come home than I am, and we would both gladly give another year to doing the Malay Archipelago and India; but my conscience says that La Farge ought to go, so I have imposed on myself the contract of taking him to England and shipping him home in October. Our Samoan friend Consul Sewall is now in Sydney, by accident, and wants to get to Singapore as we do, for we rebel at the awful voyage direct to Ceylon; so we leave here in three days, by rail, for Brisbane; there take a coastwise steamer to some northern port called Townsville; and there catch the big steamer Jumna for Batavia. From Batavia a steamer runs weekly to Singapore, where we catch the China mail steamers for Ceylon. We hope to get a week's rest at Ceylon, and then start for Paris by the Suez Canal. We have thirteen thousand miles to go, and two months to go it. I shall hope to give La Farge a few weeks run in Paris and London before trotting him down to Liverpool. Then I shall consider my own future, and not till then. Tearfully as I wish to see you again, I have no intention of returning for the winter; but when I ask myself what next, I break down. Solitary travel is a doubtful joy. At best, travel brings frightful *longueurs,* and at worst it is intolerable unless one can wreak it on a companion. If I can only find a ripe durian and mangosteen at Batavia or Singapore, I shall have no motive worth repeating so long a seasickness, and my only resource then is Central Asia and India. That journey is too big an affair to be ventured alone.

Anyway, write to me in care of Baring Brothers. I shall be somewhere in Europe, I trust, by the time your letter gets there. Once in England I shall doubtless dawdle awhile among our friends till Gladstone and the Prince of Wales bore me beyond endurance. Now that Phillips Brooks is a bishop I feel that America must be the New Jerusalem, and that life has new value; but whether even Bishop Brooks can stand a Presidential election, I doubt.[6] Let me see that doubt resolved, before I think of return, except perhaps on a visit. Lives a dentist in the world? Can he give me all the teeth I have lost in the South Seas? For such a being, I would return even to Boston—for a space.

You demand what you are pleased to call "one of my water-colors." Know that three months ago I threw away my paints and brushes in disgust, and have not the daub of a pencil to bestow on a millionaire. The task of trying to do the undoable is even more mortifying in color than in printer's ink. I cannot conceive how even the best painters bear up against hourly humiliation, and when I found that I was learning little tricks and clever dodges to please my vanity and lose the solitary merit of childlike ignorance and fatuity, I stopped short. To be clever was too base.

Give my love to Mrs Hay and all the lobsters. Also to King if he wants it. Tell him that at least I have learned in the South Seas the vanity of geology, and how the Silurian conglomerates were made.

Ever Yrs   Henry Adams.

MS: MHi
1. *Henry V*, II, iii.
2. T. B. Read, "Drifting."
3. John E. Erskine (1806–1887), *Journal of a Cruise among the Islands of the Western Pacific* (1853).
4. HA refers to the South Sea Bubble, an English speculative scheme that failed disastrously in 1720.
5. Billerica, a farming village between the Concord and Merrimack rivers, northwest of Boston.
6. Phillips Brooks (1835–1893), HA's second cousin, had been rector of Trinity Church, Boston, since 1869 when, on April 29, 1891, he was elected Episcopal bishop of Massachusetts by a diocesan convention. Conservative churchmen throughout the country challenged his election on the grounds of latitudinarianism. The issue was in doubt until July 10 when his election was confirmed by a majority of bishops.

To Charles Francis Adams, Jr.

Sydney. 3 Aug. 1891.

Dear Charles

I find on arriving here your kind letter of May 3 on the subject of St Gaudens's figure. It is natural that St Gaudens should be nervous about the impression I might get of it, for I was myself so nervous about his success that I refused even to meet him from the moment he began the model, and persisted in the refusal till I left. As my friends are determined that I shall be satisfied with the work, I am at least relieved of a heavy anxiety on their account, though I cant help still looking forward with a little dread to my own first sight of it, not because I doubt that his artistic rendering of an idea must be better than my conception of the idea, but because the two could hardly be the same, and what is his in it might to me seem to mix badly with the image that had been in my mind. No doubt, time and familiarity with the work would set me right, but the first sense of jar might be nasty. If you and Sturgis Bigelow and Dwight agree about it, just so much anxiety is off my mind; but I would rather still wait for the opinion of a sterner critic than any of you,—Ned Hooper. If he approves, without reserves, I shall begin to feel at ease about my own opinion.

I am very glad, too, that La Farge's window satisfies you. I read him what you said about it, which gratified him much, especially for the sake of his son Grant.[1] Somehow Grant always seems to me to be Tom Perry's son, and I never get quite used to him as a La Farge;[2] but I suppose he may be clever for all that. Tom is clever too. As for La Farge, I am now dragging him to Liverpool like a truant, to ship him over to his poor son Bancel who is scared out of his front teeth by the old man's prolonged absence. I had meant to put in another year here, to do the Malay Archipelago and India, before going up to China; but if I were to stay in the Malay Archipelago, La Farge would stay too, and kick square out of all traces; and though I should like no better than to keep on indefinitely as we have been going, I have enough bowels of mercy to wish not quite to ruin his poor sons. I want him, too, to do some more windows before he goes to perdition, and I have besides a comforting conviction that unless I mean to go wholly to pieces, I must get myself a little patched at Paris or New York. So we shall leave here in a few days for Batavia and Singapore, and after a little rest at Ceylon, I hope to reach Paris early in October. The journey is a trifle of about fifteen thousand miles, most of which is solid seasickness and infernal discomfort, but one must pay for being contented, and my extravagance in that way is debauched. Every sea has received my contributions, and the more oceans I cross, the more seasick I am. Up and down the Pacific, for uncounted thousands of miles, I have groaned and sworn I never would go on water again, but still it goes on, and the finer the weather, the worse I am.

We have really had a most amusing and entertaining year of wandering, with fearful intervals of being bored, and with the usual traveller's miseries, but always varied by episodes of great entertainment. Our last was at Fiji where we have been guests of the British Governor, and have been carried in great form through mountains and tribes hardly known to geography. Our three weeks of travel through Fiji were highly entertaining; as good as Central Africa, and much less trouble. Still, I am not eager to pass many years at Fiji, or even at Tahiti or Samoa, which were much more attractive. We were quite ready to move on, when the steamer came for us, though we had to endure another week of unutterable nausea. So we turned up in Australia a few days ago.

Australia never tempted me, and I am in a hurry to get back to the tropics. Our steamer has already gone, but we linger here to get a few jobs done, and then catch it by rail and mail somewhere in the north. Indeed we expect to go so fast that by the time you get this letter, say September 10th, we hope to be inspecting Buddhist temples in Ceylon, and preparing for the frosts of Paris. I have given no thought yet to my movements after La Farge goes home. I am by no means tired of travel, but I don't hanker to travel alone in wild countries, and I must make new combinations if I am to return to the east.

I have followed American affairs, in the newspapers, out here, much more carefully than I have done at home for many years. Everywhere I have been, I have found the world going to the devil, and am the less troubled to observe that America seems well on her way to the same destiny. At our age we can afford to take it coolly. If America likes it, it suits me. Only I no longer feel the ardor of twenty years ago to set it right, and I opine that even you must by this time have come to the resigned conclusion that the planetary dance had better go its own cussed way.

I know not when you will see me again, but I am a babe of impulse, and anything is possible.

Ever Yrs   Henry Adams.

MS: MHi
1. John La Farge had entrusted the completion and installation of his window for CFA2's Boston house to his architect son, Christopher Grant La Farge (1862–1938).
2. Thomas Sergeant Perry was Christopher Grant La Farge's maternal uncle.

To Henry Cabot Lodge

Sydney, New South Wales. 4 August, 1891.

My dear Cabot

Your letter of March 23 reached me on my arrival here a few days ago, which was more good-fortune than falls to the lot of some letters, which have never reached me at all, but must be cruising about the Pacific like Wandering Epistles of Hebrews. I hope they do not suffer from seasickness as I do.

Thanks for your summary, political and social. Since leaving America, I have taken again to reading American newspapers, and am wonderfully well posted on current topics. In the middle of the Pacific Ocean all things assume a curiously level grade of interest. The political and social status of a few half-naked Samoans, Tahitians and Fijians, seems just as important as the doings of Australia, the card-play of the Prince of Wales, or the speeches of Benjamin Harrison.[1] I am far from assigning to each of these subjects even a relative standard of importance, but I am struck with the curious perspective which equalises the little with the big. For a year I have been living in communistic societies such as are the ideal of reformers, and such as I used to lecture about so learnedly. Samoa and Fiji are both of them almost pure communisms where private property is either unknown or disregarded. I found the system rather a pleasant one. On the whole, it suited me better than our own. It is intensely aristocratic, and gives enormous influence to the individual; it is indolent and pleasure-seeking; and it is perfectly indifferent to everything except women and war. Australia seeks to rival Polynesia with some success. The antipathy to work, and the love of amusement, are something like Samoa, and follow at a long distance the more perfect arrangements of Fiji; but I do not regard Australia as a success. It is neither one thing nor the other, and the people shirk work without getting real happiness in idleness.

On the whole I have been greatly entertained. The South Seas swarm with laughable satires on everything civilised, and especially on every known standard of morality. They flourished in outrageous defiance of every known moral, economical, social and sanitary law, until morality and economy were taught them, and then they went, promptly and unanimously, to the devil. Nine in every ten perished of virtue, among all the islands and races, little and big; and they go on perishing with a unanimity quite conclusive. I do not undertake to draw a moral from their euthanasia. Only the wise draw morals, and I am one of the foolish, who grow foolisher every day, and less able to see six inches before their noses; but I suppose there is a moral somewhere. Evidently the savages needed legislation.

La Farge and I have just finished Fiji. Thanks to Governor Thurston whose guests we were, we saw it in a way new to travellers, and we know it, I think, nearly as well as we know the smaller groups of Tahiti and Samoa. As financial investments, none of the Pacific islands, except the Sandwiches, are worth touching. They are not worth any one of the West Indies, if you lumped them all together. In fact, they are worth less than nothing, for they require large expenditures. Nevertheless Germany, France, Australia, New Zealand, and the Lord knows what other countries and governments, are squabbling for the possession of these wretched little lava-heaps; and such is now the dead-lock that no one dare tell the Solomon Islanders to stop murdering and eating Englishmen.

The European in face of the tropics is a sweet study. He admits himself to be an abject failure there; he can make nothing of it; he can't work; he can't digest; he can't sleep; he gets disease, and he grumbles without ceasing; but he wont let anyone else go there. He bars the Chinaman, hates the negro, and keeps sharp watch on the Indian Cooly. He wont let anyone alone. He cant keep his hands off of stray land, even though he can do nothing with it. I find no fault with him; on the contrary, he does only what he must do in the nature of nature; but what the deuce can he make of it?

On the whole, I am satisfied that America has no future in the Pacific. She can turn south, indeed, but after all, the west coast of South America offers very little field. Her best chance is Siberia. Russia will probably go to pieces; she is rotten and decrepit to the core, and must pass through a bankruptcy, political and moral. If it can be delayed another twentyfive years, we could Americanise Siberia, and this is the only possible work that I can see still open on a scale equal to American means.

Australia and New Zealand are not likely to change very much. They can go little further, for they have nowhere to go. Things are already fixed in grooves here, and the grooves are pretty shallow. I think they would do better on the long run, if there were no such thing as steamers or rapid communication. They might then develop character.

La Farge and I are going up to Paris. Not that we are at all tired of rambling, but that La Farge really must go home, and I am not disposed to travel alone. My future movements are uncertain, but my teeth need lots of attention. Give my love to your wife and Constance. Perhaps they will come over to see me, if I can't get to them. I don't suppose they hanker after a Presidential election much more than I do.

Ever Yrs   Henry Adams.

1. The presence of the Prince of Wales on the scene of the baccarat scandal that broke in early June created a furor in the press; he was severely criticized for illegal gaming. President Harrison made 140 speeches on a tour through the South and to the Pacific coast, April 14 to May 21.

To Elizabeth Cameron

August 12, 1891.

Here we are, on the "Jumna"! but if you are an exact individual, and want to know where we are, I'm afraid you must consult a pretty good Atlas. I know that the North Queensland coast is about a hundred rods ahead, and we are just slowing up to drop a mail at some small settlement which, on special inquiry of an officer, I learn is called Port Douglas. The captain tells me we are in 17° south latitude. I think we have come about two thousand miles from Sydney, or six thousand from Tahiti, which leaves eleven thousand still to do. I dare not ask when we shall reach Batavia, or how we are to get to Singapore, or whether we can hope to make Ceylon in time to reach England before you sail, since I don't know when you are to sail anyway. I am only well content to have got so far, so well.

Our stay in Sydney, after my last big despatch was mailed, which is now hurrying to you by the southern route, offered not a particle of interest. Australia and the Australians bore me. They are second-rate United States, when viewed from the tourist's standpoint, and even if they were first-rate, they are not what I came to see. We were not expected. We had not an acquaintance, and were not anxious about making one. I was only eager to be off, and rejoiced hugely when at half past six o'clock on the evening of Thursday the 6th, we scrambled into our sleeping-car and started—Sewall, La Farge and I, with the *impayable* Awoki. Then at last I began to understand how huge Australia is. We travelled all night and all the next day—twentyeight hours—more than seven hundred miles, through a country very like California, only to reach Brisbane, which, on the map, is next door to Sydney. At Brisbane we slept, and at noon, Saturday the 8th, we went aboard the steamer "Wodonga," and sailed—and sailed—and sailed—three days, until yesterday—Tuesday the 11th—at noon, we came to anchor off Townsville. Never mind what a deuce of a time we had in getting ashore, or how we lost a trunk, or what Townsville was like. Always California or Mexico! We did get ashore, and eat some native oysters, and got aboard a tender, and were carried out five miles to the "Jumna," and started north again at dark. On the whole, none of us have been more disagreeable than nature made us, unless I was a shade more offensive than usual; and, considering that our tempers were severely tried by the bad management of the steamers, this modified praise speaks loud in our favor. In one respect we are greatly pleased. The voyage is like steaming on a river. Not only are we always in smooth water, within the great Australian barrier reef, but we are generally behind islands, and both islands and coast are extremely pretty, especially in the soft sunlight. The weather is again warm, and grows warmer every day. The journey is a real enjoyment, barring the inevitable discomforts of travel. I wonder that I never heard of the charms of this route, but every charm has some blemish, and this particular amusement is tempered by what tempers so many of our best sources of virtuous happiness—its danger. Everyone on board, from the Captain to the cook, is thinking of the "Jumna's" companion-ship the "Quettah," which tore out her bottom on a sharp rock in Torres Straits, and went down with all on board, except one woman who swam a week or two, and was saved. Another great steamer of the same line had the same fate before. Torres Strait, which we enter two days hence, is one of the most dangerous navigations in the world, but if the steamers risk it, we can, and since we have seen that Governor le Marquis de la Cascade of Tahiti, was wrecked in the Paumotus in the "Volage" on the trip to the Marquesas which he invited us to make with him, we think we have lost our chance of shipwreck. Anyway we sail merrily on, and as I am an oriental fatalist, I accept whatever is to be. Our fellow passengers are, as on the Atlantic, chiefly Jews. The rest are mostly colonials and uninteresting. One or two offer possibilities of humanity. We shall know more of them, perhaps, and, if not, then we shall do without. The sky is blue; the sea is green; the shore is opaline; and white clothes are a luxury.

I wish only I could hear from you, but that is near a month away. Why could I not have known my route? Yet I did hear from you through John Hay, in a way that made me almost laugh aloud in the New South Wales express railway-train. La Farge had bought the July Scribner, and, as we were rattling over the Australian mountains towards Brisbane, he handed it to me with the remark that John Hay had something in it. I looked and saw—Two on a Terrace!; but, Great Kung-fu-tse! what two? which two? for were we not four? or did I dream it? and the kiss![1] I can swear that the pair to which I belonged, knew nothing of any kiss. If kissing there was, the other two were the sole parties to it! Is the kiss to be regarded as poetic, or is it attributed on trust to me, or was it—oh no! it would be naughty even to think it. I never could have believed that John should so compromise a trusting and lovely female. What must she think? and Mrs Hay? I say nothing of myself, or, what is more important, of my "two"; yet even there—! And can John have been shown my own poetic crime on the same topic?[2] I never showed it. If he saw it, as his verses seem to suggest by echo, he got it from lovely female, No. 2.

Sunday, 16 August. If you by chance read my weary letters, and have any notion where they take you, I shall have done something for Martha's education, for you know by this time more geography than ever I did. Here I am told is Sunday. We have been ten days travelling, by rail and steamer, and only a few hours ago got clear of Australia. At this rate I need not worry about finding you in England; at a ripe old age I shall die on the ocean, and I trust I shall make a quicker voyage to the next world. That "Quettah" affair, which did in fact hurry considerably the ultramondane travels of the passengers, has to answer for delaying us twentyfour hours, for, when we approached Torres Strait, we pulled up every evening at dark, and anchored for the night. This was always my ideal of ocean travel, and as far as that sort of comfort is concerned, nothing ever equalled going to sea in Australia; but one's progress is slow. Our captain, who is a young man, commanded the "Quettah," and has spoken to me several times of his wreck. The ship struck and went down in three minutes, before anything could be done, but a boat of more or less naked people, hardly alive, got ashore the next morning, and the captain was among them. We passed the spot, and anchored near it, night before last. Naturally the Captain does not hanker after hitting more unknown rocks in the night; and nothing is more possible, for the bottom is seldom more than one or two hundred feet deep, and a good-sized paving-stone on edge would be a danger. We did not clear the Strait until yesterday morning, and then we had to stop at Thursday Island, and pass the day taking pearl-shell on board. Thursday Island—our twothousandandfourhundredandfiftyoneth island—is the last outlying fragment of Australia. I suppose it is the limit of the Pacific ocean, and that, on this side of it, we are perhaps in the Malay Archipelago. New Guinea is only a couple of hundred miles to the northward, but as I'm not going there, I cared more about Thursday Island, which is the dreariest of dreary English settlements, on a bare burned shore of sand and granite, for all the world like New England in a July drought. We went ashore for the day. The Australian navy was there—seven gunboats just come out from England, and roaring regattas for the pleasure of the seamen and a score or two of whites who think they live here. "The second richest place in Queensland," said the indignant shop-keeper resenting some remark of Sewall's. Much pearl-oyster is fished up in or about these reefs, and every black scoundrel one sees, slips out of his pocket a paper of pearls which he offers you for sale at prices which, for all that I know, may be dirt-cheap, but are rarely worth the attention of one who does not know a good pearl from a bad one. La Farge and the females of the ship seemed to think none were good. On the other hand I was half-tempted to buy the whole lot at a bargain, and try selling them in Paris. None seemed suited for you, and the only one that approached such a standard was held firmly at £30. One or two smaller ones were good in shape, but I was told were off-color. Generally the color is a little steeley and hard; but I know not what color is right, and to my mediaeval-archaic mind the most ornamental pearls are the irregular ones, which leave something to the imagination. Of course, this taste is not only bad, but ignorant, foolish, extravagant, vicious, wicked and perfectly ridiculous; but I am not maintaining it against you; I do not suggest anyone's wearing barbaric pearls; and only in the recesses of the Malay Archipelago I venture to think that though I prefer women's necks to be round and white, I see no necessity for insisting that their ornaments should match. Anyway I bought no pearls, and was very weary of Thursday island in a very brief time. Of all the dreary spots I have seen since August last (say August 13, 1890; I happen to remember the date for a reason that I will tell you some other time) I have seen nothing so depressing as Thursday island; and all because of the settlement; for the islands at a distance are not bad, and the colors of the water are wonderful. We left there, deeply depressed, the only woman who interested me on our ship; a Mrs Rowan, of Melbourne; a curious animal, quite female in species, very intelligent with paint and piano, and the nearest approach to refinement we have met among the antipodeans.[3] She had taken a wild fancy for coming up here to meet her brother-in-law, Lord Charles Scott, who is admiral of the fleet; but when she saw the place, she nearly wept, and I think we could have induced her to go away with us to Batavia or anywhere else, had we been in search of adventures. I wonder whether one should be sorry to lose the taste for mischief. These steamers are made for it, and are very dull without it. Lots of women, and a sufficiency of young men; not a husband within two thousand miles; blue skies; bluer seas; warm, moonlight nights; and constant association for weeks; what is such a life for, but mischief. I cannot without effort conceive even of talking half an hour with anyone on the ship, and yet—. After all, I am not so *ennuyé* but that I could get into mischief if I could select my own companions.

Friday, August 21. We have stopped for an hour or two at Bali, the island next to Java, and La Farge and Sewall have gone ashore in the boat, to see what they can, and to send a telegram to Batavia if possible. The place is pretty; a broad plain with a range of forest-clad mountains behind it, all seen through opaline haze. To my fancy the small Dutch town looks better from the water than it would probably look in its own light, and as its temperature, under an almost vertical sun, promises to be something cordial, I have preferred shade and the sea-breeze and a monologue with you. Our voyage has been encouragingly successful. By Sunday we shall have run off four thousand miles since Sydney; eight thousand since Tahiti; and, for the first time, a long voyage has been really pleasant. All the way from Brisbane we have been in calm water, like a river, with land generally in sight; perfect weather; divine moonlight; and, these last two days, grand volcanic mountains to watch as we ran by the long chain of islands on our left. I wonder that no one ever told us of the charm of this route, and I am still more astonished at my own gross ignorance, for until within six weeks or so I was still under the impression that Torres Strait was a path rarely used, and that no traveller ever came that way. Had I been told that it was an impassable labyrinth, I should have believed it. Instead, I find it the regular route of large steamers, and, except for a few awkward places, a perfect Paradise of navigation. My only worry, which greatly interferes with enjoyment, is that we are behind time. We should have reached Ceylon by Sept. 1st, but shall barely reach Singapore. In two days we get to Batavia; then we must wait for a steamer to Singapore, where we must wait for another steamer to Ceylon. You will know, long before this letter reaches you, the time of our arrival at Ceylon, for I shall telegraph at once from Colombo; but you must remember that from Ceylon to Europe is three weeks of hard travel. I have lost hope of arriving in Paris before October 15 under the most favorable conditions. When—oh, when do you sail? If you had waited till Nov. 1, I should certainly have caught you. As you are to sail in October, I have the worst fears; and you can imagine that a journey of so many thousand miles is no joke if it is to meet with so sharp a disappointment at the end. I made La Farge write to his friend Johnston in Paris to take us rooms there, so that I could, if necessary, leave La Farge, and hurry over to England immediately. If you do not sail before the 25th, I cling to the hope that I shall have at least a few hours with you.—Sewall and La Farge have returned, and we are off again. They brought a peck of mangosteens aboard, and so I have eaten my first mangosteen, and accomplished half my object in going round the world. The other half—the *durian*—was not to be had here, but we are promised it at Batavia and Singapore. This is grand! Had I returned to America without eating the mangosteen and durian, life would have been unendurianable. I must have come back here to eat the durian and die. As for the mangosteen, it is certainly a good fruit,—has admirable points, no doubt,—but as yet I do not quite feel its poetic side enough to understand why it should be thought so supremely superior to the mango, our old staff of life. Probably further experience will enlighten my taste.

Saturday. 22 August. Early tomorrow morning we are to reach Batavia, and I shall let this letter go on with the ship to Aden, as it may reach you a week earlier than it would by way of the regular mail. Our voyage thus far has been a great success, and the world contains few humble individuals who are so grateful as I am for such pleasures as ocean travel gives. We have had nothing but the loveliest weather, the calmest blue seas, and the most charming bits of scenery. You ought to rejoice too, at escaping for once from the wails of seasickness. If such luck could only last! Otherwise I have nothing to tell you. As far as concerns our fellow-passengers, the record is a blank. I have not been energetic enough to exchange a dozen words with anyone beyond our own party. Every year I grow more lethargic and socially hopeless. This is hard on you, who are commonly the chief sufferer from my dulness, but it is hardest on myself who am painfully conscious of the weariness that seems to paralyse brain and tongue the moment a social effort becomes necessary. The Lord, who presumably made us, knows best why he made us stupid; but I wish, in my case, he had not added to the stupidity the unnecessary load of dread which is inspired by the thought of facing society. What a comfort it is to me to think that you have a genius for entertaining people, so that I can get, at second-hand, through you, the amusement of society without its ennui! This alone makes my return to Washington seem possible. I have naturally thought much about it in the long watches of the last three months, and even in the pangs of seasickness I have never been able to face the idea of return except with your help; so you have no end of work cut out for you, and I will bet a cart-load of bric-a-brac against a pair of old gloves that you will break down, and have to send me away again to give you a chance of life. I ought to reach Europe within three weeks after this letter arrives, and this letter ought to arrive before the end of September. We shall be detained at Batavia, Singapore and Ceylon, by making connections. I allow a week for each detention. Hurrying as fast as steamers and La Farge will let me, I hope to reach Paris at last, and to land La Farge in some hostelry selected by his friend Johnston. If haste is necessary, enclose me a line under cover to John Johnston Esq., 59 Rue Vaugirard, or in care of Drexel Harjès &Cie, 31 Boulevard Haussman, Paris. If haste is not urgent, direct to me, in care of Hottinguer &Cie. I shall telegraph from Ceylon, and from the first European port we reach. Can I do more? I wish I could. Above all, I wish I were a fortnight further on, as I had hoped and planned; but a journey of seventeen thousand miles is no trifle, and as yet only eight thousand are done; at least I measure only that. Hang on for three weeks more, if you only can!

MS: MHi
1. In Hay's poem "Two on the Terrace" the speaker, alone with his love on the terrace of the Capitol in Washington on a moonlit evening, evokes "future lovers meeting / On far-off nights like this, / Who . . . Shall meet, clasp hands, and kiss."
2. The evening recalled by Hay's poem, when Clara and John Hay, HA and Elizabeth Cameron had been together at the Capitol, had apparently also inspired HA's sonnet "The Capitol by Moonlight":

> Infinite Peace! The calm of moon and midnight! Where
> The marble terrace gleams in silvery light,
> Peace broods. Drugged by the brooding night
> The crowded tree-tops sleep in passionless air.
> Look up, where like a God, strong, serene, fair,
> The pale dome soars and slumbers, shadowy, white,
> Endymion, dreaming still that on his Latmian height
> He feels Selene's breath warm on his eyes and hair.
> Infinite Peace! Yet, bending from the West,
> Flash out the fierceness and the fire of Mars,
> While there beneath, straining to touch the stars
> The obelisk mocks us with its sweet unrest,
> And even this soft air of the terrace throbs
> With some low moan—sigh of a heart that sobs.

3. Marian Ryan Rowan (1847–1922), known as Ellis Rowan, Australian painter of wild flowers. Her sister was the wife of Lord Charles Scott (1839–1911), commander in chief on the Australian station 1889–1892.

To Charles Milnes Gaskell

Steamer "Jumna." 17 August, 1891.

Dear Carlo

Your letter, dated I don't know when, for it is locked up in some trunk in the hold, reached me on my arrival at Sydney about three weeks ago. I have wandered now over a vast amount of oceans, and the worst part of oceans is that one might as well be in one as another, for all looks much alike, and has the uniformity of the seasickness which is for me its single invariable pleasure. Up and down the Pacific for many grey weeks, my friend La Farge and I have paraded our ennui, freshening, at intervals of rest, on the little green islands that dot that sea of misery, like very small stars in a very big sky. We passed most of your winter in Samoa; the spring in Tahiti, and part of the summer in Fiji, where we were guests of Sir John Thurston at the Government House, and tramped with him through the remotest recesses of his small empire, guests of ancient cannibals now ornaments of human nature. I will say no more of my travels, because I am now on my way to England where I expect to arrive within a month after this letter reaches you. Where I now am, I do not know; but, somewhere within the vagueness of the Malay Archipelago, I am lounging along towards Batavia where we are due a week hence. These seas are all vast. Two thousand miles is the regular measure of distance between points of departure and arrival—except when it's four thousand. We left Tahiti, June 5, and went two thousand miles to Fiji. We left Fiji, July 23, and sailed two thousand miles to Sydney. We left Sydney, August 6, and came two thousand miles along the eastern coast of Australia to Thursday Island in Torres Straits. We left Torres Straits and Thursday Island thirtysix hours ago, and have two thousand miles to do to Batavia. Then Singapore; then Ceylon; and then I dare not ask how many thousand miles to Brindisi or Naples or Marseilles.

With all this, we are well, in good spirits, pleased with our adventures, and not in the least anxious to return to the world. As La Farge cannot help himself, and as I need some patching, we shall turn our steps to Paris and London, but my future movements are vague, and will depend on my own waywardness. Enough of that! If you are in England in October, or say about Nov. 1, drop a line to me—Baring Brothers, Bishopsgate Street, or Hottinguer &Cie, Paris,—to let me know your whereabouts, and I will come to you. Please remember that I never go into society; that I never dine out, except in the most domestic familiarity; that I am nowadays horribly bored by "people"; that I never try to amuse, and am easily satisfied by being amused; and that as far as I know, all the society of Europe contains no one whom I particularly care to know. Let this discharge your mind of all responsibility about me, and all care for my entertainment. I will go anywhere you say in order to be with you and your wife, but unless you can recall those whom we used to love to meet—your father and mother, your aunt Charlotte, your uncle Sir Francis, Lord Houghton and the associations of five-and-twenty years ago, you can do mighty little to make England gay to me.

Talking of Houghton and his world, I have just read the "Life." I am rather disposed to be harder on it than you are. The man who writes it is a feeble twaddler, but that I could to a degree overlook.[1] He has not a qualification for his task; he has not a particle of wit, yet undertakes to write of men who were wits by profession; he has not a spark of humor, yet mangles one of the most genial humorists of the century; and his acquaintance with his victim was too late to help him except to mislead. All this is bad enough, but I object still more to the slovenly way the work is done. Can no one any longer do literary work thoroughly? England seems to me to be the worst sinner now going in the literary way. I see nothing but *décadence.* No doubt I am wrong; somewhere something competent must exist, but the trashy way in which people for the most part seem pleased to work, grates on my literary nerves which were never very steady. If Houghton had read his own Life, he would have needed all his own good-nature to bear it without murdering his biographer. In fact, unless one or two biographers are assassinated, no considerable man can hope for peace in Heaven—or, for that matter, in Hell. Self-defence is a natural right, and what should be done with a wretch who kills your soul forever, and piles feather-bolsters on it till eternity becomes immortal struggling for breath and air. I hate to growl, but Lord Houghton was one of the best subjects for biography that our time has produced, and to throw it away like this is to throw away the lighter and gayer part of our age. Almost any one of the innumerable visitors at Fryston would have given a better idea of it than this book does. Indeed except Carlyle's visit, no idea at all is conveyed. You yourself could tell more than the two volumes contain. Even I, who was never but once at Fryston, and that in my youngest days, could give a better account of it from memory at thirty years distance, though my memory is as bad as the Life is. I do not complain because I miss the presence of the persons I knew best, and who, in my associations, were and are inseparable from Lord Houghton. Most of them are dead, and very likely left little trace of their talk or their intimacy. What annoys me is the want of art; the lack of a sharp outline, of moving figures and defined character; the washed-out feeling as though the author sponged every one's face; the slovenly way in which good material is handled; above all, the constant attitude of defence, almost apology, and the complaints of non-appreciation which are worse than stupid. If Houghton never understood himself, this is no excuse for his biographer's not understanding him. The greatest men generally pride themselves on qualities which the world denies them; but their biographers do not accent the weakness. Houghton as a statesman was a failure; as a poet, he was not in the first rank; as a social centre for the intelligent world he was an unrivaled and unapproachable success; but the biographer proves only the two introductory axioms.

The moral seems to be that every man should write his own life, to prevent some other fellow from taking it. The moral is almost worse than the vicious alternative, and, after all, the sacrifice would not ensure safety. I know no other escape except to be so obscure as not to need gibbeting at all; but who is safe even then? Poor Lawrence Oliphant was not a conspicuous man; only his insanities were such as to claim passing notice; yet his unlucky life must be ripped up in two volumes to amuse the subscribers to circulating libraries.[2] Had he told the story himself, it might have been good as literature, and instructive as a warning against high living and pure thinking; as it stands, I shrink from reading it. I thought W. E. Forster's Life shockingly poor, and dipped into Earl Russell's with the same result. On the other hand, your uncle Sir Francis, who took the biographic bull by the horns, gave us all something really himself.[3]

The world wants so much to be amused, or thinks it does, that, if every known figure in the Men and Women of the Time is to be made to dance and grimace and grin and blubber to entertain it, at least the utmost possible entertainment ought to be got out of the unlucky actor.[4] I hate botched work. Our American way of doing things is more conscientious, but not much more entertaining. Did you look into the Life of Motley? Did ever "brilliant" historian write such letters?[5] I remember his telling me once that an English dinner was the perfection of human society. He seems to have carried out his theory to the point of thinking that lists of English dinner-parties were the perfect letter-writer's companion. He failed only in omitting the *menus,* which often must have been more interesting than the company.

All this is selfish, because I am mortified at seeing what a mean figure my time will present hereafter. We have Horace Walpole, Doctor Johnson, Fanny Burney, all master-pieces for the last century. Nothing could be said against the way Walter Scott has been put before us. Byron was well-done.[6] Yet I know not one good picture of the society of the middle of our century. Perhaps George Trevelyan's Macaulay is the best. No very representative characters except Gladstone and Tennyson remain to do. Gladstone is sure to be treated politically, and I fear Tennyson's life has been too secluded to be representative. Strange, too, how dull everyone became from the moment her present majesty mounted the throne. Even Greville from that instant seems to yawn like a Queensland crocodile.[7] One is almost grateful to the Prince of Wales and his baccarat. One hour of the Prince Regent is worth a cycle of Prince Albert. In history, nothing amuses but the vicious.

You owe this literary essay to the enforced leisure of the Malay Archipelago. I am weary of reading; I have done little for a year except watch the wine-dark sea; the people on board this ship are quite impossible; I have thought out all my thoughts long ago; so you fall a victim to my need for taking life of some sort. Wreak it on the grouse who are innocent like yourself! Surely Tennyson indulged his Lotos-eaters in a dark-blue sky, vaulted o'er a dark-blue sea! What authority had he for it? If Homer or the Greeks ever said it, I should like to see the passage. I have seen more blue sky vaulted over dark-blue sea than was ever seen by any lotos-eater, Greek or Egyptian; but the peculiarity is that no matter how dark-blue the sea is, the sky is in my experience always light-blue. The sea seems to water it, and wash out the color. This explains its effect on me. I am washed-out, like the sky. I've not an energy left; all has yielded to sea-sickness and Polynesia. I know not why I am so simple an idiot as to pass my life on water when I detest it beyond expression; but really the world contains so very little travelable land, that, after all, I have not given the ocean anything near its proportion of my time.

Should you see the amiable and perfectly virtuous baronet, you had better tell him that I am coming; but I do not know of anyone else whom I care to notify. I should merely be put to the odious necessity of refusing invitations, if anyone cared enough to invite me, or to the mortification of receiving no invitations to refuse. You know of old the precise frame of mind. With me, the refusal is no longer an affectation of indifference or industry. I have been so long a recluse, that a party of mixed acquaintances would be a trial that I am a little afraid to attempt. Total strangers I mind less, for I can turn my back and go home if I like. I can't talk. Nothing is more fatiguing. I never drink champagne except when I feel like it. Finally, although quite willing to admit with Motley that an English dinner-party is the perfection of human society, I have for so long a time been accustomed to prefer the imperfection of my own dinner-table that I have debased my taste and must be left to wallow in my trough.

At the same time, certain persons must be still living whom I should go to see. In a general way I assume that everyone is dead, for I never open a newspaper or a book without noticing the ascension of some former acquaintance, or at least some one more or less known to me. I imagine that not a house in London is now open,—to me—into which I ever entered in former days. Still, here and there, probably, old acquaintances or friends are stranded whom I should express interest in, to the extent of a call. Try and think them over. Annotate them. Make memoranda of their diseases, the dates of their first husband's deaths, and their children's convictions for sodomy or card-cheating. Get a list ready for me in case I should stay more than a week in England. Luckily I come when London is empty, and society is as dull as the weather, and probably I shall be gone long before any old friend can recover from the effects of her or his last fit of gout or lethargy, enough to hear or think of me.

Positively the tropics are not bad. I have not had half bad fun; but damnably and middle-agedly respectable and correct.

Ever Yrs   Henry Adams.

MS: MHi

1. Thomas Wemyss Reid (1842–1905), editor of the Leeds *Mercury* 1870–1887, author of *Life, Letters, and Friendships of Richard Monckton Milnes* (1890).

2. Margaret Oliphant, *Memoir of the Life of Laurence Oliphant and of Alice Oliphant, His Wife* (1891).

3. T. W. Reid, *Life of the Right Hon. W. E. Forster* (1888). Sir Spencer Walpole, *The Life of Lord John Russell* (1889). Sir Francis Doyle, *Reminiscences and Opinions of Sir Francis Doyle, 1813–1885* (1886).

4. *Men and Women of the Time, A Dictionary of Contemporaries*, 13th edition (1891).

5. *The Correspondence of John Lothrop Motley*, ed. G. W. Curtis (1889).

6. Frances Burney, Madame D'Arblay (1752–1840), *Diary and Letters* (1842–1846) and *Early Diary* (1889). John Gibson Lockhart, *Memoirs of the Life of Sir Walter Scott* (1837–1838). Thomas Moore, *Letters and Journals of Lord Byron: With Notices of His Life* (1830).

7. Charles C. Fulke Greville (1794–1865), acute political observer as clerk of the privy council 1821–1859, was the most important English diarist of his generation; the first three (1875) of his eight volumes end with 1837, Victoria's accession.

To John Hay

My dear John

Did you ever happen on the Malay Archipelago when taking the children to walk? I ask only because I have come across it, and am rather struck by its merits as a variety. We are now passing the island of Bali, which is a continuation of Java. I don't exaggerate in saying that the islands here have merits, and the climate at this season might be worse. Tomorrow will be a fortnight that we have been at sea, from Brisbane. We were joined at Sydney by Sewall, our Samoan Consul General, so that we are three; the weather has been just divine; our course has lain either inside the Australian barrier-reef, or inside the long range of Malay islands, or at any rate in perfectly smooth water, all the way, so that even I, who am now seasick when I look at a bucket of water, and who suffer beyond endurance till I get ashore, no matter how long the voyage, have in this case done three thousand miles, and smoked my pipe as regularly as ashore. In my illusions of youth, I fancied the Pacific Ocean to be like this, and my bitterest disappointment was to learn the colossality of my error; but at last I really have come on an ideal summer sea where the wind is always fair and fresh, the sky always blue, the full moon always shines, and a big volcanic peak, ten thousand feet high, is always smoking a few miles to windward. Why did no one ever tell me of this route, which I fell into, almost by accident, in chasing the mangosteen and durian? To my humiliation I find that it is the habitual route of a great steamship line. The "Jumna," which has the honor of carrying us, is a five-thousand-ton ocean steamer, and one of a fleet which makes the voyage once a month or so. We escape the fearful P. & O. route round the south of Australia and save at least three thousand miles of concrete seasickness besides gaining weather, scenery, and mangosteens; for La Farge and Sewall have just been ashore at Bali, and brought back a basket of mangosteens. You know—at least I have often told you,— that the object of my projected voyage, round the world, was to eat the mangosteen and durian. I have at last hunted them to their lair. At Honolulu they were unknown, but I was pacified by the mango. At Apia, they were not to be found, but the mango soothed my sadness. At Papeete they did not exist, but still we had the mango. At Fiji I found neither mangosteen nor mango, and we became riotous and cannibalistic. At Sydney we hoped to find them in Queensland. In Queensland—oh, no!—they were still beyond the sunset and the baths of the western stars.[2] At last—at last—not an hour ago, I eat my first mangosteen, and the durian is positively promised for Batavia day after tomorrow. My mission in life may then be considered as finished, and I have but to write a poem to immortalise it. I am now reflecting on the metre. Durian offers difficulties of rhyme, and must be approached cautiously for other reasons—but I have got there all the same.

Kandy, Sept. 10. A long jump since the above was written; a jump from Java to Ceylon, with a foot-rest at Singapore. We stopped a week in Java, and eat the durian at last, but my chase was as funny as anything in Alexandre Dumas. The *durian* is taboo in good society, and the combination of durian and dutchman led me into scrapes that were pure farce. At Buitenzorg, the hotel-keeper, who was an illegitimate but very close blood-relation of Weckerlin in manner and appearance,[3] and whose reputation is notorious even among the Dutch, very nearly kicked us out of the hotel because I had a durian which I wanted to put in a neighboring field, where I could taste it. I became haunted by the ghost of the durian, which is about like a good-sized pine-apple with spikes. The refined and delicate Dutch seemed to regard the durian as a crime worse than atheism and stronger than their own canals and cabbage. Luckily some Dutchmen are less Dutch than others, and in the end I got all the *durian* I wanted, and gave it my most sympathetic attention. Not once only, nor only in one place or on one kind, but under the most favorable variety of circumstances, La Farge, Sewall and I tried the durian. La Farge's judgment was the least severe; he thought he could learn to like it with time and practice. My opinion is wholly against it; the taste is diseased; a mere vice of the palate like strong cheese or high-meats; but as far as lusciousness or fruity joy is concerned, the durian is a fraud, for which Wallace deserves to lose his whole reputation as an authority in science.[4] I regard the durian and the alligator pear as two shameful disgraces to humanity; but the durian is a vice, while the alligator pear is a slimy subterfuge,—a meanness.

The mangosteen redeems the Malay archipelago from every sin, and covers every crime. Otherwise I find man as vile as the Bishop thought.[5] Java was a disappointment; it is a Mahommedan hive of insect-humanity, without arts or antiquities, and systematically trained to Dutch purposes. Picturesque as the east always is, its intellectual monotony may be stifling. I could see nothing but rice-fields to look at, even on the mountaintops, and although I have been obliged to forego my long-planned journey in China for the present, I was not eager to see China mirrored in Java. So I came away, more than satisfied with a week,—and a durian.

Singapore is an English city, inhabited by Chinese. Nothing there calls for admiration, except the variety of ways of escape. We chose the French variety, and came on to Ceylon last week in a Messageries steamer, with the Rajah Brooke of Saráwak.[6] Colombo was awful; a vapor bath in an exhausted receiver; and we fled instantly to Kandy, where every prospect pleases, but man is deadly dull.

Anuradhapura, 13 September. We have tracked Buddhism to its lair, in an ox-cart drawn by two little trotting humped oxen, with us stowed close together inside, barely able to peer out over our boots at the moonlight on the jungle. I have no idea what part of Ceylon we are in, for I have seen no map, but by distance we are about eighty miles from Kandy and in time we are about three thousand years from Cleveland. I suspect it would amuse you, but it is parlous hot, and this plain has had no shower since April. Luckily the local governments build and run rest-houses, which are very good little inns, and we are as cool as we can be, under a vertical sun near sea-level, in dry seasons. After tramping several hours in the morning, I am keeping under shady cover till four o'clock, with another ox-cart in view for tonight. From appearances I judge this place to be now a remote, poor, thinly populated and unhealthy district, but about the time when the Romans conquered Britain, it was the capital of the Buddhist world, and about as magnificent as Rome in a way. I don't know that I like the way. My opinion of Buddhism has not been raised by seeing what a business-affair it must have been even from the start. In Japan I could see that, once or twice, the Buddhists must have put their whole heart into their work, and must have built and painted for Heaven and not for money; but here I can see no Heaven worth money. Here are the ruins of six or eight huge temples, like the biggest ecclesiastical foundations, with enormous piles of brick, like the Castle of St Angelo run mad, and with acres of stone-tanks, temples and palaces; but not a square inch of really religious art. Occasionally the carvings are fairly good, though always mechanical. All the structures are good in scale and proportion; the bathing-tanks, I think, the best; but none of the work is conscientious or religious in feeling. It resembles more the religion of the Roman empire than the Buddhism of Japan. Except the huge dagobas which were bell-shaped or domed masses of solid brick, no structure, except in wood, rose more than one storey. All the stone-work is foundation-work, stair-ways, or carved supports. The real structure, which was wood, has perished; the stucco, over the brickwork, has dropped off; the tanks, being cheaply built, have caved in from the weight of earth; the pillars, barely stuck into the ground, have sagged; the dagobas, having lost their stucco, are overgrown with grass and shrubs; everything has tumbled about, and nothing looks really dignified. Compared with an Egyptian ruin, these are mean in conception and cheap in execution. I should not care for the disappointment, if it were not for the revelation the place seems to offer of the hopelessly formal and mechanical condition of Buddhism itself from the very start. Not a trace of inspiration have I struck. Even the statues are stupid, and precious few of them.

I've a notion that Palmyra is this sort of thing. Don't you want to get up a little party to go there next spring? Say, "the family," to escape grippe? I find that I can have colds as well on the equator as anywhere, but they are quite different in character, and I can hardly recognise them. As I am by no means tired of travel, but really do not know where to go, now that China is shut, you can come to my rescue and take me somewhere.[7] This little touch of India in Ceylon rather satisfies me of what I always felt in my bones, that India would disappoint me. I have never been able to hit on anything like soul in Indian art, and as for its literature, I can study it better at home. I mean to become a Brahman, for I admit that King is right in holding that Brahmanism contains Buddhism and a good deal more; but I doubt whether I could develope into a sufficient Brahman in India. As a new Avatar I must start far off. Still, I might try a year or two of it, to see. The Malay Archipelago does not tempt me, now that I have been through it; and Ceylon, though better, is not enough to draw me back. India, Central Asia and China are my only hopes, and without China I find Asia unmanageable. I am astonished to find how relatively rich Japan was in every way. From Tahiti to Ceylon I have seen nothing whatever, old or new, in art or nature, that has tempted me to get it. Except a few *sarongs,* or native printed cotton loin-cloths, in Java, I have bought not a sainted memory of a dud. I have not a suggestion of a memory of travel to give you on my return. Even the avaricious La Farge, who wants everything that can be converted into a possible picture, has seen nothing to buy, except of course the infernal photographs which kill what poetry or art the subject has. I have sought and questioned and looked, but no art exists, or ever did exist in these countries, that is worth collecting now. Of course, I am not talking of India but of the islands, and especially of Ceylon where I expected better things. So do not look for new revelations, or for chests such as Japan furnished; for we return bare-handed without even a pearl or a cat's-eye or a moonstone. Everything is better in New York.

Red Sea. September 29. Shall I close this letter, and send it from Marseilles ten days hence to say we've reached Paris? I think so; for you know the rest—the Suez canal, the Mediterranean, and the Messageries steamer, and the old, old European grind. You know that I'm hot; that the thermometer is 92 ° by day, and 88 ° by night; that fellow-travellers are always bores, and that Mecca is somewhere over there to leeward, as I write, with my inkstand on the Djemnah's stern-rail. In fine, the play is played, and the curtain drops on Pharaoh in the Red Sea and fauns in Pacific islands. Henceforth I'm a Frenchman—or something as common—till I find a new engagement.

Ever Yrs.

MS: MHi

1. Ha sailed from Bali August 21; he evidently added "Kandy" later.
2. An allusion to Tennyson's "Ulysses."
3. G. F. H. von Weckerlin, minister to the United States from the Netherlands 1882–1889.
4. According to Alfred Russel Wallace, inside a house the smell of a durian is "often so offensive that some persons can never bear to taste it." As for the taste: "A rich butter-like custard highly flavored with almonds gives the best general idea of it, but . . . with it come wafts of flavor that call to mind cream-cheese, onion-sauce, brown-sherry, and other incongruities . . . In fact, to eat durions, is a new sensation worth a voyage to the East to experience" (*The Malay Archipelago* [1869], pp. 85–86).
5. Bishop Heber's hymn "From Greenland's Icy Mountains."
6. Sir Charles A. J. Brooke (1829–1917), rajah of Sarawak.
7. Rioting against foreigners reached such proportions in mid-1891 that the U.S. minister to Peking, Charles Denby, reported to the secretary of state that no city was safe, not even Shanghai.

To Elizabeth Cameron

26 August, 1891.

We landed at the port of Batavia last Sunday (23d) at noon, and were received instantly by the custom-house officers with an announcement that cholera had broken out, that it was likely to spread rapidly, and that we had better be careful. Both La Farge and I have run the gauntlet of cholera too often to be much affected by knowing its neighborhood, but I was deeply depressed by the thought of possible quarantines to face at Singapore, Ceylon and Naples or Marseilles. If we are caught in that way, we shall see Paris only in the wild winter. I was tempted to escape by returning on board the "Jumna" and sailing at once for Aden, but La Farge is so eager about Java that he is more likely to fling up all his duties and stay here, than to hurry away. Indeed, if by any means, I were to learn now that my visit to Europe would be useless, and that you had changed your mind about my return, and if I were to announce to La Farge my intention of staying for two years in these parts, I am confident he would stay too, and let his affairs go to the dogs. I only wish his feeling for travel were a little more energetic in his own line, so as to leave some artistic record; but I have not seen him touch a brush since we left Tahiti, near three months ago, except for two or three trifling sketches almost worse than none. Luckily I am as conscienceless as he;—more so, for he really does at times feel, or thinks he feels, remorse; whereas I long ago satisfied myself that no gratuitous aid to one's fellows results in anything but harm to them, and in supporting La Farge so long I am quite aware that he, not I, is the person at whose expense the journey is really made. In the long run, what costs me only a few thousand dollars, must cost him much that he lived for, and can never recover. Just now my plans happen to accord with his duties, so I shall drag him to Paris and send him home; but he will never forgive me. His delight with Java from the first glimpse of its Dutch marsh at Priok, the port, was much greater than mine. Hot, dusty, windy, we had to drive an hour over a fever-stricken marsh, along a ridiculous Dutch canal which gave one a mental somersault as though it were all a pantomime, and I was morose and gloomy as I am condemned to be, only more so, but La Farge was radiant with delight, and so he has been ever since, never tired, never complaining, and never even warm. Batavia amused him vastly, and it is really a droll place, as though the Hague had been overrun by hordes of Malays and Chinamen in a midsummer drought. I strolled out of our hotel that Sunday afternoon alone, for La Farge had gone out driving with Sewall; and luck led me to tumble into the Sunday-afternoon performance of the military band. The scene was enough to compare with a full-dress reception at the Royal Academy in high-art days; and that was the funniest spectacle ever man saw on this small planet. Batavian life is not so queer as that, but the show was decidedly entertaining, especially the Malay coachmen in red liveries, with tall stiff European hats and cockades on top of turbans or powdered hair. The crowd was bright with colors and a sort of hotch-potch of races, but my only acquaintance was the eternal Jew fellow-passenger, a very respectable Cohen pair, with whom I had not exchanged so much as a bow on ship-board, but who were not resentful on that account. The next day, Monday, was almost wholly lost in getting our passages by the Messageries boats to Singapore and Colombo, but I was consoled to find that by schedule-time, we should reach Colombo by Sept. 7, which is well, and promises success. In the evening we all—La Farge, Sewall and I—came up by rail forty miles to Buitenzorg—Sans Souci—the Saratoga of Batavia. As I come round the world, as you have so often heard me say, only to eat two fruits, the *durian* and mangosteen, I thought it well to lose no time, and got our landlord at Batavia to send out and procure me a durian, which was brought me just before starting; a sort of spiked, pineapple-shaped thing, slung in leaves. I had to take it with me, and the smell was very decided though not even La Farge found it at first overpowering. If I ever write a roaring farce, I shall choose for my subject, not like Dumas the Chasse aux Chastres, but the Chasse au Durian.[1] From the start we were in the worst social odor with the Dutchmen. The conductor informed us that the durian must go in the baggage-wagon, and bore it off with ill-concealed surprise at our tastes. We arrived at the Hotel Bellevue at Buitenzorg. The landlord received us at best without enthusiasm, and showed us his rooms as though he would rather kick us than have us enter them, but when he caught sight of the durian among the luggage he burst into fury, and became as offensively Dutch as Limburg cheese, and far more so than the durian. As he talked in Dutch-German, with extreme roughness of voice and manner, and would not listen to any remarks or even apologies, but flatly forbade the durian and ordered it to be removed in state by the Malay servants; and as I make a rule of never bandying words with— Dutchmen, we lost our durian and our tempers,—or, at least mine—but we enjoyed the joke even of our landlord. Buitenzorg in the evening was cold and dreary, and as I felt enough insulted, I agreed with La Farge to come on to Garoet, some two hundred miles in the interior, a long railway journey of ten hours, starting at eight o'clock in the morning and arriving at six at night, or rather, at dusk. Sewall left us to join another friend going to Anjar, but La Farge and I actually came to Garoet yesterday, and probably return tomorrow. The two hundred miles of country was a total surprise to me, as usual. We were promised beautiful scenery, and I imagined something wild, dense and mountainous. Nothing of the sort. More or less distant mountains lined our track on both sides all the way, but they bore no tropical forest; the landscape was bare or slightly wooded, and burned, except in the valley and terraces where every foot of land was given up to rice. China cannot beat Java in cultivation. This island contains twentytwo million people, and down to the last baby they must all have worked on the terracing of these rice-fields. As I never loved a paddy-field, and easily tire of cultivation, I was soon weary. The villages were not much better. I expected signs of old civilisation, but not a bit. Not a temple or a shrine or a trace of thought; no architecture except huts less interesting than the Fijian or Samoan; no nothing. Only rice, and Malays as like as rice-grains, picturesque enough, but monotonous. Java seems to be a big factory of rice and coffee. Somewhere the people must have a life of ideas, traditions, dances, songs or art, and superstition or religion perhaps, but we have no time to seek it. On the outside, the Dutch have wiped out whatever trace ever existed of whatever could interest me. I never before met a people, least of all, Mahomedans like all these, who showed no sign of having even a sacred grove to worship. Java is Japan without everything that makes Japan interesting. La Farge of course wants to get all the photographs, cloths, silks, and costumes, he sees; but on that point, and as far as I know, only on that, his natural balance of judgment is wanting. He covets any rubbish he sees, because some day, as his imagination never fails to suggest, he may have to make a window filled with Javanese peasants hoeing rice-fields,—or Japanese bar-maids washing parrots—or what you like. The passion approaches a *tic* with him. He conceals it from me now, because I have not concealed from him my opinion of it; but it has really nothing to do with the interest of the place he is in; it is only the interest of a possible picture in his fancy. I don't think Java would please him long, especially if he could not escape the Dutch. Meanwhile we have sent for durians, and have religiously opened and tasted them. The comedy was not closed by the eating. A somewhat dry, sweet rind round a horsechestnut smelling of bad cheese, is all I can make out of it. If I were not disappointed, I should laugh more than ever, for I cannot believe that what I have eaten is what Wallace described, though the description tallies in all but the supposed quality of the flavor. The mangosteen is delicious; a poem in fruit; a white sonnet of delight, shut in a lovely case of pink Japanese lacquer with a purple exterior like a small pomgranite. Truly the mango is but a coarse and common food compared with the refined and soul-compelling elevation of the mangosteen; but the durian will remain for ever a mystery and a doubt.

August 28. We came back from Garoet yesterday to our Batavia Hotel, and sail tomorrow morning for Singapore. At Garoet we had but one day, and were frozen at night. We saw the hot baths and the swarming people, and we had a little dance in the evening, when two very small dancing girls went through various meaningless steps to the music of four instruments, with singing that pierced the brain. We see Japan everywhere, but it is Japan without the fun, and the dancing was even more conventional than that of the Kioto geishas. Luckily for us, we found a young Dutchman at the hotel, who spoke a little English and was civil and helped us. In Batavia we cannot get an interpreter or commissionaire or servant who understands any language, even Dutch, and we are at our wit's end to do anything. My idea of the Dutch is now fixed forever, and who do you think is my typical Dutchman?—Weckerlin! I meet him everywhere, and he is odious; but yesterday, all through a very hot, dusty day on the railroad, we had the society of women of the Dutch species, and they were another revelation. A very distinguished middle-aged woman, evidently the wife of the Resident at Badong, overwhelmed us, with three daughters; all in one small first-class compartment, the only one on the train. I never understood how flesh could be pitchforked onto girls, till then; and how clothes could be stuck over the flesh. The effect of square corsets was wonderful. The four drank beer and eat hard-boiled eggs or other refreshments at rapid intervals all day. They were innocuous, but superb specimens of Batavian grace. On the whole I want to see no more Dutch colonies. While willing to admit that the only ultimate object of our race is to be born, to feed, and incidentally to die, the world so organised fails to interest me, and industry devoted solely to that purpose is distinctly a bore. As our last experiment, we have once more tried the *durian,* and given it every chance in its favor; but to me the result is sadness. I cannot understand its merits, and it will remain, like the alligator pear, one of my solemn life-mysteries. Nevertheless, the object of my long journey is accomplished. Nothing remains but to return to the simple roses, and to you!

September 1. According to schedule, I should have reached Ceylon today; but I have not done badly in reaching Singapore yesterday morning; and, by going on today, by the Messageries steamer, I reach Ceylon next Monday (7th), which is satisfactory. At that rate I ought certainly to be with you by October 10, and I expect you to be very highly pleased by my triumph. We had only two days of sea from Batavia, and always the tropic beauty of the Malay waters; no motion; warm weather, growing hot as we passed the equator; indolent days and nights on deck; plenty of room; and, as the steamer was French, a fairly eatable table. Sewall joined us again, and we had chance acquaintances,—colonial, English, German and French; no Dutch. The parting from Batavia was not sorrowful; the arrival at Singapore was almost commonplace. A year ago La Farge and I were thrilled by excitement at reaching Honolulu, and now we are so hardened to novelties, that we hardly see a novelty in the most chaotic city in the world. Singapore would have fed our imaginations for a month if we had come here first, for it is a sink of races; a sort of eddy where the east and west whirl about in a wild particolored walz, and Asia performs all her parts at once, on top of all. If you do not care what Singapore is, you can always utilise it for Martha's education; so tell her some day that if she were with me, she would see a big city beautifully laid out, on the water, with charming drives, and a famous botanical park, and any number of country-houses or cottages, like Beverly; and this fine English city is just crammed with Chinese, Malays, Hindus, and every kind of Asiatic creature, with turbans and without; with shaved heads, or long wild hair; with clothes of every imaginable color and kind, or with no clothes at all; and the streets sparkling with variety of colors, lines, and movement, till one's eyes are tired of watching it; especially as the atmosphere is like a vapor bath. The Japanese are also here. The jinrickshaw skitters in every direction; humped cattle, or buffalo, draw the heavy carts and drays; Chinese houses, with their hollow roof-lines, show by contrast how good the Chinese architecture is; and a Gothic, stone church, with one or two bronze statues of English work, show how bad our art is. On the whole, as La Farge remarked on driving up yesterday morning, the chief use of such a place is to make one feel *how* bad artists we are. One always doubts a little in Europe or America, whether a statue, a picture or a building may not, after all, have some one good point that might save it from sweeping damnation; but here one *feels,* without reasoning or wasting time about it, that our art is wholly, in big and in small, artificial and hopeless. One does not even care to discuss the matter. In a place like this, where one feels all or nothing, discussion is as bad as art. With all Asia dancing up and down before one's eyes, one has not superfluous energy enough to argue about London and Paris. As Sydney Smith said to Venables: by all means, consider it damned, and go on with the story.[2] The story is short, for we have less than two days here. Sewall led us into a dinner last evening at our Consul's. Probably you never heard of a youth from Idaho named Wildman, who married a niece of Nevada Stuart named I forget what, but who was educated for the stage, and married Wildman.[3] I had never heard of either party until I was led last evening into their house, and as I have eaten their curry I will say nothing against them. Sewall says that Wildman is the damnedest fool living; but perhaps he exaggerates. Mrs Wildman is not a fool,—I guaranty. Perhaps the stage has left rather more trace on her make-up than is thought the best style in England, but the climate of Singapore is fatal to color and complexion, so that no reasonable gentleman can object to counter-agents. She was rather a startling revelation to me here in Singapore, and I watched her with some interest and curiosity; but I was foolish to accept her invitation, for I detest false relations, and any relations at all must be false, between me and Wildmans. Yet I enjoyed the dinner; I liked the other guests—two or three gentlemen of the English colony; I laughed much, and talked more; and I drank champagne! Here is a list of half-a-dozen follies of which I am glad because they are true follies, though so small as to be useless for any sensible good or harm; but the trace of moral headache this morning is distinct, and takes a curious form, which seems to me, as well as I can think it out, to be a little entreaty repeating itself:—Please, please, *please,* don't, don't, *don't,* paint your eyes!

Sunday morning, Sept. 6. Ceylon in sight, and two thousand miles more run off since Batavia;—ten thousand since Tahiti. Fairly more than half, at last; for London can hardly be more than six thousand miles ahead. We shall not be able, I fear, to get our letters at Colombo today, and I shall let this fragment go on by the "Melbourne" to Marseilles, to tell you that in another week or ten days, if you have kept your plans as exactly as I have kept mine, you may expect to see me walk into your parlor. Tomorrow I shall telegraph exactly when we shall leave Ceylon and reach Europe; so what I say here matters not a jot; but sha'n't I be sold if I get a letter or telegram from you to tell me that you will have sailed before I can arrive?

In that case I think I shall play Evangeline, and go up to India to become Brahmin; for that is my last religion.[4] On this voyage, I have combined the study of Brahma with that of Walter Savage Landor and Charles Dickens. Of the three, I much prefer Brahma. Dickens frets one's temper beyond endurance by his cockneyism. Landor drives one to mania by his commonplace classicism, which is doubly trying, because it is both dogmatic and second-rate.[5] Brahma alone is everything at once—the universe as you like to take it—and includes Buddha and Christianity, Mahomet and Joe Smith, and even Laurence Olifaunt, as easy as crocodiles include sucking babies.[6] If you fail me, I shall fly to Brahma. Just now, I am pretty miserable. We left Singapore Tuesday evening on the Messageries steamer "Melbourne" with few passengers, and none, except Rajah Brooke, that we knew. To the Rajah, Sir Julian had given me a letter, and I made his acquaintance at once. He is a quiet, rather shy man of sixty or thereabouts, and is alone. Apparently he has as little knack for acquaintance-making, as we have. Our first two days were very fine and perfectly calm; but when we got beyond the protecting shore of Sumatra, and struck across the Indian Ocean, we quickly became acquainted with what is called the Southwest monsoon, which is uncommonly like our Southeast trade-wind in the Pacific, and blows so hard and dead ahead, as to make my life a burden even on this large ship. It obliges us to close our ports, and then the heat is so great below that I cannot stay more than a few minutes in my cabin, even to dress. Everyone sleeps on deck in half a gale of wind. I am seasick and half-and-half all the time, and have caught cold, and cough by way of exercise. La Farge is better, but I don't see that he gets much advantage out of it. My only consolation is that I'm not a woman with a brace or two of young children; for their lot, when seasick, seems to make mine gay by excess; and one poor little Dutchwoman—even without children—is so bad that, if she weren't Dutch, she would die. Never mind! here is Ceylon, wrapped in mist or cloud mostly, and showing as little outline as she can; but still enough to tell me that by night I shall have forgotten the steamer, and shall have made acquaintance with my last island. This is triumph. I feel like a new incarnation of Krishna or somebody, when I think that I have really seen all those islands that I have told you about since this time last year. After this, if I can only return home contentedly, and help Cabot Lodge and Teddy Roosevelt to save the country, what more has life to offer? For the soul of Siva, how many islands are necessary for me, if all these are not enough? All the same, oceans are a bore. I have nothing to tell you about the Indian ocean that differs from other oceans, which accounts for my having nothing to tell you at all. Everywhere the same watery blues and grays, and not even a fine sunset to amuse us. We are running just north of the equator, and the sun is directly over our heads, but it's a watery kind of sun, and has no merit but its watery heat. How I wish we had got at least to the Red Sea; there I could reflect on Moses and look out for Sinai; but a dismal ten days of monsoon lies between Ceylon and Aden. Breakfast is ready! In a week, look out! I am nearly there!

MS: MHi

1. In Dumas père's comedy *La Chasse au chastre* (1850) the hero obsessively pursues a rare bird.

2. Sydney Smith (1771–1845), Anglican minister, one of the founders of the *Edinburgh Review,* known for his wit. HA's allusion is probably to a version of an anecdote about damning the North Pole (see Oct. 2, 1890, note 1.)

3. William M. Stewart (1827–1909), senator from Nevada 1864–1875, 1887–1905, whose house in Washington was known as "Castle Stewart" (see HA to MHA, April 11, 1885). Rounseville Wildman was consul in Singapore 1890–1893.

4. The heroine of Longfellow's *Evangeline* (1847) becomes a Sister of Mercy in Philadelphia after years of fruitless wandering in search of her betrothed.

5. Walter Savage Landor (1775–1864), English poet and essayist whose *Imaginary Conversations* (1824–1829) includes a series of Greek and Roman dialogues.

6. Joseph Smith (1805–1844), founder of the Church of Jesus Christ of Latter-Day Saints. Laurence Oliphant, former disciple of the "prophet" Thomas Lake Harris, set forth his own brand of spiritualism in *Scientific Religion* (1888) and other works.

To Elizabeth Cameron

Tuesday, September 8, 1891.

I hope to bring you this letter just a month from today at Paris, but to provide against accident I will go on with the story so that, in case I am delayed, I can let you know all about it by just putting the sheets into an envelope.

We landed at Colombo at eight o'clock Sunday evening, in a temper and with feelings of the most depraved sort. Although we were the only passengers to Colombo, the Messageries officers, stewards and all, totally neglected us, gave us no notice when, where or how to land, and after causing us to lose two hours of light, deliberately let us go off at last as we could, at our own expense, in a native boat, handling our own luggage, without apology, although our situation was again and again, with the utmost civility, made known to them, with the request, not for aid, but only for information. I do not think we do this sort of thing in America, but it has happened twice to us since leaving Brisbane, and is, I think, the rule in the east. Steamers do not land passengers, but forget them. Had I been in my usual form, I should not have cared, but I had a cracking headache and a cold, and could not eat all day, and was exhausted by the moist heat, and generally felt more like a dead beetle than ever before since I bade you goodbye. When we got to a hotel, I crept to bed, and tried to find a spot on my pillow where my head would lie without cracking open, and so dozed till morning with the prospect of the long-expected fever at last. In the morning the headache departed, but I was left very weak, and terribly oppressed by the damp heat of Colombo,—a rice-field heat—which has made me think that if Bishop Heber had known more of the matter he would have made an improvement in his poetry, and would have altered it to: "What though the ricey breezes, blow damp oer Ceylon's isle!" Spice, I know not, but Colombo is in a big rice-swamp, and I felt as though I were in a Turkish bath, and could not get out. All this was owing, I am sure, to something eaten on the "Melbourne,"—I suspect the Camambert cheese—and to being obliged to pass the nights on deck with little sleep and no comfort. Steamers in the tropics are made just like steamers in Greenland. I have not yet seen one—except the American line to Australia—constructed with any reference to the passengers' comfort, or any means of making them comfortable; and if I could hang a few constructors, I would certainly do it in memory of the suffering I have seen them cause to women and children; but the stupidity of the European man is quite radiant, and no one proclaims it louder than the officers who are condemned to command European ships. Between French cheese and French cabins, my life was not worth taking; but my life is a trifle; and I wanted to take some Frenchman's when I saw what happened to others. A delicate little English girl, about Martha's age, was on board; colorless and thin, like all these tropic birds, but talking broken Malay, and rather interesting. On our last night on board, the heat in the cabin was great; the child was taken very sick, and while her mother was examining her, at the table in the saloon, by the light, the little creature fell flat on her face in a dead faint. She was not seasick, but exhausted; and the mother was not allowed to change cabins, or to have air, or to give the child any relief, though the ship was empty, until in a state of ferocity, she went to the Captain. She was howling furious about it, and I gave her what sympathy my sufferings tended to rouse.

Of course our first act, Monday morning, was to seek the Consulate, which I found at eleven o'clock in charge of a small native girl who was then sweeping it, but who seemed to divine my character, for she pointed to a pigeon-hole where I found letters; two from you, one written on the "Teutonic," mailed at Queenstown, and forwarded from Samoa; the other, your dear brief note of August 10, written after receiving my Sydney telegram. You are a wonderful shot with letters, but you never hit a mark closer than this. The letter was just what I wanted to set me up. Perhaps one or two are still missing, but I shall get them, and nothing important can have escaped. Had not your note been very encouraging, I think I should have broken down and gone to bed; for I was grievously disappointed about steamers. I felt too used-up to start again before Saturday the 12th, and wanted a good boat to sail between the 12th and 15th; but the devil forbade any boat at all between the 10th and 17th; and then gave only the P. & O. "Paramatta"; an old ship, of comparatively small tonnage, and of a line I wished to avoid. Instead of reaching Brindisi October 1, we shall be lucky to arrive October 5, and, if not quarantined, reach Paris October 8. Yet, I shall be well-pleased, even with this success.

Colombo seemed to furnish nothing for us, beyond your letter, and I was quite feverish to escape; so we hurried off our small jobs, and took the railway-train at two o'clock for Kandy. A meaner man than I, when I dropped on my seat in that train, I care not to meet; but I could not even lie down without fearing to faint, the oppressiveness of the want of air, and the heavy heat, though only 81° or 82°, were so deadly to me. Two or three times in the day, I had been scared by vertigo, and obliged to steady myself. A weary wight I was when the train began to move, and an impatient one for the next two hours while we jumbled over a rice-swamp where humped cattle lay with their noses just above water, and naked natives paddled in the freshet of the young monsoon; but the green was intense, and the country, even there, was interesting. By the time we had reached the hills, at four o'clock, I had revived; and the next two hours, to Kandy, when the rail rises 1700 feet through superb scenery, made me well. Ceylon is certainly the most interesting and beautiful island we have seen, taking its many-sided interests into account. In one way, Hawaii is grander; in another, Tahiti is more lovely; but Hawaii is a volcano and Tahiti a dream; while Ceylon is what I supposed Java to be, and it was not:—a combination of rich nature and varied human interest, a true piece of voluptuous creativeness. We have seen nothing to approach the brilliancy of the greens and the luxury of the vegetation; but we have been even more struck by the great beauty of the few girls we have caught a glimpse of; especially their eyes, which have a large, dark, far-off, beseeching look, that seems to tell of a coming soul—not Polynesian.

September 10. Kandy is pretty—very; and the surrounding country is prettier still, full of hills and valleys, flowers, elephants, palms and snakes. Monkeys are here also, but I have seen none wild. Another Paradise opens its arms to another son of Adam, but the devil of restlessness, who led my ancestor to the loss of his estate, leads me. I cannot stay three days contented. Socially Kandy seems as impossible as are all these colonial drearinesses, and intellectually man is indubitably vile, as the bishop justly says. In all Ceylon I cannot buy or beg a book on the Ceylon art, literature, religion or history. Of all that has been published on India, not even a stray volume of Max Müller have I seen here, except in the little library of the Sacred Tooth, the Buddhist Temple where the true faith is now alone taught by aid of our master's Tooth, or Tusk—for it is said to be ivory. Of course we visited the famous temple at once, for here is now the last remaining watchfire of our church, except for Boston where Bill Bigelow and Fenollosa fan faint embers. The Temple—Dalada Maligawa, Palace of the Tooth,—was a sad disappointment after the Japanese Temples. The art is poor, rather mean, and quite modern, and even the golden shrine of the Tooth had little to recommend it except one or two cat's-eyes. Occasionally a refined piece of stone carving,—a door-way or threshhold,—built into a coarse plaster wall, shows where some older temple has been used for modern ornament, and gives an idea that Ceylon had refinement in the thirteenth century. Hence our tears, or rather our restlessness; for photographs tell us of immense ruined cities in the jungle, a day or two distant; cities as old or older than our aera, where Buddhism flourished like the wicked, more than two thousand years ago. To get there, we must travel day and night in ox-carts; but what of that? We swallow the oxen more willingly than the fevers, snakes, leeches and ticks, with which the deserted cities are said to be now inhabited. So we start tomorrow for Anuradhapura, and, if possible, for Polonnaruwa, and shall return only just in time to take our steamer, the seventeenth. I hope my telegram of the 8th arrived promptly, and was intelligible. "Start seventeenth. Brindisi fifth." After all, I am not at all certain of starting the 17th, for I will not go on the Paramatta without ample comforts and space; I would rather wait a few days more; but my message was as exact as I could make it at a dollar a word, and a ten dollar address. I had half a mind to send you this sheet by the steamer which goes today, but I shall follow so soon that the information would be useless; and I can telegraph both from Suez and from Brindisi in advance of any letter. Almost I hope for another line from you by the mail due here today; but probably you could not calculate so nicely. Only I hope that at breakfast this morning, six hours from now, you will receive my big Sydney letter, and will see that I have behaved like a very nice little boy, and deserve a good mark. Indeed, if it were not for this unreasonable delay here, I would have reached Europe by October 1st as I told you from Tahiti I would try to do. So now for the ox-cart, and the dreadful voyage to Suez; and then—I shall have much to say.

Anuradhapura, Sunday, 13 Sept. The ox-cart was funny, but not bad, if one must pass nights in these hot regions. We have come about eighty miles from Kandy, and have passed portions of two days inspecting this very sacred city, which is very much out of the world, in a burned jungle, with perfect roads, an excellent government-inn, or Rest-house, and a poor native village, much fever-stricken, infested by jackals, with no whites except government officials in the whole district. I wanted to see the island, and this is it, I suppose, or at least the dry part of it, and sufficiently undisturbed by Europeans, of whom only a few travellers ever come here. I have looked through the inn-book, and found not a name known to me, during a record of eight or ten years; but, for that matter, since leaving San Francisco I have come across no one I ever knew before, so I could not count on finding them here. Yet Ceylon is a place where vast numbers of travellers come—or at least pass—and these ruined cities are the chief interest of the island; so they are visited by about one Englishman a month, thank Buddha, and praise to Siva and Vishnu, not even the photograph-fiend is here. As for the ruins, they are here, beyond question, and we have duly inspected them. Do you want my impressions? I don't believe you do, but it is noon; the day is scorching; we have just breakfasted; I am lying on my bed, trying to keep cool, out of the glare; and why should I not talk to you, even if you go to sleep as I should do in your place. Please imagine a great plain, covered with woods. Dumped on this dry plain are half a dozen huge domes of solid brick, overgrown with grass and shrubs; artificial mounds that have lost their architectural decorations and their plaster covering, but still rise one or two hundred feet above the trees, and have a certain grandeur. Each of these dagobas represents an old temple which had buildings about it, stone bathing-tanks, and stone statues of Buddha, chapels and paved platforms decorated with carved or brick elephants-heads, humped oxen, lions and horses. When Buddha flourished here, two thousand years ago, vast numbers of pilgrims came to worship the relics supposed to be hidden under the dagobas, but still more to pray at the sacred bo-tree, which is the original shoot brought here more than two thousand years ago from the original bo-tree under which Buddha attained Nirwana.—This, then, was Anurajpura; the bo-tree; six dagobas with relics; and one or two temples more or less Brahmanic, that is, rather for Siva or Vishnu than for Buddha, though Buddhism ran here a good deal into Brahmanism. As long as Buddhism flourished, Anurajpura flourished, and the kings went on, building tanks, both for bathing and for irrigation, some of the irrigation tanks being immense lakes, with many miles of embankment. When Buddhism declined, the place went gradually to pieces, and nothing but what was almost indestructible remains. Of course we cared little for the historical or industrial part of the affair, but came here to see the art, which is older than anything in India, and belongs to the earliest and probably purest Buddhist times; for Anuradhapura was the centre of Buddhism even then. I expected—never mind what—all sorts of things—which I have not found. To my surprise and disappointment, all the art seems to me pretty poor and cheap. Compared with Egypt or even with Japan, Ceylon is second-rate. The huge brick-dagobas were laid out on a large scale, with a sense of proportion that must have been artistic, but the want of knowledge or use of the arch makes the result uninteresting. The details are not rich; the stone carving is not fine; the statues are not numerous or very imposing even in size; and all the stone-work, even to the bathing-tanks, is so poorly and cheaply done, without mortar, rivetting or backing, that it can't hold itself up. I have hunted for something to admire, but except the bigness, I am left cold. Not a piece of work, big or small, have I seen that has a heart to it. The place was a big bazaar of religion, made for show and profit. Any country-shrine has more feeling in it than this whole city seems to have shown. I am rather glad the jackals and monkeys own it, for they at least are not religious formalists, and they give a moral and emotion to the empty doorways and broken threshholds. Of course we went at once to the sacred bo-tree, which is now only a sickly shoot or two from the original trunk, and under it I sat for half an hour, hoping to attain Nirwana. La Farge says I am always trying to attain Nirwana, and never get near it. I don't know. Sometimes I think that intellectually I am pretty close to it, if isolation from the world's intellect is Nirwana; but one or two personal interests or affections still bar the last leap to total absorption and silence; even under Buddha's most sacred tree, I thought less of him than of you; which was not the Nirwana that Buddha attained. Probably I am not the first to go through that experience on that spot; though I imagine this to be the first time that the intrusive Siva has been incarnated in you. I left the bo-tree without attaining Bhuddaship. Towards evening we got an ox-cart; a real cart with two wheels, and two slow, meditative, humped oxen, who are also sacred cattle, and who have the most Bhuddistic expression in their humps and horns that ever was reached by God's creatures. The cart was hooped over with thatch, and we put two chairs inside, and were slowly driven by a naked Tamil, as though we were priests or even Hindu deities, through the woods, every now and then clambering out to inspect some stone tank or temple among the trees, and in secret deadly terror of ticks, leeches and cobras, not to speak of centipedes and scorpions. Dusk came on just as a family of monkeys scampered up the trees and jumped across above our heads. I felt no sense of desolation or even of remoteness; sensations have palled on me; but the scene was certainly new, and in a way beautiful, for the evening light was lovely, and the ruined dagobas assumed a color that art never gave them. This evening we resume our travelling ox-cart, with the dainty little trotting oxen, more like deer than cattle; and travelling all night, we reach Dambulla in the morning where we have to look at some rock-temples. I have no longer any hope of finding real art in Ceylon; even the oldest looks to me mechanical, as though it were imported, and paid by the superficial area; but we want to be sure we have seen all the styles, and the rock-temple is a style. I would rather travel by night than by day, even when packed tight in a cart, with my boots sticking out behind. The moon is sweet, and the air exquisite, jackals and all.

September 15. Before leaving Anuradhapura, we had a dance, after the traditional style of Ceylon. Four men, ornamented with brass arm-plates, silver bangles, and other decorations belonging to their profession, and making music for themselves by thrumming small hand-drums, danced for us, before the Rest-house. They danced well, their training was good, and the dance itself was in a style quite new to us, with a good deal of violent physical exertion at times; but it did not interest me much, and I could see no trace of meaning in it; not even the overlaid, solemn elaboration of Chinese or Japanese movements, which no one can any longer explain. We paid what seems here, among these terribly poor people, rather a high price for the show,—fifteen rupees, or a little more than a sovereign; but we always encourage native industries. At about eight o'clock in the evening, our mail-cart came for us, and we started on the return-journey. I think the night-travel amused me more than the ruins did. The night-air is pleasantly cool, and the moon was bright. We lay on our backs on a mattrass, with just room—and barely—for us two. Our little white oxen, with their mystical straight horns, and their religious sacred humps, tripped along, sometimes trotting and sometimes running, their bells tinkling in the quaintest way; and the two-wheeled cart, which luckily had springs, tipped about, as though it enjoyed the fun. I slept a good deal, smoked a little, and watched the moonlight on the road and the jungle. We did twentyeight miles in seven hours, reaching a Rest-house at three o'clock in the morning, where we had to change into a less comfortable horse-coach. We knocked up the keeper of the Rest-house, and while he boiled water and made tea, we sat in the dark on the porch, listening to the creak of ox-mills, and to the wierd cries of the jackals, which seemed to fill the woods, and which are the uncanniest night-sound I ever heard. We were on the road again long before dawn, but at six o'clock we reached Dambulla, and climbed up to the Rock-temple, about a mile away. When we got there, the priest and the keys were away, and we had to send back for them, while we sat on the rocks and looked over miles and miles of forest-jungle, to distant mountains. The cave-temples were an exasperating disappointment, mean outside, and stupid within. Not stupid, La Farge insisted, but priestlike; long rows of dirty cotton curtains ran round each temple, carefully hiding the statues in order, no doubt, to extort money for showing them. The statues or figures have no merit as art, but are only conventional Indian Buddhas, sitting or reclining, and coarsely colored; their only value is as decoration, and of course their effect was not only lost but caricatured by concealing them. I think La Farge was angrier than I; but anyway I should not have cared much for the temples which are mere rough holes, without architecture or form. We hurried back to the Rest-house, and kept H.M.'s mail waiting for us till we had breakfasted; then at eight o'clock were on our way again, and at two in the afternoon were in Kandy, which seems deliciously cool and moist after the dry, hot, weary parchment of the plains. We like Kandy as much as though we were children, and it were assorted. The walks and drives are charming, and the peace is almost as ideal as that of Papeete.

Colombo, 18 September. The Parramatta went off last night, but we did not go in her. When I try to explain even to myself how it happened that this steamer, which we had taken every possible trouble to catch and with which we had apparently nothing to do, except to go aboard, should have managed to lose us, I am really puzzled. Everyone in the east would say simply that I should not have tried to go by the P. & O. which is the most unpopular corporation in the celestial system. Not a good word have I ever heard man speak for it, and my own experience fully bears out the prejudice. Yet the P. & O. people must have a certain genius, if they could get rid of passengers so firmly bound as we were. No victim ever entered their slaughtering-pen more resigned than we were when we went to the office yesterday. All we asked was to know whether our cabins were comfortable and where they were to be. The agent could tell us nothing except that the ship was empty; eightyfive vacancies to some sixty berths occupied; but he had no idea what special cabins were vacant; he made a rule not to keep plans of the ships in the office, and therefore could not show me where the cabins were, or what were their numbers or their sizes; his office would close at five o'clock, and the ship would sail in the night. Not disgusted by this cavalier treatment, as soon as the ship arrived, at half past three o'clock in the afternoon La Farge and I pulled out to her, a mile down the bay, and went aboard. A less inviting steamer I have read of, but seldom seen. An atmosphere of Scotch-English-Colonial middle-class grime pervaded the ship and all its arrangements. Dirt, clumsiness and stupidity were its only recommendations. All the same, we got the steward, looked at the rooms said to be vacant, selected two, and hurried back to the town. La Farge, as usual, was very busy buying photographs, for which my hatred has now become a real photo-phobia, and left me to secure the passages. I reached the office just at five. The agent was closing his desk. I gave him the numbers of the rooms chosen. He explained that both were otherwise engaged, but I could have two neighboring ones. He had no ship's plan to show where these were. I suggested that I could not make a decision without consulting La Farge which would take ten or fifteen minutes. He turned his back and went on locking his drawers. I turned my back, and walked gently down stairs. Such is the tale. I admit only to have been, after the first shock of surprise, excessively glad to escape from the P. & O. and its ships. This morning we mean to secure cabins on the Messageries Steamer Djemneh which sails next, three days after the Parramatta, and which will land us at Marseilles October 10, as I shall telegraph you from Aden or Suez. So we have three days more at Colombo, with nothing to do. I have already looked at all the cat's-eyes, and find none worth having at less cost than a thousand dollars, which would, I think, buy as good or better in London. No pearls; moonstones by the bushel, but little different from *nacre;* and only what are called star-stones, or star-sapphires, rather amusing. I like all the stones that appeal to the imagination, like opals and cat's-eyes; and the Asteria, or star-stones, have to me the additional charm of not being in the fashion. Yet I enjoy looking at most gems, and really delight in buying them, except that the pleasure is too costly for my means. You must take me, in Paris and London, to see gems. I must go with you to Phillips's in Cockspur Street. Here I have seen nothing fit for you.

September 27. Two thousand more miles run off—twelve thousand since Tahiti. I feel as though the journey were done, for we have seen the last of the Indian Ocean, and tonight we reach Aden. The voyage has been very quiet and pleasant, all but yesterday when the motion made me so seedy that, as they will not serve anything to eat on deck, I declined to eat at all. At sea, when sick, I can go three days without eating, but yesterday improved and I got dinner. The nights are hot—about 80°—and I passed them mostly on deck. The steamer is the Messageries Djemnah, an old boat, like the Melbourne but smaller. The passengers are few and usual. Some Dutch swine whom I am condemned to sit next; some Portuguese pecora; some French, as unsocial as myself; some English, rather better than common; and some hybrids. Their chief merit is that they are few and quiet. I read much; sleep much; and enjoy the fine weather and the tropic sea,—although for that matter one sea is like another to me except in its good or bad temper.[1] Our last days at Ceylon were rather thrown away. We went out for a night to a hotel on the sea at Mt Lavinia; pretty and slow. We got a juggler who did tricks. I was very warm. Voilà tout!

29 September. I went ashore yesterday at Aden, and sent you my telegram, which will, I hope, prevent your writing to Brindisi, and will bring me a note to Marseilles. La Farge and I telegraphed recklessly—ten pounds worth—all round the universe, to divert our minds from the heat. Aden should mean oven. Only the camels seemed baked enough to suit it. The sun hits one like a base-ball. On board, my thermometer stood at 92° all day; on shore I know not what. My cabin was above 90° all night; but I was not in it—not much. I lay on a chair on deck where it was about 86°, with air; and very pleasant. I like the Red Sea today, though it is 91° without rest, and thirteen hundred miles long. The water is smooth, like a canal, which is just my style of ocean wave, and it is not red but blue, with porpoises, and now and then a bit of bare, baked rock, but generally no land in sight. Before dawn this morning the sailors fairly hunted me down below with their deck-washing, so I took a shower-bath in the dark, and, to my alarm, little fire-flies seemed to play all over me; but it was only phosphorous and didn't bite. We are all languid with the heat; but the sun is going to set soon, very soft and saffrony, as though it were gentle and childlike—fraud as it is,—and we shall have dinner with champagne and ice and punkahs, and my Dutch hog on one side, and a poor Frenchman on the other, whose child died this morning, I think; for I passed the cabin at the time and caught a glimpse of that white horror which becomes so terribly familiar as life goes on; but on board ship no one is supposed to die. Nothing is said, and I do not venture even to ask. The family came on board only yesterday at Aden, and are not known to us.

Saturday, Oct. 3. We entered the Suez Canal at ten o'clock last night, and this morning at seven were stopped by a steamer aground ahead of us. The delay will cost us a day, I fear, and I shall see you so much later; but the weather is beautiful, the temperature charming, (80° in my cabin at two P.M. and 70° last night), and we are patient, though very dull. If we get through by this evening, we shall still be in Alexandria tomorrow morning. This is our only excitement, and I note it only to bar reflections on my slowness.

Thursday, October 8. We should have reached Marseilles today, but our detention in the Suez Canal lasted twenty hours; we passed the greater part of Sunday at Port Said; reached Alexandria Monday morning at six; sailed again at half past eight, and for the last three days have run steadily ahead, with beautiful weather and a calm sea, until now we are well through another brace of thousand miles from Aden, and have but some nine hundred more to Paris. Last evening, after dark, we came through the straits of Messina which were like a French boulevard between the rows of gas-lights on either side. Tonight we pass between Corsica and Sardinia. Tomorrow afternoon at about five o'clock we should reach Marseilles. The voyage has been charming, though as quiet as a Pacific island. We have found no exciting society and nothing to tell about. I have read a volume a day, and thought abominably about the future, which will not arrange itself or let me alone. For the first time I am beginning to feel that the long journey, which seemed interminable, is really ended, and that all the old perplexities, with plenty of new ones, are going to revive. The pleasure of seeing you once more overbalances everything else; but in the depths of my cowardice I feel more than ever the conviction that you cannot care to see one who is so intolerably dead as I am, and that the more you see of such a being, the more sorry you will be that you ever tried to bring him back to life; but, as for this, you are the best judge, and, anyway, you can always send me back to the east again by a word. Yet how can I manage not to bore you? If I only knew that, I should feel quite master of the world; but a whole year of vegetation in lonely corners of the ocean, where no social effort was required, and where I have not met one person whom I ever saw before, is shocking bad training for Paris and London. Poor La Farge has been my only victim, and on his sufferings I could look with a calm countenance, or even with a certain amount of sardonic amusement; but I could not bear yours. Men are certainly the most successful invention the devil ever made, and when they arrive at a certain age, and have to be constantly amused, they are even harder to manage than when they are young, mischievous and tormenting.

Marseilles. 9th. On shore at last, and answered your letter by telegraph at once. Perhaps I shall see you before you receive this closing despatch.

MS: MHi

1. HA omitted mentioning that on this voyage he composed "Buddha and Brahma," a meditative poem in blank verse. He sent a copy to Mrs. Cameron, April 26, 1895, and he finally published it in the *Yale Review* 5 (Oct. 1915), 82–89.

To Lucy Baxter

Red Sea, September 30, 1891.

My dear Miss Baxter

I have quite forgotten when I last wrote, but, as well as I can guess, the letter cannot be more than a month ahead of me, for it is only two months since I landed at Sydney, and since then I have done nearly a month of travel in the same direction as the mail. The more I think of it, the more appalling this long journey from Fiji to London becomes; but one never knows what to think of travel, for this immense journey of fifteen thousand miles or so, in two months, has been, since leaving Sydney, very enjoyable. Of course, it is mere skimming the surface, globe-trotting, and getting there, but it is divine touring, always perfect weather, quiet seas except for two or three slightly uncomfortable days, and beautiful variety of scene. Nothing could be pleasanter in ocean travel than the two thousand miles of Malay Archipelago. We had a week's rest in Java, which was hard work enough, for we not only had to see Batavia, but had to travel as far as the railway went, which was eleven uncommonly hot hours into the mountains. Unluckily the railway did not go to any place particularly interesting to us. Ruins, temples and even scenery, I hope, are off the line, and nothing but terraced rice-fields and innumerable villages are on it. I could not have believed that we could travel two hundred miles or more anywhere in the east without seeing more than we saw in Java; but then Java is all Mahommedan, and the Mahommedans make clean work of older religions; while on top of the Mahommedan came the Dutchman, and if all Rome, Greece, Syria, Egypt and the Himmalayas were there, they would flatten out under such a combination as that of Mahommedan and Dutchman. Since leaving San Francisco a year ago, I have learned one or two large generalisations, and one is the Dutchman. He is typical, and Java made the present condition of the east clear to me, from Constantinople to Tahiti. Java is a Dutch factory, and its twenty-odd million natives exist solely for Holland to trade with; a mere mechanism from which all intellectual existence is excluded with care. The English are much better, but the object is the same. The whole east exists for Europe to trade with. Indeed, the whole world stands only in that relation to Europe, and in the whole world are only two nations of whom you never will hear a good word spoken among residents in the east. The two are China and the United States, and the reason is the same, that both think they exist for other purposes besides only that of European trade.

This sounds ill-natured, but it is the ill-nature of two hundred years of history such as no decent European dares even to apologise for. Portuguese, Dutch, French and English have all been at it, and now even the Germans, who carried it on until they ran against us at Samoa and got a rap on the head for trying to do what has been done everywhere else on a scale a thousand times greater. I am a free-trader in economy and politics, but if I did not think American strong enough to defy Europe anyhow, I vow I would support a total prohibition of trade rather than accept what the east is.

Now they are going to try and break up China, so my travels there must be abandoned; so, from Batavia I came on to Singapore, a British trading-factory, quite pretty and deadly dull; and thence direct to Ceylon, where we rested a fortnight before beginning the last, long, five-thousand-mile pull to London. Ceylon is lovely and most interesting; a charming island in every way, and I never put in a fortnight to better purpose than there. Colombo, the port, is a hole, which has little beauty except the sea, and no interest whatever, unless perhaps one likes to look at cat's-eyes and star-sapphires, which are found in the mountains and sold by dealers at Colombo. I adore these mysterious oriental stones, whose light seems alive inside them like an *âme damnée*, but a moderate cat's-eye costs a thousand dollars even there, and the star-sapphire, though cheap enough, is hardly worth getting in any numbers. Still, we looked at all the stones we decently could ask to see, and soon exhausted the resource. This was on our return to Colombo, for on our arrival there I was wretched with a head-ache, and so used up by the moist heat, that I hurried La Farge, after one inevitable night, up to Kandy.

About Kandy I am very enthusiastic. If Europe must do the octopus-business, which is doubtless only its destiny as it was that of Rome, it could not be better done than at Kandy. There is the centre of the enormous Buddhist church, and at the same time a lovely hill-country. The British have not harmed the church, and have made the country safe and accessible with roads and government rest-houses or post-inns. I took real delight in walking about Kandy, merely for the walks, a thing I have not tried for years. The place has the other charm of entire dulness; not even an effort at gaiety or society seems to be made, and I could see no residents about, even in the pretty houses which are plenty. One was quite solitary in walking, and almost so in the public reading-room. The hotel was good, and the people at it were better than common. The nights were cool enough for sleep, and even the days not intolerable. As a specimen spot where tropics are, so to speak, on show, nothing equals Kandy.

Of course we were interested in the Buddhist part, which is like that of Rome in the Catholic church; but as far as show goes the Buddhist makes not much. The temple of the Sacred Tooth, where a tusk supposed to be Sakya Muni's is kept and worshipped, is a modern affair with a few carvings and ornaments of older work. The other temples are even more modern and poorer. The town of Kandy itself is but a village and never was more. When we came to look up the matter, we found that properly Kandy was not the religious centre, and had become so only because the old and true capital, Anuradhapura, had been destroyed several centuries ago, but that the ruins of Anuradhapura were still the real object of reverence to every true Buddhist.

After this, of course we had to abandon Kandy and hunt up Anuradhapura; for although I am no longer a Buddhist, but a Brahman, and have greatly changed my views as to the relative superiority of Buddhist revelation, I feel that my new duties to Brahma, not to mention Vishnu and Siva, require me to study Buddhism too. Anuradhapura was eighty miles from Kandy; we must travel at night, in an ox-cart; it lay in a jungle, hotter than the next world, and reeking with fever; all which we took mildly, as we always do with tales of terror; and off we started for Anuradhapura.

Decidedly the journey was worth making, but as I discovered, on my return to Kandy, an illustrated article on the subject in the very last number of Harper's, I will refer you to that for all particulars.[1] The article is exact enough in a magazine kind of way that would take the fun out of a hippopotamus, and after it Shakespeare would leave it alone. Anyway we hunted Buddha fairly into the jungle, inspected his dagobas and his rock-temples and his own private Bo-tree, under which he attained the perfect life; and finally, for my own part I may say that I returned to Kandy with a poor opinion of Ceylon Buddhism, and a settled determination to devote myself in future to Brahma.

Devotion either to Buddha or Brahma or even to J. G. Blaine is peculiarly difficult in Ceylon because no one seems to care a rupee for any religion except tea,—coffee having proved a false prophet,—and neither men nor books are to be found to instruct the wicked like me. So I had to postpone further study till I should reach London, which I regretted because on this interminable voyage I could have learned by heart all the Vedas and the whole Ramayana, in the original. Yet this will always furnish something to look forward to, so I can charter the British Museum and use the winter.

I parted from Kandy and Ceylon on the 21st with regret, partly because I had enjoyed the island, and partly because I could not again eat the mangosteen, which for a whole month consoled me for every disappointment, and even for my worst blow, the disillusionment of the *durian*. When one has nourished a dream for twenty years, and wakes to find it a durian, adversity has no more bitterness. To the mangosteen I owe a double debt of gratitude, for it was itself a dream of delight, and it softened the bitterness of the durian. With Ceylon I bade farewell also to tropic land, for no one could have the face to speak of Aden as a land, and we touch at no other in the tropics. We stopped at Aden two days ago, and went ashore with the thermometer at 92° on shipboard. I looked at the shore, and returned on board. What will not nations do for trade, and where will men not live if paid?

We cross the tropic within twentyfour hours, I suppose, and in ten days shall be in Paris. I am greatly torn by conflicting emotions. To Paris I must in any case go, or go to pieces, for I need much patching, especially in teeth; but what then? Shall I come back to India, since China is impossible? Can I make up my mind to try another spell of home, from which I shrink more than from the dentist? This long year of tropical life, during which I have never met a being whom I knew before, has broken the old habits of life and given me new ones. Much of it has been terribly dull, but none has been despondent or unhappy, and much has been excessively amusing. You can imagine how you would feel, if you had been through the experience, and I am quite clear that nothing but my increasing horror of the sea will prevent my wandering.

Meanwhile ever affectionately yours   Henry Adams.

MS: MH
1. Joseph Ricalton, "City of the Sacred Bo-tree (Anuradhapura)," *Scribner's* (not *Harper's*) 10 (Sept. 1891), 319–336.

To William Hallett Phillips

Steamer "Djemnah" near Corsica.
8 October, 1891.

My dear Me-and-the-rest-of-you

In my portfolio is a letter of yours dated May 13, which reached me at Sydney, August 1. As I was coming this way, more or less with the mail, I kept it on hand, and answer it now because I am near the stopping-place. News I can't give you. My travels are already old; but I must not forget to say that, at Sydney, finding a lot of old Travels in Polynesia, I bought enough volumes to make up a box, and had the box invoiced to you. As an excuse, I put into it a bundle of stone implements from the Fiji group. You can keep the books, as long as you like, if you care to read them, and you can add the implements to your collection. The axes are fairly representative of the Fijis, and I guaranty the genuineness of most of them; for some I got in the native villages in the interior of Vanua Levu, where no travellers have ever been before us; and some I myself found in searching the sites of destroyed towns. The variety is not great, but I believe it is all they had. Stone implements are already very scarce there as everywhere else, and I think were never common as with your people. Bows were all of wood and little used; spears were wood or tipped with bone or shark's-teeth; sharp cutting instruments were usually teeth; apparently mortars were not made; squid were caught with shell; and nets weighted with rough stones. The only wrought stone were those I sent.

I did not visit the Solomons or the groups known as Melanesian. Fiji quite satisfied me that I had no affinity with the darker races. Although Fiji is certainly half-Polynesian, the Fijians are whole brutes, and have none of the fascination of my own Tahiti race, or of the Samoans; yet the blacks made better stone implements than were made by my people, except perhaps in Hawaii, and the disgusting cannibals certainly had more sense of art. Possibly the New Zealanders owed their artistic sense to their taste for each other. This is an abstruse subject, too large for a letter.

We were five weeks in Fiji, guests of the Governor, and were taken by him on two expeditions, one of which lasted three weeks, and resembled Stanley in Africa. Of course we lived in native houses, and saw none but natives, for no whites are allowed in the interior; and excepting English officials, none have much gone there. Until within fifteen years, a white man would not willingly have risked being eaten for any pleasure which the mountain-tribes had to offer. In fact, the whole interior of Fiji was a sort of howling hell, in which every village kept watch at night in expectation of being attacked and eaten before morning. These people are now quiet, and I doubt whether at any time they were brave. Certainly the Tongans had no trouble in beating them all over the place; and the Tongans are certainly not as good warriors as the New Zealanders; but anyway we saw the whole show, including ancient cannibals by the hundreds; and also the island, straight across valleys, mountains and forests; and I do not hesitate to say that I left it without regret. My regard for the archaic man does not extend to the Melanesians. They may go where they like, and the best that can be done with them is precious little. Yet they had a good war-dance, which I was glad to see.

The next savage race I visited was that of the Australians. These are very light in color, and live in cities, two of which, Sydney and Brisbane, I saw. The people are totally without interest; they have no arts, dances or manners of their own, and I left them as soon as possible.

The group known as Malay was my next point. God alone knows his own

Malay children. As for me, I own to being quite in the dark as to what or where the Malay is. I passed a week in Java, and there I found several races. I suppose they are Malays, but in essentials they are Hindustanee, and live in rice-fields. There are twentytwo million Javanese. Many centuries ago, the Mahommedan Arabs came along and conquered them, which made them all Mahommedans. When a race has been cleaned out by Mahomet, little is left of it. Then the Dutch came along, and sat on top of the pile. When a Dutchman sits on a Mohammedan, who is lying on a Malay, you can believe, without my affidavit, that the Malay is squashed as flat as Holland. I could see nothing left of the Malay.

I stopped at Singapore only to give up the Malay business; and as China seemed just now unsuited to archaic hospitality, I came to Ceylon, and investigated the Singhalese. They are rather interesting, but not in the least archaic. In fact they have been damnably civilised these two thousand years, and have been overrun by every dominant race in that time, so that precious little is left worth our attention. Still I found things very much better than in Java.

I am now on my way to visit for a short time one or two low and degraded races in Europe. My companion La Farge must go home, so I shall go as far as England to see him off. Then I shall sit down and reflect. If you have any advice to give me, direct it care of Baring Brothers &Co. London.

Since leaving Brisbane, two months ago today, my journey has been quite divine. Such weather, such calm seas, such interesting islands, and such variety, I had not supposed to exist on this poor globe. I think better of it than I did. Ten thousand miles of ocean without seasickness are to me ten thousand sources of perfect satisfaction. I feel rich. Tomorrow we expect to land at Marseilles, and in two days more we should reach Paris. This, for the moment, closes my journey, and obliges me to take a new start. If nothing calls me home, I've a notion that Asia is my next destiny; but at all events I have got round the world, and must either stop or turn back. I've a sort of vague idea that before Asia, I would like to give a season or two to our own Indians and our wild regions; but as yet I am only certain of the extreme ignorance which prevents me from getting thoroughly in sympathy with any race, even the poor, degraded European. Devil take man's stupidity! He can't even learn a language short of a lifetime.

Of course you will apply to Dwight for the charges on the box. Should you want anything in Europe, let me know. Although nothing European is worth having, one finds there archaic work at times for sale.

Ever Yrs   Henry Adams.

My regards to the other lunatic.

Paris. October 13. Here I find your wail of September 18. I am rather surprised not to find you too, and all your friends and relations. All

America is here, including Rebecca Dodge and my own particular young woman Martha. Of course I shall clear out as soon as I can, but whither I know not. Probably a month will decide, and meanwhile I shall go to England. Once more, save your soul!

H.A.

MS: MH

To Elizabeth Cameron

Sunday. 10 A.M. [11 Oct. 1891]

Arrived at midnight, and wait only to know at what hour one may convenablement pay one's respects to you. The bearer waits an answer.

MS: MHi

To Charles Milnes Gaskell

Paris 27 Oct. 1891.

Dear Carlo

Your letter of the 22d reached me last night. Before you receive this letter, I shall be in London where I have written for rooms at the Hotel Bristol in Clifford Street. I must have a week in London to get an overcoat and my senses; but on the 4th November, I will go down to you, or with you, anywhere you like, except to sea, of which I have had momentarily enough. I shall be delighted to see the Clarks, if they want us; and will, if you like, invade every country house up to John o'Groats, provided we do not have to face parties and make society-talk for young women. If the Baronet will join, we will renew all the blossoms of our youth.

Ever Yrs   Henry Adams.

MS: MHi

To Charles Milnes Gaskell

Bristol Hotel. Thursday. [29 Oct. 1891]

Dear Carlo

J'y suis,—as our ancient friend M. Henri de Lagardere used to remark.[1] Your note of yesterday finds me promptly. As now advised, I am at your orders for next Wednesday.

I will drop a line to Seymour Street on the chance that Robert is in town.

I need hardly tell you that London seems somewhat of a ghostly world to me as yet. A few days will set it right.

Yrs ever   Henry Adams.

MS: MHi

1. Henri de Lagardère is the hero of the historical romance *Le Bossu* (1857) by the French author Paul Féval. *J'y suis* (I am here) is Lagardère's motto repeated with ludicrous frequency. HA may be referring to a dramatized version first produced in 1862.

To Elizabeth Cameron

Wenlock Abbey, Nov. 5, 1891.

A long, lowering, melancholy November day, the clouds hanging low on Wenlock Edge, and stretching off to the westward where you are streaming along the Irish coast and out to sea; for I am writing in the hour before dinner, and you must be just losing sight of land. I have shivered over the fire, chatting feebly, and this afternoon have ridden for two hours over the sodden fields, in the heavy air, talking with Gaskell in our middle-aged way about old people, mostly dead; but always mentally wandering from the talk and the dim landscape to you and your ship. As fate sometimes does temper its sternness with pity, the day, sad as it was, has been calm, as though the storm and strain were over. I was glad for your sake, and a little on my own account, for, as usual, I have passed a bad *quart d'heure* since bidding you good-bye in your Hansom cab across the darkness of Half Moon street. I ought to spare you the doubtful joy of sharing my pleasures in this form; but you, being a woman and quick to see everything that men hide, probably know my thoughts better than I do myself, and would trust me the less if I concealed them. You saw and said that my Paris experiment was not so successful as you had meant it to be. Perhaps I should have done better not to have tried it, for the result of my six months desperate chase to obey your bidding has not been wholly happy. You do not read Mrs Browning. No one does now. As a collegian I used to read Aurora Leigh and Lady Geraldine's Courtship and the Swan's Nest on the River, and two lines have stuck:

> "Know you what it is when Anguish, with apocalyptic *Never*,
> To a Pythian height dilates you, and Despair sublimes to Power?"[1]

The verse is charmingly preposterous and feminine, for a woman never recognises an impossibility; but an elderly man, when hit over the head by an apocalyptic *Never,* does not sublime to Power, but curls up like Abner Dean of Angels, and for a time does not even squirm;[2] then he tumbles about for a while, seeing the Apocalypse all round him; then he bolts and runs like a mad dog, anywhere,—to Samoa, to Tahiti, to Fiji; then he dashes straight round the world, hoping to get to Paris ahead of the Apocalypse; but hardly has he walked down the Rue Bassano when he sees the apocalyptic *Never* written up like a hotel sign on No. 12; and when he, at last leaves London, and his cab crosses the end of Cork St, his last glimpse of No. 5A shows the Apocalyptic *Never* over the front door. More than once today I have reflected seriously whether I ought not at once to turn round and go back to Ceylon. As I am much the older and presumably the one of us two who is responsible for whatever mischief can happen, I feel as though I had led you into the mistake of bringing me here, and am about to lead you into the worse mistake of bringing me home. Not that I take a French view of the matter, or imagine you to be in the least peril of falling into the conventional dilemmas of the French heroines; but because, no matter how much I may efface myself or how little I may ask, I must always make more demand on you than you can gratify, and you must always have the consciousness that, whatever I may profess, I want more than I can have. Sooner or later the end of such a situation is estrangement, with more or less disappointment and bitterness. I am not old enough to be a tame cat; you are too old to accept me in any other character. You were right last year in sending me away, and if I had the strength of mind of an average monkey, and valued your regard at anything near its true price, I should guard myself well from running so fatal a risk as that of losing it by returning to take a position which cannot fail to tire out your patience and end in your sending me off again, either in kindness or in irritation; but I cannot sublime to power, and as I have learned to follow fate with docility surprising to myself, I shall come back gaily, with a heart as sick as ever a man had who knew that he should lose the only object he loved because he loved too much. I am quite prepared to have you laugh at all this, and think it one of my morbid ideas. So it is; all my ideas are morbid, and that is going to be your worst trouble, as I have always told you. Yet I would give you gladly as many opal and diamond necklaces as Mr Cameron would let you wear if I could only for once look clear down to the bottom of your mind and understand the whole of it. I lie for hours wondering whether you, out on the dark ocean, in surroundings which are certainly less cheerful than mine, sometimes think of me, and divine or suspect that you have undertaken a task too hard for you; whether you feel that the last month has proved to be—not wholly a success, and that the fault is mine for wanting more than I had a right to expect; whether you are almost on the verge of regretting a little that you tried the experiment; whether you are puzzled to know how an indefinite future of such months is to be managed; whether you are fretting, as I am, over what you can and what you cannot do; whether you are not already a little impatient with me for not being satisfied, and for not accepting in secret, as I do accept in pretence, whatever is given me, as more than enough for any deserts or claims of mine; and whether in your most serious thoughts, you have an idea what to do with me when I am again on your hands. I would not distress you with these questions while you were fretted, worried and excited by your last days here; but now that you are tossing on the ocean, you have time to see the apocalyptic Never which has become yours as well as mine. I have dragged you face to face with it, and cannot now help your seeing it. French novels are not the only possible dramas. One may be innocent as the angels, yet as unhappy as the wicked; and I, who would lie down and die rather than give you a day's pain, am going to pain you the more, the more I love.

Nov. 6. Another dark, still day. We had a meet of the hounds this morning, and I rode to it with the Gaskells, and capered over the muddy fields on a pulling poney till my back is sore as never before, and some muscle is so gone wrong that I almost howl every time I rise from my chair. The hunt left us, and we rode home and killed a fox in the Abbey grounds as though the fox had meant to pay me a personal attention. This afternoon I wandered alone across Wenlock Edge and through miles of soaked meadow. The air is still calm, and I thought always of you, but you are near a thousand miles away already, and this weather is no longer yours. Curiously enough, I feel rather peaceful and contented in this dank, dark, dripping, dreary atmosphere, where the hills melt or freeze into dim outlines of mist and cloud. For the moment the world seems stationary, and I can stop too. Nothing has changed here since I first came in the year '64. For once I find perfect stability and repose; even Gaskell seems hardly altered. My long, tearing, wild jaunt of the last five months, ends here in a sense of ended worlds and burnt-out coal-and-iron-universes. Tomorrow I am going over to Birmingham to pass Sunday with the Chamberlains. I have offered myself to Mrs Dugdale—don't be alarmed! only for a call. I go to Tillypronie next week. Am I not social and human? I try to be civil, because you tell me I'm rude, and I want to please you. In secret I dread returning to the solitude of hotels and the weariness of self—self—self, and the temptation to commit any folly that would give amusement or change.

Highbury. Sunday, November 8. Here I am with the Chamberlains in their big house with a suburb of greenhouses and forests of orchids. They—Chamberlains and orchids—are charming hosts, and Madame, younger than ever, and like the younger sister of her step-daughters, quite shines with new light as a *grande dame.*[3] Only a few young people are here, and all seems serene and happy. The girls are decidedly agreeable, and my host is admirable in the domestic relation. I feel quite like your brute when I see how gentle and deferential he is. How I wish you would make me a social gem; but you neglect your duties. We have strolled about the place, and the sun actually shone. My virtue shines too, for I suddenly burn with interest for English politics, and talked till near two o'clock last night with my Right Honorable friend on the prospects of the coming general election. With his usual frankness he announced his expectation of the defeat of his party.[4] What ought I to have said? In truth I cared much more to know

Nov. 6. Another dark, still day. We had a meet of the hounds this morning, and I rode to it with the Gaskells, and capered over the muddy fields on a pulling pony till my back is sore as never before, and some muscle is so gone wrong that I almost howl every time I rise from my chair. The hunt left us, and we rode home and killed a fox in the Abbey grounds as though the fox had meant to pay me a personal attention. This afternoon I wandered alone across Wenlock Edge and through miles of soaked meadow. The air is still calm, and I thought always of you, but you are near a thousand miles away already, and this weather is no longer yours. Curiously enough, I feel rather peaceful and contented in this dank, dark, dripping, dreary atmosphere, where the hills melt or freeze into dim outlines of mist and cloud. For the moment the world seems stationary, and I can stop too. Nothing has changed here since I first came in the year '64. For once I find perfect stability and repose; even Gaskell seems hardly altered. My long, tearing, wild jaunt of the last five months, ends here in a sense of ended worlds and burnt-out coal-and-iron-universes. Tomorrow I am going over to Birmingham to pass Sunday with the Chamberlains. I have offered myself to Neil Dugdale — don't be alarmed: only for a call. I go to Tillypronie next week. Am I not social and human? I try to be civil, because you tell me I'm rude, and I want to please you. In secret I dread returning to the solitude of hotels and the weariness of self — self — self, and the temptation to commit any folly that would give amusement or change.

A page from Henry Adams' serial letter of November 5, 1891, to Elizabeth Cameron

The Adams memorial by Augustus Saint-Gaudens, Rock Creek
Cemetery

how your voyage was getting on and whether you were as cold as I am; but the weather is still so very fine and calm that I hope for the best. How I wish you were here with us, and how I should have enjoyed a peaceful Sunday with you among the orchids, admiring *Odontoglossum grande,* if that is its name! I should have had nothing to say to you; I never have anything; but you could have gone to sleep among the palms and ferns, and I could have read to Martha.

Monday. Nov. 9. Wenlock again this evening. Mrs Dugdale telegraphed that she was at Ascot or London or some such neighborhood, so I was spared that effort. This morning I made a special inspection of the Chamberlains' heating and lighting apparatus. Joseph has five big boilers and a gas boiler; a big and little dynamo, and so on. I would like to resemble him in this as in other matters; apparently he takes no thought of money, but he takes less thought of his house, which he leaves to wife and son; and he declared that no one had ever asked to see his boilers before. Then Mistress Mary drove me to the town to show me, also at my request, her portrait now on exhibition there. I thought it much better than I expected. Millais, whatever his weaknesses, is neither a fool nor a lunatic.[5] On the whole Mistress Mary is lucky, and I would give much to see an equally pleasant portrait of you and Martha. How good it might be! Then she took me to church to see Burne Jones's glass, which is—not so bad as I expected.[6] Then we went to the Art Museum to see an exhibition of Pre-raphaelitic pictures—Burne Jones, Holman Hunt, Rosetti, &c,—and these, on the whole were fully as bad as I expected.[7] Then we parted and I came back to Wenlock. I am waiting only to hear of your safe arrival, to mail this letter, probably just as I start for Scotland on Thursday or Friday. Last night the wind blew violently, but you were two thousand miles away, and that gust, at least, could not harm you. I wish you were here with us. You would have to sleep all day, or ride in fields soaked with mud. I am still stiff as a martyr on a gridiron.

Tuesday, 10th. All day out doors, walking or riding, either along muddy roads or through fields and lanes like sloughs. I rather like it still. I feel as though I had reached harbor, and the dull, wet skies and brown foliage leaves me more cheerful than I was in the most perfect tropics. Yet I was tired this evening, and after dressing for dinner I was waiting before the fire in the Abbott's room for Gaskell and Lady Catherine to come down, when a footman brought me a bundle of shirts forwarded by my order from the Hotel Bristol, and in the bundle was a lot of letters, among them your sweet note from Queenstown. Did I not just feel like a horrid brute? No! the fruit and butter came not from me; I hesitated and said to myself that you didn't want them. No! I did not even send a farewell telegram to Queenstown! I hesitated and said to myself that you didn't want it. No! I was glad not to have gone with you to Crewe! I hesitated, and said to myself that you did not want me, and I had suffered already enough in parting. Always when I reach the desperate stage you say or write something that makes me feel unreasonable and brutal, and ashamed of everything but loving you. Why send you what I have written in this letter? I know it cannot give you pleasure, and is likely to give you pain. Yet it is all true, and the pain is actually mine, not yours; your position is right enough, and easily held; mine is all wrong and impossible; you are Beauty; I am the Beast, and until I turn into somebody else I cannot with propriety lead a life fit for you to associate with. I must be a nuisance to you and myself—like Hamlet or Prince Bulbo.[8] But I am really annoyed that you thought my good-bye abrupt, and had no idea it was to come then. I thought I had told you in the afternoon that my good-bye was intended to be our last words in your rooms, for, later, I should have no chance for more than a mere word of farewell. After all, it was only of a piece with my whole visit,—fragmentary, interrupted and unsatisfactory. The fault is mine; you are as gentle, obliging and thoughtful as ever, and nothing remains for me but to be sorry after all is over. Yet I wish—I wish—I wish, I could see clear through your mind. You have a nature like an opal, with the softest, loveliest, purest lights, which one worships and which baffles one's worship.

Thursday, 12 November. The Times today announces the arrival of your Teutonic at New York yesterday morning; less than six days therefore from Queenstown. I feel greatly relieved, for I can at least hope that the voyage was good. The relief was the greater because a change of weather set in here on Sunday which has culminated in a violent storm, and had your ship been delayed, I should have feared that you might have passed through this gale, and suffered. I suppose La Farge sailed from Queenstown today into the teeth of the gale; at any rate I did for him what I was too low-spirited to do for you,—I both telegraphed and wrote farewell. We had been so long together, and had intended to meet again in London, but missed it! We have never had a quarrel, or even a disagreement, which surely proves that he must have a wonderfully sweet disposition. Apart from this, he is the only man of genius I now know living, and though he had seven devils, I would be his friend for that. If I could only give him a big window to do, like Chartres or Amiens![9] So I am now all alone for the first time; you gone; he gone; and myself the gonest of the lot. I still linger at Wenlock, partly because the Clarke's have set Saturday for Tilliepronie, partly because I feel at home here, as though I were in hiding. Lady Catherine is very nice indeed; she has grown simpler and more natural than in the old sun-flower days, and is very gentle and sympathetic; but I think my true source of repose here is not so much in her or in her husband as in the place itself. At atmosphere of seclusion and peace certainly lingers in these stones, and I have thought much of the life I should certainly have led here had I come with the same experiences five hundred years ago, to the same retreat. Progress has much to answer for in depriving weary and broken men and women of their natural end and happiness; but even now I can fancy myself contented in the cloister, and happy in the daily round of duties, if only I still knew a God to pray to, or better yet, a Goddess; for as I grow older I see that all the human interest and power that religion ever had, was in the mother and child, and I would have nothing to do with a church that did not offer both. There you are again! you see how the thought always turns back to you. Goodbye now! I shall post this letter tomorrow on my way north. My next will follow in about a fortnight. To the last moment I doubt the wisdom of sending this letter; but: Kismet! Let fate have its way.

MS: MHi

1. HA quotes from "Lady Geraldine's Courtship" (1844). He mistitles "The Romance of the Swan's Nest" (1844). Elizabeth Barrett Browning's narrative poem *Aurora Leigh* (1857) was an immediate and continuous success, going into a 17th edition in 1882.

2. Abner Dean's fate in the Bret Harte poem (see HA to Elizabeth Cameron, June 28, 1891, note 2): "He smiled a kind of sickly smile, and curled up on the floor / And the subsequent proceedings interested him no more."

3. Chamberlain, twice widowed when he married Mary Endicott, had six children by his previous marriages. His eldest daughter was the same age as his young wife.

4. The Liberal Unionists.

5. Sir John Everett Millais (1829–1896) was much in demand as a portrait painter.

6. Sir Edward Burne-Jones, a native of Birmingham, designed stained-glass windows at St. Martin's and St. Philip's.

7. Joseph Chamberlain as mayor of Birmingham 1873–1875 virtually rebuilt the city center and began the expansion of the museum, which had in 1885 moved into new quarters. Its notable collection of Pre-Raphaelite paintings includes major works by Burne-Jones, William Holman Hunt (1827–1910), Dante Gabriel Rossetti, and Millais, founders of the Pre-Raphaelite Brotherhood.

8. A ridiculous lovesick character in Thackeray's *The Rose and the Ring* (1855).

9. La Farge had written from Brittany about his study of medieval cathedral windows and his wish that he could do the stained glass for a large building (La Farge to HA, Nov. 10, 11, 1891).

7·

"Coming to Life Again in a Dead World"

1891–1892

With Elizabeth Cameron's departure, Adams resumed his professedly antisocial social life. He went to the Gaskells at Wenlock, and with Gaskell to Sir John and Lady Clark's at Tillypronie in Aberdeenshire. He attended to bodily repairs, with minor surgery in London and dentistry in Paris. In London and Paris he renewed archival research to fill gaps in the period just before the *History*, assuming that, despite the lack of current professional scrutiny, future critics might put him to the test.

In his channel passage back to England, Adams railed against the lack of progress in comfort and efficiency, connecting personal experience to historical generalization in a way that would soon become characteristic. Yet his devotion to progress applied to technology only. In Paris he reacted to new French writing and art and theater with vigorous scorn. In London he caught up on old friends and reported with affectionate irony: "Much has gone, but thank the British Constitution, nothing new has come, and I sleep in peace with all the Georges and Queen Anne."

But the past was no more dead for him than the future. When he sailed for home on February 3, 1892, Adams' farewell letters to Cunliffe and Gaskell had a tone, not of finality, but of continuance.

To Elizabeth Cameron

Tilliepronie, Nov. 14, 1891.

I put my last, or first, letter into the mail yesterday at Wellington as we started to catch the Scotch express at Crewe, and I hope that by this time it is already on its way down the Irish channel. I wished it were written in a pleasanter tone, and promised a cheerfuller outlook; but enough of that! I will be as cheerful as I can in this one. Gaskell and I caught the Express at about two, and rattled all day northwards. The skies were black; the fields were under water; the air was rough and raw; but we had engaged a compartment and brought our own dinner, so, with much talk, the hours slipped away until at eleven at night we reached Aberdeen and in due time went to bed. This morning we rambled about Aberdeen, looking at Scotland as it ought to be, then took the Deeside train to Dennit, and drove eight miles up the hills to Sir John Clarke's house of Tilliepronie. Did you meet Sir John? If not, Hay will tell you all about him and Lady Clark. For several reasons, I was willing, if not glad, to come back here; but chiefly because I thought it would please the Clarks, to whom I owe many kindnesses which I cannot repay. So Gaskell also, poor fellow, has dragged himself from his wife and fireside, to travel three or four hundred miles in wintry weather, to please the kind laird and lady. Here we are, and I use my hour before dinner to tell you of our safe arrival, while I think of you as probably having reached Washington. Once more, how far away!

November 19. We have passed five days on this hill, more than a thousand feet above sea-level. The view is superb, a grand sweep over valley and hill, but the weather has been atrocious. Some days we have not left the house, and until today our utmost venture was a mile or two down the road. Only this morning I got a two-hour stretch up over the moor and the heather, and I enjoyed the intense solitude of the brown hills where nothing spoke except the fresh wind and the occasional bark of a startled grouse; but the moors are saturated with water and I had to be shy of bogs. Gaskell was out with a gun killing rabbits, an amusement he does not greatly love; and Sir John can neither walk nor shoot, but takes a turn on a poney. Naturally in such a retreat I have little to write about. Our table is far too good, and we have to cut down our gormandising, for fear of evil. Of course we talk a great deal, mostly of people, but I am rather surprised to find scandal less extensive than formerly, and the fast set much less notorious. Apparently society is scared, and keeps its soiled linen in the domestic laundry. I have read laboriously, working up my French literature, since I can find no English. I have written up my correspondence. I have telegraphed to Mary Charlton, offering myself for Sunday, and received reply that she would be away;[1] so I shall stop over Sunday at Acton with the Cunliffes, and go up to London on Monday to begin work, already a fortnight late. Tell

Spring Rice that we often speak of him and charge him with all the crimes we can. We are all going fast to democracy, and gloom pervades the Union.

Acton. Nov. 21. We bade good-bye to our Scotch hosts yesterday morning. They have been affectionate as possible, and in our parting talk Sir John amused me by another demonstration of the old-old wish, so familiar to me from my women friends, that I might find a *Frou-frou,* as he puts it,—a companion; he would like to see me marry; and how can I say that in forty years of search, I have never met but one woman who met me all round so as to be a real companion? He would say that this was my delusion; but I don't see that he would better the matter by that. So I hold my tongue, and say that one must not make a bad matter worse. How I pity at times that imaginary lady, my possible wife! what a gay time she would have of it, and how quickly and comfortably I would suck the blood out of her;—unless she were sensible enough to save herself in time, more or less after the manner of my old friend Wentworth Beaumont's new companion.[2] Yet all women would look on with approval, and encourage me, if I had the supreme selfishness to sacrifice some innocent victim to my *ennui.* Honestly, is not central Asia out of all comparison more respectable than such a resource?; yet everyone combines to dissuade me from Asia, and almost conspires to sacrifice some new Iphigenia to secure my safe return home; while I, who do not want to sacrifice any woman, least of all an Iphigenia, dangle here, cursing myself for indecision. Truly, men are poor creatures, and though I quite admit that I am perhaps the best of the lot, I do not pique myself even on that. Marry I will not; no woman is good enough for me; not even the lovely member of the British aristocracy who came down with us today from Carlisle, and had not only a coronet and a husband, but an ounce or two of solid paint on her slightly weather-worn cheeks. My friends are so respectable and retired that none of them knew this habit of high society, and I was able to affect acquaintance with hig' lif' on the strength of your gossip. Otherwise we finished our journey without incident, sleeping at Carlisle, parting at Warrenton, and Gaskell returning to Wenlock while I reached Wrexham for lunch. Here is only the family, and I talk only general election with Robert. You would smile melodiously could you hear me talk politics. Solemnly, I think I seem to talk it all right, and my remarks are always received as though they conveyed a meaning. This proves nothing, I admit, except that externally I appear no madder than my neighbors; but in America I should think even that a triumph. Do write me the political gossip! Here it will give me a sort of air of reasonability; perhaps it may save me just the margin of lucidity I need; for, as now constituted, I am as likely to nominate George Washington as Benjamin Harrison, and elect him too. There! I must dress for dinner. Good-bye!

Sunday, 22d. A big function at church today to instal the new Lord Mayor of Wrexham. I went to it to pass the time and to hear the Bishop preach, as I like to study Bishops when I can, much as I have inspected coral polyps.

Otherwise a very quiet Sunday; a short stroll; much talk with Robert, and a general vague sense of wonder what is to become of me. Tomorrow to London.

Monday, 23 Nov. Here I am again, just arrived at my old quarters at the Brunswick, for the first time absolutely alone, and rather more solitary than if I were in Yarkand;[3] but the first of a pack of letters on my table is a telegram from you, which came ten days ago, but perhaps is more welcome at this particular moment because it hits the solitary lame duck. You have so often made me grateful in this way that I feel remorse at the thought that you are probably at the same moment receiving my letter from Wenlock. All the same, my letters, though not bad on the whole, are not wholly cheering. Always at this season of the year I am in a panic, because, almost as regularly as the shortest days come, for years past, I have had some more or less crushing disaster, until I hardly dare breathe before New Year's day has passed. Today, which has been one of my most unlucky days of late years, I have had no very bad news, but still enough to make me solidly uncomfortable. I shall wait anxiously to hear from you what you have to tell about Hay and Washington. Every motive, except that of seeing you and him, urges me not to come back, but these two overbalance all others, and I shall come, though with much sinking of the heart; but pray do not betray my intention to anyone at all, for I want to reserve my plans to myself for reasons that belong to my family affairs. Tomorrow I shall go to Phillips's to see what he has done with my star-sapphire; if possible also to Woolner's to see his water-colors. The birthday has passed, but has not been celebrated, and among the many little matters that occupy me here, this is my only real pleasure.[4]

Tuesday, 24th. My campaign today has fairly ended in the conclusion that I must go home anyhow to get teeth and body patched up, for nothing but the direst necessity would warrant my doing it here; so you may expect me in February at latest; but do not betray me. Please keep it quite to yourself. Probably I must postpone Spain till next time; but I must try to bag Holland, and must anyway go back to Paris. I ought to be glad to be decided; perhaps I am; but certainly I took more pleasure in going to Woolner's and selecting your water-color. The one I chose is a Turner, and a pretty blooming nice one, in my opinion, though it costs me nothing, and you need not feel uncomfortable on that account. It is a great sweep of land and sky with a dash of trees and a pool; quite the easy thing I would do myself if it were not easier to do something else; but done in his later and slappier style, like a Frenchman more or less. Shall I frame and send it, or bring it? I hardly like to send it because I must then make a certain degree of talk about it, and people always exaggerate the value of such things; yet I could send it direct to you, not as a birthday present but as bought by your order on commission, and you could send me a check for it. Suit yourself! From Woolner's I went to Phillips's, and saw the star-stone in its new setting which Phillips is delighted with, and which will, I think, please you. I'll not describe it, but will try to send it next week through the Legation, and will put with it a little baby-pin for Martha. I am having an intaglio arranged for Lady Katty, so you need not think you are the only one who gets presents.

Thanksgiving Day. 26th. Yesterday your letter arrived, only about a week old. Naturally I was pleased, for it was all good news, as your letters always are; whereas mine are so disagreeable, egotistic and yawpy that I quiver at the thought of their existence, and entreat you, in mere kindness to me, to burn them. With yours, I received a long despatch from my brother Tati at Tahiti, full of Tahitian news. He talks of coming in '92 to America, and I think he is like me,—he must come, to be patched up. You will have to be very kind to my dear big brother, and come in to breakfast and dine with him every day. You will like him best so, rather than in your own house with frivolous jesting youth like Blaine and Morton. No! once more; I did not send the butter and fruit, and am glad of it since some one else did. What is more, I fear I cannot send the ring. Lars will try to get it into the bag, but is not sure.[5] The picture is still more troublesome, for I want you to have it, and it will take forever through the custom-house, besides duties.[6] *Que faire?* Must I come myself? Tonight Lars and I eat a Thanksgiving turkey in his rooms, and go to some theatre. If he is half as glad as I am not to be alone, he can give thanks with reason. No one at all is in town, and I cant make up my mind to seek out the few exceptions. Lecky, on whom I counted, is in bed with influenza; Wemyss Reid, whom I was to know, is on the continent. Lars and I are quite alone, for I daren't face Harry James after treating his play as I did;[7] but you can judge of the situation when you see me with Lars for my closest companion.

Saturday, 28th. Our dinner turned out very well; Lars and I eat up the whole of an excellent turkey, with suitable cranberry sauce, and made an evening of it, painting the town red. Lars is a lucky appointment for me. I am not a little obliged to the State Department for this favor, which for once serves my turn better than any other could have done. This morning I have taken the small package to him, containing your ring and a little pin for Martha at Christmas. I told him that you had left a small commission with me, with orders to send it to you through the bag; and if it failed, he need not expect the Senate to confirm his appointment. He took it, and I earnestly trust that Sevellon Brown will let you have it within a few hours after you receive this. Phillips and I are now close friends; I am sure he would like to take me into partnership, and I seriously think I should get more pleasure from fussing over gems than I shall ever get from any pursuit of happiness in other directions. I delight in trying experiments on them. Just now I chiefly want you to take the pleasure, so I am anxious to have them reach you. Only I wish you could make me some presents; as it is, you see, my presents must serve for both; for I can think of nothing in the world—that you can give—that I want. Tomorrow I lunch with Harry James after all; and shall get Lars to dine with me. Monday I dine with Woolner. Just now I am going to call on Mrs Lecky, Mistress Alice Mason, and May Lacaita. Surely some of them will be at home. I shall post this letter as I go.

MS: MHi

1. Mary Campbell, a friend of HA and MHA, married in 1873 William Oswald Charlton (1850–1894), a secretary of the British legation in the 1880s. After MHA's death she became, along with Mary Endicott and Mary Leiter, one of the "three Marys" who often graced HA's breakfast table.
2. Wentworth Beaumont (1829–1907), a widower, married Lady Edith Althea Hamilton Colley (d. 1927) in February. She was the widow of Maj. Gen. Sir George Pomeroy-Colley, who had been killed in action in South Africa in 1881.
3. A city at the western end of the Takla Makan Desert in China.
4. Nov. 10, 1891, was Mrs. Cameron's 34th birthday.
5. Larz Anderson (1866–1937), second secretary of the U.S. legation in London 1891–1894, son of Nicholas Longworth Anderson, HA's Harvard classmate and Washington friend.
6. Art objects were not on the duty-free list at this time; the duty would have been 20 percent ad valorem.
7. *The American,* James's first play, based on his 1877 novel, opened in London on Sept. 26 and ran for 70 nights in spite of generally unfavorable reviews.

To John Hay

Tillypronie, Tarland, Aberdeenshire.
14 Nov. 1891.

My dear John

I use this paper to show you more quickly where I am. At this season Scotland is not greatly sought, but you will appreciate the motives which have led Gaskell and me all this way. They are unselfish all round.

I have now been rather more than a month in Europe, and at this point touch my northernmost limit. From Sydney to Aberdeen is a long swing, but the journey has been well worth making. Even Paris had a certain interest. I could find nothing new that pleased me either in art or literature, and as for society nothing of the satisfactory sort was within the bounds of my imagination; but a fortnight or so passes quickly even if nothing is the result, and perhaps some particles of dust of nothing may save the result from absolute nothingness. Then I had La Farge, Mrs Cameron, Miss Cameron, and the engrossing Martha, to beguile my ennui at intervals. I haunted the theatres, operas and concerts. In orchestral music Paris has made a great stride; in opera she has gone off; and her theatres were living on *reprises.* Réjane was admirable in the Cigale; I went twice to see her.[1] No other actor or actress affected me much. The plays were very indecent, but not more so than formerly, and they were certainly funny. I did some real laughing, and enjoyed it.

Reid was civil and very properly asked me to dinner, which I very improperly begged off.[2] The rage for declining invitations is a form of madness which is in no way a pleasure to me, but such a genuine horror always seizes me now at the vision of a party of any sort, that I violate all decency in trying to escape. Luckily I was not bothered that way in London. No one seemed to be in town, and as pretty nearly everyone was dead, my loss would anyway have been small. The Camerons sailed on the 4th, and I chose the same moment to beguile my solitude by going down to Wenlock Abbey where the Gaskells were expecting me. Of course the weather was like the devil run to deluge. Nothing but black skies and soaked fields met my eyes, but I mind weather less than people, and I was quite contented at Wenlock with Gaskell and his wife, and even lived constantly in the open air, rather wondering only at the English passion for riding in a foot of mud through stubble for pleasure. Gaskell mounted me on a poney, took me to a meet of the hounds, killed me a fox, and capered me, with Lady Catherine, through all the mud in sight of Wenlock Edge.

I passed Sunday at Birmingham with the Chamberlains. Our Mary was extremely pretty, sweet, decidedly improved, and apparently very happy. She took me to see her portrait, which I thought a happy escape; also to see Burne Jones's windows, and an exhibition of pre-Raphaelitic pictures. Chamberlain showed me his orchids and told me what he expected from Gladstone's new administration, for he admits the coming defeat of the Unionists. The Chamberlain house is very big, very costly, and rather American than English. The girls seemed to me pleasant, bright, and well-mannered, and nothing can surpass the perfection of Chamberlain's manner to his wife and family. I deeply regretted that you and my other friends should be so very deficient in these respects.

Gaskell and I next made a desperate effort and got up here. The intervening country seemed to be drowned out, and was so dark and dismal that I hardly saw it; but we found the Clarks wonderfully bright, considering their frightful infirmities, and not much changed. Indeed the table is, if possible, even better than it used to be, and there are more new books than ever, and more people to talk about. I find English society rather scared into decency. At least Sir John has no special scandals to feed me on, and except for the Prince of Wales and Lady Brooke, an old affair, I am led to believe that the world has purged and lives cleanly.[3] Everyone talks politics. The Unionist gentry, like other mugwumps, must now bid farewell to Parliament. The deluge is coming, and the Church and State are sinking beneath the waves. Selah! For myself, I care but slightly, yet the approaching fate of Chamberlain affects me deeply on account of his young wife. Let us hope he will be electrocuted, not hung.

My thoughts turn sadly to you at times, especially because you are hourly mentioned here, and tender messages impressed on me at stated intervals. I would you were with us, for we are fairly merry even without you, and I have won success by some of your very oldest stories. Of my own plans I know almost less than my friends know. At one moment I feel quite resolved to run over to Washington in February for three or four months. A few hours afterwards I find myself planning for letters of introduction to India, and a start instans. The hesitation has been somewhat trying, not to say painful; but seems no nearer settlement than at first. If I decide for Washington, I shall be chiefly influenced by the wish to see you; but in the meanwhile I am going back to the continent in order to get homesick if I can. I have fixed on Dec. 1 for my crossing.

England, though singularly commonplace and quite phenomenally *fin de siècle* in a sense unknown to France, suits me fairly well for the moment, and I breathe rather more peacefully here than elsewhere. If you were only here, and we had a nice country-house for Mrs Hay and the children and me, with poneys and an orchid and rose house, for all which we would get Chamberlain to pay, I should be quite happy, and we would combine and write literary notices of French novels for the Tribune and Evening Post. This is my scheme for our declining years.

My love to all yours.

Ever affely Henry Adams.

MS: RPB

1. Gabrielle Réjane (1857–1920), one of the outstanding French actresses of the century, played in a revival of *La Cigale,* a comedy by Henri Meilhac and Ludovic Halévy.
2. Whitelaw Reid was U.S. minister to France 1889–1892.
3. Lady Brooke (1861–1938), formerly Frances ("Daisy") Maynard, wife of Francis Greville, Viscount Brooke.

To Lucy Baxter

Tillypronie, Aberdeenshire 16 Nov. 1891.

My dear Miss Baxter

Your letter of October 25 reached me the other day when I was staying with one of my old friends in Shropshire. I wonder how this sort of thing would suit you. For my own part I can imagine few things more gloomy than England at this season, drenched and soaked with rain, and dark with clouds of a peculiar black quality which lower over the landscape in a temper that excludes hope and sun together; yet my spirits are unusually good here,—better than in the sunshine and warmth of the tropics; and I feel quite as though I had reached port. I have not. I am painfully at a loss what to do next. The decision frets me and I put it off from day to day; but in the meanwhile I am quite contented to sit by the fire with a few old friends, and abuse creation in general and the present time in particular. I find England superficially little changed, but evidently on the verge of great changes. Many of my old friends have grown older, but otherwise seem to me much what they were. England is much less smart; much more American, and decidedly less queer and old-fashioned than it used to be; but I found my Abbey in Shropshire absolutely the same, and all the country, for miles around it, seemed hardly to have seen a change of season since I first stayed there twentyseven years ago. Indeed I doubt whether, if I had last seen it in the days of Queen Elizabeth, I should have noticed much alteration. The noblemen and country gentlemen are poorer, entertain little, and economise all they can. The grand style has almost wholly disappeared. The footmen no longer wear powder, or stand behind the chariots with their long canes in hand. The railways are bigger and more crowded, but more third-class in respect of passengers than ever. Coming democracy casts its shadow before.

I left my Abbey at Wenlock to pass a Sunday with the Chamberlains at Birmingham. You remember that Mrs Chamberlain was Mary Endicott, one of my Washington girls, and I wrote to ask to see her. I found her mistress of a big, new house on the verge of Birmingham, with everything as costly as one could wish, and with greenhouses enough to satisfy even me. She was looking very young, fresh and happy, and was a charming hostess, greatly improved, I thought, in every way. Her husband too looked very young, especially when I reflected that he is two years older than I am, and that while I have closed my account with the world, he considers himself to be only opening his. I envied him his orchids, if nothing else, and the four hot-water boilers that warm his winter-garden, and give him a very fair bit of tropics where he can smoke his pipe when he likes.

My friend Gaskell and I came up to Scotland last Saturday to pass a few days with Sir John and Lady Clark, two old friends of ours, who are now obliged by their increasing infirmities to pass the whole year in their house more than a thousand feet up on the mountain-side some ten or twelve miles from Balmoral, looking over a magnificent range of valley and mountain just now soaked in water or crowned with snow. We are alone here with the Clarks, who are invalids; and as the weather is wet and cold, we have little to do but to discuss other people and to eat Lady Clark's breakfasts, lunches and dinners, which are incomparably good, not because of the cook but because of the mistress. The Clarks are not rich but are fond of people, of books, and of the world; and they keep up their interest surprisingly. I look with wonder at the courage and energy with which they face the ills and cares of life, and keep a fresh interest in everything, even in Americans and American books with which their house swarms. We leave here next Friday when I expect to return to London, and in due time to Paris, whence I shall presently take train for the south of Europe.

La Farge is now on the ocean. At least I suppose so, for I have cut off communication with the world, and have left my letters to accumulate in London. He went to Brittany when I came to England, for he had to visit his aunts and cousins there. I fear he is having a bad voyage, for he left Liverpool in the worst of the worst storm of the season. The Camerons have already reached Washington, I suppose. I have no other American friends to fall back upon, and am rather at a loss for company.

From home, except for your letter, I have heard almost nothing. If

Dwight has written within the last six months, I have not received his letters, and am wholly unable to account for the sudden stoppage of his correspondence. Probably I am in some occult way the offender, but I know not how, and naturally do not care to ask. Doubtless I shall learn quite soon enough. Mabel Hooper writes regularly; at least, I think her latest letter was not long ago. Of course I do not expect letters from the family, as I never write to them. Probably John's brief announcement of Frank Brooks's death, which reached me last week, was the only news of the season, for, of three or four letters that came then, not one contained any news,—not even yours.[1] So I have no excuse for coming home, since nothing happens, and no one needs me.

On the whole I am a good deal disappointed to find that ten or twelve years have produced so very little in Europe that seems to be worth seeking. In art I can hear of positively nothing; even La Farge had to give up the search after long and patient inquiry. In literature, the field offered to me by my friends is quite barren. Except Stevenson and Rudyard Kipling, who are both in the South Seas from whence I have only just emerged, I hear of neither poet, novelist, historian, essayist or philosopher of note, and criticism is very low. This is what I am told; if my own search discovers anything, I shall let you know.

Take great care of yourself. Health grows scarce now'a'days.

Ever Yrs   Henry Adams.

London, 23 Nov. On arriving here I find a letter from Dwight, so my speculations on that head may be regarded as cancelled. At the same time, my perplexities in that connection are not diminished but rather increased. I really do not know what to say or do, and am cowardly enough to want to stay away on that account if on no other. Otherwise the news from home seems to be tolerably good, and you are all so kind in wishing my return that I feel ungrateful and brutal in dreading to come; but you must make allowance for a chicken so singed as I am. After three weeks passed in visiting old friends, I have come back to London to look after various small matters, and when these are finished, I must return to Paris. As a matter of pleasure I should prefer to stay in London until I make my next decided move, but I have left many unfinished odds and ends in Paris, and have no choice. London is curiously homelike to me, even after so many years of absence, and though I am for the first time quite alone. I hope you will manage to come out here next year. I am sure it would amuse you, and I think it would do you good. You and I are not the most high-spirited of beings, but here at least one is not worried by being obliged to affect good spirits, and one can look on at this show without feeling obliged to care what becomes of it. After all, this is nearer the spirit of the time—the *fin-de-siècle* as the French now call it—than any other.

MS: ScU
1. Francis Boott Brooks, son of HA's cousin Edward Brooks.

573

To Theodore F. Dwight

London, 24 Nov. 1891.

Dear Dwight

I was glad to receive yesterday your letter of Nov. 9. My movements have been so rapid and steady in the direction of the mail that I have neglected to write until I should reach some stopping-place. At present I have come to a stand, undecided what to do next, and waiting till I find myself decidedly turned in one direction or another.

I judge from your letter that nothing in special requires my presence at home. For the moment I am somewhat occupied here in directing searches in various archives to fill gaps in my collection of papers. I have thought it wise to go back a few years before 1800, to make sure that I have everything which can throw light on my period. As no one yet seems to have taken the trouble to criticise me, and as I have grave doubts whether anyone has ever read me seriously with a view to testing my accuracy, my present task seems a work of supererogation, but as I can never tell what may happen, the precaution seems worth taking.

Literature is pretty dead here, especially in the historical way. With the exception of Lecky I know no one, and hear of no one whom I want to know. Many of my old friends are still lively, and if I cared for general society I could have any quantity. As it is, I am content to stay quiet.

So little Possum has followed Marquis to the next world. I am glad I had not to see him go, but as I expected it soon, I am not surprised. Indeed I wish only that Prince and Daisy might also have a peaceful end, as they are too old ever to be used again. Whenever I come back, I would rather begin perfectly fresh, with as little as possible of decrepitude. I like youth about me now that I have not to carry its anxieties.

La Farge has got home at last, I hope the better for his long vacation. The Camerons also are established at Washington again, and I hope the cold weather will set Hay on his legs. Probably I shall soon get letters telling me about my Washington circle who are very good in keeping me in their memory.

I trust that you are hard at work, and have made good progress with the papers. That is now one of my chief remaining interests. I want to see the family records thoroughly arranged and made serviceable as my last contribution to the concern. You can hardly do it too well or too completely. The task is a long and tedious one, but it requires only patience and labor, and I hope, whenever I return, to find it far advanced. This is the only labor that is now much on my mind.

Ever Yrs   Henry Adams.

T. F. Dwight Esq.

MS: MHi

To Anna Cabot Mills Lodge

London, 25 Nov. 1891.

My dear Sister Anne

Your modesty is at least as great as are your many other virtues; but I trust that all my friends may not imitate you, admirable though their model is; for in that case I should fare ill for correspondence, and should even be myself reduced to the painful inquiry whether anyone, cleverer at the work than myself, were among the envious crowd who compete to hear from you. Yet I'll not reproach you, for you have not yet arrived at the fascinating age. The mark of that period of life is when people become more interesting in pen than in person. Until then we all have the right to shirk letter-writing. Hay and I have arrived there, and must write; but you have much still to learn.

Of course I sympathised fully in your feelings about Constance.[1] The truth is that in all the real trials of love, nothing can be said to any good purpose. One must bear or break; and the marriage of a daughter, even as young as Constance, has got to be borne. I could say nothing to make it easier; but I hope that by this time it hurts less.

You are all so lovely about wishing me back that I shall never dare come for fear of diminishing my popularity. If I were wildly amusing myself by travel, I should feel horribly selfish and heartless, but the single merit of travel is that it offers a variety of ways of boring oneself, whereas at home one is reduced to boring one's friends. I can at a pinch endure my own sufferings, but I cannot bear inflicting them on others. The English, when bored, kill something. I always feel as if I, too, were putting up a grouse or a pheasant when I stalk a friend to inflict my dreariness on him. I am sure that I caused Hay's collapse by this kind of diabolic chase.

If Hay really proves to be seriously ill I shall come home to be with him, but I hope the autumn will restore his strength, and that now, as before, his weakness will turn out to be nervous. Perhaps my hesitation to return is partly due to the fear that I might make him worse rather than better. What I seriously prefer is that all the family should come over here next summer, and take a princely establishment somewhere within reach of London, for which Hay should pay; and which should provide amusement for all the husbands—if Cabot could reconcile himself, to anything English beyond reach of presidential elections—while I should be properly and suitably petted and cared for by all the wives. Surely this is a modest want which you will all be glad to gratify, and I have only to suggest it in order to secure an immediate adoption of the idea.

In the meanwhile I am not too excessively bored by London, which seems uncommonly homelike and foggy. At times I admit that everything is intolerable; but at other times I find a certain amount of society, and a few old friends who are not wholly decrepit. Most of them too have become somewhat more pessimistic than I myself, and make me feel hopeful in comparison. They assure me that art, religion, literature, philosophy and poetry are all as dead as Achilles and Agamemnon, and can never revive; in short they are *plus fin de siècle que les plus fins (de siècle)*, and see nothing before mankind except infinite ennui diversified by vice. As I have found a way out, I listen with patience, for, like Sturgis Bigelow, I have taken to religion. For your life don't betray me to him; he would never quite forgive me; for, finding Buddhism a trifle flat and unsatisfactory I have become a Brahmin and, like Krishna Mulvany, am going in for a new Avatar.[2] We shall come to it some day, and what a pity it is that we cannot make my dear cousin the Bishop our new incarnation of Brahma! He looks it so well.[3]

You will have heard all possible news of me long ago. Since the Camerons went home, nothing has happened. Deserted by them and by La Farge, I exist in a solitude indescribably dreary, brightened at times by flashes of hope. Duty calls me back to Asia, and sooner or later that destiny will accomplish itself, for Brahma waits me; but pleasure calls me home; and what to decide I know not. You happy creatures, who can get the meat and drink of eternal life out of a presidential election—why can't you give it to me? Just elect me member of Congress, and see what credit you will do yourselves! Give me an office! Everyone that has an office is all right, and I feel quite sure that if I had an office I should live happily ever after. Hay and I are both dying for no other reason than that we are not made to go to our office every day, and write letters to people who have not got offices but want them.

Yet I should worry on very happily if I had you and the rest of the family over here to amuse me, and I think you all very selfish not to come. Perhaps you might have some plausible excuse for not going with me to the South Sea islands, but you can have none for leaving me alone here. If I were myself acting selfishly in staying here, you might have some defence, but I am here solely for your good; for I came all this way in search of a new young man to take the place of Spring Rice now grown up. New young women are always on hand; in thirty years I have never known them to fail; but a new young man is the rarest of game. For near a month I have searched, travelled, inquired, advertised in "Truth"[4] and the "Saturday Review," to no purpose. I can hear of no new young man, and I am regularly planted; for, without him, life is quite too too utter. I can neither go to Asia nor go home till I have found him; when found, his boots shall be my care; I will brush his clothes and pay his tailors; yet even this does not produce him.

Love to Cabot and Mr Blaine, as well as to Mr Reed (whom I am not so intimate with as I am with the other two); also to Constance to whom I sent a little remembrance through Mrs Cameron, which has probably by this time reached her. I should have sent one to you but was afraid Cabot would think it the mark of a trifling and negative mind, and would not permit you to receive it. Yet it was pretty nice, all the same, and I was sorry you missed it. London still has some fairly nice things in it, though the supply does not increase.

Ever Yrs   Henry Adams.

Mrs H. Cabot Lodge.

MS: MHi
1. Constance Lodge, who was 18, was engaged to Augustus Peabody Gardner. They were married on June 14, 1892.
2. Terence Mulvaney in Kipling's *Soldiers Three* (1888), after his enlistment in the Indian army expired, found he had lost touch with England; to the astonishment of his soldier friends, he returned to India as a mere civilian.
3. Phillips Brooks.
4. *Truth* was Henry Labouchere's radical weekly.

To Elizabeth Cameron

Hotel Bristol. 1 Dec. 1891.

I have cheated you and deceived you; but I did not go to do it; I meant to tell the truth. One object in coming to Europe was to get rid of a sort of wen that for years past has perched on my shoulder, and that I feared might make me look like a camel if I left it alone. Of course I might have had it attended to anywhere, but as it seemed a sort of excuse for a journey, I brought it here, hoping that a little blistering would be all that was needed. So last week I went to see a surgeon, who told me that blistering would do no good; he had better cut it out, and this, though not a serious affair, would require my shutting myself up in a private hospital for ten days or more. At this I kicked, and said that, if I must be shut up, I preferred to be shut up in my own house at home, and would wait till I got there. In this spirit I wrote last to you. Then I endured two days of black fog, gloom such as the north pole at this season must compare cheerfully with; and almost total solitude. A week more was in store before I could get away. So suddenly, in the middle of the night, I decided to seize the moment and finish up the job. Today was the day fixed, but my surgeon sent word this morning that he was unwell and couldn't. Tomorrow therefore I am to move into my hospital quarters, and be carved. I begin to half understand how a woman feels who is going to have a baby, though mine is such a very small one as not to be worth talking about; but I suppose a week must pass before I shall be allowed to write much, and more before I can wear a coat.

December 4. 17 Upper Wimpole Street. Sure enough, on Wednesday afternoon, punctually at the minute fixed, I lay down on the operating board, and snuffed in their beastly cloroform. You of course know the sensation, but it was new to me, and I tried hard to watch it; but the impression is too quick for study. One moment of cerebral fireworks, and the next thing one knows is a sort of putting one's head through a bit of death, and catching life by the tail again. For once the experience amused me. I felt a certain pleasure in not being bored. Of the operation I know nothing except that it was "such a small affair" as the nurse said, that I was rather ashamed of it; but really I didn't want to let a thing grow to be a second head on my shoulders, and I become like the two-headed calf in the Cigale.[1] The worst is that in order to extract a wretched sort of corn from one's shoulder, one must go through the paraphernalia of extracting all one's insides. Here I am, all up and dressed and writing, but trussed like a turkey, and shut up for another week, I suppose. I have let no one but Larz into the secret of where I am; they all think me in Paris. Larz himself is bunged up with a tooth, but comes to see me every day. Yet secrecy is not so easy as one might think. I find that my landlady-hostess who turns her house to use in this way, is intimately acquainted or related with half my London friends. Meanwhile I have your Turner to look at; and Earl Russell's matrimonial adventures to read about.[2] I expect soon to be out again, and off for Paris. I should not have told you my story of seclusion, except that you were bound to hear it somehow. Don't tell it. People exaggerate so.

Sunday, Dec. 6. Still in hospital, though perfectly restored, dressed and as well able to be about as ever I was. The surgeon seems to want to restore my childhood before letting me out. Strange that I am quite contented and happy to stay, and for the first time since reaching Paris I have not suffered a moment's depression. I write letters and read all day, but see no one except my nurse, my landlady and my surgeon. Even Larz is out of town or somewhere, and no one else knows my whereabouts. I have just written a long letter to my beloved Tati, in Tahiti, urging him to bring Marau with him to America next year when he comes. You know that King Pomare, her husband that had been, died just a week after I left Tahiti, and so, the royal line being extinct, our family is pretty near all the royalty and nobility that is left. Marau would be great fun as my guest in Washington, but I fear that, like Mrs Jack, she is afraid of compromising herself. I want much to get her memoirs printed, if she only won't be too proper. Nowadays London and Paris are the only places where impropriety has free play; our poor dear islanders are not only decent compared with the people here, but the women cannot begin to rival these English women in beauty. I am bewildered and aghast to see the improvement in the dress, style and even the stature of the upper-class demi-monde in London. The commoner type of the music-halls has changed little, but the swell women are a totally new order of being. The old simplicity of vice has given place to the strangest apeing of high life. You see I am falling into bad ways. You had better make me come home. Luckily I am no longer very easily led away.

Monday eve. 7th. Just as I was sitting down to struggle with my sixth solitary hospital dinner and evening, your letter of Nov. 27 arrived. My conscience told me that it had an ugly look; it seemed thin and beetle-browed; and I did not dare read it. As I'm cut off from wine and tobacco I could not nerve myself much; but at last, after hanging as long as I could over my baked apple, I resolutely stuck my legs on the fire, and opened the envelope!

Well! I knew it beforehand, and could have mind-read it all without winking. Ought I to reproach myself! If I should make you feel better by it, I would reproach myself to the world's end; but I felt and feel ever-so-much worse about it than you do, or than you ever will feel; for you at least have Martha, and I have nothing—your Goddess of Liberty being, as far as I know, only a negation. You can get on—I can't. The world amuses you—it bores me beyond surgery. You are obliged to drag your cart—I am at liberty to kick mine over. So I will not make myself more wretched than I am by remorse at making you wretched; and as soon as my shoulder is well, and my teeth patched up, say in about six weeks, I will take a steamer and come home. Then I will try my poor best not to bore you too much, though this little premonition of the future tells me what is coming. At worst I can always go into a hospital, and that seems to be the only refuge that gives me cheerfulness and repose of mind. I am now at liberty to go out, but I sit all day before the fire, reading, and listening to the storm outside. Upon my soul, I dread release.

Wednesday, 9 Dec. Hotel Bristol. Released today. In fact I was discharged yesterday, but the weather was bad, and I was rather glad to stay peacefully in my retreat. Except that I find myself a little weak, I should have forgot in five minutes that I had been seven days in hospital. Immediately I set about clearing up my odds and ends, so as to go to Paris on Sunday; and while about it, I stopped at the White Star office, and studied the winter arrangement. What say you to the Teutonic on February 3? This will bring me to Washington February 10 or 11. I shall probably take Stateroom W for that passage, and if I cannot get away so early, I shall shift to the Majestic a fortnight later. Please keep this secret. You know how I hate to announce a plan unless certain of carrying it out, and I want to reserve the liberty of change down to the last moment. There are also family reasons why I prefer to keep my plans to myself. No one but you need know. Two months hence, then, I shall probably be with you, and shall bring your Turner with me. In the interval I shall leave it with Larz, as a picture bought for you on commission, and belonging to you. I expect to send your plays direct from Paris next week, in a box of books I have bought on my own account. Do you want anything else? If so, write at once to me at Paris,—Hottinguer &Cie, Rue de Provence,—for I hope to be back here within a month, and you will have none too much time. Of course I give up Spain for the present. Grubb scares me.[3] For the matter of that, everything scares me; but I can run away no further.

Thursday, 10 Dec. Today I have been to Eton with Robert Cunliffe to see his boy Fossie (Foster) and Gaskell's boy Evelyn. The weather was awful;

blowing great guns with heavy showers of rain, and of course gloomy and muddy as you please; but it has never at any time since you left been so cold and raw as when we came over from France into the east wind. We went down at eleven o'clock and picked up the boys, both of them nice, natural, simple fellows, and the small Gaskell a sweet cherub, only with a complexion so exquisite that I should fear he might turn delicate. We took them to lunch with us, and went with them about the place, to hear the evening roll-call, and see a game of football in six inches of trampled mud. Nothing is more English than love of mire and cold. Why is it that in every English countryhouse one has a fire to go to bed by, but never a fire in the morning to dress by;—at least at this season. Eton was very quaint and perfectly unchanged; the same streets; the same buildings; the same pink-cheeked boys in the same tall silk hats, big white collars and tailless jackets; the same everything as thirty years ago. I wonder whether it will go on just the same in the next world. We wanted one of the boys to get birched for our amusement, but, though whipping is still practiced, they thought even their best manners unequal to that. We tipped them half a sovereign apiece when we came away, just as one did, no doubt, in the reigns of the Tudors. It was like a play, so quaint and innocent of real life. Is it not wonderful that boys and girls still exist in this weary, worn-out, elderly, gray-haired world?

Saturday, 12 Dec. So I have settled it. Yesterday, besides various other small matters, I made deposit for stateroom W on the Teutonic for February 3. Tomorrow I go over to Paris, expecting to remain there till Jan. 15, and then to return here for a fortnight before sailing. Once more, at the risk of exasperating you, I repeat that you are the only person who is to be told of this intention. I do not make secrets; I have none; as far as I know, my life has never had a secret of any consequence, not even a love-affair or a political bargain for office; but I am dead to the world;—dead as Adam and Eve, only just not yet buried; and I have been hoping, and still try to hope I may come to life again. I am making pitiable efforts to do it, and just train on raw beefsteak and eggs to read through the Times sacrilegiously every morning. Sometimes I talk so glibly about the day's news and Gladstone and Balfour and John Morley that I feel almost a glimmer of a hope by play-pretending very much and very steadily I may get to look at Ben Harrison as though he might be a real man, and even a senator might not be a phantasm.[4] Until I feel sure of this—say, until I find I can pinch Ben Harrison and he squeals—I hate to go about as though I were real. Pretending to be alive is a positive swindle on Cabot Lodge and Teddy Roosevelt, for we cannot possibly all be real. Either they are phantasms or I am. Respect my phantasmodesty, I implore, and let me slink back to my place like a ghost, to find out in silence and peace whether I am still a little bit alive.

I stopped in Half Moon Street to inquire whether Mary Charlton had come up. You know she was to start for Egypt just now. The servant said that Charlton was there, but not his wife, and thought she was ill. I left my card, but have not seen Charlton. I hope she is not too weak for the journey, but she looked horribly fragile. Robert Cunliffe and I dined quietly together at the Club. Today I have been to the Legation and given my last blessing to White.[5] I have also been to 38 Clarges Street where Larz Anderson lives, and have engaged a floor there from January 10. There I shall leave your Turner, so if I am drowned on the channel, send and get it. Gussy Jay crossed three or four days ago in the last gale but one; he and his boat were flung smash on the end of the pier, and nearly sunk; then turned back and made Dover after ten hours on the channel, and got to Paris at last after being thirtysix hours on the way.[6] This beats all my long experience to small chips. The weather has been fearfully windy, and this evening another gale seems coming on for the steamer to go with this letter.

There! I have given you a most minute account of my nothingness for the last fortnight. One would think I might do better in a place like England, but solitude is solitude even in London, and somehow I cannot catch on to anything else. Evidently the social faculty, which never was strong, is pretty well lost in me; otherwise I should be living with all the nobility and gentry. Don't let my imbecility bore you too much.

MS: MHi
1. In *La Cigale* the heroine describes how she was pursued by a two-headed calf.
2. John Francis Stanley (1865–1931), 2nd Earl Russell, was being sued by his wife for separation on the charge of cruelty.
3. A widower when he went to Spain as U.S. minister in 1890, Edward Burd Grubb (1841–1913) met Violet Sopwith, an Englishwoman, and was married within the year.
4. Arthur James Balfour (1848–1930), chief secretary for Ireland 1887–1891, on Oct. 17 became first lord of the treasury and conservative leader in the House of Commons. John Morley (1838–1923), liberal journalist, biographer of Burke and Cobden, chief secretary for Ireland 1886, 1892–1895, supported home rule; his *Life of Gladstone* (1903) became a major source for the *Education.*
5. Henry White (1850–1927), first secretary of the U.S. legation in London 1886–1893, 1897–1905.
6. Augustus Jay (1850–1919), second secretary of the U.S. legation in Paris, married to Emily Astor Kane Jay.

To Rebecca Dodge Rae

London, 5 Dec. 1891

My dear Friend

So you at last are left alone and are entitled to attention![1] I am sorry for it. Nothing troubles me more than to have my friends on my mind because then I know they are in a mess. Yet you have naturally a cheerful temper, and, as long as that lasts, everything must come out right. Anyway, write me a line to tell me about it. Direct to Hottinguer &Cie, 38 Rue de Provence, Paris.

However deserted you may feel, you are certainly a heap gayer than I am, for at best this season is not one that I hanker for, and London is not a lively place to pass it. Everyone has gone home. Larz Anderson and I are left quite alone in London. A few million other people are scattered about, but we don't mind them. The theatres are dreadful. I have called on a dozen people, who, I was assured, wanted to see me; but they had all left town yesterday for several weeks. I have not sought the Yates Thompsons because I suspected that they might wish to amuse me, which would have been too terrible. I am waiting for a dozen new shirts, and a pair of new shoes; when they are ready and I am dead beat,—say a week hence—I shall go to Paris again, though I dread it, for Paris is worse than London. Yet I must have my teeth ruined by some dentist before I can go anywhere; and what is the use of starting anywhere before spring? Even Washington is no good in January. You are all absorbed in dinners and balls, and never come near me.

What a pity it is that present matrimonial arrangements are so restrictive. You might come over and take care of me, as you are not allowed to take care of your husband; but the world, as at present constituted, gets to be a bigger absurdity every day, and I suppose the blooming nonsense will outlast me. The South Seas are the only region where such things are understood; but you would wear too much cocoanut oil there to be a good housekeeper. So I shall have to see this excellent opportunity lost by all the ladies of my breakfast-table; who would, under any sensible form of society, enjoy immensely keeping house for me here, and who are deprived of such a vacation by the ridiculous rules of custom. I am sorry for you, but what can I do?

Dwight wrote to me under your dictation, but did not tell me what sort of voyage you had, nor had he much to say. Curious trait of nature! A low-spirited person cannot abide other persons in low spirits. What business has Dwight to be low in his mind? He gets on my nerves as bad as I do myself. One fool is enough at a time, and if I play fool, I can't have another fool about me. Don't tell him so! With your usual frankness—which I always enjoy when it is applied to me—you are quite capable of saying all this to him, and I doubt the benefit of such a douche. You had better administer all the proper correctives to me, and say nothing about it to anyone else. Thus far in life I have made it a rule to trust all my secrets to women, and as few as possible to men. I never caught any woman in betraying a confidence, but I am not sure that I ever found a man who kept one. This accounts for my remarks to you on Dwight; so mind you keep them to yourself. Poor Dwight is a worse moral dyspeptic than I am; which is saying much. He is greatly to be pitied, too; and I do not want to make him—or myself—worse by attempts to make either of us better. Willy Phillips is a third lunatic; but he does not inflict his disease so much on others, at least outside the domestic circle. All such people should be carefully isolated and put under certain restraint.

As I have studied the temper of Dwight enough to be satisfied that the only good I can do him is to give him independence, I do not feel as though I needed more light on that subject; but you are to a certain extent my almoner, and can tell me whenever it happens that I could do any good to anyone. You used to say that if you had money, you could do so many kindnesses with it![2] Do your kindnesses, and with your own money, and I will make it good. Of course I cannot do them directly, or be known to do them indirectly; but as I thoroughly believe that I never yet did a charity without doing harm, and sometimes far more harm than good, I am not particularly anxious to be charitable and much less to be known for such. I am willing to let you try your hand at it, if you like, and if you really have any strong cases, you will certainly make use of me. If you succeed in doing any good, or even in giving any pleasure that has no counter-balancing harm, you will win a double success.

You will also, I hope, look in on William and Maggy from time to time, and tell them that you expect me back next week. They need to be kept awake. I've half a mind to run home just for one night to scare them, but the sea is so beastly sick. How could you stand it!

Mrs Cameron and Martha were a great comfort to me as long as they stayed, though I saw much more of the two Miss Camerons than of Mrs Cameron. Rachel and Martha were two very jolly and amiable companions, just about suited to my youthful wants. I got along nicely with them, and wish they would come back and take care of me. Mrs Cameron is no good. She has too much to do, and lets everybody make use of her, which pleases no one because of course each person objects to other persons having any rights that deserve respect. As long as she lives, it will always be so, and she will be everybody's slave and get no thanks. If it greatly amused her, or if she did it on calculation and for the return it brings in social popularity, I should think it all right; but of all the mysteries that have perplexed my life and driven me to absynthe for relief, the greatest and most hopeless mystery has been my friends' friends, and the tie that unites my friends with their friends. The same problem crops up with each, and I can well understand one *âme damnée*; but a dozen *âmes damnées* floor me. Original sin is a trifle to it.

With my best love to your mother ever sincerely Yrs

Henry Adams.

MS: MH
1. Her husband, Charles Rae, was on sea duty.
2. Rebecca Rae was associated with various charity groups in Washington.

To Elizabeth Cameron

Folkestone, Sunday, 13 Dec. 1891.

Improvement and rapidly approaching perfection are deeply stamped on every part of modern society. One never can enough wonder at the astonishing strides of our recent civilisation. This morning at ten o'clock I left

London, and here I am already, not indeed at Paris as I expected, but in the Pavilion Hotel at Folkestone, with nothing on earth to do but to talk to you. On arriving at Folkestone, the authorities told us in the most usual kind of way, as though I were Caractacus or Henry the First, that no boat would start today. I might have gone on to Calais, but the gale was so violent that I felt no eagerness to go out into it, and so I even stopped and waited like my old friend *rusticus* for the river to flow past,[1] and I fear with the same result, for the gale slams ahead as wildly as it did in Early English History. If it does not moderate, I shall go on to Dover and cross by the Calais mail which *must* go, under contract; but I cling to the hope that the gale will blow out tonight. My only occupation has been to walk a mile or two along the cliff westward to the Martello tower. The wind struck and pounded me like a bully, and the channel was seething. The air was a caldron of thin mist, and all was whirling up the channel in a mixed and churny state of sea and air. The only cheerful object was the three masts of a big ship sticking straight out of the water under the cliff. The hull went under last week in the storm. Well! it blew sometimes in the South Seas too.

Paris. 15 December. Midnight. I crossed Monday at noon; the wind was still stiffish and we wobbled much as when we crossed six weeks ago, but we had no delays, and reached Paris at six, where I am established for the time in a huge white-and-gold sitting-room at the Continental. Paris is as dark, muddy and desolate as London. Today has been my first campaign, and my first are always my brightest, so I can form a guess at what is coming. The only bright spot was that I found your plays all packed up, ready to start this week. As they were wrapped in paper in a big box filled with other books of mine, I could not examine them to see whether the binding was right, but I hope you will like it and them. The box will be addressed to Willy Phillips. I also called at the Legation on business, and there saw Gussy Jay who seemed to think Paris about as dull as I did. Apparently nothing has happened in it since you left. At all events no one is here that I know, and I am in for three weeks of dreary solitude. In an access of energy this evening I went off and dined at a restaurant across the river. Not another person was there, and I dined alone; it was worse than Vefour's in the Palais Royal where I had one companion the last time I tried it,—I don't mean you, but an unknown man. Then I went to the Odeon to see Réjane in *Amoureuse*, advertised as a comedy, but a comedy *à la fin de siècle*, which is ghastly tragedy that made me sick and sorry I went.[2] Always marriage! I am so deadly weary of the whole menagerie; but Réjane was very good. At least I rather think so, though she made me turn green with horror.

Thursday, 17 Dec. Come, by the mother of Vishnu, I have done good work these two days! My dentist is already busy with me, and I am already busy with my archives. First I fill a tooth; then I read a manuscript; then I wallow for an hour in a volume of Jules Lemaitre to teach me what has been doing in all these years;[3] then I call on Mrs Gussy Jay for an hour—

oh, dear!—and now I am going to take some dinner and go to the Variétes to see Mamselle Nitouche. I do not know who Mamselle Nitouche is, but she is an old success, and one of the plays in your lot, so you can soon learn whether my morals are safe.[4] I doubt, knowing the ways of the Variétés which are very amusing and colossally improper; but it will average right, for I went last night to the Palais Royal to see Céline Chaumont in Monsieur l'Abbé, which was even moral and idyllic, so that I would have spared some decency to have had Céline twenty years younger. She was never too delicate, but her style was better suited to twenty than to forty years old.[5] Ah, but I am positively overcome with occupation! How tired you must be of hearing about me; but what and how then! Since I have spoken to not a being except Mrs Gussy Jay! what do you want? shall I send you observations on the weather,—which, by the way, is now charming? I can make an abstract of my documents or the bill of fare; but otherwise I must talk of my excessively familiar self.

Midnight. Nitouche was charming and made me happy. Only I wish you had been with me, and we had taken a bit of supper afterwards, like other good people, at the Maison d'Or.

Saturday, 19 Dec. Decidedly I am made for solitude. Happiness will be my lot, after all; for I've seen not a known face for two days, and yet feel like a gaudy boy. And *so* busy! Your twenty-five volumes of plays are already on their way to you, in a big box of books addressed to Willy Phillips, which should reach Washington in time if so please Brahma and the New York custom-house; for they go to Georgetown, and New York never hurries to benefit rivals. Then I am rushing through archives by the ton, and so, by the bye, is Paul Ford, Dwight's *bête noir,* who is having archives copied by the mile, and seems to mean to do what I mean to do. One or the other will be sad, and it will not be maw-même, as Charles Sumner used to say; for I don't care, but probably he does. Then pretty nearly all my teeth are in a manner taken to the shop to be repaired, and I hope they will come back some day wagging their tails behind them. I feel proud, like a man-of-war that has cruised three years and gone into dock for repairs. As for my shoulder, I cannot detect even a scar. You could not find my double-head if you tried. In short, I am rushing like a November meteor through the frosty air—for it has turned sharp cold now;—but this is mere trifling, and I must be serious. Last evening at seven o'clock I found at the office your letter of the 8th, three days earlier than I had expected a letter, which was smart of you, and gave me a certain respect for your good sense, as my brother Brooks might say. I tucked the letter into my pocket with as much care as though it were a big diamond for my white necktie, and then I walked out into the world, and along the Rue de la Paix and up the Boulevards—all the way thinking what a pleasant evening I was going to have with the letter en tete-à-tête—until I came to the Passage des Princes—do you know where it is? up next the Rue Richelieu?—and there I turned into a bijou restaurant, and sat down in a bright corner on a blue velvet sofa, and eat my bouillabaisse as though I were Thackeray, who, poor devil, had not begun to reach my age, and had not half as pretty a letter to keep him company—not even if Mrs Brookfield did write it.[6] The bouillabaise was very good, and the partridge was not bad, and the Bordeaux was fair though they always will serve it too cold; but the letter was charming society, for I could speculate all through my dinner what was in it; which is more than one need do with most good society. Then the garsoon brought me some coffee and a cigar; and I opened the letter.

You liked the ring—truly? I hope so, for I wanted it to please you, and the setting was my own, after an old pattern. I thought the stone became quite tender and moony under the influence of the pearls, and looked as though it were not at all out of conceit of its own charms. Martha's pin I care less about, because it is Phillips's doing, but I was anxious that the ring should please, because it was my responsibility. Now, if the plays suit you I shall be at ease, for I have no fear about the picture. Turners can take care of themselves. I read the letter, and then I read it over again, and then I smiled all by myself. So Brooks calls his wife idiot from hell, does he? Brooks is a lad of great natural discernment and affection, and yet he is not always so happy as that. Upon my word, something is in it. Womankind is impayable. Now, you! just look at it! In one letter you talk about marriage with bitterness such as I never use about anything,—for I am not bitter, only just bruised and scared till I daren't lift my head,—and in your next you say that I ought to marry, for it might take some of the bitterness out of *my* veins—mine, when for years I have defended marriage vehemently against your cruel denunciations. Ah, well! You know better, and are only making a little fun of my sentimentality; but all the same it is a true feminine inversion of roles. I am past marriage, more's the pity! I would not marry now—no! not even you—if I could. Is that a fair return for your scratch? Only with me, as you know, when I say this, I mean that life has for me no more interest or meaning; and never had any except in marriage.

Having smiled and finished my cigar, I walked on to the Gymnase and saw Mon Oncle Barbassou; the first act, as usual, and even the second, quite amusing, but draggy in the last half.[7] As usual, too, a droll commentary on marriage. Like you, these French fins de siècle can't get on with it, and can't get on without it—in fact are as *bêtes* as I am on the subject.

December 23. Hang the dentistry! it is infernal and every day grows worse. I am now repenting my toothache of a year ago, in Samoa. You don't remember it, but the sufferer never forgets that kind of debauch. To think that one feels remorse for wickedness and not for toothache! How absurd a thing morality and conscience are. No vice could hurt so much as teeth do, but one never treats toothache and seasickness as a subject for moral lessons. They don't affect one's social position. I wish I could send you news, but I have not exchanged a word with a cat. I live like an anchorite on truffles and champagne, without seeing a human reptile. This is not my fault. I have called on everyone I could think of, including Lord Vernon, and all were away.[8] This moment I am astounded at receiving an invitation to dinner on Sunday from Mrs Gussy Jay. I have accepted it. The truth is, I have exhausted the theatres, and my evenings have become dreary. By the bye, I saw Nos Intimes at last. Jane Hading was good, but the role is not a happy one. I am sorry we did not see the play together; it is highly moral and domestic; another example of the French appreciation of marriage. Read it![9] You will find it among my French plays, though I used to prefer the Faux Bonshommes.[10] Sunday afternoon I went to the Chatelet Concert, and sat near where we sat together two months ago, and heard Beethoven's Ninth Sinfony as we then heard the first;—eight weeks, is it? Rien que ça! Then I went to the Ambigu and saw the chief lover strangle the heroine on the stage, and toss her body about, with its admirably naturel look of strangulation on the face.[11] It was very improving, and like all these French plays, it was wholly to show how much better virtue and marriage are than vice and cocotterie. I was quite convinced by the demonstration. The French are very droll. They all stand at the street-corners and howl that man is a sordid brute; that life is a vile orgy; and that the universe is a stupid cloud of dust; and they tell how hopeless they are and how wretched; and not one of them ever had the sense to prove it by holding his tongue, which they would certainly all do if they suffered as much as they pretend. Instead, they write pessimism for a living, and call it art, or paint it, which is worse. Do you know your Musset? He began it. Read the Letter to Lamartine! "C'était dans une rue étroite et tortueuse."[12] I daren't say, read Rolla, for Rolla is vicious.[13] I have read neither for thirty years, and now they seem to me like childs'-play; but Zola and Maupassant are only more brutal, not more mature.[14] I am going through a regular study of the whole, and feel as though the drollest experience of modern history were that all these people should—like Victor Hugo, Lamartine and Leconte de l'Isle—take themselves au sérieux.[15]

Christmas Eve. I have dined at the antique Lion d'Or with only some Champagne of '74 to keep me company, and the idea of how pleasant it would be if you were of the party; but it would be hard on you. Tomorrow this monologue must go to the post. À revoir bientôt!

MS: MHi

1. The fable of the country bumpkin in Horace, *Epistles,* I, 2.

2. *L'Amoureuse* (1891) by Georges de Porto-Riche concerns a neglected wife who takes a lover though she still loves her husband.

3. Jules Lemaître (1853–1914), literary critic, *Impressions de théâtre* (1888–1898), *Les Contemporains* (1886–1899).

4. *Mam'selle Nitouche* (1883) by Henri Meilhac and Albert Millaud.

5. Céline Chaumont (1848–1926) played the part of a prudish mother-in-law in the comedy *Monsieur l'Abbé* (1891) by Henri Meilhac and Albert de Saint-Albin.

6. Thackeray was a gastronome and wrote on Parisian cuisine in his "Memorials of Gourmandizing." He died at the age of 52 (HA was 53 at this time). His letters to

Jane Octavia Elton (Mrs. William Henry) Brookfield (1821–1896), to whom he had been deeply attached, were published by her in 1887.

7. *Mon Oncle Barbassou* (1891), adapted by Emile Blavet and Fabrice Carré from a novel by Mario Uchard.

8. George William Henry (1854–1898), 7th Baron Vernon, was married to Frances Margaret Lawrence (d. 1940) of New York.

9. Jane Hading (1859–1934) in *Nos Intimes* (1861), by Victorien Sardou.

10. *Les Faux Bonshommes* (1856) by Théodore Barrière and Ernest Capendu.

11. *L'Auberge des mariniers* (1891) by Emile Moreau.

12. "C'était dans une rue obscure et tortueuse / De cet immense égout qu'on appelle Paris" (It was in a dark and crooked street / Of this huge sewer they call Paris); Alfred de Musset, "Lettre à M. de Lamartine" (1836).

13. In Musset's poem "Rolla" (1833) the loss of religious faith, attributed to Voltaire's teachings, leads to debauchery and prostitution.

14. Emile Zola and Guy de Maupassant (1850–1893), identified with literary naturalism, were at the height of their careers.

15. Victor Hugo (1802–1885), Alphonse de Lamartine (1790–1869), and Charles Leconte de Lisle (1818–1894), poets of the Romantic and Parnassian movements.

To Marian Fell

Paris. Dec. 15. [1891]

My lovely little Marian[1]

Your beautiful letter reached me today. I wish I could come to you at Christmas, for I am all alone in this great city, and have no little girl to speak to; but I am so far away from you that if I started now, and traveled as hard as I could, I am afraid I could not get to you in time. I hope that this letter may manage to go so fast that you will get it at Christmas, so that you will know how sorry I am to be so far.

You write so much better than I do that I am almost ashamed to have you see my letter but now that you write so well, you will often sit down and write to me. I want to know what you are doing, and what you play, and who you play with. You know that your mamma cannot write such letters as you do, or make such nice pictures, so she is afraid to write to me.

Perhaps some day I shall come home to see you. I meant to have gone to China to see the people who wear their hair braided in pigtails, as little girls sometimes wear theirs, but they say I must not go to China, and so I do not know where to go. If I come home you must be very kind to me. I will tell you about all the places I have been at, and the queer people I have seen, and the sharks and the monkeys and the parrots, and you shall tell me all that you have seen.

I am so far away that all I can send you for Christmas is my love. Good bye. Dont forget to write to me again.

Henry Adams.

MS: MHi

1. HA inscribed this letter in block capital letters.

To William Hallett Phillips

Paris, 20 December, 1891.

My brave Barbarian

Behold, I send you another box of books, and a big one. Do me the sublime favor to rescue it from the maw of the custom-house. I believe it is free of duty, being not only in foreign tongue, but instruments of my trade, and I being an American artisan temporarily residing abroad. Nevertheless, if the Honorable sir Mac Kinlé should insist upon taking toll on my poor tools in order to support the orgies of Benjamin Harrison and J. G. Blaine, even pay what is required, as you have done heretofore, and suffer in silence, for man is born to suffer.[1] Let the box be taken to my house, and opened. On the top you will find a small volume for yourself; the Daphnis and Chloé of Longinus in its old French costume; a book which I love for its illustrations; but, for the sake of your social dignity, do not show it to any female without explaining in advance the meaning which the engraver attached to his last plate.[2] In fact, you had better not call indiscriminate attention to the book anyway.

Among the contents of the chest, please pick out twentyfive volumes of French plays bound in various colors, and tell William to take them over to Mrs Cameron to whom they belong.

The rest is rubbish of my own which William can carry up stairs and deposit on the floor of my bed-room, or anywhere else out of the way.

As you see, I am in Paris which is not exactly the South Seas, though a good deal more solitary. I am patching up my carcase which has somewhat gone to pieces in the Gardens of Eden where dentists are unknown. If I were five-and-twenty years younger, Paris would amuse me; in fact, it did. As I am five-and-twenty years older, and know not a human imbecile here, I am but moderately entertained. In fact, I should be much better off at home or in Central Asia or for that matter in Central America; but I am tied here for three weeks more, and then I must return to England for a space, when I shall decide what to do next. The world is my oyster, no doubt; but I have already opened it and eaten so much of it that the rest is not so fresh as it was, and I am somewhat troubled by its smell. Especially here in Paris, I should say, it is very far gone.

All the same, I work hard to improve my mind, for my morals are already educated. I shall soon be thoroughly saturated with all that is best in French decadence, especially the farces which leave little or nothing to be desired in the way of morality and art. The last show is a rape and abortion to be performed on the stage at the Theatre Libre.[3]

Thanks to your savage virtues, you are safe from such civilised blessings. Pity my lapse of virtue.

Ever Yrs   Henry Adams.

MS: MH
1. William McKinley (1843–1901) of Ohio, Republican representative 1876–1891, sponsor of the high protective tariff bill passed in 1890. He was governor-elect of Ohio.
2. Evidently the reference is to Longus' *Daphnis and Chloe* as translated by Jacques Amyot in 1559, but which illustrated edition is not apparent.
3. The sexual performance, which resulted in the arrest of the director and the closing of the theater, was at the Théâtre Réaliste, not at André Antoine's Théâtre Libre.

To John Hay

Paris, 21 December, 1891.

Mon Cher

I expect a letter from you soon. That is the reason why I select this vast canvas of paper. I wish to do honor to the letter which ought to be entering my republic. Also I have nothing to do this evening. I have been here a week, which has just served to exhaust all the theatres, and the night is so cold that I shiver at the idea of beginning on the Cafés Chantants. For the first time in my life I am in Paris without society of any kind, as solitary as the sun or the moon. I converse with no one but my dentist and my bookseller, and when I am not squirming in the dentist's chair, I am burrowing on the archives of the Ministère des Affaires Etrangères, discovering blunders that adorn my history. Would that you were here! You would be bored to extinction, which would make you excellent company for me.

Naturally, with such inducements, I have taken arduously to improving my mind, and to picking up the lost pieces of broken crockery scattered over twenty neglected years of French manufacture. As yet, the painting and the sculpture have made me only sea-sick; with all the good-will in the world I have not been able to face the terrors of French art, but I will still try, mon ami,—I will try. In the theatre I have done better. To be sure, the theatre is weaker than I ever knew it before, and I am, I find, a severer critic than one should be; but I have got pleasure out of Réjane, and I find Jane Hading fairly satisfactory. The Palais Royal and the Variétes are very amusing—almost as much so as they used to be. Generally the acting averages well, but I am pained to see that no distinctly first-rate actor or actress is on the stage, and as yet nothing approaching a first-rate new play has met my anxious eyes. At the Français—a theatre which irritates my sensitive nerves—I have seen the old Monde où l'on S'ennuie, and was considerably overcome at finding that, with all its wit, it impressed me as being saved from failure only by the visible efforts of the actors; its intrigue is excessively commonplace, and it hangs together very loosely.[1] At the Vaudeville I have seen the reprise of Nos Intimes, and felt to the full extent the admitted weakness of its last Act. At the Variétés, the Cigale and Nitouche were delightful, but there too the last Acts were not good enough for the first. All these plays are reprises, and some of them from a long way back. The new plays are faulty the other way; they are better constructed; the climax is well worked up, and the last Act is the strongest; but, oh, my blessed virgin, what situations! Nothing so revolting and horrible ought to be allowed to be seen. I have not been to the Théatre Libre, where I observe by the Figaro that a rape and abortion are to be given on the stage at an approaching performance, but I would as lieve see either or both as see some of the situations I have seen. At the same time I am not so much impressed by indecency as I expected; in fact it seems to me no worse than in old times.

Curiously enough the thing that pleases me most in Paris is the newspapers. Think of that! I can read them. They are uncommonly well written, especially the feuilletons which seem to me better than ever. Jules Lemaitre is delightful. Anatole France is always good. Sarcey you know of old.[2] I kept his yesterday's comments on Ibsen, thinking that I would send them to you, as they seemed to express our views with excellent fooling; but I don't know;—shall I, or shall I not? These things hardly keep their aroma through a sea-voyage. I know of nothing else to send, unless it is Jules Lemaitre's last volume of causeries. Books by the score are poured out, but Maupassant and Loti are the fashions of the day, and you know them both. I am keeping the Goncourt's journal for my next long voyage.[3]

The Opéra here strikes me as poor both at the Grand and the Comique. I have endured Ambroise Thomas until flesh, to ignore blood entirely, rebelled. Lohengrin is better, but that damned swan bores one at last; and why should we not at least have Wagner in some less familiar form! Melba I heard only in Hamlet which is an intolerably commonplace opera.[4] On the other hand Paris is immensely strong in concerts, and on Sunday one can choose between three big orchestras of the first class, all playing Beethoven, Wagner and Berlioz, and all crowded with audiences so respectable that Boston is fin de siècle compared with them.

As for the restaurants—well! I am shaving fiftyfour and things don't taste as they used to do. Perhaps the Café Anglais is as good as ever; but I should say that the cuisine had fallen off. Not but what it is good; only it wants go. I have made superhuman efforts to try all the restaurants far up the boulevards, where foreigners are unknown, and I much prefer them; but the cuisine is the same old story, or even more so. I prefer Delmonico.

December 25. Forgive me! it was not a rape; it was a "prise de possession." I enclose an account of it in this morning's paper.

I can tell you nothing of the world of society. I have seen absolutely no one. The last time I went to the Legation, I was told that the minister was about to depart for Spain. I did not see him because he was not at the office. I did see Gussy Jay; also I called on his wife. This represents my whole acquaintance. If anyone else is here whom I ought to call upon, I do not know it. I trust that whenever you come here to educate Helen and Alice, you will find society such as the world elsewhere cannot offer. For my own part, Apia and Papeete were socially gay compared with Paris.

I have an idea for the amusement of our future lives. Let us get possession of an evening newspaper, and write alternate feuilletons once a week. I think I could do it for a time with some enjoyment, if I were exempted from writing under my own name. If we were indecent enough, we could always make a success, and French literature would supply us with indecencies to perpetuity. Reflect on this! I am sure it has possibilities.

No letter from you. Gredin, va! While you are butterflying in the salons of Washington, I am grubbing in the desolation of Paris, and you do not give me a thought. If you have nothing to say, why not say it? À revoir! My love to all yours.

Ever   Henry Adams.

MS: RPB
  1. *Le Monde où l'on s'ennuie* (1881) by Edouard Pailleron.
  2. Lemaître, drama critic for the *Journal des Débats;* Anatole France (1844–1924), fortnightly columnist and literary editor of *Le Temps;* Francisque Sarcey (1827–1899), drama critic for *Le Temps.*
  3. The *Journal* of the brothers Edmond and Jules de Goncourt (1822–1896; 1830–1870) was being selectively published in nine volumes, 1887–1896.
  4. Charles Ambroise Thomas (1811–1896), composer of *Mignon* (1866), a staple of the Opéra Comique repertory, and of *Hamlet* (1868). *Lohengrin* (1850), by Richard Wagner, was new to Paris; it was first performed there Sept. 16, 1891. Nellie Melba was the stage name of Helen Porter Mitchell Armstrong (1859–1931), Australian soprano.

To Lucy Baxter

Paris, 22 Dec. 1891.

My dear Miss Baxter

I expected a letter from you today at the latest, and am rather uneasy at not receiving it, from fear that you may be ill. For some reason Polly Hooper has not written lately, and I feel cut off from my Boston correspondents, but as far as concerns the Hoopers I am not anxious because Edward wrote to me at Thanksgiving. Of you I have no news since a long time— October, I think, for I have lost or mislaid the last. My own last letter to you was more than a month ago if I recollect right, from Scotland. I shall not be quite at ease till I hear from you.

Of myself I have little more to say than that I have been occupied in doing what I came back for; that is, in getting myself patched up for my next movements. I came over to Paris ten days ago and have been devoted to my dentist for a week. Dentistry is never one of the exuberant joys of life, and I am far from recommending it as an amusement of travel; but even at my age I am unwilling to have false teeth or to go toothless, so I bear the martyrdom with heroism. I expect to be free in time, and to return to England about Jan. 10. Then I must decide what next.

My great difficulty is the being entirely alone which seems a serious obstacle to any considerable journey, such as India or central Asia, between which I must choose if I am to start again. Even in Paris I am in absolute solitude. For the first time in my life I am here without a companion, and for a week I have not exchanged a word with anyone except the people at the Legation. This is dull. Yet I do not greatly object to solitude in Paris for a time. I have many years of arrears to pick up; a vast amount of reading to do; all the theatres to exhaust; and a good deal of reading of archives, to ascertain how many blunders I have foisted into history. Paris is an interesting place, and I am quite as much alive to its interest now as I was thirty years ago. Even the restaurants entertain me, and if I had anyone to show me what I want to see, I should wish no better than to be here.

At the same time Paris is by no means at its best. In fact even I, who have fallen into a stupid way of regarding myself as quite dead and beyond human interest, am youthful and buoyant in many ways, compared with the life of Paris. For the last thirty or forty years,—in fact, since the time of Alfred de Musset—the intellectual tone of Paris has gone from one stage of despondency to another, until now it is fairly impossible. They have adopted the phrase *fin de siècle* to describe the time; or occasionally *décadance;* and nothing interests me so much as to see how the best writers—like Renan, Jules Lemaitre, and the feuilletonistes in general,—struggle with it and yield to it.[1] The outbursts of rebellion against this pessimism are innumerable, in the church, among the young, in the press, at the theatres; but it gains power steadily, and has made tremendous headway in the last ten years. In fact it now controls pretty nearly all the art of France,—the literature and painting,—and I find nothing free from it except the music. As yet Beethoven, Berlioz and Wagner are supreme here, and, every Sunday, three great orchestras give classical concerts to crowded audiences. Last Sunday I heard Beethoven's Ninth Sinfony with the choruses, some three hundred performers, vocal and instrumental. Luckily the French are very slow to adopt new ideas in music, but the décadance will come there too, and the impressionist in music will be something unutterable.

At the same time I find something very droll and French in the naïveté with which all these poets, novelists and painters are showing their genius in describing how unutterably bad and hopeless the world is, and especially how vile and brutal human nature is. Overwhelming despair is the substance of all their art, and yet everyone knows that the mark of real despair and deepest sense of abandonment is silence. One who is thoroughly knocked on the head has nothing to say. He is only too glad to lie still. These French pessimists howl their despair on every possible street corner, and if they cannot make money by it, they make or try to make notoriety which they like rather better. They have not got anywhere near the stage of real pessimism, and as long as they turn it into what they call poetry, or tell it in novels and stories, they are quite safe. On the whole I suspect that

America will reach real pessimism sooner than France will. The Americans are melancholy by nature.

As no new books or plays or pictures of any consequence have lately been produced, I have had time to catch up to some extent with the older works of the last twenty years; but it is a pity that so few of them are possible for women to read or enjoy. The Frenchman is apt to be either a saint or a brute, and both are unsuited to our modes of thought. I make much more violent efforts to swallow French literature and art than I ever had to make to swallow Polynesian raw fish, but, do what I will, the gorge rises. The Frenchman frankly says he is a beast, and so he is.

This is rather a literary essay, but naturally I cant go into particulars. On the whole, I prefer my South Sea Islanders, who at least never made a parade of brutality, but were simple in wickedness, which deprived it of half its vice. I shall soon tire of the show, which, in truth, is not refreshing. I wish I could find one spot in the world where one could frankly enjoy.

Write soon.

Ever affely Yrs   Henry Adams.

MS: ScU

1. Ernest Renan (1823–1892), historian of the origins of Christianity, lost his chair at the Collège de France because his *Vie de Jésus* (1863) rejected the claim of divinity. *Feuilles détachées* (1891) reaffirmed his scientific skepticism and vaguely evolutionary piety.

To Elizabeth Cameron

Paris, Monday, 28 December, 1891.

Coming back as usual at four o'clock from my afternoon séance with the associates of Robespierre and Barrère, I find on my table a petit bleu from Hottinguer containing Martha's Christmas telegram, which is vastly better literature than anything in French, not even excepting Racine, unless you insist on it. I will not reply by the same channel because I send quite enough letters and things to you without calling extra attention by telegraph; so Martha must wait three weeks to learn that her wishes for my Merry Christmas resulted in a warm rainy day, during which I sat before the fire and read, barely looking out of my window from hour to hour to see whether the files of spindle-trees in the Tuileries Gardens were dripping, and whether the top of the Eiffel tower were in the clouds.[1] At eight o'clock, I wandered up to the Café Anglais, which was totally empty, and so sepulcral and dreary that I caught cold over my modest pint of Champagne; and then came back to my big white-and-gold saloon to devour more French literature. On the whole, the Christmas was not bad—for Christmas. Saturday was lovely and springlike, so to enjoy it I went to hear Melba sing Marguerite, and was less exasperated than usual in that high temple of bad art.[2] Sunday afternoon I went to the Conservatoire, and heard at last a part of Berlioz's Faust. Somehow, I was a little disappointed, which annoyed me, because I dislike to feel myself judging what is good; I try to judge only what is not good; towards the real artists I take no attitude except that of staying quiet on my knees, as I do before Shakespeare and Rembrandt and George Washington and you. After walking back from the Boulevard Poissonnière through an interminable throng of sight-seeing Parisians, I went to dine with the Gussy Jays, where I met Mrs Griswold Gray, and Mr & Mrs Teddy Wharton. Enfin! but after a month of talking to oneself, one does not object to talking to some one else. Mrs Wharton surprised me by her knowledge, especially of Paris on the literary and artistic side; she is very intelligent, and of course looks as fragile as a dandelion in seed; an American product almost as sad to me as M. Puvis de Chavannes.[3] The talk was mostly about Americans in Paris, of whom the number seems sufficient, but among them none that are likely to take pleasure in my acquaintance or to seek it. Evidently solitude is my lot.

29 December. Midnight. This afternoon a letter from John Hay, dolorous with deaths and sicknesses and disappointments.[4] I felt quite as though I were the spoiled child of destiny that you and King and sister Anne and all the family should be going to funerals and having illness, and suffer from all the ills of life, while I have only to snuffle and ache in the peaceful solitude of the Hotel Continental, and have a dentist to keep me lively, and a chronic consciousness of being dead without the merit of keeping quiet. So to change the atmosphere I went down to the table-d'hôte, which is ghastly but quick; and hurried off to the Opéra Comique to perform an act of piety to the memory of my revered grandfather. Some people might think it a queer place for the purpose, and the association of ideas may not be obvious even to you, but it is simple. A century ago, more or less, Grétry produced his opera: Richard Coeur de Lion.[5] A century ago, more or less, President Washington sent my grandfather, before he was thirty years old, as minister to the Hague, and my grandfather was fond of music to such an extent that, if I remember right, he tried to play the flute. Anyway he was so much attached to Grétry's music that when he was turned out of the Presidency he could think of nothing, for days together, but "Oh, Richard! oh, mon roy, l'univers t'abandonne"; and as I had never heard the opera, I thought I would see it now that it has been revived at the Opéra Comique. Nothing more delightfully rococo and simple could well be, than the music of Grétry. To think that it was fin de siècle too—and shows it in the words—and led directly into the French Revolution. I tried to imagine myself as I was then—and you know what an awfully handsome young fellow Copley made me—with full dress and powdered hair, talking to Mme Chose in the boxes, and stopping to applaud "Un regard de ma belle."[6] Unluckily the Opera Comique which used to be the cheerfullest theatre in Paris, is now to me the dreariest, and poor Richard howled mournfully as though time had troubled him. Unluckily for me, too, the next piece was the Lakmé by Delibes, modern enough, no doubt;[7] but if I abhor the French more in one genre than in another, and find their fatuity more out of place in any other part of the world than in that where I happen to be, my abomination of them is greatest when they try to escape from themselves, and especially when they become oriental. I forgive them for making me wring my teeth with despair at their Greeks and Romans, their English and Americans; but I cannot stand them when they get south of Marseilles and the Suez Canal. After sitting through a bayadère dance that ground me into the dust, I came away with the last verse in my ears: "Dieu protège nos amours!" As far as I can see, this is all God has to do in Paris anyhow.

New Years Day. 1892. One word of Happy New Year to Martha. I hunger and thirst to have her with me, for, though I am duly impressed with the happy destiny which has showered on me all those blessings that you congratulate me for possessing, occasionally I cannot help so far feeling a lack of something,—say a cat or a dog or a monkey, and Martha might serve for any of them—as to wish that some of my blessings were convertible into others that would amuse me. So wish her a Happy New Year, and tell her that the Champs Elizzie look very natural; at least I suppose so, though I never go there now. In fact I go nowhere, for I have a vile cold, and yesterday was so shaky and achy that after dragging myself to the dentist's and back, I lay before a fire and lived on quinine and bouillon all day. The régime suited me, for I woke this morning much better, but have ventured out for only half an hour. Swine that I am, I blush to think that I owe this infliction to drinking Champagne, which always poisons me; and I drank it—yes, I did—like a wicked, wicked profligate, only for the sake of a little exhileration from the fiz. I am happy to think that all of you too have your colds and megrims, and this is all I have to tell you.

4 January. Drat the cold; it hangs on like despair. I thought it done and gone, and then I felt so weak that I had to take once more to a diet of quinine and bouillon, and there I am today. Curious! I find that any little illness now makes me feel weak. Is it years—or virtues? I hope it's not grippe, at all events, for in that case I should be hard pressed to get off by the 3d. Luckily I have exhausted all the Paris I can do single-handed, and can devote myself conscientiously to reading. I call it a poor day when I don't finish at least one volume. Imagine my state of happiness, surrounded by a pile of yellow literature, skimming a volume of Goncourt, swallowing a volume of Maupassant with my roast, and wondering that I feel unwell afterwards. These writers have at least the merit of explaining to me why I dislike the French, and why the French are proper subjects for dislike. Even I, who do not love the French, and who, as you know, have never been able even to swallow my friends' Frenchmen, should hesitate to believe that human nature, except in the Solomon Islands, could be quite so mean and monkey-like in its intellectual cruelty as the naturalists and realists describe their fellow-countrymen to be, unless I read every day in the police-reports the proof that they do not exaggerate. At every interval of years I come back here with a wider experience of men and knowledge of races, and always the impression becomes stronger that, of all people in the world, the French are the most gratuitously wicked. They almost do me good. I feel it a gain to have an object of dislike. At least that is real, and I can kick it. Next to having an object to like, I am duly grateful for having an object to detest.

Still no letter from you! I suppose your New York deranged it. Will it come tomorrow? After answering this one, you will, I hope, have no more letters to write.

Just now the errand-boy comes in with a letter,—not from you. My sister Anne writes on the 18th, and her letter has taken seventeen days to reach me.

5 January. Here you are, your Christmas letter! Just as I supposed! I knew exactly what was in it. Apparently I have lost no gaiety by remaining in hospital here for the last two months. You do not wear aureoles of joyfulness on your side, much. I am sorry. I wish I were there. I feel sometimes as though, when people are in trouble, I can do something; I know what they want; and the more trouble they are in, the more I know of it. With the contented ones, I have always to act a little, and two or three hours tire me; but I can always be natural with people who suffer. Allons! Four weeks from tomorrow I should be starting, and glad I am, for never before in my life have I passed a month of perfect solitude; and although I am greatly pleased to have succeeded in doing it, and not to have gone mad and cut my throat, as Guy de Maupassant has just done,[8] yet I have reached the point where the sound of my own voice startles me, and I seem to be suffocating for want of sound of other people's voices. A diet of quinine, too, lacks succulence. I lost my appetite weeks ago, from eating alone, which is always fatal to me, but I never bargained for supplying the place of mutton with quinine. I think the cold is going off, but I cannot do without the quinine which gives me nerves to be tortured by the dentist. Another five days, and I trust to be back in London; and, Oh! Lucifer son of the Morning![9] if I could only express the extravagance of my intensity of hatred for this good city of Paris!

January 7. Tomorrow is my mail-day, so I have not much more to say. My cold is decidedly better, I should say, well; but I am still very careful, leave my room very little, never go out at night, and stick to quinine. The idea of illness here in Paris is more than I can face. All my horizon is now limited to getting to London on Sunday, and every day that brings me nearer to it is a load off my mind. My search in the archives is finished. My dentist promises to release me—tant bien que mal—on Saturday; and although I have escaped better than I expected, you can imagine that I've had a parrot of a time. So tomorrow—Friday—I begin to get things into travelling shape. My heart leaps at the thought; for, in my journey of eighteen months round the world, among the remote and melancholy islands where I have been for four months at a time imprisoned, unable to escape, never have I felt anything like the effect of nightmare that I have got from four weeks in Paris. Talk about our American nerves! they are normal and healthy compared with the nerves of the French, which are more diseased than anything on earth except the simple Norwegian blondes of Mr Ibsen. In all Paris,—literature, theatre, art, people and cuisine—I have not yet seen one healthy new thing. Nothing simple, or simply felt, or healthy; all forced even in its effort to be simple—like Maupassant, the flower of young France,—all tormented, and all self-conscious. I'm sorry you got your clothes here; they must be bad. Hosannah! am I not just glad to think that in three days I shall be back among those poor drivelling idiots of English, who are stupid enough to be beasts in the field, and whose good old conventional ideas are as restful as Moses in the bulrushes; and that in six weeks I shall be back with you and Martha in the pays bleu where the rest of the world may be flat as a monthly magazine, and I not care an antipyrine.

January 8. I have just come in from paying bills and breakfasting with Whitelaw Reid, and now this letter must go. I am quite overcome by the unusual excitement of going into society. To be sure, the society consisted only of Whitelaw Reid and his wife, but he seemed the most agreeable of men, and she the most engaging of women. He talked all the time, and with the utmost openness about everything, and of course, to give an air of probability to the local color, Meredith Read came in.[10] At last Roustan was announced, and I fled. The chief subject of interest and discussion is always Mr Blaine. As Mr Blaine suits me quite as well as Mr Chose or any other subject, I find prodigious interest in expressing my opinion about his health and prospects. Be sure to have lots to tell me about him when I get home. I can't do without him. He's as active a conversational solvent as old man Gladstone in England.

Now I am going to set to work overhauling my trunks; tomorrow I have my last interview with my dentist; and Sunday I cross to London. My cold still hangs on, confound it! Ordinarily I should not mind it; but with the movements of the next month before me I want to be perfectly well. La Farge writes me that he and all his people have been ill for a fortnight with grippe. Over here it rages gaily too, though the winter has been very mild and much as it was when you left. The theatres are still imbecile; not a good play has been brought out, and the opera is worse and worse. I am reduced to playing solitaire again, when rendered desperate by reading. One might almost as well play solitaire in Washington.

MS: MHi
  1. The Eiffel Tower was the world's tallest structure.
  2. Melba was singing in Gounod's *Faust*.
  3. Pierre Puvis de Chavannes (1824–1898), best known for his delicate religious and allegorical murals.

4. May Hoyt, a cousin of Mrs. Cameron, had died, as had the fiancée of George Howland. Henry Cabot Lodge was confined with a bronchial infection. Clarence King had accepted the hospitality of HA's Washington house where he hoped in a few days to dash off an important addendum to his geological study of upheaval and subsidence, but he found that the research on geothermal topography which he had instituted at the Geological Survey did not confirm his theory of subterranean fusion.

5. André Grétry (1741–1813), *Richard Coeur de Lion* (1784).

6. The oval portrait of JQA at age 28, by John Singleton Copley (1738–1815), was painted in 1796 and was much liked by the Adams family. CFA2 currently owned it; it is now at the Museum of Fine Arts, Boston.

7. Léo Delibes (1836–1891).

8. Maupassant, in an advanced stage of syphilis, attempted suicide Jan. 1.

9. Isaiah 14:12.

10 John Meredith Read (1837–1896), after ten years in the U.S. foreign service, had lived in Paris since 1879.

To Charles Milnes Gaskell

Hotel Continental Paris, 31 Dec. 1891.

Dear Carlo

If things go by the clock, I should reach London in ten days, say Sunday 10th, and go into lodgings at 38 Clarges Street where my young friend Anderson, our second Secretary, has rooms. This will make it necessary for me to have a club. The St James's would be as good as any, I suppose. Can you get me an invitation there, or, for that matter to any other respectable haunt?

This week I am shut up with a vile cold, as everyone else is. It hangs on like any other vice, but is much more unpleasant than any ordinary wickedness.

My stay in England will be a short one, probably not much beyond the month of January.

Give my regards to miladi and the children. I fear that, if I get to Thornes at all, it will not be till the last week in January, so I may not see the Eton daisy.

Ever Yrs   Henry Adams.

MS: MHi

To John Hay

Paris, 9 Jan. 1892

My dear John

On this last night of my imprisonment "dans cet immense égout qu'on appelle Paris," my suppressed rage feels the necessity of explosion.[1] I will come home, and immediately, if you will join me in writing, under any assumed name or character you please, a volume or two of Travels which will permit me to express my opinion of life in general, and especially of the French, their literature and their art. I wont do it alone. Such a book, to be amusing needs variety of treatment and experience. The world is too big for one—or even for two. If King could be induced to join, so much the better; but I would do it with you alone, and put into it all the vinegar, pepper and vitriol necessary to make it a success of scandal if nothing else. I am fairly tired—bored beyond endurance—by the world we live in, and its ideals, and am ready to say so, not violently, but kindly, as one rubs salt into the back of a flogged sailor, as though one loved him.

I have said and stick to it, that I will never again appear as an author, but I don't mind writing anonymously as one does in the newspapers, and Travels that say anything are nowadays read. Of course I should not touch the South Seas; I could not without betraying myself. We could start with San Francisco and go through America to England and France, which is a big mouthful enough.

If you want me to come home, try this experiment, which is only our old scheme revived and enlarged.

Without some such occupation I can't hold out long anywhere; and the occupation must be joint, in order to keep me going. My notion of Travels is a sort of ragbag of everything; scenery, psychology, history, literature, poetry, art; anything in short, that is worth throwing in; and I want to grill a few literary and political gentlemen to serve with champagne.

London. Monday, 11th. The comforts of European travel in winter fill me with admiration for America. Yesterday I came over from Paris. Being still off my correct form, with a cough and general poorness of condition, I felt the effort more than usual. Actually thirty years ago I did the same thing without a sign of change. The Calais steamer is now somewhat larger than then; otherwise, not a shadow of improvement or alteration. Wedged into the old compartment with the old crowd, shivering over cold foot-warmers of the last century, I got to Calais, with nothing to eat, and went on the steamer in an icy fog that froze my back-bone. I shook with cold. Seizing a stateroom and shutting myself up, I wrapped every coat and rug I had, or could find, round me, and lay down under a heap, and rang for hot tea. Slowly I recovered warmth enough not to shiver, but was too cold to sleep. Yet surely a steamer might be warmed. At Dover again the old English compartment with its foot-warmer, freezing; and at Charing Cross half an hour of custom-house in a chill like salted ice. Everything on this main mail route was identical with what it was when I first knew it, except that the terminus was then at London Bridge. I can understand that their art should be bad and their literature rotten and their tastes mean, but why the deuce they should inflict on themselves cold and hunger and discomfort, hang me if I can understand. Actually, in Europe I see no progress—none! They have the electric light, voilà tout!

This is the end! If nothing more has been done in these last thirty years, that have produced our Atlantic steamers and our railway system in America, nothing more need be expected from Europe. The people are stupid. They grow stupider and coarser as their aristocracies disappear. They have no longer even the refinement of manners and tastes of their old society.

Then, I have arrived. The end is here, and I have seen all there will be to show. One can't mistake a drift of thirty years. I am furious and astonished, like a bull that has butted a brick wall, and reflects.

13th   London is lovely; just a rich brown tone, and nothing else. Occasionally a red ball glows in the southern sky, and once or twice has cast a shadow. I thrive in it, and have already recovered my appetite and wax fat. As for people, I know little indeed. I sat with Harry James an hour or two yesterday afternoon, and found him in double trouble between the death of his friend Balestier and the steady decline of his sister.[2] Everyone is still out of town. Everyone has influenza, or has had it, or expects to have it. As yet I've not discovered a single English acquaintance, and shall have to begin laboriously knocking at doors from street to street to ask where everyone is. Did I tell you that my last act in Paris was to breakfast with Whitelaw Reid. I liked his wife; she seemed very simple and sympathetic.[3] Whitelaw drank white wine, and in consequence talked like three Frenchmen. He was extremely civil and cordial, had much to say about you, and generally seemed to me greatly improved, with the air of one who has arrived, and need bother no more to be long-haired.

Lincoln is in bed with influenza, and when I went to the office yesterday, White had gone off to nurse him. The Whites are still in the country.[4]

Larz Anderson and I are in the same house, in Clarges Street, and breakfast together, and go about dining at the various clubs and haunts of fashion. I have learned to drink Champagne and read Truth. No, that's a lie! I can't read Truth yet, but try and hope. Meanwhile I read Mr Blowitz and the Times, and feel a deep interest in Maupassant, whose mental condition in his healthiest state worried me greatly because he seemed totally unconscious whether he wrote excessively funny or excessively stupid things.[5]

A revoir bientôt! I want to visit Truxton at Teheran but can find no companion.[6]

Ever Yrs   Henry Adams.

MS: RPB

1. HA quotes from Musset's "Lettre à Lamartine" (see HA to Elizabeth Cameron, Dec. 13, 1891).

2. Charles Wolcott Balestier (1861–1891), American novelist and publisher based in London, contracted typhoid while visiting at Dresden and died Dec. 6. Alice James (1847–1892) died in London of cancer March 6.

3. Elisabeth Mills Reid (1858–1931), New York social leader and philanthropist, chiefly active in hospitals and the Red Cross.

4. Henry White and his wife Margaret Stuyvesant Rutherfurd White (d. 1916) had a country house in Berkshire.

5. There was extensive newspaper coverage of Maupassant's attempted suicide and his subsequent confinement to a hospital for the insane.

6. Truxtun Beale (1856–1936), brother of Emily Beale and Lafayette Square neighbor of HA, U.S. minister to Persia 1891–1892.

To Charles Milnes Gaskell

Monday, 11th. [Jan. 1892]

Dear Carlo

On arriving here last evening I found your letter and the club-invitations waiting me in the most punctual and satisfactory order. A thousand thanks!

I would I were a mouse, and could hybernate. Winter always was hateful to me, and has become more so since escaping it for a time. Winter and civilisation go together; they have no business in a happy home and contented mind.

I am torpid as a snake in the mud. My energies refuse to act. I don't know why I came here, or what to do next. I detest going out doors, and can't stay in. All this means only that my cold hangs on.

My regards to miladi.

Ever Yrs   Henry Adams.

38 Clarges St.

MS: MHi

To Elizabeth Cameron

London, Jan. 11, 1892.

Back again in England, shuddering at all the horrors of the last four weeks, and swearing frightful invocations of evil on myself if I ever do that again. The journey yesterday added a parting horror to France, and I shivered all the way to Calais in an iced transport of joy, varied by violent outbreaks of barking, at my escape. The channel was calm—so calm that I felt not a motion—and so cold, cold, cold, and iced fog, that I shut myself up in a private cabin and shook and shivered within half a dozen coats and blankets. Thirty years have not made a change in the discomforts of European travel; I should not have known, from anything but the electric light, that our war was over, and that I had ceased to belong to the London legation. The Frenchman and Englishman are just where they were thirty years ago, with a certain halo of vulgarity and commonness added to their stupidity. If they had taste! but what little taste they then had has vanished and vulgarised. Thank Christopher Columbus and George Washington who gave us a country where there was nothing to spoil and where man can play what antics he likes without disturbing the ghost of an artist. Well! I am here at last, in Clarges St, with three inches of thick mud everywhere, and Larz Anderson for a companion. After my long solitude I love him like the sun and moon and planets and Sirius on top of all. We shall dine at the club tonight, and I shall feel young like him, or he old like me. Tomorrow must begin work, for I have only three weeks left; and just think, after all, I have done neither Spain nor Holland, nor made the studies I intended here. I need a year for it, and shall have to return some day.

Friday, Jan. 15. Your letter of Jan. 5 arrived before breakfast, and now that breakfast is finished and Larz gone to see how his chief is, I sit down to read your news, which is at least harmless. Here we are influenzad out of all patience. No one talks of anything else, and now that it has on one day killed an heir apparent and a cardinal, the panic is at its height.[1] I would rather not have it just now, but, if I do, you will have to wait another fortnight or so before I get home, which will be well enough, since you will all be dancing like grasshoppers gay at that time, and I shall be superfluous. Life here is of the quietest. My cough is now pretty well gone but I have thought best to nurse it, and not go to balls much. So Larz and I have dined at some club every evening, and gone to bed at eleven o'clock. The régime suits us. I have recovered my appetite and cheerfulness, and rather enjoy the life. I have seen no one except Harry James and Alice Mason who has just arrived from Scotland and a tremendous struggle with influenza at Balburnie, and double pneumonia. The Gaskells do nothing but write and telegraph me to come to Yorkshire, but I am packing up your Turner to send it in advance so that I may not be bothered in the Custom House. Three big boxes will go in this way, so that I may have only my sea-trunk with me, and may pay duties properly to support President Harrison's riot. So I do not go to Yorkshire, and find London more attractive, though the clubs are solitary and the houses pestilential. After Paris it seems to glow with welcome. I've not seen Harry White who is always talking about my going to the country with him, but who persists in staying in the country, where I don't want to go. Lincoln is in bed. As for the myriad English-people whom one has known, or who have fed at one's table, I believe they must be dead, for I hear not even their names. As I have a rule of never calling on men if I can help it, but only on women, the range of my socialities is limited. I cannot hear of anyone whom I want to know, unless perhaps Arthur Balfour, nor do my friends speak of anyone new as counting for anything in their lives. So I am happy and contented to think that at all events I am not bored by Andrew Lang, and Gosse and Sydney Colvin, and the swarm of writers for magazines, and that I have not a fashionable acquaintance in the world.[2] Unless you are fashionable?—but that can't be, for if you were fashionable you would never write me such long and angelic letters.

Monday, Jan. 18. Gaskell came up on Saturday, and we have been knocking about town renewing our old acquaintances who are packed away into odd corners out of sight like broken bric-à-brac. None are fashionable; a few are respectable and well-to-do; some are struggling under the heels of the horses. We dined with May Lacaita, the daughter of our old uncle Sir Francis Doyle, a favorite cousin of ours, and still full of Irish charm. She declares she once sat next John Hay at a dinner at the Farrars, and he gave her a book. We sat an hour yesterday with Augusta Hervey who now gives music lessons; but is, I think, rather better off than her cousins the Bristols who are obliged to let Ickworth as well as the house in St James's Square, and live on husks in the dark. I have just come from an effort of piety—a call on old Thomson Hankey, my contemporary, now eightysix years old, with a memory gone to the bowwows, who succeeded at last in remembering my father, but still is hazy as to my identity, and persists in repeating that I am a professor at Harvard College. He was delighted at telling how he had buried all his contemporaries. I have also sat an hour with the Woolners, to bid them good-bye. Queer sensation, this coming to life again in a dead world. People are rather glad to see one; ask no questions; slide silently over all that has come between, as though all the ghosts were taking tea with us, and needed no introductions; and so we rattle on about today and tomorrow, with just a word thrown in from time to time to explain some chasm too broad to be jumped. I feel even deader than I did in the South Seas, but here I feel that all the others are as dead as I. Even Harry James, with whom I lunch Sundays, is only a figure in the same old wallpaper, and really pretends to belong to a world which is extinct as Queen Elizabeth. I enjoy it. Seriously, I have been amused, and have felt a sense of rest such as I have not known for seven years. These preposterous British social conventions; church and state, Prince of Wales, Mr Gladstone, the Royal Academy and Mr Ruskin, the London fog and St James's Street, are all abstractions which I like to accept as I do the sun and the moon, not because they are reasonable but because they are not. They ask me no questions and need no answers. Just the opposite of Paris and the French, they do not fret me with howling for applause because they are original. My only sorrow is to see no footmen in powder, no small-clothes and silk-stockings; no yellow chariots, and no fat coachmen in three-cornered hats. Much has gone, but thank the British Constitution, nothing new has come, and I sleep in peace with all the Georges and Queen Anne.

January 21. A lovely dark day, black as night, and full of refined feeling. Larz and I have breakfasted, and he has gone to his diplomatic duties, while I wonder whether, if I go out, I can find my way in the streets. My boxes are packed, and ready to go as freight by the next steamer. I have nothing more to do. I have called on all the old people. I have dined with various octogenarians, and buried the Duke of Clarence. As yet I have seen nobody and heard nothing worth remembering. Influenza is the chief topic of conversation, as monotonous as London topics are apt to be, and at the clubs I hear nothing but inquiries whether the other fellow has had it, and replies specifying the rheumatism or the gout or the bronchitis that the other fellow has had. Mrs Harry White has had a bad time of it, and is still very far from well. Minister Lincoln is not yet out of his room. Last evening came a letter from John Hay about the Bonaparte ball and you and Mrs Lodge. I wish I had been in the pantry to look in and see you in your black dress dancing with the Turk. Well! I should properly be there three weeks hence, and will begin merrily the old dance; but I fear terribly that you are all mistaken in thinking that I can add anything to your pleasure. We all want too much, and I am the worst of the lot, and the others all catch the disease from me. Rebecca writes me that she too is influenzed, and is going to take her mother south. Please be careful and keep well—you and Martha. Or if you must be ill, let me take you somewhere, or come over to me, and set up No. 1603 as a quarantine hospital. I look out of my window in 38 Clarges Street at a sky absolutely black, and an invisible cab below, and I wonder what sort of a morning is dawning on La Fayette Square.

Saturday, Jan. 23. So the time has come for closing and sending off my last letter. On Monday I go down to Yorkshire to pass the week with Gaskell, and on my return I shall have only a day here to close up and go. London is still quiet, muddy and dark. Last night I went to Sir Charles Halle's concert with Augusta Hervey and a friend of hers.[3] The hall was only half full, and the big orchestra seemed a majority. I believe I have done all my social duties as far as the season and the influenza allow. The little society I have found has offered a curious contrast to my former experiences here, when the days were hardly long enough to meet the engagements. Now I seem to be the oldest inhabitant, and forgotten by time. I should not mind except that sometimes the feeling of being less than half my old self becomes rather trying. I have seen nothing worth buying, which is another great change; and have heard of no one whom I care to meet. Still, London is in its way rather pleasant and quieting. I am not anxious to get away, and the absence of clatter and fashion is on the whole pleasanter than being surrounded by a swarm of society that is wholly strange. Tomorrow, as usual on Sundays, I lunch with Harry James, who is chiefly excited by the marriage of his friend Rudyard Kipling with the sister of another friend, Balestier, an American who was half publisher, half author, and whose sudden death at Dresden a month ago, was a sad blow to James, who depended on him for all his business arrangements.[4] I imagine Kipling to be rather a Bohemian and wanderer of the second or third social order, but he has behaved well about his young woman and has run in the face of family and friends who think him a kind of Shakspeare, and wanted him to marry the Queen or the Duchess of Westminster. I believe his wife is a perfectly undistinguished American, without beauty or money or special intelligence. They were married very privately and almost secretly last week. James had confided it all to me last Sunday, which is the cause of my happening to know about it. James also confided to me his distress because Sergent, the painter, had quarreled with a farmer down at the place, wherever it is, where the Abbey-Millet-Parsons crowd now pass their winters,[5] and after riding up and down his fields of spring wheat, had been wrought to such frenzy by being called no gentleman, that he went to the farmer's house, called him out, and pounded him; for which our artist-genius in America would certainly get some months of gaol, and may get it even here, which much distresses Henry who has a sympathetic heart. This too was confided to me, and has not yet got into the newspapers. As Sergent seems not to distress himself, I see no reason why James should do so; but poor James may well be a little off his nerves, for besides Balestier's death, the long, nervous illness of James's sister is drawing slowly to its inevitable close, and James has the load of it to carry, not quite alone, for Catherine Loring is here in charge of the invalid, but still the constant load on one's spirits is considerable.[6] I wish I could help him. His sister now keeps her bed, and is too weak to think of anything but her nerves. I sat two hours with Miss Loring yesterday.

I suppose that the Teutonic will somehow get me across that dreary ocean and land me at New York in due time. I think about it as little as possible, and shall certainly be much surprised at finding myself there. As you will know almost the hour to expect me, I shall not telegraph, but shall take the first train, day or night, and appear at my own door, I hope, on Thursday, Feb. 11, at latest. Please write a little line, and leave or send it, so that I may find it on my arrival, to tell me that you and Martha are well; and in giving it to William or Maggy you might hint to them that the cook had better be on hand Thursday noon. They need not know this before Wednesday evening, and can, I suppose, keep it to themselves. I do not care to make any concealment from my friends in Washington, but I can't tell them without letting my people in Boston know; and I want to get back before they know anything about it. This is by no means in order to amuse me or them, but for private and personal reasons. Should I get influenza, or be prevented from sailing, or have more last words to say, I shall write again a week hence. If you get no letter Monday, you can count on my probable arrival Thursday; but as John Hay writes me that he can't see you for the cloud of dagos and other moths always fluttering in the light and warmth of your presence, I do not expect you to retire into seclusion on my arrival. By all means, singe the dagos. As for me, I am singed enough. I am *censé* to come home only to organise a new party for Central Asia. After all, it is sure to come to that. Meanwhile I am yours.

MS: MHi

1. Albert Victor, duke of Clarence (1864–1892), elder son of the Prince of Wales, and Henry Edward Manning (1808–1892), cardinal of the Roman Catholic church and archbishop of Westminster, both died Jan. 14.

2. Edmund William Gosse (1849–1928), critic, biographer, and poet. Sidney Colvin (1845–1927), art and literary critic, keeper of prints and drawings at the British Museum 1883–1912.

3. Sir Charles Hallé (1819–1895) conducted the Manchester orchestra and chorus at St. James's Hall.

4. Caroline Starr Balestier (1862–1939) married Rudyard Kipling (1865–1936) on Jan. 18.

5. The village of Broadway in Worcestershire.

6. Katharine Peabody Loring (1849–1943), of Beverly, Mass., Alice James's friend and companion.

To Charles Francis Adams, Jr.

London, 20 Jan. '92.

Dear Charles

I have just received your letter postmarked Jan. 8.

Obviously, if the arrangement with Dwight is not to be extended over another summer, he should receive immediate notice.

I neither have, nor should have, any voice in the matter. You must do whatever is your judgment, without regard to me.

My return in any case would be greatly eased by finding the thing settled; but my movements are likely, for some years, to be too erratic to warrant my assuming responsibility in a matter where I am not personally engaged.

Anyway Dwight should have notice.

As for me, pray dismiss the idea that I want to have anyone live with me.

Ever Yrs   Henry Adams

MS: MHi

To Sir Robert Cunliffe

Thornes House, Wakefield.
Sunday 31 Jan. [1892]

My dear and only Baronet

For ages past, I have said to myself three times each day that I was going to write you a letter full of valuable advice and information, but an enormous increase of business consequent on the Rossendale election and the report on Asylums to the County Council, as well as a series of addresses I am now making to the infant schools on the important subject of education for the aged (a subject which I mean to bring before Parliament at the earliest opportunity),—all these, and many other smaller demands on my time have prevented me from writing as I wished.

Surely I should have come to nurse you at Acton if my public duties had not detained me, and if I had known you were ill, and if I had not known that you would wish me in the Red Sea first. So I remained in London, very happy, the only man not in bed being Charles Robartes, and the clubs being all my own. As I live by prayer I vow that London is not half bad when it is invisible, and I am quite disposed to wonder that no one lives there. Naturally of a jealous and envious nature, I was glad to see that no one was more fashionable than I, and that I was no more bored than my neighbor.

At last I came down here for rest, after the extreme strain of London. Between ourselves I admit that I had another motive; I wished to study the eight hours question with a view to a great speech in support of the Bill when I introduced it,[1]—assuming always that Gladstone gives me the Home Department as everyone expects, for I wont be fobbed off with India. A week's work has pretty well finished that job and I return to town this evening.

Before Parliament meets I must run over to America for a few days, so I have taken passage on the Teutonic which sails Wednesday. As I shall have one or two trifles to attend to in London, I shall take a late train to Liverpool Tuesday night, arriving there only in time to go to bed, and going on board before noon the next day. I should have offered myself at Acton for Tuesday night if I could have managed it, but shall now wait till my return. If you care to run across the Atlantic with me, I will take you in my stateroom, and will see that Mr Blaine gives you a correct opinion of President Harrison. You can always get back in time to see the Grand Old Man smash your party, and rise to his apotheosis, with his benevolent hands giving you his blessing.

I imagine that at Liverpool a Station Hotel exists which will be good enough for a radical eighthourian like me. Till then I am at 38 Clarges Street.

So much for serious business. If I were in a jesting humor I should say how sorry I am for your new influenzation. The devil is in it. Still, I hope and believe that the worst is over.

Thanks for your interest in the Spectator's civility.[2] My conscience reproaches me bitterly to think that the too amiable British spectator cannot always be expected to understand what he is pleased to call "well-bred irony" and thinks I am flattering Canning by saying he was born a cad.

My love to yours Ever truly Henry Adams.

MS: MHi

1. A bill limiting the working day of miners to eight hours was in fact introduced in Parliament and defeated March 23.

2. HA's *History* was reviewed in the London *Spectator* 66 (May 23, 1891), 726–727.

To Charles Milnes Gaskell

R M S "Teutonic" 3 Feb. 1892.

Dear Carlo

Here I am, sure as eggs is addled, wobbling down the Irish channel on the big ship, and bound, beyond recall, to a week's misery, and the new world. Robert came over to see me off, which was just what I needed to cheer me; and he had hardly gone when I fell into the arms of Rudyard Kipling and his new wife, and wife's sister, and wife's mother, and so have once more attached myself to the immortals.[1] Henry James is responsible for this last variation on my too commonplace existence.

In London I found my youth Anderson suddenly departed, like everyone else, for Cannes; so I was alone for two days, except a parting dinner with James at a restaurant.

Unless Bumpus is a liar and a thief, Molly should by this time have received three fairy-books from me. I count much on aiding her education which, like everyone else's, should be exclusively useful and not ornamental. I know nothing so useful as fairies.

My toes are beastly cold and I expect never, never, to be warm again, for the northwest wind blows like Boreas the brawler that he is. My two hundred fellow-travellers are Jews. I am going to my cabin to turn on the electricity and the steam, and read a good book, and try to play that I am enjoying the best of possible oceans.

Farewells to all yours, and more than thanks for all your kindness. Hasta mas vista.

Ever truly   Henry Adams

MS: MHi
 1. Josephine Balestier and Anna Smith Balestier (Mrs. Henry Balestier).

Index

Adams, Henry Brooks (*cont.*)
"The slow dawn comes at last,"
III:340

Adams, Herbert Baxter, II:493
—letter to, II:330
Adams, Isaac Hull, I:216, 312; II:131;
III:176, 177
Adams, John, I:213; II:56, 319, 412, 468;
III:54–56; political quarrels, I:209;
II:267, 291, 317; *Discourses on Davila,*
II:323
Adams, John (of Samoa), III:335, 374
Adams, John (son of CFA2), II:233;
III:66
Adams, John Quincy, II:196, 241, 297,
317, 319, 323, 506; and Grétry's opera,
III:594; writings, II:194, 226, 338, 457;
III:54, 55–56
Adams, John Quincy II, I:5, 6, 45, 266,
374; II:276, 554; III:145; social life,
I:15, 35, 48, 77, 88, 191; engagement,
I:137, 141, 180, 183; political activities,
I:509–510, 512, 557; II:6, 16, 150–151;
HA's financial agent, I:516, 524–525;
political integrity, I:525, 528, 533;
II:444
—letters to, I:524; III:50
Adams, John Quincy III, I:286; II:58, 276
Adams, Louisa Catherine (Mrs. JQA),
I:373; II:25
Adams, Louisa Catherine (HA's sister):
see Kuhn, Louisa Adams
Adams, Louisa Catherine (daughter of
CFA2), II:125; III:289–290
Adams, Marian Hooper, II:135, 153, 199,
200–201, 362; III:481; engagement,
II:131–135 passim; wedding,
II:139–140, 141, 146; begins wedding
trip, II:141; characterized, II:133, 137,
140, 608; III:565; and *Democracy,*
II:412, 413, 488; photography, II:507,
511–512, 517, 526, 527, 557, 558; vigil
at father's deathbed, II:578–609 pas-
sim; depression, II:614, 617, 623, 634,
635, 636, 639; death, II:640–645;
III:358; namesakes, III:35n, 107, 263
—letters to, II:498, 579(2), 580, 581,
583, 584, 585, 586, 587, 588, 592, 594,
595, 597, 598, 599, 601, 603(2), 605,
606
Adams, Mary (HA's sister): *see* Quincy,
Mary Adams
Adams, Mary Hellen (Mrs. John Adams;
HA's aunt), II:5, 39, 81
Adams, Mary Hone Ogden (Mrs.
CFA2), I:487, 488–489, 506, 549
Adams, Mary Ogden (daughter of
CFA2): *see* Abbott, Mary Adams
Adams, Molly: *see* Abbott, Mary Adams
Adams, Samuel, II:196–197, 412

Adams monument, III:146, 160, 263,
287, 379, 406, 415–416; first reports of,
III:480–481, 484, 494, 496; *see also*
Saint-Gaudens, Augustus; White,
Stanford
Addison, Joseph, II:46
Adee, Alvey A., II:479
Adee, David G., II:479
Adler, Felix, II:192
Aenga, Princess (of Samoa), III:314, 316,
317–318, 327, 383
Agassiz, Alexander, II:312, 455, 493, 587
Agassiz, George R., III:146
Agassiz, Ida: *see* Higginson, Ida A.
Agassiz, Louis, I:569
Albani, Francesco, II:355
Albert of Saxe-Coburg, Prince Consort,
I:97, 271
Alcott, Bronson, II:566
Alderson, Florence, I:553, 568; II:52, 54
Alexander, Charles B., III:107
Alexander, Harriet C. (Mrs. Charles B.),
III:107
Alexander, Mark, II:318
Alexandra, Princess of Wales, I:317, 333
Alice, Princess, I:306–307
Allegre, Sophie: *see* Gallatin, Sophie Al-
legre
Allen, Charles A., I:462
Allen, Elisha H., II:488
Allen, William F., II:202
—letter to, II:262
Alley, John B., I:205, 210, 220, 232
Allison, William B., II:92
Alma-Tadema, Laura (Mrs. Lawrence),
II:542
Alma-Tadema, Lawrence, II:542
Alston, John J. P., I:346
Alvensleben, Count Frederick J., II:580
Alward, Dennis R., II:586
Amberley: *see* Russell, John, Viscount
Amberley
American Academy of Arts and Sciences,
II:242
American Historical Association, II:553,
623, 624, 625, 626, 627–628; III:9
American Social Science Association,
II:261, 308
Ames, Frederick L., II:554; III:74n
Ames, James Barr, II:155, 156
Amis, Betty, I:76, 81, 83, 90, 94
Amis, Sally, I:76, 83
Amory, Thomas C.
—letter to, II:220
Amory, William, I:209, 212
Anderson, James H.
—letters to, I:318, 320
Anderson, Larz (1803–1878), I:223–224
Anderson, Larz (1866–1937), III:567
Anderson, Nicholas L.: in Germany, I:3,
5, 8, 29, 71, 76; Civil War service,

Wadsworth, Evelyn P. (Mrs. Craig),
II:481
Wadsworth, Herbert, III:316
Wadsworth, William Austin, III:260
Wagner, Richard, III:590, 592
Wakea, Princess (of Samoa), III:289–290,
291
Waldegrave, Frances Braham, Countess,
I:438, 534
Wales, Prince of: see Edward VII
Walker, Francis A., II:12, 418, 425
—letters to, II:259, 335, 427
Walker, Robert J., I:350
Wallace, Alfred Russel, III:531, 536; Is-
land Life, III:341–342
Wallop, Lady Catherine: see Gaskell,
Lady Catherine
Walpole, Horace, I:204; II:52
Walpole, Sir Robert, II:52, 197
Walpole, Sir Spencer: Life of Russell,
III:527
Ward, Anna B. (Mrs. Samuel G.)
—letter to, II:644
Ward, Artemus (Charles Farrar Browne),
II:233, 584
Ward, Edward M., I:354
Ward, Mary A. (Mrs. Humphry), II:467;
III:150, 181
Ward, Samuel ("King of the Lobby"),
II:28
Ward, Samuel Gray (N.Y. banker),
I:244; II:158; III:226
Warder, Benjamin H., II:589n, 594
Waring, George E., II:613
Warner, Charles Dudley, II:472
Warren, John B. L., II:77
Warren, Mabel Bayard (Mrs. Samuel
D.), II:486
Warren, Margaret: see Cowell-Stepney,
Lady
Warren, Samuel D., II:486
Washburn, Cadwallader C., I:205, 211,
225
Washburn, Emory
—letter to, II:215
Washburn, Israel, Jr., I:204
Washburn, Mary W. (Mrs. Israel, Jr.),
I:204
Washburn, William, II:130, 198
Washburne, Elihu B., II:12, 253, 272,
273
Washington, George, II:241, 291, 319,
323, 330, 451; III:594
Watterson, Henry, II:192n
Watts, Thomas, I:259
Weber, Karl Maria von, I:16, 57; III:278
Webster, Daniel, I:208; II:46, 506
Weckerlin, G. F. H. von, III:531, 536
Weed, Thurlow, I:212, 284, 288, 297,
314, 409, 496; II:425; political go-be-
tween, I:218, 220, 225; Union publicist

in England, I:266, 268, 269, 274, 275,
278, 301
—letter to, I:273
Weitzel, Godfrey, I:490
Welles, Gideon F., I:217, 220
Welling, James C., II:452
Wells, David A., II:10, 12, 19, 26, 68, 88,
91, 425; revenue reports, II:11, 98;
NAR contributor, II:85, 223; Robinson
Crusoe's Money, II:262; "Reform of
Local Taxation," II:262
—letters to, II:11, 85, 98, 222, 223, 262,
282
Wensleydale, Lord, I:426
Western Reserve University, II:475
Wetmore, George P., II:554, 558, 564,
570
Wharton, Edith (Mrs. Edward R.),
II:596; III:594
Wharton, Edward R., II:596
Wheeler, Joseph
—letters to, III:236, 240, 245
Wheeler, William A., II:206
Whistler, James Abbott McNeill, III:250,
251
White, Andrew D., II:625, 628
White, Henry, III:580, 600
White, Horace, II:88, 91, 191, 217, 259,
434
White, Margaret (Mrs. Henry), III:600,
603
White, Richard Grant, II:473
White, Stanford, III:126, 137, 406, 415,
494; see also Adams monument
Whitman, Walt, II:46
Whitney, Dorothy, III:59
Whitney, Flora P. (Mrs. William C.),
II:579, 580
Whitney, Josiah D., II:113
Whitney, William C., II:577; III:89
Whitney, William D., II:268
—letters to, II:85, 96, 113, 192, 201, 209,
245, 265, 294, 295
Whittier, John Greenleaf, II:46
Wilde, Oscar, II:511
Wilkes, Charles, I:343; III:405
Willamov, Grégoire de, II:480
William III, II:197
Williams, Sir Charles Hanbury, II:52
Williams, George H., II:19
Williams-Wynn, Charles W., II:146
Williams-Wynn, Charlotte, II:32n;
III:526; writings, II:104, 106, 109, 134,
303
Williams-Wynn, Frances: Diary of a Lady
of Quality, II:49
Wilson, Bluford, II:255, 342
Wilson, Charles L., I:232, 236, 275
Wilson, Charles Rivers, II:363
Wilson, Henry, I:11, 198, 217, 222, 557;
II:151

DATE DUE

HIGHSMITH 45-102   PRINTED IN U.S.A.